T0305365

ALTERNATIVE INVESTMENTS

The *Robert W. Kolb Series in Finance* provides a comprehensive view of the field of finance in all of its variety and complexity. It covers all major topics and specializations in finance, ranging from investments, to corporate finance, to financial institutions. Each volume is written or edited by a specialist (or specialists) in a particular area of finance and is intended for practicing finance professionals, graduate students, and advanced undergraduate students. The goal of each volume is to encapsulate the current state of knowledge in a particular area of finance so that the reader can quickly achieve a mastery of that discipline.

Please visit www.wiley.com/go/kolbseries to learn about recent and forthcoming titles in the Kolb Series.

ALTERNATIVE INVESTMENTS

Instruments, Performance, Benchmarks, and Strategies

Editors

H. Kent Baker

Greg Filbeck

The Robert W. Kolb Series in Finance

WILEY

Cover Design: Levia-Sposato
Cover Image: © CactusSoup/iStockphoto

Published by John Wiley & Sons, Inc., Hoboken, New Jersey.
Published simultaneously in Canada.

Library of Congress Cataloging-in-Publication Data:

Alternative investments : instruments, performance, benchmarks, and strategies / H. Kent Baker and Greg Filbeck, editors.
pages cm. – (The Robert W. Kolb series)
Includes index.
ISBN 978-1-118-24112-7 (cloth); ISBN 978-1-118-28518-3 (ebk); ISBN 978-1-118-28334-9 (ebk); ISBN 978-1-118-28258-8 (ebk)
1. Investments. 2. Asset allocation. 3. Investment analysis. I. Baker, H. Kent (Harold Kent), 1944- II. Filbeck, Greg.
HG4521.A48 2013
332.6–dc23

2012039746

Printed in the United States of America.

10 9 8 7 6 5 4 3 2 1

Contents

Acknowledgments

Bringing *Alternative Investments: Instruments, Performance, Benchmarks, and Strategies* from the idea stage to publication involved many individuals. Although we cannot thank everyone who played a role in this process, we would like to recognize some major players. We appreciate the support provided by Bob Kolb and Kevin Commins in gaining approval of this book. The chapter authors deserve special thanks for their excellent work. Our expert team at John Wiley & Sons exhibited professionalism in bringing the manuscript to final form, especially Claire New, the production editor. The Kogod School of Business at American University and Penn State Behrend provided financial support. Linda Baker deserves special thanks for her careful review of parts of the manuscript as well as for her patience and encouragement. Janis, Aaron, Kyle, and Grant Filbeck deserve special thanks for their support and encouragement. The authors dedicate this book to Linda Baker and Janis Filbeck.

PART I

Introduction

CHAPTER 1

Alternative Investments: An Overview

H. KENT BAKER
University Professor of Finance, Kogod School of Business, American University

GREG FILBECK
Samuel P. Black III Professor of Insurance and Risk Management, The Behrend College, Penn State Erie

INTRODUCTION

Given historically low interest rates coupled with severe equity bear markets, interest in alternative investments has recently soared. Because sophisticated investors viewed the resulting investment environment for traditional investments as low return, many turned to alternative investments as a way of meeting their return objectives and, perhaps to a lesser extent, as a means of controlling risk. That is, alternative investments provide an opportunity to earn a reasonable return with manageable risk. Some alternative investments offer good opportunities to participate in different markets and to apply investment strategies that are unavailable to the general investing public. Thus, investors and portfolio managers who understand alternative investments have a substantial advantage over those who do not. Chen, Baierl, and Kaplan (2002), Amin and Kat (2003), Chen, Ho, Lu, and Wu (2005), and Anson (2006) find superior performance for the inclusion of alternative investments on a stand-alone basis or as a part of a portfolio consisting of traditional assets.

What are so-called "alternative investments"? *Alternative investments* refer to many asset classes that fall outside of traditional investments, such as stocks, bonds, and cash. Broadly speaking, anything else in which an individual or institution can invest may be called an alternative investment. Because alternative investments encompass a wide range of offerings, limiting the discussion of the various types to a few major categories is helpful. Yau, Schneeweis, Robinson, and Weiss (2007) place such investments into two broad categories:

1. Traditional alternative investments
   - *Real estate*: Ownership interests in land or structures attached to land. Investors may participate in real estate directly or indirectly. Direct ownership involves investment in residences, commercial real estate, and

agricultural land. Indirect investment includes investing in companies engaged in real estate ownership, development, or management; real estate investment trusts (REITs); commingled real estate trusts (CREFs); and infrastructure funds.

   - *Private equity*: Ownership interests in publicly traded companies. Although private equity involves an array of investment activities, among the most important fields of private equity activity are venture capital (equity financing of new or growing private companies), closely held companies, and buyout funds (the buyout of established companies through private equity funds).
   - *Commodities*: Agreements to buy and sell a tangible asset or an actual physical good that is generally relatively homogeneous in nature. The three major classes of commodities are energy (e.g., crude oil and coal), metals (e.g., gold, silver, platinum, copper, and aluminum), and agricultural products (e.g., coffee beans, corn, orange juice, soybeans, sugar, and wheat). Commodities are essential building blocks of the global economy.

2. Modern alternative investments
   - *Managed futures*: Private pooled investment vehicles that can invest in cash, spot, and derivative markets for the benefit of their investors and that have the ability to use leverage in a wide variety of trading strategies. Managed futures offer the potential for reduced portfolio volatility and the ability to earn profit in any economic environment. Managed futures accounts can take both long and short positions in futures contracts and options on futures contracts in the global commodity, interest rate, equity, and currency markets.
   - *Hedge funds*: Loosely regulated and actively managed pooled investment vehicles that use a wide variety of investment strategies, such as taking aggressive long and short positions and using arbitrage and leverage. Because hedge funds can take many forms, no precise legal or universally accepted definition is available. Nonetheless, the primary goal of most hedge funds is to reduce volatility and risk while attempting to preserve capital and deliver positive (absolute) returns under all market conditions.
   - *Distressed securities*: Securities of companies or government entities that are either already in default, under bankruptcy protection, or in distress and heading toward such a condition. The most common distressed securities are bonds and bank debt. As investments, distressed securities are usually very risky because the company might not recover.

Although each of these alternative investments has unique characteristics that require a different approach by investors, alternative investments have some common characteristics. For example, they may be relatively illiquid and may involve relatively high costs of purchase and sale compared to stocks and bonds. Appraising the performance of alternative investments is often difficult because of problems associated with determining the current market value of the asset and the complexity of establishing valid benchmarks. Limited historical risk and return data may be available.

Further, many alternative investments are unavailable or unsuitable for the general public due to their complexity or structure. The complexity associated with alternative investments is a limiting factor for the average investor because such investments may require due diligence and a high degree of investment analysis before buying. *Structure* refers to how the investment is offered. Many alternative investments are private offerings available only to sophisticated investors. Not surprisingly, the major investors in alternative investments are high-net-worth individuals (accredited investors) and institutional investors. According to Securities and Exchange Commission (SEC) guidelines, an accredited investor, in general terms, must have a net worth of at least $1 million in assets, or have income over $200,000 per year (last two years and expectation of the same for the current year), or both. Some offerings require investors to have more than $5 million in assets to qualify. Yet, the potential risk-diversification benefits of alternative investments offer broad appeal across investor types. This is because of their generally low correlation with traditional financial investments.

Purpose of the Book

The purpose of *Alternative Investments—Instruments, Performance, Benchmarks, and Strategies* is to examine the many and varied areas that are now viewed as alternative investments. The survey nature of this book involves trade-offs given the vast footprint that constitutes alternative investments. Although no single book can cover everything associated with this topic, this book highlights key topics. Readers can gain an in-depth understanding of the major types of alternative investments and the latest trends within the field. Empirical evidence about each type of alternative investment is featured. Cited research studies are presented in a straightforward manner, focusing on the comprehension of study findings, rather than the details of mathematical frameworks. Authors contributing chapters consist of a mix of academics and practitioners.

Although each chapter is self-contained, the chapters are organized into five sections: (1) introduction, (2) real estate, (3) private equity, (4) commodities and managed futures, and (5) hedge funds. These topics not only incorporate the major types of alternative investments discussed by Yau et al. (2007) but also expand upon their list. Within each category, the book provides a discussion of such topics as the market for the investments, benchmarks and historical performance, specific investment strategies, and issues about performance evaluation and reporting.

Features of the Book

Alternative Investments—Instruments, Performance, Benchmarks, and Strategies has several distinguishing features.

- Perhaps the book's most distinctive feature is that it provides a detailed discussion of alternative investments, including empirical evidence and practice within the various topics covered. The book attempts not only to blend the conceptual world of scholars with the pragmatic view of practitioners, but also to synthesize important and relevant research studies in a succinct and clear manner and to present recent developments. Thus, the book reflects the latest trends and cutting-edge research involving alternative investments.

- The book contains contributions from numerous authors, ensuring a variety of perspectives and a rich interplay of ideas.
- Each chapter ends with a summary and conclusions section that provides the key lessons of the chapter.
- When discussing the results of empirical studies that link theory and practice, the objective is to distill them to their essential content so that they are understandable to readers, including theoretical and mathematical derivations to the extent to which they may be necessary and useful to them.
- The end of each chapter contains at least four discussion questions that help to reinforce key concepts. Guideline answers are presented at the end of the book. This feature should be especially important to faculty and students using the book in classes.

Intended Audience

The book's unique set of features should be of interest to various groups, including practitioners, investors, academics, and students. Practitioners can use this book to navigate through the key areas in alternative investments. Individual and institutional investors will also benefit as they attempt to expand their knowledge base and apply the concepts contained within the book to the management of their portfolios. Academics can use this book in their undergraduate and graduate investment courses and as a source for understanding the various strands of research emerging from this area. The book also has the potential for being used in the Chartered Alternative Investment Analyst (CAIA) program because the topics included in the book closely mirror those required by the CAIA program.

STRUCTURE OF THE BOOK

The remaining 27 chapters of the book consist of five sections. A brief synopsis of each chapter by section follows.

Part I. Introduction

Alternative investments include real estate, private equity, commodities, managed futures, and hedge funds, among others. These investments have the potential to enhance the risk-adjusted performance of existing portfolios of traditional investments. Chapter 2 highlights the role that alternative investments play in strategic asset allocation. Chapter 3 explores long-term trends that have emerged in alternative investments because of the financial crisis of 2007–2008. Because many alternative investments operate in private markets under less regulated conditions, Chapter 4 points out the increased importance of investor due diligence when including alternative investments within a portfolio.

Chapter 2 The Role of Alternative Investments in Strategic Asset Allocation (Douglas Cumming, Lars Helge Haß, and Denis Schweizer)
This chapter introduces a framework for strategic asset allocation using alternative investments along with traditional investments. The approach accounts for time series biases with alternative asset indices. A strategic asset allocation model is used that is flexible enough to capture the risk-return profile adequately, as well as to incorporate real investor preferences. The empirical results show that bonds are highly important in all portfolios, but defensive portfolios tend to use stocks of large U.S. firms. In all portfolios, emerging markets gain in relevance with decreasing risk aversion. For alternative investments, all portfolios use the maximum allocation of hedge funds and a medium allocation of commodities. Private equity is comparatively more important in defensive portfolios, whereas REITs gain in importance as risk aversion decreases.

Chapter 3 Trends in Alternative Investments (Erik Benrud)
The market for alternative investments has changed considerably since the financial crisis of 2007–2008. This chapter examines those changes and posits which ones reflect important, long-term trends that emerged from the turbulence of the crisis. The most important overall trend is an increase in the responsiveness of managers to the demands of investors in an effort to keep capital invested. This trend has led to more specific trends, such as an increase in transparency and liquidity in existing products and the introduction of new products with more investor-friendly properties. Although these trends will likely have positive effects, they may also have undesirable implications for the returns on alternative investments.

Chapter 4 Alternative Investments and Due Diligence (Gökhan Afyonoğlu)
Alternative investments such as hedge funds, private equity funds, real estate funds, timberland and commodity funds are drawing ever-increasing amounts of attention and capital. Alternative funds are private investment vehicles that are subject to less regulation than traditional asset classes. From an investment perspective, managers of such investments typically use sophisticated and opaque investment strategies; trade complex instruments such as derivatives; utilize leverage; and invest in illiquid assets. These factors, in addition to risk/return characteristics that differ from those of traditional investments, make analyzing and assessing alternative investments more challenging and elevate the importance of thorough due diligence. Furthermore, the entrepreneurial nature of many investment advisers coupled with a lack of transparency necessitates extensive business or operational due diligence in order to ascertain that firms have adequate organizational structure, governance mechanisms, and checks and balances to safeguard investors; minimize operational risks; and comply with laws, regulations, and industry best practices.

Part II. Real Estate

Investors can gain exposure to real estate in various ways. Chapter 5 introduces the section and points out that this exposure can occur in a variety of ways, including direct investment in private real estate markets (both commercial and residential) or public equity markets through REITs. Chapters 6 and 7 provide expanded coverage on commercial real estate. Chapter 6 investigates ways of analyzing returns, whereas Chapter 7 offers empirical evidence of how commercial real estate performs through investments in REITs. Chapter 8 discusses how real estate mortgages serve as the collateral for mortgage-backed securities (MBS) and how the increased complexity of MBS played a key role in the recession emerging from the financial crisis of 2007–2008. Chapter 9 shows the role that real estate can play in the private equity markets. Chapter 10 provides a discussion of methods available to value real estate. Chapter 11 concludes the section by discussing three different approaches to assessing real estate performance.

Chapter 5 REITs and the Private Real Estate Market (Shaun A. Bond and Qingqing Chang)

Financial economists have long been interested in the dual-market nature of real estate. Real estate is in a unique position among alternative asset classes in that an active market transacting commercial and residential real estate assets exists alongside the public pricing and trading of REITs on the stock market. This chapter summarizes past research on how these two markets are connected and whether investors in REITs receive a return consistent with the direct real estate market. To investigate this issue, an analysis is conducted using multivariate cointegration techniques on a data set that includes the financial crisis of 2007–2008 and a carefully matched set of control variables. Researchers have previously used matched controls to address this issue. The findings suggest that REITs and the private real estate market adjust together toward a long-run equilibrium. Evidence also indicates that the financial markets lead movements in the real estate market.

Chapter 6 Commercial Real Estate (Peter Chinloy)

This chapter develops the return to holding commercial real estate. That return is examined for the four main property types: apartments, industrial, office, and retail. Commercial real estate has a return consisting of the sum of an income yield or cap rate and capital gains. Interestingly, expected capital gains over the long term are equal to the rate of inflation. The real return to real estate is consequently the income yield or capitalization (cap) rate, which acts as the real discount rate. The cap rate differs between investors even for the same asset because of agency and contract issues. The agency issues concern operating expenses, capital expenses, and revenues. Because apartment tenants differ in ability to operate and lack scale, landlords bear these costs. Leases are offered with full service to tenants. Industrial tenants are on site, so landlords offer triple net leases and pay no maintenance. Office tenants are unsure about capital expenses and demand them up front as tenant improvements. Retail tenants offer to share revenues with landlords to ensure upkeep.

Chapter 7 Real Estate Investment Trusts (Brad Case)

This chapter focuses on the return characteristics of commercial real estate investments made through REITs. REITs enable investors to access the commercial real estate asset class indirectly through ownership of equity shares in a company whose assets consist primarily of commercial properties or mortgages and whose revenues derive primarily through commercial property leases or mortgage payments. Investments in equity shares of listed REITs preserve liquidity while exposing the investor to short-term fluctuations not related to property market developments. Historical performance data suggest stronger risk-adjusted returns for investments in listed REITs than for other real estate investments. This result may be attributable to differences in principal–agent issues, financing practices, and capital market discipline.

Chapter 8 Mortgage-Backed Securities (Eric J. Higgins)
MBS are a financial repackaging of the interest and principal payments on mortgages that are sold to investors. The repackaging of these mortgage payments is known as *securitization*. Mortgage securitization relies on the knowledge of the cash flows to be received from the mortgages, including prepayments. The MBS market in the United States reached a peak of over $9 trillion in 2007. The current MBS market had its genesis in the late 1960s, but two previous MBS markets existed in the United States in the late 1880s and the 1920s. The increasingly complex mortgage securities created in the recent MBS market helped fuel a real estate boom that ultimately led to the worst U.S. recession since the Great Depression.

Chapter 9: Mezzanine Debt and Preferred Equity in Real Estate (Andrew Berman)
This chapter discusses mezzanine loans and preferred equity investments, which are two types of nontraditional real estate financing providing capital and liquidity to real estate owners. Unlike traditional mortgage loans, these nontraditional methods of financing have complex structures and different risks and benefits. Mezzanine loans are debt transactions in which the lender's collateral is in the form of the mezzanine borrower's ownership interests in other entities that own income-producing property. Preferred equity transactions are structured as equity investments in an entity that owns real property. These equity investments are structured as capital contributions to the entity; in return, the investor receives a preferred return on its investment. The investor's preferred return is the economic equivalent to interest on a mezzanine loan. Although each of these financing vehicles is structured differently (one as debt and the other as equity), both allow property owners to obtain funds in excess of the typical senior mortgage loan, increase the property owner's leverage, and provide liquidity. This chapter discusses the unique structure of these financings and examines both the opportunities and risks for real estate owners, mezzanine lenders, and preferred equity investors.

Chapter 10 Real Estate Appraisal and Valuation (Jeffrey D. Fisher and Demetrios Louziotis, Jr.)
This chapter explains why appraisals are necessary for the valuation of private real estate investments. The traditional approaches to valuation are explained, including a discussion of their advantages and disadvantages. Emphasis is placed on the income approach, because income tends to be most relevant for income-producing real estate. The income approach may be based on direct capitalization (value in perpetuity), discounted cash flow (DCF) analysis, or both. DCF uses a discount rate to estimate the present value of projected future cash flows from operations and resale of the property at the end of its holding period. The relationship between

the discount rate and cap rate is also discussed. The cap rate is used in direct capitalization and is the ratio of the first year net operating income (NOI) to the value of the property. It is often used as a general guideline for how commercial real estate is being priced relative to its current earnings. The sales comparison and cost approaches are alternative methods for estimating value and provide a check on the results of the income approach. The final value estimate reconciles the individual value estimates from each approach used.

Chapter 11 Performance of Real Estate Portfolios (David Geltner)
This chapter describes the three major approaches to measuring the investment returns within the real estate asset class or portfolios of commercial properties: indices based on appraisals, transactions, and stock prices. Appraisal-based indices are the traditional approach, but suffer from lagging and smoothing bias, questions about their subjectivity, and the limited population of properties that are regularly appraised. Transaction-based indices, a major innovation during the past decade, address many of these shortcomings. Yet, they provide only price change, not total return, and are difficult to trade or invest in directly. The newest innovation is stock market–based indices that provide more frequent and leading information and greater tradability but do not directly reflect private property market pricing.

Part III. Private Equity

Private equity consists of the four components discussed within this section: venture capital, mezzanine capital, buyout funds, and distressed debt. Chapter 12 discusses venture capital, which is most closely associated with financing for privately held startup companies. Mezzanine capital, as discussed in Chapter 13, offers investors higher return opportunities within debt securities in exchange for a subordinated position within debt issues. Chapter 14 introduces buyout funds, which consist of publicly held firms taken private, often for the purposes of increasing firm efficiency and restoring entrepreneurial spirit without being under the microscope of the public markets. Distressed debt, discussed in Chapter 15, offers opportunities for investment returns from positions taken in a recovering firm or through appropriate positions in the bankruptcy process for a deteriorating firm. In Chapter 16, the holistic performance of private equity is assessed on a stand-alone and risk-adjusted basis. Chapter 17 further extends this analysis through assessment of systematic and abnormal performance of private equity.

Chapter 12 Venture Capital (Tom Vanacker and Sophie Manigart)
This chapter introduces venture capital, which is a subset of the private equity asset class that focuses on investments in new or growing privately held companies with high growth potential. It specifically addresses why venture capital investors exist beside traditional financial intermediaries, such as banks; what the different venture capital models are; what venture capitalists do; how venture capital investors influence the development of their portfolio companies; and how venture capital as an asset class may create value for investors. For this purpose, the chapter relies on an extensive and growing, but largely fragmented, stream of research on venture capital from the finance, entrepreneurship, and management fields.

Chapter 13 Mezzanine Capital (Sameer Jain and Phillip Myburgh)
Mezzanine securities represent privately-negociated instruments with a cash flow and collateral priority ranking in the middle of a borrower's capital structure, senior to common or preferred equity but subordinated to senior secured debt. The ongoing dislocation in global credit markets creates an environment where liquidity and capital resources are expected to remain scarce. The senior secured syndicated loan market has contracted substantially, and both the second-lien bank debt and high-yield markets are generally only accessible by seasoned issuers typically raising large amounts with relatively conservative capital structures. These prevailing market conditions create a particularly attractive environment for mezzanine investors, because mezzanine capital is required to bridge the funding gap in many transactions that require borrowers to raise leveraged finance. This chapter analyzes mezzanine capital's investment characteristics, distinguishes between mezzanine capital and high-yield debt, explores supply and demand factors driving mezzanine pricing, reviews similarities and differences in mezzanine's usage in the United States and Europe, and highlights important investing considerations.

Chapter 14 Buyout Funds (Christian Rauch and Mark Wahrenburg)
What are buyout funds, how are they run, and how do they create value for investors? What is the current state of the buyout industry, and how did fund managers deal with the adversities they faced during the financial crisis of 2007–2008? Which challenges await the industry in the future? This chapter attempts to answer these questions. To do so, the chapter explains the economic features and major value drivers of buyout funds. It also discusses how the recent financial crisis crippled these value drivers and how the subsequent regulatory scrutiny might have the potential to change the buyout industry in the future.

Chapter 15 Distressed Debt Investing (Michelle M. Harner, Paul E. Harner, Catherine M. Martin, and Aaron M. Singer)
This chapter discusses the phenomenon of distressed debt investing. Hedge funds and private equity funds, as well as other investors, increasingly seek returns through debt or equity securities of troubled companies. These investments present various strategic and legal considerations with which courts and investors themselves continue to wrestle. For example, gaps in information often exist for distressed debt investors, especially if the company issuing the relevant debt or equity is private. Distressed debt investors are ultimately placing a bet about the appropriate level in the capital structure in which to invest as the likely "fulcrum security." Investors also face the risk that the claims they purchase may be valueless based on avoidable transfer theories or other, similar principles. This chapter discusses these and other related issues and provides illustrative case studies to describe the potential legal ramifications of distressed investments.

Chapter 16 Performance of Private Equity (Christoph Kaserer and Rüdiger Stucke)
This chapter gives an overview on the performance of private equity, the different performance-measurement methods, as well as evidence from the recent literature and a database with current performance numbers. First, the chapter explains why the calculation of time-weighted returns is extremely difficult for private equity

funds. As a result, alternative performance measures have been developed that are based on the observable cash flows from a fund investor. On this basis, the internal rate of return (IRR), the modified IRR, and the money multiple, as well as the public market equivalent are introduced. Second, methodological as well as operational problems associated with these methods, the adjustment for risk, and the challenges in obtaining reliable performance data are discussed. Finally, the chapter gives an overview on the empirical findings in the literature on private equity performance, and presents recent performance numbers for three subasset classes of private equity.

Chapter 17 Private Equity: Risk and Return Profile (Axel Buchner, Arif Khurshed, and Abdulkadir Mohamed)
This chapter examines abnormal performance and systematic risk of private equity investments around the world. The methodology extends the standard IRR approach and allows the estimation of systematic risk and abnormal returns of a cross-section of private equity investment cash flows. The empirical results show that the systematic risk (beta) for the venture and buyout investments is significantly different from 1.0, while abnormal returns (as measured by alpha) are significantly positive for both types of deals. Buyout investments are characterized by lower systematic risk and higher abnormal performance than venture capital investments.

Part IV. Commodities and Managed Futures

Commodity investments often serve as a hedge against inflation, offering diversification benefits in a portfolio context. Managed futures strategies, which include commodity and financial futures, incorporate active management and leverage to take advantage of opportunities that exist in capital markets. Chapter 18 gives an overview of the performance of commodities and the role they play in a portfolio context. In Chapter 19, commodity performance is further analyzed through various strategies. Chapter 20 introduces methodology to assess the role that commodities play in strategic portfolio allocation. Chapter 21 discusses managed futures strategies. Chapter 22 reports and analyzes their historical performance.

Chapter 18 Investing in Commodities (Claudio Boido)
Policies of asset allocation have changed substantially in the last decade, and many asset managers have varied their choices of asset classes within a portfolio. Research shows that commodity futures returns often exhibit a negative correlation with equity markets. In recent years, two major changes have taken place in commodity markets. First, world demand for commodities has been sustained due to large variations in the price of some commodities. Historically, the real prices of crude oil and equities have increased in tandem only during episodes of growth in world demand for industrial commodities. Second, financial institutions have sharply increased their share of open interest in commodity futures markets. This chapter examines commodities as a financial asset and reviews the recent literature on the correlation between commodities and traditional asset classes with a view on how to select a portfolio.

Chapter 19 Performance of Commodities (Andrew Clark)
This chapter discusses the history of commodity trading, commodity trading basics, commodity futures, the basics of commodity exchange-traded funds (ETFs), and commodity investing via managed futures. It also examines contango and backwardation and their associated roll yields and, finally, the intermediate-term outlook for commodities. The chapter focuses on how to trade commodities through futures, ETFs, and commodity-trading advisors (i.e., managers of managed futures accounts). In particular, the following areas are discussed: costs of carry; margin accounts; leverage issues, especially as they occur in ETFs; the hows and whys of spreading; delta-neutral hedging; nondirectional trading; and trading programs such as trending and market-neutral strategies.

Chapter 20 Commodity Futures and Strategic Asset Allocation (Yongyang Su, Marco Lau, and Frankie Chau)
This chapter analyzes the role of commodities in the process of strategic asset allocation. It emphasizes computing the optimal weighting of commodities relative to the traditional assets in a multiperiod portfolio choice setting and offers some plausible explanations on why commodities are an important asset class beyond the traditional portfolios of stocks and bonds. From the perspective of U.S. investors, the analysis shows that investors have a relatively strong and stable intertemporal hedging demand for commodities for long-term horizons despite their increasingly easy and inexpensive access to the global equity and bond markets. Overall, the results lend support to those institutional investors who believe that commodities are an important asset class and continue to include such assets in their strategic portfolio allocation process.

Chapter 21 Managed Futures: Markets, Investment Characteristics, and Role in a Portfolio (David Accomazzo)
The modern investor faces increasingly complex financial markets. Globalization, exceptional international monetary policies, fragmentation of trading venues, rapidly changing technology, and an unstable regulatory framework contribute to instability and to the shattering of some long-held investing convictions. Crises seem to occur more frequently and with increasing magnitude, and traditional diversification does not seem to provide the advantages witnessed in the past. This chapter provides an overview of an alternative investment strategy called managed futures that can improve portfolio construction. The overview includes an introduction to the industry, an analysis of the current state of the sector, and the role of this strategy in a portfolio. Particular attention is dedicated to the dynamic of choosing a Commodity Trading Advisor (CTA). Furthermore, a case study about the recent collapse of MF Global—one of the largest brokers in the industry—is included due to its far-reaching consequences and likely changes that may result in the industry because of it.

Chapter 22 Performance of Managed Futures: 1983 to the Post-2008 Crisis Period (Kai-Hong Tee)
The growth of the managed futures industry increased dramatically in the late 1970s after the introduction of the world's first financial futures contracts (foreign currency futures) by the Chicago Mercantile Exchange in 1972. The first published

academic research on the performance of managed futures appeared in the 1980s. Researchers who adopted similar performance metrics to assess managed futures in different time periods also reach similar conclusions as earlier studies about the benefits of managed futures. Some recent studies address the issues of performance persistence and market-timing ability of managed futures traders. Following the onset of the financial crisis of 2007–2008, researchers also reassessed the diversification benefits of managed futures and the low correlations of their returns with those of stocks and bonds. Evidence reaffirms that the favorable characteristics of managed futures investments are useful for investors looking for a "crisis alpha" for their portfolios in periods with high market volatility.

Part V. Hedge Funds

Hedge funds encompass a wide variety of strategies that run the gamut from those that alter systematic risk exposure to those that focus exclusively on mispricing by eliminating systematic risk altogether. Chapter 23 offers an overall introduction to hedge funds, explaining the dynamics of the markets in which they operate and biases associated with performance measurement. Chapter 24 focuses on the performance of various hedge fund strategies, indicating that adding hedge funds to traditional portfolios offers enhanced returns and reduced risk. Chapter 25 presents risk management measures in assessing the complex risk exposures undertaken by hedge funds. Chapter 26 discusses the role hedge funds may have played in the financial crisis of 2007–2008 and the regulatory framework in which hedge funds operate. Chapter 27 introduces replication strategies as a basis of mimicking the dynamic nature of hedge fund strategies. Chapter 28 explores the tradeoff of the benefits of managerial expertise in creating these funds with the added expense of an additional layer of fees.

Chapter 23 Investing in Hedge Funds (Hunter Holzhauer)

This chapter provides an introduction to the extensive field of hedge fund investing, which has grown over the last 60 years to become a major influence on the financial markets. As this influence grows, new pillars of empirical research are raised to shine more light on the hedge fund industry from every angle, including performance, risk management, market impact, and fund of funds strategies. Detailed analysis of each area of empirical research can be found in the following chapter. However, to firmly support these pillars of research, this chapter builds a solid foundation based upon the history and purpose of hedge funds. Thus, this chapter builds upon more foundational themes for hedge funds, including their structure, history, data biases, strategies, and future.

Chapter 24 Performance of Hedge Funds (Dianna Preece)

Hedge funds pool private capital and engage in a wide range of investment and trading activities. Fund managers take long and short positions and use leverage and derivatives to accomplish the return objectives of the fund. Actions of fund managers, rather than those of market forces, tend to drive hedge fund returns. Funds are limited to accredited investors who generally are high-net-worth individuals and institutional investors. Substantial research examines hedge funds during the last 15 years. Studies show that hedge funds have negatively skewed returns with positive excess kurtosis. Hedge fund returns exhibit low correlation with stock and bond returns, making them an attractive addition to a portfolio of traditional assets. Studies also indicate that adding hedge funds to portfolios of traditional assets tends to reduce risk and increase returns.

Chapter 25 Hedge Funds and Risk Management (Theodore Syriopoulos)

Hedge funds have exhibited not only fast growth rates and increased assets under management but also losses and failures. The dynamic investment strategies employed and the complex risk exposures undertaken have turned the issue of efficient risk management into a critical priority. This chapter contributes a concise discussion and critical evaluation of the advantages and limitations of the most appropriate risk tools to apply to hedge funds, such as the variance-based approach, value-at-risk, expected shortfall, extreme value theory, tail analysis, and generalized Pareto distribution. The empirical approaches most widely employed to calculate risk measures are also introduced, including parametric models, Monte Carlo and historical simulations, scenario analysis, stress tests, and copulas.

Chapter 26 Hedge Funds and the Financial Crisis (Jing-Zhi Huang and Ying Wang)

Hedge funds suffered their worst year on record in 2008, during the financial crisis of 2007–2008. Yet, the crisis brought more attention to the so-called shadow banking system, which includes hedge funds among other players. This chapter focuses on two important issues that received extensive coverage in the wake of the financial crisis: the role of hedge funds in the crisis and the regulation of hedge funds. In particular, this chapter reviews recent studies that examine trading activities of hedge funds during the crisis and also reports some recent developments on how to extract the information about systemic risk from hedge funds.

Chapter 27 Hedge Funds: Replication and Nonlinearities (Mikhail Tupitsyn and Paul Lajbcygier)

Hedge funds were once considered to derive returns only from managers' superior skill for security selection and market timing as well as their ability to find and quickly exploit arbitrage opportunities in the market. Recently, researchers have challenged this view when academic studies revealed that a large part of hedge fund returns stems from systematic risk premiums rather than abnormal performance or alpha. As a result of the revelation that an alternative beta exists and drives hedge fund returns, many researchers have been motivated to determine if hedge fund returns can be replicated inexpensively, similar to index fund replication, such as Vanguard's S&P 500 product. So far, researchers have proposed several approaches to replication. However, the task is still a work-in-progress in terms of successful implementation. Hedge funds' dynamic investment strategies and flexibility to trade derivatives lead to complex nonlinear exposures to systematic risk, which existing linear models fail to capture. Until these nonlinear features are taken into account, any replication model is unlikely to succeed and evolve into a viable alternative to direct hedge fund investing. Therefore, this chapter introduces a new nonlinear model of hedge fund returns that paves the way toward nonlinear replication.

Chapter 28 Fund of Funds: A Tale of Two Fees (Kartik Patel)
The role of a hedge fund asset class in institutional portfolios has increased in popularity because of its ability to deliver high risk-adjusted performance while maintaining a low correlation to traditional asset classes, such as stocks and bonds. A fund of funds (FOF) provides exposure to a diversified portfolio of hedge funds for institutional investors. FOFs add value through strategic allocation and manager selection to construct portfolios. Selecting the number of funds in a portfolio depends on the investor's risk appetite. Although a small number of funds in a portfolio has a potential of earning high returns, it poses a risk of underperforming benchmarks required for institutional mandates. Selecting a FOF depends on identifying managers with both a strong operational due diligence team and a strong investment team.

SUMMARY AND CONCLUSIONS

Alternative investments include a wide variety of assets that do not fall within the context of traditional investments. This book explores real estate, private equity, commodities and managed futures, and hedge funds within the universe of alternative investments. As a group, alternative investments allow for the possibility of enhanced risk-adjusted performance through the possibility of enhanced returns, reduced risk, or both.

Having a better understanding of the role these investments play in a portfolio context offers advantages to investors, especially when that knowledge also includes investment strategies that are implemented in the private markets. This awareness should include an understanding of the lack of normality and the potential illiquidity that exist within these markets. Some strategies attempt to eliminate market risk completely in an attempt to exploit mispricing, often with leverage (e.g., market-neutral hedge fund strategies), whereas other strategies attempt to provide a hedge against inflation (e.g., commodity futures). Throughout this book, readers can expect not only to gain a better understanding of each of the types of alternative investments presented, but also to understand how their inclusion may better achieve portfolio objectives. Enjoy the journey.

REFERENCES

Amin, Gaurav S., and Harry M. Kat. 2003. "Hedge Fund Performance 1990–2000: Do the 'Money Machines' Really Add Value?" *Journal of Financial and Quantitative Analysis* 38:2, 251–274.

Anson, Mark J. P. 2006. *Handbook of Alternative Assets.* Hoboken, NJ: John Wiley & Sons, Inc.

Chen, Peng, Gary T. Baierl, and Paul D. Kaplan. 2002. "Venture Capital and Its Role in Strategic Asset Allocation." *Journal of Portfolio Management* 28:2, 83–89.

Chen, Hsuan-Ch, Keng-Yu Ho, Chiuling Lu, and Cheng-Huan Wu. 2005. "Real Estate Investment Trusts: An Asset Allocation Perspective." *Journal of Portfolio Management* 31:5, 46–55.

Yau, Jot K., Thomas Schneeweis, Thomas R. Robinson, and Lisa R. Weiss. 2007. "Alternative Investments Portfolio Management." In John L. Maginn, Donald L. Tuttle, Dennis W. McLeavey, and Jerald E. Pinto, *Managing Investment Portfolios—A Dynamic Process*, 3rd ed., 477–578. Hoboken, NJ: John Wiley & Sons, Inc.

ABOUT THE AUTHORS

H. Kent Baker is a University Professor of Finance in the Kogod School of Business at American University. Professor Baker is an author or editor of 19 books, including several textbooks such as *Understanding Financial Management—A Practical Guide*. His most recent books include *Portfolio Theory and Management, International Finance: A Survey, Socially Responsible Finance and Investing, Survey Research in Corporate Finance, The Art of Capital Restructuring, Capital Budgeting Valuation, Behavioral Finance, Corporate Governance,* and *Dividends and Dividend Policy.* As one of the most prolific finance academics, he has published more than 150 refereed articles in such journals as the *Journal of Finance, Journal of Financial and Quantitative Analysis, Financial Management, Financial Analysts Journal, Journal of Portfolio Management,* and *Harvard Business Review.* He has consulting and training experience with more than 100 organizations. Professor Baker holds a BSBA from Georgetown University; an MEd, MBA, and DBA from the University of Maryland; and an MA, MS, and two PhDs from American University. He also holds CFA and CMA designations.

Greg Filbeck holds the Samuel P. Black III Professor of Insurance and Risk Management at Penn State Erie, the Behrend College, and serves as Program Chair for Finance. He formerly served as Senior Vice-President of Kaplan Schweser and held academic appointments at Miami University (Ohio) and the University of Toledo, where he served as the Associate Director of the Center for Family Business. Professor Filbeck is an author or editor of four books including his latest, *Portfolio Theory and Management*, and has published more than 70 refereed academic journal articles that have appeared in journals such as *Financial Analysts Journal, Financial Review*, and *Journal of Business, Finance, and Accounting*. Professor Filbeck conducts consulting and training worldwide for candidates for the Chartered Financial Analyst (CFA), Financial Risk Manager (FRM™) and Chartered Alternative Investment Adviser (CAIA®) designations, as well as holding all three designations. Professor Filbeck holds a BS from Murray State University and a DBA from the University of Kentucky.

CHAPTER 2

The Role of Alternative Investments in Strategic Asset Allocation

DOUGLAS CUMMING
Professor and Ontario Research Chair, York University

LARS HELGE HAß
Assistant Professor of Accounting and Finance, Lancaster University

DENIS SCHWEIZER
Assistant Professor of Alternative Investments, WHU–Otto Beisheim School of Management

INTRODUCTION

Alternative investment funds have become increasingly important to institutional investor portfolios. This chapter introduces a framework for strategic asset allocation that incorporates the special characteristics of alternative investments.

Investors wanting to build exposure to alternative investments must choose an appropriate strategic asset allocation. This allocation choice is ultimately the most critical decision in the investment process because it determines a portfolio's return variability, and thus its investment performance (Brinson, Hood, and Beebower, 1986, 1991; Hoernemann, Junkans, and Zarate, 2005).

Alternative investments typically suffer from data biases such as appraisal smoothing and stale pricing for private equity. Furthermore, their return distributions have higher moments (skewness and kurtosis) that are not captured by their standard deviation measures. Thus, every standard method for portfolio optimization that uses alternative investments is likely to be inaccurate to some extent (Fung and Hsieh, 1997, 2001; Martin, 2001; Brooks and Kat, 2002; Popova, Morton, Popova, and Yau, 2003; Agarwal and Naik, 2004; Jondeau and Rockinger, 2006). Furthermore, institutional investors tend to have different objective functions than individual investors (Cumming and Johan, 2006; Morton, Popova, and Popova, 2006; Cumming, Fleming, and Johan, 2011; Groh and von Liechtenstein, 2011; Nielsen, 2011).

The framework introduced in this chapter corrects for data biases in the time series returns of some alternative investments (i.e., private equity and hedge funds). The method uses a mixture of two normal distributions to replace empirical return distributions that often exhibit skewness and positive excess kurtosis. This approach ensures that the best-fit return distributions will exhibit higher moments closer to their empirical pendants. An optimization procedure is then performed using these distributions. To derive the strategic asset allocation, a goal function is applied to examine real investor preferences for risk aversion. The investor's objective function maximizes the probability of outperforming a benchmark return, while minimizing the probability of underperforming another benchmark.

In this portfolio optimization approach, systematic risk factors, such as beta, are relevant for traditional equity allocation. For alternative investments, however, the focus is on alpha, or outperforming the risk-adjusted benchmarks. One of the key elements of this approach is the definition of the relevant benchmark, with different adjustments to account for any alternative investment data biases.

Previous literature on asset allocation with alternative investments focuses on the effects of adding one investment class to a traditional mixed-asset portfolio. Research shows positive portfolio effects for adding hedge funds (Amin and Kat, 2002, 2003; Lhabitant and Learned, 2002; Gueyie and Amvella, 2006; Kooli, 2007) and private equity (Chen, Baierl, and Kaplan, 2002; Schmidt, 2004; Ennis and Sebastian, 2005). Studies also show that real estate investment trusts (REITs) increase portfolio performance (NAREIT, 2002; Chen, Ho, Lu, and Wu, 2005; Hudson-Wilson, Fabozzi, Gordon, and Giliberto, 2005; Lee and Stevenson, 2005; Chiang and Lee, 2007).

However, Huang and Zhong (2012) are a notable exception to the findings within this literature. Their work shows that commodities, REITs, and Treasury inflation-protected securities (TIPS) provide positive diversification benefits to investor portfolios. For commodities, no consensus yet exists on whether these securities increase investor value. Gorton and Rouwenhorst (2006) and Conover, Jensen, Johnson, and Mercer (2010) find positive effects, while Erb and Harvey (2006) and Daskalaki and Skiadopoulos (2011) find no such effects.

The results reported in this chapter find that only defensive portfolios use stocks of large U.S. firms as part of the traditional asset classes. In all portfolios, however, bonds are of great importance and should be added to the maximum possible allocation restriction. The evidence also finds a negative correlation between emerging markets and risk aversion.

For alternative investments, the results show a negative correlation between REITs and risk aversion. In contrast, commodities have comparatively more stable medium allocations in all portfolios. Hedge fund allocations are comparable to bond allocations because they are integrated with the maximum portfolio allocation into virtually all optimal portfolios. By comparison, private equity is particularly important in defensive portfolios.

In summary, the evidence shows that alternative investments are important for the strategic asset allocation of institutional investors such as endowments, family offices (i.e., private companies that manage investments for a single wealthy family), pension funds, and high-net-worth individuals with sufficient time horizons and investment capital. However, not all alternative investment classes are of equal importance. They are inappropriate as substitutes for traditional asset classes and may serve better as complements to achieving the desired risk-return profiles.

The rest of this chapter proceeds as follows. The next section describes the data set and how to correct the data biases that can arise when using alternative investments. The chapter then explains an optimization procedure, describes the results, and discusses potential extensions to the current approach. The final section presents a summary and a discussion of the results.

DATA SET

Since Markowitz's (1952) seminal paper on portfolio theory, most research confirms that diversification can increase expected portfolio returns while reducing volatility. However, investors should not blindly add another asset class without carefully considering how it will affect their portfolios. A naïvely chosen allocation to the newly added asset class may not improve the risk-return profile and can even worsen it. Against this context, investors need to determine whether alternative investments really improve the risk-adjusted performance of a mixed-asset portfolio, and whether they should be included in the strategic asset allocation.

The analysis in this chapter uses the following indices as proxies for each asset class: two traditional asset classes (proxy indices in parentheses)—stocks (the S&P 500 Total Return Index and MSCI Emerging Markets Total Return Index) and government bonds (the J.P. Morgan U.S. Government Bonds Total Return Index)—and four alternative assets—private equity, subdivided into buyouts (U.S. Buyout) and venture capital (U.S. Venture Capital) (both indices based on the Thomson Reuters VentureXpert database); commodities (the S&P GSCI Commodity TR Index); hedge funds (Hedge Fund Research, Inc., or HFRI, Fund of Funds Composite); and REITs (the FTSE EPRA/NAREIT Total Return Index). Exhibit 2.1 describes these asset classes and proxies. All time series in the study are on a monthly basis (except the private equity time series, which is on a quarterly basis), and all span the period January 1999–December 2009.

The study uses an investable fund of funds (FOF) index as the proxy index, in contrast to stand-alone hedge funds, which have historically higher performance. For the choice of all "representative" asset class benchmarks, a "market portfolio" is used that best describes the respective risk and return characteristics. In this context, this study follows Fung and Hsieh's (2000) argument that a fund of hedge funds represents typical investors in hedge fund portfolios, generally with an available net-of-fees performance history.

Examining the experience of hedge fund investors seems suitable for estimating the investment experience of hedge funds. Noninvestable index data may exhibit biases such as liquidation bias, survivorship bias, attrition rate bias, and selection bias. Estimates for survivorship bias, for example, vary from 0.16 percent (Ackermann, McEnally, and Ravenscraft, 1999) to 6.22 percent (Liang, 2002) across different hedge fund styles and data vendors.

Before discussing the descriptive statistics of the asset classes, several potential biases are examined that could distort the inherent risk-return profile. For example, appraisal-based private equity indices exhibit distortion through smoothed returns, which result from deformation. This phenomenon can lead to appraisal

Exhibit 2.1 Data Description of Asset Classes and Proxies

Asset Class	Proxy Index	Frequency	Inception Date	End Date	Additional Information
U.S. Stocks	S&P 500 Composite—Total Return Index	Monthly	Jan 99	Dec 09	standardandpoors.com
Emerging Markets	MSCI Emerging Markets—Total Return Index	Monthly	Jan 99	Dec 09	datastream.com
U.S. Government Bonds	JPM U.S. Govt. Bond—Total Return Index	Monthly	Jan 99	Dec 09	datastream.com
Real Estate Investment Trusts	FTSE EPRA NAREIT—Total Return Index	Monthly	Jan 99	Dec 09	nareit.com
Commodities	S&P GSCI Commodity—Total Return Index	Monthly	Jan 99	Dec 09	datastream.com
Hedge Funds	HFRI Fund of Hedge-fund Composite Index	Monthly	Jan 99	Dec 09	hedgefundresearch.com
Buyout	Thomson Reuters VentureXpert	Quarterly	Jan 99	Dec 09	thomsonreuters.com
Venture Capital	Thomson Reuters VentureXpert	Quarterly	Jan 99	Dec 09	thomsonreuters.com

This exhibit reports the proxy indices for each asset class. The frequencies, inception dates, end dates, and additional information sources are given for the proxy time series.

Exhibit 2.2 Autocorrelation Structure of the Appraisal Value-Based Private Equity Indices

Private Equity	Lag 1	Lag 2	Lag 3	Lag 4
U.S. Buyout	**0.3561**	**0.2945**	0.2178	0.1903
U.S. Venture Capital	**0.6153**	**0.4988**	**0.3897**	0.0559

This exhibit shows the autocorrelation coefficients for the quarterly distribution of returns for the appraisal value-based private equity indices (U.S. Buyout and U.S. Venture Capital), based on Thomson Reuters VentureXpert database from January 1999 through December 2009 for lags 1 to 4. Numbers in boldface are statistically significant at the 0.05 level.

smoothing, lack of quarterly data availability, and/or stale pricing and cause a statistically positive autocorrelation, as shown in Exhibit 2.2. These relationships are commonly seen among illiquid investments, such as private equity and individual hedge fund strategies, as shown in Exhibit 2.3 and as described by Avramov, Kosowski, Naik, and Teo (2008). Smoothed returns can arise due to irregular price determination, overly long periods between price determinations, and the use of book value rather than market prices (Geltner, 1991; Gompers and Lerner, 1997). The resulting positive autocorrelation leads to a significant underestimation of risk and market exposure (Asness, Krail, and Liew, 2001) due to the smoothed returns when naïvely using raw data.

Exhibit 2.2 shows that private equity exhibits a significantly positive autocorrelation of 0.6153 in the first of four lags for U.S. venture capital. In contrast, as presented in Exhibit 2.3, hedge funds do not show any significant autocorrelation

Exhibit 2.3 Autocorrelation Structure of the Monthly Return Distribution of Selected Asset Classes

Lags	S&P 500 Index	MSCI Emerging Markets	JPM U.S. Government Bonds	FTSE EPRA/ NAREIT	S&P GSCI Commodity	HFRI Fund of Funds
Lag 1	0.1008	0.2096	0.1236	0.0039	0.1762	0.0854
Lag 2	−0.0160	0.1845	0.0567	**−0.3224**	0.0963	0.1219
Lag 3	0.0195	0.0489	0.0858	0.1381	0.1258	0.0997
Lag 4	0.0260	−0.0176	−0.1206	**0.3031**	0.0171	−0.1228
Lag 6	0.0241	−0.0603	0.0542	−0.0707	0.0239	0.0451
Lag 7	−0.1282	−0.1060	−0.0681	**−0.2712**	−0.0079	0.0791
Lag 8	0.0900	0.0513	−0.0067	0.0636	−0.0608	0.0813
Lag 9	0.1304	0.0125	−0.1007	0.1748	−0.0189	**0.1839**
Lag 10	0.1732	0.0950	−0.0395	0.0012	−0.0385	**0.2078**
Lag 11	0.0184	0.0160	0.0989	**−0.2226**	0.0374	0.1185
Lag 12	−0.0435	−0.0097	0.0517	0.1047	0.1719	0.0352

This exhibit shows the autocorrelation coefficients for the monthly return distributions of the S&P 500 Index, MSCI Emerging Markets, JPM US Government Bonds, FTSE EPRA/NAREIT, S&P GSCI Commodity, and HFRI Fund of Funds from January 1999 through December 2009 for the monthly lags 1 to 12. Numbers in boldface are statistically significant at the 0.05 level.

in the first four lags because they are represented by a FOF index instead of by single hedge fund strategies. Thus, adequately capturing this asset class's risk-return profile requires correcting the private equity time series.

To adjust for appraisal smoothing, stale pricing, and illiquidity and to obtain an unbiased data set, the private equity time series is unsmoothed by using Getmansky, Lo, and Makarov's (2004) method. This procedure incorporates the entire autocorrelation structure of the return distribution. As discussed further in Cumming, Haß, and Schweizer (2011), this method improves on Geltner's (1991) approach because the entire lag structure is considered simultaneously. No need exists for an unsmoothing parameter (Byrne and Lee, 1995). Next, the private equity return series is rescaled from quarterly to monthly data (Cumming, Haß, and Schweizer 2011).

Furthermore, some scholars stress that hedge fund time series are subject to a considerable survivorship bias that is typically estimated in the 2 to 3 percent range (Brown, Goetzmann, and Ibbotson, 1999; Fung and Hsieh, 2000; Anson, 2006). Because an investable fund of hedge funds index is used, survivorship bias does not affect performance. Therefore, no adjustments are made.

Exhibit 2.4 gives the descriptive statistics after adjusting for the aforementioned distortions of the risk-return profile. The statistics show that the risk, measured by standard deviation, of both private equity segments increases after the return unsmoothing. For U.S. Buyout (U.S. Venture Capital), the standard deviation increases by a factor of 1.79 (1.45). Note also that emerging markets have the highest mean return (1.21 percent), but only the third highest standard deviation (6.96 percent), followed by REITs, with a mean return of 0.81 percent and the highest standard deviation of 7.30 percent.

The higher moments (skewness and kurtosis) are additional potential sources of risk. Hedge funds exhibit the largest negative skewness (−0.519), with kurtosis of (6.728), whereas REITs exhibit skewness of −0.300, with the largest kurtosis (13.162) among all asset classes. Therefore, hedge funds and REITs show the most unfavorable higher-moment properties because negative skewness in combination with positive excess kurtosis indicates that more outliers are on the lower tail of the return distribution and that they occur more often than expected under normal distributions. This is known as *tail risk.* Private equity also exhibits large positive kurtosis of up to 7.183, whereas excess kurtosis (defined as kurtosis reduced by a value of 3) for other asset classes is closer to zero.

Analyzing the higher moments of the return distribution for the asset classes shows that some return distributions do not follow a normal distribution. In this case, the Jarque-Bera test (Jarque and Bera, 1980) rejects the null hypothesis of a normally distributed return distribution for REITs and venture capital at the 0.01 level. Thus, relying on a simple mean-variance framework and ignoring the higher moments does not adequately capture the risk-return profile. Failure to consider higher moments increases the probability of maintaining biased and suboptimal weight estimations, as well as underestimating tail losses.

Exhibit 2.5 provides insight into the diversification potential of each asset class. Hedge funds have a high diversification potential because their correlation with all other asset classes is statistically indistinguishable from zero. A similar diversification potential exists for government bonds, which also have a correlation with all other asset classes that is statistically indistinguishable from zero (except for

Exhibit 2.4 Descriptive Statistics from the Monthly Return Distribution of All Asset Classes

	S&P 500 Index	MSCI Emerging Markets	JPM U.S. Government Bonds	FTSE EPRA/ NAREIT	S&P GSCI Commodity	HFRI Fund of Funds	U.S. Buyout	U.S. Buyout (desmoothed)	U.S. Venture Capital	U.S. Venture Capital (de-smoothed)
Mean	0.05%	1.21%	0.33%	0.81%	0.73%	0.33%	0.31%	0.32%	0.42%	0.43%
Standard Deviation	5.11%	6.96%	2.99%	7.30%	7.07%	3.14%	1.83%	3.27%	3,70%	5.37%
Kurtosis	4.478	2.976	4.791	13.162	4.252	6.728	3.24	2.834	6,91	7.183
Skewness	−0.462	−0.315	−0.001	−0.300	−0.510	−0.519	−0.19	−0.135	1,63	1.441
Minimum	−14.14%	−19.53%	−8.24%	−32.87%	−22.66%	−10.74%	−4.49%	−7.89%	−5,33%	−12.42%
Maximum	10.62%	16.88%	9.46%	28.93%	18.03%	9.32%	4.48%	8.32%	14,83%	23.01%
Median	0.48%	1.83%	0.35%	1.37%	1.29%	0.28%	0.20%	0.35%	−0,09%	−0.16%
25th Percentile	−2.94%	−3.26%	−1.76%	−2.81%	−3.63%	−1.74%	−0.70%	−1.92%	−1.38%	−2.25%
75th Percentile	3.15%	6.07%	2.10%	4.69%	5.79%	1.96%	1.55%	2.49%	1.38%	2.37%
LPM	1.96%	2.24%	1.01%	2.08%	2.44%	1.04%	0.56%	1.14%	0.97%	1.58%
CVaR	−11.03%	−14.06%	−5.48%	−17.96%	−14.94%	−6.02%	−3.83%	−6.77%	−5.07%	−8.78%
MaxDD	61.58%	56.08%	24.51%	69.36%	62.39%	24.18%	34.33%	43.83%	63.29%	69.85%
Jarque-Bera	16,707***	2,189	17,646***	569,887***	14,337***	82,390***	1.085	0,556	142.293***	141,932***

***, **, and * indicate statistical significance at the 0.01, 0.05, and 0.10 levels, respectively, based on monthly returns.

This exhibit shows the mean, monthly standard deviation, skewness, kurtosis, minimum, maximum, median, 25th percentile, 75th percentile, square root of lower partial moment 2 with threshold 0 (LPM), conditional value at risk (CVaR) at the 0.95 confidence level, and the maximum drawdown (MaxDD) of the monthly return distributions of the S&P 500 Index, MSCI Emerging Markets, JPM US Government Bonds, FTSE EPRA/NAREIT, S&P GSCI Commodity, HFRI Fund of Funds, U.S. Buyout (original and desmoothed), and U.S. Venture Capital (original and desmoothed) from January 1999 through December 2009. Private equity (U.S. Buyout and U.S. Venture Capital) return time series with significant autocorrelation are considered after an autocorrelation adjustment using Getmansky et al.'s (2004) method. All indices are total return indices or earnings are retained. All discrete returns are converted into logarithmic returns. Finally, the assumption of a normal return distribution is supported via the Jarque-Bera (1980) test.

Exhibit 2.5 Correlation Matrix of the Monthly Return Distribution of All Asset Classes

	S&P 500 Index	MSCI Emerging Markets	JPM U.S. Government Bonds	FTSE EPRA/ NAREIT	S&P GSCI Commodity	HFRI Fund of Funds	U.S. Buyout	U.S. Venture Capital
S&P 500 Index	**1.000**							
MSCI Emerging Markets	**0.275**	**1.000**						
JPM U.S. Government Bonds	−0.183	−0.044	**1.000**					
FTSE EPRA/NAREIT	**0.648**	0.153	−0.067	**1.000**				
S&P GSCI Commodity	**0.305**	−0.020	−0.102	0.189	**1.000**			
HFRI Fund of Funds	0.157	0.172	−0.176	0.161	0.184	**1.000**		
U.S. Buyout	0.103	**0.292**	**−0.241**	−0.061	−0.082	0.088	**1.000**	
U.S. Venture Capital	0.077	**0.337**	−0.144	−0.127	−0.043	0.049	**0.720**	**1.000**

This exhibit shows the correlations between the asset classes from Exhibit 2.2. The following are: the S&P 500 Index, MSCI Emerging Markets, JPM U.S. Government Bonds, FTSE EPRA/NAREIT, S&P GSCI Commodity, HFRI Fund of Funds, U.S. Buyout, and U.S. Venture Capital from January 1999 through December 2009. Numbers in boldface are statistically different from zero at the 0.05 level.

U.S. Buyout). No statistically significant negative correlation occurs between asset classes.

After reviewing the descriptive statistics of the return distributions, determining a priori whether one asset class is a suitable substitute for another is impossible. Therefore, all the asset classes are considered for the portfolio construction. To create optimal investor portfolios, the model considers the asset class characteristics.

METHODOLOGY AND RESULTS

In addition to discussing the descriptive characteristics of the various alternative asset classes and potential biases, this chapter also concentrates on correcting any biases from the raw return series and explaining their statistical properties. Some of the resulting return distributions are not normally distributed, and thus may exhibit skewness and excess kurtosis. Assuming investors do not have quadratic utility functions (and therefore ignoring higher moments of the return distribution), a simple Markowitz (1952) mean-variance framework will likely result in an inefficient portfolio composition and an underestimation of tail risk.

As a way to capture higher moments, the literature offers several alternatives to the normal distribution. For example, the multivariate student t-distribution is well suited for fat-tailed data, but it does not allow for asymmetry. The noncentral multivariate t-distribution also has fat tails and is skewed; however, the skewness is linked directly to the location parameter, making it somewhat inflexible. The lognormal distribution has also been used to model asset returns, but its skewness is a function of its mean and variance, not a separate parameter.

Thus, to capture higher moments of non-normally distributed returns, a distribution that is flexible enough to fit the skewness and the kurtosis is needed. Following recent finance literature (Jondeau and Rockinger, 2000; Liu, Shackleton, Taylor, and Xu, 2007), a combination of two geometric Brownian motions is used to generate a mixture of normal diffusions. The normal mixture distribution is an extension of the normal distribution and has been successfully applied in various research fields.

The idea of "mixing" two distributions to approximate empirical distributions is commonly used in other fields, such as statistics. In this context, the mixture model is a probabilistic model that illustrates subpopulations within an overall population, but without requiring that the observed data set identify the subpopulation to which the individual observations belong.

Financial applications have also frequently used mixture models, especially as alternatives for modeling jumps to incorporate crises in catastrophe models. They have been applied to such diverse problems as modeling complex financial risks (Alexander, 2001, 2004; Brigo and Mercurio, 2001, 2002; Buckley, Comezana, Djerround, and Seco, 2004; Tashman and Frey, 2008; McWilliam, Loh, and Huang, 2011), risk management (Venkataraman, 1997), asset allocation (López de Prado and Peijan, 2004; Venkatramanan, 2005; Kaiser, Schweizer, and Lue, 2012), stochastic processes (Brigo, Mercurio, and Sartorelli, 2002), and asset returns during crises using a mixture of gamma distributions (Bekaert and Engstrom, 2011).

The normal mixture distribution is chosen primarily for its flexibility and its tractability in capturing asymmetric return distributions, a particularly important feature for alternative investments (Ding and Shawky, 2007; Metrick and Yasuda,

2010, 2011). The approach outlined in this chapter is similar to that of Popova, Morton, Popova, and Yau (2007).

Exhibit 2.6 shows the empirical distributions of the monthly returns for each asset class, as well as the two normal distributions that are combined to the overall fitted distribution. As already discussed in the descriptive statistics shown in Exhibit 2.4, the empirical distribution of all asset classes shows significant tail risk, especially for alternative investments. Therefore, the normal mixture distribution provides a better fit to the empirical distribution compared to a normal distribution.

The next step is to construct a strategic asset allocation using a broad variety of asset classes. Because the mean-variance approach is not applicable, an appropriate objective function is needed. Real-world investors looking to incorporate alternative investments into their portfolios are often family offices, corporations, pension funds, high-net-worth individuals, and large endowments. These investors typically use prespecified benchmarks (Grinold and Kahn, 1999). Standard objective functions cannot capture this relative aspect, but rather rely solely on absolute terms. Additionally, these investors generally seek higher expected returns than money market investors but tend to be more risk averse. Therefore, they are particularly attentive to downside risk because they usually make regular distributions. These investors should achieve a certain minimum return.

The objective function of the investor is as follows (Morton et al., 2006). Let r denote the random return of the portfolio, and r_1 and r_2 some benchmark returns, which can be constants or random variables. Here, the investor's objective is to maximize the function shown in Equation 2.1:

$$\Pr(r > r_1) - \lambda \Pr(r < r_2) \tag{2.1}$$

In other words, the investor wants to maximize the probability of outperforming some benchmark return while minimizing the probability of underperforming the other benchmark return. Thus, the first benchmark could be a constant, for example, 10 percent annually, or a random return of some other index, such as the S&P 500 Index, as the market return. The second benchmark is usually chosen to be 0 percent, the risk-free rate, or a government bond yield. The analysis defines the first benchmark as a constant 8 percent annually and the second as 0 percent. For reasons of robustness, two stochastic benchmarks are assumed instead: the Treasury-bill rate and the Barclays Capital Aggregate Bond Index. The results remain qualitatively stable.

The term λ is a positive constant, representing the trade-off between the two objectives. λ has a negative correlation with investor risk aversion. In other words, as λ increases, investors become less aggressive (and their risk aversion increases) because they weight the second objective more heavily and are more concerned about losses than gains. Similar to the relative risk aversion coefficient found in canonical utility functions, plausible values of λ lie between 1 and 6.

Two constraints are also considered when optimizing the portfolios numerically: (1) short selling is not permitted and (2) the maximum asset class allocation (MAA) is restricted to 20 percent. The aim of this restriction is to avoid having the portfolio dominated by a single asset class. When a minimum diversification

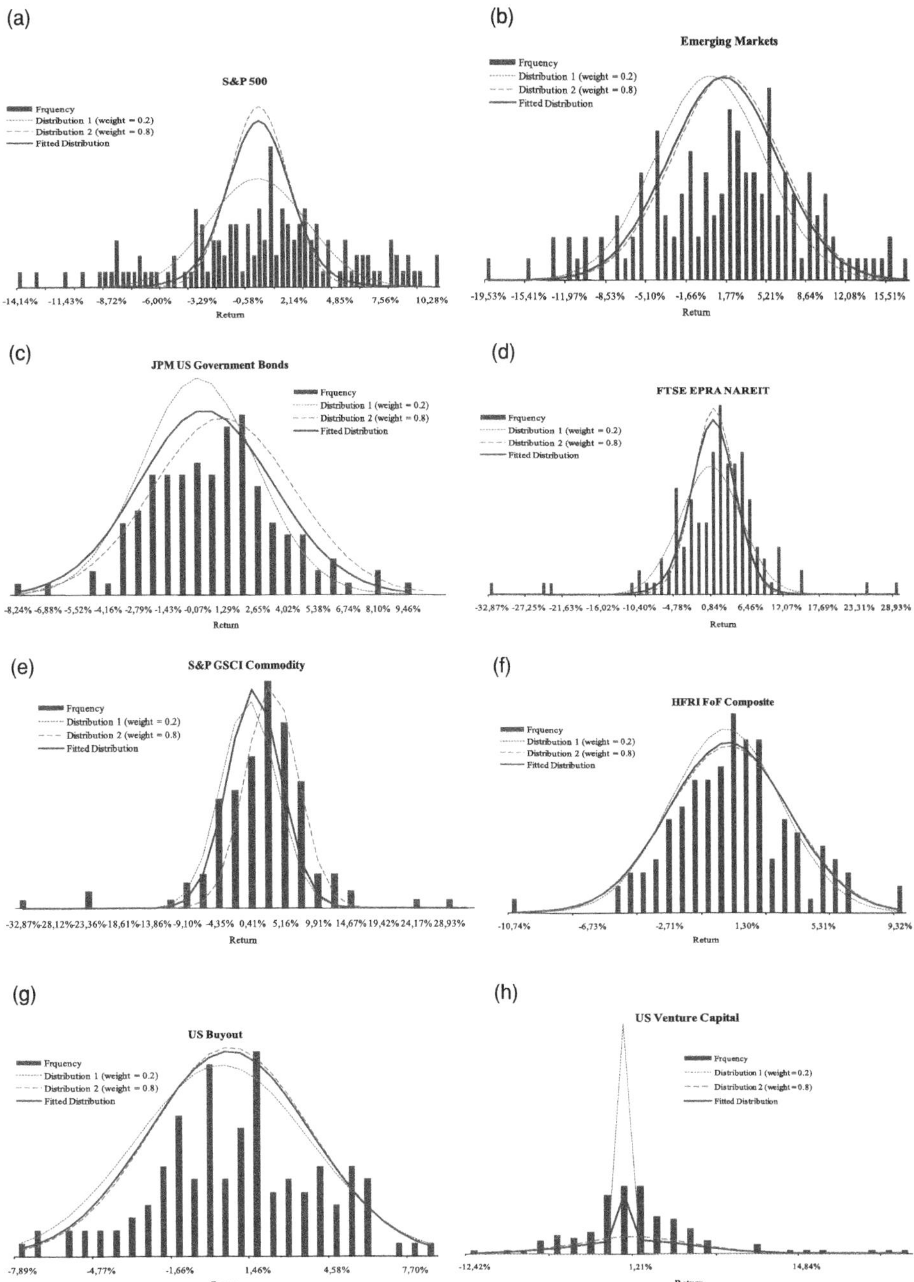

Exhibit 2.6 Histograms and Fitted Distributions for All Asset Classes

This exhibit shows the monthly return histograms of the eight asset classes and the corresponding fitted return distribution for each strategy from January 1999 through December 2009. The fitted return distribution is composed of two auxiliary distributions—distributions 1 and 2—weighted with factors 0.2 and 0.8, respectively.

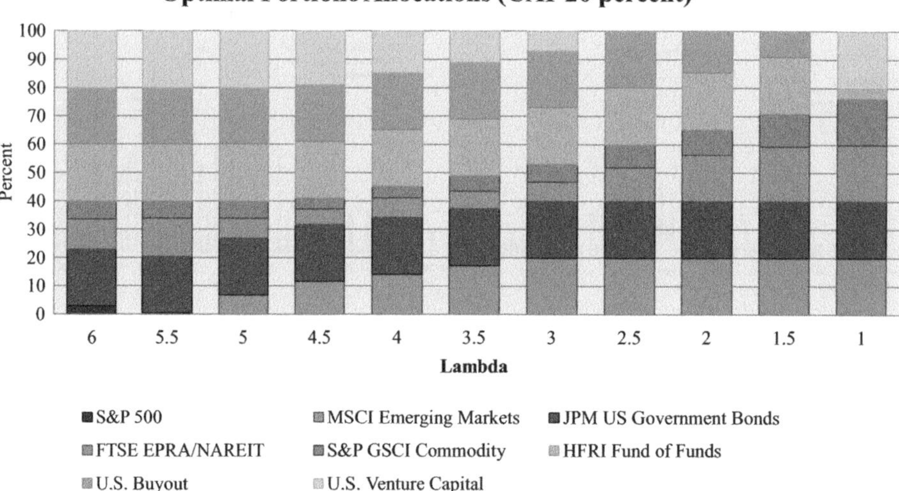

Exhibit 2.7 Optimal Portfolio Allocations (CAP 20 percent)
This exhibit shows the relationship between the risk aversion factor and the corresponding optimal portfolio allocations for the asset classes with a maximum weight restriction per asset class of 20 percent (CAP). The sample period is January 1999 through December 2009.

restriction is imposed, the results are not as prone to optimization because optimal portfolio allocations do not rely comparatively on the past performance of the respective assets. Using these constraints and the objective function in Equation 2.1, the optimal hedge fund portfolio is calculated for different values of λ. All asset classes are incorporated into at least one optimal portfolio, but the allocations naturally vary by strategy and are not of equal importance.

Exhibit 2.7 shows that traditional asset classes and stocks of large U.S. firms (using the S&P 500 Index as a proxy) are considered only in the optimal portfolios for defensive risk-averse investors ($\lambda = 6$). In contrast, stock investments in emerging markets increase in importance as risk aversion decreases, up to a 20 percent MAA for λ greater than 3.5. Furthermore, bonds are of great importance and are added to a MAA of 20 percent in all portfolios because they can provide downside protection for institutional investors to achieve higher than minimum returns.

For REITs, the first analyzed alternative investment, the allocation in the optimal portfolios, increases up to 20 percent with decreasing risk aversion. Not surprisingly, allocations to REITs can vary somewhat in defensive portfolios because REITs exhibit the highest historical standard deviation and the most unfavorable higher moment properties of all the considered asset classes. In contrast, commodities have a comparatively stable allocation in all portfolios of between 6 percent and 15 percent.

Hedge fund allocations are comparable to those of bonds because they are integrated into all optimal portfolios at a 20 percent allocation (except for $\lambda = 1$). Private equity is also very important, especially in defensive portfolios, and is allocated to the maximum 40 percent in a portfolio (buyout and venture capital) until $\lambda = 4.5$. At that point, the allocation decreases, and, for a value of 2.5, venture capital drops out of the portfolio. When summing up the allocations, alternative investments have a cumulative weight of about 60 percent in offensive and performance-oriented portfolios ($\lambda = 1$) and about 77 percent in defensive portfolios ($\lambda = 6$).

The results show that traditional and alternative investments form substantial portions of investor portfolios. This result holds for the sample independent of the level of investor risk aversion. Only a combination of both asset class categories leads to the highest investor utility. Therefore, traditional and alternative investments are not substitutes but rather complements.

EXTENSIONS

This chapter introduces a new asset allocation approach that is especially suited for incorporating alternative investments. Common indices are used to represent the different asset classes. A natural extension would be to consider various hedge fund styles and the types of commodities that comprise the indices.

Using indices offers several advantages over using individual assets (single hedge funds or hedge fund styles/different commodities). First, by using indices, no need exists to account for liquidity differences. Furthermore, trading costs at the index level are more comparable. Portfolio allocation models at an individual asset level must account for liquidity and trading costs because they are not comparable across different types of alternative investments.

Second, indices are calculated net of fees and taxes, making them particularly attractive. Using portfolio allocations based on specific underlying assets, in contrast, requires accounting for the different fee and tax structures that are specific to the particular asset. However, despite the additional complexity, promising advantages are present. Hedge funds and, to a lesser extent, private equity funds have many different styles with vastly different strategies and risk-return profiles. Additionally, commodities and their risk-return profiles also vary. Using aggregated indices for these asset classes results in losing the possibility of combining individual assets to achieve the best investor-specific risk-return profile. This problem can be even more severe because individual assets in alternative investments exhibit higher moments that can be used in the suggested approach to achieve superior portfolio diversification. This relationship is also true for derivative securities, which may be worth considering in future extensions of the current approach.

Another promising avenue for extending the present approach is the introduction of dynamics. Incorporating higher moments in dynamic asset allocation models and using a dynamic objective function are both potentially exciting areas for future research.

SUMMARY AND CONCLUSIONS

Although investors use Markowitz's (1952) classic mean-variance approach for strategic asset allocation, it fails to capture further risk factors, such as skewness and kurtosis. This drawback becomes important when considering alternative investments because the return distributions of hedge fund strategies are usually not normally distributed. This can lead to nonoptimal strategic allocation suggestions.

This chapter introduces a mixture of traditional methods, which are more flexible ways to individually incorporate the higher moments of different alternative investment return distributions. These distributions are used to determine strategic asset allocations for investors with differing degrees of risk aversion and preferences. The method discussed in this chapter also incorporates stochastic and static benchmarks.

In the proposed portfolio optimization approach, systematic risk factors such as beta are relevant for traditional equity allocation. For alternative investments, however, the focus is on alpha, or outperforming risk-adjusted benchmarks. Key components of the approach are defining the relevant benchmark and using different adjustments to account for the data biases that are inherent in alternative investments.

Moreover, in the proposed method, investors choose one benchmark to outperform while simultaneously choosing a second benchmark for minimum acceptable performance. After defining the goal function, the optimization problem is solved for a set of risk parameters and very stable portfolio allocations are obtained, regardless of the level of λ.

This approach also incorporates the heterogeneity of different asset classes and individual investor preferences to deliver robust results for institutional investors' strategic asset allocation. The results are generally superior to those obtained with Markowitz's (1952) classic mean-variance approach, particularly when markets face regime switches, such as during the financial crisis of 2007–2008. At these times, a robust and reliable strategic asset allocation method is crucial.

DISCUSSION QUESTIONS

1. Which biases can distort the risk-return profile of alternative investments?
2. Why is a mixed-normal distribution suited to capture the risk-profile of alternative investments?
3. Why are traditional utility functions unsuitable for asset allocation with alternative investments?
4. Why are traditional investments and alternative investments complements rather than substitutes?

REFERENCES

Ackermann, Carl, Richard McEnally, and David Ravenscraft. 1999. "The Performance of Hedge Funds: Risk, Return, and Incentives." *Journal of Finance* 54:3, 833–874.

Agarwal, Vikas, and Narayan Y. Naik. 2004. "Risk and Portfolio Decisions Involving Hedge Funds." *Review of Financial Studies* 17:1, 63–98.

Alexander, Carol. 2001. "Option Pricing with Normal Mixture Returns." ISMA Centre Research Paper.

Alexander, Carol. 2004. "Normal Mixture Diffusion with Uncertain Volatility: Modeling Short- and Long-term Smile Effects." *Journal of Banking & Finance* 28:12, 2957–2980.

Amin, Gaurav S., and Harry M. Kat. 2002. "Diversification and Yield Enhancement with Hedge Funds." *Journal of Alternative Investments* 5:3, 50–58.

Amin, Gaurav S., and Harry M. Kat. 2003. "Hedge Fund Performance 1990–2000: Do the 'Money Machines' Really Add Value?" *Journal of Financial and Quantitative Analysis* 38:2, 251–274.

Anson, Mark J. P. 2006. *Handbook of Alternative Assets*. Hoboken, NJ: John Wiley & Sons, Inc.

Asness, Cliff S., Robert Krail, and John M. Liew. 2001. "Do Hedge Funds Hedge?" Available at ssrn.com/abstract=252810.

Avramov, Doron, Robert Kosowski, Narayan Naik, and Melvyn Teo. 2008. "Investing in Hedge Funds when Returns Are Predictable." Paper Presented at the American Finance Association, New Orleans.

Bekaert, Geert, and Eric C. Engstrom. 2011. "Asset Return Dynamics under Bad Environment-Good Environment Fundamentals." Available at ssrn.com/abstract =1440226.

Brigo, Damiano, and Fabio Mercurio. 2001. *Interest-Rate Models: Theory and Practice*. Berlin: Springer-Verlag.

Brigo, Damiano, and Fabio Mercurio. 2002. "Lognormal-Mixture Dynamics and Calibration to Market Volatility Smiles." *International Journal of Theoretical and Applied Finance* 5:4, 427–446.

Brigo, Damiano, Fabio Mercurio, and Giulio Sartorelli. 2002. "Lognormal-Mixture Dynamics under Different Means." Working Paper, Banca IMI.

Brinson, Gary P., L. Randolph Hood, and Gilbert L. Beebower. 1986. "Determinants of Portfolio Performance." *Financial Analysts Journal* 42:4, 39–48.

Brinson, Gary P., L. Randolph Hood, and Gilbert L. Beebower. 1991. "Determinants of Portfolio Performance II: An Update." *Financial Analysts Journal* 47:3, 40–48.

Brooks, Chris, and Harry M. Kat. 2002. "The Statistical Properties of Hedge Fund Index Returns and Their Implications for Investors." *Journal of Alternative Investments* 5:2, 26–44.

Brown, Stephen J., William N. Goetzmann, and Roger G. Ibbotson. 1999. "Offshore Hedge Funds: Survival and Performance, 1989–95." *Journal of Business* 72:1, 91–117.

Buckley, Ian, Gustavo Comezana, Ben Djerroud, and Luis Seco. 2004. "Portfolio Optimization When Asset Returns Have the Gaussian Mixture Distribution." Working Paper, Imperial College London.

Byrne, Peter, and Stephen Lee. 1995. "Is There a Place for Property in the Multi-Asset Portfolio?" *Journal of Property Finance* 6:3, 60–83.

Chen, Peng, Gary T. Baierl, and Paul D. Kaplan. 2002. "Venture Capital and Its Role in Strategic Asset Allocation." *Journal of Portfolio Management* 28:2, 83–89.

Chen, Hsuan-Ch., Keng-Yu Ho, Chiuling Lu, and Cheng-Huan Wu. 2005. "Real Estate Investment Trusts: An Asset Allocation Perspective." *Journal of Portfolio Management* 31:5, 46–55.

Chiang, Kevin C. H., and Ming-Long Lee. 2007. "Spanning Tests on Public and Private Real Estate." *Journal of Real Estate Portfolio Management* 13:1, 7–15.

Conover, C. Mitchell, Gerald R. Jensen, Robert R. Johnson, and Jeffrey M. Mercer. 2010. "Is Now the Time to Add Commodities to Your Portfolio?" *Journal of Investing* 19:3, 10–19.

Cumming, Douglas J., Grant Fleming, and Sofia A. Johan. 2011. "Institutional Investment in Listed Private Equity." *European Financial Management* 17:3, 594–618.

Cumming, Douglas J., Lars Helge Haß, and Denis Schweizer. 2011. "Private Equity Benchmarks and Portfolio Optimization." Available at ssrn.com/abstract=1687380.

Cumming, Douglas J., and Sofia A. Johan. 2006. "Is It the Law or the Lawyers? Investment Covenants around the World." *European Financial Management* 12:4, 553–574.

Daskalaki, Charoula, and George S. Skiadopoulos. 2011. "Should Investors Include Commodities into Their Portfolios after All? New Evidence." *Journal of Banking & Finance* 35:10, 2606–2626.

Ding, Bill, and Hany A. Shawky. 2007. "The Performance of Hedge Fund Strategies and the Asymmetry of Return Distributions." *European Financial Management* 13:2, 309–331.

Ennis, Richard M., and Michael D. Sebastian. 2005. "Asset Allocation with Private Equity." *Journal of Private Equity* 8:3, 81–87.

Erb, Claude B., and Campbell R. Harvey. 2006. "The Strategic and Tactical Value of Commodity Futures." *Financial Analysts Journal* 62:2, 69–97.

Fung, William, and David A. Hsieh. 1997. "Empirical Characteristics of Dynamic Trading Strategies: The Case of Hedge Funds." *Review of Financial Studies* 10:2, 275–302.

Fung, William, and David A. Hsieh. 2000. "Performance Characteristics of Hedge Funds and Commodity Funds: Natural vs. Spurious Biases." *Journal of Financial & Quantitative Analysis* 35:3, 291–308.

Fung, William, and David A. Hsieh. 2001. "The Risk in Hedge Fund Strategies: Theory and Evidence from Trend Followers." *Review of Financial Studies* 14:2, 313–341.

Geltner, David M. 1991. "Smoothing in Appraisal-based Returns." *Journal of Real Estate Finance & Economics* 4:3, 327–345.

Getmansky, Mila, Andrew W. Lo, and Igor Makarov. 2004. "An Econometric Model of Serial Correlation and Illiquidity in Hedge Fund Returns." *Journal of Financial Economics* 74:3, 529–609.

Gompers, Paul A., and Joshua Lerner. 1997. "Risk and Reward in Private Equity Investments: The Challenge of Performance Assessment." *Journal of Private Equity* 1:2, 5–12.

Gorton, Gary B., and K. Geert Rouwenhorst. 2006. "Facts and Fantasies about Commodity Futures." *Financial Analysts Journal* 62:2, 47–68.

Grinold, Richard C., and Ronald N. Kahn. 1999. *Active Portfolio Management: A Quantitative Approach for Producing Superior Returns and Controlling Risk.* New York: McGraw-Hill.

Groh, Alexander P., and Heinrich von Liechtenstein. 2011. "The First Step of the Capital Flow from Institutions to Entrepreneurs: The Criteria for Sorting Venture Capital Funds." *European Financial Management* 17:3, 532–559.

Gueyie, Jean-Pierre, and Serge P. Amvella. 2006. "Optimal Portfolio Allocation Using Funds of Hedge Funds." *Journal of Private Wealth Management* 9:2, 85–95.

Hoernemann, Jeffrey T., Dean A. Junkans, and Carmen M. Zarate. 2005. "Strategic Asset Allocation and other Determinants of Portfolio Returns." *Journal of Private Wealth Management* 8:3, 26–38.

Huang, Jing-Zhi, and Zhaodong Zhong. 2012. "Time-Variation in Diversification Benefits of Commodity, REITs, and TIPS." *Journal of Real Estate Finance and Economics*, forthcoming.

Hudson-Wilson, Susan, Frank J. Fabozzi, Jacques N. Gordon, and S. Michael Giliberto. 2005. "Why Real Estate?" *Journal of Portfolio Management* 30:5, 12–25.

Jarque, Carlos M., and Anil K. Bera. 1980. "Efficient Tests for Normality, Homoscedasticity and Serial Independence of Regression Residuals." *Economics Letters* 6:3, 255–259.

Jondeau, Eric, and Michael Rockinger. 2000. "Reading the Smile: The Message Conveyed by Methods Which Infer Risk Neutral Densities" *Journal of International Money and Finance* 19:1, 885–915.

Jondeau, Eric, and Michael Rockinger. 2006. "Optimal Portfolio Allocation under Higher Moments." *European Financial Management* 12:1, 29–55.

Kaiser, Dieter G., Denis Schweizer, and Wue Lue. 2012. "Efficient Hedge Fund Strategy Allocations—A Systematic Framework for Investors that Incorporates Higher Moments." *Financial Markets, Institutions & Instruments* 21:5, 241–260.

Kooli, Mather. 2007. "The Diversification Benefits of Hedge Funds and Funds of Hedge Funds." *Derivatives Use, Trading & Regulation* 12:1, 290–300.

Lee, Stephen, and Simon Stevenson. 2005. "The Case for REITs in the Mixed-Asset Portfolio in the Short and Long Run." *Journal of Real Estate Portfolio Management* 11:1, 55–80.

Lhabitant, Francois, and Michelle Learned. 2002. "Hedge Fund Diversification: How Much Is Enough?" *Journal of Alternative Investments* 5:3, 23–49.

Liang, Bing. 2002. "Hedge Funds, Fund of Funds, and Commodity Trading Advisors." Working Paper, Case Western Reserve University.

Liu, Xiaoquan, Mark Shackleton, Stephen Taylor, and Xinzhong Xu. 2007. "Closed-Form Transformations from Risk-Neutral to Real-World Distributions." *Journal of Banking and Finance* 31:5, 1501–1520.

López de Prado, Marcos M., and Achim Peijan. 2004. "Measuring Loss Potential of Hedge Fund Strategies." *Journal of Alternative Investments* 7:1, 7–31.

Markowitz, Harry M. 1952. "Portfolio Selection." *Journal of Finance* 7:1, 77–91.

Martin, George. 2001. "Making Sense of Hedge Fund Returns: A New Approach." In Emmanuel Acar, ed., *Added Value in Financial Institutions: Risk or Return*, 166–182. New York: Prentice-Hall.

McWilliam, Noel, Kar-Wei Loh, and Huan Huang. 2011. "Incorporating Multidimensional Tail-dependencies in the Valuation of Credit Derivatives." *Quantitative Finance*, 11:12, 1803–1814.

Metrick, Andrew, and Ayako A. Yasuda. 2010. "The Economics of Private Equity Funds." *Review of Financial Studies* 23:6, 2303–2341.

Metrick, Andrew, and Ayako A. Yasuda. 2011. "Venture Capital and Other Private Equity: A Survey." *European Financial Management* 17:4, 619–664.

Morton, David P., Elmira Popova, and Ivilina Popova. 2006. "Efficient Fund of Hedge Funds Construction under Downside Risk Measures." *Journal of Banking & Finance* 30:2, 503–518.

NAREIT. 2002. "Diversification Benefits of REITs: An Analysis by Ibbotson Associates." Available at nareit.com.

Nielsen, Kasper M. 2011. "The Return to Direct Investment in Private Firms: New Evidence on the Private Equity Premium Puzzle." *European Financial Management* 17:3, 436–463.

Popova, Ivilina, David P. Morton, Elmira Popova, and Jot Yau. 2003. "Optimal Hedge Fund Allocation with Asymmetric Preferences and Distributions." Available at ssrn.com/abstract=900012.

Popova, Ivilina, David P. Morton, Elmira Popova, and Jot Yau. 2007. "Optimizing Benchmark-based Portfolios with Hedge Funds." *Journal of Alternative Investments* 10:1, 35–55.

Schmidt, Daniel M. 2004. "Private Equity-, Stock- and Mixed-Asset Portfolios: A Bootstrap Approach to Determine Performance Characteristics, Diversification Benefits and Optimal Portfolio Allocations." Working Paper, Center of Private Equity Research.

Tashman, Adam, and Robert Frey. 2008. "Modeling Risk in Arbitrage Strategies Using Finite Mixtures." *Quantitative Finance* 9:5, 495–503.

Venkataraman, Subu. 1997. "Value at Risk for a Mixture of Normal Distributions: The Use of Quasi-Bayesian Estimation Techniques." *Economic Perspectives* 3:1, 2–13.

Venkatramanan, Aanand. 2005. "American Spread Option Pricing." Working Paper, University of Reading.

ABOUT THE AUTHORS

Douglas Cumming, CFA, is a Professor of Finance and Entrepreneurship and the Ontario Research Chair at the Schulich School of Business, York University. His research interests include entrepreneurship, entrepreneurial finance, venture capital, private equity, IPOs, law and finance, market surveillance, and hedge funds. He is a coeditor of *Entrepreneurship Theory and Practice*. He has published 80 articles in leading refereed academic journals since completing his JD/PhD in 1999, including papers in the *Journal of Financial Economics*, *Review of Financial Studies*, *Journal of Banking and Finance*, *Journal of International Business Studies*, and the *Economic Journal*, among others. He is also the coauthor of books with Elsevier (2009) and Oxford University Press (2012), and editor of two handbooks with John Wiley & Sons (2010), three handbooks with Oxford University Press (2012), and two handbooks with Springer (2012). He has consulted for private and governmental organizations in North America, Europe, and Australasia.

Lars Helge Haß is Assistant Professor of Accounting and Finance at Lancaster University Management School, Lancaster University (United Kingdom). His research interests include asset allocation, alternative investments, asset pricing, and market-based accounting research. He has published in *European Financial Management*, *International Review of Financial Analysis*, and the *Journal of Real Estate Finance and Economics*. He holds a PhD in finance from WHU–Otto Beisheim School of Management, as well as master's degrees in computer science (RWTH Aachen University), business administration (University of Hagen), and economics (University of Hagen).

Denis Schweizer is Assistant Professor of Alternative Investments at WHU–Otto Beisheim School of Management. His research interests include alternative investments and their economic consequences. He has published in such journals as *European Financial Management*, *International Journal of Theoretical and Applied Finance*, and *Journal of Corporate Finance*. From September 2011 until January 2012, he was a visiting scholar at New York University. Before joining WHU, he studied business administration at the University of Frankfurt am Main and worked for UBS Investment Bank and as a research assistant at European Business School (EBS). He received a PhD from the European Business School (EBS).

ACKNOWLEDGMENTS

This work has benefited greatly from comments from John Doukas, Greg N. Gregoriou, Dieter G. Kaiser, Harry M. Kat, Lutz Johanning, Christian Koziol, Rainer Lauterbach, Michael McDonald, Mark Mietzner, Juliane Proelss, and Maximilian Trossbach. We are very grateful to the editors, H. Kent Baker and Greg Filbeck, for very useful comments and suggestions. An earlier version of this work appears as Douglas Cumming, Lars Helge Haß, and Denis Schweizer (2012), "Strategic Asset Allocation and the Role of Alternative Investments," *European Financial Management*.

CHAPTER 3

Trends in Alternative Investments

ERIK BENRUD
Clinical Professor of Finance, LeBow School of Business, Drexel University

INTRODUCTION

> If you can look into the seeds of time
> And say which grain will grow and which will not,
> Speak then to me, who neither beg nor fear
> Your favors nor your hate.
>
> —Shakespeare, 1986, I. iii. 58–61

Such is the request made to supernatural apparitions by Banquo, a fellow nobleman of the title character in Shakespeare's *Macbeth,* after a bloody battle. The apparitions respond by saying Banquo will be great and not great and happy and not happy. Similarly, this chapter reports on trends in alternative investments that offer forecasts with both positive and negative implications. The main theme is that the financial crisis of 2007–2008 brought about many changes, which over a period of years have led to a new equilibrium between investors and the institutions in the alternative investment markets. In some instances, those changes may be described as a maturing process. The new equilibrium is setting the course for future trends, which include a higher level of responsiveness by financial institutions to the demands of clients in terms of services and products. However, it may also include costs in terms of lower returns and reduced opportunities for diversification.

The alternative investment market is diverse, and the trends are different for each sector in that market. Also, some markets predate others, and each is in its own state of development. Real estate has been around for millennia, for example, and changes in that market reflect changes not only in the tastes of investors but also in the trends in the needs of the end users, such as the increased demand for rental units relative to single-family homes. Commodity markets are also ancient; for example, a sophisticated futures exchange appeared as early as the eighteenth century in Japan (Schaede, 1989). Yet, in response to investor demands, institutions are offering new commodity indices (MarketWatch, 2012). Private equity has been an investment category since the early days of capitalism. Yet, in the past decade, private equity fund managers have accommodated the demands of investors with the development of the club deal and the secondary buyout model (Anson, 2006). Whether the term *maturing process* applies in all cases, one common feature in most markets is the offering of new products as part of the financial industry's recognition that being responsive to investors' demands is crucial to keeping capital invested.

Real estate, commodities, and private equity are certainly important sectors. Consistent with the case of the relative investment weights in most portfolios of alternative investments, this chapter devotes the largest allocation to hedge funds for several reasons. First, the hedge fund market is the youngest of the sectors and has recently experienced important changes. Many of the changes in the hedge fund market are representative of the changes in the other markets. Second, developments in the hedge fund market tend to be much more prominent in the media. Surveys of participants in alternative investment markets tend to focus on hedge funds, and the analysis of recent surveys is an essential part of any assessment of current and future trends.

This chapter includes information from several published surveys. Other sources of information include summaries of survey results that appear in the news and other types of reports. News reports also provide information concerning changes in regulations, estimates of capital flows and amounts invested, returns on indices, and the developments of new products. In order to acquire the most recent information, this chapter relies partially on Internet sources. Most of the cited Internet sources are associated with widely recognized news organizations such as *The Wall Street Journal* and Reuters.

The remainder of the chapter has the following organization. The next section, which gives an overview of common trends in most sectors, is followed by an examination of the trends in each specific sector. The hedge fund sector receives the most attention and has its own section. The summaries of trends in other sectors are in subsections of the section following the material on hedge funds. Those summaries make references to the sections on common trends and hedge funds. The final section provides a summary and conclusions.

COMMON CURRENT TRENDS

In any given year, reports on trends in alternative investment markets appear from sources with varying reputations. Usually the reports appear around the beginning of the calendar year and make prognostications for the year ahead. The goal of this chapter is to offer an assessment of longer-lasting trends in the alternative investment markets, including a discussion of how the trends developed. Yet, in order to better understand the possible paths of future developments, there is value in looking at some of the more recent common trends and developments across sectors.

Lewin (2011) reports four trends that are reshaping alternative investments: (1) increased transparency, (2) greater regulation, (3) increased outsourcing, and (4) more hybrid investment structures. She asserts that governments around the world are passing laws to protect investors, increase transparency, and enhance liquidity. These laws often focus on alternative investments. In the United States, the passage of the Dodd-Frank Act of 2010 has led to the most significant changes in the financial industry since the Great Depression. This legislation has special provisions for alternative investments. The European Commission passed the Directive on Alternative Investment Fund Managers, which has many of the same goals as the Dodd-Frank Act. Both pieces of legislation are the result of the financial crisis of 2007–2008.

The risks revealed during the financial crisis made managers recognize the importance of a dedicated expertise in managing operations. This recognition has led fund managers to seek specialists outside the firm. Despite the potential for new counterparty risks, fund managers are increasingly outsourcing operational activities for improved efficiency, risk management, and performance.

The trends in outsourcing and regulation are important, but they are likely to be transitory. The level of severity of regulations in financial markets has changed over time. Some goals of the Dodd-Frank Act may not be reached, and that regulation may retreat from some of the goals that have already been achieved. As for outsourcing, fund managers can outsource a limited number of tasks. Furthermore, fund managers may eventually reverse the outsourcing trend by hiring the experts as full-time employees. The other two trends of increased transparency and types of products reflect more important developments in that they embody fundamental changes that are likely to have long-term implications.

Agnew (2012) and Steinbrugge (2012) cite the 10 hedge fund industry trends announced in early 2012 by Agecroft Partners, which is a third-party marketing group based in the United States:

1. Pension funds being the largest contributor to growth in assets under management.
2. Endowments increasing allocations.
3. Family offices staffing up.
4. A decline in fund of funds.
5. Consultants coming under pressure.
6. A large rotation of assets between managers.
7. Larger allocations to small and midsize managers.
8. More allocations to managers with strong brands.
9. An increase in fund closures offset by a larger number of new launches.
10. More hedge funds focusing on the retail market.

Although evidence supports all of these trends and their importance for 2012, some are likely to be transitory. There will be a limit to how much pensions and endowments can invest, for example, and the number of staff a family office can hire. The section of this chapter that focuses on hedge funds asserts that the ability to rotate among managers and the preference for small and midsize funds, which are more flexible and reactive, are indicative of the longer-term trends.

Many of the longer-term trends, such as increases in transparency, the offerings of new hybrid products, and the ability of investors to move more freely among funds, are positive for investors. They reflect an increase in the responsiveness of alternative investment fund managers to the demands of their clients. Investors are likely to have more product choices, more information to make the choices, and a greater ability to act on those choices and compose better portfolios.

Investors can compose better portfolios with more accurate data. Progress has been made in improving the accuracy of asset valuation and the measurement of returns. Regulatory changes have prompted some of the improvements. The Financial Accounting and Standards Board instituted SFAS 157, Fair Value Measurements, which has the goal of improving how accounting statements report the value of assets, particularly those in alternative investment portfolios. Although important, passing such measures is not a new trend in itself, and, just like the laws associated with the Sarbanes-Oxley Act, questions exist about the costs of compliance relative to the benefits. Passing the regulation does reflect the more permanent trend of making the markets more accommodative to investors, as does the fact that institutions are providing detailed guidance in publications such as the American Institution of Certified Public Accountants' (AICPA) *Alternative Investments—Audit Considerations: A Practice Aid for Auditors.* A clear trend exists in dealing with the fact that "Valuing alternative investments may encompass a wide array of methodologies that may involve many assumptions and the exercise of professional judgment" (AICPA, 2011, p. 7).

An increasing number of academic journal articles are focusing on various aspects of the alternative investment markets, including the accuracy in the reporting of returns and value. This topic is part of a more general theme in the literature where researchers examine issues that directly aid investors in making choices. For example, Agarwal, Daniel, and Naik (2009) find that funds with superior performance usually have greater managerial incentives, such as high-water mark provisions and a larger portion of the invested capital coming from the general managers.

Researchers have investigated alternative investment performance relative to the performance of conventional assets. In the first decade of the twenty-first century, for example, several articles addressed this topic with respect to private equity. In this case, the controversy moved from the performance comparisons to the accuracy of the data. Early research provides evidence that would question the assumption that private equity offers most investors the opportunity for higher risk-adjusted returns relative to conventional assets (Conroy and Harris, 2007). However, subsequent studies reveal problems with the data used (Harris, Jenkinson, and Kaplan, 2012). After correcting for data problems, later studies reverse the unfavorable conclusions about private equity contained in earlier works. The attention from the academic community is likely to increase as portfolio allocations to alternative investments increase, operations change, and new products emerge.

The attention devoted to alternative investments is evident in the number of reports on trends in alternative investment markets each year. Momsem (2011) offers a list of the top five alternative investment trends for 2011: (1) an increase in regulation and transparency,(2) more managed accounts, (3) further middle-office outsourcing, (4) growth in Asia, and (5) a reduction in operational risk. In September 2011, *Financial Advisor* posted an article titled "Trends That Are Shaping the Alternative Investments Industry" that identified three trends: (1) liquidity, (2) hedge fund replication strategies, and (3) transparency and control (Meek 2011). Although Lewin (2011) does not include all the trends listed in the other two reports, it serves as a good basic reference for starting discussions and making comparisons because of its detail and explanations. Most of the trends listed in these reports reflect the underlying and lasting trend of accommodating investor demands in all sectors of the alternative investment market. Not all specific trends will be the same, however, and there will be similar and unique ways that each alternative investment market sector develops and accommodates investors.

HEDGE FUNDS

Dramatic changes have occurred in the hedge fund market since the turbulent events of 2008. After massive amounts of capital left the market and many hedge funds shut down during and immediately after the financial crisis, market participants and outside experts looked forward with speculation and skepticism concerning "which grain will grow and which will not." This section summarizes some of the initial forecasts and the actual changes that occurred in the hedge fund market and how those changes have developed into new trends. The root of most changes seems to be the emergence of a new understanding between investors and managers. The understanding is that investors are no longer going to take terms as given by the managers, and managers now have to accommodate investor demands to keep capital invested in the market. Investors have been expressing concerns over fees, liquidity, transparency, and other issues, and managers have reacted in various ways. In general, the accommodation has taken the form of offering more choices, which keeps investors of various tastes in the market even in the face of situations such as the financial crisis of 2007–2008 and the poor hedge fund performance of 2011.

"Considering the battering that alternative investment funds took in 2008 and 2009, it's not surprising that many pundits predicted a long, slow recovery of the asset class, if not its outright demise" (Momsem, 2011). Titles from news articles from that time include "Hedge-Fund Investors Remove Record $152 Billion" (Kishan, 2009) and "Hedge Fund Withdrawals Keep Rising" (Kouwe, 2009). The Deutsche Bank (2009) survey reports that investors intended to reduce allocations to hedge funds and other alternative investments dramatically in 2009.

The capital outflows soon reversed, however, and by the end of 2010 assets under management were within a few percent of the highest levels ever achieved (Momsem, 2011). By the end of 2011, hedge fund assets achieved new highs at levels that exceeded $2 trillion. In 2010 and 2011, the number of hedge funds grew by 500 after accounting for closings (Authers, 2012).

What brought investors and their capital back into the hedge fund market? One obvious reason was the avoidance of a complete meltdown and the beginning of a recovery. According to the National Bureau of Economic Research, the recession ended in June 2009. Although such an announcement made some investors more venturesome, changes occurred on the supply side of the market. In other words, investors returned not only because of higher expected returns associated with an economic recovery, but also because of expectations of a higher level of responsiveness from hedge fund managers to their tastes. As early as December 2008, many prominent managers and experts recognized the new bargaining power of investors and changing environment in which "everything is on the table for negotiation, including fees" (Holt, 2008).

The trend toward an eventual equilibrium concerning hedge fund fees serves as a good example of the new investor—manager relationship. An important and symbolic aspect of the old relationship and the complacency of investors is the fact that up until 2007 only one fee structure was prevalent. Despite the rapid increase in the supply of hedge funds from 1990 to 2007, the typical arrangement was a 2 percent management fee and a 20 percent performance fee. When faced with the decline in demand for fund shares in 2008, many experts predicted that hedge fund fees would soon decline (Phillips, 2009; *The Economist*, 2009).

Eisinger (2011) and Foster (2012) point out that fees eventually declined slightly a few years after the financial crisis. However, the trends concerning fees that began in 2008 have been more complicated than a simple decline. Managers began offering investors choices with respect to fees and lockup periods. Grene (2008) and Terzo (2008) commented on the trend soon after the crisis. Hu (2008) and Strasburg (2008) cite specific funds and the tiers of fee/lockup choices they offered to investors. Johnson (2009) cites survey evidence indicating that more than three out of four managers would be willing to offer discounts in return for investors agreeing to lock up their assets for three years.

Soon after the crisis, surveys indicated that investors had heterogeneous preferences with respect to the trade-off between fees and lockup periods (Deutsche Bank, 2009; Phillips, 2009; Johnson, 2009). Subsequent surveys find the same results. The Deutsche Bank (2011) survey indicates that 17 percent of those polled believed that a longer lockup period is the strongest argument for lower fees. More than half of those who responded to the Credit Suisse (2011) survey indicated that they believed that funds should lower fees for investors who agree to longer lockups. This diversity of tastes is important because, as Benrud and Chang (2011) demonstrate, offering more fee/lockup choices to investors with diverse tastes concerning lockups can prevent the outflow of capital even when the number of potential investors is declining.

Managers again faced outflows of capital in 2011 when investors exercised their new assertiveness in response to poor hedge fund performance that year. Large net withdrawals followed reports of turbulence in hedge fund returns in the third quarter of 2011 (Eder, 2011). Another indication of investor assertiveness is their propensity to move among managers, and managers are letting them do it. During the period of poor performance in 2011, Williamson (2011) and Cruise (2011) report how institutional investors are carefully evaluating hedge fund benefits and that they will move more quickly to a new manager or fund than they have in the past.

As Steinbrugge (2012) notes, the much-cited Agecroft Partners 2012 forecasts of industry trends predicts that major inflows will come from pension funds, endowments, and foundations, which means that institutional investors will still be the major players. Agecroft Partners also predicts that the rotation between managers will continue, because investors will no longer be complacent to stay with an underperforming manager. Investors will still want the exposure of hedge funds, but they will quickly punish a manager who does not perform well.

Investors will continue to show a preference for small and midsized managers that can be more flexible. According to Per Trac (2011), over the years 1996 to 2010 small funds (assets less than $100 million) generally outperformed midsized funds (asset between $100 and $500 million), which outperformed large funds. The Agecroft Partner study predicts that the trends, many of which reflect the accommodative nature of hedge fund managers, will keep money flowing into hedge funds despite poor performance (Steinbrugge, 2012).

The results in the Credit Suisse (2011) and Deutsche Bank (2011) surveys indicate that liquidity and transparency were at the top of investor concerns in 2011. According to a late 2011 study conducted by Preqin (2011), hedge fund managers have been giving in and offering more liquidity and transparency. The Preqin study hypothesizes that managers' willingness to increase liquidity and transparency may have been why institutional investors have remained committed to investing in hedge funds to date and predicts that the assets under hedge fund management will reach new highs.

Managers are not only offering increased transparency and liquidity in existing products but are also creating new products to have these specific properties. The list of such products includes funds in compliance with the Undertaking for Collective Investment in Transferable Securities (UCITS), 40 Act Funds, and replicating funds. UCITS are funds launched in Europe that conform to specific regulations so that they have liquidity and transparency, and they target the retail investment market. Such funds have been very popular. In 2010, UCITS made up only 7 percent of the hedge fund universe but accounted for 20 percent of the inflow and were called "the biggest thing in the hedge fund industry" (Jones, 2010).

In the United States, the counterparts to UCITS are 40 Act Funds, which are traditional hedge funds structured as mutual funds so that they offer greater transparency and liquidity. By registering as a 40 Act Fund, a hedge fund distributes net asset value (NAV) reports at least semi-annually and provides daily liquidity. However, it can engage in many of the traditional hedge fund strategies with a few restrictions concerning the use of derivatives and leverage (Faiola, 2011; Margulies, 2011). Another choice is the increasing array of replicating funds. These are mutual funds that combine conventional assets in such a way that they attempt to duplicate the returns of hedge funds. Replicating funds have had mixed success, and some skepticism exists about their usefulness (Fieldhouse, 2008; Spence, 2009; Haslett, 2010). Skepticism is also surfacing about the fund of funds sector, and the inflow of funds to that sector has slowed (Deutsche Bank, 2011; Agnew, 2012). Apparently the increase in transparency and investor assertiveness is leading to an increased scrutiny on established products. If it is not clear that fund of funds are worth the second layer of fees, investors are likely to rotate away from that sector just as they do from nonperforming managers.

With the increasing transparency and liquidity and the proliferation of new products comes a downside that may have contributed to the poor performance of hedge funds in 2011. That downside is the likely decline in the returns of any asset or strategy from the trends outlined here. Also, correlations may be increasing, which can reduce the potential for diversification.

The proliferation of vehicles such as 40 Act Funds and UCITS represents the declining distinction between traditional and alternative assets, which could lead to a lower potential for diversification (*The Economist*, 2011). Furthermore, managers of funds that focus on goals other than absolute return are likely to see returns suffer. In the case of UCITS, for example, the returns on those funds were lower than those reported by hedge funds in 2010. According to Westbrook (2011), the average UCITS return was 6.9 percent compared with an 11 percent return reported by hedge funds.

Future research is likely to investigate the relationship between the trends outlined here and returns. In the meantime, investors should remember that only so much alpha is available and that net alpha across products and strategies is zero. With more products, many of which make their strategies increasingly transparent, the prospects of harvesting the level of hedge fund benefits for excess returns seen in the pre-2007 era could be dwindling.

OTHER ALTERNATIVE INVESTMENT SECTORS

As noted previously, Lewin (2011) identifies four trends that are reshaping the alternative investment industry: (1) increased transparency, (2) greater regulation, (3) increased outsourcing, and (4) more hybrid investment structures. Each trend pertains to hedge funds and at least one of the other major sectors of alternative investments: private equity, managed futures, and real estate. This section of the chapter discusses the recent changes and longer-term trends in the other sectors using the list in Lewin (2011) as a starting point and then examines the unique and longer-lasting trends in those sectors.

Private Equity

Because private equity and hedge funds share several qualities, private equity is the first sector to examine. The legal and accounting concepts for hedge funds and private equity are similar. New legislation that targets alternative investments will typically have a similar impact on both hedge funds and private equity. As of September 19, 2011, for example, the Securities and Exchange Commission (SEC) has new rules concerning who can be charged a performance fee, or *carried interest*. The rules are the same for hedge funds and private equity funds (Spangler, 2011).

Lewin (2011) predicts an increase in hybrid securities. In recent years, hedge funds have been making investments in private equity (*Businessweek*, 2007). Private equity firms have been adopting hedge fund characteristics, for example, liquidity within three years and no capital calls (FINalternatives, 2012). This trend is likely to continue with the development of new types of funds to accommodate the tastes of investors.

Similar to the managers of hedge funds, private equity managers will have to accommodate the trend of increasing investor assertiveness. In reference to the published results of the *SEI Private Equity Survey: Turning Client Knowledge into a Competitive Advantage* (SEI, 2011a), Ross Ellis, Vice President and Head of the SEI Knowledge Partnership for SEI's Investment Manager Services division, offers the following conclusion:

> Managers are facing greater performance pressure, greater fee pressure, and greater transparency expectations. They have to increase their operational effectiveness if they hope to meet the greater demand for value and compete in the "Era of the Investor" (SEI, 2011b).

According to the results of the SEI survey, 59 percent of private equity firms indicate they increased transparency to retain and/or attract new capital in the years following the financial crisis of 2007–2008. More than one-third of the firms report having lowered management fees, and more than 10 percent reported having lowered incentive fees. The hedge fund market shares all of these trends.

As in the hedge fund market, investors may have to lower return expectations. Reasons for this include increased competition for deals, the existence of fewer deals with turnaround prospects with the potential to generate high returns, and less access to bank lending to achieve adequate leverage for high returns (Or, 2011). A trend following the financial crisis is private equity firms reinventing themselves in the face of the bleak landscape and the lower level of bank lending (Pricewaterhouse Coopers, 2008; *The Economist*, 2012). Despite possible problems, the responses to the SEI survey indicate that investors see private equity as having the best prospect for returns among the alternative investment sectors.

Two other noteworthy trends in the private equity sector are the use of club deals, which employ a syndication strategy, and environmentally conscious funds. Anson (2006) points out that club deals were increasing in the years before the financial crisis of 2007–2008. Porter (2011) and Pinto (2012) indicate that this trend has recently increased despite some concerns, such as the additional fees of the club deal and the ability to manage risk. Although the club deal may fall from popularity, the phenomena itself is indicative of a trend in innovations to offer investors other ways to invest in the market.

Cumming and Johan (2007) state that, as with club deals, increased interest in socially responsible investing occurred before the financial crisis. In the years following the crisis, new sustainability funds began regaining popularity (Davis, 2010). Of all alternative investment funds incorporating environmental, social, and governance (ESG) criteria, private equity has seen much more growth in combined assets than hedge funds (Humphreys, 2011). An increase in ESG criteria in financial products is likely to be a long-lasting trend.

Managed Futures and Commodities

Generally, institutional portfolio managers have taken positions in commodities and managed futures to increase diversification. In times of crisis, when volatility increases, futures markets have historically earned higher returns, which offset the losses in traditional assets. Both the perception of the role of managed futures as an investment vehicle and the properties of its returns may be changing, however, in that investors are also seeking returns in addition to diversification. Recent statistics show that the properties of the returns in the managed futures sector may be changing.

The year 2011 was not a good one for most types of investments, including commodities and managed futures. A report issued by Attain Capital Management (2012) indicates that the low return occurred in a year of high volatility, which is an aberration from the traditional pattern. Determining whether the historical relationship between managed futures volatility and returns has changed requires more observations than a single year. Managers are likely to be interested in investigating this because, as in other sectors, investors in managed futures and commodities are voting with their capital flows. A recent report from Barclays Capital notes that inflows into commodities in 2011 were more than 70 percent lower than in 2010 and were the lowest in nine years. The market has "matured" so that investors are interested in more than diversification (Anjum and Sheppard, 2012; Kolesnikova, 2012). Despite the disappointments of 2011, the 2012 market began with optimism and a positive but rocky start (Attain Capital Management, 2012; Plevin, 2012).

Institutions have also been introducing new products in this sector. In 2008, *Morningstar Advisor* noted that more financial advisers will have the opportunity to invest in commodities through exchange-traded products and mutual funds (Kaplan, 2008). The trend in new products continues. One example is a new commodity index for buy-and-hold investors offered by Direxion. Not only does it attempt to lower downside risk, but it also has lower fees (MarketWatch, 2012). Another example is an increased selection of exchange-traded funds (ETFs), such as the U.S. Commodity Index FD–ETF (USCI), which became available in August 2010. Institutions have issued many other ETFs, which offer more opportunity to gain commodity exposure, especially to retail investors (Dutram, 2012). As with various innovations in the other markets, such as club deals and replicating funds, time is needed to determine their worth. As with the other markets, the trend of being more responsive to investors' demands is likely to continue.

Real Estate

Given the many types of real estate investments, the trends are different for each type and can vary from region to region. As of 2012, all real estate investments are still recovering from the downturn of 2008, and are likely to do so in the years ahead. Most recently, announcements of optimism and improving trends have emerged mingled with reports of further price declines and hidden inventory that has not reached the market. In the long term, people need structures in which to live and work, and more investment opportunities will eventually emerge. The short and intermediate trends are continued uncertainty for the general market and an increased emphasis on finding key types and areas in which to invest.

Unlike the other alternative investment sectors, real estate does not share the trend of financial institutions inventing new products and enhancing existing ones to accommodate the demands of investors. This may be because investors still have a strong taste for real estate, but they are holding back for the one characteristic that financial institutions cannot guarantee in a product: adequate returns. A report from the Urban Land Institute and Pricewaterhouse Coopers (Miller, 2012) says that the stock market volatility and low bond yields have investors looking at real estate closely, but that they are "unsettled in the face of limited property investment opportunities." In general, for 2012, "U.S. real estate players must resign themselves to a slowing, grind-it-out recovery following a period of mostly sporadic growth, confined largely to 'wealth island' real estate markets" (Miller, 2012, p. 1).

Real estate investors are also cautious about most world markets. According to a report published by Jones Lang LaSalle, the United Kingdom commercial property market is likely to see mixed fortunes in 2012. Yet, the market is likely to be better in 2012 than in 2011, and this positive trend should continue through 2013 (Burrell, 2012).

According to reports, the outlook for real estate investment trusts (REITs) is positive. Equity capital flowed into REITs over the years 2009 to 2011. According to the National Association of Real Estate Investment Trusts, REITs issued $37.5 billion in initial and additional common and preferred shares in 2011, which is a

32 percent increase over 2010 and the largest ever inflow to the market. Managers largely used the capital to reduce debt and restructure balance sheets, which puts REITs in a strong financial position for making acquisitions (Pruitt, 2012).

At any point in time, a consensus is unlikely to exist about the single best type of real estate in which to invest. At the beginning of 2012, most public sources agreed that apartments appear among the most promising targets for investments in real estate (Vincent, 2012; MortgageOrb, 2012). As the real estate market continues to evolve from the turbulence of the first decade of the twenty-first century, some types are likely to replace others in the list of best performers.

SUMMARY AND CONCLUSIONS

The primary theme of this chapter is that institutions and managers in most sectors of the alternative investment market are attempting to retain and attract investor capital by offering more attractive features to their existing products and by offering new products and services. Although this seems like a positive trend that should make the market greater and investors happier, negative consequences may result that may make the market less great and investors not so happy. The basic law of economics is that nothing is free, and the efforts to appease investors in the ways outlined here may very well lower returns and have hidden dangers. Yet, on a higher level, the improvement in manager and investor relations could have positive effects, such as more efficient markets and greater opportunities for wealth creation.

Who among private equity investors can complain about lower fees, higher levels of liquidity, and more transparency? One answer is those investors who saw private equity returns plunge in the third quarter of 2011 (Cambridge Associates, 2012) or those who earned negative returns for 2011, such as those delivered by Kohlberg Kravis Roberts (KKR). Another answer is those investors who think that the industry is not doing enough. According to the SEI (2011a) survey results, investors and managers have different perceptions about how well the industry is accommodating investor demands. The results indicate that 85 percent of fund managers believed that investors have access to all needed information, for example, while only 43 percent of investors and only 10 percent of consultants share that belief.

As for the lower returns of private equity and hedge funds in 2011, time is needed to determine whether it is the result of managers having diverted their attention to appeasing investors in other ways rather than just focusing on returns. On a deeper level, it is useful to look back in time to address a more dangerous result than lower returns under normal conditions. One of the causes of the financial crisis of 2008–2009 was the demand from institutional investors for highly rated investment products that paid a high return. Financial institutions went to great lengths to develop products such as collateralized debt obligations with insured senior tranches to meet this demand, and they apparently went too far. As the current trends in alternative investments continue over time, are similar disastrous seeds being planted? The optimistic answer is that the financial industry learned its lesson from 2008 and that the trends in transparency included with the other trends will prevent the growth of a new generation of potentially toxic assets or other such disastrous outcomes.

Also, on a deeper level, at least one possible favorable outcome may take extensive analysis and time to detect. That outcome is the overall increase in connections of the suppliers of capital with productive, wealth-creating end users. Although net alpha is zero and the available alpha to alternative investments may be harder to earn for any given fund, alpha is the excess return above the required return given the exposure to risk. Thus, lower alpha is not in itself bad because the current trends may increase the returns from risk exposure. After all, for a given risk-free rate, an asset with a beta of one and no alpha will earn a higher return when the market risk premium is 10 percent than an asset with a beta of one and an alpha of 2 percent when the market risk premium is 7 percent.

An old adage says that a rising tide lifts all boats. If being lifted higher is good, then all benefit even if fewer can rise above the new higher level of the sea. If the trends lead to higher economic growth, then the story of trends in alternative investments and capital markets in general, despite recurring crises, is more than simply "a tale told by an idiot, full of sound and fury, signifying nothing" (Shakespeare, 1986, V.v.26–28).

DISCUSSION QUESTIONS

1. Compare the choices that investors in hedge funds had with respect to fees before and after the financial crisis of 2007–2008. How did the changes after the crisis compare to what experts had forecasted would happen to fees during and shortly after the crisis?
2. What are UCITS funds? Discuss their popularity and how their characteristics and performance reflect the trends posited in this chapter.
3. With respect to the size of hedge funds, what are the predicted trends in relative performance and investor preferences? What explains this?
4. List three reasons that earning high returns in private equity has become more difficult.
5. List two factors that occurred in 2011 that have important implications for the trends in the commodities and managed futures sectors.

REFERENCES

Agarwal, Vikas, Naveen Daniel, and Narayan Naik. 2009. "Role of Managerial Incentives and Discretion in Hedge Fund Performance." *Journal of Finance* 64:5, 2221–2256.

Agnew, Harriet. 2012. "Financial News: Ten Trends for Hedge Fund Flows in 2012." *The Wall Street Journal*. Available at http://online.wsj.com/article/BT-CO-20120103-706424.html.

AICPA. 2011. *Valuing and Reporting Plan Investments*. Washington, DC: American Institute of Certified Public Accountants (AICPA). Available at www.aicpa.org/InterestAreas/EmployeeBenefitPlanAuditQuality/Resources/PlanAdvisories/DownloadableDocuments/EBPAQC_Plan_Sponsor_Adv_lowres.pdf.

Anjum, Naveed Anjum, and David Sheppard. 2012. "Commods Investment Almost Ground to Halt in 2011." Reuters. Available at www.reuters.com/article/2012/01/26/us-commodities-investment-barclays-idUSTRE80P1NH20120126.

Anson, Mark. 2006. *The Handbook of Alternative Assets*. Hoboken, NJ: John Wiley & Sons, Inc.

Attain Capital Management. 2012. "Managed Futures 2012 Outlook/2011 Review." Attain Capital Management. Available at www.attaincapital.com/alternative-investment-education/managed-futures-newsletter/investment-research-analysis/457.

Authers, John. 2012. "Hedge Funds Have Grown Too Big and Need Pruning." *Financial Times*. Available at www.ft.com/intl/cms/s/0/3ac1846c-4810-11e1-b1b4-00144feabdc0.html#axzz1lzsnYGwb.

Benrud, Erik, and Beryl Chang. 2011. "A New Decision for Hedge Fund Managers: Longer Lockups for Lower Fees." *Financial Decisions* 23:2. Available at http://financialdecisionsonline.org/current/BenrudChangWinter2011.pdf.

Burrell, Andrew. 2012. *Jones Lang Lasalle Property Predictions 2012*. Chicago: Jones Lang LaSalle. Available at www.joneslanglasalle.com/MediaResources/EU/Marketing/UnitedKingdom/Property_Predictions/2012/JLL_Property_Predictions_2012_Full_110112.pdf.

Businessweek. 2007. "Hedge Funds Jump into Private Equity." *Bloomberg Businessweek*. Available at www.businessweek.com/magazine/content/07_09/b4023048.htm.

Cambridge Associates. 2012. "U.S. Private Equity and Venture Capital Funds Posted a Loss in Q3 2011, Ending a String of Nine Consecutive Quarters of Positive Returns." Cambridge Associates. Available at www.cambridgeassociates.com/about_us/news/press_releases/48.%20US%20PE%20and%20VC%20Funds%20Posted%20a%20Loss%20in%20Q3%202011,%20Feb%202012.pdf.

Conroy, Robert, and Robert Harris. 2007. "How Good Are Private Equity Returns?" *Journal of Applied Corporate Finance* 19:3, 96–108.

Credit Suisse. 2011. *Separating Fact from Fiction in the Hedge Fund Industry: The 2011 Credit Suisse Global Survey of Hedge Fund Investor Appetite and Activity*. Credit Suisse.

Cruise, Sinead. 2011. "Hedge Fund Exits Rose in Stormy September." Reuters. Available at www.reuters.com/article/2011/10/12/uk-globeop-capital-idUSLNE79B00Q20111012.

Cumming, Douglas, and Sofia Johan. 2007. "Socially Responsible Institutional Investment in Private Equity." *Journal of Business Ethics* 75:4, 395–416.

Davis, Phil. 2010. "Sustainable Funds Regain Popularity." *Financial News*. Available at www.efinancialnews.com/story/2010-11-01/sustainable-funds-regain-popularity.

Deutsche Bank. 2009. *2009 Alternative Investment Survey—A Closer Look at the Hedge Fund Industry*. Deutsche Bank Hedge Fund Capital Group.

Deutsche Bank. 2011. *Ninth Annual Alternative Investment Survey—Investor Insights on the Changing Hedge Fund Landscape*. Deutsche Bank Hedge Fund Capital Group.

Dutram, Eric. 2012. "Inside the Managed Futures ETFs." Zacks Investment Research. Available at www.zacks.com/stock/news/68391/Inside+The+Managed+Futures+ETFs.

Eder, Steve. 2011. Hedge Funds Face Investor Pruning." *The Wall Street Journal*. Available at http://online.wsj.com/article/SB10001424052970203911804576649030922283532.html.

Eisinger, Jesse. 2011. "Credibility Shaken, Hedge Funds Are Punished by Investors." Deal Book, *The New York Times*. Available at http://dealbook.nytimes.com/2011/02/16/credibility-shaken-hedge-funds-are-punished-by-investors/.

Faiola, Allison. 2011. "A New Market for 40 Act Funds." Brighton House Associates. Available at http://www.brightonhouseassociates.com/investor-monitor/2011/08/a-new-market-for-40-act-funds/.

Fieldhouse, Stuart. 2008. "Hedge Fund Replication: A Revolution in the Making?" *The Hedge Fund Journal*. London: State Street Global Advisors Limited. Available at www.thehedgefundjournal.com/special-reports/replication/hedge-fund-replication-a-revolution-in-the-making-.php.

FINalternatives. 2012. "Hedge Fund Launches Hybrid Private Equity Vehicle." FINalternatives. Available at www.finalternatives.com/node/3820.

Foster, Mike. 2012. "Hedge Fund Skills Have Evaporated, Fees Are Next." *Financial News*. Available at www.efinancialnews.com/story/2012-01-23/hedge-fund-skills-have-evaporated-fees-are-next?mod=sectionheadlines-PE-AM.

Grene, Sophia. 2008. "Funds Slash Fees to Pull in Cash." *Financial Times Weekly Review of the Hedge Fund Management Industry*. Available at http://media.ft.com/cms/17427d0c-bd8a-11dd-bba1-0000779fd18c.pdf.

Harris, Robert, Tim Jenkinson, and Steven Kaplan. 2012 "Private Equity Performance: What Do We Know?" Darden Business School Working Paper No. 1932316, University of Virginia.

Haslett, Walter. 2010. "Get a Grip on Hedge Fund Replication." *Financial Times*. Available at www.ft.com/intl/cms/s/0/21fb3a20-cd89-11df-9c82-00144feab49a.html#axzz1nWxfsJ1l.

Holt, Christopher. 2008. "Hedge Fund Fees: The Shape of Things to Come." *Seeking Alpha*. Available at http://seekingalpha.com/article/109727-hedge-fund-fees-the-shape-of-things-to-come.

Hu, Bei. 2008. "Hedge Funds Lower Fees, Lengthen Lockups on New Funds." *The Financial Express*. Available at www.financialexpress.com/news/hedge-funds-lower-fees-lengthen-lockups-on-new-funds/394401/1.

Humphreys, Joshua. 2011. *Sustainability Trends in US Alternative Investments 2011*. Washington, DC: US SIF. Available at http://ecoadata.com/home/wp-content/upLoads/2011/10/EcoAnalytics_SIFReport_AlternativeInvestments1.pdf.

Johnson, Steve. 2009. "Hedge Fund Managers Resigned to Falling Fees." *Financial Times*. Available at www.ft.com/cms/s/0/26a7a8fe-de90-11dd-9464-000077b07658.html.

Jones, Sam. 2010. "US Hedge Funds Embrace the Benefits of UCITS." *Financial Times*. Available at www.ft.com/intl/cms/s/0/77d8731a-a0b9-11df-badd-00144feabdc0.html#axzz1nzOcgTNS.

Kaplan, Paul D. 2008 "Forging a New Commodity Index." *Morningstar Advisor*, Summer, 26.

Kolesnikova, Maria. 2012. "Investors Look for 'Active' Commodity Exposure, Hermes BPK Says." Bloomberg. Available at www.bloomberg.com/news/2012-01-23/investors-look-for-active-commodity-exposure-hermes-bpk-says.html.

Kishan, Saijel. 2009. "Hedge-Fund Investors Remove Record $152 Billion." Bloomberg News. Available at www.bloomberg.com/apps/news?pid=20601087&refer=home&sid=aL3fOSkanqs8.

Kouwe, Zachery. 2009. "Hedge Fund Withdrawals Keep Rising." *The New York Times*. Available at http://dealbook.blogs.nytimes.com/2009/04/21/hedge-fund-withdrawals-keep-rising.

Lewin, Marina. 2011. *Alternative Investments Adapt: Four Trends Reshaping the Industry*. New York, NY: Bank of New York Mellon Alternative Investment Services. Available at www.bnymellon.com/foresight/pdf/alternativeinvestments.pdf.

Margulies, Elana. 2011. "'40 Act Funds Fill a Gap in US Investor Demand." *Hedge Fund Manager Week*. Available at www.hfmweek.com/blogs/the-long/1682137/40-act-funds-fill-a-gap-in-us-investor-demand.thtml.

MarketWatch. 2012. "Direxion Modifies Commodity Fund's Strategy with Change to Next Generation Commodity Index." *The Wall Street Journal*. Available at www.marketwatch.com/story/direxion-modifies-commodity-funds-strategy-with-change-to-next-generation-commodity-index-2012-01-30.

Meek, Ed. 2011. "Trends That Are Shaping the Alternative Investment Industry." *Financial Advisor*. Available at www.fa-mag.com/online-extras/8682-trends-that-are-shaping-the-alternative-investment-industry.html.

Miller, Jonathan. 2012. Emerging Trends in Real Estate 2012. Washington, DC: Urban Land Institute and New York, NY: Pricewaterhouse Coopers. Available at www.uli.org/~/media/Documents/ResearchAndPublications/EmergingTrends/Americas/2012/ET_US2012.ashx.

Momsem, Chris. 2011. "Top Five Alternative Investment Trends for 2011." Advent on HedgeFund.net. Available at http://news.hedgefund.net/default.aspx?story=12311.

MortgageOrb.com. 2011 "PwC: Apartment Sector Could Dominate Commercial Real Estate in 2012." MortgageOrb.com. Available at http://mortgageorb.com/e107_plugins/content/content.php?content.10576.

Or, Amy. 2011. "Private Equity Battling Downward Return Trend," MarketWatch, *The Wall Street Journal*. Available at www.marketwatch.com/story/private-equity-battling-downward-return-trend-2011-06-16.

Per Trac. 2011. *Impact of Fund Size and Age on Hedge Fund performance: Fifth Annual Update for 2010 Performance, with a 2011 Review*. New York: Per Trac. Available at www.pertrac.com/assets/Uploads/PerTrac-Impact-of-Fund-Size-and-Age-on-Hedge-Fund-Performance-September-26-2011.pdf.

Phillips, Maha K. 2009. "Cross Roads." *CFA Institute Magazine* 20, 32–34.

Plevin, Liam. 2012. "Comeback Kids: Corn, Oil, Tin Battered Just Weeks Ago, Resources Shake Off Global Fears." *The Wall Street Journal*. Available at http://online.wsj.com/article/SB10001424052970203920204577195103805679334.html.

Pinto, Genevieve. 2012. "M&A Activity—Interesting Trends from 2011 and Insights for 2012." Canadian M&A Perspectives. Available at www.canadianmergersacquisitions.com/2012/02/21/ma-activity-interesting-trends-from-2011-and-insights-for-2012/.

Porter, Kiel. 2011. "'Club Deals' on the Rise Despite Worries over Model." *Financial News*. Available at www.efinancialnews.com/story/2011-06-28/dealogic-club-deals-dealogic-securitas-direct.

Preqin. 2011. "Preqin: Liquidity Tops Concerns Among Institutional Hedge Fund Investors." Preqin. Available at www.preqin.com/item/preqin-liquidity-tops-concerns-among-institutional-hedge-fund-investors/102/4174.

Pricewaterhouse Coopers. 2008. "Private Equity Firms Reinvent Themselves in Challenging Credit Environment." Available at www.pwc.com/us/en/press-releases/private-equity-firms-reinvent-themselves-in-challenging-credit-environment.jhtml.

Pruitt, A.D. 2012. "REIT Firms Set for Acquisitions." *The Wall Street Journal*. Available at http://online.wsj.com/article/SB10001424052970204368104577138692466847570.html.

Schaede, Ulrike. 1989. "Forwards and Futures in Tokugawa-period Japan: A New Perspective on the Djima Rice Market." *Journal of Banking & Finance* 13:4-5, 487–513.

SEI. 2011a. *SEI Private Equity Survey: Turning Client Knowledge into a Competitive Advantage*. Oaks, PA: SEI.

SEI. 2011b. *SEI Survey: Investors' High Hopes for Private Equity Come with Higher Expectations for Managers*. Oaks, PA: SEI. Available at www.seic.com/enUS/about/6154.htm.

Shakespeare, William. 1986. *The Tragedy of Macbeth* in *William Shakespeare the Complete Works*. Stanley Wells and Gary Taylor editors. New York: Oxford University Press. 1099–1126.

Spangler, Timothy. 2011. "Performance Fees for Hedge Funds, Private Equity Funds Restricted." *Forbes*. Available at www.forbes.com/sites/timothyspangler/2011/07/13/performance-fees-for-hedge-funds-private-equity-funds-restricted/.

Spence, John. 2009. "Hedge Funds without the '2 and 20?': Indexed ETFs Geared to Copy Hedge-Fund Performance." MarketWatch, *The Wall Street Journal*. Available at www.marketwatch.com/story/etfs-try-to-duplicate-hedge-funds-performance.

Steinbrugge, Donald A. 2012. "Key Trends for 2012: Agecroft." *The Hedge Fund Journal*. London, UK. Available at www.thehedgefundjournal.com/news/2012/01/05/key-trends-for-2012-agecroft.php.

Strasburg, Jenny. 2008. "Hedge Funds' Capital Idea: Fee Cuts." *The Wall Street Journal*. Available at www.efinancialnews.com/story/2008-09-09/hedge-funds-capital-idea-fee-cuts.

Terzo, Gerelyn. 2008. "A Changing World for Hedge Funds." *Investment Dealer's Digest*. Available at http://web.ebscohost.com/ehost/pdf?vid=9&hid=115&sid=7a02e369-afe9-4927-989f-66b96d0a4088%40sessionmgr103.

The Economist. 2009. "Hedge Funds: One-and-Ten." *The Economist*. Available at www.economist.com/node/15955358.

The Economist. 2011. "Yale May Not Have the Key." *The Economist*. Available at www.economist.com/node/18335141.

The Economist. 2012. "Bain or Blessing?" *The Economist*. Available at www.economist.com/node/21543550.

Vincent, Roger. 2012. "Investors See Commercial Real Estate as a Good Bet." *Los Angeles Times*. Available at http://articles.latimes.com/2012/jan/02/business/la-fi-property-report-20120102.

Westbrook, Jesse. 2011. "UCITs Fund Assets Tripled to $90.5 Billion in 2010, Survey Finds." Bloomberg. Available at www.bloomberg.com/news/2011-04-06/ucits-fund-assets-tripled-to-90-5-billion-in-2010-survey-finds.html.

Williamson, Christine. 2011. "Turbulence Hits Hedge Fund Returns in 3rd Quarter." *Pension and Investments*. Available at www.pionline.com/article/20111017/REG/111019904.

ABOUT THE AUTHOR

Erik Benrud, CAIA, FRM, CFA earned his PhD from the University of Virginia and is a member of the finance faculty at LeBow College of Business at Drexel University. He teaches alternative investments, mentors students in the CAIA and CFA programs, and recently helped make the LeBow College of Business an academic partner with the CAIA Association. He is the lead coauthor of *Derivatives and Risk Management* with Greg Filbeck and Travis Upton and has published in a dozen different journals, including the *Journal of Alternative Investments* and *Journal of Financial Services Research*. His activities have won him several teaching and research awards from AACSB-accredited universities. In recent years, Professor Benrud has given alternative investment seminars and delivered lectures on the topic to the business community in Philadelphia and in New York.

CHAPTER 4

Alternative Investments and Due Diligence

GÖKHAN AFYONOĞLU*
Vice President, Investment Risk Analyst, Investment Risk Management Group, PNC Bank

INTRODUCTION

Alternative investments such as hedge funds, private equity funds, real estate, commodities, and timber have received much attention from both investors and the general public worldwide in recent years as the promise of superior risk-adjusted returns and diversification benefits for investors' portfolios draws increasing amounts of capital into these assets. Global hedge fund assets under management (AUM) grew to $2.1 trillion in the second quarter of 2012 from $39 billion in 1990 (HFR, 2012); private equity assets increased to nearly $2.4 trillion at the end of 2010 from under $1 trillion in 2003 (Maslakovic, 2011). Despite their allure, alternative investments present unique challenges that require investors to conduct thorough due diligence, which is an in-depth examination of both financial and nonfinancial aspects of an investment opportunity.

ALTERNATIVE INVESTMENTS

Alternative investments are those that are outside of traditional asset classes (i.e., publicly traded equities, fixed-income securities, and cash and cash equivalents) and include hedge funds, private equity funds, real estate funds, and commodity and infrastructure funds. Hedge funds are by far the most popular type of alternative investment and span a diverse array of strategies. Private equity comprises various categories, such as leveraged buyout, venture capital, distressed investments, mezzanine finance, and growth capital. Commodity and natural resource funds invest directly in commodities such as oil, gold, corn, soybeans, or derivative instruments tied to these commodities.

---

*Disclosure: The views expressed in this chapter are those of Gökhan Afyonoğlu individually and should not be construed to be the position of PNC Bank, National Association, or any of its affiliates.

Characteristics of Alternative Investments

Alternative funds are offered as private placements, which are not subject to the same level of regulatory oversight as traditional investments. Mutual funds, for example, are registered with the Securities and Exchange Commission (SEC) and are strictly regulated to ensure restricted use of leverage, daily pricing of securities at fair value, high liquidity, public disclosure, and regular reporting of holdings. Alternatives have historically been exempt from these rules; however, the Dodd-Frank Act adopted in 2010 enhances the regulatory oversight of these funds.

Alternative investment funds characteristically use a variety of asset classes, markets, strategies, and capital structures unavailable in traditional investments with the objective of generating absolute returns that do not necessarily track a defined benchmark (The Greenwich Roundtable, 2009). In addition to stocks, bonds, and cash instruments, hedge funds trade options, forwards, swaps, foreign exchange and interest rate derivatives, preferred stock, and convertible bonds. They use short selling to take advantage of overpriced securities or falling markets and employ leverage to boost returns. Investing in illiquid assets and using financial leverage play an important role in alternative investment strategies: Leveraged buyout funds acquire majority stakes of mature firms employing debt, and real estate funds invest directly in commercial properties that will generate steady rental income and appreciate in value.

To be able to purchase shares in alternative investment funds, investors must be qualified as accredited investors or qualified purchasers by satisfying specific requirements with respect to net worth and annual income. The rationale of this rule is that only investors who are presumed to be "sophisticated" can "fend for themselves" given the complexity and the lack of transparency and regulatory reporting in alternative investments (Donohue, 2010). Investment firms that manage alternative investment funds as "general partners" (GP) usually charge a 2 percent annual management fee on AUM and a 20 percent performance or incentive fee on profits. A *high-water mark* condition prevents the manager from charging performance fees until the asset level reaches a previous peak. A *hurdle rate* is a minimum return threshold that the manager must exceed before collecting an incentive fee.

Liquidity in alternative investments has two aspects: liquidity provisions of the fund and liquidity of the fund's underlying investments. Managers usually set terms such as lockups, notice and redemption periods, gates, and side pockets that restrict investors' ability to redeem their shares. The rationale for these provisions is to fulfill redemption requests without having to liquidate assets at distressed levels. Alternative investments generally have poor liquidity: A one-year initial lockup period during which no withdrawals are allowed and quarterly redemptions thereafter with 45- to 60-day notice have been historically common for hedge funds. Private equity and real estate funds typically have a life span of 10 years. Additionally, due to investor qualification requirements (i.e., as a high-net-worth or institutional investor) minimum amounts to invest are relatively high. For example, a $500,000 to $1 million initial minimum investment is typical for high-net worth individuals investing in a hedge fund.

The diversity of instruments, techniques, markets, and strategies used in alternative assets allows investors to gain exposure to risk factors that differ from those found in traditional investments. Thus, their returns are expected to be, by and large, uncorrelated to traditional equity and bond markets, which provides diversification benefits and enhances risk-adjusted performance of the overall portfolio. Besides enhancing portfolio returns, strategies such as private equity and venture capital enable investors to access new investment opportunities and markets that are unavailable in traditional investments (Schneeweis and Georgiev, 2002).

Academics and practitioners have conducted extensive research on the performance of various alternative investment strategies and their benefits to portfolios with a conventional asset allocation to stocks and bonds. Although findings mostly confirm higher risk-adjusted returns and diversification benefits, they also reveal higher than expected volatility and correlations with traditional markets for certain strategies. Schneeweis, Karavas, and Georgiev (2002) report that hedge fund and illiquid private equity/debt based alternative investments combined with traditional stocks and bonds provide maximum risk and return benefits in a portfolio. Ackermann, McEnally, and Ravenscraft (1999) find that hedge funds consistently outperform mutual funds but not necessarily standard market indices; nevertheless, they generate more volatility than both mutual funds and market indices. Amenc, Martellini, and Vaissié (2002) demonstrate that hedge fund strategies offer varying degrees of diversification benefits, with some having a higher correlation with the market, such as distressed securities, emerging markets, event driven, or global macro, and others having low to negative exposure to market risk, such as convertible arbitrage, fixed income arbitrage, market neutral, and short selling. In sum, investors must be aware of the unique risk-return characteristics that alternatives present.

Beyond less strict regulatory disclosure requirements, opaqueness of investment process, especially in certain hedge fund strategies, has traditionally been an issue for investors. Academic research shows that notwithstanding the justification of protecting proprietary trading strategies, secrecy can be a source of alpha generation. Green and Glode (2008) analyze how secrecy helps private equity partnerships generate returns. Disclosure of a fund's strategy to potential investors may cause information spillover to competitors, which leads to a reduction in partnership profits. In a study of Form 13F filings, Aragon, Hertzel, and Shi (2012) contend that confidential positions of fund advisers earn positive and significant abnormal returns over the postfiling confidential period. Confidentiality becomes especially important for illiquid positions in order to prevent competitors from front running. Another instance emblematic of transparency debate surrounding alternative investments is hedge funds' secrecy on their short positions. Hedge funds are very sensitive about their short books because a short squeeze may cause them to suffer outsized losses. Lastly, systematic global macro and managed futures managers have a reputation for maintaining secrecy around their proprietary quantitative investments processes.

Legal and Regulatory Aspects

Alternative investments as privately owned capital pools that are structured as limited partnerships (LP) are a legal concept rather than an asset class in and of themselves. In fact, hedge funds, private equity funds, and venture capital funds are legally indistinguishable (Donohue, 2010). A private partnership's shares are not offered publicly, and the type and number of investors that can participate in such a partnership are restricted. Domestic alternative investment funds are usually structured as limited partnerships or limited liability companies (LLC). A master-feeder fund structure is commonly used to simultaneously accommodate various types of investors such as taxable U.S. investors, U.S. tax-exempt investors, and non-U.S. investors.

Recent blowups in alternative investment funds, including the well-publicized Madoff scandal, have put the insufficiency of regulatory oversight of alternative investments in the spotlight. With the passage of the Dodd-Frank Act, the SEC has adopted new rules that require alternative investment advisers managing more than $150 million in assets to register with the agency and to adhere to new reporting requirements. The change affects hedge funds and private equity funds and excludes venture capital funds (SEC, 2011c). The new regulation obliges investment advisers to make disclosures on Form ADV about their firms, products, clients, and service providers (e.g., auditors, administrator, prime brokers, custodians, and legal counsel). Form ADV is the information form used by investment advisers to register with both the SEC and state securities authorities.

ALTERNATIVE INVESTMENTS DUE DILIGENCE

Due diligence is the research, examination, and analysis conducted to evaluate an investment opportunity. The process involves examining investment aspects (i.e., the fund's strategy; historical performance and volatility; portfolio construction; market opportunity; correlations with markets and other asset classes; investment terms; and risk factors, such as credit, liquidity, and market risks, and other risks relevant to the strategy; as well as investment team and research process). Due diligence also focuses on noninvestment aspects, such as the firm, organizational structure, personnel, risk management, information technology, compliance, and legal functions. Overall, due diligence helps to determine whether an opportunity is suitable to the investor's objectives and needs.

Alternative investment shops, particularly hedge funds, have traditionally been entrepreneurial in nature, with the vast majority of them consisting of relatively small teams. Smaller scale in conjunction with lighter regulatory oversight raises the question of adequacy of the organization and of its investment and risk management process, internal controls, and financial reporting functions necessary to ensure investor protection and adherence to laws and regulations. This is where operational, as well as business or enterprise, due diligence comes into the picture. Operational due diligence, henceforth referred to as *business due diligence*, ensures that the investment firm has a stable organization, robust infrastructure, requisite investment and risk management process, efficient operations, and complies with all laws, rules, and regulations, as well as industry best practices. In fact, Brown, Fraser, and Liang (2008, p. 17) report that operational due diligence is an important source of alpha in hedge fund investments; its value lies in avoiding "hedge funds that underperform or go out of business than it does in selecting top performing hedge funds."

The large blowups of alternative investment managers over the last two decades created upheaval in the markets and led to large losses not only for high-net-worth investors, but also for institutional investors, such as pension funds and endowments, which are considered relatively sophisticated. Amaranth Advisors, Tiger Funds, Long-Term Capital Management, Bernard Madoff, Bayou Group, and Pequot Capital Management are cases in point (McEnery, 2011). Some of these collapses occurred due to investment-related decisions, and others were associated with operational blowups or frauds. Adding to these failures the fact that hundreds of hedge funds close every year mostly due to poor performance, the importance of due diligence becomes self-evident. Although the new registration and disclosure rules mandated by the Dodd-Frank Act will increase overall transparency, due diligence will remain critical for investors to eliminate operationally weak firms and select good investment opportunities.

In summary, the nature of alternative strategies necessitates a thorough and extensive effort to make a successful investment decision. This effort must focus both on the fund from an investment perspective and the firm from a business and operational perspective. Without proper coverage of both of these aspects, due diligence will remain incomplete.

Due Diligence Methodology

The quantity and depth of the areas to cover render due diligence on alternative investments a lengthy and laborious process, which calls for a well-thought-out plan and a coordinated effort by a team of subject-matter experts. Due diligence is an iterative rather than a linear process and involves conducting document reviews, phone calls, face-to-face meetings, and on-site inspections.

The search for a fund should ideally start from a larger set of options and proceed to a smaller list of candidates through elimination, yielding a candidate that will undergo a deep dive or a full-fledged examination. The process starts with idea sourcing to identify a broad set of available options and subsequently involves initial screening to narrow down the list to a handful of alternatives to ultimately identify a finalist, which will be examined more closely in full review.

A due diligence project may take up to a few months to perform, depending on various factors, such as firm size, number of locations, legal structure and jurisdictions of the funds, quality of information obtained from the manager, and extent of reference and background searches that will be conducted. The professional standing of third-party service providers is also an important factor: The scope of examination should be broadened to review any third-party service providers that are not well known.

Clear segregation of business due diligence from investment due diligence is a *sine qua non,* as per industry best practices: Each must be performed independently by separate teams with independent veto power over the investment decision. Although investment due diligence has historically been predominant, the focus on business aspects of due diligence has intensified in recent times.

Idea Sourcing and Initial Screening

Investing in an alternative investment fund can be part of a broader portfolio allocation, be it a fund of funds portfolio or an alternatives bucket within a diversified institutional portfolio. Alternatively, the process can be a one-off allocation within a portfolio that contains traditional assets. Within broader portfolio objectives, an *investment mandate* defines the parameters of an allocation, including an investment class, strategy, and target geography, such as a global macro strategy, a buyout fund specializing in mid-market companies, or a real estate manager focusing on class-A commercial office properties in first-tier central business districts. The investment mandate can have other qualitative and quantitative criteria, such as minimum firm size and strategy AUM, minimum length of track record, and minimum team size.

An investment officer at a pension fund, for example, initiates a search based on the investment mandate. For idea generation, investors usually turn to a variety of sources, including internal and commercial databases, investment consultants, broker/dealers, placement agents, other investors, and professional networks. Frequent cold calls from established firms as well as up-and-coming managers about new funds are commonplace; institutional investors often find sorting through the maze of innumerable sales and marketing pitches challenging. Ultimately, the importance of using professional contacts and networks for idea sourcing cannot be overemphasized.

Next, the officer needs to define an investment universe based upon the investment mandate. An *investment universe* comprises the broader set of available investment vehicles in a given strategy/style, such as European equity long/short hedge funds; an equivalent in the traditional world would be Japanese small/midsize companies in equities or a U.S. large-cap value equity fund in mutual funds. The search process can vary considerably from mandate to mandate. For some strategies, such as single-strategy hedge funds, commercial databases containing thousands of entries are available. Professional networks, consultants, and internal databases that are developed over time prove more useful for searches that involve asset classes for which third-party databases may not be as readily available.

In case of a hedge fund mandate, for instance, an investment officer usually runs a search on the predetermined investment universe in a commercial, or third-party, data repository such as Hedge Fund Research, eVestment, EurekaHedge, or Morningstar. Besides strategy/style, a search incorporates parameters such as AUM levels, performance track record, age of the fund, and volatility and risk measures. A database search can also have other parameters, such as domicile of the fund, geographic focus, currency, minimum subscription amounts, management and performance fees, and liquidity terms. Using quantitative/statistical analysis, the investment officer looks into numerous risk and return metrics, such as annualized and rolling-period returns, percent positive months, standard deviation, downside deviation, drawdown, beta, skewness and kurtosis, and various other risk-adjusted return measures, such as the Sharpe ratio (excess return per unit of standard deviation) and the Sortino ratio (excess return per unit of downside deviation). This analysis helps the analyst determine how the fund has performed in the past not only in absolute terms but also relative to peers; relevant strategy benchmarks (e.g. the HFRI Macro Systematic Diversified Index) and other market indices (e.g. the S&P 500 Total Return Index). By refining the search criteria, the investment officer narrows the result set down to a few options that satisfy the guidelines of the mandate, obtaining what is called an initial *shortlist*, also known as a *focus list*.

A search for an illiquid alternative fund—buyout, venture capital, or a real estate funds—may not be as quantitatively oriented as a hedge fund search. When sourcing deals in these strategies, where much less data and information are publicly available than on hedge funds, investment officers often resort to internal pipelines—or databases—that are developed through contacts with consultants, other investors, placements firms, fund managers, and professional networks. Press reports and industry publications also help identify prospective teams. In illiquid alternative strategies, top-tier managers far outperform the rest of the pack. As Swensen (2009) reports, the return differential between first-quartile and third-quartile managers is 9.2 percent for real estate funds, 13.7 percent for leveraged buyout funds, and a dramatic 43.2 percent for venture capital funds, whereas the differential is 0.5 percent for U.S. fixed-income managers and 1.9 percent for U.S. equity managers. Therefore, access to top-tier teams is the primary determinant of outperformance in illiquid alternatives.

In initial screening, investors weed out those funds that do not fit the risk-return criteria as well as other broad measures of the mandate due to, for instance, excessive historical volatility, prohibitively high subscription amounts, or unacceptable liquidity provisions. From an operational viewpoint, lack of independent risk management, self-administration, or use of an unknown firm as an auditor can be showstoppers. The next step is to collect detailed information on the managers in the shortlist. Upon reviewing numerous documents, investors hold preliminary phone calls and meetings with the firms. Focusing mostly on investment aspects, and to some degree on high-level business aspects, initial screening serves to identify a fund that will be subject to a full-fledged review.

Full Review

Full review involves an exhaustive and in-depth examination of all investment and business aspects. Additional interviews with investment team and operational personnel, on-site visits, reference checks, and background searches are conducted. The logic of the full-fledged review is to permeate beyond "marketing glitz" and to verify the information provided by the firm, identify the strengths and weaknesses of the strategy and the organization, and uncover any potential problem points.

A crucial step during the full-review phase is the due diligence questionnaire (DDQ). DDQs help investors collect more granular information on the offering than is available in the marketing presentation and other manager-supplied materials. Although some investment managers distribute a precompleted generic DDQ to all prospective investors, institutional investors mostly use their custom-tailored DDQs.

Document Review

Documents that investment advisers make available include performance data, a private placement memorandum, a limited partnership agreement, subscription documents, and regulatory filings. Some documents, such as the marketing materials and the pitch book, will have already been supplied during initial screening.

The private placement memorandum (PPM), also known as an *offering memorandum,* provides information about different topics, including the fund's investment objectives, strategy, legal structure, investment team, risk factors, conflicts of interest, service providers, fund operations, profit and expense allocations, fees, withdrawals, and tax matters. The stated investment objective and investable securities listed in the PPM must be compatible with the investment mandate. A long/short equity fund, for example, should not be investing in commercial mortgage-backed securities. The subscription agreement contains the representations, warranties, and covenants of limited partners who would like to purchase shares in the fund. The PPM and the subscription agreement must be carefully reviewed both from investment and legal perspectives.

The limited partnership agreement for a fund that is set up as an LP is the legal governing document of the fund. The corresponding document for an LLC is an operating agreement. An LP agreement establishes the rights and responsibilities of investors (i.e., limited partners) and the fund manager (i.e., general partner). The terms and provisions stated in this document deal with the fund's organization, the manager's powers and authority, fee calculations, limitations on liability, capital contributions, profit and loss allocations, distributions, withdrawals, accounting and administrative aspects, and dissolution.

For a registered investment adviser (RIA), investors should check the Form ADV Part 1 and Part 2 and 13F filed with the SEC. Form ADV Part 1 provides information about the adviser's business, ownership, clients, employees, business practices, affiliations, and any disciplinary events of the firm or its employees. Part 2 contains information on advisory services offered, fee schedule, disciplinary information, conflicts of interest, and the educational and business background of key personnel (SEC, 2011b). Larger investment managers (those managing more than $100 million) report their long-only positions on Form 13F with the SEC. Short positions, mutual funds, and securities that trade on non-United States exchanges are excluded. Additionally, holdings are reported with a 45-day lag and are aggregated by issuer at the firm level (SEC, 2011a).

Investment and Business Aspects

Although due diligence is asset-class specific, a common step across all asset classes is to investigate the following investment and business aspects.

Firm Management and Investment Team

Alternative assets are essentially bets on individuals' talent and their abilities to make the right calls. Besides exhibiting investment savvy, a management team has to demonstrate that it is capable of running a business successfully on a sustainable basis. Investment process, research, and idea generation are usually products of founding partners' expertise and experience. Therefore, understanding the background of founders, partners, and portfolio managers is essential for assessing the firm's investment process. Meeting key investment staff in person is imperative; senior personnel's willingness to meet and answer questions is indicative of the firm's transparency.

Investors should review the experience and qualifications of team members, including analysts. Team expertise should be consistent with the strategy; the launching of a merger arbitrage fund by a team with primary experience in equity long/short strategy, for instance, should raise questions. Teams having a track record of working together and running successful funds are highly desirable. Although a newly established fund lacks a demonstrable history, the team's previous experience running other funds in the same strategy will serve as a yardstick to make a forward-looking assessment. Looking at the past successes, investors must determine whether the team follows a replicable investment process that can be applied to and succeed in varying market conditions.

Investors should strive to evaluate the investment team as a whole and compare it to peer organizations. Soft factors, such as cohesion and collaboration between investment officers, provide a measure of how teamwork oriented the culture of the firm is. Low turnover, especially among senior-level personnel, is usually a reliable indicator of team stability, compensation structure effectiveness, and alignment of interests within the firm.

Corporate Structure and Governance

Corporate structure (i.e., the way a firm is organized) and corporate governance (i.e., the system by which a firm is managed) are important from an operational risk perspective. Corporate structure is usually a function of a firm's size: Larger firms have requisite staffing, middle- and back-office operations, and infrastructure, along with departments or teams responsible for specialized functions. Larger firms also rely on committees, policies, procedures, and systems that enable effective operations and establish an adequate framework of checks and balances.

Boutique-style investment shops that mainly comprise a core investment staff and a few support personnel, by contrast, do not usually have the wherewithal to ascertain sufficient separation of duties, independent risk management and operations, and strong internal controls that institutional investors regard as indispensable. In case of smaller hedge funds, for instance, the portfolio manager, who happens to be the founder, may simultaneously perform the duties of chief executive officer (CEO), chief operating officer (COO), and chief risk officer (CRO). Such concentration of critical duties in one individual is a red flag from a business or operational risk perspective.

A committee-based corporate structure decentralizes the decision-making process and enhances governance. Formal participation and signoff authority of multiple parties in investment and business management help improve the soundness of the overall decision-making process. Additionally, risk management, operations, compliance, and accounting should be clearly segregated from investment management and should report to a board of directors, the CEO, or the COO. Such a segregation of functions, independence from the investment team, and committee-based decision mechanisms establish a solid basis for proper corporate governance.

Succession planning is critical from the perspective of an organization's longevity. Larger organizations usually have formal succession plans and rely on periodic hiring and promotions to fill their leadership pipelines. In smaller firms where a principal or a portfolio manager makes investment decisions, investors demand key man insurance or provisions to orderly liquidate the fund and return capital to investors if this individual is incapacitated to perform portfolio management duties. Last but not least, the ownership structure of an investment firm is also material to operational risk. Firms that are majority or wholly owned by large organizations such as banks or bigger asset managers can rely on the holding company's financial backing during difficult economic times as well as the parent's operational and compliance oversight capabilities.

Investment Process and Strategy

The investment process involves strategy, idea generation, research, investment selection, portfolio construction, execution, and exit. The manager should be able to articulate a streamlined investment process. A black box approach to which some managers, especially in the quantitative hedge fund space, have traditionally resorted with the justification of protecting proprietary investment techniques nowadays does not find a sympathetic ear among investors. Specifically, sophisticated institutional investors demand to gain thorough insight into the details of how a strategy is implemented.

A manager should demonstrate the uniqueness and superiority of his particular strategy that is under consideration. The competitive advantage of the investment team should be hard to replicate and sustainable over the long term. Internally produced proprietary research can be an important competitive advantage because generation of original investment ideas or unique methods of identifying investment opportunities will likely be difficult for competitors to copy. An established investment process that has consistently produced successful risk-adjusted returns is more desirable than having a couple of "stars" in the investment team who generate superior performance without following a repeatable process.

Although investment strategy analysis varies for each alternative strategy, common points across asset classes are noteworthy. Investors should have a solid understanding of the markets, geographies, asset classes, securities, and capital structures that a strategy uses. Detailed analysis of liquidity terms is necessary in order to determine how the investment will affect the liquidity profile of the investor's portfolio. Increasing capital inflows into a strategy usually leads to diminishing investment returns. Hence, investors should assess the scalability of the strategy and the methodology that the manager uses to calculate the market size and the strategy capacity.

Style drift is a change in the strategy, such as using different instruments, techniques, or markets from what was stated in the offering documents. This critical risk factor is undesirable because the manager steps outside of his area of expertise and thus causes exposure to unnecessary risks. At least as important as investment selection is the manager's selling discipline and how it has been exercised in the past. Sell decisions can be more prone to investment mistakes, and consistently applied discipline in exiting investments is a sound way to control downside risks. Selection and disposing of individual investments should be considered within the context of the portfolio construction and management process. Asset mix, position sizing, and portfolio rebalancing are important topics to address. Investors should discuss leverage, including historical use of leverage by the fund and the types of leverage employed. Leverage must be evaluated in conjunction with the nature of the strategy under consideration.

For illiquid strategies, understanding the deal-sourcing process as well as the way a manager generates economic value is essential. Leveraged buyout funds, for example, may add value by increasing operational efficiency in underlying portfolio companies or by using financial engineering. Institutional investors prefer to work with teams that have improved operations, and not by leveraging and deleveraging. Investors should attempt to understand how a buyout team worked against adversity to take advantage of growth opportunities. The way the GPs took on challenges in the past will be an important predictor of how they will perform in the face of future challenges. Given the long life span of illiquid strategies, assessing whether the partnership's past successes is replicable in the future and whether the GPs' strategy is scalable with larger amounts of capital is crucial (Afyonoğlu, 2010).

Performance Analysis

During initial screening, investors use the performance track record to select funds from the investment universe and to create a shortlist. During a full review, however, performance is analyzed quantitatively and qualitatively to gain deeper insights into risk-return characteristics of the strategy. The ultimate objective is to quantify the economic value that a manager has created and to determine how the investment would improve the existing portfolio's risk-adjusted returns.

Studying exposure information regarding strategy, industry, subsector, geography, and market exposures will help identify risk factors that contributed to past returns. Style analysis, originally developed by William Sharpe in 1992 to analyze mutual funds, can be applied to a hedge fund strategy to verify the style followed by the manager, notwithstanding the limitations of applicability to this asset class (Fung and Hsieh, 1997; Dor and Jagannathan, 2002). Another useful analytical method is *attribution analysis*, which helps quantify the portfolio's active return with respect to a benchmark and helps explain the manager's skill in allocating into asset classes versus selecting individual securities. Analysts can use various methodologies, such as the capital asset pricing model (CAPM), historical variance, peer index, or factor-based models, to measure alpha, or excess return, attributable to manager skill versus beta, attributable to market return (Schneeweis, Kazemi, and Martin, 2001). If returns generated by a strategy are mostly due to market exposure, investors can achieve similar results by investing in index funds, mutual funds, or individual securities without incurring the excessive fees of a hedge fund. High historical returns due to favorable market conditions or a one-off opportunity do not carry substantial predictive value for evaluating a manager's investment skills.

Investors should engage in a discussion with the manager about how the strategy fared during past market cycles, such as the 1997 Asian financial crisis, the dot-com crash, or the 2008 global financial crisis, and how it is expected to behave in favorable or adverse market environments in the future. Periods of peak-to-valley drawdowns should be evaluated and compared with market indices. Further, asking what mistakes the manager made in the past few years is critical. Clear answers about which investments failed, why they failed, and what the manager learned from these incidents demonstrate the candidness and transparency of the manager. By extension, a manager's reluctance to admit mistakes or elaborate on them is a major red flag.

Another goal to achieve in this stage is to determine the fit of the investment to the portfolio. Modern portfolio theory asserts that a portfolio can attain higher returns with a lower aggregate risk by combining assets that have not only higher risk-adjusted returns but also lower correlations with each other. Investors should study correlations of the prospective fund with other assets in the portfolio as diversification benefits materialize through lower realized correlations. Likewise, studying correlations of the fund with major market indices such as the S&P 500 Index or Barclay's Aggregate Bond Index will reveal how the investment is expected to perform in the face of market fluctuations and whether it will provide the uncorrelated returns that investors seek in alternative investments.

Nevertheless, because correlations between major asset classes and indices notably change during times of high volatility, periods of market downturns should be carefully examined to understand the performance of the fund in contrast to the markets.

Private equity and real estate investments are measured in internal rate of return (IRR) and cash multiples. A distinction should be made between gross IRR and net IRR, with the latter being the more appropriate measure for investors. Geography, industry, strategy, stage, and vintage year are relevant exposure dimensions to consider. When analyzing individual investments, entry/exit pricing and timing, transaction structuring, as well as underlying valuation assumptions should be reviewed. Attribution analysis helps measure performance by individual partner, industry, vintage year, geography, and other factors. According to Meyer and Mathonet (2005), investors should inquire about how much of the previously managed portfolios is realized (i.e., sold) and unrealized and publicly traded. Additionally, the authors also note that investors should verify realized performance, review the valuation of unrealized investments, and investigate key portfolio companies as case studies. Beyond the few top-performing investments, analyzing how the rest of the portfolio fared provides useful insights into a manager's skill in value creation. Investors prefer to see consistently good performance across investments in a buyout portfolio. Conversely, the proportion of successes to failures will differ in a venture capital portfolio in which one or two "winners" with numerous "losers" may be acceptable (Afyonoğlu, 2010).

Assets under Management and the Investor Base

AUM should be reviewed at a firm, strategy, and fund level. A fund level–only view will likely not give a holistic picture, because the majority of assets of a strategy may be in separately managed accounts run by the team that is running the LP that the investor is considering. The manager should provide a breakdown of AUM by investor type, such as corporate and public pension funds, foundations, endowments, sovereign wealth funds, funds of funds, and retail, and by geographical region. Because institutional money tends to be "sticky," the dominance of institutional investors in the investor base provides stability to asset levels and is usually indicative of the operational quality of the manager. Another critical aspect to consider is the concentration risk that may be induced by the investors with the most shares in the asset base. If, for example, the top investor constitutes 40 percent of a strategy's assets, a full redemption by that investor will cause a large shrinkage in the AUM, leading to negative repercussions for the firm as well as for other investors whose investments will become more concentrated in the asset base.

Finally, investors should inquire about asset growth, recent withdrawals, and subscriptions. How much further the asset base can grow is related to the capacity of the overall strategy. Aggressive asset gathering may hint at a manager's desire to increase the fund's management fee base instead of striving to outperform the markets. Investors should beware of firms that show tendencies to become asset gatherers.

Investment Terms and Conditions

Terms and provisions of the offering include subscription and redemption terms, gates and lockups, fee structure, expenses, and others set in the offering documents. Besides compatibility with the liquidity requirements of investors, a fund's liquidity terms have to align with the liquidity profile of its underlying holdings. An example of a liquidity mismatch is a fund investing in relatively illiquid assets, such as distressed debt or asset-based securities, while offering monthly redemptions.

Side pockets, which are segregated accounts that hold illiquid assets, allow the manager to refrain from selling illiquid assets at the most inopportune time and to wait until the markets and valuations improve. Thus, side pockets serve to protect investors in case of a "run on the fund." The manager should explain under what conditions the fund would create a side pocket, which assets may be held in a side pocket, and whether the fund has created a side pocket in the past. In-kind redemptions enable the manager to pay investors using in-kind securities instead of cash in dire times when illiquid assets cannot be sold. Investors should ask if the fund allows in-kind payments and whether it has made such payments historically.

A discussion of the fee structure should focus on management and incentive fees, calculation methodology, hurdle rates, high-water marks, clawback provisions, and any differences between fee calculations for onshore and offshore funds. Fee calculations should be comparable to peer funds and in line with industry standards. Managers sometimes give preferential treatment to other investor or share classes with *side letters* (i.e., separate agreements signed with some investors granting them rights that differ from those in the fund's governing documents), usually in the form of increased liquidity, more transparency, and reduced fees. Investors should inquire to see any side letters given to other investors and engage in negotiating similar terms.

Transparency and Investor Reporting

Expectations of investors for transparency have risen well beyond periodic performance reporting to encompass such information as gross/net market exposures; liquidity levels; capital inflows and outflows; investor base breakdown and concentration; risk and return attribution; exposure by geography, industry, and asset class; risk measures; and even underlying portfolio holdings. Despite known secrecy about short positions, investors expect managers to at least talk about their short books in a broad sense.

Investors should be able to access investment personnel not only during initial due diligence but also on an ongoing basis after making an allocation. Equally important is transparency with respect to mid- and back-office functions and access to non-investment staff, including personnel in risk management, accounting, compliance, and information technology. The due diligence process should serve as an opportunity to evaluate the openness and responsiveness of the manager firsthand and verify findings with current and former clients of the fund.

Reviewing all regular client communications and reports, investors should assess the quality of information provided. As part of ongoing reporting, the manager should provide updates on major changes, such as staff departures or additions, or changes with respect to third-party service providers, organizational structure, investment or risk management process, strategy, investment terms, and valuation policies. Additionally, the manager should inform investors of any legal or regulatory proceedings or actions that may involve the fund or key personnel, disciplinary events, or any material operational issues. Disclosure of all counterparties, leverage providers, and credit lines is essential.

Investors should request risk reports and verify that the risk factors measured are in line with the manager's strategy. An FAS 157 report from the audited financial statements gives insight into valuations and liquidity levels of assets, which should be commensurate with the fund's strategy. For example, a long/short domestic equity manager should not have a considerable amount of the portfolio assets in the *Level 3 category* (i.e., assets that have inputs with no observable market prices and hence are the most difficult to value). In the case of private equity funds, cash flow information of investments in the manager's previous funds and data on current portfolio companies, valuations, exposures, and leverage levels are key items that investors should review.

Alignment of Interests and Compensation Structure

Alignment of interests relates both to limited partners and fund staff. A substantial participation by the firm's principals and personnel in the fund relative to their personal net worth provides assurance to investors that the team is "putting its money where its mouth is." Investors should inquire not only about personal investments of the staff, but also how their investments have changed over time, and whether the firm will report to investors any major change in these investments.

Compensation structures that encompass equity ownership and/or deferred compensation provide for a strong incentive mechanism to retain critical personnel and attract top talent. Spreading of equity ownership beyond the founders to the investment team and even to operational roles will further contribute to overall team stability. In the case of private equity funds, investors look for managers who spread their carry across team members. Equitable distribution of profits is conducive for junior members to stay with the firm and to contribute to the firm's success. Team structures with one or two dominant, legendary partners are not considered ideal for long-term viability of organizations. In sum, a compensation structure that motivates partners to collaborate for the good of all investors is more desirable for limited partners. As an industry veteran commented, track record issues can be overcome by other factors; however, "poor alignment of interest tends to be a deal killer" (Afyonoğlu, 2010).

Risk Management

Besides risks inherent in an investment strategy, investors should evaluate risk management oversight on a firm level. An effective risk management framework comprises experienced staff, clearly defined policies and procedures, and robust analytical systems to monitor, measure, and control risk exposures. Strategy-related risks are addressed as part of portfolio management. However, firm-level risk management oversight should be independent from the investment management function. Ideally, independence entails functional segregation, authority to vet new and existing investments and strategies, and power to intervene and reduce risks in portfolios when limits are exceeded. Larger organizations usually have risk committees that oversee exposures and approve policies and procedures. Compensation of risk management personnel should also be detached from performance of individual strategies.

The manager should identify relevant exposures for the strategy, including market, liquidity, leverage, counterparty credit, concentration, model, and operational risks. Policies and procedures should clearly lay out methodologies for monitoring and measuring risk factors, set the frequency of monitoring, and identify limits to which exposures will be managed. Risk should be measured in multiple dimensions, including actual and forecasted volatilities, drawdowns, correlations with assets within portfolios, correlations with risk factors, skewness, kurtosis, liquidity, concentrations, and Value at Risk (VaR). A combination of measures, such as stop-loss policies, position limits, and limits on market gross/net, long/short, industry, and geography exposures, may be used to control risk factors. Investors should review risk reports, including outcomes of stress tests or scenario analyses. In order to evaluate the performance of the VaR model, back-testing can be performed by comparing the forecasted losses with the realized losses and looking for "breaches" of VaR at the given confidence level of the model.

As part of assessing risk management, investors should investigate the following major categories of risk.

Counterparty Credit Risk *Counterparty risk* is associated with the inability or unwillingness of a counterparty in a transaction to fulfill its contractual obligations. Alternative funds' counterparties, such as prime brokers, and trading, lending, and derivatives counterparties should be financially strong and creditworthy. A counterparty risk management process consists of initial due diligence to review and approve new entities as well as ongoing monitoring of existing ones. To spread counterparty risk, investment managers should use a diverse group of organizations. Investors should inquire about exposures of the fund to and limits set for each counterparty.

Liquidity Risk *Liquidity* is the ability of an investment management firm to meet its debt obligations without incurring unacceptably large losses (Lopez, 2008). Liquidity risk differs for various strategies and instruments used. For example, hedge funds may trade highly liquid securities, such as equities and exchange-traded futures and forward contracts, or less liquid securities, such as asset backed securities, bank loans, distressed debt, and convertible securities. Leveraged buyout, venture capital, and real estate funds are by default illiquid. The strategy's liquidity should be compatible with an investor's own liquidity terms. Gate and side pocket provisions established in a fund's governing documents aim at an orderly portfolio liquidation, and the manager may suspend redemptions to prevent a fire sale of assets in case of a run on the fund. However, any favorable redemption terms granted to other investors may affect the liquidity of the portfolio if liquid assets are sold to pay out redemptions of those investors, leaving illiquid assets to assume a larger proportion of the remaining portfolio.

The manager should present a plan for portfolio liquidation, detailing what percentage of assets is forecasted to be sold over what time period. The investor should understand the liquidity risk inherent in the particular strategy and how portfolio liquidity may be affected during a market downturn. In case of a sell-off of illiquid assets, bid-ask spreads will increase and prices will plunge, causing the manager to incur deep losses when liquidating positions.

Financing provided by banks and brokerages can also affect fund liquidity. Besides margin financing provided by brokerages, managers use credit facilities from commercial banks to fulfill redemption requests. Hence, investors should review terms, conditions, and limits for margin accounts and other financing facilities of the fund and understand what conditions may cause the counterparties to revise these terms, which could potentially lead to a reduction in available financing and thus restrict the fund's liquidity.

Leverage Risk *Leveraging* can be defined as any method by which a manager increases the exposure of a fund, whether through borrowing of cash or securities or leverage embedded in derivative positions or by any other means (The European Commission, 2011). Practically, leverage is the ratio of total assets controlled by the fund to the equity capital provided by investors and is used to enhance investment returns. First and foremost, investors should understand how the manager defines leverage and how much leverage the manager uses to implement the strategy. Hedged equity managers, for instance, report leverage on a gross/net and long/short basis. Historical fluctuation of leverage used, maximum and minimum levels attained, limits set on market exposures, and how leverage is expected to contribute to the fund's risk-return profile are important points to address.

Leverage levels in a fund should be compatible with the particular strategy under consideration. Fixed-income arbitrage strategies, for example, employ relatively high levels of leverage. The use of high leverage in strategies in which it is uncommon should raise a red flag. Likewise, high leverage in funds with large amounts of illiquid investments can prove dangerous, especially in times of increased volatility. Generally, the use of leverage should be assessed in combination with other factors, such as asset types, sectors, and positions; overall liquidity of the portfolio; trading strategies; volatility of assets and trading strategies; and the crowdedness and concentration of these trading strategies (The Asset Managers' Committee, 2009).

Although leverage levels are important, so are sources of leverage. For liquid alternative strategies, a manager can generate leverage through margin borrowing from prime brokers, secured lines of credit from banks, repurchase agreements, short selling of securities, or use of derivatives. Derivatives contain intrinsic leverage, which is not necessarily reported on balance sheets. This *off-balance-sheet leverage* enables managers to attain much higher levels of exposure than is possible through margin financing or bank loans.

Illiquid alternatives, such as private equity, especially leveraged buyout funds, finance their investments with borrowed capital to increase their buying power. In contrast to hedge funds, leverage is carried by the portfolio companies in private equity funds and properties in real estate funds; consequently, each investment is insulated from the liability that other portfolio investments carry. Investors need to look at leverage levels in portfolio assets and understand the methods used for leverage, as well as any debt that is coming due.

Operational Risk *Operational* or *non-investment risk* is the possibility of losses from systems, processes, technology, individuals, or events (The Asset Managers' Committee, 2009). As opposed to investment risks, investors are not compensated for operational risks. Operational risk management encompasses middle- and back-office functions, including valuation, trade processing, accounting, legal and compliance, information technology, and financial reporting. Trade errors, technology-related losses, net asset value (NAV) calculation errors, reporting and accounting mishaps, and outright fraud are all in the realm of operational risk. Investors need to ensure that an alternative investment firm has requisite internal controls (i.e., effective and efficient operations, compliance with laws and regulations, and reliable financial reporting) that will help manage and control operational risks (COSO, 2011).

Written policies and procedures as well as segregation of duties are prerequisites of internal controls. Operational functions ideally should report to a COO who is independent from investment management. In case of hedge funds, investors should understand and check in real time the entire lifecycle of a trade from its entry into an order management system to execution, capture, and reconciliation. Trades, positions, and cash should be reconciled, usually on a daily basis, between the internal systems and data coming from prime brokers, administrators, custodians, and counterparties. Any discrepancies must be promptly resolved.

Other important topics to review are order sizing and splitting procedures, trading authorization of personnel, limits on traders, allocation of trades to accounts, fee accrual, previous trade errors, assignment of responsibility of errors, and monitoring of corporate actions. Investors should understand cash and collateral management and control process, including cash movement authorizations, levels of cash, institutions where cash is held, and implementation of cash movement and reconciliation procedures. At least two high-level signatories should be required to transfer funds, with one of them being a non-investment person, such as a CFO. Investors should inquire whether managers have undergone an SSAE 16—previously known as SAS 70—examination to demonstrate that their internal controls have been audited.

Valuation

Managers should have an established framework consisting of a clearly defined policy, governance structure, and controls around valuation. A valuation policy separate from the PPM should include pricing sources and methodologies used to value each asset or instrument type in which the fund invests. Pricing sources can range from exchange-quoted prices for listed securities to third-party valuation services, internal valuation models, or manager estimates. At least two sources should be designated for each asset type; over-the-counter (OTC) securities such as corporate or sovereign bonds should have multiple dealer quotes.

Valuation process should be independent from investment management. A valuation committee that reviews and approves valuation policies, provides oversight, and resolves conflicts is typical for funds that invest in illiquid and difficult-to-price assets and for larger organizations managing a number of strategies. An external administrator is indispensable for independently valuing holdings and calculating the fund's NAV in parallel to the manager's internal process. The Investors' Committee (2009) recommends that portfolios containing illiquid investments undergo independent valuation on a semi-annual basis and independent valuation in general should "mirror the liquidity of the fund." Additionally, fund's valuation methodology should be assessed in the context of the fund's liquidity profile and fee structure.

The valuation approach of the manager should be consistent with FAS 157, fair value measurement standards, set by the Financial Accounting Standards Board (FASB). Investors should seek disclosure of the fund's asset valuation according to FAS 157, with asset levels broken down into three categories based on how observable their prices are. Investors should closely study Level 3 assets and seek information about realized and unrealized profit and loss (P&L) that these assets generate. Managers should disclose realized and unrealized P&L information for Level 2 assets (i.e., assets that have no observable market prices but have inputs that do) in addition to Level 3 assets. This information will reveal how much of the fund's performance is coming from more difficult-to-value assets (The Asset Managers' Committee, 2009).

In evaluating private equity and real estate funds, investors should understand the valuation approach, including methodologies, such as discounted cash flow analysis, precedent transactions, and comparables, and models used, pricing discipline, and frequency of valuation of portfolio holdings. Examining financial models used in actual investments, investors should look at entry and exit values and contrast them with comparable transactions. The frequency of valuation and calculation of IRR and net-of-fees returns should be in line with industry standards. Any changes to the valuation methodology or assumptions used in valuations should be promptly reported to investors (GIPS Executive Committee, 2010).

Third-Party Service Providers

Third-party service providers include the administrator, auditor, prime broker, custodian, legal counsel, and research, valuation, accounting, and advisory service providers. Investors must ensure that third parties are independent from the manager and are reputable organizations that have expertise in the specific asset class that is under consideration. Independence of service providers is mandated by the current regulatory environment and heightened vigilance of investors about errors, inaccuracies, and outright fraud. Self-administration, for example, is no longer acceptable for established institutional investors in the aftermath of the recent hedge fund blowups.

The investment manager should have a well-defined process for conducting initial due diligence and ongoing monitoring of service providers. If the service provider is not well known, investors should conduct due diligence in order to corroborate its capabilities and professional standing. Investors must understand the full scope of the services rendered by each provider and any service level agreements in place. Equally important is determining if the manager has ever changed its service providers and, if so, what firms were used previously and why the relationships were ended.

The administrator provides such services as fund accounting and administration, trade capture and reconciliation, valuation, performance measurement, NAV, profit and loss, and fee calculations and financial and tax reporting. Relevant topics to address are flow of information with respect to trades, positions, and cash among the administrator, manager, and prime broker and the recording, settlement, and reconciliation processes. Additionally, investors should inquire about restatements of NAV, handling of processing errors, differences between preliminary and final NAV, pricing differences between the administrator and prime broker, and timeliness of NAV and performance reporting.

Prime brokers offer asset custody, trade clearing and settlement, cash management, securities lending, and financing services to hedge funds. After the collapse of Lehman Brothers, using multiple prime brokers has become commonplace in order to reduce counterparty risk although this adds to operational complexity due to the difficulty of reconciling records across multiple entities. Prime brokers should hold assets in the name of the fund, segregated from their own assets. Investors should ask if the prime broker is allowed to rehypothecate (lend) any fund assets and if any limits exist on the amount of assets that can be lent out. Investors should also review margin and collateral requirements and the circumstances under which the prime broker can change margin terms.

The auditor, just like the administrator and the prime broker, should be independent and reputable. The reasoning for using an unknown entity as auditor must be questioned. Investors should ask if the auditor is providing any other services, such as tax and advisory, to the manager and if a qualified opinion has ever been issued. Investors should contact the auditor to confirm the relationship and, if possible, obtain the audited financial statements instead of receiving them from the manager. When examining audited financial statements, footnotes, year-end asset levels, investor subscriptions and redemptions, and NAV data should be closely studied.

Technology, Infrastructure, Business Continuity Planning

A robust information technology (IT) infrastructure is a must to support effective front-, middle- and back-office operations, especially for hedge fund managers. Investors should inquire about software applications used for various functions, such as portfolio management, trade execution and processing, pricing, financial and tax reporting, corporate actions, client management, and fund accounting, as well as hardware systems, including the network and servers, and logical and physical access security. Using systems that are outdated, discontinued, or uncommon for the given asset class is a warning sign. Investors should understand what functions are outsourced, and, if so, check the reputation of the vendors. Investors should also evaluate the quality of the internal IT resources. For any internally developed applications, the firm should have the requisite development and maintenance capabilities in-house.

A well-designed business continuity and disaster recovery plan (BC/DRP) involves processes for frequent data backup and storage, designation of a recovery facility in case the primary location becomes uninhabitable, resumption of and remote access to critical systems, and alternate protocols to establish communications and connectivity. The procedures should be well defined and documented, and describe how the business will resume operations in case of a disruption or a disaster. Scenario planning and testing are important elements of BC/DRP. Investors should specifically ask to see results of any tests performed and how long it will take the manager to resume normal operations in the aftermath of a major disruption.

Compliance and Legal

Managers must demonstrate that they have adequate controls in place to ensure adherence to applicable laws, regulations, and standards of ethical behavior. An independent chief compliance officer should oversee the compliance function. A compliance oversight committee is part of appropriate governance for larger organizations, whereas a dedicated officer is required for smaller organizations. Elements of a compliance framework include a compliance manual, a written code of ethics, and monitoring and enforcement programs. A compliance manual should address such topics as conflicts of interest, anti-money laundering practices, insider trading, personal transactions, recordkeeping, reporting, and escalation mechanisms.

Investors should ask about other business affiliations of principals and key personnel and assess if such affiliations could potentially cause conflicts of interest or distract personnel away from the fund's business. Investors should understand any business relationships a manager may have with affiliated entities. For example, if a hedge fund is using an affiliated broker/dealer to execute trades, it still must ascertain best execution and also provide disclosure about the relationship to investors. The manager must disclose all *soft-dollar arrangements* (i.e., compensation of brokerage firms for research services, for example, through commissions on trades executed by the brokerage, rather than making direct payments for research) and the scope of services received in exchange. Investors should review outsourced compliance and legal functions and ensure that these parties have appropriate credentials and are in good professional standing.

Investors must inquire if the firm or any of its personnel has been subject to any legal, regulatory, or administrative investigations, proceedings, actions, or penalties. Information provided by the manager must be independently verified with background searches and legal and regulatory authorities, including the SEC, the Financial Services Authority (FSA), the National Association of Securities Dealers (NASD), the Commodity Futures Trading Commission (CFTC), or the Financial Industry Regulatory Authority (FINRA). The manager must demonstrate evidence that appropriate remedial action has been taken for any infractions that may have occurred.

Background Searches and Reference Checks

Investors should conduct background checks on principals, portfolio managers, key personnel, and any other staff authorized to trade or move cash. Using external background search firms for this purpose is commonplace. The scope of search spans criminal and civil background checks, regulatory records and proceedings, academic and employment history, professional affiliations, and credit history. Investors should be wary of any inconsistencies between manager-supplied information and information obtained from background searches.

Investors should go beyond references provided by the manager and use their own networks to confirm the reputation of the firm and its principals in the marketplace. Former investors and employees of the fund may prove valuable sources of information about potential weaknesses that may not be easily revealed by company-designated references. In private equity searches, investors should speak with current management and former employees of portfolio companies, current and former LPs, coinvestors, bankers, advisers, and attorneys and any other parties who have worked with the manager in the past.

FINAL EVALUATION

At the end of the due diligence process, investment and business due diligence teams formulate their independent assessment of the prospective fund. Any problem points or issues that are identified should be thoroughly discussed. Sometimes, investors are willing to work with what they consider to be an otherwise relatively reliable organization to remedy issues spotted during the due diligence process. Other times, red flags emerging during the examination will cause investors to forgo the opportunity altogether. In any case, both the investment team and the business due diligence team should establish their opinions and vet the investment independently. This will ensure that an opportunity is given a sound consideration from both investment and enterprise aspects.

SUMMARY AND CONCLUSIONS

Evaluating alternative investments presents challenges due to the unique characteristics of this asset class, such as targeting of absolute returns; following flexible investment mandates, using complex and opaque investment strategies, derivatives, and leverage; and investing in illiquid assets. Less strict regulatory oversight and a lack of disclosure and reporting requirements have traditionally led investors to make a substantial effort to analyze and fully understand these investments and ensure suitability with their own investment objectives. Furthermore, the entrepreneurial nature of many investment advisers coupled with a lack of transparency necessitates a thorough business or operational due diligence examination in order to ascertain that firms have adequate organizational structure, governance mechanisms, and checks and balances to safeguard investors, minimize operational risks, and comply with laws, regulations, and best practices.

DISCUSSION QUESTIONS

1. Why is due diligence important in alternative investments?
2. Briefly explain investment due diligence.
3. Explain the meaning of business or operational due diligence.
4. Briefly describe the due diligence process.

REFERENCES

Ackermann, Carl, Richard McEnally, and David Ravenscraft. 1999. "The Performance of Hedge Funds: Risk, Return and Incentives." *Journal of Finance* 54:3, 833–874.

Afyonoğlu, Gökhan. 2010. *Due Diligence on Alternative Investments: An Institutional Investor's Perspective*. Independent Study in Finance, University of Pennsylvania, The Wharton School, Philadelphia.

Amenc, Noël, Lionel Martellini, and Mathieu Vaissié. 2003. "Benefits and Risks of Alternative Investment Strategies." *Journal of Asset Management* 4:2, 96–118.

Aragon, George O., Michael Hertzel, and Zhen Shi. 2012. "Why Do Hedge Funds Avoid Disclosure? Evidence from Confidential 13F Filings." Working Paper, W. P. Carey School of Business. Arizona State University.

Brown, Stephen J., Thomas L. Fraser, and Bing Liang. 2008. "Hedge Fund Due Diligence: A Source of Alpha in a Hedge Fund Portfolio Strategy." Available at http://papers.ssrn.com/sol3/papers.cfm?abstract_id=1016904.

COSO. 2011. *Internal Control—Integrated Framework.* Committee of Sponsoring Organizations of the Treadway Commission. Durham: AICPA.

Donohue, Andrew J. 2010. *Speech by SEC Staff: Regulating Hedge Funds and Other Private Investment Pools.* Available at www.sec.gov/news/speech/2010/spch021910ajd.htm.

Dor, Arik Ben, and Ravi Jagannathan. 2002. *Understanding Mutual Fund and Hedge Fund Styles Using Return Based Style Analysis.* Cambridge, MA: National Bureau of Economic Research.

Fung, William, and David A. Hsieh. 1997. "Empirical Characteristics of Dynamic Trading Strategies: The Case of Hedge Funds." *Review of Financial Studies* 10:2, 275–302.

GIPS Executive Committee. 2010. *Global Investment Performance Standards.* Charlottesville, VA: The CFA Institute.

Green, Richard C., and Vincent Glode. 2008. *Information Spillovers and Performance Persistence in Private Equity Partnerships.* Working Paper, Tepper School of Business, Carnegie Mellon University.

HFR. (2012). *HFR Global Hedge Fund Industry Report—Second Quarter 2012.* Chicago. Hedge Fund Research.

Lopez, Jose A. 2008. *FRBSF Economic Letter 2008–33 What Is Liquidity Risk?* Available at www.frbsf.org/publications/economics/letter/2008/el2008-33.html.

Maslakovic, Marko. 2011. *TheCityUK Private Equity 2011 Report.* Available at www.thecityuk.com/assets/Uploads/PrivateEquity2011.pdf.

McEnery, Thornton. 2011. *The 10 Greatest Hedge Fund Implosions of All Time.* Available at www.businessinsider.com/the-top-10-hedge-fund-implosions-of-all-time-2011-6?op=1.

Meyer, Thomas, and Pierre-Yves Mathonet. 2005. *Beyond the J-Curve: Managing a Portfolio of Venture Capital and Private Equity Funds.* West Sussex: John Wiley & Sons, Ltd.

Schneeweis, Thomas, and Georgi Georgiev. 2002. *The Investment Benefits of Traditional Alternatives: Venture Capital, Private Debt and Private Equity.* CISDM/Isenberg School of Management, University of Massachusetts.

Schneeweis, Thomas, Vassilios N. Karavas, and Georgi Georgiev. 2002. *Alternative Investments in the Institutional Portfolio.* CISDM/Isenberg School of Management, University of Massachusetts.

Schneeweis, Thomas, Hossein Kazemi, and George Martin. 2001. *Understanding Hedge Fund Performance: Research Rules of Thumb for the Institutional Investor.* Isenberg School of Management, Center for International Securities and Derivatives Markets, University of Massachusetts.

SEC. 2011a. *Form 13F—Reports Filed by Institutional Investment Managers.* Washington, DC: U.S. Securities and Exchange Commission. Available at www.sec.gov/answers/form13f.htm.

SEC. 2011b. *Form ADV.* Washington, DC: U. S. Securities and Exchange Commission. Available at www.sec.gov/answers/formadv.htm.

SEC. 2011c. *SEC Adopts Dodd-Frank Act Amendments to Investment Advisers Act.* Washington, DC: U. S. Securities and Exchange Commission. Available at www.sec.gov/news/press/2011/2011-133.htm.

Swensen, David F. 2009. *Pioneering Portfolio Management: An Unconventional Approach to Institutional Investment.* New York: Simon & Schuster, Inc.

The Asset Managers' Committee. 2009. "Best Practices for the Hedge Fund Industry." *Report of the Asset Managers' Committee to the President's Working Group on Financial Markets*. Available at www.amaicmte.org/Public/AMC%20Report%20-%20Final.pdf.
The European Commission. 2011. "Directive 2011/61/EU of the European Parliament and of the Council of 8 June 2011." *Official Journal of the European Union*. Legislation 174: 54, 18.
The Greenwich Roundtable. 2009. *Best Practices in Alternative Investing: Portfolio Construction*. The Greenwich Roundtable. Greenwich: The Education Committee of the Greenwich Roundtable.
The Investors' Committee. 2009. "Principles and Best Practices for Hedge Fund Investors." *Report of the Investors' Committee to the President's Working Group on Financial Markets*. Available at www.amaicmte.org/Public/Investors%20Report%20-%20Final.pdf.

ABOUT THE AUTHOR

Gökhan Afyonoğlu is a Vice President and Investment Risk Analyst in the Investment Risk Management Group at PNC Bank. He assists in overseeing investment and risk management process at PNC Asset Management Group. Before assuming his current position, he conducted due diligence examinations and analysis of alternative investment managers as an Investment Portfolio Analyst at PNC. His research interests include investment and market risk management, counterparty risk management, quantitative investment analysis, global macroeconomics, enterprise risk management, analytical reporting, and software development. Mr. Afyonoğlu earned a BS in mechanical engineering from Boğaziçi (Bosphorus) University in Istanbul, Turkey, an MS in industrial engineering from the University of Florida, an MBA from the Wharton School, and an MA in international studies from the Lauder Institute at the University of Pennsylvania.

PART II

Real Estate

CHAPTER 5

REITs and the Private Real Estate Market

SHAUN A. BOND
West Shell, Jr. Chair and Director of the UC Real Estate Center, Department of Finance and Real Estate, University of Cincinnati

QINGQING CHANG
PhD Student, Department of Finance and Real Estate, University of Cincinnati

INTRODUCTION

This chapter reviews the connection between the returns of real estate investment trusts (REITs) and the private real estate market. This topic has been the subject of extensive interest in the field of real estate from both practitioner and academic perspectives. The basic question that concerns investors and researchers is whether REITs achieve a total return consistent with the returns associated with the real estate that forms the core asset holdings of the trust. Alternatively, are the returns more in line with the returns in the overall stock market? A third possibility exists that the returns on REITs is some hybrid of both a real estate return and a stock market return.

The relationship between REIT returns and the core real estate holdings of the trust is important for investors considering allocating funds to real estate. Many investors are attracted to real estate because of the potential diversification benefits the asset class is believed to offer (Bond, Hwang, Mitchell, and Satchell, 2007). However, investment in direct real estate (i.e., purchasing buildings) may be infeasible or prohibitive for many reasons. These reasons include high transaction costs, large lot size, the inability to create a sufficiently diversified portfolio of properties, uncertainty about valuation, limited experience in managing the asset, and concern about liquidity. Even investment in collective investment vehicles, such as closed or open-ended funds, might not completely overcome these obstacles to investing in direct real estate.

REITs offer a form of investment in real estate, particularly in the case of publicly listed REITs, that overcomes many of the obstacles to direct real estate investment listed in the previous paragraph. Transaction costs for publicly traded REITs are very low, information transparency is high, valuation of equity holdings is readily available, diversified portfolios can be easily created, and trading in public REITs has a much higher level of liquidity than trading in the direct real estate market. From this perspective, the case for REITs is very strong. However, the lingering concern for investors, particularly if they already have a substantial holding in equities, is whether REITs will provide the same risk and return benefits that they are hoping to achieve by investing in real estate. REITs are expected to behave substantially like the direct real estate market because, by regulation, REITs are required to have 75 percent of their assets as real estate. Furthermore, 75 percent of the gross income for the REIT must come in the form of rents or mortgage interest payments. These restrictions create a security where the underlying assets and cash flow are closely connected to real estate assets.

The remainder of the chapter has the following organization. The next section provides a review of the existing literature on the connection among the private real estate market, the stock market, and REITs. Next, the chapter presents new empirical evidence on the connection between public and private real estate markets. This analysis differs from other work in this area by drawing a control sample from the broader stock market to match the REIT sample on the basis of size and book-to-market ratio. The final section provides a summary and conclusions.

LITERATURE

Wendt and Wong (1965), Robichek, Cohn and Pringle (1972), and Smith and Shulman (1976) provide some of the earliest work on correlations between direct real estate and the stock market and on the investment characteristics of REITs. Indeed, nearly 50 years ago Wendt and Wong highlight and anticipate many of the issues that still concern researchers focused on the role of real estate in mixed-asset portfolios today. They compare the investment performance of a portfolio of multifamily properties around San Francisco to a random sample of stocks drawn from the CRSP database. Examining performance over the 1950s and early 1960s, the authors conclude that the higher (after-tax) performance of real estate investments is associated with the higher leverage employed by investors as well as tax advantages received by real estate investors.

Robichek et al. (1972) present empirical evidence on the correlation between (farm) real estate returns and domestic and foreign equities, bonds, and commodities from 1949 to 1969. Later studies often confirmed two findings emerging from this study: the apparent low volatility of real estate as an asset class and the low or negative correlations with other asset classes.

Rounding out the early published studies on real estate is a study of REIT performance by Smith and Shulman (1976) covering the period from 1963 to 1974. This study anticipated many themes that emerged in the later literature, including the advantages of REITs relative to direct investment, discounts to net asset value, and the systematic and idiosyncratic risk of REITs. In comparing REITs to a sample of closed-end funds, the authors find that REITs have lower performance relative to their control group and lower levels of systematic risk. Smith and Shulman's (p. 66) concluding comment, which recent history has probably not fully supported, casts doubt on the place of REITs in institutional investors' portfolios:

> When equity REIT's appeared on the investment scene, they seemed to offer (like high-technology growth stocks, nursing homes, conglomerates, and gold before them) substantial advantages without attendant disadvantages. Their subsequent

> performance has proved otherwise. Real estate investments have not been, and are unlikely to become, a panacea for large institutional portfolios.

Hoag (1980), Miles and McCue (1982, 1984), and Brueggeman, Chen, and Thibodeau (1984) all recognized the need for a consistent set of real estate returns data and attempted to provide this information from a limited set of commercial properties. The challenge in much of the early literature on real estate investment was constructing a historical series on direct real estate returns. Often this was done by using returns from Commingled Real Estate Funds (CREF) or obtaining access to internal data sets from large institutional investors.

The study by Miles and McCue (1982) is particularly relevant to the topic of this chapter because it directly compares the performance and portfolio composition of CREFs to REITs. An important contribution of Miles and McCue is the recognition that organization form affects the types of properties acquired by each type of investment vehicle, and this ultimately affects return outcomes. The authors also investigate the geographic diversification of fund returns. However, sample size and sample selection issues severely affect all of these early studies.

Over the next decade, research in real estate finance grew rapidly along with the development of improved data sets with longer historical time series. In particular, the development of the National Council of Real Estate Investment Fiduciaries (NCREIF) data set aided the research community. Ross and Zisler (1991) explore the characteristics of equity REITs, CREFs, and direct property investment. They notice significant differences between REIT returns and direct property investment. In considering whether REITs could substitute for direct real estate exposure, Ross and Zisler (p. 181) conclude:

> Does the EREIT index measure equity real estate returns and risks? Is it a good measure of the return and the risks than an institutional investor could, on average, expect to receive from a typical investment in equity real estate? There can be no definitive answers to these questions, but we can offer a qualified "probably not."

This conclusion is also consistent with the work of Liu, Hartzell, Greig, and Grissom (1990), who find that although REITs are integrated with the stock market, the direct real estate market is segmented from the stock market.

Giliberto (1990) and Gyourko and Keim (1992) explicitly investigated the dynamic connection between direct real estate markets and REITs. Both papers use dynamic regression models and find evidence that REIT returns appear to predict returns in the direct real estate market. This result holds after allowing for the autocorrelated nature of direct real estate return series based on the work of Geltner (1991). These papers began a stream of literature related to price discovery and asset substitutability that continues to this day.

The methodology used in these papers still forms the basis on much current research, although data availability has improved substantially over time, along with advances in econometric technology. For example, Seck (1996) uses a vector autoregression (VAR) methodology and takes into account financial and macroeconomic variables. He finds that financial market variables predominately drive REIT returns, whereas economic variables are more closely connected to the NCREIF returns. Barkham and Geltner (1995) use Granger causality tests to investigate price discovery between securitized real estate assets and the direct market in both the United States and the United Kingdom. They find that information is incorporated into securitized real estate (REIT and the property company) returns up to one year before the direct market, even allowing for smoothing in the appraisal-based direct property series. Geltner and Kluger (1998) further refined the comparison of performance between REITs and direct property investment by creating pure-play price indices that track returns in the different sectors of the real estate market based on public market pricing.

Glascock, Lu, and So (2000) use cointegration techniques to examine the long-run relationship among REITs, the stock market, and the direct real estate market. The statistical technique of cointegration identifies the existence of long-run relationships between stochastic time series. In this case, researchers are looking for the existence of a long-run relationship between REITs and measures of the direct property market. Cointegration allows for the fact that the connection between the two markets might not always hold in the short term, for example, because REIT prices might be more influenced by the overall stock market in the short term, but over the longer term investors will receive similar performance. Glascock et al.'s finding indicates that a substantial time variation could exist in the connection between REITs and the overall equity market.

Clayton and MacKinnon (2001) provide further discussion of time variation. Although stocks and REITs are cointegrated from 1992 onwards, a relationship apparently did not exist before then. Before 1992, REITs were more closely connected to the bond market than the equity market. This finding may well have been due to changes in the regulations relating to REITs in the early 1990s. Clayton and MacKinnon also find that REITs and the direct property market do have a cointegrating relationship over the period from 1977 to 1996.

Many studies have investigated this topic since the early 2000s. Generally, fewer developments have occurred regarding the methodology used by more recent research. Yet, contributions have been made concerning the more precise adjustment of the data series (Pagliari, Scherer, and Monopoli, 2005; Riddiough, Moriarity, and Yeatman 2005; Boudry, Coulson, Kalberg, and Liu, 2012), the use of international data sets (Eichholtz and Hartzell, 1996; Chau, McGregor, and Schwann, 2001; Sebastian and Schatz, 2009; Hoesli and Oikarinen, 2012; Yunus, Hansz, and Kennedy, 2012), or liquidity transmission (Bond and Chang, 2012).

Boudry et al. (2012) provide a good example of how researchers are now more carefully considering the nature of REITs, which are predominately small companies, along with more recently developed transaction-based real estate indices, such as the MIT TBI index of Fisher, Geltner, and Pollakowski (2007). Using the TBI index avoids problems associated with appraisal smoothing that are known to affect the NCREIF index. Boudry et al. (pp. 243–244) perhaps best sum up the current understanding of the connection among REITs, direct real estate, and the equity market:

> It appears that the REIT and Real Estate Markets adjust to each other and also to the financial markets. If securitized and unsecuritized real estate get out of equilibrium, both adjust back towards the equilibrium path. In this sense it appears that the financial markets informationally lead the real estate markets.

The remainder of this chapter provides an additional analysis of the connection between REITs and the direct real estate market. This analysis closely follows Boudry et al. (2012) but uses a more extensive data set, including the time period of the financial crisis of 2007–2008. Unlike other studies, the current study uses a matched-sample of stocks from the CRSP data set for comparison purposes. Drawing upon the finding that most REITs are small value stocks, the study also compares REITs to small capitalization indexes, such as the Russell 2000. This provides a more carefully matched control sample of equities from which to draw conclusions about the comovement of REITs with the stock market. To avoid problems with appraisal smoothing in appraisal-based indices, the measure of direct real estate used in this study is the MIT TBI index.

DATA

The data used for this analysis come from four sources: (1) the CRSP/Ziman REIT Database, (2) CRSP monthly stock returns, (3) the Transactions-Based Index (TBI) from the MIT Center for Real Estate, and (4) the Bloomberg database. This analysis begins with all firms on the New York Stock Exchange (NYSE), American Stock Exchange (AMEX), and NASDAQ contained in the Ziman REIT Database with available monthly return data since 1980.

The major results presented in this chapter are based on a sample from January 1994 to December 2011 and include 283 REIT firms. The analysis starts with January 1994 data because the nature of the REIT market changed substantially after the announcement of the Revenue Reconciliation Act of 1993 in August 1993.

To compare REITs shares with ordinary common shares (CRSP share codes 10 and 11), a control group sample is constructed. Fama and French (1992) contend that common stock returns are related to firm size and book-to-market ratios. Barber and Lyon (1997) document that constructing control firms by size and book-to-market ratio generates well-specified test statistics in most sample situations. As in Barber and Lyon, a REIT sample firm is matched to a control firm with the closest size and book-to-market ratio. Size and book-to-market are constructed as in Fama and French. Specifically, a control firm is chosen with the smallest absolute differences in size and book-to-market ratio; if ties occur, the closest match in size is used.

Because different property types may have different return dynamics, this chapter also investigates four types of properties for both REITs and TBI. To explore the relationship between REITs and equity markets, the S&P 500 index is used as a proxy for large-cap stocks and the Russell 2000 index as a proxy for small-cap stocks. To explore the relationship between REITs and the bond market, the J.P. Morgan U.S. Aggregate Bond Index is used as a proxy for the overall bond market. The TBI index is obtained from NCREIF, the S&P 500 index from CRSP, and the Russell 2000 and J.P. Morgan bond index from Bloomberg.

Descriptive Statistics

Exhibit 5.1 reports descriptive statistics for the data used in the analysis. Panel A reports quarterly return statistics for aggregate REITs and REIT property type (Office, Retail, Industrial, and Apartment) from the CRSP/Ziman REIT Database,

Exhibit 5.1 Descriptive Statistics for Real Estate and Financial Market Returns

Returns	Observations	Mean	Standard Deviation	Minimum	Maximum
Panel A. Quarterly sample (1994Q1–2011Q4)					
TBI	72	0.027	0.057	−0.161	0.181
TBI (Office)	72	0.026	0.056	−0.161	0.167
TBI (Retail)	72	0.028	0.060	−0.158	0.220
TBI (Industrial)	70	0.028	0.060	−0.164	0.182
TBI (Apartment)	72	0.024	0.058	−0.159	0.187
REIT	72	0.028	0.110	−0.383	0.373
REIT (Office)	72	0.028	0.122	−0.439	0.484
REIT (Retail)	72	0.030	0.126	−0.430	0.541
REIT (Industrial)	72	0.034	0.107	−0.352	0.328
REIT (Apartment)	72	0.036	0.105	−0.351	0.415
Control	72	0.033	0.115	−0.320	0.315
S&P 500	72	0.023	0.092	−0.237	0.213
Russell 2000	72	0.021	0.108	−0.265	0.230
Bond	72	0.015	0.021	−0.027	0.061
Panel B. Annual sample (1994–2011)					
TBI	18	0.113	0.110	−0.157	0.276
TBI (Office)	18	0.109	0.112	−0.174	0.257
TBI (Retail)	18	0.118	0.127	−0.132	0.421
TBI (Industrial)	16	0.115	0.121	−0.155	0.271
TBI (Apartment)	18	0.099	0.114	−0.123	0.258
REIT	18	0.121	0.236	−0.421	0.419
REIT (Office)	18	0.124	0.267	−0.492	0.540
REIT (Retail)	18	0.123	0.228	−0.436	0.455
REIT (Industrial)	18	0.140	0.204	−0.372	0.378
REIT (Apartment)	18	0.150	0.195	−0.236	0.454
Control	18	0.139	0.260	−0.458	0.683
S&P 500	18	0.099	0.204	−0.382	0.357
Russell 2000	18	0.078	0.193	−0.348	0.454
Bond	18	0.065	0.049	−0.029	0.174

This table reports descriptive statistics for the data used in the analysis. Panel A reports statistics for the quarterly sample, 1994Q1 to 2011Q4; Panel B reports statistics for the annual sample, 1994 to 2011. The aggregate REITs data and REITs property-type data (Office, Retail, Industrial, and Apartment) are from the CRSP/Ziman REIT Database. Control is the control sample constructed by matching the REIT firms with the non-REIT firms by size and book-to-market ratio. TBI is the aggregate MIT transactions-based index; TBI (Office, Retail, Industrial, and Apartment) are the MIT TBI property-type indices. S&P 500 is the S&P 500 index; Russell 2000 is the Russell 2000 value index; and Bond is the J.P. Morgan bond index.

the aggregate MIT transaction-based index (TBI) and the TBI property-type index, a control group for REITs, S&P 500 index, Russell 2000 value index, and J.P. Morgan aggregate corporate bond index over the sample period 1994Q1 to 2011Q4. Panel B reports nonoverlapping annual return statistics from 1994 to 2011.

The results indicate that REITs have more than twice the variation of the TBI, whereas REITs are slightly less volatile than the control group. Panel A shows that the quarterly average standard deviation of REITs is 0.110, compared to an

Exhibit 5.2 Correlations: 1994Q1–2011Q4

	REIT	REIT (Office)	REIT (Retail)	REIT (Industrial)	REIT (Apartment)
Panel A. Short-sample quarterly returns					
TBI	0.06	0.08	−0.02	0.01	0.10
TBI (Office)	0.02	0.06	−0.05	−0.03	0.07
TBI (Retail)	0.06	0.07	−0.01	0.01	0.10
TBI (Industrial)	0.08	0.11	0.00	0.03	0.11
TBI (Apartment)	0.03	0.04	−0.08	−0.01	0.08
Control	0.83	0.79	0.74	0.73	0.71
S&P 500	0.60	0.63	0.54	0.61	0.53
Russell 2000	0.72	0.69	0.64	0.69	0.63
Bond	−0.07	−0.08	−0.04	−0.06	−0.10
Panel B. Short-sample annual returns					
TBI	0.24	0.22	0.26	0.46	0.27
TBI (Office)	0.08	0.13	0.11	0.31	0.13
TBI (Retail)	0.29	0.23	0.34	0.52	0.33
TBI (Industrial)	0.28	0.27	0.30	0.49	0.26
TBI (Apartment)	0.45	0.45	0.43	0.67	0.46
Control	0.89	0.88	0.85	0.75	0.78
S&P 500	0.50	0.61	0.47	0.51	0.47
Russell 2000	0.73	0.73	0.69	0.69	0.69
Bond	−0.02	−0.06	−0.08	0.06	−0.12

This table reports correlations for the data used in the analysis. Panel A reports quarterly observations from 1994Q1 to 2011Q4; Panel B reports nonoverlapping annual data from 1994 to 2011. The aggregate REITs data and REITs property-type data (Office, Retail, Industrial, and Apartment) are from the CRSP/Ziman REIT Database. Control is the control sample constructed by matching the REIT firms with the non-REIT firms by size and book-to-market ratio. TBI is the aggregate MIT transactions-based index; TBI (Office, Retail, Industrial, and Apartment) are the MIT TBI property-type indices. S&P 500 is the S&P 500 index; Russell 2000 is the Russell 2000 value index; and Bond is the J.P. Morgan bond index.

average of 0.057 for TBI and an average of 0.115 for the control group. Substantial variations also exist among different property types in the REIT market but not as much for the TBI indices. Panel A shows that the average standard deviations for REIT property-type indices range from 0.105 to 0.126, whereas the average standard deviations for TBI properties range from 0.056 to 0.060. In the quarterly and annual samples, the mean and standard deviation of the returns of the control group are slightly higher than those of REITs. In general, however, the return dynamics of both variables are closely linked.

To examine the relationship between REITs and the other return series, pairwise correlations are calculated and reported in Exhibit 5.2. Panel A reports correlations of quarterly returns, whereas Panel B reports correlations of annual returns. The results show that the correlation between the aggregate REIT and TBI indices increases from 0.06 for quarterly returns to 0.24 for annual returns, indicating that REITs behave more like real estate over longer time horizons. The results are similar at the property-type level. The average correlation between the TBI and the four different REIT property types grows from 0.04 for quarterly returns to 0.30 for annual returns. Even though REITs correlate more with real estate over the longer time horizon, REITs do not necessarily correlate less with financial assets. Comparing quarterly to annual measures, only the correlations between REITs and the S&P 500 index decrease, whereas the correlations between REITs and the other financial assets increase slightly. These results make sense because the S&P 500 index represents large-cap equities, whereas REITs are generally small-cap equities.

EMPIRICAL STRATEGY

To examine the dynamics of REIT returns, a vector error correction model (VECM) developed in Johansen (1991, 1995) is estimated. To develop a VECM, consider a VAR of order p in Equation 5.1:

$$y_t = A_1 y_{t-1} + \ldots + A_p y_{t-p} + Bx_t + \varepsilon_t \tag{5.1}$$

where y_t is a k-vector of nonstationary I(1) variables (REIT, TBI, Control, S&P 500 index, Russell 2000 index, and Bond); x_t is a d-vector of deterministic variables; and ε_t is a vector of innovations. This VAR can be written as Equation 5.2:

$$y_t = \Pi y_{t-1} + \sum_{i=1}^{p-1} \Gamma_i y_{t-i} + Bx_t + \varepsilon_t \tag{5.2}$$

where $\Pi = \sum_{i=1}^{p} A_i - I$, and $\Gamma_i = -\sum_{j=i+1}^{p} A_j$.

Granger's representation theorem asserts that if the coefficient matrix Π has reduced rank $r < k$, then there are $k \times r$ matrixes α and β each with rank r such that $\Pi = \alpha\beta'$ and $\beta' y_t$ is I(0). The term r is the number of cointegrating relations, and each column of β is the cointegrating vector. The elements of α are known as the adjustment parameters in the VEC model.

ESTIMATION

To estimate a VEC model, the analysis proceeds in four steps:

1. Test for nonstationarity in the data using Augmented Dickey-Fuller (ADF) tests.
2. Select the optimal lag length for the system based on the Akaike, Schwarz's Bayesian, and Hannan and Quinn information criteria.
3. Test for cointegrating relationships in the system using trace and maximum eigenvalue tests.
4. Estimate the VECM using the optimal lag length calculated in (2) and the number of cointegrating relationships tested in (3).

Exhibit 5.3 reports the unit root (ADF) tests for the variables used in the research. The null hypothesis of the test is that the data series is nonstationary. The

Exhibit 5.3 Unit Root Tests: 1994Q1–2011Q4

	Levels		First difference	
Variable	***t*-statistic**	***p*-value**	***t*-statistic**	***p*-value**
REIT	−1.49	0.54	−9.65	0.00
REIT (Office)	−1.46	0.55	−9.28	0.00
REIT (Retail)	−1.23	0.66	−9.74	0.00
REIT (Industrial)	−0.22	0.93	−10.47	0.00
REIT (Apartment)	−1.00	0.75	−9.75	0.00
TBI	−1.41	0.57	−9.83	0.00
TBI (Office)	−1.55	0.50	−3.39	0.01
TBI (Retail)	−0.85	0.80	−9.69	0.00
TBI (Industrial)	−1.64	0.46	−9.68	0.00
TBI (Apartment)	−0.85	0.80	−5.18	0.00
Control	−1.30	0.63	−10.75	0.00
S&P 500	−1.77	0.40	−10.50	0.00
Russell 2000	−1.40	0.58	−11.79	0.00
Bond	−1.39	0.59	−9.87	0.00

This table reports Augmented Dickey-Fuller tests on the levels and first differences of the data used in the analysis. The aggregate REITs data and REITs property-type data (Office, Retail, Industrial, and Apartment) are from the CRSP/Ziman REIT Database. Control is the control sample constructed by matching the REIT firms with the non-REIT firms by size and book-to-market ratio. TBI is the aggregate MIT transactions-based index; TBI (Office, Retail, Industrial, and Apartment) are the MIT TBI property-type indexes. S&P 500 is the S&P 500 index; Russell 2000 is the Russell 2000 value index; and Bond is the J.P. Morgan bond index.

p-values reported are MacKinnon, Haug, and Michelis (1996) one-sided *p*-values. The results in Exhibit 5.3 show that the null hypotheses of nonstationarity for all the variables cannot be rejected at conventional alpha levels. However, after taking the first differences for all variables and repeating ADF tests, the null hypotheses of nonstationarity for all variables can be rejected. In sum, the results in Exhibit 5.3 indicate that all the variables are integrated of order one and are stationary in their first differences.

Exhibit 5.4 reports the optimal lag structure for the specified VAR system based on the Akaike's information criteria (AIC), the Schwarz's Bayesian information criteria (SBIC), and the Hannan and Quinn information criteria (HQIC) for the period from 1994Q1 to 2011Q4. The VAR(1) is estimated with lag equal to 0 through 4. Each VAR specification includes REITs (or REIT property type), TBI (or matching TBI property type), the control group for REITs, the S&P 500 index, the Russell 2000 value index, and the J.P. Morgan aggregate corporate bond index. In the context of VAR models, AIC tends to be more accurate with monthly data, HQIC works better for quarterly data on samples of more than 120, and SBIC works fine with any sample size for quarterly data (on VEC models). Therefore, when different optimal lag lengths are chosen by different information criteria, the results indicated by SBIC and HQIC are preferred to those suggested by the AIC. For all regressions, the SBIC and HQIC indicate an optimal lag length of one in the VAR representation or a lag length of zero in the VECM representation.

Exhibit 5.4 Optimal Lag Structure

REIT Quarterly Sample

Lag	AIC	SBIC	HQIC
0	−7.85	−7.65	−7.77
1	−20.22	−18.84*	−19.67*
2	−20.43*	−17.88	−19.42
3	−19.95	−16.23	−18.48
4	−19.72	−14.83	−17.78

REIT (Office)				REIT (Industrial)			
Lag	AIC	SBIC	HQIC	Lag	AIC	SBIC	HQIC
0	−7.49	−7.29	−7.41	0	−7.67	−7.48	−7.59
1	−19.82	−18.45*	−19.28*	1	−19.87	−18.50*	−19.33*
2	−19.99*	−17.44	−18.98	2	−20.02*	−17.48	−19.02
3	−19.44	−15.72	−17.96	3	−19.64	−15.92	−18.16
4	−19.34	−14.44	−17.40	4	−19.55	−14.65	−17.61

REIT (Retail)				REIT (Apartment)			
Lag	AIC	SBIC	HQIC	Lag	AIC	SBIC	HQIC
0	−7.22	−7.02	−7.14	0	−7.42	−7.22	−7.34
1	−19.75	−18.38*	−19.21*	1	−19.57	−18.20*	−19.03*
2	−19.77*	−17.22	−18.76	2	−19.70*	−17.15	−18.69
3	−19.23	−15.50	−17.75	3	−19.27	−15.55	−17.80
4	−18.96	−14.06	−17.02	4	−19.10	−14.21	−17.16

This table reports Akaike's information criteria (AIC), Schwarz's Bayesian information criteria (SBIC), and Hannan and Quinn information criteria (HQIC) for *p*th-order VAR models. The aggregate REITs data and REITs property type data (Office, Retail, Industrial, and Apartment) are from the CRSP/Ziman REIT Database. Control is the control sample constructed by matching the REIT firms with the non-REIT firms by size and book-to-market ratio. TBI is the aggregate MIT transactions-based index; TBI (Office, Retail, Industrial and Apartment) data are the MIT TBI property-type indices. S&P 500 is the S&P 500 index; Russell 2000 is the Russell 2000 value index; and Bond is the J.P. Morgan bond index. The selected optimal lag lengths based on each criterion are marked with an asterisk "*".

Engle and Granger (1987) point out that a linear combination of two or more nonstationary series may be stationary. If such a stationary linear combination exists, the nonstationary time series are said to be cointegrated. The cointegrated relationship between nonstationary series can be interpreted as a long-run equilibrium relationship among the variables. The purpose of the cointegration test is to determine whether a group of nonstationary series is cointegrated. The presence of a cointegrating relationship forms the basis of the VEC specification. Exhibit 5.5 reports trace and maximum eigenvalue tests for each VECM specification over period 1994Q1 to 2011Q4. The trace statistic reported in the second column tests the null hypothesis of r cointegrating relations against the alternative of k cointergrating relations, where k is the number of endogenous variables, for

Exhibit 5.5 Cointegration Tests: 1994Q1–2011Q4

Null	Trace	Critical Value	Null	Max	Critical Value
REIT					
$r \leq 0$	100.97	95.75	$r = 0$	**39.89**	40.08
$r \leq 1$	**61.08**	69.82	$r = 1$	28.06	33.88
$r \leq 2$	33.02	47.86	$r = 2$	17.43	27.58
$r \leq 3$	15.59	29.80	$r = 3$	9.30	21.13
$r \leq 4$	6.30	15.49	$r = 4$	5.87	14.26
REIT (Office)					
$r \leq 0$	159.90	103.85	$r = 0$	68.36	40.96
$r \leq 1$	91.54	76.97	$r = 1$	38.83	34.81
$r \leq 2$	**52.71**	54.08	$r = 2$	**24.41**	28.59
$r \leq 3$	28.31	35.19	$r = 3$	17.02	22.30
$r \leq 4$	11.29	20.26	$r = 4$	8.20	15.89
REIT (Industrial)					
$r \leq 0$	116.29	95.75	$r = 0$	45.83	40.08
$r \leq 1$	70.46	69.82	$r = 1$	37.37	33.88
$r \leq 2$	**33.09**	47.86	$r = 2$	**17.20**	27.58
$r \leq 3$	15.89	29.80	$r = 3$	11.03	21.13
$r \leq 4$	4.86	15.49	$r = 4$	4.71	14.26
REIT (Retail)					
$r \leq 0$	143.63	117.71	$r = 0$	54.53	44.50
$r \leq 1$	89.10	88.80	$r = 1$	40.06	38.33
$r \leq 2$	**49.04**	63.88	$r = 2$	**20.95**	32.12
$r \leq 3$	28.09	42.92	$r = 3$	11.42	25.82
$r \leq 4$	16.67	25.87	$r = 4$	9.82	19.39
REIT (Apartment)					
$r \leq 0$	141.37	103.85	$r = 0$	68.70	40.96
$r \leq 1$	**72.68**	76.97	$r = 1$	**29.40**	34.81
$r \leq 2$	43.28	54.08	$r = 2$	19.20	28.59
$r \leq 3$	24.08	35.19	$r = 3$	13.03	22.30
$r \leq 4$	11.05	20.26	$r = 4$	7.39	15.89

This table reports Johansen's trace and maximum eigenvalue tests for VECM (2). REIT refers to the VECM with the aggregate REIT return from the CRSP/Ziman REIT database; REIT (Office, Retail, Industrial, and Apartment) refers to the VECM with the aggregate REIT property-type returns from the CRSP/Ziman REIT property-type database. The VECM specification includes the matching real estate index, the aggregate MIT TBI (or matching MIT TBI property-type indices), the control group of REITs, the S&P 500 index, the Russell 2000 value index, and the J.P. Morgan aggregate corporate bond index. Data are quarterly and cover the period 1994Q1 to 2011Q4. Null is the null hypothesis under the tests, and critical values are at the 0.05 level (MacKinnon, Haug, and Michelis, 1996). The number of cointegrating vectors based on each test statistic is in bold.

$r = 0,1,\ldots, k-1$. The trace statistic for the null hypothesis of $r$cointergrating relations is computed as shown in Equation 5.3:

$$LR_{tr}\,(r\,|k) = -T\sum_{i=r+1}^{k}\log(1-\lambda_i) \tag{5.3}$$

where λ_i is the ith largest eigenvalue of the Π matrix in Equation 5.2.

The fifth column in Exhibit 5.5 reports the maximum eigenvalue statistic, which tests the null hypothesis of $r$cointegrating relations against the alternative of $r + 1$ cointegrating relations. This test statistic is computed as shown in Equation 5.4:

$$LR_{max}(r|r+1) = -T\log(1-\lambda_{r+1}) = LR_{tr}(r|k) - LR_{tr}(r+1|k) \tag{5.4}$$

for $r = 0, 1, ..., k - 1$.

For the aggregate REIT index, the trace statistic and maximum eigenvalue statistic yield conflicting results. In this case, a single cointegrating vector is assumed because the test statistic indicating no cointegrating vectors is almost rejected at the 0.05 level in the contradictory test. This finding is consistent with the results of Boudry et al. (2012). For REIT (Office), REIT (Industrial) and REIT (Retail) the trace statistic and maximum eigenvalue statistic indicate two cointegrating relationships, whereas for REIT (Apartment) the trace static and maximum eigenvalue statistic suggest only one cointegrating relationship.

RESULTS

Exhibit 5.6 reports the estimates of the cointegrating relations (β) and the adjustment parameters (α) of the VEC model. The cointegrating vector β is not identified unless some arbitrary normalization is imposed. The reported estimates of β and α are based on the normalization $\beta'^{S_{11}}\beta = I$ (S_{11} is defined in Johansen, 1995). In the case of two cointegrating relationships, the restriction is imposed such that one relationship captures the dynamics among the public real estate market, the private real estate market, and the financial markets (REIT, Russell 2000, Bond, Control, and TBI), and the other relationship captures the relationship between the private real estate market and the financial markets (S&P 500, Russell 2000, Bond, Control, and TBI).

Panel A of Exhibit 5.6 reports the results for the aggregate REITs, and Panels B through E report results for the REIT property types. For the aggregate REITs, all β coefficients are statistically significant except the one for the S&P 500 index, which makes sense because the S&P 500 index represents large-cap firms whereas REITs consist of mostly small-cap firms. The significant β coefficients suggest long-run equilibrium relationships among the public real estate market, the private real estate market, and the financial markets. As to the α coefficients, only the coefficients for REIT and TBI are statistically significant, indicating that REIT and TBI adjust to a long-run equilibrium relation when they get out of equilibrium. This evidence may also suggest that the financial markets lead the public and private real estate markets. Note that the α coefficient of Control is not statistically significant, indicating that, even though the matched firms share the similar financial situation with REIT firms (e.g., size, book-to-market ratio, return, and volatility of returns), REITs have unique features that are similar to TBI in the long run.

For REIT (Apartment) (Panel E of Exhibit 5.6), however, the results for the β coefficients suggest that only REIT (Apartment), Control, and TBI (Apartment) share a long-run equilibrium relation. Because Control is a group of non-REIT small-cap firms that share a similar size and book-to-market ratio with REIT firms,

Exhibit 5.6 Vector Error Correction Models 1994Q1–2011Q4

	α_1	t	α_2	t	β_1	t	β_2	t
Panel A. REIT								
REIT	0.21	−2.38			1.00			
S&P 500	0.00	0.02			−0.05	−0.23		
Russell 2000	−0.00	−0.03			0.95	1.90		
Bond	−0.01	−0.91			0.67	2.07		
Control	0.00	0.03			−2.39	−8.93		
TBI	−0.17	−4.33			0.73	3.89		
Panel B. REIT (Office)								
REIT	−0.34	−2.15	0.26	2.50	1.00			
S&P 500	−0.09	−0.70	0.06	0.78			1.00	
Russell 2000	−0.12	−0.83	0.07	0.76	1.12	2.29	−0.77	−1.10
Bond	−0.01	−0.53	0.01	0.54	1.79	3.13	−0.04	−0.05
Control	0.02	0.14	−0.02	−0.23	−0.75	−1.96	1.86	3.43
TBI	0.08	1.46	0.03	0.89	−2.01	−6.02	2.39	−5.08
Panel C. REIT (Industrial)								
REIT	−0.50	−2.84	0.53	3.15	1.00			
S&P 500	0.07	0.36	−0.14	−0.78			1.00	
Russell 2000	−0.05	−−0.32	0.01	0.05	0.40	1.29	−1.69	−2.15
Bond	0.03	0.14	−0.08	−0.43	0.70	2.08	−0.80	−0.95
Control	−0.04	−1.18	0.04	1.25	−1.99	−7.84	3.37	5.23
TBI	0.29	3.97	−0.01	−0.21	0.23	1.07	−2.91	−5.35
Panel D. REIT (Retail)								
REIT	−0.92	−6.20	0.05	1.57	1.00			
S&P 500	−0.14	−1.04	−0.01	−0.34			1.00	
Russell 2000	−0.23	−1.49	−0.01	−0.16	1.00	8.64	−3.68	−5.73
Bond	−0.04	−1.33	0.01	1.37	0.78	2.37	−7.71	−4.20
Control	−0.38	−2.32	−0.02	−0.54	−1.53	−14.82	4.04	7.02
TBI	0.22	3.39	0.09	5.82	−0.56	−6.23	−2.73	−5.46
Panel E. REIT (Apartment)								
REIT	−0.05	−1.58			1.00			
S&P 500	0.02	0.73			0.19	0.23		
Russell 2000	0.03	0.94			−0.10	−0.05		
Bond	−0.01	−0.95			3.89	1.48		
Control	0.04	1.24			−3.17	−3.25		
TBI	−0.06	−4.34			3.26	5.20		

This table reports estimation results for VECM (2). It also reports the standard decomposition, where α refers to the adjustment matrix and β is the cointegrating matrix. REIT refers to the VECM with the aggregate REIT return from the CRSP/Ziman REIT database; REIT (Office, Retail, Industrial, and Apartment) refers to the VECM with the aggregate REIT property-type returns from the CRSP/Ziman REIT property-type database. The VECM specification includes the matching real estate index, the aggregate MIT TBI (or matching MIT TBI property-type indices), the control group of REITs, the S&P 500 index, the Russell 2000 value index, and the J.P. Morgan aggregate corporate bond index. Data are quarterly and cover the period 1994Q1 to 2011Q4.

this evidence indicates that REITs consisting of apartment properties are similar to small stocks and the corresponding apartment private real estate market. Furthermore, the results for the α coefficients show that only TBI (Apartment) adjusts to this long-run equilibrium, indicating that in the apartment real estate market the public real estate market leads the private real estate market, at least in the long run.

For REIT (Office), REIT (Industrial), and REIT (Retail), the results from both the trace statistics and maximum eigenvalue statistics reported in Exhibit 5.5 suggest two cointegrating relations. Therefore, the restriction is imposed that one relation captures the dynamics among the public real estate market, the private real estate market, and the financial markets (REIT, Russell 2000, Bond, Control, and TBI), and the other captures the relationship between the private real estate market and the financial markets (S&P 500, Russell 2000, Bond, Control, and TBI).

Panels B through D show that the estimation results for the Office, Industrial, and Retail property types are mainly consistent. For all three property types, except for Industrial, a cointegrating relationship exists among REIT, TBI, and financial markets, suggesting a long-run relation among the three markets. For all three property types, except for Office, evidence shows that REIT and TBI adjust toward each other and the financial markets. For REIT (Office), however, the results from the α coefficient suggest that in the Office real estate market, the private real estate market is leading the public real estate market in the long run. For all three property types, a long-run equilibrium relationship exists between financial markets and TBI, which conflicts with the results found in Boudry et al. (2012), who suggest that no long-run relationship exists between the TBI and financial markets. This conflicting result might come from the fact that the second cointegrating vector contains the Control group in which the size and book-to-market ratio matched non-REIT firms could share a long-run equilibrium relation with TBI.

To examine the effect of an innovation shock of one endogenous variable to the long-run equilibrium relationship between public and private real estate markets and financial markets, the impulse response functions are computed for all the variables in each of the VEC models. Exhibit 5.7 reports the results for the aggregate REIT index. For brevity, only the results of impulse response functions for the aggregate REIT index are reported. The results in Exhibit 5.7 show shocks from REITs to the TBI and vice versa, but the magnitude is larger for the response from the TBI to REITs. Other than the effect on each other, shocks to both REITs and the TBI have an effect on the bond market (represented as JP in the Exhibit 5.7) but not to other sectors of the financial markets. Shocks to financial markets tend to have a very small effect on each other, but the bond markets seem to react to shocks from all the markets.

SUMMARY AND CONCLUSIONS

This chapter has examined the connection between public and private real estate markets. Real estate assets offer an attractive laboratory for understanding issues involving asset pricing and price discovery because substantially similar assets can be observed trading in public markets (for REITs) and private markets (the transactions of institutional investors). However, major empirical challenges exist

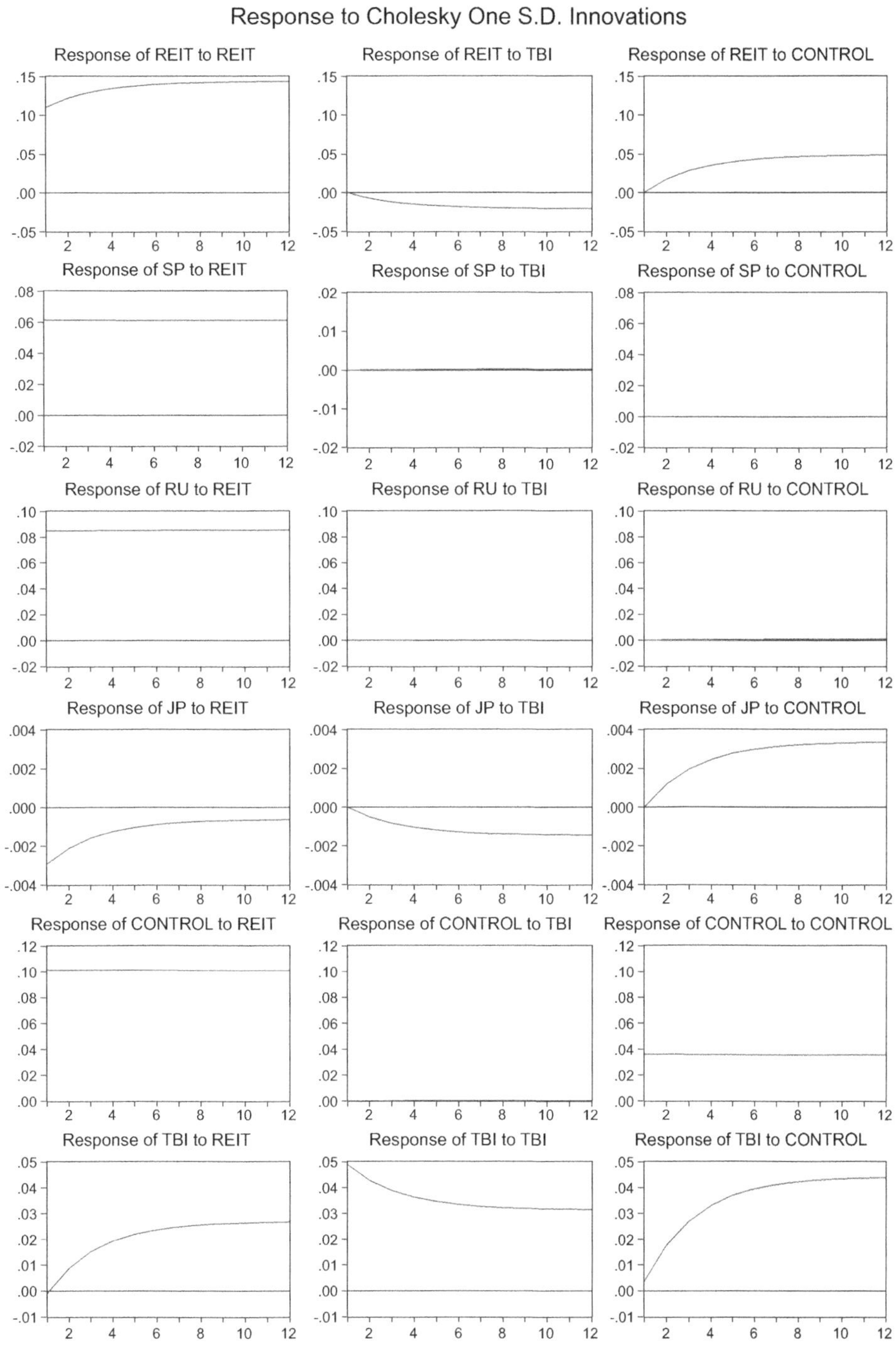

Exhibit 5.7 Impulse Response Functions (Aggregate REIT): 1994Q1–2011Q4
This figure graphs the impulse response functions for the VEC model that includes the aggregate REIT, the aggregate TBI, the Control, the S & P 500, the Russell 2000, and the J.P. Morgan bond index.

in order to fully capture the unique differences in the data sources available. Historical developments in this area largely reflect researchers grappling with these empirical challenges.

The chapter surveyed the literature covering the connection between public and private real estate markets. Almost 50 years ago researchers analyzed this topic and were aware of many important conceptual issues that needed to be addressed. These early studies were often limited in terms of the data availability, and the quantitative techniques were typically limited to simple bivariate analyses. Nonetheless, subsequent research often repeated and confirmed observations from these early studies. The development of more robust empirical analyses followed the availability of improved data sets on the returns in private real estate markets, such as the NCREIF index. Although not without limitations, this development was probably the single most important factor in the advancement of empirical research in real estate.

Improving data also coincided with advances in econometric methodology. Researchers moved from simple correlation analysis to dynamic regression models to cointegration analysis. Despite these advances, little consensus emerged on the fundamental question of the connection between public and private real estate markets. Some research indicates REITs are more properly considered to be equities than real estate. Other research finds conclusions were highly dependent on the time period used and a long-term connection to the direct market. Still other studies suggest a hybrid characteristic to REITs.

In an attempt to provide additional empirical evidence on this topic, this chapter followed recent studies by using multivariate cointegration tests to examine the connection between REITs and direct property markets. The study reported in this chapter closely followed Boudry et al. (2012) but included a data set consisting of a longer time period, which included the financial crisis of 2007–2008, as well as additional control variables. At the aggregate level, the empirical analysis shows a close connection among REITs, direct real estate markets, and the overall financial markets. However, an equilibrating mechanism appears to link REITs to the direct real estate market. At the sector level, the results for apartments differ from those of the other sectors. In particular, an equilibrium relationship between the controls, apartment REITs, and the apartment TBI index was found and suggests the close connection between apartment REITs and small capitalization stocks. For the other sectors, the results are more consistent with a long-run relationship existing among the financial market variables, REITs, and the direct real estate market. Finally, the chapter examined the size of the connections between the variables by using impulse response functions. REITs affect other financial variables as well as the direct property market. Shocks to the direct property market affect REITs but have little effect beyond that.

DISCUSSION QUESTIONS

1. Discuss the historical development of research on the connection between public and private real estate markets.
2. Explain the conceptual argument for why the returns of REITs might match that of the direct (private) real estate markets.

3. From the statistical evidence presented, explain whether the returns from private real estate are correlated with REITs or other financial market variables.
4. Explain why cointegration techniques are used to test whether REITs and private real estate markets share a long-run connection. From the evidence presented in this chapter, explain whether this is the case.

REFERENCES

Barber, Brad M., and John D. Lyon. 1997. "Detecting Long-run Abnormal Stock Returns: The Empirical Power and Specification of Test Statistics." *Journal of Financial Economics* 43:3, 341–372.

Barkham, Richard, and David Geltner. 1995. "Price Discovery in American and British Property Markets." *Real Estate Economics* 23:1, 21–44.

Bond, Shaun A., and Qingqing Chang. 2012. "Liquidity Dynamics across Public and Private Markets." *Journal of International Money and Finance*, forthcoming. Available at www.sciencedirect.com/science/article/pii/S0261560612001118.

Bond, Shaun A., Soosung Hwang, Paul Mitchell, and Stephen E. Satchell. 2007. "Will Private Equity and Hedge Funds Replace Real Estate in Mixed-Asset Portfolios?" *Journal of Portfolio Management* 33:5, 74–84.

Boudry, Walter I., N. Edward Coulson, Jarl G. Kalberg, and Crocker H. Liu. 2012. "On the Hybrid Nature of REITs." *Journal of Real Estate Economics and Finance* 44:1–2, 230–249.

Brueggeman, William B., A. H. Chen, and Thomas G. Thibodeau. 1984. "Real Estate Investment Funds: Performance and Portfolio Considerations." *AREUEA Journal* 12:3, 333–353.

Chau, K. W., Bryan D. MacGregor, and Greg Schwann. 2001. "Price Discovery in the Hong Long Real Estate Market." *Journal of Property Research* 18:3, 187–216.

Clayton, Jim, and Greg MacKinnon. 2001. "The Time-Varying Nature of the Link between REIT, Real Estate and Financial Asset Returns." *Journal of Real Estate Portfolio Management* 7:1, 43–54.

Eichholtz, P.M.A., and David J. Hartzell. 1996. "Property Shares, Appraisals and the Stock Market: An International Perspective." *Journal of Real Estate Finance and Economics* 12:2, 163–178.

Engle, Robert F., and Clive W. J. Granger. 1987. "Co-integration and Error Correction: Representation, Estimation, and Testing." *Econometrica* 55:2, 251–276.

Fama, Eugene F., and Kenneth R. French. 1992. "The Cross-section of Expected Stock Returns." *Journal of Finance* 47:2, 427–465.

Fisher, Jeffrey, David Geltner, and Henry Pollakowski. 2007. "A Quarterly Transactions-Based Index (TBI) of Institutional Real Estate Investment Performance and Movements in Supply and Demand." *Journal of Real Estate Finance and Economics* 34:1, 5–33.

Geltner, David. 1991. "Smoothing in Appraisal-Based Returns." *Journal of Real Estate Finance and Economics* 4:3, 327–345.

Geltner, David, and Brian Kluger. 1998. "REIT-Based Pure-Play Portfolios: The Case of Property Types." *Real Estate Economics* 26:4, 581–612.

Giliberto, S. Michael. 1990. "Real Estate Investment Trusts and Real Estate Returns." *Journal of Real Estate Research* 5:2, 259–264.

Glascock, John L., Chiuling Lu, and Raymond W. So. 2000. "Further Evidence on the Integration of REIT, Bond, and Stock Returns." *Journal of Real Estate Finance and Economics* 20:2, 177–194.

Gyourko, Joseph, and Donald B. Keim. 1992. "What Does the Stock Market Tell Us about Real Estate Returns?" *Journal of the American Real Estate and Urban Economics Association* 20:3, 457–485.

Hoag, James W. 1980. "Towards Indices of Real Estate Value and Return." *Journal of Finance* 35:2, 569–580.

Hoesli, Martin, and Elias Oikarinen. 2012. "Are REITs Real Estate? Evidence from International Sector Level Data." Swiss Finance Institute Research Paper Series No 12–15.

Johansen, Soren. 1991. "Estimation and Hypothesis Testing of Cointegration Vectors in Gaussian Vector Autoregressive Models." *Econometrica* 59:6, 1551–1580.

Johansen, Soren. 1995. *Likelihood-based Inference in Cointegrated Vector Autoregressive Models.* Oxford: Oxford University Press.

Liu, Crocker, David Hartzell, Wylie Greig, and Terry Grissom. 1990. "The Integration of the Real Estate Market and the Stock Market: Some Preliminary Evidence." *Journal of Real Estate Finance and Economics* 3:3, 261–282.

MacKinnon, James G., Alfred Haug, and Leo Michelis. 1996. "Numerical Distribution Functions of Likelihood Ratio Tests for Cointegration." *Journal of Applied Econometrics* 14:5, 563–577.

Miles, Mike, and Tom McCue. 1982. "Historic Returns and Institutional Real Estate Portfolios." *AREUEA Journal* 10:2, 184–199.

Miles, Mike, and Tom McCue. 1984. "Commercial Real Estate Returns." *AREUEA Journal* 12:3, 355–377.

Pagliari, Joseph L., Kevin A. Scherer, and Richard T. Monopoli. 2005. "Public Versus Private Real Estate Equities: A More Refined, Long-Term Comparison." *Real Estate Economics* 33:1, 147–187.

Riddiough, Timothy J., Mark Moriarty, and P. J. Yeatman. 2005. "Privately Versus Publicly Held Asset Investment Performance." *Real Estate Economics* 33:1, 121–146.

Robichek, Alexander A., Richard A. Cohn, and John T. Pringle. 1972. "Returns on Alternative Investment Media and Implications for Portfolio Construction." *Journal of Business* 45:3, 427–443.

Ross, Stephen A., and Randall C. Zisler. 1991. "Risk and Return in Real Estate." *Journal of Real Estate Finance and Economics* 4:2, 175–190.

Sebastian, Steffen, and Alexander Schatz. 2009. "Real Estate Equities—Real Estate or Equities?" European Public Real Estate Association (EPRA) Research Paper. Available at www.epra.com/media/EPRA˙research˙on˙Real˙Estate˙vs˙Equities.pdf.

Seck, Diery. 1996. "The Substitutability of Real Estate Assets." *Real Estate Economics* 24:1, 75–95.

Smith, Keith V., and David Shulman. 1976. "The Performance of Equity Real Estate Investment Trusts." *Financial Analysts Journal* 32:5, 61–66.

Wendt, Paul F., and Sui N. Wong. 1965. "Investment Performance: Common Stocks versus Apartment Houses." *Journal of Finance* 20:4, 633–646.

Yunus, N., J. Andrew Hansz, and Paul J. Kennedy. 2012. "Dynamic Interactions between Private and Public Real Estate Markets: Some International Evidence." *Journal of Real Estate Finance and Economics*, forthcoming. Available at http://dx.doi.org/10.1007/s11146–010–9297–5.

ABOUT THE AUTHORS

Shaun Bond holds the West Shell, Jr. Chair of Real Estate and is Director of the Real Estate Center in the Department of Finance and Real Estate at the University of Cincinnati. He held an appointment in the Department of Land Economy at the University of Cambridge and was also a visiting professor at the Pennsylvania State University and The George Washington University. Professor Bond is a member of the editorial boards of *Real Estate Economics*, *Journal of Property Research*, and *International Journal of Housing Markets and Analysis*. His research interests concern real estate finance and financial econometrics. He has published in such journals as the *Journal of Business*, *Real Estate Economics*, *Journal of Real Estate Finance and Economics*, *Journal of International Money and Finance*, *Journal of Portfolio Management*, and *European Journal of Finance*. He holds a PhD and an MPhil in economics from the University of Cambridge and an undergraduate degree in economics from the University of Queensland.

Qingqing Chang is a PhD candidate in Finance in the Department of Finance and Real Estate at the University of Cincinnati. Her broad areas of interest are empirical corporate finance, asset pricing, and their application in the real estate market. She is investigating market and idiosyncratic liquidity across different financial assets, and their relationships with stock returns. She has presented her research at both the ASSA meetings and international conferences. She has published in the *Journal of International Money and Finance*. Ms. Chang graduated summa cum laude from Renmin University of China, with a BS in management (concentration in land resource management and urban planning) and an MS in economics (concentration in real estate).

CHAPTER 6

Commercial Real Estate

PETER CHINLOY
Professor, Department of Finance and Real Estate, Kogod School of Business, American University

INTRODUCTION

Commercial real estate is an important alternative investment because of its size and potential returns. The purpose of this chapter is to examine the issues of return and asset classes in real estate investment. The return on securities is the sum of any dividend and capital gains. An analogous return in commercial real estate is the sum of the cap rate and capital gains. The *cap rate* is the ratio of net rent after operating expenses to the price of the property. The cap rate is based on rents, which are sometimes tied to inflation. The majority of the return over the long term comes from the yield. Commercial real estate has features similar to an indexed bond, but with the principal subject to appreciation. The asset is illiquid, allowing investors to capture a premium if they do not require short-term cash.

From the *National Income and Product Accounts for the United States*, the Bureau of Economic Analysis estimates a value of commercial real estate in 2010 of $6 trillion. Of this amount, $4 trillion is investable. Commercial real estate has four asset types: apartments, industrial, office, and retail. The National Council of Real Estate Investment Fiduciaries (NCREIF) is a trade association of institutional commercial real estate investors. In its *NCREIF Indices Review, First Quarter 2011*, office and retail make up about one-third each, with the remaining 25 and 9 percent divided between apartments and industrial, respectively.

Other sources document the importance of commercial real estate within a portfolio. According to Miles and Tolleson (1997), commercial real estate equity constitutes about 7 percent of the investable assets in the United States. Another 7 percent is the mortgage debt on commercial real estate. The market capitalization of U.S. stocks represents 25 percent of investable assets. Consequently, large institutional investors have taken notice of the importance of commercial real estate as an option in the portfolio selection process.

El-Arian (2008) proposes a portfolio that can generate a long-term real return between 5 and 7 percent annually. The standard deviation of the returns ranges between 8 and 12 percent annually. After constructing the efficient frontier, commercial real estate is 6 percent of the portfolio. Another 5 percent is in infrastructure assets for roads, highways, and airports. For the remainder of the portfolio, 42 percent is in stocks and 19 percent in bonds, for a total of 61 percent in traded securities. Rounding out the portfolio are private equity (7 percent), special opportunities (8 percent), and commodities (11 percent).

Real estate can also be an important part of a portfolio for endowments. For example, Swensen (2000), a Yale endowment manager, contends that cash requirements for endowments are predictable and small. Thus, the endowment should seek illiquid investments to exploit market inefficiencies and capture any associated premiums. In 2010, Yale placed 21 percent of its endowment in absolute return or hedge funds, 30 percent in private equity, and 28 percent in real assets. This allocation has 79 percent of the portfolio in illiquid assets. In its 2010 annual report, the Yale endowment noted its intention to increase the proportion of illiquid assets to 90 percent. Half of its real assets (14 percent of the portfolio) are allocated to real estate and infrastructure.

Commercial real estate is 7 percent of Yale's portfolio, similar to the findings and recommended allocations of Miles and Tolleson (1997) and El-Arian (2008). Its commercial real estate is equal to the position in domestic stocks. Domestic bonds and foreign stocks, at 4 and 10 percent, respectively, round out the portfolio, which holds no cash. The actual outcome is a real return of 6.2 percent with a standard deviation of 14.7 percent over 1990 to 2010. These estimates use returns, variances, and covariances across the assets and a Markowitz allocation.

Endowments, pension funds, retirement accounts, and life or other insurance investments with limited and predictable short-term liquidity requirements target a long-run real return. Commercial real estate's long-run return of at least 6 percent meets a target set for these funds.

Yet, these returns do not come without risks that are specific to real estate. The two major risks addressed in this chapter are barriers to entry and agency issues.

Income-producing real estate has landlords as owners and tenants. Investments in commercial real estate involve various parties. The investor owning the building has an asset manager dealing with the balance sheet and capital items. A property manager handles rent collection and expenses on the income statement. The tenant is either a household in a residential asset or a firm in a nonresidential one. The many parties involved in a real estate investment lead to conflicts of interest and agency issues. These conflicts induce separate contractual arrangements for the main categories of commercial real estate (apartments, industrial, office, and retail).

The chapter begins by discussing supply and barriers to entry. Demand for commercial real estate is by national and international investors. Supply is controlled by local governments and cultural rules, leading to variation in performance across locations. The next section examines returns to holding real estate. As with other assets, commercial real estate returns are the sum of income and capital gains. Unlike the capital gains on stocks, however, expected real estate capital gains are equal to the rate of inflation. The dividend yield of the cap rate on real estate is then the expected real return. That expected real return becomes the discount rate.

The remaining sections discuss the asset types within commercial real estate. The sequence by ascending complexity and agency goes from apartments to industrial, office, and retail. With apartments, owners carry out operating and capital expenses rather than constrained and diffused tenants. Leases are quoted with full service to the tenant. In industrial warehouses and distribution centers, tenants know their space and requirements. They operate the building and pay its expenses, and rents are triple net to tenants. *Triple net* means that tenants pay all expenses. In offices, tenants are frequently large firms and owners setting up single-asset entities to avoid contagion and asset substitution. Tenants must negotiate capital improvements up front.

Revenue from an individual tenant in a shopping center depends on the performance of adjacent stores. Tenants demand operating and capital expense concessions when their marketing and sales operations create positive externalities. These anchor tenants include department stores and supermarkets. The chargebacks of operating and capital costs are shifted among tenants. Anchors pay less of these expenses, and in-line or satellite tenants pay higher proportions. Separately, all tenants share revenue with the owner. Just as tenants face sales taxes on revenues or franchise fees, they also pay a percentage of their sales as rents. The revenue sharing offers incentives for landlords to maintain the attractiveness of the property. These issues are discussed in the remainder of the chapter.

SUPPLY AND ENVIRONMENT

This section addresses the supply and environment for commercial real estate, which differs across markets. Local restrictions govern land use, zoning, construction, and renovation. These restrictions involve barriers to entry in some markets, notably along the two U.S. coasts. Other markets have almost unlimited entry. In some markets, the high barriers to entry reduce new construction when prices or rents change. In others, the barriers are sufficiently low that construction has fewer limitations. A uniform positive demand shock, such as from lower interest rates, has different impacts across markets. In tight markets with limited supply, prices rise. In markets with limited barriers, construction rises.

With stocks and bonds, buyers and sellers arrive at the market simultaneously as traders. These parties set bid and ask prices at which they will trade. They have maximum bid and minimum asks as reserves. In illiquid markets, such as for commercial real estate, demand and supply are not coincident in time. Suppliers or sellers arrive first and set asking prices. Buyers arrive later and observe the inventory of assets for sale and space to rent.

Construction material costs are similar around the country and are available from sources such as RSMeans and Boeckh. Construction workers are mobile and move to jobs. Agriculture is a commodity, and its demand prices fall at the edges of metropolitan areas. Because agriculture is a commodity and priced identically, land use demand is similar around the country.

The implication is that the principal difference in real estate costs comes from the land eligible or entitled for construction. Glaeser (2010) indicates that the difference between entitled and agricultural land prices accounts for most of the differential in intercity real estate prices. For example, tighter entitlement restrictions have limited the construction of skyscrapers in Manhattan.

The Wharton Residential Land Use Regulatory Index combines restrictions on permitting and entitling land across jurisdictions (Gyourko, Saiz, and Summers, 2008). The nine tightest states in land use regulation border the Atlantic or Pacific oceans. These include Washington, Oregon, California, and Hawaii, four states that border the Pacific Ocean. Geographical constraints for mountains and water are additional restrictions on the proportion of land available for development. The most hemmed-in markets are in coastal California and South Florida (Saiz, 2010). The five most restrictive markets are Miami, Los Angeles, Fort Lauderdale, San Francisco, and San Diego. At the other end, Atlanta, Dallas, and Houston have limited barriers to entry.

REAL ESTATE CHARACTERISTICS

Real estate has several distinguishing characteristics, including differences in accounting, management of properties, financing, illiquidity, and as a hedge against inflation. The income received from real estate mixes current and capital revenues and expenses. Consequently, income statements become subject to interpretation and manipulation.

Real estate with long-term hold strategies involves capital expenditures. Capital expenditures and ongoing repairs are long-term investments, and the ability to manage them differs across owners. Not spending on repairs raises net operating income (NOI) and the short-term cap rate. The result is a type of reverse window dressing where a property offered for sale may under-spend or defer maintenance.

For properties generating cash flow, real estate offers borrowing without pledging other collateral or on a nonrecourse basis. For properties with mortgage debt, an important consideration is whether financing is recourse. A *recourse mortgage* means that the lender can seek repayment from sources other than the specific property in the event of a default. These sources include other property or the personal assets of a key principal or guarantor. A *nonrecourse mortgage* means that only the secured collateral serves as the source for repaying the loan.

Accounting rules are not always consistent with real estate measurement. Balance sheets measure real estate at historical cost, or the purchase price plus capital improvements. U.S. generally accepted accounting principles (GAAP) do not permit adjustments for inflation or deflation of asset prices. Thus, balance sheets do not reflect changes in asset prices. A source of difference between book and market values of firms is the implied value of real estate assets.

Accounting rules also require depreciating real estate assets at standardized rates. Since the 1986 Tax Reform Act, nonresidential properties are depreciated on a straight-line basis with a useful life of 39.5 years.

PRICES AND VOLUMES

With real estate, the price is no longer a sufficient statistic for the market valuation because the price must be adjusted for the time needed to sell the property. As in other illiquid markets, real estate clearing comes from a mixture of prices and quantities. An example comes from the housing market. An owner planning to sell a house places a listing. A certain number of houses sell, leading to a sales-listing ratio. The inverse is the time needed to sell the existing inventory. The mean price is only for the houses that sell. The *effective price* is the product of the mean price and the sales-listing ratio.

A similar situation applies in the rental market. Suppose an apartment building has 100 rental units with 90 apartments occupied with monthly rentals of $1,000 for each apartment. The vacancy rate is 10 percent. The effective rent is $1,000 times 90 percent, or $900 per month. However, this effective rent is sometimes adjusted for collection costs, including bounced checks and uncollected rent.

Both the spot market for space and the asset for the properties involve a price-quantity clearing mixture. The dynamic measure of quantities in the space market is absorption. In each period, the inventory available is the previous level plus construction less demolition. The *absorption* is the change in inventory occupied during a period, which is measured as an absolute cost, not on a percentage basis. A growth rate of the rent charge often occurs between periods, and that rent growth is negatively correlated with the vacancy rate. The *equilibrium vacancy rate* reduces the rent growth to zero. Rents can be quoted in real terms, meaning that they are adjusted for inflation. A separate and lower equilibrium vacancy rate reduces real rent growth to zero.

REAL ESTATE RETURNS

The justification for an increased weight of commercial real estate in a portfolio is its ongoing returns in excess of price inflation with low apparent volatility. The NCREIF website reports property index returns for commercial real estate and its four main components. The overall series began in 1978, and up to the third quarter of 2011 the average annual return was 8.9 percent, with a standard deviation of 7.9 percent. Over the same period, NCREIF reports the following annual returns: industrial, 9.1 percent; office, 8.3 percent; and retail, 9.2 percent. The apartment series started in 1984 and offered a mean annual return of 8.7 percent through the third quarter of 2011. The annual standard deviations for the four asset types of commercial real estate are: apartments, 7.6 percent; industrial, 7.9 percent; office, 10.0 percent; and retail, 6.5 percent. Over the same period, the Standard & Poor's 500 had a 9.1 percent annual return, with standard deviations ranging from 14 to 21 percent. Thus, measured real estate returns are comparable to those in stocks but with half the volatility. Using 4 percent as an average riskless rate, commercial real estate has a Sharpe ratio of 0.6. The *Sharpe ratio* is a measure of risk-adjusted performance that compares excess return to the total risk of a portfolio, where total risk is measured by the portfolio's standard deviation. Investors prefer higher Sharpe ratios. The Sharpe ratio of 0.6 for commercial real estate compares with 0.4 for stocks at the lowest volatility estimate.

Subsequent real estate returns have confirmed this apparent paradox of high risk-adjusted returns. NCREIF provides a return series based on properties owned by its members. CoStar and Real Capital Analytics offer alternative return series. CoStar's index is based on repeated sales of the same property. All of these indices report similar performance of commercial real estate after 2001.

Exhibit 6.1 reports average returns to holding commercial real estate after inflation. Returns are from NCREIF, and the Consumer Price Index (CPI) measures inflation. During the period 1979 to 2001, commercial real estate earned an inflation-adjusted return of 4.8 percent annually, with a standard deviation of 7.4 percent. The four property classes had the following annual returns and standard deviations shown in parentheses: apartments, 5.7 (7.4) percent; industrial, 5.1 (7.5) percent; office, 4.1 (9.2) percent; and retail, 5.3 (6.7) percent.

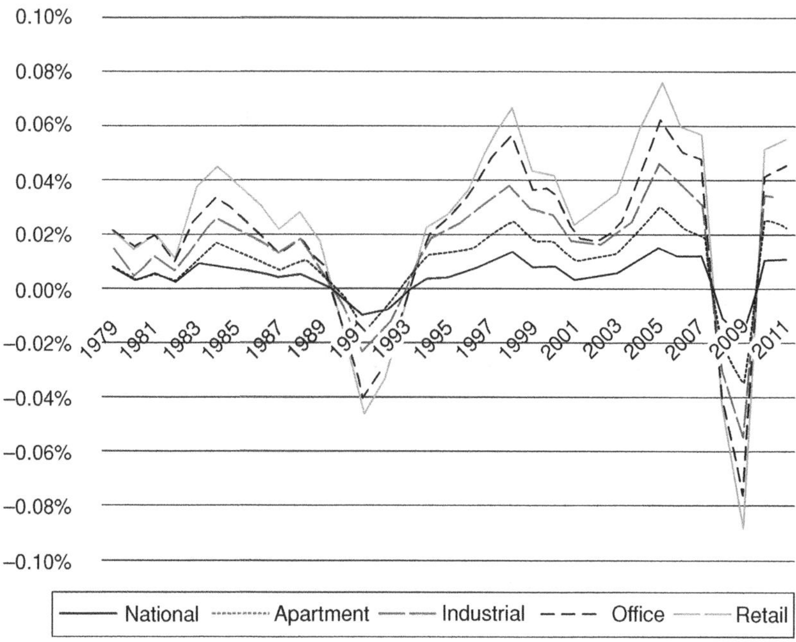

Exhibit 6.1 Inflation-Adjusted Commercial Real Estate Returns, 1979 to 2011
This exhibit presents inflation-adjusted commercial real estate returns over the period 1979 to 2011 for the following areas: national, apartment, industrial, office, and retail. Commercial real estate returns are from NCREIF at ncreif.org. Inflation is the growth rate of the Consumer Price Index from the U.S. Bureau of Labor Statistics at bls.gov. The inflation rate is subtracted from the annual return. Data for 2011 are annualized based on the first three quarters of the year.

As shown in Exhibit 6.1, the real estate returns are highly correlated with each other. The asset earned negative real returns during 1991 to 1993, after the recession of 1990 to 1991. During the financial crisis of 2008 and 2009, real estate earned negative returns but bounced back in 2010 and 2011. The overall returns indicate that real estate earned inflation-adjusted returns between 4 and 6 percent annually, consistent with targets for overall portfolios. The high positive correlation with inflation itself makes commercial real estate an inflation hedge (Miles and Mahoney, 1997).

These returns are subject to measurement errors that plague all illiquid assets. One issue is that in the data before 2001 assets were valued at the end of the year for portfolio purposes. Real estate rarely trades, so properties not selling were valued based on appraised. Appraisers do not take into account volatility and tend to extrapolate or smooth prices. The result is lower measured volatility that understates actual risk.

One response is to use only actively traded properties. The price index is based on pairing the same property registering two sells on different dates. In a regression, the logarithm of capital gains is the dependent variable. The independent variables are a set of dummies for all the time periods in the sample. For each capital gain, the second sale has a dummy variable of plus one for its date. The first sale has a dummy variable of minus one for its date. The same property is compared at different selling dates to control for other quality differences.

While real estate exhibits these return relationships, transactions are infrequent. An investor holding these assets requires knowledge at the end of a reporting year as to what they are worth. This information constitutes the balance sheet and holding of the portfolio. With real estate having few transactions, this means conducting an appraisal or opinion of value. Using repeat sales entails discarding between half and 80 percent of transactions in an already thin market.

Mean reversion in real estate returns occurs over very long time series. Hoyt (1933) examined the price of urban land in Chicago between 1830 and 1930. Over the century, the average rate of land price increase is the inflation rate. While not for commercial real estate, Eicholtz (1997) finds that house prices in Amsterdam over the period 1628 to 1973 increased at virtually the rate of inflation.

Over the period 1899 to 1999, Wheaton, Baranski, and Templeton (2009) find that the real return to office buildings in New York is the cap rate or income yield. Capital gains are at the rate of inflation. During the 1980s, New York office buildings earned a return of 40 percent cumulatively above the rate of inflation. During the period between 1981 and 1986, accelerated depreciation and the ability to deduct operating losses from real estate against any income lowered the cost of capital and raised prices. The 1986 Tax Reform Act limited depreciation to a constant basis and limited loss deductibility. The reforms were phased and effective in 1990. With the subsidies removed, office prices gave up the 40 percent premium during the 1990s.

As with any asset, the return to holding real estate is the dividend yield plus capital gains. *Dividend yield* is the net rent collected after expenses as a proportion of the price. This yield is known as the *income capitalization* or *cap rate*.

The *return to real estate* is the sum of the cap rate or dividend yield and capital gains. NCREIF reports that cap rates for office, industrial, and retail range between 6 and 9 percent annually. These rates declined to the lower range during the 2006 to 2009 period. A weighted average return on commercial real estate can be structured to yield 5 to 7 percent annually.

The *real return* is the cap rate plus the premium of real estate appreciation over general prices. Eicholtz (1997) and Wheaton et al. (2009) estimate that premium to be zero. In effect, the empirical results indicate that the inflation-adjusted return to real estate has two components. The cap rate is the long-run real return. Another component is an error term around the long-run rate of inflation. The cap rate straddles a real long-term target return between 5 to 7 percent annually.

For real estate over the long run, Equation 6.1 shows the annual return:

$$\text{Return} = \text{Cap rate} + (\text{Rate of capital gains} - \text{Inflation rate}) \qquad (6.1)$$

The bracketed term for the rate of capital gains minus the inflation rate has an expected value of zero. Thus, the cap rate is the expected long-run return and is the real discount rate applicable to commercial property.

Using data for U.S. stock markets since 1802, Siegel (2008) finds that the long-term real rate of return on stocks is 6.8 percent annually. Dimson, Marsh, and Staunton (2002) find the long-term real rate of return to be 6.3 percent annually for 1900 to 2000 over 16 stock markets.

Goetzmann and Ibbotson (2006) find that stocks have a nominal annual return of 7.9 percent from 1792 to 1925. The annual capital gains and income are 1.9 percent and 6 percent, respectively. The standard deviation is 14.6 percent, and the rate of inflation is 0.9 percent. Bonds have a yield of 4.2 percent annually. From 1926 to 2004, stocks have an annual nominal return of 12.3 percent, with a standard deviation of 20.3 percent. Capital gains are 7.9 percent, income is 4.4 percent, and inflation is 3.1 percent annually.

Equation 6.2 shows a condition for stocks that is similar to that for real estate:

$$\begin{aligned}\text{Return} = {} & \text{Capital gains} + \text{Dividend premium} \\ & +(\text{Dividend rate} - \text{Inflation rate})\end{aligned} \tag{6.2}$$

The long-run rate of capital gains is the stock return and discount rate. The dividend yield less the inflation rate has an expected value of zero. A premium above the inflation rate is paid on dividends because of transaction costs associated with realizing capital gains. This structure does not explain why dividends and capital gains reversed roles over two centuries.

The long-run stock return at 6 percent annually is similar to that for real estate except with greater volatility. Pastor and Stambaugh (2011) contend that even with centuries of data no assurance exists that the historical return is a forecast of the future. Uncertainty over the expected return outweighs mean reversion, so volatility increases over long holding lengths. Eddings (2011) reports that Treasury bonds returned 11.5 percent annually from September 1981 to September 2011, as compared with 10.8 percent for the Standard & Poor's 500 index. Bonds had not previously outperformed stocks in any 30-year period since 1861.

Real estate has in measured performance a comparable return to other assets, such as stocks, but with lower volatility. Because capital gains, on average, increase at the rate of inflation, the cap rate yield is a real rate of return.

Another characteristic of commercial real estate is that it serves as an inflation hedge. A regression of aggregate NCREIF real estate returns for 1979 to 2011 to the third quarter on U.S. CPI growth yields a coefficient not significantly different from one. Real estate returns are almost perfectly correlated with inflation.

DiPasquale and Wheaton (1995) describe a sequence of rental, asset price, and construction markets for real estate. In a static equilibrium, the rent level and the rate of vacancy clear the rental market for space. The real estate market is cleared by prices and quantities. The vacancy-adjusted effective rent is the flow to holding apartments. Households generate a downward-sloping demand for space. Supply is set by local restrictions and can be viewed as perfectly inelastic in the short run. Barring explicit controls, the rent is set above where demand and supply is equal. The result is an excess supply contributing to the vacancy. The equilibrium vacancy rate clears the market at a given rent.

Local regulations and the cost of building materials determine the amount of new construction. Construction can be viewed as a call option. The value depends on the price of existing assets, their volatility, and the time to build. When the asset price is below a strike price determined by new construction costs, no additions to inventory take place. High asset prices trigger new construction, adding to inventory during booms and bubbles.

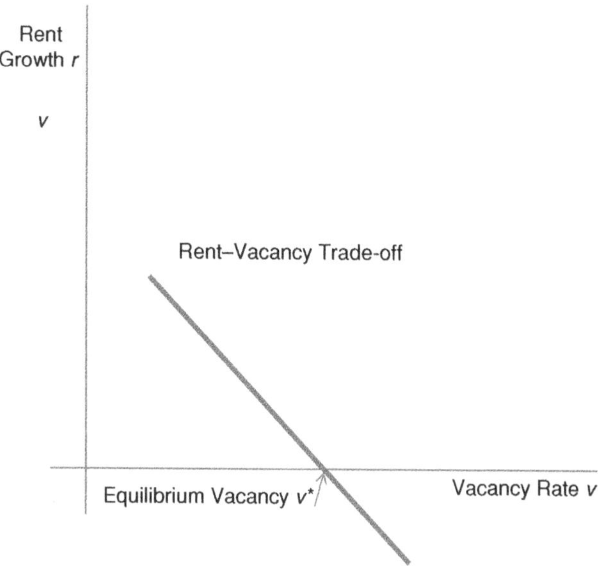

Exhibit 6.2 Rent–Vacancy Trade-off
This exhibit shows the trade-off between rent growth and the vacancy rate. A higher vacancy rate forces rent increases downward.

With loan balances fixed, default is similar to a put option held by the real estate owner. When the asset price falls below nonrecourse debt, the default put option is in the money. If owners exercise their default options, then lenders receive the properties by foreclosure.

Exhibit 6.2 shows the relationship between rental increases on the vertical axis and the vacancy rate on the horizontal axis. The solid line is the rent-vacancy trade-off, which is negatively sloped. Where the rent–vacancy trade-off intersects, the horizontal axis is the equilibrium vacancy rate, which is the rate at which rent increases are reduced to zero.

APARTMENTS

Apartment tenants are liquidity constrained and vary in their ability to maintain a property. By paying all operating expenses, the landlord offers a full-service rent to tenants. Apartments include residential apartments, student housing, and nursing homes.

In the United States, residential properties benefit from debt finance with federal entities. These entities are the Government National Mortgage Association, the Federal National Mortgage Association, and the Federal Home Loan Mortgage Corporation, which have respectively become known as Ginnie Mae, Fannie Mae, and Freddie Mac. These agencies' debt is tied to that of U.S. Treasuries, including federal guarantees. Those guarantees imply that borrowers do not have to take personal recourse. Debt financing on apartments and residential housing typically has long-term fixed interest rates and payments and is nonrecourse. Only the property serves as collateral for the loan and not assets of the key principals.

Exhibit 6.3 Residential Property

Income Statement
Rental income, rent roll
Less: Physical and economic vacancy
= Effective gross income (EGI). Full service gross (FSG) rent
Less: Operating expenses
Less: Capital expenditures (Capex)
= Funds from operations (FFO)
Valuation
Net operating income (NOI)/Cap rate = Price
Gross rent multiplier (GRM) ratio of price-to-rent roll
Household rent: Effective gross income (EGI)
Household
Mortgage interest rate after tax
Plus: Operating expenses
Less: Capital gains net of depreciation
= Cost of ownership (User cost)
Decision. A lower EGI relative to user cost leads the household toward renting.

This exhibit provides a format for conducting a financial analysis that can be used to determine the return and the household's choice between renting and owning.

For both sale and rental real estate properties, transactions involve bilateral negotiations as opposed to price-taking behavior. These negotiations and incentives give rise to agency issues, which are addressed in real estate contracts. Because contractual terms differ between parties, the cap rates of properties vary.

Real estate returns depend on the financial structure of deals and involve analyzing income statements and cash flows. Exhibit 6.3 shows a structure for residential properties and illustrates the income statement of an apartment complex and the household's choices. The rent is the gross revenue before any adjustments, such as subtracting economic vacancy. Vacancy is from physical space not being occupied and results from space occupied but where rent is not collected in full. The effective rent is the gross charge multiplied by one minus the vacancy rate. The tenant pays gross rent as a cost of being an apartment dweller.

In order from variable to fixed costs, operating expenses are management fees, utilities, repairs and maintenance, general and administrative, landscaping, insurance, and property taxes. Single-net rents involve tenants being billed for property taxes. Double-net rents have the tenants paying for property taxes and insurance. These fixed expenses do not generate disputes over usage if billed back to the tenants. In triple-net leases, tenants pay property taxes, insurance, and variable operating expenses.

Tenants pay expenses where no agency issue on maintenance or performance is present. Subtracting the operating expenses from effective rent produces NOI, which is divided by the price to produce the cap rate or yield.

Capital expenses include roofing, other structural costs, and the cost of turning the unit after a tenant leaves or arrives. These tenant improvements include painting, carpeting, and upgrades. Given agency issues with residential tenants' capabilities and constraints, the landlord pays the capital and operating expenses.

The household makes its choice between renting and owning. A rental involves paying the effective gross rent. The *effective gross rent* is the posted rate multiplied by one minus the vacancy rate. If the household views renting and owning as identical, the effective gross rent is equal to its user cost. The user cost is the cost of finance after tax, plus operating expenses, less capital gains net of depreciation. The user cost views the household as paying all the expenses of ownership. Equation 6.3 shows the formula for effective rent:

$$\begin{aligned}\text{Effective rent} &= \text{Rent}(1 - \text{Vacancy rate}) = \text{User cost}\\ &= (1 - \text{Household tax rate})(\text{Mortgage rate})\\ &\quad + \text{Operating expenses} - (\text{Capital gains} - \text{Depreciation})\end{aligned} \tag{6.3}$$

The user cost of homeownership is the after-tax cost of mortgage debt plus repair expenses, less capital gains. When the user cost increases because of higher mortgage rates or difficulty in qualifying, the tenure choice switches to apartments. When capital gains on houses decrease or become negative, the demand for rental housing increases. Because rising interest rates and falling house prices increase the demand for apartments, this asset exhibits countercyclical behavior.

In the U.S. market for houses, the household can borrow at an interest rate that has specific features. The loan rate is tied to long-term rates for Treasuries, with the 10-year note pricing 30-year fixed rate mortgages. The loan is typically nonrecourse except against the housing collateral. The loan effectively has an option to default. This option is in the money when prices fall below the loan balance. The loan is typically prepayable without penalty.

This type of debt financing is another distinguishing characteristic of apartments. The financing typically has restrictions on prepayment, including penalties or yield maintenance. The result is that financing is available for apartments when credit restrictions or downturns in the economy occur. This scenario is another condition where apartment investments are countercyclical and a hedge against output declines.

Based on the *Household and Family Statistics* of the U.S. Census in 2010, the overall homeownership rate was 66.9 percent. The remaining households are candidates for being renters. Non-Hispanic whites had a homeownership rate of 74.4 percent; the rate was 45.4 percent among black households. Hispanic households had homeownership rates of 47.5 percent and Asians 58.9 percent. Homeownership rates were 51.6 percent for household heads aged 30 to 34.

The supply of rental housing has responded sharply to incentives. Booms in U.S. rental housing construction occurred during the periods 1970 to 1975, 1981 to 1986, and after 1995. In each case, a type of tax incentive drove construction. In the most recent period, government-backed debt finance for construction together with tax credits for equity drove supply. Those tax credits are sold for cash to corporate investors.

INDUSTRIAL

An apartment building has many tenants on separate leases paying gross rents. At the opposite end of the spectrum, an industrial building usually has one tenant and minimal operating expenses. Industrial buildings include warehouses and distribution centers. For example, delivery of goods ordered online is from these warehouses or fulfillment centers. Warehouses and distribution centers are increasingly located near port facilities. The dominant market is the Inland Empire of Riverside-San Bernardino. This distribution center is near the Los Angeles-Long Beach ports that account for almost half of inbound container traffic in the United States. In 2010, absorption, or the change in occupancy, in the Inland Empire was more than 9 million square feet, or 75 percent of the national total.

Nonresidential commercial real estate includes office, industrial, and retail. A firm has a choice between owning and leasing its space. With the lessee paying operating expenses, the lease is triple net to the lessor. The lease rent per dollar of the property is the cap rate.

An operating lease satisfies other operating and accounting regulations. By satisfying certain conditions, an operating lease in the United States becomes off-balance-sheet financing. The lease does not appear as a liability on a firm's balance sheet while occurring in footnotes to the financial statements. A capital or finance lease is a liability, and thus it appears on the lessee's balance sheet. A capital lease satisfies at least one of four conditions regarding ownership, a bargain option, estimated economic life, and fair value. In the United States, the Financial Accounting Standards Board (1968) developed these provisions.

Under FASB 13, *Accounting for Leases*, a lease is classified as a finance lease if it meets any one of the following four criteria:

1. The title to the leased asset is transferred to the lessee at the end of the lease.
2. A bargain purchase option exists to purchase the leased property (i.e., the bargain price strike is sufficiently below fair market value that option exercise is assured).
3. The lease period is at least 75 percent of the estimated economic life of the property.
4. The present value of the lease payments is at least 90 percent of fair market value.

With firms as the tenants, the agency cost of operating expenses is resolved by shifting operating costs from the owners to the tenants. The tenants pay all operating expenses as triple-net leases. The owner's rental is the NOI. The firm makes a choice between renting or leasing and owning. The decision is based on a per-dollar basis of the property value comparison. Equation 6.4 determines whether a firm should own or lease its real estate:

$$\begin{aligned}(1 - \text{Lessee tax rate})(\text{Cap rate}) = {} & (1 - \text{Lessor tax rate})(\text{Mortgage rate}) \\ & -(\text{Capital gains} - \text{Depreciation})\end{aligned} \tag{6.4}$$

Equation 6.4 establishes a condition as to the business entity that owns and the one that leases. The party with the lower tax rate tends to be a lessee. From Equation 6.4, lessors tend to be lower-tax entities, such as endowments, pension funds, and insurance companies.

OFFICE MULTI-TENANT

An apartment building has many tenants who are liquidity constrained and not in business. An industrial building with a single tenant has one focused user, better able to carry out its repairs and operation. A different case is where one building has several business tenants. In offices, typically no sales and transactions are delivered to customers, but business is conducted. The agency issues have to do with allowing tenants to manage and customize their spaces. The landlord does not monitor or observe sales of the tenants in a professional space at medicine, law, and consulting firms. Firms have back-office support space in offices generating no revenues.

The owner, even if institutional, typically sets up a single-asset entity owning one building and possessing an uncertain time horizon. A tenant with a high credit rating and a long horizon wants to be assured that the landlord pays the capital and operating expenses. A solution to agency issues with the leasing contract is to have the landlord pay up-front capital expenses at the time of the lease. These tenant improvements and leasing commissions cover the transaction costs of moving and address agency costs.

The rent paid by the tenant covers both operating and capital expenses. These expenses are divided into categories for base rent, bumps, core factor, expense pass-through, and the recovery of the capital costs of tenant improvements. The *base rent* is a rent quoted per square foot per year. Upward adjustments, known as *bumps*, are additions for inflation over the term of the lease. A *core factor* is a proportional addition for space that is in common areas, such as elevators and hallways. An *expense pass-through* is an item for which the landlord receives the bill but is reimbursed by the tenant.

As Equation 6.5 shows, the gross rent on a multi-tenant commercial property, such as an office building, is:

$$\begin{aligned}\text{Gross rent} = {} & \text{Base rent} + \text{Bumps} + \text{Core factor} + \text{Expenses} \\ & \text{pass-through (Operating)} \\ & + \text{Tenant improvement recovery (Capital)}\end{aligned} \tag{6.5}$$

Equation 6.6 shows the net rent collected by the owner:

$$\begin{aligned}\text{Funds from operations (FFO)} = {} & \text{Gross rent}(1 - \text{Vacancy}) - \text{Operating} \\ & \text{expenses} - \text{Capital expenses}\end{aligned} \tag{6.6}$$

From the owner's perspective, the value of the lease is the present value of the gross rents paid by the tenant over the term, less the up-front tenant improvements and leasing commissions. The *nominal discount rate* is the cap rate plus the expected rate of inflation. The landlord will carry out, at a minimum, leases with a positive net present value (NPV).

As an example, a property has a \$30 per square foot base rent in the first year with 50 cent annual bumps and a 15 percent core factor. Its operating expenses are \$9 per square foot, and similar leases are offered to all tenants. The tenant improvements recovered in added rent are \$12.50 on \$50 of tenant improvements made for five years. In the initial year, the rent is the base of \$30 plus a core factor add-on

Exhibit 6.4 Nonresidential Property

Income Statement
Rental income
Less: Physical and economic vacancy
= Effective gross income
Less: Operating expenses
= Net operating income (NOI)/Cap rate = Price
Less: Capital expenditures
= Funds from operations (FFO)
Tenant (lessee) pays: Net rent = NOI, triple net lease
Tenant (lessee) after-tax cost: NOI after tax
2. Investment
Loan-to-value ratio (LTV) Loan/Price
Debt service coverage ratio (DSCR) NOI/Debt service
Depreciation benefits
Capital gains
Landlord (lessor) after-tax user cost = After-tax cost of capital + Capex – Depreciation benefits – Capital gains.
Equilibrium condition: Lessee after-tax rent = Lessor after-tax user cost

This exhibit provides a format for conducting a financial analysis that can be used to determine the return and the firm's choice between leasing and owning.

of 1.1, which results in an actual rent of $33. Adding the tenant improvements, the revenue on the lease is $45.50 per square foot per year. The building loses $8 per square foot for vacancy and bad debt, reducing effective gross income to $25 annually per square foot. Subtracting the $9 per square foot in operating expenses from the effective gross income, NOI is $16 per square foot annually. At a 10 percent cap rate, the building has a value of $16/0.10, or $160 per square foot.

The value of the lease is the present value of the effective rent less the tenant improvements and leasing commissions. Equation 6.7 gives the performance of the building:

$$\begin{aligned}\text{Rental income} - \text{Physical and economic vacancy} &= \text{Effective gross income}\\ &\quad -\text{Operating expenses} = \text{NOI}\end{aligned} \tag{6.7}$$

The value of the building is the NOI divided by the cap rate. The nominal cap rate is the rate of discount. Exhibit 6.4 summarizes the conditions for nonresidential property.

The agency risk of the overuse of maintenance and high operating expenses, including utilities, is managed by the base stop. *Base stop* expenses deal with differences in electricity use, including information technology equipment. The tenant is responsible for its share of these costs going forward, but not for previous operating expenses. The multi-tenant building causes externalities. Medical offices have high foot traffic through the building. Tenants vary in their requirement for parking or access to transportation facilities. They also differ in the density or the number of square feet required per employee.

Apartment buildings have Treasury-related callable debt financing. Single-tenant industrial buildings have bondlike features. Once a long-term lease is in place with a reputable tenant, they trade based on the credit rating of the occupier rather than the features of the building. Multi-tenant commercial real estate has a separate type of debt market. The building qualifies for debt financing based on its loan-to-value ratio and its debt service coverage ratio. The *loan-to-value ratio* is the maximum loan available divided by the price of the property. The *debt service coverage ratio* is for the net operating income after reserves divided by the payment. In booming markets, such as the one that existed between 2003 and 2007, the loan-to-value ratio exceeded 80 percent and the debt service coverage ratio was as low as 1.1. When credit conditions are tight, the loan-to-value ratio can be 60 percent or lower and the debt service coverage ratio 1.4 or higher.

The *unleveraged return* is the sum of the cap rate plus the capital gains rate. This return is equal to the riskless rate plus a premium for holding multi-tenant commercial real estate. The leveraged return subtracts the product of the loan-to-value ratio and the interest rate to obtain the cash flow. The *leverage return* is the cash flow divided by one minus the loan-to-value ratio. Access to locked-in, nonrecourse financing allows the portfolio size to be increased, even if the investor cannot take advantage of tax benefits from deducting interest. By using a 50 percent loan-to-value ratio, the investor can hold twice as many properties.

A risk exists that the tenant defaults or has a reduction in credit. This risk is magnified because of landlord payments for tenant improvements. The risk is reduced by a security deposit or letter of credit. The single-asset structure prevents asset substitution. Lenders prefer this arrangement to protect their loan.

RETAIL

Retail properties have revenue and sales that are tied to a specific asset. Retail properties include big box stores and shopping centers. Big box tenants such as Walmart, Home Depot, and Lowe's are considered similar to industrial users. They are single-tenant operators, usually leasing the store from an institutional real estate investor. Shopping centers include strips or neighborhood locations in local and regional malls. Other assets where sales are specific to one location are hotels and restaurants. Shopping centers are either anchored or not. An *anchor* is a tenant such as a department store occupying extensive space, usually at the entry end of the center. Other types of retail property are community centers, sometimes anchored by supermarkets and drugstores.

The anchor argues that its size and advertising attract traffic, raising demand for the other tenants, known as *in-line tenants* or *satellites.* In exchange, the center offers rents that are equal only to marginal operating costs. The International Council of Shopping Centers (2008) in its *Dollars & Cents of Shopping Centers* estimates that the average rent that anchors pay is $5 per square foot per year. This cost only covers operating expenses and none of the capital expenses of the center. Those capital expenses are shifted in higher rents to the in-line tenants.

The demand for retail space depends on the rent. The demand shifts depending on consumer sentiment, the mix between large and small tenants and the number of households in the local retail area.

Some tenants create a positive externality by increasing demand for products sold by others. Department stores carry out advertising and marketing, have longer hours, and are located at the entrances to shopping centers. They are willing to take large and extensive spaces within these malls. By encouraging customers to visit, these anchors are driving tenants to the remaining in-line stores. For this positive externality, the anchor tenant demands lower rent.

Operating expenses have fixed and variable components. Fixed operating expenses include the net-net portions for property taxes and insurance, as well as landscaping and snow removal. Variable operating expenses include management fees, utilities, repairs and maintenance, and general and administrative (G&A) costs. Anchors are only willing to pay for variable operating costs. Another operating expense is common area maintenance (CAM) for the parking lot, roof and structure, hallways, front entrance, and elevators. Anchor tenants frequently demand to be excluded from the CAM charges.

Landlords face additional risks from anchors. Anchors take advantage of the low rent to become sublandlords. The ground floor of a department store is often a shopping center. The jewelry department is a triple-net sublease to a contractor. Signet and Zale's are the major jewelry chains and operate several store platforms. Cosmetics firms provide advertising support, subleases, and subsidies to the salaries of the makeup artists. Jewelry and cosmetics tend to be located in the center aisles. Along the walls, brand-name designers set up boutiques within the stores, being offered tenant improvements. JC Penney has set up Sephora boutiques inside the store, as has Sears with Lands' End. These actions mean that the landlord has a large, low-cost competitor that was initially subsidized.

Another risk with retail is that the up-front demand for tenant improvements includes funding for custom finishes and restaurants and other stores. The tenant demands the up-front capital payments to hedge against landlord spending in the future. The landlord has similar risks about the tenant. A discount retail chain could demand extensive up-front cash and subsequently default.

With a multi-tenant format, retail has a similar structure to office. If landlords sign negative NPV leases with anchor tenants, they must sign positive NPV leases with the in-line stores. An additional risk is that some of these stores are chains themselves wanting tenant improvements and subsidized rents.

A further issue is that revenue is tied to the store location. Local governments levy sales taxes. The implication is that retailers report sales at an individual store. Tenants want landlords to maintain and upgrade their building. In exchange, tenants are willing to offer a percentage of their sales as additional rent. The percentage rent manages the agency issues of management and maintenance.

As an example, a retailer expects \$400 in sales per square foot per year. The percentage rent is 5 percent of sales above this figure. In this case, the *natural breakpoint*, or base rent, is 5 percent of \$400, or \$20 per square foot per year. Percentage rent is a call option bought by the landlord and sold by the tenant. Its payment is contingent on the success of the retail space. Equation 6.8 shows the individual rent for each tenant:

$$\begin{aligned}&\text{Gross tent} = \text{Base tent} + \text{Bumps} + \text{Core factor} + \text{Common area maintenance}\\&+\text{Tenant improvement recovery (Capital)}\\&+\text{Percentage rent (Revenue)}\end{aligned} \tag{6.8}$$

The landlord constructs the present value of cash flows for each lease after accounting for up-front tenant improvements. For anchors, this calculation gives a negative NPV to be recovered from in-line stores.

A problem for this recovery is that some in-lines benefit little from anchor externalities. In 2011, the sales tracking firm RetailSails reported the sales per square foot for the 160 largest retail chains. The leader was Apple at $5,626 in annual sales per square foot. Upscale retailers Tiffany and Coach, athletic apparel maker Lululemon, and game store GameStop completed the top five. None of the top five are department stores or supermarkets, and need not depend on their traffic. These in-line retailers have choices of unanchored locations such as along main street configurations, where no cross-subsidization of rents occurs.

SUMMARY AND CONCLUSIONS

This chapter has examined rates of return to holding real estate. The conclusion is that real estate has historically provided inflation-adjusted returns of between 4 and 6 percent annually. The asset offers a hedge with a high positive correlation with inflation. There are different asset classes within real estate for apartments, industrial, office, and retail. The leases and management structures reflect agency issues for each asset. They create returns that differ among the owners. Those who understand and manage the conflicts obtain higher returns.

In contrast with traded financial markets, real estate is illiquid but allows borrowing. The ability to borrow against real estate collateral alone creates a nonrecourse obligation. That nonrecourse borrowing allows investors to take long and short positions in real estate by adjusting debt sizes.

DISCUSSION QUESTIONS

1. What determines whether tenants want to rent or buy?
2. How can an industrial lease be converted into an indexed bond?
3. In multi-tenant office buildings, what are the agency issues with capital expenses?
4. How does a supermarket get compensated for bringing traffic to smaller stores in a shopping center?
5. What are the differences in returns to commercial real estate, and what is the value of commercial real estate in an overall portfolio?

REFERENCES

DiPasquale, Denise, and William Wheaton. 1995. *Urban Economics and Real Estate Markets*. Englewood Cliffs, NJ: Prentice Hall.

Dimson, Elroy, Paul Marsh, and Mike Staunton. 2002. *Triumph of the Optimists: 101 Years of Global Investment Returns*. New York: Princeton University Press.

Eddings, Cordell. 2011. "Say What? In 30-Year Race, Bonds Beat Stocks." *Bloomberg News*, October 31. Available at www.bloomberg.com.

Eicholtz, Piet. 1997. "A Long Run House Price Index: The Herengracht Index 1628–1973." *Real Estate Economics* 25:2, 175–192.

El-Arian, Mohammed. 2008. *When Markets Collide*. New York: McGraw-Hill.

Financial Accounting Standards Board. 1968. *Financial Accounting Standards Board 13, Accounting for Leases*. Norwalk, CT: Financial Accounting Standards Board.

Glaeser, Edward. 2010. *The Economics of Agglomeration*. Chicago: University of Chicago Press.

Goetzmann, William N., and Roger G. Ibbotson. 2006. *The Equity Risk Premium*. New York: Oxford University Press.

Gyourko, Joseph, Albert Saiz, and Anita Summers. 2008. "A New Measure of the Local Regulatory Environment for Housing Markets: The Wharton Residential Land Use Regulatory Index." *Urban Studies* 45:3, 693–729.

Hoyt, Homer. 1933. *One Hundred Years of Land Value in Chicago*. Chicago: University of Chicago Press.

International Council of Shopping Centers. 2008. *Dollars & Cents of Shopping Centers*. New York: International Council of Shopping Centers.

Miles, Mike, and Joseph Mahoney. 1997. "Is Commercial Real Estate an Inflation Hedge?" *Real Estate Finance* 14:1, 31–45.

Miles, Mike, and Nancy Tolleson. 1997. "A Revised Look at How Real Estate Compares with Other Major Components of Domestic Investment Universe." *Real Estate Finance* 14:1. 11–20.

Pastor, Lubos, and Robert Stambaugh. 2011. "Are Stocks Really Less Volatile in the Long Run?" *Journal of Finance*, 67, 431–478. www.retailsails.com. www.asymco.com/2012/04/18/apple-stores-have-seventeen-times-better-performance-than-the-average-retailer/

Saiz, Albert. 2010. "The Geographic Determinants of Housing Supply." *Quarterly Journal of Economics* 125:3, 1253–1296.

Siegel, Jeremy J. 2008. *Stocks for the Long Run*. New York: McGraw Hill.

Swensen, David. 2000. *Pioneering Portfolio Management*. New York: Free Press.

Wheaton, William C., Mark S. Baranski, and Cesarina A. Templeton. 2009. "100 Years of Commercial Real Estate Prices in Manhattan." *Real Estate Economics* 37:1, 69–83.

ABOUT THE AUTHOR

Peter Chinloy is a Professor in the Department of Finance and Real Estate at the Kogod School of Business, American University, Washington DC. His research interests include real estate equity investment, mortgage securities, and agency. His teaching includes real estate development and finance, corporate finance, and business economics. Professor Chinloy has published in the *American Economic Review, Real Estate Economics, Journal of Real Estate Finance and Economics,* and *Journal of Real Estate Research.* He has taught at Cornell University, University of Southern California, Santa Clara University, University of British Columbia, and University of Western Ontario. He has a MA and PhD in economics from

Harvard University and an undergraduate degree in accounting from McGill University.

ACKNOWLEDGMENTS

The author acknowledges John Benjamin, Wendy Liu, Eric Maribojoc, Maury Seldin, Bruce Thompson, Jon A. Wiley, and Joe Williams and the editors. The support of the Homer Hoyt Institute at American University is gratefully acknowledged.

CHAPTER 7

Real Estate Investment Trusts

BRAD CASE
Senior Vice President, NAREIT

INTRODUCTION

As defined in the United States, a real estate investment trust (REIT) is a company that meets all of the following criteria:

- A corporation (for federal tax purposes) with transferable shares held by at least 100 different shareholders, with the largest five shareholders collectively owning no more than 50 percent by value (the *ownership test*).
- At least 75 percent of assets are real estate, such as real property or loans secured by real property (the *assets test*).
- At least 75 percent of income is from real estate, such as rents from real property and interest on loans secured by real property (the *income test*).
- At least 90 percent of taxable income is distributed to shareholders (the *distribution test*).
- Elects REIT status when filing federal income tax returns.

Congress created REITs in 1960 for the purpose of making real estate investment returns accessible to investors lacking the resources to buy property directly. Because property owners are subject to personal but not corporate income tax, REITs deduct distributions from taxable income in computing corporate income tax liability. The ownership test ensures that the deductibility of distributions benefits the intended investors, whereas the asset, income, and distribution tests ensure that REIT returns closely approximate what those investors would have earned by investing directly in the underlying assets.

REITs are typically differentiated by type of ownership (listed, public nonlisted, and private) and by type of assets (equity REITs own primarily real property, whereas mortgage REITs own primarily residential or commercial mortgages). At the end of October 2012, the listed REIT industry encompassed 138 equity REITs, of which 92 (representing 54.8 percent of all listed REITs by market capitalization) invested primarily in the core apartment, industrial, office, and retail property types. The remaining 46 equity REITs (34.4 percent of all listed REITs by market capitalization) invested primarily in noncore property types, including health care properties, hotels, timber lands, infrastructure, self-storage facilities, and data centers. Listed equity REITs were valued at $521 billion in aggregate market capitalization and held about $825 billion of assets, perhaps 13 to 15 percent of investable commercial property in the United States. There were also 33 mortgage REITs, of which 19 (9.1 percent of all listed REITs by market capitalization) invested primarily in residential mortgages. The remaining 14 mortgage REITs (1.7 percent of all listed REITs by market capitalization) invested primarily in commercial mortgages. With leverage averaging 82.2 percent, the aggregate market capitalization of $63 billion implies that mortgage REITs held some $75 billion in underlying assets.

Public nonlisted REITs (PNLRs) are subject to requirements applicable to all public securities, including filing financial reports with the Securities and Exchange Commission (SEC). As of the third quarter of 2011, on the basis of SEC filings compiled by SNL Financial, the National Association of Real Estate Investment Trusts (NAREIT) had identified 63 PNLRs with $97 billion in total assets. Corporate tax returns filed with the Internal Revenue Service (IRS) indicated about 6,000 private REITs in 2010. Data on operating and investment performance by PNLRs and private REITs are much less available than for listed REITs. The remainder of this chapter uses data only for listed equity REITs.

The main purpose of this chapter is to summarize REIT investment characteristics. The chapter first considers arguments for and against including REITs as an alternative investment in the real estate asset class, focusing especially on the correlation of REIT returns with unlisted property returns. The next sections examine historical REIT returns, including their division between income and capital appreciation, as well as REIT volatility and risk-adjusted returns. The next section discusses several aspects of the REIT business model that may explain the superior returns of REITs relative to unlisted real estate investments, and the final section summarizes the chapter.

REITS AND THE REAL ESTATE ASSET CLASS

Chapter 5 identifies illiquidity as among the distinguishing characteristics of commercial property as an alternative investment. Claims on commercial properties held through stock in a listed REIT, however, are fully liquid, with daily share trading averaging about $4 billion. The fact that listed REITs are traded through the stock market has led some to suggest that listed REITs do not provide exposure to the returns of the real estate asset class, a suggestion that, as noted by Gyourko and Keim (1992), deserves scrutiny.

The most commonly employed measure of unlisted commercial property returns is the NCREIF Property Index (NPI), published quarterly by the National Council of Real Estate Investment Fiduciaries, with data beginning in 1978. The contemporaneous correlation between quarterly gross total returns measured by the NPI and by the FTSE NAREIT Equity REITs Index for 1978Q1–2012Q3 is just 0.153, suggesting little commonality in exposures. Such a facile conclusion should be examined more closely, however, given that both indices measure returns derived from similar sets of underlying assets.

Error Correction and the Investment Horizon

Because REITs are traded through the stock market, factors unrelated to the underlying property market may affect REIT stock prices. For example, investors trading stocks through a mutual fund or exchange-traded fund (ETF) following a broad market index (such as the S&P 500) or a broad sector index (such as the S&P Financial Sector) will also trade REITs—because they are included among the constituents of both indices—even if the trading decision had nothing to do with property market conditions. The trading process can cause "error" in the sense that REIT stock prices may diverge from their intrinsic value, and REIT return indices will reflect those valuation errors.

An analogous error process, namely, the use of appraised property values, affects returns as measured by the NPI. Cannon and Cole (2011) find that appraisal errors in the NPI database exceed 12 percent on average. For unlisted property, the valuation process causes "errors" in the sense that measured values diverge from true values, and indices such as the NPI will reflect those valuation errors.

In both markets, an error correction process exists that should tend to bring measured values closer to intrinsic values. For listed REITs, if stock prices move away from their intrinsic values, then buying and selling by knowledgeable investors should correct the under- or overvaluation. For unlisted properties, if the appraisal misrepresents a property's actual value, then the error should be corrected through subsequent transaction or reappraisal. In either case, the error correction process should cause measured values and returns to approximate intrinsic values and returns more closely over time.

Exhibit 7.1 shows correlations between the NPI and the FTSE NAREIT Equity REITs Index for 1978Q1–2012Q2 with the period over which returns are measured increasing from the standard 1 quarter to periods of 2 through 20 quarters. The correlation increases from 0.153 for the shortest period to 0.504 for a 20-quarter

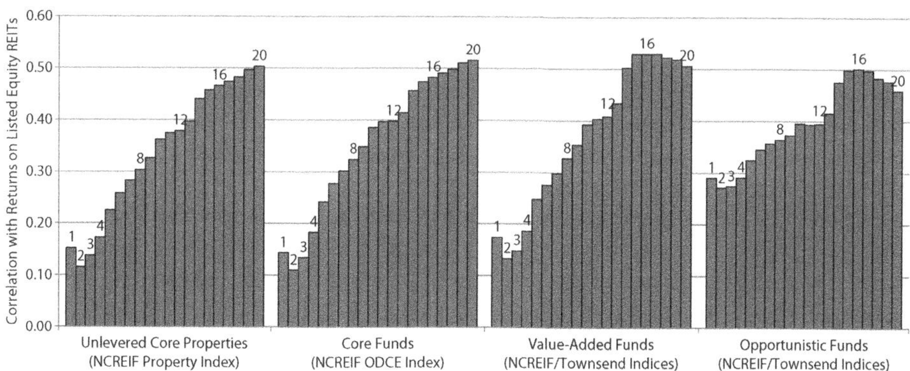

Exhibit 7.1 Correlations between Listed and Unlisted Property Returns by Investment Horizon (in quarters)

This exhibit shows the correlations between listed and unlisted property returns based on the investment horizon. The results indicate that the correlations between listed REITs and four measures of unlisted property investments increase sharply when measured over longer investment horizons.

period, suggesting that the error correction process does cause measured returns to listed REITs and unlisted properties to track each other more closely over longer horizons. These results are especially relevant because property investors generally have investment horizons of at least five years. Exhibit 7.1 shows similar patterns of correlations between REIT returns and returns measured by the NCREIF Open-End Diversified Core Equity (ODCE) Fund Index and by the NCREIF/Townsend Fund Indices for funds following value-add or opportunistic strategies. Core funds generally seek steady, bondlike income through ownership of fully leased high-quality properties, whereas opportunistic funds generally seek opportunities to achieve capital appreciation, often by purchasing poorly leased or even unfinished properties; value-add funds typically seek fairly steady income with some opportunity for capital appreciation.

Oikarinen, Hoesli, and Serrano (2011) address the same question using a more sophisticated cointegration analysis. A finding of cointegration between two series implies that their correlation approaches one as the investment horizon is extended. Indeed, Oikarinen et al. (p. 75) find "a tight long-run relationship between NCREIF and NAREIT total return indices" and conclude that "REITs and direct real estate are substitutable in the mixed-asset portfolios of a long-horizon buy-and-hold investor."

Effects of Illiquidity Lag and Appraisal Lag

The liquidity of the stock market suggests that new information bearing on the intrinsic value of property should generally be incorporated immediately into measured REIT stock prices and returns. In contrast, the illiquidity of the property market suggests that the same new information will be incorporated into measured returns only after a lengthy process of revelation through transactions and then appraisals.

Illiquidity lag refers to the passage of time before changes in property values are revealed by completed transactions, whereas *appraisal lag* refers to the passage of additional time before the information revealed by transactions is incorporated into appraisals on nontransacting properties. Illiquidity lag appears to average around two quarters (during which the properties are marketed, terms are negotiated, and the transactions are closed), whereas appraisal lag appears to average an additional two quarters (partly because typically only a portion of the portfolio is appraised during any given quarter).

Exhibit 7.2 shows the correlations between REIT returns and returns measured by the four indices of unlisted property investments over 20-quarter investment horizons, with REIT returns lagged by 0 to 8 quarters. Incorporating a lag of four quarters increases the measured correlation between REITs and the NPI from 0.504 to 0.623 and has a similar effect on correlations with the other unlisted property investment measures.

Effects of Illiquidity Smoothing and Appraisal Smoothing

The process of measuring asset values and returns in the property market, which is characterized by infrequent transactions of differentiated products, results in

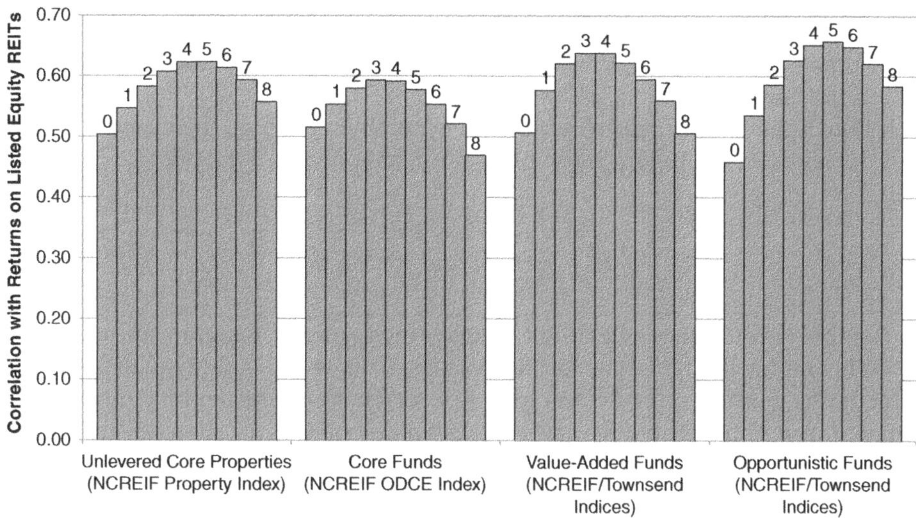

Exhibit 7.2 Long-Horizon Correlations between Unlisted Property Returns and Lagged REIT Returns

This exhibit shows the correlations between unlisted property returns and lagged REIT returns. Using four measures of unlisted property, the results indicate that correlations increase sharply when REIT returns are lagged by four to five quarters to match the illiquidity and appraisal lag in measuring unlisted property returns.

smoothing of the measured historical series. *Illiquidity smoothing* (also called *temporal aggregation*) results because transactions occurring over a discrete period, generally one month or one quarter, are aggregated for the purpose of producing the index for that period. In contrast, the return for liquid assets such as REITs is measured using the last transaction in each period.

Appraisal smoothing results from two facts. First, typically only some of the assets in a property portfolio are appraised in a given quarter, whereas "stale" appraisals may be used to value the other assets. Second, appraisers are subject to the behavioral bias known as *anchoring*, which is the tendency to place undue weight on previous values. For example, if unlevered property values decline sharply in a given quarter, appraisers may be uncomfortable recognizing the entire actual decline immediately.

To the extent that smoothing affects measured returns, it may be detected by examining the autocorrelation of the historical index series. For example, Equation 7.1 expresses the reported return on commercial property as a weighted average of the true return and the previous period's reported return, with the weight on the previous period equal to the first-order autocorrelation coefficient:

$$R_t^{reported} = (1 - \rho)\, R_t^{actual} + \rho R_{t-1}^{reported} \qquad (7.1)$$

where $R_t^{reported}$ is the reported return during time period t; R_t^{actual} is the actual return during time period t; $R_{t-1}^{reported}$ is the reported return during the previous time period; and ρ is the first-order autocorrelation coefficient.

If Equation 7.1 accurately describes the smoothing process, then knowing the value of ρ enables solving for the actual return, as shown in Equation 7.2:

$$R_t^{actual} = \frac{\left(R_t^{reported} - \rho R_{t-1}^{reported}\right)}{1-\rho} \tag{7.2}$$

The first two columns of Exhibit 7.3 show the quarterly total returns reported for REITs and for the NPI over the 40 quarters 2002Q4–2012Q3 (plus 2002Q3 for unsmoothing purposes). The first-order autocorrelation coefficient for the NPI is estimated at 0.852, indicating very substantial smoothing. In contrast, the first-order autocorrelation coefficient for REIT returns is just 0.164, and statistical testing cannot reject the hypothesis that its true value is zero. Equation 7.2 can be used to estimate unsmoothed versions of both historical series, as shown in the third and fourth columns of Exhibit 7.3. REIT data are unsmoothed for comparability, although statistical tests fail to indicate that unsmoothing is appropriate.

Note that the average annualized return of each unsmoothed series (14.6 percent per year for REITs and 7.5 percent for the NPI) is similar to the corresponding value of each smoothed series (14.4 percent for REITs and 7.1 percent for the NPI). Smoothing and, therefore, unsmoothing do not affect the average reported long-term returns except through *end point bias*, which is starting or ending with an abnormally high or low value.

In contrast, smoothing generally has a marked effect on both the reported volatility of a data series and the reported correlation between two data series. The volatility of the unsmoothed REIT return series is only slightly higher than the volatility of the original series (30.8 percent vs. 26.1 percent), reflecting the small first-order autocorrelation coefficient for REITs. For the NPI, however, the unsmoothed series shows 254 percent more volatility than the smoothed series (22.1 percent vs. 6.25 percent), reflecting the very large first-order autocorrelation coefficient and the very dramatic smoothing of the reported returns. The correlation of the unsmoothed series is nearly twice as large as the correlation of the smoothed series (0.533 vs. 0.273).

REITs and the Stock Market Asset Class

Because REITs are traded through the stock market, their prices may be affected by trades done through broad-market instruments such as ETFs on the basis of information unrelated to the property market. Over longer investment horizons, however, any resulting mispricings will tend to be corrected through countervailing transactions by knowledgeable investors. Of course, investments in any other segment of the stock market are subject to the same error and error correction processes.

Exhibit 7.4 shows for each of 10 stock market sectors identified in S&P's Global Industry Classification System (GICS) the correlation between returns for that sector and for the broad market as measured by the Wilshire Total Market Index.

Exhibit 7.3 Unsmoothing of Data for Unlisted Property and Measurements of Volatility and Correlation

	Reported		Unsmoothed	
YearQ	**EqREITs**	**NPI**	**EqREITs**	**NPI**
20023	−9.16%	1.50%		
20024	0.28%	1.38%	2.14%	0.70%
20031	0.55%	1.60%	0.60%	2.82%
20032	12.97%	1.80%	15.41%	2.97%
20033	9.38%	1.69%	8.68%	1.04%
20034	9.83%	2.48%	9.92%	7.03%
20041	11.88%	2.28%	12.29%	1.12%
20042	−5.93%	2.84%	−9.43%	6.07%
20043	8.10%	3.14%	10.85%	4.85%
20044	15.09%	4.37%	16.46%	11.48%
20051	−7.17%	3.22%	−11.54%	−3.37%
20052	14.31%	5.05%	18.53%	15.55%
20053	3.71%	4.15%	1.62%	−0.99%
20054	1.42%	5.14%	0.97%	10.82%
20061	14.60%	3.33%	17.19%	−7.08%
20062	−1.71%	3.72%	−4.92%	5.98%
20063	9.14%	3.22%	11.27%	0.34%
20064	9.33%	4.23%	9.37%	9.99%
20071	3.34%	3.34%	2.16%	−1.77%
20072	−9.16%	4.31%	−11.61%	9.88%
20073	2.46%	3.28%	4.74%	−2.64%
20074	−12.79%	2.92%	−15.78%	0.87%
20081	1.27%	1.31%	4.04%	−7.95%
20082	−5.05%	0.28%	−6.29%	−5.68%
20083	5.42%	−0.46%	7.48%	−4.69%
20084	−38.90%	−8.57%	−47.60%	−55.27%
20091	−31.97%	−7.61%	−30.61%	−2.09%
20092	28.70%	−5.48%	40.61%	6.77%
20093	33.12%	−3.60%	33.99%	7.21%
20094	9.26%	−2.40%	4.58%	4.56%
20101	9.89%	0.47%	10.01%	16.98%
20102	−4.18%	3.02%	−6.94%	17.70%
20103	12.69%	3.57%	16.00%	6.74%
20104	7.30%	4.33%	6.24%	8.71%
20111	7.37%	3.07%	7.38%	−4.20%
20112	2.78%	3.65%	1.87%	6.97%
20113	−15.18%	3.01%	−18.71%	−0.67%
20114	15.12%	2.68%	21.07%	0.77%
20121	10.36%	2.30%	9.42%	0.13%
20122	3.87%	2.40%	2.60%	2.95%
20123	2.13%	2.05%	1.79%	0.08%
Ann Avg	14.4%	7.1%	14.6%	7.5%
Volatility	26.1%	6.25%	30.8%	22.1%
Correlation	0.273		0.533	

This exhibit shows the use of quarterly returns from REITs and unlevered core properties (NPI) to correct for smoothing by estimating the first-order autocorrelation coefficient. Unsmoothing has little effect on average measured historical returns but a marked effect on measured volatility of unlisted real estate, as well as on the measured correlation between listed REITs and unlisted real estate.

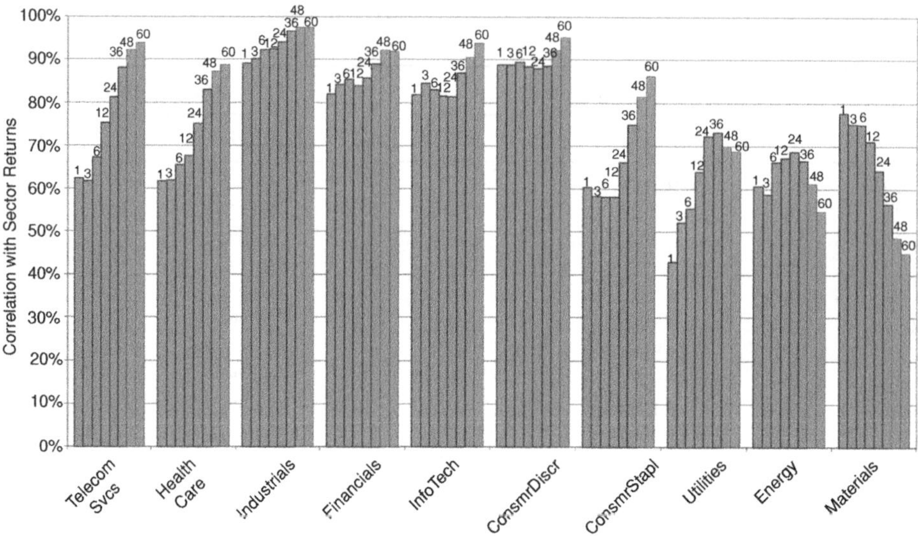

Exhibit 7.4 Correlations between Stock Market Sectors and the Broad Stock Market by Investment Horizon (in months)

This exhibit shows that the return correlations between most sectors of the stock market and the broad stock market increase when returns are measured over longer investment horizons.

As in Exhibit 7.1, the correlations are computed for investment horizons increasing in length (from 1 month to 60 months). Of particular note is that in 8 of the 10 sectors correlations over longer horizons are higher than correlations over shorter horizons. This is the same pattern observed in Exhibit 7.1 for correlations between REITs and unlisted property returns.

For example, the correlation of the telecommunications services sector with the broad stock market is just 0.615 when measured using one-month returns, suggesting that over short horizons the returns of telecom stocks are affected by different factors than those that affect the rest of the market. Over longer horizons, however, the correlation increases to 0.936, suggesting that long-term returns to telecom stocks differ little from long-term returns to other stocks. As in the property market, increasing correlations over longer investment horizons suggest that returns arising from short-term trading (or appraisal) behavior differ from returns arising from long-term earnings drivers. In the short term, factors unique to the telecom industry may affect telecom stocks. In the long term, however, the state of the overall domestic economy affects stock returns regardless of whether the investor is exposed to the overall economy through telecom stocks or other sectors.

The two exceptions to the general rule occur with the energy and materials sectors. These results are consistent with the overall interpretation of correlation over longer investment horizons. Companies in the energy and materials sectors give investors indirect exposure to the commodities market, which is typically recognized as an asset class separate from the stock market, with returns affected by different drivers.

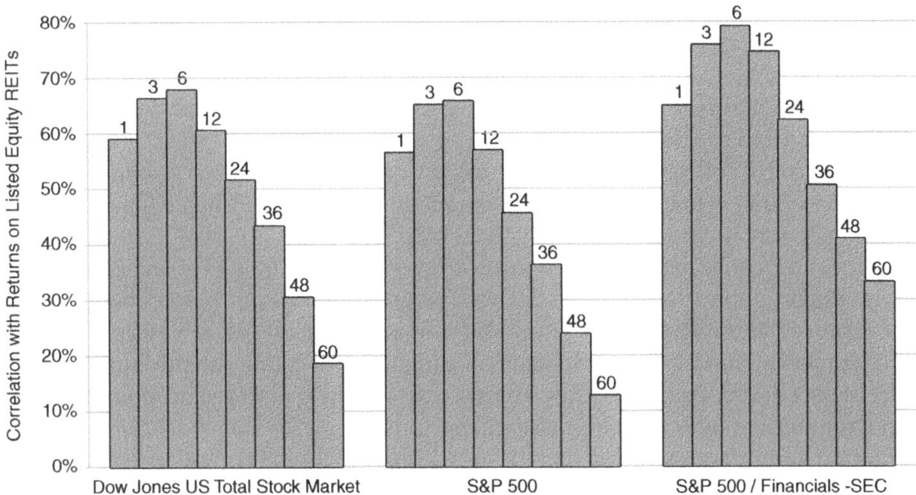

Exhibit 7.5 Correlations between Listed REITs and the Broad Stock Market by Investment Horizon (in months)

This exhibit shows that the return correlations between REITs and the broad stock market decline when returns are measured over longer investment horizons.

Exhibit 7.5 presents the same analysis but shows the correlations between REITs and the broad stock market. Very strikingly, the pattern is reversed: The correlation over short horizons is relatively high (0.590 using 1-month returns) whereas the correlation over longer horizons is dramatically lower (just 0.185 using 60-month returns). This result is consistent with the interpretation that REITs, although traded through the stock market, provide exposure to the real estate asset class rather than to the stock market; that is, the long-term drivers of REIT returns differ substantially from those of returns to other stocks.

Exhibit 7.5 also shows correlations between REITs and the financial sector, in which GICS classifies REITs. As with the broad market, the correlation between REITs and the financial sector is relatively high using one-month returns as the basis for measurement. This is not surprising given that trades motivated by information about, say, banks may be executed through financial-sector ETFs. Over longer investment horizons, however, the drivers that determine long-term REIT returns have little in common with the drivers of financial company returns.

HISTORICAL REIT RETURNS

According to monthly total returns data from January 1972 through October 2012 from the FTSE NAREIT Equity REITs Index, REITs have produced a long-term geometric average return of 12.06 percent per year. Yet, common practice is to focus on the "modern REIT era" that began roughly in late 1991 with the initial public offering (IPO) for Kimco Realty Corporation. During the 20 plus years from the end of 1991 through October 2012, the geometric average return for REITs was

11.24 percent per year. This compares favorably with other equity assets, including large-cap stocks (8.18 percent from the S&P 500), small-cap stocks (8.75 percent from the Russell 2000), and foreign stocks (4.90 percent from the MSCI EAFE), as well as with bonds (6.44 percent from the BC US Aggregate) and commodities (3.66 percent from the S&P GSCI).

Comparing REIT returns with returns on other property investments raises three issues. First, returns may be measured on an unlevered basis (as with the NPI) or they may include the effects of leverage. The FTSE NAREIT Equity REITs Index, for example, is a stock return index that reflects REITs' use of leverage, typically averaging about 40 percent. Second, returns are often reported on a gross basis, whereas fees and expenses may differ sharply for different ways of investing in property. Third, because returns on unlisted real estate are measured with illiquidity lag and appraisal lag, the analyst must be aware of the end point bias in comparing returns over limited historical periods.

Exhibit 7.6 addresses two of these issues—differences in fees and unlisted market lagged data—in comparing returns among unlevered core properties (NPI), core funds (ODCE), value-add and opportunistic funds (NCREIF/Townsend), and

Exhibit 7.6 Performance of Listed REITs and Unlisted Property Investments over the Full Market Cycle

			Full Cycle (Peak to Peak)		Bull Market Only (Trough to Peak)	
Form of Real Estate Investment	**Typical Leverage (%)**	**Fees and Expenses (basis points)**	**Duration (Years)**	**Net Total Returns (%)**	**Duration (Years)**	**Net Total Returns (%)**
Unlevered Core Properties (NCREIF Property Index)	0	115	17.75 90q3–08q2	266 7.6/year	15 93q2–08q2	322 10.1/year
Core Funds (NCREIF ODCE Index)	25	107	17.75 90q3–08q2	272 7.7/year	15 93q2–08q2	341 10.4/year
Value-Add Funds (NCREIF/Townsend Indices)	55	131	17.25 90q3–07q4	318 8.6/year	14.5 93q2–07q4	430 12.2/year
Opportunistic Funds (NCREIF/Townsend Indices)	60	221	17.25 90q3–07q4	621 12.1/year	14 93q4–07q4	964 18.4/year
REITs (FTSE NAREIT Equity REITs Index)	40	50	17.5 89q3–07q1	802 13.4/year	16.5 90q3–07q1	1,041 15.9/year

This exhibit compares net returns from listed REITs with four measures of unlisted property investments over a full property market cycle from 1989–1990 to 2007–2008.

listed REITs. Specifically, Exhibit 7.6 avoids end point bias by comparing returns over a full market cycle, identified by a cyclical market peak in 1989 or 1990 and by a second cyclical market peak in 2007 or 2008. As the "Full Cycle—Duration" column indicates, the commercial property market cycle lasted for 17.5 years, plus or minus one quarter, but the cycle dates differed between listed and unlisted investments. REITs reached a market peak in 1989Q3, while all four measures of the unlisted market reached their peak four quarters later in 1990Q3; REITs then reached their second market peak in 2007Q1, while the four unlisted measures reached their peak either three or five quarters later (2007Q4 or 2008Q2).

In comparing returns over the full market cycle, Exhibit 7.6 avoids differences in fees and expenses by reporting net returns. Fees and expenses are assumed to average 115 basis points (bps) per year for unlisted core property investments and 50 bps per year for REITs; the other three indices report net returns. The estimated fees for REITs represent a characteristic fee structure for actively managed domestic REIT portfolios, whereas the return data for REITs represent passive investments in the REIT index.

As the "Full Cycle—Returns" column shows, net through-the-cycle cumulative returns were 802 percent for REITs compared to 621 percent for opportunistic funds, 318 percent for value-add funds, 272 percent for core funds, and 266 percent for unlevered core properties. Because the cycle durations were nearly identical, returns can also be compared on a per-year geometric average basis. REIT net returns averaged 13.4 percent per year compared to 12.1, 8.6, 7.7, and 7.6 percent, respectively, for the other four measures. Returns have not been adjusted for differences in leverage, so they do not by themselves indicate different degrees of success in executing a property investment mandate. Nevertheless, the magnitude of the differences in returns between REITs and both unlevered core properties and core funds is far too great to be explained by differences in leverage. With respect to value-add and opportunistic funds, the fact that REITs produced substantially greater returns is striking given the substantially greater use of leverage by the unlisted funds.

The comparison shown in Exhibit 7.6 suggests that REITs did, in fact, perform sharply better at executing their property investment mandate than the various investments represented by the unlisted real estate indices. Several researchers make more careful comparisons of REITs with unlevered core property returns by adjusting for the actual use of leverage by individual REITs, and also by adjusting for differences in the mix of property types represented by the different indices. Riddiough, Moriarty, and Yeatman (2005), Pagliari, Scherer, and Monopoli (2005), Tsai (2007), and Ling and Naranjo (2012) all find that REIT returns generally exceed core property returns on an unlevered basis over various historical time periods, although none adjust for lag in the unlisted markets and the differences between the markets are sometimes quite small.

Income and Capital Appreciation

Exhibit 7.7 separates the average through-the-cycle net total return for each of the five ways of investing in property into its income component and its capital appreciation component. Fees and expenses are assumed to be paid out of income, as is reported by the ODCE Index. Value-added and opportunistic funds provide relatively low income (not surprising, given that they typically take leasing risk in

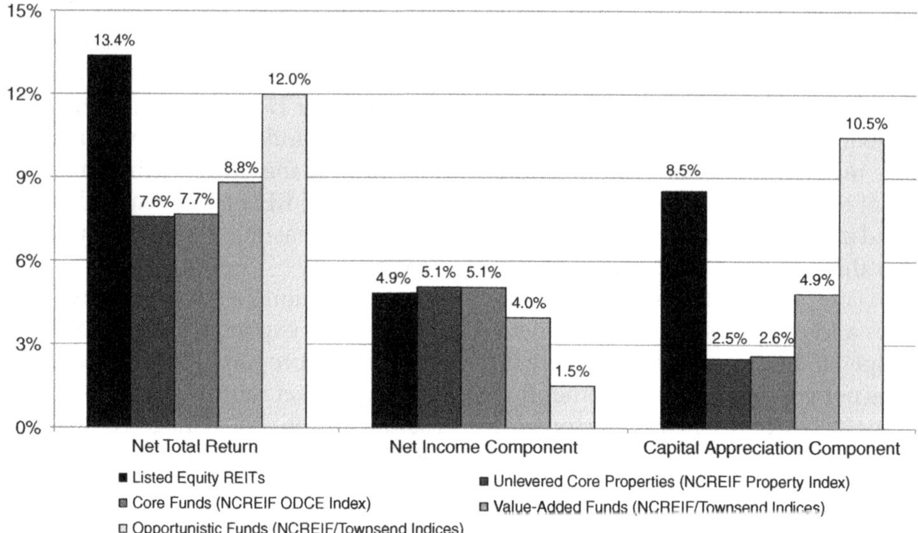

Exhibit 7.7 Division of Full-Cycle Property Returns into Income and Capital Appreciation Components

This exhibit compares the income and capital appreciation components of total returns from listed REITs and four measures of unlisted property investment.

the hope of generating superior capital appreciation) but the income components of net investment returns for the other real estate investment strategies are quite similar at 5.07 percent per year for unlevered core properties and core funds, and 4.86 percent per year for REITs. The NPI and ODCE indices indicate that unlevered core properties and core funds produced little capital appreciation during the 17.5-year market cycle at 2.50 and 2.61 percent per year, respectively. In fact, measured capital appreciation was negative in real terms after subtracting inflation that averaged 2.7 percent per year. Value-added funds and especially opportunistic funds and REITs, however, achieved substantial capital appreciation averaging 4.85 percent, 10.47 percent, and 8.53 percent per year, respectively.

Manager Selection

Institutional investors typically invest heavily in identifying private equity fund managers who are expected to produce superior risk-adjusted returns (positive alpha) and for this reason sometimes expect to receive better returns than the average represented by an index. Empirical evidence supporting such an expectation is scanty, especially in real estate. Hahn, Geltner, and Gerardo-Lietz (2005) and LaFever and Canizo (2005) find evidence of return persistence, whereas Tomperi (2010) and Bond and Mitchell (2010) do not. A recent study by Cici, Corgel, and Gibson (2011) finds that REIT fund managers are able to use superior security-selection abilities to generate significant positive alpha.

Analysts should also note that the NCREIF and NCREIF/Townsend indices do not reflect the entire universe of unlisted property investments or investment managers. Rather, they represent those investments that institutional investors selected after the process of identifying superior investment managers. In contrast, the FTSE NAREIT Equity REITs Index represents every listed equity REIT that meets FTSE's standard liquidity and market capitalization criteria.

REIT VOLATILITY AND RISK-ADJUSTED RETURNS

Monthly total returns data from the FTSE NAREIT Equity REITs Index indicate that the annualized volatility of REIT investments has been 17.3 percent per year. During the 20 plus years of the "modern REIT era," volatility averaged 19.7 percent per year. Those figures are slightly higher than for large-cap stocks (15.6 percent and 14.9 percent), comparable to small-cap stocks (20.0 percent and 19.4 percent) and foreign stocks (17.5 percent and 16.9 percent), slightly lower than for commodities (20.4 percent and 21.3 percent), and, of course, sharply higher than for bonds (5.6 percent and 3.7 percent).

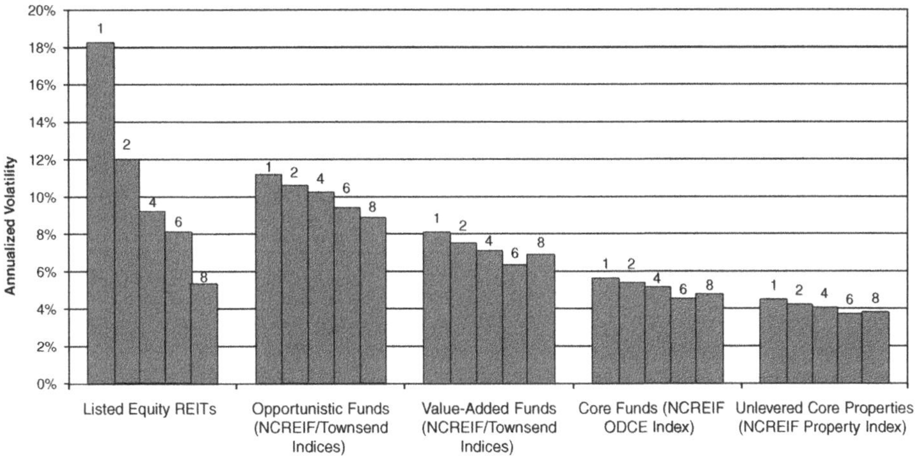

Exhibit 7.8 Volatility of Listed and Unlisted Property Returns by Investment Horizon (in quarters)
This exhibit shows that measured volatility declines when returns are measured over longer investment horizons, especially for listed REITs.

Two issues must be kept in mind when comparing REIT volatility with volatility of other property investments. First, illiquidity smoothing and appraisal smoothing in the measurement of returns on unlisted property investments mean that their true volatility is not fully measured, whereas true volatility is fully measured for REIT returns. The data shown in Exhibit 7.3 suggest that unsmoothing using the estimated first-order autocorrelation coefficient increases the estimated volatility of the NPI by 254 percent, compared to just 18 percent for REIT returns.

Second, investment characteristics computed on the basis of short-horizon data (such as quarterly returns) are not strictly relevant for investors with long time horizons, including property investors. Exhibit 7.8 shows estimated volatility for REITs and the four indices of unlisted property investments measured over investment horizons increasing from 1 to 8 quarters. For every type of property investment, volatility declines over longer investment horizons as short-term fluctuations in asset values are "averaged out." The decline in volatility is, however, dramatically greater for REIT investments than for any of the four unlisted property investments. This is because the "natural smoothing" that occurs in asset returns over longer investment horizons has largely been incorporated into quarterly returns through the ("unnatural") effects of illiquidity smoothing and appraisal smoothing.

Over most longer investment horizons, the volatility of REIT returns is less than the volatility of returns on value-add or opportunistic funds, though greater than the volatility of returns on unlevered core properties or core funds. This result should be expected. In fact, volatility figures that fail to show this pattern should be considered suspect. All five indices reflect the underlying returns on commercial property assets but incorporate the effects of differing degrees of leverage, which increases both returns (provided that asset returns exceed the cost of capital) and volatility. REITs typically employ less leverage than value-add or opportunistic funds but more leverage than unlevered core properties or core funds.

Exhibit 7.9 shows risk-adjusted performance as measured by the Sharpe ratio (i.e., annualized average net returns in excess of the risk-free rate divided by annualized standard deviation) for the five property investment indices over investment horizons increasing from 1 to 8 quarters. The use of longer-horizon data does not affect return calculations, so the fact that volatility declines through "natural" smoothing means that risk-adjusted returns are stronger when measured

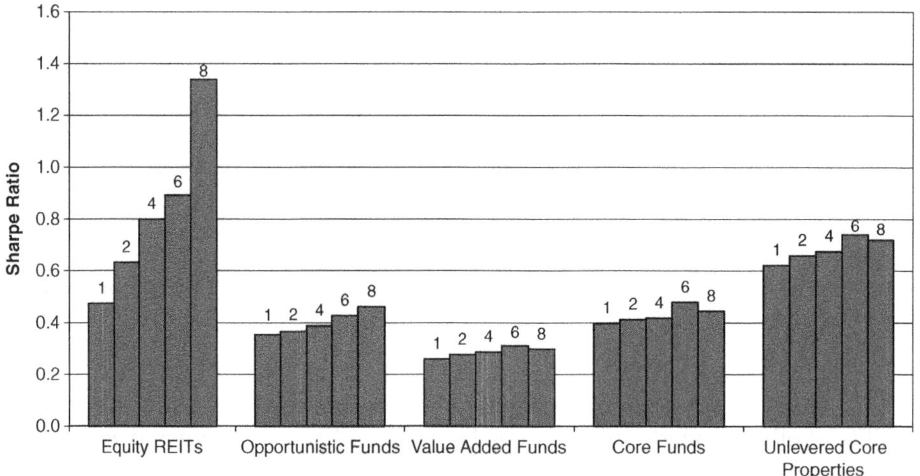

Exhibit 7.9 Sharpe Ratio of Listed and Unlisted Property Returns by Investment Horizon (in quarters)

This exhibit shows that risk-adjusted returns are greater when returns are measured over longer investment horizons, especially for listed REITs.

Exhibit 7.10 Volatility of Unlevered Returns Measured from REIT Stock Price Changes and from Property Transactions

Total Return Measure		Apartment (%)	Industrial (%)	Office (%)	Retail (%)	Composite (%)
NCREIF Transaction-Based Index	Volatility	12.72	11.46	11.80	12.47	11.82
	ρ	25	26	11	36	22
FTSE NAREIT PureProperty® Index	Volatility	11.05	13.34	11.32	11.55	10.85
	ρ	10	21	−7	20	9

This exhibit compares volatility of listed REITs and unlisted properties after removing the effects of leverage and appraisal smoothing.

over longer investment horizons. As the exhibit shows, the effect is especially pronounced for REITs.

Volatility Estimated from Unlevered Transaction-Based Return Indices

The FTSE NAREIT PureProperty® Indices, published starting in June 2012, provide estimates of the unlevered return since 1999 on properties owned by listed equity REITs. Thus, they reflect the volatility of unlevered property investments that are valued by the market through REIT stock transactions. A high-quality corollary in the unlisted property market is the Transaction-Based Index (TBI) initially developed by the MIT Center for Real Estate and now published by NCREIF, which is based on transactions of properties included in the NPI data set. Estimates of property volatility based on the TBI are free from the enormous problem of appraisal smoothing, although not from the smaller problem of illiquidity smoothing (Lin and Vandell, 2007).

Exhibit 7.10 compares the volatility of total returns on commercial property for the four property types included in the TBI over the period 2000–2011 for which PureProperty® data are available. For each data source, a "composite" index has also been constructed (adapted from unpublished analysis conducted by David Geltner, MIT Center for Real Estate). The data show that the volatility of unlevered property-level total returns is actually slightly less for REIT-owned properties than for unlisted properties in three of the four property types (apartments, office, and retail) as well as in the composite of all property types. The exhibit also shows that the first-order autocorrelation coefficient on total returns is smaller for the PureProperty® indices than for the TBI. This result suggests that TBI-estimated returns still reflect illiquidity smoothing (and therefore that their measured volatilities underestimate their true volatilities), although none of the estimated coefficients is significantly different from zero. In short, the data suggest that the volatility of REIT investments is actually less than the volatility of unlisted property investments after controlling for differences in leverage and for smoothing in the measurement of unlisted property returns. This result may reflect the superior information efficiency of the stock market.

THE REIT BUSINESS MODEL

REITs invest in the same asset market as the unlisted investment managers whose returns are summarized by the NPI, ODCE, and NCREIF/Townsend indices. Thus, finding that REITs provide returns that appear to be so much stronger, even on a risk-adjusted basis, is surprising. Although several possible explanations for this discrepancy can be offered, published academic research offers some support for five explanations:

- Transparency of REITs relative to non-REIT property investments.
- Liquidity of REIT investments relative to non-REIT property investments.
- Closer alignment of interests between investors and REIT decision makers.
- Limited free cash arising from the REIT distribution test.
- Better sources of financing for REITs relative to non-REIT investments.

Transparency

Bushman and Smith (2003, p. 66) define *transparency* in the corporate context as "the widespread availability of relevant, reliable information about the periodic performance, financial position, investment opportunities, governance, value, and risk of publicly traded firms." Rawlins (2008, p. 74) describes transparency as "having these three important elements: information that is truthful, substantial, and useful; participation of stakeholders in identifying the information they need; and objective, balanced reporting of an organization's activities and policies that holds the organization accountable."

As publicly registered investment securities, REITs are subject to the same reporting requirements as other listed companies, including regular publication of financial statements adhering to generally accepted accounting principles (GAAP). Moreover, REITs are scrutinized by dedicated REIT equity (and debt) analysts who publish investment recommendations based on analysis of each REIT's financial situation and operating performance. In contrast, non-REIT property investment managers are not generally subject to SEC requirements for GAAP reporting, either to investors or to noninvestors, and are not subject to public scrutiny from disinterested analysts.

Several studies, including Botosan and Plumlee (2002) as well as Lambert, Leuz, and Verrecchia (2007), support the notion that greater transparency promotes superior investment performance through greater capital market discipline and lower capital costs. Specifically with respect to REITs, An, Cook, and Zumpano (2011, p. 429) report the following:

> Using a panel data set of REITs, we find corporate transparency to be positively associated with REIT growth. These results suggest that greater transparency facilitates firm growth by relaxing information-based constraints on external financing. … Moreover, the sensitivity of investment to cash flows is decreasing in transparency, evidence that transparency relaxes liquidity constraints. Finally, we find more transparent REITs are less likely to crash.

Liquidity

Stock liquidity—that is, the ease of trading equity shares without large transaction costs—provides another form of capital market discipline that, like transparency, can improve investment decision making and performance. Indeed, transparency and liquidity generally work together. For example, poor investment decisions by a listed REIT may trigger a downgrade in analyst ratings, in turn triggering stock sales, which would both increase the cost of capital and reduce executive incentive compensation.

Amihud and Mendelson (2005) and Butler, Grullon, and Weston (2005) find that liquidity, like transparency, reduces the cost of capital. Fang, Noe, and Tice (2009, p. 150) report that

> Firms with liquid stocks have better performance as measured by the firm market-to-book ratio. Liquidity increases the information content of market prices and of performance-sensitive managerial compensation.

Several studies focus on liquidity specifically in the REIT market, in many cases comparing REITs with illiquid property investments. Marcato and Ward (2007, p. 599) find that "the development of REITs has increased liquidity and has therefore contributed to improved operational efficiency in real estate markets." Benveniste, Capozza, and Seguin (2001, p. 656) report that "exchange trading increases shareholder wealth by around 10–15 percent at the margin compared to the relatively illiquid real estate market."

A frequently cited reason for investing in unlisted property rather than REITs is to capture an *illiquidity premium*. Theoretically, because liquidity is of value to investors, they would be unwilling to invest in illiquid assets unless they were compensated in the form of higher risk-adjusted returns. Although some support is available in the empirical literature for the existence of the hypothesized illiquidity premium within the stock market, some studies, such as Fang et al. (2009), imply the opposite result: Better performance is associated with liquidity rather than illiquidity.

Investment decision makers should be cautious not to confuse the required return on an asset with its expected return. The *required return* compensates the investor for taking on increased risks or costs, and is higher for investments that expose the investor to those additional risks and costs (including opacity as well as illiquidity). The *expected return* embodies the investment manager's (including the corporate executive team's) success in producing net returns for the investor, and is lower to the extent that investment returns are inferior because of factors such as increased capital costs or inhibited responsiveness of investment manager decision making to incentive compensation.

Alignment of Interests between Investors and Investment Managers

Although various methods are available to align the interests of investment managers with those of investors, perhaps the most important are governance and incentive compensation. As with transparency and illiquidity, effective governance can bring discipline to investment decisions. Bushman and Smith (2003, p. 79), for example, identify as one form of transparency "the use of financial accounting information in corporate control mechanisms that discipline managers to direct resources toward projects identified as good and away from projects identified as bad," a process that could be termed *effective governance*.

Several studies investigate the effects of governance on returns specifically in the REIT industry. Hartzell, Kallberg, and Liu (2004, p. 539), for example, find that "firms with stronger governance structures have higher IPO valuations and better long-term operating performance than their peers." Institutional Shareholder Services (a subsidiary of MSCI) annually ranks stock market sectors according to the average Corporate Governance Quotient (CGQ) awarded to each company reflecting investor-aligned governance structures. The real estate industry, including REITs, has repeatedly been ranked second behind only public utilities.

The other main way of aligning investors' with investment managers' interests is through effective managerial compensation. Two-thirds of listed REITs offer managerial incentive compensation that is composed entirely of restricted stock ownership, which by definition aligns the interests of managers perfectly with those of shareholders. In contrast, the incentive compensation packages offered by unlisted property investment funds typically provide optionlike payoffs that align the interests of investment managers very poorly with those of investors. In particular, the typical fee structure of a private equity fund is composed of a management fee on committed capital that is insensitive to investment performance, plus a *promote*, typically computed as 20 percent of returns in excess of a *hurdle rate* commonly set at 8 percent.

Under this fee structure, managers—unlike investors—share in high returns but not in losses and are rewarded for taking greater risks than may be in shareholders' best interests. For example, the compensation structure encourages managers to use excessive leverage because the incentive is based on levered rather than unlevered returns. Moreover, if poor initial investment decisions reduce a fund's returns below its hurdle rate, the fee structure provides no incentive for managers to work to correct the fund's returns unless they can reasonably expect to bring returns above the hurdle rate. Finally, the fact that management fees are tied to assets under management gives managers an incentive to expand assets under management even if by doing so they reduce investor returns. In contrast, the use of restricted stock ownership in REIT incentive compensation packages gives REIT executives an incentive not to increase assets under management except through earnings-accretive investments.

The Free Cash Problem

One way in which poor alignment of interests can damage investment returns is the free cash problem identified by Jensen (1986, p. 323):

> Payouts to shareholders reduce the resources under managers' control, thereby reducing managers' power, and making it more likely they will incur the monitoring of the capital markets which occurs when the firm must obtain new capital. Financing projects internally avoids this monitoring . . .

To summarize, the *free cash problem* refers to retaining earnings and deploying them in ways that benefit managers while avoiding capital market scrutiny.

In contrast, investors' interests are served by disgorging earnings to ensure that investment financing is subject to capital market scrutiny and is therefore more likely to benefit investors.

The distribution test—the requirement that REITs distribute at least 90 percent of their taxable income—while not eliminating the free cash problem, certainly reduces its potential scope. Because REIT managers cannot retain earnings to the same extent as other investment managers, REITs generally establish and maintain access to every part of the capital market so that when profitable investment opportunities present themselves REITs can quickly and inexpensively obtain financing even while undergoing capital market scrutiny. Campbell, Devos, Maxam, and Spieler (2008, p. 200), for example, find that REITs tend to establish lines of credit (LOCs) in anticipation of accretive investment opportunities: "unlike conventional firms, REITs use LOCs primarily to fund major capital investments," and "REITs announcing LOC agreements have superior operating performance as measured using net income over total assets."

In contrast, the business model of unlisted property investment funds, such as those represented by the ODCE and NCREIF/Townsend indices, is first to amass capital and then to deploy it without further capital market scrutiny. This model can result in investment decisions that are not in investors' interests. For example, during 2007 transaction prices in the commercial property market were elevated with abnormally low cap rates even relative to low risk-free rates of return. In such a "frothy" market, investors' interests would generally have been served by selling rather than purchasing assets—and, in fact, by returning committed capital to investors rather than deploying it, since acquisitions generally would not be accretive.

As Exhibit 7.11 shows, however, unlisted property investment managers became enormous net purchasers of assets during 2006 and 2007 by acquiring some $190 billion more properties than they sold. Furthermore, they undertook many of these acquisitions with abnormally high leverage. For example, the NCREIF/Townsend Fund indices indicate that the average leverage in 2008Q4 was 67.1 percent for opportunistic funds and 57.3 percent for closed-end value-added funds. Given the low acquisition cap rates and the slim prospects for either growth in net operating income or capital appreciation, managers apparently sought to reach hurdle return rates primarily by taking on additional risk in the form of higher leverage, even if a subsequent decline in asset values might leave investors with negative net returns.

Sources of Financing

Contrasting with the free cash problem—that is, the availability of profitable investments when capital is abundant—is the availability of capital when profitable investments are abundant. As Exhibit 7.11 also shows, unlisted property investment managers were net sellers of properties both before the market peak (2002–2004) and after it (2009–2010), even though both would have been favorable periods for acquisitions. In effect, unlisted property investment managers exhibited "buy-high, sell-low" behavior. In contrast, REITs were net buyers both before and after the peak, becoming huge net sellers during the peak. This behavior can plausibly be attributed to differences in the sources of capital for the REIT and non-REIT segments of the property market. Specifically, REITs have access to public

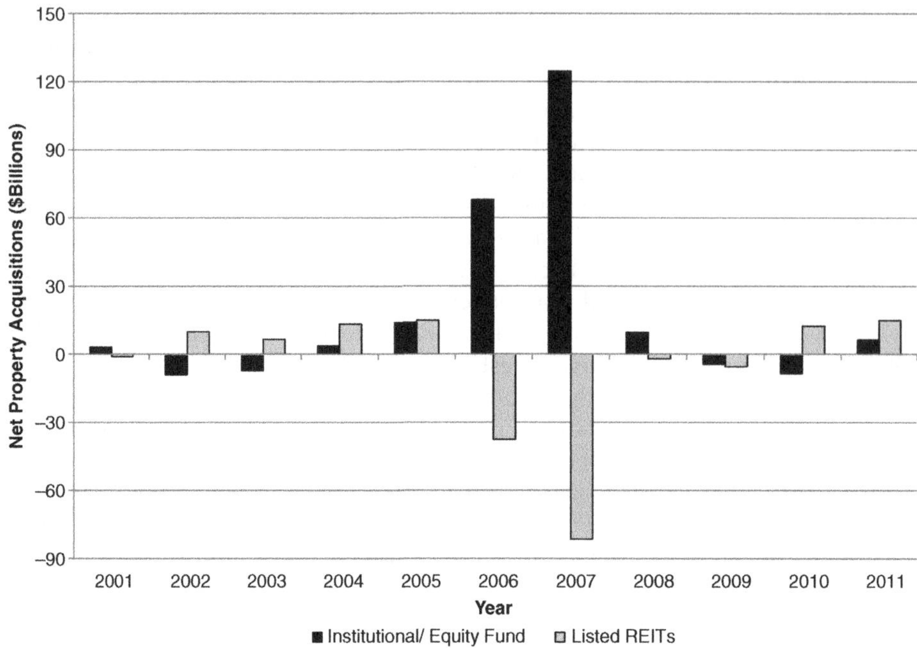

Exhibit 7.11 Net Property Acquisitions by Year, 2001–2010
This exhibit shows that REITs were net sellers of assets during the market peak and net buyers both before and after the peak, whereas unlisted property investment managers were net buyers during the market peak and net sellers both before and after the peak. Source: Real Capital Analytics.

markets for equity and debt financing, whereas unlisted property investment managers have access only to private equity and private debt. As MacKinnon (2011, p. 15, 17) notes:

> A lack of capital means reduced competition in the bidding for available properties, including distressed properties coming to market. Investors having access to capital when others do not could be positioned to take advantage of such market conditions, potentially creating value. With access to the public markets, REITs have a built-in advantage in times of constrained credit through the ability to raise capital via seasoned equity or unsecured bond issues.
>
> If REITs are able to bid on properties at a time of decreased competition, and at a time when owners of property may be forced into distressed sales because of their own capital constraints, then REITs may obtain properties at advantageous prices and thereby create value for shareholders.

Open-end unlisted property funds face an additional disadvantage relative to REITs. Just as capital inflows (the free cash problem) may motivate them to purchase assets near market peaks, capital outflows may prevent them from purchasing assets near market troughs and may even motivate them to sell assets. Open-end funds typically maintain a *cash buffer* (i.e., uninvested cash, generally 3 to 5 percent of assets) to meet redemption requests, but when a large number of investors seek to redeem shares, fund managers may have to forego investment opportunities to protect the cash buffer. Such managers may even be motivated to raise additional cash, perhaps by selling assets, to protect the cash buffer.

SUMMARY AND CONCLUSIONS

Equity shares of REITs represent ownership in the commercial properties owned by the REITs. Therefore, REITs provide exposure to the real estate asset class. The fact that REITs are traded in a liquid environment through the public stock market has led some to argue that they do not provide real estate returns and do not constitute an alternative investment. Trading through the stock market introduces short-term return variation that is unrelated to the real estate market. Yet, the long-term returns to REITs are very closely tied to the long-term returns to other forms of property investment; that is, REIT returns have a high correlation with unlisted property returns and a low correlation with stock market returns.

Historical investment performance data show that REITs have provided returns superior to those provided by unlisted property investments, including core properties held directly or in separate accounts, as well as unlisted property investment funds following core, value-add, or opportunistic strategies. The five available measures of returns suggest that REITs provide income returns similar to those of the other investments, along with capital appreciation rivaled only by those of opportunistic funds.

Volatility is fully measured for REIT investments, but for unlisted investments is disguised by illiquidity smoothing and appraisal smoothing. Over longer investment horizons, the measured volatility of REIT returns is consistent with the measured volatility of unlisted property returns, and risk-adjusted returns are far superior for REITs. Moreover, comparison of unlevered transaction-based property returns data suggests that REIT volatility is essentially identical to, and perhaps even less than, the volatility of unlisted property investments.

Superior investment performance by REITs may be explained by at least five aspects of the REIT business model. First, REITs benefit from substantially greater transparency, which reduces capital costs and imposes capital market discipline. Second, REITs benefit from liquidity, which has the same effects. No empirical evidence suggests an illiquidity premium in property investments. Third, REIT governance and executive incentive compensation align the interests of REIT managers closely with those of investors. Fourth, the distribution requirement ameliorates the free cash problem under which executives tend to use available cash to make investments that are not in investors' interests. Fifth, REITs' access to public as well as private equity and debt markets—and the fact that REIT investors make decisions by buying and selling existing shares rather than by committing capital and redeeming shares—means that investment criteria rather than capital flows drive REIT investment decisions.

DISCUSSION QUESTIONS

1. Which tests determine eligibility for REIT status?
2. What are the main arguments for and against including REITs as an alternative investment in the real estate asset class?

3. What are illiquidity smoothing and appraisal smoothing, and what are their effects on the measured volatility of unlisted real estate investments relative to REIT volatility?
4. What are the effects of illiquidity lag, appraisal lag, illiquidity smoothing, and appraisal smoothing on the measured correlation between listed and unlisted property investments?
5. Which aspects of the REIT business model may cause REIT returns to differ from unlisted property returns?

REFERENCES

Amihud, Yakov, and Haim Mendelson. 2005. "The Liquidity Route to a Lower Cost of Capital." *Journal of Applied Corporate Finance* 12:4, 8–25.

An, Heng, Douglas O. Cook, and Leonard V. Zumpano. 2011. "Corporate Transparency and Firm Growth: Evidence from Real Estate Investment Trusts." *Real Estate Economics* 39:3, 429 454.

Benveniste, Lawrence, Dennis R. Capozza, and Paul J. Seguin. 2001. "The Value of Liquidity." *Real Estate Economics* 29:4, 633–660.

Bond, Shaun A., and Paul Mitchell. 2010. "Alpha and Persistence in Real Estate Fund Performance." *Journal of Real Estate Finance and Economics* 41:1, 53–79.

Botosan, Christine A., and Marlene A. Plumlee. 2002. "A Re-examination of Disclosure Level and the Expected Cost of Equity Capital." *Journal of Accounting Research* 40:1, 21–40.

Bushman, Robert M., and Abbie J. Smith. 2003. "Transparency, Financial Accounting Information, and Corporate Governance." *FRBNY Economic Policy Review* 9:1, 65–87.

Butler, Alexander W., Bustavo Grullon, and James P. Weston. 2005. "Stock Market Liquidity and the Cost of Issuing Equity." *Journal of Financial and Quantitative Analysis* 40:2, 331–348.

Campbell, Robert D., Erik Devos, Clark L. Maxam, and Andrew C. Spieler. 2008. "Investment, Liquidity, and Private Debt: The Case of REIT Credit Facilities." *Journal of Real Estate Portfolio Management* 14:3, 195–201.

Cannon, Susanne Ethridge, and Rebel A. Cole. 2011. "How Accurate Are Commercial Real Estate Appraisals? Evidence from 25 Years of NCREIF Sales Data." *Journal of Portfolio Management* 35:5, 68–88.

Cici, Gjergji, Jack Corgel, and Scott Gibson. 2011. "Can Fund Managers Select Outperforming REITs? Examining Fund Holdings and Trades." *Real Estate Economics* 39:3, 455–486.

Fang, Vivian W., Thomas H. Noe, and Sheri Tice. 2009. "Stock Market Liquidity and Firm Value." *Journal of Financial Economics* 94:1, 150–169.

Gyourko, Joseph, and Donald B. Keim. 1992. "What Does the Stock Market Tell Us about Real Estate Returns?" *Journal of the American Real Estate and Urban Economics Association* 20:3, 457–485.

Hahn, Thea C., David Geltner, and Nori Gerardo-Lietz. 2005. "Real Estate Opportunity Funds." *Journal of Portfolio Management* 31:5, 143–153.

Hartzell, Jay C., Jarl G. Kallberg, and Crocker H. Liu. 2004. "The Role of Corporate Governance in Initial Public Offerings: Evidence from Real Estate Investment Trusts." *Journal of Law and Economics* 51:3, 539–562.

Jensen, Michael C. 1986. "Agency Costs of Free Cash Flow, Corporate Finance, and Takeovers." *American Economic Review* 76:2, 323–329.

LaFever, Robert A., and Luis Canizo. 2005. "Revisiting Performance Persistence in Real Estate Funds." Working Paper, Center for Real Estate, Massachusetts Institute of Technology.

Lambert, Richard, Christian Leuz, and Robert E. Verrecchia. 2007. "Accounting Information, Disclosure, and the Cost of Capital." *Journal of Accounting Research* 45:2, 385–420.
Lin, Zhenguo, and Kerry D. Vandell. 2007. "Illiquidity and Pricing Biases in the Real Estate Market." *Real Estate Economics* 35:3, 291–330.
Ling, David C., and Andy Naranjo. 2012. "The Dynamics of Returns and Volatility in Public and Private Real Estate Markets." Working Paper, Hough Graduate School of Business, University of Florida.
MacKinnon, Greg. 2011. "Do REITs Have an Advantage When Credit Is Tight?" *Journal of Real Estate Portfolio Management* 17:1, 15–25.
Marcato, Gianluca, and Charles Ward. 2007. "Back from Beyond the Bid-Ask Spread: Estimating Liquidity in International Markets." *Real Estate Economics* 35:4, 599–622.
Oikarinen, Elias, Martin Hoesli, and Camilo Serrano. 2011. "The Long-Run Dynamics between Direct and Securitized Real Estate." *Journal of Real Estate Research* 33:1, 73–103.
Pagliari, Joseph L., Kevin A. Scherer, and Richard T. Monopoli. 2005. "Public versus Private Real Estate Equities: A More Refined, Long-Term Comparison." *Real Estate Economics* 33:1, 147–187.
Rawlins, Brad. 2008. "Give the Emperor a Mirror: Toward Developing a Stakeholder Measurement of Organizational Transparency." *Journal of Public Relations Research* 21:1, 71–99.
Riddiough, Timothy J., Mark Moriarty, and P. J. Yeatman. 2005. "Privately versus Publicly Held Asset Investment Performance." *Real Estate Economics* 33:1, 121–146.
Tomperi, Ilkka. 2010. "Performance of Private Equity Real Estate Funds." *Journal of European Real Estate Research* 3:2, 96–116.
Tsai, Jengbin Patrick. 2007. "A Successive Effort on Performance Comparison between Public and Private Real Estate Equity Investment." Working Paper, Center for Real Estate, Massachusetts Institute of Technology.

ABOUT THE AUTHOR

Brad Case is Senior Vice President, Research and Industry Information at the National Association of Real Estate Investment Trusts (NAREIT®) in Washington, DC. His research has been published in *Review of Economics and Statistics*, *Real Estate Economics*, *Journal of Real Estate Finance and Economics*, and *Journal of Portfolio Management*. He holds patents for both the PureProperty® index methodology and "backward-forward" trading contracts. Dr. Case earned his BA at Williams College, MPP at the University of California at Berkeley, and PhD in economics at Yale University. He also holds the CFA and CAIA designations.

CHAPTER 8

Mortgaged-Backed Securities

ERIC J. HIGGINS
von Waaden Chair of Investment Management, Kansas State University

INTRODUCTION

On July 10, 2007, Moody's downgraded more than 400 securities created from home equity loans. The total face value of the securities downgraded was in excess of $5 billion. Standard & Poor's followed two days later with 612 downgrades of securities with a face value in excess of $7.5 billion. These massive downgrade events began the downward spiral of the mortgage-backed securities market that had grown from nothing in 1970 to a value of over $9 trillion by 2007. Before 2007, terms such as *securitization* and *tranches* and acronyms such as *MBS* (mortgage-backed securities), *CDOs* (collateralized debt obligations), and *CDS* (credit default swaps) were unfamiliar to most individuals. However, as the crisis deepened, the MBS market became the epicenter of the financial crisis, and many questions began to arise. How can so many securities be created from a pool of simple home mortgages? How did the U.S. government and its related agencies become so involved in the housing market? Did MBS cause the turmoil that led to the 2007–2008 financial crisis?

The purpose of this chapter is to provide answers to these and other questions that surround the MBS market. The chapter begins by examining how MBS are created and reviews some of the various types of MBS. Next, the chapter provides a historical perspective on the MBS market and the factors that led to its rapid growth. The role of MBS in the recent financial crisis is explored. The chapter concludes with some thoughts on the future of the MBS market.

HOW ARE MORTGAGE-BACKED SECURITIES CREATED?

MBS are created through a process known as securitization. *Securitization* is the transformation of an asset into an investment by selling claims against the expected future cash flows of the asset. Any asset with a stream of expected future cash flows can be securitized. The most widely known asset-backed securities (ABS) are MBS, but many other assets have been securitized, including credit card receivables, auto loan receivables, and student loan receivables. One of the most unique securitizations occurred in 1997 when rock star David Bowie securitized the rights to all future revenues from his song portfolio. The bonds created from his song portfolio,

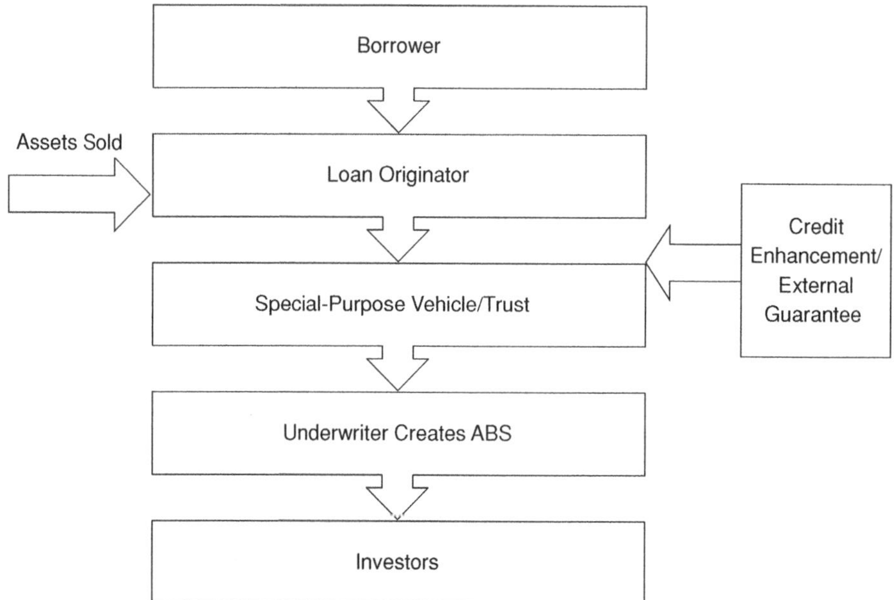

Exhibit 8.1 The Securitization Process
This diagram shows the process of securitization from the origination of the loan to the ultimate packaging of the loan into a security that is sold to investors.

known as Bowie Bonds, sold for $55 million and were purchased by the insurance company Prudential.

The essential component of securitization is risk sharing. The issuers of the ABS are transferring the risk of holding the assets to the investors in the ABS. The investors are willing to bear the risk given that they earn an appropriate rate of return. In theory, securitization benefits both issuers and investors. Issuers get access to liquidity and to a reliable funding source that may better match their liabilities. Investors get access to asset markets that may otherwise be unavailable to them, and they are better able to manage risk by investing across a broader range of asset classes.

Exhibit 8.1 shows a basic diagram of the securitization process. Borrowers seek credit from financial institutions who sell the loans made to borrowers to a special-purpose vehicle (SPV). The SPV is also known as the *conduit*. The SPV pools assets together to form the collateral for the ABS that will be issued. As the assets are pooled by the SPV, certain guarantees or credit enhancements may be added to the mortgage pool to reduce risk. For example, in the case of securities sponsored by Government National Mortgage Association (Ginnie Mae), all mortgage payments coming into and out of the SPV are guaranteed by the government. Once the assets have been pooled and all credit enhancements and guarantees have been added, the securities to be sold are created with the help of an underwriter and are sold to investors. The SPV remains the ultimate holder of the assets and passes all payments to investors. The originator of the assets will often retain the rights to service the assets and will pass the borrowers' payments to the SPV.

Investors in any ABS face three common risks: interest rate risk, default risk, and sponsor risk. As a debt instrument, an ABS promises some future interest rate over a set period of time to investors. As interest rates in the market increase, the value of the ABS decreases. The effect of changes in the prevailing market rate of interest on bond values is called *interest rate risk*. Because an ABS is created from the expected future payments on an asset, a possibility exists that the payments may not be received, thereby creating default risk. Hence, *default risk* is the risk that a bond will fail to make promised or scheduled payments (either interest or principal payments). For example, a home owner may default on his mortgage or an individual may not repay his credit card debt. Finally, an ABS issue is only as good as the institution that creates the issue (the sponsor). If the sponsor of the issue were to go bankrupt, guarantees provided by the sponsor may not be honored, causing a negative impact on the value of the ABS. Gorton and Souleles (2006) model and empirically show how sponsor risk directly affects the value of credit card ABS issues. Using data from mortgage securitizers during the recent financial crisis, Faltin-Trager, Johnson, and Mayer (2011) find a direct relationship between ABS sponsors and subsequent performance of their ABS issues. Also, the investor in the ABS relies on the sponsor to provide accurate and honest information about the assets held by the SPV. If investors are misled about the nature of those securitized assets, they are unable to appropriately evaluate the risk of the ABS. For example, if the sponsor claimed to follow a set of strict underwriting criteria for the loans that were placed into a SPV, investors assume something about the quality of those loans. According to Bethel, Ferrell, and Hu (2009), many lawsuits resulting from the 2007–2008 financial crisis centered on the underwriting standards followed by mortgage securitizers. If the actual underwriting standards are less than what the sponsor reports, the ABS investor will have inappropriately assessed the risk of the assets held by the SPV.

MBS are a specialized subset of ABS created through the securitization of residential mortgage loans. Besides the general risks that investors face in holding ABS, MBS investors also face prepayment risk. *Prepayment risk* arises due to the fact that a mortgage holder may repay their mortgage early; that is, *prepayments* are principal repayments in excess of those required on amortizing loans, such as residential mortgages. Prepayment risk is higher when interest rates go down, which is the opposite effect of interest rate risk. Several other factors besides interest rate movements affect prepayment risk, including refinancing incentives built into mortgage contracts, the age of the mortgage, seasonality (summer is the peak season for home sales and prepayments), and the previous paths of interest rates.

The percentage of prepayments made annually is known as the *conditional prepayment rate* (CPR). The CPR is used to calculate the *single monthly mortality rate* (SMM), which is simply the percentage of loans in a given pool that will repay each month. CPRs are generally estimated in one of two ways. First, CPRs can be estimated using data from the Federal Housing Authority (FHA). The FHA tracks all of the loans it guarantees and has a large database of prepayment data upon which estimates of CPRs can be made. Second, CPRs can be estimated using the convention set by the Public Securities Association (PSA). The PSA convention assumes that the CPR is equal to 6 percent $\times$ $(t/30)$, where t is the number of months since loan origination for the first 30 months of the life of the loan pool and is a constant 6 percent thereafter. Prepayments are typically modeled by investors in terms of a percentage of the FHA or PSA prepayment rates. For example, a 200 percent FHA prepayment would use a CPR that is double the standard FHA prepayment rates. Utilizing multiples of prepayment rates allows investors to examine different risk scenarios in order to be able to accurately assess the expected payments from a MBS.

The simplest form of MBS is a pass-through security. In a *pass-through security*, mortgages are pooled and all principal and interest payments on the mortgages are passed directly to investors. Although pass-through securities are popular, they have several limitations that many investors do not like. Pass-through securities have long maturities and subject investors to increased interest rate risk. Unlike most mortgage bonds, pass-through securities pay both interest and principal to investors, creating more reinvestment risk for investors in pass-through securities relative to regular bonds. Mortgage prepayments, which can be estimated, pose problems for investors because prepayments are uncertain and create even more reinvestment risk. Finally, the pass-through market is typically limited to mortgages that are backed by the government or that are conforming mortgages. A *conforming mortgage* is a mortgage that meets certain criteria that are set by government-sponsored entities (GSE) such as Ginnie Mae. This structure limits the amount of underlying collateral that could ultimately be securitized. Collateralized mortgage obligations (CMOs) were developed to overcome these limitations.

The person hailed and later vilified as the creator of CMOs was Lewis Ranieri of Salomon Brothers. In 2004, *BusinessWeek* recognized Ranieri as one of its "greatest innovators of the past 75 years" (McNamee, 2004). By 2008, however, Nobel Prize–winning economist Robert Mundell described Rainier as one of the four villains of the mortgage crisis. Although the perception of Ranieri's contributions to society is in the eye of the beholder, one fact exists—Ranieri and Salomon Brothers helped create the first CMOs, including the first CMO issued by a GSE, the Federal Home Loan Mortgage Corporation (Freddie Mac).

The logic behind the creation of CMOs is essentially the same as the logic behind the creation of pass-through securities: They take the cash flows from an asset and package them together to be sold to investors. The difference between pass-through securities and CMOs is the nature of the packaging. Pass-through securities can be thought of as the "plain vanilla" of the MBS world. CMOs opened up a world of flavors to the MBS market.

The key to creating CMOs is a thorough understanding of the payments received on mortgages. A mortgage payment has only two cash flows: principal payments and interest payments. Principal payments may occur early or the borrower may default on his mortgage. The belief of the CMO creators was that if prepayments could be estimated with relative certainty and default could either be estimated or controlled, a myriad of different and complex securities could be created from a pool of mortgage loans. The different securities created in a CMO are commonly referred to as *tranches.* A tranche in a CMO has the same characteristics as a bond: a face value, a promised coupon rate, and a promised term to maturity or a repayment schedule. The only difference between a CMO tranche and a bond is that the coupon and principal payments come from the interest and principal payments received on the pool of mortgage loans.

To see how a CMO can be created, consider the example presented in Exhibit 8.2. Panel A of Exhibit 8.2 contains an amortization schedule for a $1,000,000 pool

Exhibit 8.2 Example of Loan Amortization and CMO Creation

Panel A. Amortization for $1,000,000 in loans, 5 years to maturity, 6 percent interest, and 10 percent prepayment

Year	Beginning Balance	Loan Payment	Interest	Principal	Prepayment	Ending Balance
1	$1,000,000	$237,396	$60,000	$177,396	$100,000	$722,604
2	722,604	208,537	43,356	165,181	72,260	485,163
3	485,163	181,504	29,110	152,394	48,516	284,252
4	284,252	155,041	17,055	137,986	28,425	117,841
5	117,841	124,911	7,070	117,841	0	0

Panel B. Hypothetical sequential CMO with two tranches, an IO notional, and a residual claim

Year	Tranche A Interest	Tranche A Principal	Tranche B Interest	Tranche B Principal	IO Notional Payment	Residual Payment
1	$15,000	$23,750	$277,396	$0	$21,250	$0
2	6,678	23,750	222,604	14,837	12,928	0
3	0	23,008	0	200,910	6,102	0
4	0	12,963	0	166,411	4,092	0
5	0	4,642	0	92,842	2,428	25,000

This exhibit shows the amortization of a $1,000,000 loan in Panel A and a hypothetical securitization of the loan receivables in Panel B.

of mortgage loans that has five years to maturity, offers a 6 percent interest rate, and makes annual payments. In this example, the assumption is that 10 percent of the mortgages will be repaid each year. Thus, the mortgage pool has a CPR of 10 percent. Creating the amortization schedule involves the following steps:

1. Using the beginning balance of the mortgage pool, find the required mortgage payment given the 6 percent interest rate and the number of years left until maturity. In the first year, the required mortgage payment is $237,396.
2. Compute the required interest payment, which is $60,000 in the first year.
3. Compute the principal payment (total payment – interest payment), which is $177,396 in the first year.
4. Compute the amount of mortgage prepayments by multiplying the prepayment rate by the beginning mortgage balance, which is $100,000 in the first year.
5. Repeat the steps 1 through 4 until the mortgage pool is fully amortized.

As Panel A of Exhibit 8.2 shows, getting an accurate estimate of the interest and principal payments expected in the mortgage pool is possible based on the given prepayment assumptions. In the world of the CMO, the 10 percent CPR assumption becomes the base case upon which the CMO will be built. The base case is typically referred to as the 100 percent prepayment case. The prospectus that accompanies the CMO will detail various permutations of prepayment assumptions on the base case such as 50 percent and 200 percent so that investors will have an understanding of the possible ranges of the value of their securities.

The principal and interest payments that are derived from the amortization table will be used to create the CMO. The first consideration in creating a CMO is to determine the number and type of tranches that are to be created from the mortgage pool. In theory, the only limitations on the number and type of tranches that can be created are set by the characteristics of the mortgage pool. For example, the mortgages being securitized in the example have five years left to maturity. Thus, creating a security that has a maturity of greater than five years is impossible. In reality, however, the market will determine the types of securities that are created. If no demand exists for one-year MBS, there is no reason to create them. Typically, the following factors are considered when creating the tranches of a CMO:

- *Demand at various points on the yield curve.* In order to create as much demand for the CMO tranches as possible, issuers will want to offer a variety of maturities.
- *Credit risk protection.* Some investors in CMO tranches will desire low-risk, highly rated securities, whereas others will desire higher yielding securities. The CMO issuer must create tranches that will be able to achieve the bond ratings that are demanded by investors.
- *Reinvestment risk protection.* Fixed-income investors are used to having predictable repayments of their bonds. Thus, CMO issuers will often create tranches that have some protection against the prepayments that occur in the mortgage pool.

The CMO issuer must balance all of these issues in order to create securities that will fit within the limitations of the mortgage pool and will be desired by investors.

The next consideration in creating a CMO security is to determine the total face value of the tranches that will be issued from the mortgage pool. In the example in Exhibit 8.2, the total face value of the mortgage pool is $1,000,000, so theoretically a total face value $1,000,000 of CMO tranches could be issued. If the mortgages that are being securitized are backed by a government agency such as the FHA, the mortgage pool is insulated from the possibility that mortgage default will decrease the value of the pool, and the whole $1,000,000 face value of the mortgage pool could be issued as CMO tranches. If a possibility for mortgage default exists, the face value of the CMO tranches will likely be less than the face value of the mortgages. This situation is known as *overcollateralization.* Overcollateralization is used to control the credit risk of the CMO tranches.

Panel B of Exhibit 8.2 lists the proposed CMO structures and payments. For this CMO, four securities will be created: an A tranche, a B tranche, an interest only (IO) notional tranche, and a residual (R) tranche. The A tranche will have a shorter term to maturity and the B tranche will have a longer term to maturity. Creating the differing maturity structures involves using a sequential payment structure. Sequential payment structures are the most common tool in the CMO issuer's tool box. In a sequential structure, the tranches have varying maturities based on the allocation of principal payments to investors. The tranche with the shortest term to maturity receives all principal payments in a mortgage pool until the security is paid in full. Subsequent tranches receive principal payments in a sequential manner until all tranches are paid in full. The A tranche in the example is structured so that it will be repaid by the end of the second year and the B tranche is structured so that it will be repaid by the end of the life of the mortgages (five years).

The example in Exhibit 8.2 assumes that the mortgages in the pool are not government insured and may experience defaults. Given that this is the case, the CMO issuer has two choices: issue $1,000,000 face value of securities to the A and B tranche holders and let them bear the potential default risk or overcollateralize the CMO and provide some protection to the A and B tranche holders. In the example, the CMO is overcollateralized. The decision to provide overcollateralization drives the choice of the face values of the A and B tranches. In the first two years, the CMO is expected to provide principal payments of $514,837, and over the last three years the CMO is expected to provide principal payments of $485,163. Thus, to provide protection for the A and B class investors, the face value of the A tranche is set at $500,000 and the face value of the B tranche is set at $475,000, meaning that this CMO issue has $25,000 of overcollateralization. The overcollateralization of the CMO issue gives rise to the residual class security.

The residual class security will only receive payments after the A and B tranche securities are paid in entirety. Thus, the residual class security is known as a *subordinated security*. In CMO issues, subordinated securities are common and are used to control the risk of the mortgage pool and provide protection for senior tranche holders. The coupon rates on the A and B tranches are market driven given their risk characteristics and their maturities. The CMO issuer does have to give some consideration to the prepayment and default characteristics of the mortgage pool to ensure that sufficient interest payments will be present to cover all of the promised coupon payments. In the example, the coupon rate of the A tranche is set at 3 percent and the coupon rate of the B tranche is set at 5 percent. The interest rates on the two tranches are less than the 6 percent coupon rate that the mortgage collateral is currently paying. Thus, assuming no defaults, residual interest can be distributed. This residual interest creates the IO notional tranche. Because the IO notional tranche does not have an actual face value, the nomenclature *notional* is used to define the tranche. Typically, the IO tranche has a promised coupon rate that is based on the expected overages in interest payments received. The notional principal amount is derived from the promised coupon rate.

Given that the structure of the CMO issue has been set, the cash flows to the three tranches can now be analyzed. In the first year of the security, the A tranche holders receive interest payments of $500,000 × 3 percent = $15,000 and the B tranche holders receive interest payments of $475,000 × 5 percent = $23,750. Given the sequential nature of the CMO tranches, the A tranche receives all of the $277,396 in principal payments made. The A tranche will now have a balance of $222,604, which represents the difference between the original face value of the tranche and the principal payments made. Assuming no defaults, the IO notional tranche will receive the excess interest payments of $60,000 − $38,750 = $21,250.

In the second year, the A tranche receives interest payments of $222,604 × 3 percent = $6,678. The B tranche continues to receive interest payments of $23,750. The A tranche receives $222,604 of principal payments and the B tranche will then receive $237,441 − $222,604 = $14,837 of principal payments. The IO notional tranche continues to receive the excess interest payments.

During the last year of the securitization, the residual tranche will receive the excess principal payments that arise due to the overcollateralization, which equals $1,000,000 − $975,000 = $25,000. The A tranche has a weighted average life of ($227,396/$500,000) × 1 year + ($222,604/$500,000) × 2 years = 1.345 years. The weighted average life of the B tranche is 3.71 years. Weighted-average lives are always reported in the CMO prospectus and are analyzed for different prepayment scenarios.

The analysis in this example is based upon the assumed CPR of 10 percent and no defaults. If these parameters change, the value of the tranches will change. For example, assume that the prepayment rate is 400 percent, four times the base-case scenario, or 40 percent in the first year. In this case, the total principal payments in the first year will be $177,396 + $400,000 = $577,396. This scenario would mean that the A tranche will completely repay in year 1 and the B tranche will have a $77,396 reduction in face value in year 1. This increase in prepayments would drop the total return to both the A and B tranches and changes the IO notional payment structure. As this example illustrates, investors should understand the different tranches that are being offered so that they can adequately assess risk. The next section reviews some different classes of MBS that exist in the market.

A REVIEW OF THE DIFFERENT CLASSES OF MORTGAGE-BACKED SECURITIES

Despite a seemingly endless number of different types of MBS, they can generally be classified into two types. This section reviews both types of securities using the prospectuses from actual ABS transactions.

Pass-Through Mortgage Securities

The most common MBS are agency pass-through securities. Ginnie Mae, the Federal National Mortgage Association (Fannie Mae), and Freddie Mac create agency pass-through securities. Ginnie Mae does not directly purchase the loans that are used to create its pass-through securities, but it does guarantee the payments of interest and principal in its mortgage pools. Ginnie Mae only securitizes pools of government-guaranteed loans, thereby eliminating default risk. Given that the U.S. government directly backs Ginnie Mae securities, no sponsor risk exists. Fannie Mae and Freddie Mac purchase mortgage loans directly from financial institutions to create pass-through securities and securitizes both government-guaranteed loans and conforming mortgage loans. Fannie Mae and Freddie Mac both guarantee the mortgage payments on the loans that they securitize but, unlike Ginnie Mae, the U.S. government does not directly back their guarantees. Thus, investors in Fannie Mae and Freddie Mac securities could face both sponsor risk and default risk on conforming mortgage loans. All three agency issuers charge fees for providing their pooling and guarantee service, which are deducted from the mortgage cash payments before distribution.

Ginnie Mae first issued pass-through securities in 1968, followed by Freddie Mac in 1971 and Fannie Mae in 1981. Ginnie Mae pass-through securities tend to

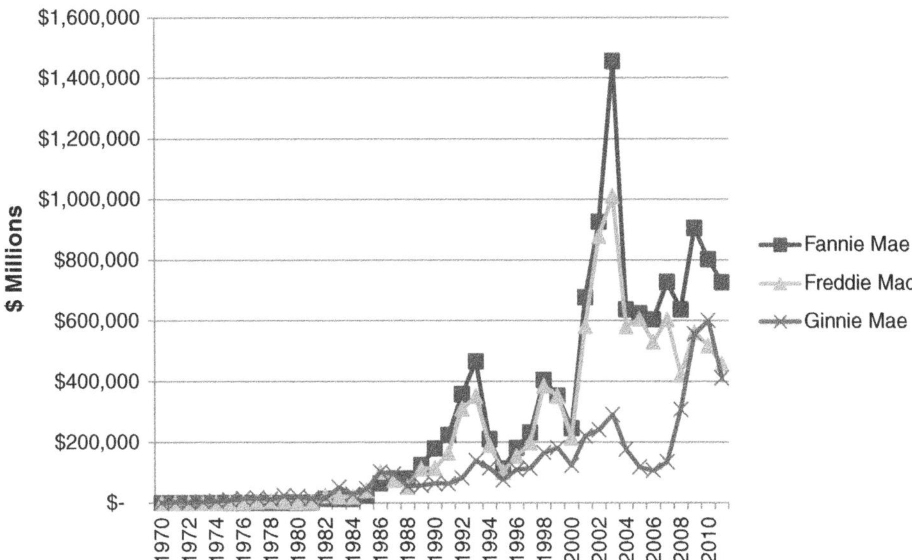

Exhibit 8.3 Annual Issuance of Agency Pass-Through Securities from 1970–2011 as Reported by the Securities Industry and Financial Markets Association (SIFMA)
This diagram shows the total annual issuance of agency securities in millions of dollars as reported by the Securities Industry and Financial Markets Association (SIFMA).

have lower prepayment risk than Fannie Mae and Freddie Mac due to the relative homogeneity in the loans guaranteed by Ginnie Mae. Currently, Ginnie Mae has two active programs from which it sponsors pass-through securities. The Ginnie Mae I program creates pools of mortgage loans that are very similar in terms of interest rates and maturities and primarily services large financial institutions that will be selling large volumes of loans. The Ginnie Mae II program was created in 1983 and was designed to allow financial institutions with smaller loan volumes to participate in the Ginnie Mae securitization program. Ginnie Mae II loan pools are more diverse in terms of interest rates and maturities. Thus, these pass-through securities have a greater degree of uncertainty in their prepayment rates relative to Ginnie Mae I securities. Fannie Mae and Freddie Mac pass-through securities are created from pools of residential mortgages, multifamily housing mortgages, and other pass-through securities. The loans in the Fannie Mae and Freddie Mac pools tend to be more heterogeneous and have more prepayment risk than Ginnie Mae securities. Salomon Brothers pioneered nonagency pass-through securities (also known as *private label pass-through securities*), which first appeared in 1977.

Exhibit 8.3 shows the total volume of agency pass through securities issued by agencies as reported by the Securities Industry and Financial Markets Association (SIFMA). As Exhibit 8.3 shows, the amount of agency pass-through securities grew dramatically in the first decade of the 2000s. Lower interest rates and a rapidly growing (and some would say overheated) real estate market fueled much of that growth. Much of the rapid growth in agency securities came from Fannie Mae and Freddie Mac.

Exhibit 8.4 Tranche Offerings from the Fannie Mae REMIC Trust 2012–53

Class	Loan Group	Face Value ($)	Security Type	Interest Type	Interest Rate (%)
CZ	1	51,270,000	SUP	FIX/Z	4.00
FP	1	48,370,000	PAC/AD	FLT	LIBOR + 35 BPS
PA	1	145,110,000	PAC/AD	FIX	2.00
PL	1	20,250,000	PAC/AD	FIX	4.00
PI	1	NTL	IO	FIX	4.00
SP	1	NTL	IO	INV	6.65 – LIBOR
A	2	160,000,000	PT	FIX	2.00
AI	2	NTL	IO	FIX	3.50
EA	3	66,030,000	SEQ	FIX	1.75
EL	3	4,970,000	SEQ	FIX	3.00
EI	3	NTL	IO	FIX	3.50
IE	3	NTL	IO	FIX	3.50
CD	4	92,595,901	PT	FIX	1.50
CI	4	NTL	IO	FIX	3.00
AP	5	40,735,246	SC/PT	FIX	2.00
PF	5	27,156,830	SC/PT	FLT	LIBOR + 40 BPS
PS	5	NTL	IO	INV	6.40 – LIBOR
BK	6	184,521,368	PT	FIX	1.75
BI	6	NTL	IO	FIX	3.50
R	ALL	—	RESIDUAL	—	0.00
RL	ALL	—	RESIDUAL	—	0.00

This exhibit contains the tranche offerings from the Fannie Mae REMIC Trust 2012–53 created from information contained in the prospectus for this offering.

Two main reasons explain the rapid growth. First, Fannie Mae and Freddie Mac were not constrained to purchasing only government-insured mortgages. Second, their government-sponsored status allowed Fannie Mae and Freddie Mac to obtain capital at lower rates resulting in rapid growth. Both Passmore (2005) and Eisenbeis, Frame, and Wall (2007) find that Fannie Mae and Freddie Mac had excessive leverage, presumably due to their government subsidy, and that they posed a substantial risk to the financial system. Interestingly, Ginnie Mae security issuance fell dramatically in the period from 2004 to 2007. This time period corresponds to the rapid growth in the subprime mortgage market. Two ways of viewing this drop off in issuance by Ginnie Mae are that either financial institutions focused on making subprime loans due to the high demand for that product or most of the good loans that could be insured by the government had already been made. Either way, this trend should have been a warning signal of the problems to come.

Collateralized Mortgage Obligations

In order to try to provide some idea of the many different types of CMO securities tranches, the deal structures of three actual CMO issues are reviewed. Exhibit 8.4 shows the tranches of the Fannie Mae REMIC Trust 2012–53 taken from the prospectus. Exhibit 8.5 shows both the tranches of the Countrywide Alternative

Exhibit 8.5 Tranche Offerings from the Countrywide Alternative Loan Trust 2005-J13

Class	Loan Group	Face Value ($)	Security Type	Interest Type	Interest Rate (%)	Initial Rating
1-A-1	1	20,000,000	PT	FLT	LIBOR + 30 BPS	AAA
1-A-2	1	NTL	IO	INV	7.20 – LIBOR	AAA
1-A-3	1	20,000,000	PT	FIX	4.50	AAA
1-A-4	1	5,169,000	PT	FIX	6.00	AAA
1-X	1	NTL	SUP	FLT/Z	—	AAA
2-A-1	2	34,000,000	PT	FLT	LIBOR + 70 BPS	AAA
2-A-2	2	NTL	IO	FLT	4.80 – LIBOR	AAA
2-A-3	2	34,000,000	PT	FIX	5.50	AAA
2-A-4	2	8,060,000	PT	FIX	5.50	AAA
2-A-5	2	40,000,000	PT	FLT	LIBOR + 42 BPS	AAA
2-A-6	2	NTL	IO	FLT	5.02 – LIBOR	AAA
2-A-7	2	19,335,732	PT	FIX	5.50	AAA
2-A-8	2	996,268	PT	FIX	5.50	AAA
2-A-9	2	30,000,000	PT	FLT	LIBOR + 50 BPS	AAA
2-A-10	2	NTL	IO	FLT	5.00 – LIBOR	AAA
2-A-11	2	26,854,000	PT	FIX	5.50	AAA
2-X	2	NTL	SUP	FLT/Z	—	AAA
PO	ALL	107,697	PO	FIX	—	AAA
A-R	ALL	100	RES	FIX	5.50	AAA
M	ALL	6,020,000	SUB	FLT	0.00	AA
B-1	ALL	2,257,500	SUB	FLT	0.00	A
B-2	ALL	1,254,500	SUB	FLT	0.00	BBB

This exhibit contains the tranches and initial bond ratings for the Countrywide Alternative Loan Trust 2004-J13. This information comes from the prospectus for this transaction.

Loan Trust 2004-J13 and finally, Exhibit 8.6 shows the deal structure for the ABACUS 2007-AC1 synthetic CDO, both taken from their prospectuses.

Before reviewing each of these CMO issues individually, a few common elements are worth noting. First, as previously emphasized, each of these exhibits came from the prospectuses of the respective CMO issues. An investor in a CMO must thoroughly review an issue's prospectus. The prospectus provides an investor with a complete description of each tranche in the issue, provides a thorough description of the collateral that supports the CMO, and details the representations and warranties being made about the collateral that supports the CMO. These pieces of information are absolutely critical for an investor to digest in order to be able to make an informed investment decision. Second, each of these issues represents one of many CMOs issued by each issuer during the year, thus the year and identifier nomenclature. Finally, each of these issues is held in a specific trust from which the underlying collateral is pooled and then distributed to investors.

The Fannie Mae REMIC Trust 2012–53 CMO shown in Exhibit 8.4 is typical of most CMOs issued by the three government agencies. The trust is structured as a real estate mortgage investment conduit (REMIC). REMICs were created as a result of the 1986 Tax Reform Act. Before the creation of REMICs, institutions that issued CMOs were required to keep the assets held in the CMO trust on their

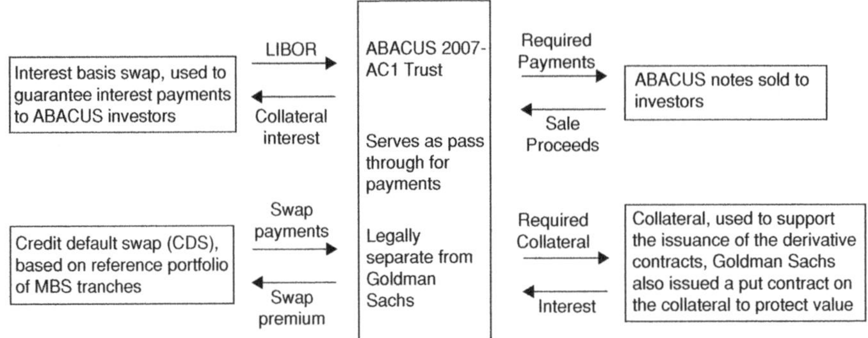

Exhibit 8.6 Deal Structure for Goldman Sachs ABACUS 2007-AC1 Trust
This exhibit illustrates the transactions that take place to create the ABACUS 2007-AC1 Trust created based on information contained in the prospectus for this transaction.

balance sheets. REMICs are structured to allow institutions the ability to remove any assets sold to the REMIC from their balance sheets. Almost all CMOs issued are structured as REMICs. Exhibit 8.4 shows the Fannie Mae REMIC trust, which is actually composed of six different mortgage pools even though the issue is controlled by only the 2012–53 REMIC trust. This grouping of mortgage pools in a single trust is common and is done to best match the characteristics of the underlying collateral in the various groups. The total size of the issue is $841,009,345 and, given Fannie Mae's guarantees, is backed by a like amount of collateral. The collateral in this CMO consists of Fannie Mae pass-through securities and a tranche from a previously issued Fannie Mae REMIC. Even though the deal contains no overcollateralization, potential returns for the residual tranche still exist. The residual tranche will receive any interest payments that are earned by the trust during the time between the mortgage payments are received by the trust and by the time that the payments are distributed to investors. As Exhibit 8.4 shows, all of the mortgage groups have notional (NTL) IO tranches. NTL IO tranches generally exist when the coupon payments on the underlying collateral are expected to be larger than the promised coupon payments on the CMO tranches. Thus, the NTL IO tranches will receive any excess interest payments after all promised coupon payments have been made. The face value of the NTL IO tranches simply reflects the face value that would have to exist to support the promised coupon.

The tranches in group 1 of this CMO are known as a *planned amortization class* (PAC) of securities. In a PAC, the securities are structured such that principal payments are passed to security holders on a regular schedule, eliminating excess prepayment risk. The scheduled payments are designed to be maintained within a certain range of prepayments, known as the PAC band, which is defined in the prospectus. To help provide protection for the PAC securities, a supporting class of security (typically known as a Z class security) is created, which in the example in Exhibit 8.4 is the CZ tranche of the group 1 securities. The supporting tranche absorbs excess prepayments and will not receive principal payments when prepayment shortfalls exist, which means that the supporting tranches have a highly variable weighted-average life. Another type of scheduled repayment CMO is a targeted amortization class (TAC) security. In contrast to a PAC, a TAC has a fixed prepayment rate as opposed to a prepayment range. TACs, therefore, will have greater cash flow variability relative to PACs.

The PAC classes in group 1 pay both fixed interest rates (FIX) and floating interest rates (FLT), also known as a *floater*. The addition of floating-rate securities in the CMO issue enhances the marketability of the issue. When a floater is created, an inverse floater (INV) is created that has a notional principal that is the same as the floater. In Exhibit 8.4, the FP tranche is the floater and the SP tranche is the inverse floater. In CMO securities, the floater will have an interest rate cap. An *interest rate cap* sets an upper limit on the rate that can be earned on the floater. The cap is necessary due to the fact that the mortgage collateral typically pays a fixed rate. Thus, large increases in interest rates would lead to a funding shortfall for the floater. The INV is an IO security that pays out the difference between the interest rate cap level and the promised rate on the floater. Inverse floaters are risky securities and tend to be sold to sophisticated investors, such as hedge funds.

The tranches in groups 2, 4, and 6 are pass-through (PT) tranches with a corresponding IO tranche. The PT tranches behave just like regular pass-through securities except that the interest rate paid on the PT tranche is set at a fixed rate lower than the actual interest payments on the underlying collateral. The lower fixed rate on the PT tranche allows for the creation of a fixed-rate IO tranche.

The tranches in group 3 are sequential tranches. The EA tranche receives principal payments first and the EL tranche receives principal payments next. The underlying collateral for the group 3 securities are 15-year, mortgage pass-through securities (note the last payment date of 2027 in Exhibit 8.4). Given the relative sizes of the tranches, the EL tranche will behave much like a regular bond. The EL tranche is scheduled to receive only interest payments until 2024, at which point the principal will be returned in 2025, 2026, and 2027.

The tranches in group 5 are interesting because the underlying collateral in group 5 is actually a tranche from another Fannie Mae REMIC trust. The tranche underlying the securities in group 5 is a PT tranche with an IO fixed-rate tranche. This tranche is then repackaged into both a fixed-rate PT tranche and a floating-rate PT tranche with a corresponding inverse-floater tranche. This type of repackaging is sometimes referred to as a *re-REMIC*.

Exhibit 8.5 shows the deal structure for the Countrywide Alternative Loan Trust 2005-J13. This deal is interesting due to the collateral that underlies the deal. This deal was created by pooling what are known as Alt-A loans issued by Countrywide. *Alt-A loans* are loans that do not meet the criteria to be considered conforming loans but were issued to borrowers that were deemed to be good credit risks. These loans, along with subprime loans, were at the center of the 2007–2008 financial crisis. Of course, in retrospect, saying that these loans should not have been securitized is easy. However, as Exhibit 8.5 shows, Standard and Poor's gave an AAA rating to all of the senior tranches of this CMO. How could securities created from these lower quality loans be rated AAA? The answer lies within the structure of the CMO.

The total face value of the securities offered in this CMO was \$248 million, and the amount of collateral supporting the CMO was \$250 million. Thus, the deal offered about \$2 million in overcollateralization. Besides the overcollateralization, the deal offers protection to the senior tranches by adding several subordinated tranches. The subordinated tranches in the deal (Classes M, B-1, and B-2 in Exhibit 8.5 and three privately placed tranches) represent 4.9 percent of the total face value of the deal. Thus, this CMO included about $12 million dollars of subordinated securities. The subordinated tranches support the senior tranches by being the first securities to absorb any losses from the default of the mortgages in the pool. Subordinated tranches are often referred to as *first-loss tranches.* With the addition of the $2 million of overcollateralization, the pool could suffer a default rate of about 5.6 percent and still be able to pay the principal to the senior note holders.

In addition to the residual tranches that support the entire loan pool, both loan groups have a supporting security class (1-X and 2-X) that function like the Z class security in the Fannie Mae REMIC Trust. The supporting tranches are designed to support the "nondiscount" mortgages that are in the trust. A *discount mortgage* is a mortgage that offers a lower interest rate for a set period of time.

During the mortgage boom, many nonprime variable rate mortgages featured reduced variable rates for the first two or three years of the mortgage. Many of the loans in this deal were discount variable rate mortgages. These mortgages are likely to have lower prepayment rates during the discount period. Thus, the 1 X and 2 X tranches are designed to compensate for the fact that the nondiscount mortgages in the pool were likely to prepay at a greater frequency than the discount mortgages. The interest rates paid on the 1-X and 2-X tranches are variable based upon the prepayment rates of the nondiscount mortgages.

Again, more recent history would suggest that this was not nearly enough protection for the senior security holders, but a review of the market in 2004 might suggest differently. Sengupta (2010), who provides an excellent review of Alt-A mortgage performance, finds that in 2004, when this deal was issued, default rates on Alt-A mortgages were relatively low. Additionally, no one really expected these mortgages to actually remain Alt-A. The presumption was that as long as real estate prices continued to increase, which they had for the previous 30 years, homeowners would either refinance or the Alt-A mortgages would eventually become conforming.

The structure of the Countrywide deal is rather standard. Most of the tranches are PT securities with both fixed and floating coupon rates that are lower than coupon rates on the underlying mortgage pool. The lower coupon rates allow for the creation of both fixed-rate IO securities and floating-rate IO securities with a corresponding inverse floater. The Class 2-A-7 and 2-A-8 securities are a variation on the traditional PT security. These securities are known as nonaccelerating senior (NAS) securities. NAS securities have a lockout period in which the securities are fully protected from prepayments. This deal also offers some support for the floating-rate securities. The trust purchased an "interest rate corridor" from Bear Stearns that provides protection against interest rate increases and helps offset the higher costs of the floating-rate securities. The trust also contains a principal only (PO) tranche. As the name suggests, the PO tranche only pays out principal. The pairing of IO and PO tranches (called *strips*) is very common, because the interest and principal payments come from the actual required mortgage payments. Prepayments are generally not included in the strips. This PO tranche, however, is serving as a nonsubordinated buffer to the other senior tranches. The PO tranche takes losses before the senior tranches, but the losses are deferred and are promised to be paid later.

Any chapter on MBS would be incomplete without a brief discussion of the CDO market. Exhibit 8.6 contains a diagram of the deal structure for perhaps the most infamous CDO of all time, the Goldman Sachs ABACUS 2007-AC1 trust. The ABACUS deal eventually led the Securities Exchange Commission (SEC) to fine Goldman Sachs $550 million. CDOs function much like re-REMICs in that they are a simple repackaging of existing tranches of CMO issues or of other debt instruments. The ABACUS deal takes the whole notion of repackaging one step further, because it is a synthetic CDO. As Exhibit 8.5 shows, a *synthetic CDO* uses a variety of derivative contracts, such as CDS, to replicate the cash flows generated from an underlying "reference portfolio." The reference portfolio is the collateral upon which the synthetic CDO is built. The cash flows that are generated from the derivative contracts are passed on to the investors, but the trust does not actually hold the underlying reference portfolio. The reference portfolio for the ABACUS deal was a portfolio of lower rated tranches from subprime mortgage CMOs. Basically, the ABACUS deal was a credit derivative that was betting on the value of the subprime mortgage market. If the subprime market stayed solvent, investors in the ABACUS deal would make money. If the subprime market failed, the counterparties to the derivatives that comprised ABACUS' cash flows would make money. So, in a sense, the actual value of the reference portfolio was irrelevant to the ABACUS deal, what mattered was the amount of credit risk in the subprime mortgage market.

Any time that a disparity occurs between the assets that underlie a derivative security and the value of the derivative security, speculation is encouraged. In this case, synthetic CDO buyers were chasing higher yields in the subprime mortgage market. The issuers of CDOs were betting that the subprime mortgage market would fail. Neither party particularly cared about the actual mortgages themselves. This dynamic meant that those creating the mortgages could take liberties with traditional underwriting standards because they knew that a ready market existed for any mortgage labeled as subprime. This situation, in turn, created pressure on the real estate market. This pressure is the essence of Gorton's (2008) argument that highly complex derivative securities helped precipitate the 2007–2008 financial crisis. As can be seen from the discussion of CMO securities, a definite progression of complexity in the MBS market occurred: pass-through securities to CMOs to CMOs written on weak collateral to CDOs to synthetic CDOs. Gorton's argument can be supported by looking at the development of the MBS market place. The next section explores the 2007–2008 financial crisis and tries to understand more completely the role that MBS played in the crisis.

THE ROLE OF THE MBS MARKET IN THE 2007–2008 FINANCIAL CRISIS

Understanding the role that MBS played in the 2007–2008 financial crisis involves knowledge of the long and rather checkered history of the MBS market. The modern MBS market began in 1970 when Ginnie Mae issued its first pass-through security. Contrary to popular belief, the modern MBS market was not the only MBS market in the financial history of the world. According to Snowden (2010b), U.S. agricultural mortgage brokers in the 1880s placed mortgages in trusts and sold securities that used those mortgages as collateral. Today, this type of security would be known as a mortgage-backed bond. According to Snowden, banks in Europe had been issuing this type of security for many years before the introduction of agricultural-based mortgage bonds in the Unites States. This market, much like the current MBS market, fell apart during a financial crisis, specifically the depression of 1893.

The MBS market began to reemerge in the period before the Great Depression. The MBS market that developed during this time period was very similar to the current MBS market. In the 1920s, a major expansion of both residential and commercial real estate development occurred in the United States. Easier access to credit for individuals fueled much of this expansion.

Snowden (2010a) discusses two financial innovations that helped fuel the mortgage debt boom in the 1920s, both of which are familiar features in today's mortgage market: mortgage insurance and participation certificates. Private mortgage insurance provided the financial guarantee that allowed mortgage lenders in the 1920s to sell mortgages to create liquidity and then issue more mortgages. As Snowden notes, private mortgage insurance was so vilified during the Great Depression as a cause of the real estate crisis that it was not seen again until the 1950s. While the majority of loans backed by private mortgage insurance were sold individually to investors, some loans were pooled together and participation certificates were issued against those loans. The participation certificates gave holders the rights to the interest and principal payments made on those loans. These securities were very similar to the mortgage pass-through securities that exist today.

The 1920s MBS market came to a crashing halt during the Great Depression. Snowden (2010a) notes that many of the mortgage insurance companies that were engaged in selling mortgage participation certificates undertook the same deceptive practices, relaxed underwriting standards (e.g., Countrywide), asset substitution (Higgins and Mason, 2004), and inadequate guarantee funding (e.g., AIG) that plagued the mortgage industry in the period immediately before the beginning of the financial crisis that began in 2007.

The seeds for the current MBS market were sown in the aftermath of the Great Depression. Although a myriad of changes occurred to the financial system as a result of the Great Depression, two changes stand out as important in the development of the current MBS market: the creation of FHA mortgage insurance and the creation of Fannie Mae. FHA mortgage insurance was created during the Great Depression to encourage commercial banks and other financial entities to reenter the housing market. The program created standardized loan terms and sizes for mortgages that would qualify for FHA insurance. The program was also a precursor to other government mortgage guarantee programs, such as the Department of Veterans Affairs (VA) loan program, the Rural Housing Service (RHS) loan program, and the Office of Public and Indian Housing (PIH) loan program. The creation of government guarantees on loans, much like private mortgage insurance in the 1920s, allowed for the creation of a secondary market in mortgage loans. Fannie Mae was created in 1938 with the purpose of buying government-insured mortgages. As Snowden (2010a) discusses, the National Housing Act authorized the creation of National Mortgage Associations that were to be private entities authorized to purchase FHA insured loans and funded by mortgage backed bonds. Because of little private interest in the National Mortgage Association program, Fannie Mae was created as a government-backed entity.

Fannie Mae was the only purchaser of government-backed mortgages until 1968. The Housing and Urban Development Act of 1968 split Fannie Mae into two entities. Fannie Mae was now chartered as a privately held entity that had access to a government credit line [thus, the origin of the term *government-sponsored entity* (GSE)]. Fannie Mae continued to directly purchase government-backed loans. Ginnie Mae was created to guarantee the timely payment of FHA- and VA-backed mortgage loan pools and was, and still is, backed by the U.S. government. Freddie Mac, a GSE, was created in 1970 as a competitor to Fannie Mae, and both Fannie Mae and Freddie Mac were allowed to purchase conforming mortgage loans that were not government insured. Conforming loan limits and terms were set by the Department of Housing and Urban Development and continue to be set by the Federal Housing Finance Association, the current overseer of Fannie Mae and Freddie Mac.

Three main factors drove the creation of Ginnie Mae, Fannie Mae, and Freddie Mac. First, Fannie Mae had grown to a large size by 1968 and its debentures represented a major liability of the federal government. To get out of the mortgage market, the government essentially moved the assets of Fannie Mae "off balance sheet" (a technique later used by private securitizers) by creating the legally separate, privately held entities that are known today. Second, the government wanted to increase home ownership rates in the United States and to offer home loans to more low- and moderate-income families. Finally, the government also wanted to create an active secondary mortgage market to support the goal of increasing home ownership. Ginnie Mae's guarantee of timely mortgage payments on FHA and VA loans created an active market for pass-though securities very similar to those created in the 1920s. These pass-through securities allowed financial institutions to clear their balance sheets and make more loans. The creation of Fannie Mae and Freddie Mac expanded the pool of loans that could be purchased from financial institutions and again allowed the financial institutions to make more loans.

With the creation of Ginnie Mae, Fannie Mae, and Freddie Mac, the stage was set for rapid growth in the housing market. New home sales from 1970 to 2007 increased at a rate much higher than the growth rate in the population in the United States, real estate values grew at an annually compounded rate of 5.9 percent per year from 1970 to 2007, and home ownership rates increased from 64 percent in 1970 to a peak of 69 percent in 2005. The creation of these three entities also ushered in a new era of financial innovation that began with the securitization of home mortgages. In 2007, the overheated real estate market imploded, new home sales became nonexistent, and, as of April 2012, home ownership rates were at their lowest levels in 15 years.

Besides complex financial structures, three factors seemingly led to the 2007–2008 financial crisis. First, the 1999–2000 recession prompted the Federal Reserve to cut interest rates to what, at that time, were historically low levels. Interest rates were held at low levels until mid-2004. The low levels of interest rates spurred financial institutions to become increasingly aggressive with mortgage lending as the demand for housing (obviously buoyed by the rapidly growing MBS market) continued to increase and mortgage rates remained high relative to the cost of funds in the market. The lower interest rates also spurred investors to chase yield and seek riskier alternatives. The convergence of these two factors spurred the rapid growth of the subprime lending market. Again, the fact that lenders could remove the loans from their balance sheets through securitization buoyed this market.

The second environmental factor that created problems in the MBS market was the true sale assumption. The creation of REMICs after the 1986 Tax Reform Act allowed institutions that were securitizing assets to legally remove those assets from their balance sheets. In practice, however, securitizations closely resemble typical firm financing arrangements. Sponsors of securitized assets maintain representations and warranties, servicing contracts, and repeated reliance on a relatively small market of buyers for future securitizations that continually link buyers and sellers, rendering the notion of true sale obsolete.

Empirically, Higgins, Mason, and Mordel (2012) find evidence that the market treats securitizing firms as actually holding much more debt than they actually hold and that this treatment is related to their use of off-balance-sheet securitizations. These results are consistent with classifying securitizations as financings rather than sales, despite accounting and regulatory classifications to the contrary. If the securitizations are actually financings, then much more leverage exists in the financial market than what appears on the balance sheets, which was certainly evidenced during the financial crisis.

Finally, a liberal regulatory climate characterized the period before the crisis. The deregulation of banks, including the removal of interstate branching restrictions and the allowance of bank holding companies to own securities firms, led to massive consolidation in the banking industry and spurred the growth of incredibly complex financial institutions. The large, complex financial institutions were greeted with regulatory ambivalence on issues such as violations of true sale (Higgins and Mason, 2004) and were encouraged to leverage as capital requirements actually declined. Both regulators and the market in general also discounted the massive degree of interdependence in the financial markets. The large, complex financial institutions had become systemically important to the entire global financial market place, and all financial institutions were making the same bet—home prices would continue to increase.

The introduction of complex financial structures into this financial and regulatory climate produced disastrous consequences. MBS, CMOs, CDOs, and synthetic CDOs became the fuel from which the real estate market fed, ultimately leading to the greatest recession since the Great Depression.

SUMMARY AND CONCLUSIONS

Mortgage-backed securities have been hailed as one of the greatest advances in financial markets and blamed for causing the worst recession since the Great Depression. The reality is that the creation of the current MBS market began with a noble purpose, which was to increase mortgage market liquidity in order to increase home ownership rates in the United States. The MBS market saw a rapid expansion, growing from nothing in the 1970s to an over $9 trillion market by 2007. An expansive monetary policy and a lax regulatory environment aided the rapid growth in the market. These factors led to the creation of ever more complex securities that ultimately led to the downfall of the MBS market.

Many questions surround the future of the MBS market. After the collapse of the MBS market in 2007, private-label MBS issues have become nonexistent.

Recent changes by the Financial Accounting Standards Board (FASB) restrict the ability of financial institutions to use SPVs to facilitate the sale and removal of assets from their balance sheets, casting doubt upon the viability of the private label MBS market altogether. Fannie Mae and Freddie Mac continue to issue pass-through securities and CMOs even though they are currently held in receivership. The U.S. government has and continues to spend billions of dollars supporting Fannie Mae and Freddie Mac and, implicitly, has made supporting the U.S. housing market an unfunded federal mandate. How long this mandate will last and what will become of Fannie Mae and Freddie Mac are unclear. The government could move to privatize Fannie Mae and Freddie Mac. If the history of the Great Depression is any indication, private investors will be unlikely to step in and fill the role of these two mortgage entities. This scenario opens the real possibility that the current MBS market may cease to exist, bringing markets again full circle.

DISCUSSION QUESTIONS

1. Outline the steps used to create the tranches of a CMO.
2. Define the following CMO tranche types: planned amortization class (PAC), target amortization class (TAC), interest only (IO), principal only (PO), and inverse floater.
3. Discuss the previous MBS markets that existed in the United States.
4. Identify the three factors, in conjunction with the growth in complex financial structures, that helped trigger the 2007–2008 financial crisis.

REFERENCES

Bethel, Jennifer E., Allen Ferrell, and Gang Hu. 2009. "Legal and Economic Issues in Litigation Arising from the 2007–2008 Credit Crisis." In Yasuyuki Fuchita, Richard Herring, and Robert Litan, ed., *Prudent Lending Restored: Securitization after the Mortgage Meltdown*, 163–235. Washington, DC: Brookings Institution Press.

Eisenbeis, Robert A., W. Scott Frame, and Larry Wall. 2007. "An Analysis of the Systemic Risks Posed by Fannie Mae and Freddie Mac and an Evaluation of the Policy Options for Reducing Those Risks." *Journal of Financial Services Research* 31:2–3, 75–99.

Faltin-Trager, Oliver, Kathleen Johnson, and Christopher Mayer. 2011. "Sponsor Risk and the ssPerformance of Asset-Backed Securities." Columbia Business School Working Paper No. 11–6. Available at http://ssrn.com/abstract=1916311.

Gorton, Gary. 2008. "The Panic of 2007." In "Maintaining Stability in a Changing Financial System." *Proceedings of the 2008 Jackson Hole Conference*, 131–262, Federal Reserve Bank of Kansas City.

Gorton, Gary, and Nicholas S. Souleles. 2006. "Special Purpose Vehicles and Securitization." In René Stulz and Mark Carey, ed., *The Risks of Financial Institutions*, 549–602. Chicago, IL: University of Chicago Press.

Higgins, Eric J., and Joseph R. Mason. 2004. "What Is the Value of Recourse to Asset-Backed Securities? A Study of Credit Card Bank ABS Rescues." *Journal of Banking and Finance* 28:4, 857–874.

Higgins, Eric J., Joseph R. Mason, and Adi Mordel. 2012. "Asset Sales, Recourse, and Investor Reactions to Initial Securitizations: Evidence Why Off-Balance Sheet Accounting Treatment Does Not Remove On-Balance Sheet Financial Risk." Working Paper, Kansas State University.

McNamee, Mike. 2004. "Your Mortgage Was His Bond." *BusinessWeek*, November 29. Available at www.businessweek.com/magazine/toc/04–48/B3910magazine.htm.
Passmore, Wayne. 2005. "The GSE Implicit Subsidy and the Value of Government Ambiguity." *Real Estate* Economics 33:3, 465–486.
Sengupta, Rajdeep. 2010. "Alt-A: The Forgotten Segment of the Mortgage Market." *Federal Reserve Bank of St. Louis Review* January-February, 55–71.
Snowden, Kenneth A. 2010a. "The Anatomy of a Residential Mortgage Crisis: A Look Back to the 1930s." NBER Working Paper, No. 16244.
Snowden, Kenneth A. 2010b. "Covered Farm Mortgage Bonds in the Late Nineteenth Century US." NBER Working Paper, No. 16242.

ABOUT THE AUTHOR

Eric Higgins is the von Waaden Professor of Investment Management at Kansas State University. Before coming to Kansas State in 2001, Professor Higgins was at Drexel University. His research has been published in such journals as the *Journal of Banking and Finance, Financial Review, Journal of Financial Research, Journal of Business Finance and Accounting,* and *Business and Society.* Professor Higgins has presented his research at the Bank Structure Conference and at research seminars and conferences hosted by the Federal Deposit Insurance Corporation, Federal Reserve Bank of Philadelphia, Federal Reserve Bank of Kansas City, and Federal Reserve Bank of Minneapolis. His research has also been quoted in publications such as *The Wall Street Journal, American Banker,* and CNBC. Professor Higgins received his undergraduate degree in finance from Kansas State University and his PhD in finance from Florida State University.

CHAPTER 9

Mezzanine Debt and Preferred Equity in Real Estate

ANDREW R. BERMAN
Professor of Law and Director, Center for Real Estate Studies, New York Law School

INTRODUCTION

In the last 10 years, the commercial real estate market has witnessed drastic changes in the types and volume of nontraditional financing methods. Before the recession that began in late 2007, unprecedented growth took place in two types of nontraditional financing: mezzanine debt and preferred equity. During that time, real estate borrowers had easy access to capital with loan-to-value ratios that sometimes exceeded the value of the property, and lenders could earn high interest rates and fees from these riskier financings. In the years following the 2008 recession recession, however, traditional mortgage lenders imposed tighter underwriting standards, and real estate owners and developers competed for the limited sources of available capital. As a result, the need for alternative funding sources increased. This provided an opportunity for a new group of lenders to enter the market to provide liquidity and additional capital. These nonbank financial institutions and hedge funds (many with billions of dollars under management) looked for opportunities to provide real estate financing during the volatile time period immediately following Lehman's collapse and the ensuing financial meltdown and continue to do so now.

With mezzanine debt and preferred equity investments, real estate owners could obtain much needed capital, and nonbank financial institutions and hedge funds could enter the finance markets and earn high interest rates and fees from these riskier and nontraditional financings. Real estate investors and scholars view these nontraditional financings (i.e., preferred equity and mezzanine debt) as a major way to fill the "financing gap" between the senior mortgage debt and the owner's equity. This chapter discusses the risks and opportunities of these two types of nontraditional real estate financings. It also examines how investors effectively manage the inherent risks of, and create opportunities with, mezzanine loans and preferred equity investments.

This chapter is organized as follows. The first part focuses on mezzanine loans and describes the legal and economic structure of mezzanine financings, along with the investment opportunities, and the business risks, of mezzanine loans. The second part focuses on preferred equity investments and also examines the legal and economic structure of these equity investments, along with the investment opportunities and risks of preferred equity.

MEZZANINE LOANS

In the real estate industry, *mezzanine financing* is a type of secured loan where the lender's collateral consists of the borrower's equity interests in other entities. With a traditional mortgage loan, the borrower owns the underlying income-producing real estate itself and grants the lender a mortgage lien on the property. However, a mezzanine loan is not directly secured by real estate because the mezzanine borrower does not actually own any income-producing property or other tangible assets. Mezzanine borrowers typically only own equity interests in other subsidiary entities, and these subsidiaries actually own the income-producing real estate. From both an economic and legal perspective, Berman (2007, p. 995) states that the "value of the mezzanine borrower's collateral derives solely from its indirect ownership of the underlying mortgaged property."

Mezzanine borrowers typically pledge as collateral all of their equity interests in the underlying subsidiaries that control, directly or indirectly, the mortgage borrower and the ultimate owner of the underlying real property. Because of this unique legal structure, Fisch, Freidus, and McOwen (2011) explain that mezzanine lenders are structurally superior to equity holders of the borrower, but at the same time they are structurally subordinate to the senior mortgage lender. The mezzanine loan is situated between the more secure senior mortgage loan and the equity investors. The highly leveraged mezzanine loan brings with it both risks and rewards for the parties. The following sections discuss the investment opportunities and risks of mezzanine lending in real estate.

Mezzanine Loans: Investment Opportunities

The growth of mezzanine loans is to some extent directly linked to the growth of commercial mortgage-backed securities (CMBS). In 2009, national credit rating agencies such as Standard & Poor's and Moody's required that any mortgage loan included in a CMBS offering prohibit the mortgage borrower from incurring any additional mortgage debt on the income-producing property. Because of this requirement, Rubin (2009) explains that the underwriting guidelines issued by the rating agencies effectively eliminated junior mortgage financing. As a result, the market demanded other types of financing to fill the gap left by the absence of junior mortgages. Lefcoe (2009) explains that mezzanine financing became an attractive form of financing, quickly replacing traditional junior mortgages and growing exponentially. According to Rubock (2007), the amount of mezzanine loans included in commercial real estate (CRE) collateralized debt obligations (CDO), for example, increased from just a few million dollars to over $3 billion annually.

Mezzanine loans are also popular with real estate owners because many mezzanine lenders offer accrual features that defer portions of the interest payments until the mezzanine loan reaches maturity (balloon payment). The unique structure of this loan reduces the burden on current cash flow and consequently has a positive effect on the borrower's debt coverage ratios. Furthermore, senior mortgage lenders frequently permit borrowers to obtain mezzanine loans because the loan proceeds often provide the required capital for property improvements and renovations, and these renovations increase the market value of the mortgage lender's collateral. Consequently, real estate owners and developers often seek mezzanine loans to replace traditional junior mortgages and to provide the required capital to close the financing gap between the senior mortgage debt and common equity.

Leverage

Recently, senior mortgage lenders have adopted conservative lending practices, leaving borrowers with lower loan-to-value (LTV) ratios. Fass, Shaff, and Zief (2011) maintain that as a result of the Dodd-Frank Act of 2010 and the financial regulations that have since been adopted, lending practices now also require higher debt coverage ratios (DCR). The DCR represents a property's net operating income divided by the annual debt service. Because owners are reluctant to inject additional equity into projects, Saft (2011a) contends that mezzanine loans provide these owners with capital to increase their LTV ratios without further encumbering the property with an additional mortgage. Saft also states that although a mezzanine lender is technically a secured creditor of the borrowing entity, credit agencies and senior mortgage holders generally treat mezzanine loans as a form of equity rather than debt, thereby permitting borrowers to increase their financial leverage.

Arnold (2011a) provides that mezzanine loans require higher yields than traditional junior mortgages because the collateral is a "weaker" form of security. For example, Arnold (2011b) asserts that the rapid growth of mezzanine loans in commercial real estate finance has caused lenders to assume more risk in exchange for higher returns. As Duell (2012) observes, mezzanine loan transactions frequently have internal rates of return (IRR) in excess of 20 percent. Dehncke-McGill (2012) states that mezzanine lenders' target rates of return fluctuate with the quality of the property and the stability of their cash flows. In determining the necessary IRR for mezzanine loan transactions, lenders consider the property location, rating, and length of tenant leases, rental income, and the amount of equity at risk.

Maturity of Existing Debt

In the past, mezzanine loans successfully provided real estate investors with methods to reorganize their capital structure without "watering down" their equity or negatively affecting the senior debt. Duell (2012) states that "[b]oth 2005 and 2006 were big years for conduit lending, and most of those loans had seven to 10-year terms." Lee (2011) provides empirical evidence showing that approximately $2.8 trillion in commercial real estate mortgages will be maturing between 2012 and 2020, with nearly $1.8 trillion in debt maturing between 2012 and 2015. With a large volume of original senior mortgage debt set to mature within the next few years, property owners need financing sources to refinance their debt obligations and fund the gap between debt and equity. Analysts foresee an opportunity for mezzanine lenders to provide owners with additional capital to refinance these loans.

In the next several years, many opportunities will be available for mezzanine lenders and borrowers. In describing a recent transaction, *Commercial Mortgage*

Alert (2012) illustrates some of the benefits of combining mezzanine loans and preferred equity investments along with traditional senior secured mortgages:

> The 1,013-room property, called Parc 55 Wyndham, has $211.5 million of outstanding debt that matured yesterday. The Rockpoint team is trying to pay it off by lining up a $90 million senior mortgage, $60 million of mezzanine debt and $50 million of preferred equity. It would also kick in about $10 million of fresh equity itself. . . . As Rockpoint scrambles to arrange fresh financing, high-yield investors are jockeying to buy the existing junior mezzanine debt on the hotel, in order to position themselves to take a run at the property if the refinancing fails. Market pros value the hotel at $210 million to $220 million, meaning that the Rockpoint team has little or no equity remaining in the property.

As this example illustrates, the mezzanine borrower can use the loan proceeds to meet certain financial and legal obligations under the existing senior mortgage and to limit the amount of cash equity at stake. Furthermore, the mezzanine lender earns high interest rates while at the same time holding collateral. However, the collateral is actually the mezzanine borrower's equity interests in the underlying entity that indirectly owns the income producing property.

Shifting the Risk through Securitization

Berman (2005) states that the growth in mortgage securitizations led to the creation of new real estate financing options, such as mezzanine loans and preferred equity. Similarly, Hughes (2011) asserts that the rise in mezzanine loans has been a function of the growth in securitization itself. Lenders use securitized mezzanine loans to raise money through the capital markets in order to fund additional loans to borrowers. Although mezzanine lenders typically experience the first dollar loss if a borrower defaults, mezzanine lenders protect their credit position by shifting the risk to secondary market investors through securitization. Because securitized mortgage facilities prohibit borrowers from acquiring junior mortgages, the structure of mezzanine loans provides borrowers with extra capital without negatively affecting the credit rating of the senior mortgage.

Furthermore, Rubock (2007, p. 1) states that, "[b]ecause of the CRE CDO alternative, mezzanine loans now have a natural capital market, and Moody's rates them in their own right, not viewing them merely as an impediment to higher rating on the senior secured debt." Thus, by packaging mezzanine loans in diverse securitization pools, lenders can shift the risks of real estate projects to investors in the secondary market and raise funds to finance additional real estate projects.

UCC Article 9 and Title Insurance

As Berman (2007) discusses, mezzanine lenders often find it difficult to enforce their rights and remedies if borrowers default. However, Rubock (2007) notes that mezzanine loans have distinct advantages compared to mortgage financing. For instance, a foreclosure of the collateral in a mezzanine loan under the Uniform Commercial Code (UCC) is considerably quicker than a mortgage foreclosure. Further, with a speedy mezzanine loan foreclosure, highly capitalized mezzanine lenders can inject funds into distressed properties more easily and quickly than traditional junior mortgage lenders.

Although mezzanine loan foreclosures are relatively quick, lenders still face many risks because of the unique nature of mezzanine loan collateral. Because the mezzanine lender's collateral (i.e., the equity interest in the mortgage borrower) is technically considered personal property, the UCC governs the foreclosure process rather than traditional mortgage law. As a result, Fisch and Simkin (2008) explain that the mezzanine lender's legal interests in the equity collateral need to be properly "perfected" under applicable UCC law.

UCC Article 9

Prendergast (2011) confirms that since mezzanine lender's collateral is considered personal property under state law, Articles 8 and/or 9 of the UCC applies depending on certain circumstances. Berman (2007) states that mezzanine lenders need to ensure "attachment" and "perfection" of the security interest in the lender's collateral in order to protect the lender's right to foreclose upon a default. With proper legal drafting, a mezzanine lender can easily structure the transaction so that Article 8 of the UCC governs these issues, and the lender can physically take possession and control of the "stock" certificate evidencing the equity serving as collateral. In the alternative, the lender's collateral may be classified as a "general tangible" under Article 9. Under this provision of the UCC, the secured lender perfects its security interest in the "general intangible" by filing a UCC-1 financing statement in the state where the debtor and collateral are located. In either case, according to Saft (2011a), once the security interest is created, attached, and perfected, mezzanine lenders' lien priority and collateral interest are generally superior to that of third-party lien holders.

If Article 8 of the UCC does not govern the transaction, disputes with other lien holders may arise because the determination of priority is based on the "first to file" the financing statement. Consequently, Berman (2007, p. 1004) asserts that perfection by possession or control typically "ensures a first priority lien over another lien holder who previously perfected by filing a financing statement even if the later secured party knew of the filing by the previous secured lender." As a result, mezzanine lenders often manage these risks by requiring, as a condition to the issuance of the loan, that the mezzanine borrower opt-in to Article 8 of the UCC and deliver physical control of the certificates to the mezzanine lender.

Title Insurance

In what began as an attempt to mitigate the risks associated with perfecting security interests, mezzanine lenders now routinely require borrowers to obtain mezzanine loan title insurance. Mezzanine lenders want to ensure that the quality of the title to the underlying property is free and clear from undisclosed liens and other defects. Typically, the closing of the mezzanine loan is conditioned upon the borrower's delivery of a special endorsement to the existing title policy of the mortgage borrower. Consequently, the endorsement provides the mezzanine lender with the right to receive payments otherwise payable to the underlying mortgage borrower.

Mezzanine lenders also frequently obtain "title" protection under UCC Article 9. With this relatively new title insurance product, mezzanine lenders are insured against defects in the attachment, perfection, and priority of the lender's lien in the mezzanine loan collateral. The most important protection that a mezzanine lender receives from this type of title policy, however, is that the title company will pay for all legal fees, costs, and expenses incurred in the defense of the lender's security interest in the collateral. Murray and Scott (2006) assert that these title insurance products help insure the quality of the mezzanine borrower's collateral.

Intercreditor Agreement between the Senior Mortgage Lender and the Mezzanine Lender

The intercreditor agreement is the most important document governing the relationship between the senior mortgage lender and the subordinate mezzanine lender because it governs the parties' respective rights and liabilities in the event of default under the mortgage or mezzanine loan. Although the senior mortgage lender may seriously affect the value of the mezzanine lender's collateral, the mezzanine lender can defend against some of these risks with various protections contained in an intercreditor agreement. Fawer and Waters (2007) state that mezzanine lenders typically modify the standard intercreditor agreement so that the mezzanine lender has (1) the right to receive notice of mortgage default and the opportunity to cure defaults, (2) the right to foreclose on its collateral, (3) the right to purchase the senior mortgage loan, and (4) approval rights over material modifications of the senior loan.

Right to Receive Default Notices and Cure Defaults

Mezzanine lenders typically require the senior mortgage lender to send them notices of any material default. After receiving a default notice, a mezzanine lender has only a short period of time to decide whether to remedy the default under the mortgage loan. If the default is not remedied, however, the mezzanine lender might lose the value of its collateral because a mortgage foreclosure would result in the sale of the underlying mortgaged property to the successful bidder at foreclosure. Although the mezzanine borrower would still technically own the equity interests in the underlying entities, these entities will no longer own the mortgaged property.

Under a typical intercreditor agreement, mezzanine lenders often have the same time period as the mortgage borrower to cure any defaults under the senior mortgage. Fileti (2012) contends that the standard form of the intercreditor agreement provides "stand-still obligations" on the senior lender following a default under the senior loan. For mezzanine lenders, these provisions provide a right to cure monetary and nonmonetary defaults before the senior mortgage lender takes any enforcement actions, including mortgage foreclosure. Arnold (2011a, p. 2) contends that, "senior lenders [might] welcome the role of the mezzanine lender, [because mezzanine lenders] have an incentive to cure defaults by the borrower in order to prevent a foreclosure and any resulting loss to the mezzanine lender." A mezzanine lender will generally only exercise its right to cure defaults under the senior mortgage when the underlying property's value is greater than the sum of all the outstanding liens on the property or if they believe they can take control of the property and increase its value.

Right to Foreclose

The mezzanine lender's primary remedy is the right to foreclose the mezzanine borrower's pledged equity interests. The ability to exercise this remedy depends largely on how broadly the relevant intercreditor agreement defines the term *Qualified Transferee*. Fawer and Austin (2011, p. 2) argue that the "more broadly the term 'Qualified Transferee' is defined, the more liquid the mezzanine loan and the pledged equity become." At the minimum, therefore, the mezzanine lender needs to be a Qualified Transferee so that if the mezzanine lender is the winning bidder at a foreclosure sale, this lender would be protected against the senior mortgage lender challenging the transfer of equity and related change of control. Furthermore, mezzanine lenders ought to protect against the risk that a successful UCC foreclosure will trigger a "due-on-sale" clause under the senior mortgage (because most mortgages define a "sale" to include a change of control of the mortgage borrower).

Right to Purchase the Senior Loan

If a default exists and the senior mortgage loan has been accelerated, mezzanine lenders usually have the right to purchase the senior mortgage. Fawer and Austin (2011) contend that mezzanine lenders ought to have the option to purchase the senior mortgage after a default until some outside date after the senior mortgagee commences its mortgage foreclosure. Accordingly, mezzanine lenders typically ensure a "right of first refusal" on the senior mortgage at a price that is equal to the outstanding amount due under the mortgage, but that does not require the mezzanine lender to pay any late fees, default interest, or prepayment penalties under the senior loan.

Mezzanine Lender's Rights and Remedies upon Borrower Default

When a default occurs under the mezzanine loan but there is no default under the senior mortgage, a mezzanine lender's primary remedy is generally to foreclose on the pledged security interest and take over ownership rights of the underlying property. Although Article 9 of the UCC requires a foreclosure sale to be "commercially reasonable," requiring delivery of notice and standard marketing procedures, Fisch et al. (2011) state that mezzanine lenders can usually complete a UCC foreclosure sale in 60 days or less.

In order to protect their rights after a foreclosure, mezzanine lenders normally restrict the mezzanine borrower's right to cause the mortgage borrower to prepay, modify, refinance, or grant additional collateral to the senior mortgage lender. This restriction helps to protect mezzanine lenders from changes under the senior loan that could inhibit the mezzanine lender's remedies. Similarly, Fileti (2011) recommends that the mezzanine lender should perform extensive due diligence of all material contracts relating to the property and/or the mortgage borrower as another safeguard, because after foreclosure the mezzanine lender, in essence, will own and control the property entity subject to those agreements.

As a practical matter, Fass et al. (2011) state that when there are defaults under both the senior mortgage and the mezzanine loan, the mezzanine lender's principal options are to either remedy the default under the senior mortgage or to purchase the mortgage loan. Berman (2007, p. 1022) contends that most senior mortgage loans provide for some type of purchase option. Mezzanine lenders also face the risk that foreclosure of the mezzanine loan collateral would trigger the "due on transfer" clause under the senior mortgage. As discussed previously, senior mortgage documents typically restrict transfers of the equity in the mortgage borrower or the transfer of the underlying real property. Thus, mezzanine lenders typically draft provisions protecting against the risk that any changes in control of the borrower will not trigger any "due on transfer" clauses under the senior mortgage.

Protection against Bankruptcy Risks

Some risk exists that the mezzanine or mortgage borrower might file for or become subject to an involuntary bankruptcy. In these cases, there are substantial risks of substantive consolidation, the imposition of the automatic stay limiting the mezzanine lender's ability to act, and the setting aside of pre-bankruptcy transactions as "fraudulent" transfers. In response to these risks, mezzanine lenders generally require that the mezzanine borrower is a bankruptcy-remote special-purpose entity (SPE). Fisch et al. (2011) contend that in a bankruptcy of the mezzanine borrower, the mezzanine lender would typically be able to obtain relief from the automatic stay and exercise its rights and remedies.

INVESTMENT RISKS OF MEZZANINE LOANS

As discussed in the previous section, mezzanine loans offer tremendous investment opportunities in today's commercial real estate market. However, if care is not taken, mezzanine lenders might suffer the financial consequences of these risky investments, especially because mezzanine loans do not have many of the typical mortgage protections. Berman (2007) contends that mezzanine lenders often lack protections customary to mortgages. For example, mortgage lenders have the following rights: to appoint a receiver, to protect against waste, and to foreclose the borrower's equity of redemption. In addition, basic property law ensures that a mortgage lien will bind future owners of the mortgaged property.

The investment risks involved with mezzanine loan transactions generally occur at four points in time: (1) prior to the origination of the mezzanine loan when the parties assess leverage, the response of the securitization market, and the relative costs and benefits of the investment ("high-yield" issues); (2) at the point of creation, attachment, and perfection of a security interest in, and the economic evaluation of, the mezzanine loan collateral; (3) when negotiating the intercreditor agreement with the senior mortgage lender; and (4) when the mezzanine borrower defaults and the mezzanine lender needs to enforce its remedies. This section discusses in greater detail these investment risks.

Leverage, Securitization, and High-Yield Issues

According to Duell (2012), one of the biggest impediments to a robust mezzanine lending market in 2011 was the high price of mezzanine money. As a result, mezzanine lenders responded to stagnant market conditions by offering accrual/balloon payment options and by lowering their interest rates somewhat. Nevertheless, even lower interest rates have not overcome hesitations to incur further debt obligations.

In the basic mezzanine loan transaction, the mezzanine lender is often subject to the liens of the senior mortgage. Berman (2007, p. 999) asserts that "[s]ince only the bottom-tiered entity (the mortgage borrower) actually owns real property, the mezzanine borrower's entire net worth, cash flow, and value of its collateral is derived solely from its (direct or indirect) equity in the entity that owns the underlying income-producing property." Accordingly, even if a mezzanine lender has a perfected security interest in the mezzanine borrowing entity, a mezzanine lender is still junior to any liens that the mortgage borrower has incurred. Thus, if the cash flows from a real estate project are insufficient to cover the borrowers' debt service, the mezzanine lender will absorb the financial loss before any other mortgage lenders.

Furthermore, Moody's rating agency views securitized mezzanine loans as a "weaker" form of security than the traditional second mortgage. Rubock (2007, p. 7) asserts that "Moody's views [mezzanine loans] as having a lesser negative effect on the senior debt, and therefore logically it must bear a greater portion of the expected losses when the total loan leverage defaults." Consequently, in a situation where the mezzanine loan is structured with multiple tranches, the mezzanine lender at the bottom tranche will be forced to either inject more capital into the distressed project or walk away from a failed investment.

Title and Collateral Risks

Mezzanine loans also carry special title risks because the mezzanine lender's collateral consists of equity, which is legally classified as personal property, rather than the typical real estate collateral with a mortgage loan. Because the lender's ability to foreclose upon personal property collateral depends on adherence to a different body of law, the mezzanine lender needs to take additional precautions to enforce its remedies and foreclose on its collateral.

As discussed previously, mezzanine lenders often require mezzanine borrowers to "opt-in" to Article 8 under the UCC in order ensure that the collateral becomes a "security" under Article 8 and an "investment property" under Article 9. If mezzanine lenders do not require this further protection, the security interest is merely considered a "general intangible" under UCC Article 9. As a result, the evaluation of mezzanine loan collateral differs somewhat from ordinary real estate collateral in a mortgage loan.

Limitations on Rights and Remedies under the Intercreditor Agreement

Berman (2007, p. 1018) contends that "mezzanine loans are also typically contractually subordinated to the related senior mortgage loans pursuant to the terms of an intercreditor agreement entered into between the senior mortgage lender and the mezzanine lender." The intercreditor agreement severely limits and restricts the ability of the mezzanine lender to foreclose or enforce some of the rights under the mezzanine loan. Steiner and Samton (2011) assert that mortgagees and mezzanine lenders often have disagreements if the "value of the [underlying] property drops to or below the amount of the outstanding first mortgage loan, as a result leaving the mezzanine lender with a de facto unsecured debt to a company that, in all likelihood, has no other assets." Accordingly, frequent conflicts and sometimes litigation occur if the underlying property becomes distressed and insufficient income is available to cover the annual debt service.

Limitations to the Right to Cure

One of the most important limitations provided in the intercreditor agreement is the provision that the mezzanine lender is required to remedy all defaults under the senior mortgage before initiating a foreclosure action against the mezzanine borrower. In *Bank of America, N.A. v. PSW NYC LLC* (commonly referred to as the "Stuyvesant Town" case), the New York Supreme Court prohibited the mezzanine lender from foreclosing on the borrower's pledged equity without first curing or repaying the outstanding indebtedness under the senior mortgage. The court's decision was based on its interpretation of the "Foreclosure of Separate Collateral" provision under the intercreditor agreement. The court held in the Stuyvesant Town case, similar to *Highland Park CDO I Granter Trust, Series A v. Wells Fargo Bank, N.A.*, that because the senior mortgage had been accelerated, "[the] Intercreditor Agreement bars [junior lender] from recovering on the mezzanine loan until the senior loan is repaid in full."

The Stuyvesant Town case clarifies that a mezzanine lender needs to understand and adhere to all of the express obligations under the intercreditor agreement before it takes any remedial action against the borrower. Furthermore, a mezzanine lender is likely to expend an enormous amount of resources to protect its interest in the event of a default under the senior mortgage. Fawer and Austin (2011, p. 2) claim that "[m]ezzanine lenders should therefore strive to avoid any limitation on the exercise of their right to foreclose, and to make sure that any such foreclosure should never be an event of default under the terms of the senior loan." Accordingly, mezzanine lenders should negotiate provisions that permit a foreclosure of the mezzanine collateral before being required to cure any defaults under the senior mortgage.

Transfer Restrictions

Intercreditor agreements also usually require that the mortgage borrower be controlled by (and that the mezzanine or mortgage collateral can only be transferred to) a "Qualified Transferee" (QT). A definition of a QT often includes the mezzanine lender itself and an institutional investor who meets minimum "net worth" or "liquid asset" requirements. Prendergast (2011, p. 20) contends that "[a] breach of this requirement by selling to a purchaser that does not meet the standard will probably result in a default under the senior mortgage debt thereby shifting the bargaining power to the senior lender." The QT restrictions limit the availability of potential purchasers of the mezzanine collateral at a foreclosure sale, thereby making the collateral less liquid and potentially less valuable.

Replacement Guaranty

In general, most senior mortgage holders will negotiate a provision in the intercreditor agreement requiring the mezzanine lender, in the event of a mezzanine loan foreclosure and subsequent purchase of the mezzanine collateral, to provide a replacement guarantor under the senior loan. The theory behind the replacement guaranty is based on the fact that mortgage borrowers are usually obligated under the senior loan to guaranty the loan, assuming any liabilities for acts that the borrower has committed, such as fraud and misrepresentation. If the mezzanine lender purchases the mezzanine collateral at a UCC sale, and steps in as the owner of the mortgage borrower, parties often disagree whether the mezzanine lender (new mortgage borrower) should be obligated to replace the guarantor under the senior loan. Steiner and Samton (2011) explain the issues that mortgagees face if mezzanine lenders do not replace the guaranty under the senior loan:

> The concern and uncertainty that many mortgage lenders are facing is the ability to enforce such guarantees if a mezzanine lender has foreclosed and, therefore, controls the mortgage borrower. The guarantor, who is no longer in control of the borrower, would argue that the clear intention of the non-recourse carve-out guaranty is to hold the individual (or equity owner) that makes decisions on behalf of the borrower liable if such borrower commits a proscribed act. If, however, the guarantor is no longer in control of the mortgage borrower (after a mezzanine foreclosure) when, for example, it files for protection under bankruptcy laws, will a court still hold such guarantor to the obligations of the guaranty?

Limitations to Rights and Remedies Upon a Mezzanine Borrower Default

The mezzanine lender often has difficulty foreclosing on the borrower's equity interests after an event of default. This difficulty arises because of the need to comply strictly with the UCC, including the provision stating that foreclosure sales must be commercially reasonable. Mezzanine lenders are also sometimes restricted by limitations set forth in the intercreditor agreement, as well as certain requirements set by the rating agencies. As a result, mezzanine lenders are often under tremendous time pressure to exercise their remedies before the senior mortgage holder completes a mortgage foreclosure. Berman (2007, p. 1023) asserts that "[o]nce the senior mortgage lender completes its foreclosure, the underlying mortgage borrower will no longer own the income-producing property, and the mezzanine borrower will own equity in an entity with no assets."

Moreover, because the mezzanine lender does not have a direct legal relationship to the land, mezzanine lenders generally do not have any direct rights against the mortgage borrower or its equity owners for monetary defaults. Even in situations where the mezzanine lender can foreclose on the pledged equity interests, it simply steps into the shoes of the equity owners of the underlying mortgage borrower. The mezzanine lender is, therefore, in no better position than the previous mortgage borrower—it is still subject to the existing senior mortgage, other outstanding liens, and real estate taxes. Unlike the senior mortgage, the mezzanine lender has no special right to foreclose on any of these other liens and interests attached to the underlying property. Frequently, the mezzanine lender's only true remedy is to refinance the property subject to any prepayment penalties pursuant to the senior mortgage or to buy out the senior lender at par value.

Another potential risk that mezzanine lenders face, in the event of a default under the mezzanine loan, is a "cash sweep" under the senior loan. Rubin (2009, p. 42) describes a *cash sweep* as a provision "that permits the mortgage lender to trap all cash flow from the property to pay its debt, property expenses and fund reserves, leaving little or no money to pay the [mezzanine] lender."

Commercially Reasonable

If a mezzanine lender seeks to foreclose on its equity collateral, it must comply with many of the provisions of UCC Article 9 and sell the collateral either at a private or public sale. Berman (2007, p. 1016) contends that mezzanine lenders cannot effectively dispose of the collateral at a private sale, "[s]ince there is no established market, no standardized price quotations, and mezzanine loan collateral is extremely complicated." Thus, mezzanine lenders cannot "buy" the collateral itself at a private sale because mezzanine loans are not the type of collateral customarily sold on a recognized market or subject to standardized price quotations.

As a result, mezzanine lenders will typically have to sell the pledged collateral at a public sale. However, even a public sale can result in formidable risks because no established market is available for this type of collateral. Accordingly, mezzanine lenders are often left with no choice other than to "buy" the collateral at the public foreclosure sale.

Under UCC § 9–610, the transferability of collateral at a public sale must be "commercially reasonable." Furthermore, some jurisdictions also require lenders to prove that the public disposition of the mezzanine collateral was "commercially reasonable" in order to claim a deficiency judgment. One risk is that some doubt still exists about the exact meaning of "commercially reasonable" in this context. UCC § 9–627 provides that "a disposition of collateral is 'commercially reasonable' if it is made: in the usual manner on any recognized market; at the price current in any recognized market at the time of the disposition; or otherwise in conformity with reasonable commercial practices among dealers in the type of property that was the subject of the disposition." The risk for mezzanine lenders is that, other than the two statutes cited above, the UCC provides little guidance on what constitutes a commercially reasonable sale.

If the foreclosure sale does not meet the requirements for "commercial reasonableness," then the borrower or guarantor may sue the mezzanine lender or be released from any recourse liability. Consequently, mezzanine lenders ought to ensure that they have complied with these provisions.

Bankruptcy and Workout Risks

In general, the mortgage lender will take action to forbid the mezzanine lender from becoming a secured creditor of the property owner (mortgage borrower). Berg and Gogliomella (2010) contend that so long as an outstanding senior mortgage loan exists, the mezzanine lender is prohibited from causing or influencing the senior borrower to file for bankruptcy or other insolvency proceedings. Rubin (2009) asserts that if the property owner files for bankruptcy, the mezzanine lender typically would not hold a claim to the property owner's assets and would not have voting rights regarding reorganization plans.

In effect, should a plan for reorganization require a transfer of the property from the property owner, the mezzanine lender could be left owning equity in a worthless entity. Berg and Goliomella (2010) conclude that if the mezzanine lender is treated as a creditor in the bankruptcy of the mortgage borrower, the mezzanine lender will be prohibited from taking any action in the bankruptcy proceeding without the senior lender's consent, and the senior lender will be authorized to exercise its remedial power against junior creditors. Thus, in order to protect its collateral interest in the borrowing entity, the mezzanine lender might need to invest additional capital into the mortgage borrower for a workout or, alternatively, negotiate a purchase of the mortgagee's interests.

PREFERRED EQUITY

Preferred equity is another type of nontraditional real estate financing used by property owners to obtain additional capital. Unlike mezzanine loans, where a clear creditor/debtor relationship exists, preferred equity transactions are not structured as debt. Rather, in a preferred equity transaction the investor/lender makes a capital contribution in a special-purpose entity (borrower). This entity normally owns the underlying income-producing real property and is also the mortgage borrower. Fisch et al. (2011) assert that due to restrictions set forth in standard senior mortgages, preferred equity transactions are most often made to borrowing entities that indirectly own the underlying property (instead of the mortgage borrower entity itself).

In exchange for its capital contribution, the investor becomes an equity owner in the mortgage borrower with special "preferred" rights. As Berman (2005) notes, these rights often include: (1) the right to receive a special (or preferred) rate of return on its capital investment and (2) the right to an accelerated repayment of its initial capital contribution. In effect, the preferred rate of return reflects the interest component of a conventional loan, and the accelerated repayment of the investor's capital is analytically similar to the repayment of outstanding principal in a loan.

As structured, preferred equity investors ("preferred members") are structurally subordinate to all of the borrower's creditors (secured and unsecured) but are senior to common equity owners ("common members"). Fisch et al. (2011, p. 1) claim that the biggest difference between the structure of mezzanine loans and preferred equity investments is that:

> [I]n general, investments intended to have a simple structure with current payments of interest and a fixed maturity date (with or without extension options) are usually structured as mezzanine loans, while investments with more complicated features, such as a cash distribution "waterfall" that allows the owner/developer to receive some cash flow distributions while the junior capital is still outstanding, or the capital provider sharing in the "upside" on top of its promised return, lend themselves more readily to a preferred equity structure.

Further, preferred members do not have any foreclosure rights, and typically the borrower or borrowing entity does not pledge its equity interests or other assets as collateral. Instead, preferred members have superior contractual rights (compared to the common equity investors) with respect to cash distributions or dividend payments. Preferred members also have specific contract remedies set forth in the organizational documents of the entity in the event of a financial delinquency or a "Change of Control Event," which is discussed in the next section.

Preferred equity investments are commonly made when senior mortgage lenders prohibit mortgage borrowers from incurring any further debt. Arnold (2011c) asserts that preferred equity investments are also used when "a property is generating insufficient cash flow to service a junior or mezzanine loan." Although investing in distressed property carries high risks, the structure of preferred equity transactions allows for capital to be injected into these properties without incurring additional debt obligations. Saft (2011b) contends that because preferred equity investors acquire direct equity ownership with the property, they can better protect their capital investment and perhaps obtain higher rates of return if a project is successful. The next section discusses the opportunities and risks of preferred equity investments in real estate.

Preferred Equity Opportunities

As discussed previously, a preferred equity investor usually makes a capital contribution in the underlying mortgage borrower or a newly formed borrowing entity that indirectly owns the underlying income-producing property. Saft (2011b, p. 1) states that preferred equity transactions have "typically [been] structured as joint venture transactions between the property owner and a capital provider, who enter into an agreement with each other to form . . . a limited liability company." In return for its investment, a preferred equity investor receives preferred equity interests with a preferred return, while the other equity investors receive common equity interests with no preferred return.

Preferred members also normally receive any cash distributions or dividend payments before any common equity members. Arnold (2011c) asserts that the right to receive a preferred distribution—at times as much as 18 percent—on the invested equity amount is a key aspect of preferred equity transactions. Although preferred members (as equity) take subordinate positions to all secured and unsecured creditors of the mortgage borrower, preferred members are able to collect high rates of returns, especially when the underlying property is profitable. Furthermore, if the property is underperforming, the preferred member might have the right to take over control of the mortgaged property, or the right to remove voting and control privileges from the common member.

Right to Receive Regular Dividend Payments

Arnold (2011c) states that real estate investors who are seeking higher rates of return and who are not overly concerned with exit strategies can structure their senior equity position as a "preferred equity member." Although preferred equity transactions can be structured in a variety of ways, a preferred member will usually receive, in exchange for its capital contribution, a preferred rate of return on its investment and an accelerated repayment of its capital. Accordingly, a preferred member normally receives cash payments before any common equity member (property owner). Thus, a preferred member generally receives the repayment of its initial investment before any other equity members and also receives a preferred rate of return. Moreover, if a real estate project is profitable, a preferred member may also receive a percentage of the excess cash flow, thereby sharing in any upside appreciation.

In general, the organizational documents provide the preferred rate of return, which is expressed as an annual rate and accrues from the time of the preferred member's initial capital contribution. A common method of cash flow distribution is the "waterfall" method. The waterfall method generally provides the common and preferred members with a distribution structure for any available cash flow after all debt obligations and operating expenses have been paid. According to Spyksma (2011), a typical preferred equity waterfall distributes available cash flow as follows:

- First, to the preferred member in satisfaction of the preferred return on the preferred member's equity investment.
- Second, to the preferred member in an amount sufficient to return the preferred member's initial equity investment (capital contribution).
- Third, to the common member in an amount sufficient to return the common member's capital contributions.
- Finally, the balance of any available cash will be distributed between the preferred member and the common member according to a predetermined percentage.

This relatively straightforward waterfall distribution illustrates that the preferred member receives both a preferred rate of return (the interest component) and a preferred return on its capital investment (the principal component), even before any excess cash flow is distributed to the common equity member. Accordingly, the preferred member has tremendous leverage because it will either receive a preferred rate of return when a project is successful or take over full control of the property if the common equity member fails to pay the preferred return or if the project is otherwise failing. In the final step of the above waterfall structure, the preferred member can negotiate the right to share profits or residual interests after the preferred equity "borrower" makes all of its mandatory payments to investors.

Redemption Rights

The organizational documents of these entities normally provide the preferred equity investor with the right of redemption of its entire capital contribution, preferred return, and additional cash flow by an agreed-upon date (similar to the maturity date of a loan). If the common members, who manage the day-to-day operations, fail to fully redeem the preferred member's interests by this predetermined date, the organizational documents declare that a "Change of Control Event" has occurred (similar to an event of default in a typical loan transaction). Although common members might have an opportunity to extend the set date for mandatory redemption, a "Change of Control Event" typically gives the preferred members full day-to-day control of the mortgage borrower and the underlying property. Additionally, Fileti (2011, p. 1297) contends that some preferred members "may [even] have certain 'springing' control rights that give it authority to sell or refinance the underlying real estate asset or exercise full rights of a managing partner if its position is not redeemed on the anticipated redemption date."

Moreover, if the common members want to redeem the preferred members' interests in advance of the redemption date, the preferred members usually receive some additional compensation (similar to a prepayment premium in a loan). The amount of this additional fee is often based on whether (and when) the preferred return or initial investment has been (or will be) paid back. Thus, by including a redemption provision in the organizational documents of the relevant entity, preferred members can obtain automatic, self-exercising remedies.

Right to Control and Manage

In general, preferred members do not have a day-to-day managerial role and only have the right to approve major decisions of the entity. For instance, Fileti (2011, p. 1297) asserts that preferred members retain the following approval rights:

> [The right] to consent to any additional capital contributions or admission of additional equity holders; to consent to any filing for bankruptcy or appointment of a receiver; and to consent to major decision such as additional debt; major contracts; affiliate transactions; mortgage loan prepayments or amendments; refinancing; property management arrangements; and modifications to organizational documents.

However, in the event of a failed payment of preferred return, or if the common equity member breaches any provisions of the operating agreement, the preferred member can acquire full or substantial control of the entity. Because a preferred member's financing is structured as an equity investment rather than secured debt, preferred members lack foreclosure rights, but can gain day-to-day control through enforcing its remedies after a "Change of Control Event." Accordingly, Saft (2011b, p. 1) reasons that "[i]f the management of the LLC [borrowing entity] fails to pay the preferred member the promised return, the old management (common members) is ousted and the common members lose their voting rights, dividends, and right to the distribution of any profit."

Furthermore, in some situations a preferred member can force a sale of the property or can purchase the common members' stake to become the sole owner of the underlying property, subject to any outstanding mortgages or other debt obligations. Thus, similar to mezzanine lenders, once the preferred member takes control of the mortgage borrower, the preferred member will have effective control to manage the day-to-day operations of the mortgage borrower and owner of the underlying income-producing property.

Transfer Rights and Bankruptcy

Senior mortgages often contain due on sale clauses triggered by change of control or transfers of majority interests in the mortgage borrower. However, Saft (2011b, p. 1) states that this is usually not an issue because "many mortgages permit borrowers to make limited transfers of ownership interests in the property owner without the existing lender's consent, usually so long as certain individuals or entities retain either a minimum level of ownership and/or managerial control over the asset." In order to comply with the senior mortgage and still enforce its preferred rights under the organizational documents, preferred members should allow the common members to retain a minimum level of equity ownership or obtain confirmation from the senior lender that the preferred member is a "Qualified Transferee" for the same reasons as discussed above. If these steps are taken, the preferred member will not have to obtain the approval from the senior lender in order to enforce its remedies after a "Change of Control Event" occurs. Further, if the borrowing entity files for bankruptcy, preferred members typically want to be characterized as preferred equity holders rather than as secured debt because they do not want to be subject to the automatic stay or other constraints imposed under bankruptcy law.

PREFERRED EQUITY RISKS

As discussed in the previous section, because of their unique structure preferred equity investments offer the preferred member many benefits. Nevertheless, this unique structure also presents certain risks. This section discusses in greater detail some of the common risks with preferred equity investments.

Limitations as a Preferred Equity Member

As discussed in the previous section, preferred members do not normally receive any special collateral. Rather, they have to rely on only the specific contractual provisions contained in the organizational documents between the common member(s) and preferred member(s). Although preferred members have contract rights and remedies, Fisch et al. (2011) warn that the preferred member's ability to enforce these rights and remedies can be quite complex, slow, and uncertain. For instance, Fileti (2011, p. 1297) states that "a [preferred member] may need to enforce its rights through contractual and partnership-type remedies that may involve squeeze-downs; buy-sell provisions; conversion from non-managing member (or limited partner) to managing member (or general partner) status; fiduciary principles; requirements for state court dissolution; and other complications." Even determining whether a contract provision or a "Change in Control Event" has been breached can result in time-consuming and costly litigation. Accordingly, because preferred equity investors have no rights to collateral or any security interest to foreclose, preferred equity investors usually have greater exposure to risk than mezzanine lenders.

Limitations on the Right to Receive Cash Distributions

In return for its investment, a preferred member obtains preferred shares of equity and a preferred rate of return. The preferred member acquires a senior position to the common member to any cash distributions (only after the debt service has been paid). Hudgins (2008) contends that preferred equity investments are particularly costly to the common members (mortgage borrower) due to internal interest rates as high as 20 percent. Although preferred members have a right to receive regular cash distributions in respect to its senior position to the common member, Fass et al. (2011) assert that preferred members are generally unsecured and rank below all of the borrower's creditors, including the mortgage lender and mezzanine lenders. Accordingly, given these structural drawbacks, a preferred equity member is likely to receive its preferred rate of return and repayment of its original investment only if the underlying real estate project meets its initial projections and generates sufficient cash flow after paying off outstanding debt obligations.

Limitations under the Senior Loan

As discussed in the previous section, many senior mortgages prohibit a change in the control of the mortgage borrower and/or a transfer of more than 50 percent of the equity therein. Spyksma (2011. p. 110) asserts that mortgage lenders, especially if the mortgage loan is destined for a securitization, want to enforce strictly these approval rights because the mortgage lender is rightly concerned with the financial wherewithal and the "operational capacity and experience" of the new equity holders. The mortgage lender usually includes restrictive covenants and default provisions limiting the ability for a preferred member to take over control of the mortgage borrower after a "Change of Control Event" occurs. If a preferred member obtains control of the mortgage borrower as a result of a "Change in Control Event," this is likely to trigger an accelerated default clause under the senior mortgage.

However, Saft (2011b. p. 1) proposes that "[w]hile a preferred equity structure may potentially run afoul of the ownership transfer restrictions often contained in senior mortgage documents, many mortgages permit borrowers to make limited transfers of ownership interests in the property owner without the existing lender's consent, usually so long as certain individuals or entities retain either a minimum level of ownership and/or managerial control over the asset." Furthermore, a preferred member can also obtain confirmation from the mortgage lender in advance that the preferred member is a permitted "Qualified Transferee."

Bankruptcy Risks

In a bankruptcy proceeding of the borrowing entity, a preferred member will generally be treated as an equity investment. Nevertheless, if a preferred member displays characteristics of a creditor (e.g., requiring the borrower to pledge collateral in return for the investment), a bankruptcy court may recharacterize the preferred equity transaction into a loan and the preferred member as an unsecured creditor. Additionally, if the mortgage borrower files for bankruptcy, the preferred member has the added risk of substantive consolidation. Substantive consolidation is an equitable doctrine that characterizes separate legal entities as a single-debtor entity. Therefore, a court would possibly not only treat preferred equity investment as debt, but a bankruptcy judge might also order substantive consolidation of the "separate" entities, and the automatic stay would restrict a preferred member's ability to enforce its right to control the borrowing entity. Berman (2005, p. 120) concludes that

> preferred equity investors are perhaps unrealistically confident that their transaction documents are actually enforceable, that a bankruptcy court would not order the substantive consolidation of borrower's assets with another bankrupt debtor or void certain transfers as a fraudulent preference, and that the lenders and investors can effectively and quickly enforce their rights and remedies under the transaction documents and obtain control of the underlying property.

Accordingly, although a preferred member may be able to enforce certain control rights, this member also faces the risks of recharacterization, substantive consolidation, and the automatic stay.

SUMMARY AND CONCLUSIONS

This chapter has discussed two types of nontraditional real estate financings: mezzanine loans and preferred equity investments. Although each of these financing vehicles is structured differently (one as debt and the other as equity), both allow property owners to obtain funds in excess of the typical senior mortgage loan and to limit the amount of its own equity at risk in a real estate project. Given the unique structure of these financings, real estate owners are able to substantially change the capital stack and its cost of funds. With these opportunities come risks for both the real estate owners and lenders/investors.

DISCUSSION QUESTIONS

1. What is the rationale for choosing mezzanine loans over traditional junior mortgages?
2. Discuss the legal structure of mezzanine loans. Why are mezzanine loans sometimes considered to combine aspects of debt and equity transactions?
3. Discuss why developers and senior lenders like mezzanine loans.
4. In the event that a mezzanine borrower defaults, identify the remedies available to a mezzanine lender. Discuss the risks that the mezzanine lender faces when enforcing its remedies.
5. Discuss the structure of preferred equity investments. How do they differ from mezzanine loans? How can a preferred equity member gain managerial control of the underlying property?

REFERENCES

Arnold, Alvin. 2011a. "Short-Term and Medium-Term Financing: In General—The Mezzanine Loan." *Real Estate Investor's Deskbook*, 3rd ed., §5:47. Valhalla, NY: Warren, Gorham & Lamont.

Arnold, Alvin. 2011b. "Short-Term and Medium-Term Financing: In General—The Mezzanine Loan—The Growth of Mezzanine Loans." *Real Estate Investor's Deskbook*. 3rd ed., §5:50. Valhalla, NY: Warren, Gorham & Lamont.

Arnold, Alvin. 2011c. "Short-Term and Medium-Term Financing: In General—Preferred Equity." *Real Estate Investor's Deskbook*. 3rd ed., § 5:49. Valhalla, NY: Warren, Gorham & Lamont.

Berg, Mitchell, and Salvatore Gogliomella. 2010. "Rights and Restrictions in Intercreditor Agreements; Real Estate." *New York Law Journal*, October 20. Available at http://realestateclips.blogspot.com/2010/10/rights-and-restrictions-in.html.

Berman, Andrew R. 2005. "Once a Mortgage, Always a Mortgage—The Use (and Misuse) of Mezzanine Loans and Preferred Equity Investments." *Stanford Journal of Law, Business, and Finance* 11:1, 76–125.

Berman, Andrew R. 2007. "Risks and Realities of Mezzanine Loans." *Missouri Law Review* 72:4, 993–1030.

Commercial Mortgage Alert. 2012. *Rockpoint Scrambling to Refinance SF Hotel*. February 10. Available at www.cmalert.com/headlines.php?hid=155890.

Dehncke-McGill, Melissa. 2012. *Private Equity: Who's Ahead. NYC Real Estate Private Equity Players Weigh in on Where They're Raising Capital and What Kinds of Investments They're Eyeing This Year.* March 1. Available at http://therealdeal.com/issues_articles/private-equity-whos-ahead.

Duell, Jennifer. 2012. "Mezzanine Lenders Look Forward to a Big Year." *National Real Estate Investor*. February 2. Available at http://nreionline.com/finance/mezzanine_lenders_big_year_02022012/.

Fass, Peter M., Michael E. Shaff, and Donald B. Zief. 2011. "Commercial Mortgage-Backed Securities and Commercial Debt Obligations." *Real Estate Investment Trusts Handbook*. §1:39.

Fawer and Austin. 2011. "Intercreditor Agreements 2.0: Lessons Learned in the 'Tranches.'" *New York Law Journal*, November 21. Available at www.dicksteinshapiro.com/files/Publication/8f66682f-c446-4936-abdd-00a9337fc76e/Presentation/PublicationAttachment/84baa7fb-ab1d-4f40-a320-b9a89c0d4ed0/Lessons_Learned_Tranches.pdf.

Fawer, Mark S., and Michael J. Waters. 2007. "Mezzanine Loans and the Intercreditor Agreement: Not Etched in Stone." *Real Estate Finance Journal*, Spring, 79–85. Available at www.dicksteinshapiro.com/files/Publication/427b6314-e547-40de-9e31-5e0e18a69c7a/Presentation/PublicationAttachment/f0db8de8-3e64-44dd-ab40-aa956023f0a9/Mezzanine%20Loans%20and%20the%20Intercreditor%20Agreement.pdf.

Fileti, Thomas R. 2011. "Subordinate and Mezzanine Real Estate Financing." *The American Law Institute* ST005 ALI-ABA 1485–1499.

Fileti, Thomas R. 2012. "The 'CMBS FORM' of Intercreditor Agreement—Time for a Fresh Look?" *Commercial Real Estate Financing 2012: Getting Back to Business* 2, 29–54.

Fisch, Peter, Harris B. Freidus, and Micah J. B. McOwen. 2011. "Preferred Equity and Mezzanine Loans as Subordinate Financing Tools." *New York Law Journal*, November 30. Available at www.paulweiss.com/media/109627/nylj_30nov11.pdf.

Fisch, Peter E., and Steven Simkin. 2008. "Foreclosing on a Mezzanine Loan under UCC Article 9." *New York Law Journal*, May 7. Available at http://ul.firstam.com/assets/DFBEBD5D-3183-4C27-B9D6-9D595A02FE61.pdf.

Hudgins, Matt. 2008. "Catch-22 in Mezzanine Lending." *National Real Estate Investor*. Available at http://nreionline.com/finance/investors/real_estate_catch_mezzanine_lending/.

Hughes, Heather. 2011. "Securitization and Suburbia." *Oregon Law Review* 90:2, 359–412.

Lee, Evelyn. 2011. "Teeing Up Debt." *CBRE*. Available at http://www.cbreglobalinvestors.com/aboutus/mediacenter/capitalmarketscommentary/Documents/mediacoverage/Teeing%20Up%20Debt.pdf.

Lefcoe, George. 2009. *Real Estate Transactions, Finance, and Development*, 6th ed. New York: LexisNexis.

Murray, John C., and Randall L. Scott. 2006. *Title Insurance for Mezzanine Financing Transactions*. Available at www.firstam.com/title/resources/reference-information/jack-murray-law-library/title-and-ucc-insurance-for-mezzanine-financing-transactions.html.

Prendergast, James D. 2011. "Real Estate Mezzanine Lending Collateral Foreclosure: Insurance Tailored to the Operation of the U.C.C. Is Not a Luxury—It's a Necessity." *Practical Real Estate Lawyer* 27:6, 11–31.

Rubin, Paul. 2009. "Strategic Thinking for the Mezzanine Lender." *American Bankruptcy Institute Journal*. 28:8, 42–43, 88.

Rubock, Daniel B. 2007. *Moody's Investors Service, US CMBS and CRE CDO: Moody's Approach to Rating Commercial Real Estate Mezzanine Loans.* March 29. Available at http://dirt.umkc.edu/attachments/MDYMezz%20Loans.pdf.

Saft, Stuart M. 2011a. "Lessons Learned from the Crash: Improving Mezzanine Financing." *New York Law Journal,* March 14. Available at http://174.143.32.93/~/media/Files/inthenews/2011/20110321_LessonsLearned.ashx.

Saft, Stuart M. 2011b. "Preferred Equity Investor." *Commercial Real Estate Workouts,* 3rd. ed., § 6:13. New York: McGraw-Hill.

Spyksma, Sarah V. J. 2011. "Joint Ventures as a Financing Vehicle." *Commercial Real Estate Financing 2012: Getting Back to Business.* 2, 105–120.

Steiner, Jeffrey B., and Zachary Samton. 2011. "Intercreditor Dis-Agreements." *New York Law Journal,* July 20. Available at www.newyorklawjournal.com/PubArticleNY.jsp?id=1202503351990&Intercreditor_DisAgreements.

ABOUT THE AUTHOR

Andrew R. Berman is Professor of Law and Director at the Center for Real Estate Studies at the New York Law School. Professor Berman teaches real estate transactions and finance, property, real estate transactional skills, and other advanced real estate courses. Before joining the faculty at New York Law School in 2002, he was a partner at Sidley Austin LLP's New York Real Estate Group. Professor Berman was in private practice nearly 15 years. He is an expert on various aspects of real estate law, including real estate finance, sales and purchase contracts, real estate development, and commercial leasing. Professor Berman is often interviewed by national press and called upon to be an expert witness and consultant on major litigation cases and transactions. He received an AB from Princeton University from the Woodrow Wilson School of Public and International Affairs and holds a JD, cum laude, from New York University School of Law.

ACKNOWLEDGMENTS

The author thanks his student research assistant, Jeffrey Kahn (NYLS, Class of 2013) for his invaluable assistance with the preparation and research of this chapter.

CHAPTER 10

Real Estate Appraisal and Valuation

JEFFREY D. FISHER
Professor Emeritus, Indiana University Kelley School of Business, and President, Homer Hoyt Institute

DEMETRIOS LOUZIOTIS, JR.
Senior Vice President, Global Real Estate Solutions Group, ARGUS Software, Inc.

INTRODUCTION

An accurate estimate of the value of real estate is important for various reasons. For example, investors may use the valuation estimate to determine if the purchase price is fair. Lenders, in turn, use the valuation estimate as a basis for underwriting a loan on the property being used as collateral. After the property is purchased, investors may want to track the performance of the property over time based in part on how its value changes. This process requires periodic appraisals. Some real estate funds are structured to allow investors to buy or sell shares in the fund based on the appraised value of the properties. These funds are usually appraised quarterly, although in recent years several funds have started to conduct daily valuations of the properties (Wincott, 2012). Developers estimate whether the value created by development exceeds the costs associated with the development. These are a few reasons that value is important for real estate income-producing and development projects.

The purpose of this chapter is to discuss why appraisals are used to estimate the value of commercial real estate and to illustrate how the value is estimated. The remainder of the chapter is organized as follows. The next section explains why appraisals rather than transaction prices are necessary. The types of value estimated by an appraisal are discussed. This section is followed by a discussion of the various approaches that appraisers use to estimate value, including the income approach, the cost approach, and the sales comparison approach. The last section before the conclusion discusses the risks and additional factors that must be considered when valuing development projects.

APPRAISALS

For publicly traded assets such as stocks and bonds, frequent transaction prices are available that reflect the value investors are currently placing on these assets. In contrast, commercial real estate, such as an apartment or office building, trades infrequently. For example, a particular building might sell once in a 10-year period. Thus, transaction activity for a particular property is unreliable as an indication of how its value changes over time. As estimates of value, appraisals are used for infrequently traded assets such as real estate properties.

Whenever an appraiser starts a new assignment, the first step is to define the problem. This process involves determining what question the appraiser is supposed to answer. This requires an understanding of the purpose of the report, the rights being valued (fee simple—no encumbrances, or leased fee—subject to in-place leases), and what definition of *value* is to be used. The focus of an appraisal is usually on the market value of the property. The *market value* can be thought of as the most probable sale price. It is what a typical investor is willing to pay for the property and the price at which a seller would sell. Other definitions of value differ from market value. For example, *investment value* is the value to a particular investor. This value could be higher or lower than the market value depending on the particular investor's motivations and how well the property fits into the investor's portfolio, the investor's risk tolerance, and the investor's tax circumstances. For example, an investor who is seeking to have a globally well-diversified portfolio of real estate that does not already have investments in New York and Shanghai may place a higher value on acquiring a property in either of those locations than investors who already have properties in these locations in their portfolios.

A potential seller and buyer care about the market value because it is useful to know when negotiating price. The market value may differ from the value that the potential buyer or seller originally placed on the property and from the ultimately agreed-upon price. A seller in distressed circumstances may be willing to accept less than market value due to liquidity needs, and a particular buyer (investor) may be willing to pay more than market value because the investment value to that buyer exceeds the value to a typical investor. A lender also usually cares about market value because if a borrower defaults on a mortgage loan, the market value less transaction costs is the maximum that the lender can expect to receive from the sale of the property.

Although market value is typically the basis for the appraisal, the appraiser must also distinguish if the market value is on a stabilized, as-is, or prospective basis. The market value on a *stabilized* basis means that the property is valued as if it were operating at or very near its full productive capabilities (e.g., at a normal level of occupancy for the market). The market value on an *as-is* basis starts with a stabilized value estimate to which adjustments are made to reflect the current productivity of the property, if necessary (e.g., if the property has a higher than normal vacancy rate because of poor management, then the value would be reduced compared to the stabilized value). The stabilized and as-is values could be the same, but when they are not a buyer or lender often wants to know both. A market value on a *prospective* basis is an indication of what the value will be in the future assuming some changes are made to the property (e.g., a major renovation).

This value relates to the discussion of development project appraisals later in this chapter.

INTRODUCTION TO VALUATION APPROACHES

Appraisers generally use three different approaches to estimate value: (1) the income approach, (2) the cost approach, and (3) the sales comparison approach. In brief, the income approach considers what price an investor would pay based on prospective cash flows of the property and an expected rate of return (discount rate) that is commensurate with the risk of the property. The value estimated with this approach is the present value of the expected future income from the property, including proceeds from resale at the end of a typical investment holding period.

The cost approach considers the cost to buying land and constructing a new building on the site (or comparable site) that has the same utility or functionality to the user as the property being appraised. Adjustments are made if the property is older or is not of a modern design, if constructing a new property is infeasible in the current market, or if the location of the property is not ideal for its current use. The concept is that an investor should not pay more for a property than the cost of buying vacant land and developing a comparable property.

The sales comparison approach considers what similar or comparable properties (*comparables*) transacted for in the current market. Adjustments are made to reflect differences in the comparables from the property being appraised (referred to as the *subject property*), such as size, age, location, and condition of the property, and to adjust for differences in market conditions at the times of sale. The concept is that an investor would not pay more than what others are paying for similar properties. More formally, the comparables approach and the cost approach are based on the theory of substitution, which suggests that value is based on the cost of purchasing or constructing a substitute property that provides the same benefits to the user.

The three approaches are unlikely to result in the same value because they rely on different assumptions and availability of data to estimate the value. Ideally however, the results from the three approaches should not vary widely. If the result from one approach varies greatly from the other two approaches, this may indicate that the approach is based on weaker or inappropriate data. The idea is to triangulate the market value by approaching the estimate three different ways. The appraiser may have more confidence in one or more of the approaches depending on the availability of data for each approach. The appraiser then tries to reconcile the differences in the estimates of value from each approach and develop a final estimate of value for the subject property. Hodges (1993) provides a discussion of the evolution of the three approaches to value.

THE INCOME APPROACH

Appraisers use the income approach because it best reflects the potential productivity of a property. The starting point is usually an estimate of the net operating income (NOI) for the property.

Net Operating Income

The NOI is a measure of the income from the property after deducting operating expenses for items such as property management, property taxes, insurance, maintenance, utilities, repairs, and insurance. The NOI is calculated before deducting any costs associated with financing and income taxes. Income taxes and financing costs are important to an investor's cash flows but are deducted from the NOI to calculate after-tax cash flows for the equity investor.

Capital expenditures (*capex*) are akin to a sinking fund for replacing longer-life items such as a roof or heating and air conditioning equipment that may also affect cash flow calculations. Sometimes this cost is accounted for by including a "reserve allowance" as one of the expenses. The reserve allowance spreads the cost of the capital expenditure over time. Other times, the expenditure may be deducted from the NOI in the year it is expected to occur.

Appraisers may also need to account for tenant improvement allowances and leasing commissions. Often a property owner will provide a contribution toward the finishing of a space (commonly referred to as *fit out*) for a new tenant that is moving into a property. This allowance is an up-front cost that must be reflected in the analysis. An owner will also typically have to pay a leasing commission to a broker who leased the vacant space.

In some situations, the lease on a property requires the tenants to be responsible for some or all of the operating expenses, so they would not be deducted when calculating the NOI. Alternatively, such operating expenses might be deducted when calculating the NOI, but any additional income received from the tenants due to the reimbursement of these expenses would also be included as income when calculating the NOI. Of course, when the tenant must pay the expenses the rent is expected to be lower. Considering specific lease terms is also necessary when estimating the NOI. A general calculation of the NOI follows:

Rental income at full occupancy
+ Other income (such as parking)
= Potential gross income (PGI)
− Vacancy and collection loss
= Effective gross income (EGI)
− Operating expenses (OE)
= Net operating income (NOI)

Application of the Income Approach

Two ways to apply the income approach to value a property are available. The approaches differ in how they incorporate expected growth in the NOI. The first is referred to as the *direct capitalization method,* and it is based on dividing the current or first-year NOI by a *capitalization rate*, or *cap rate*, that implicitly reflects expected future growth in the NOI. The NOI growth rate is implicit in the cap rate. The cap rate can be viewed as the reciprocal of a price-earnings (PE) ratio. It expresses the relationship between a single year's income and the asset value. Properties with higher growth expectations will tend to have lower cap rates just as stocks with higher growth expectations will have higher PE ratios. Investors will pay a higher price relative to current income the more that income is expected to grow in the future. Lennhoff (2011) provides further discussion of direct capitalization.

The second general way of applying the income approach is the *discounted cash flow (DCF) method*. With this methodology, the NOI is projected each year over an investment holding period, after which the property is assumed to be sold. Some may also use NOI after deducting for capex, the tenant improvement allowance, and leasing commissions. The growth in the NOI (or net cash flow (NCF)) is explicit in the projected future NOI (or NCF). Value is estimated by taking the present value of the projected NOI or NCF and the present value of the projected resale proceeds.

The DCF method can be applied in a number of different ways depending on the complexity of the income received from the property being valued. But no matter how the approach is applied, the concept is that the real estate value is based on discounting the cash flows, typically represented by the NOI. The discount rate should reflect the risk characteristics of the property and the expected holding period.

When the property has many different leases with different expiration dates and complex lease provisions, appraisers using the income approach often use spreadsheets or software such as ARGUS Valuation DCF or ARGUS Enterprise. The website ARGUSSoftware.com provides further information about ARGUS Valuation DCF and ARGUS Enterprise. At the other extreme, when simplifying assumptions can be made about the pattern of future income, simple formulas often can be used to estimate the value.

The Direct Capitalization Method

As noted previously, the direct capitalization method divides the current or first-year NOI by a rate known as the capitalization rate (cap rate). The cap and discount rates are closely related but are not the same. The *discount rate* is the return required from an investment, and it comprises the risk-free rate plus a risk premium specific to the investment. The cap rate is lower than the discount rate because it is calculated using the current or first-year NOI. Thus, the cap rate is similar to a current yield for the property, whereas the discount rate is applied to current and future NOI that may be expected to grow. In general, when income and value are growing at a constant compound growth rate the cap rate is as shown in Equation 10.1:

$$\text{Cap rate} = \text{Discount rate} - \text{Growth rate} \tag{10.1}$$

Defining the Cap Rate

The cap rate is an important measure for valuing income-producing real estate. The cap rate is defined as shown in Equation 10.2:

$$\text{Cap rate} = \text{NOI}/\text{Value} \tag{10.2}$$

where the NOI is usually based on what is expected during the current or first year of ownership of the property. Sometimes the term *going-in cap rate* is used to clarify that it is based on the first year of ownership when the investor is going into the deal. The *terminal cap rate* is based on the expected income for the year after the anticipated sale of the property.

The value used in Equation 10.2 is an estimate of what the property is worth at the time of purchase. Rearranging Equation 10.2 and solving for value results in Equation 10.3:

$$\text{Value} = \text{NOI}/\text{Cap rate} \tag{10.3}$$

Thus, knowing the appropriate cap rate permits estimating the value of the property by dividing its first-year NOI by the cap rate.

Equation 10.1 may be used to calculate a cap rate from a discount rate. Another approach is to determine the cap rate by observing the prices for which other similar or comparable properties are selling. Assuming that the sale price for a comparable property is a good indication of the value of the subject property, Equation 10.4 shows the formula for the cap rate:

$$\text{Cap rate} = \text{NOI}/\text{Sale price of comparable} \tag{10.4}$$

Relying on the price for just one sale to determine the cap rate would be inappropriate. Instead, a more appropriate procedure would be to observe several sales of similar properties before drawing conclusions about what cap rates investors are willing to accept for a property. As will be discussed later in this chapter, the cap rate is likely to differ for different properties based on, for example, the property's future income potential (i.e., how it is expected to change after the first year). This distinction is important, because the cap rate is only explicitly based on the first-year income. However, the cap rate that investors are willing to accept depends on how they expect the income to change in the future and the risk of that income. These expectations are implicit in the cap rate. Differences in the riskiness of properties can also cause cap rates to differ for riskier properties having higher cap rates and higher discount rates.

The cap rate is like a snapshot at a point in time of the relationship between the NOI and value. As noted previously, this relationship is somewhat analogous to the PE multiple for a stock except that it is the reciprocal. The reciprocal of the cap rate is price divided by the NOI. Just as stocks with greater earnings growth potential tend to have higher PE multiples, properties with greater income growth potential have higher ratios of price to the current NOI and thus lower cap rates. An important factor with PE multiples is to understand if it is based on trailing 12 months results or the projection for the next 12 months (i.e., a forward multiple). Equally important is understanding which NOI is being used when deriving cap rates from comparables.

Stabilized NOI

When the cap rate is applied to the forecasted first-year NOI for the property, the implicit assumption is that the first-year NOI is representative of what the typical first-year NOI would be for similar properties. This value may differ from what is actually expected for the first year if that income is not representative of what the property will earn in the future. Under these conditions, the appraiser uses a "stabilized NOI" for the purpose of property valuation. This distinction is important when using direct capitalization because the cap rate applied to that income has the expected future growth in income implicit in the cap rate, as previously discussed. If the first-year income is unusually high or low, the appraiser will make an additional adjustment to the value after estimating it using the stabilized NOI. For example, a new development project may take a year or two to lease up to stabilized NOI. Thus, it will have lower than typical occupancy for a year or two until leased up. The appraiser could first estimate the value of the property as if it were already stabilized and then deduct an allowance for the loss in value due to the lower income during the lease-up period. When using the DCF method (discussed in the next section), this approach is unnecessary, because the actual cash flows for each year, including the lease-up period, can be explicitly projected and discounted. Parli and Fisher (2010) provide further discussion of dealing with above- or below-market occupancy.

THE DCF Method

The direct capitalization method typically estimates value by capitalizing the first-year NOI at a cap rate derived from market evidence. In contrast, DCF analysis projects the future NOI or NCF for the property and estimates the value by discounting the future NOI or NCF and expected resale price.

The Relationship between the Discount Rate and the Cap Rate

As discussed previously, if the income and value for a property are expected to change over time at the same compound rate, such as 3 percent per year, the relationship between the cap rate and discount rate is shown in Equation 10.1. To see the intuition behind this, solve for the discount rate in Equation 10.5, which is the return that is required to invest in the property.

$$\text{Discount rate} = \text{Cap rate} + \text{Growth rate} \tag{10.5}$$

Recall that the cap rate is based on the first-year NOI. The growth rate captures how NOI is expected to change in the future along with the property value. Thus, the investor's return (discount rate) comes from the return on the first-year income (cap rate) plus the growth in income and value over time (growth rate). Although income and value may not always change at the same compounded rate each year, this formula provides insight into the relationship between the discount rate and the cap rate. Essentially, the difference between the discount and cap rates involves growth in income and value.

Intuitively, given that both methods start from the same NOI in the first year, investors would pay more for a growing income stream compared with one that was constant. So, the price is higher and the cap rate is lower when the NOI is growing. This relationship is what is meant by the growth being implicit in the cap rate. If the growth rate is constant, Equation 10.3 can be extended using Equation 10.1 to give Equation 10.6:

$$V = NOI/(r - g) \tag{10.6}$$

where r is the discount rate (required return) and g is the growth rate for income (assuming constant growth in income and that value grows at the same rate).

This relationship is analogous to the constant dividend growth model applied to stocks (i.e., $P_0 = D_1/(k - g)$, where P_0 is the current stock price, D_1 is next year's dividend, k is the required rate of return, and g is a firm's expected constant growth rate). If NOI is not expected to grow at a constant rate, then NOIs are projected into the future and each period's NOI is discounted to arrive at a property value. Rather than project NOIs into infinity, NOIs are typically projected for a specified holding period and a terminal value (sale price) at the end of the holding period is estimated.

For example, suppose the NOI is expected to be $80,000 the first year and to increase at a 2 percent rate annually for the foreseeable future. The property value is also expected to increase by 2 percent annually. Investors expect to receive a 10 percent internal rate of return (IRR) given the level of risk; therefore, the value is estimated using a 10 percent discount rate. The value of the property today (at the beginning of first year) is: $V = NOI/(r - g) = \$80{,}000/(0.10 - 0.02) = \$80{,}000/0.08 = \$1{,}000{,}000$.

The Terminal Capitalization Rate

When a DCF methodology is used to value a property, an important input is usually the estimated sales price of the property at the end of a typical holding period. This is often referred to as the *estimated terminal value.* Estimating the terminal value of a property can be challenging in practice, especially when one realizes that the purpose of the analysis is to estimate the value of the property today. But if the value of the property is unknown today, how can one know what it will be worth in the future when sold to another investor? Thus, some method is needed for estimating what the property will be worth when sold in the future.

In theory, this value is based on the present value of income received by the next investor. Usually the NOI is not estimated for another holding period beyond the initial one. Rather, the direct capitalization method is employed using the first-year NOI of ownership for the next investor and a cap rate. The cap rate used to estimate the resale price or terminal value is referred to as a *terminal cap rate.* It is a cap rate that is selected at the time of valuation to be applied to the NOI earned in the first year after the property is expected to be sold to a new buyer. In a sense, direct capitalization is used to estimate the future resale price.

The selection of a terminal cap rate is challenging. Recall that the cap rate equals the discount rate less the growth rate when income and value are growing constantly at the same rate. Whether constant growth is realistic or not, the cap rate will be higher (lower) if the discount rate is higher (lower). Similarly, the cap rate will be lower if the growth rate is expected to be higher, and vice versa. These relationships also apply to the terminal cap rate as well as the initially calculated cap rate.

The terminal cap rate could be the same, higher, or lower than the initially calculated cap rate depending on expected discount and growth rates at the time of sale. If interest rates are expected to be higher in the future and push up discount rates, then terminal cap rates might be higher. The growth rate is often assumed to be a little less because the property is older at the time of sale and may not be as competitive. This would result in a slightly higher terminal cap rate. Uncertainty about what the NOI will be in the future may also result in selecting a higher terminal cap rate; that is, the objective is to select a cap rate today to apply to NOI when the property is sold at some point in the future. More uncertainty is associated with estimating NOI in the future when the property is projected to be sold. Thus, all else being equal, a cap rate applied to income in the future will generally be higher than a cap rate applied to current income. Therefore, the terminal cap rate will tend to be higher than the going in cap rate that would be applied to current NOI. The point is that the terminal cap rate may differ from the cap rate that would be applicable to NOI at the time of the appraisal.

Advanced DCF: Lease-by-Lease Analysis

Using a DCF approach for real estate income-producing properties is intuitively appealing, especially when properties have many tenants and more complex leases. The general steps to a DCF analysis are as follows: (1) project income from existing leases; (2) make assumptions about lease renewals, operating expenses, capital expenditures, and absorption of any vacant space; (3) estimate resale value (reversion); and (4) select the discount rate to find the PV of cash flows.

Existing Leases

Projecting income from existing leases involves capturing the start and end date for each lease and the various determinants of rent under the lease, such as the base rent, projected increases in the base rent (steps), and adjustments that may occur because the lease is linked to an index, such as a CPI adjustment. The projected income from existing leases would include income from expense reimbursements on leases that provide for the tenant being billed for some portion of the operating expenses because it is a net lease or a gross lease but has a provision for pass through of expenses to the tenant if they exceed a certain amount.

Lease Renewals

An appraiser also needs to make assumptions about what will happen when a lease comes up for renewal, which is often referred to as *market leasing assumptions.* That is, does the appraiser think the lease will be renewed? One assumption involves estimating a probability that the lease will be renewed, which is referred to as the *renewal probability.* For example, for a particular tenant or group of tenants, the appraiser might assume a 60 percent chance that the lease will be renewed and a 40 percent chance it will not be renewed. This estimate obviously involves some judgment, but it will be based on historical experiences with different types of tenants as well as consideration of economic conditions likely to exist at the time of the lease renewal.

The assumption about lease renewal probabilities affects cash flows in several ways. First, the assumption about the rent to be received from an existing tenant that renews the lease may be lower than that expected from a new tenant found to lease the space if the existing tenant does not renew. This situation may occur because the owner may be willing to accept a lower rent from an existing tenant that is already in place and has been paying rent on time, and the space will not be vacant until a new tenant is found. Second, a new tenant is more likely to ask the owner to provide a tenant improvement (TI) allowance to help finish or refinish the tenant's space. Third, finding a new tenant is likely to involve paying leasing commissions to a broker, whereas the commissions might be avoided or be less if an existing tenant renews.

In conjunction with making assumptions about the lease renewal probability, the analyst would also indicate how many months are required to lease the space if the lease is not renewed. This estimate is usually conducted by specifying the number of months vacant if a lease is not renewed.

Operating Expenses

Operating expenses involve items such as property taxes, insurance, maintenance, management, marketing, and utilities that the owner must pay. Even if the tenant is responsible for paying some or all of the expenses, the owner often initially pays these expenses and then is reimbursed by the tenant. Thus, operating expenses would be additional *reimbursement income* to the owner from tenants who are ultimately responsible for paying such expenses.

Operating expenses are often categorized as fixed, variable, or a hybrid of the two. Variable expenses depend on the level of occupancy, whereas fixed expenses do not. Fixed expenses can still change over time. Most expenses, including fixed expenses, change over time due to inflation. But some expenses also depend on the occupancy of the property, such as the management fee, which is often a percent of income collected from tenants. Insurance and property taxes are more likely to be fixed and not vary with occupancy. Utilities may be a hybrid. Utility expenses are likely to increase with the number of tenants. Yet, some fixed amount of utility expense typically occurs even for a building that is almost empty. Common areas such as lobbies and hallways must still be heated/air conditioned and adequately lit. Thus, utilities might be considered to be partially fixed and partially variable.

Capital Expenditures

In addition to the operating expenses discussed in the previous section, expenditures may be incurred for items that are not ordinary annual expenses, such as a new heating and air conditioning system or a roof replacement. These items, as described earlier, are referred to as *capital expenditures* (or *capex*), and they also affect cash flows. Funds used to improve a tenant's space for a new lease are also considered capital expenditures, as are funds spent to renovate the building. These capital expenditures are deducted from the NOIs to calculate cash flows that would be discounted when doing DCF analysis. These expenditures differ each year and are sometimes "lumpy" by nature. Sometimes analysts estimate, on average, what the annual amount of capital expenditures will be and have an annual deduction for capital expenditures rather than attempt to project exactly when the expenditures might occur. The capex should still be a deduction from NOIs, although some analysts include it along with other operating expenses and call it a *replacement reserve.* Regardless of how the capex is determined, the present value of the cash flows should be essentially the same.

Absorption of Any Vacant Space

The property being valued may also have some space that is currently vacant and available for lease. Analysts must make an assumption as to when the space is likely to be leased, which could involve several leases starting at different points in time in the future. Until the space is leased, it will be reflected in the vacancy rate for the property, as will space vacant as a result of the lease renewal assumptions previously discussed.

Resale Value (Reversion)

When preparing a DCF analysis, the usual practice is to make an assumption as to how long the initial investor will hold the property. For example, an assumption might be that the property will be held for 10 years and then sold to another investor. An alternative holding-period assumption could be based on a projection of cash flows for the entire economic life of the property, although the land normally has value after the building is ready for demolition.

Projecting future cash flows becomes increasingly difficult the longer the projection period, so for practical purposes a holding period of about 10 years is typically used. This holding period allows capturing the details of existing leases and what will happen when most if not all of them renew if the lease term of the longest lease is 10 years or less. Having a holding period that goes beyond when existing leases expire can ease estimating the resale price at the end of the holding period because all leases will be at market rents and have normal rent growth thereafter. In contrast, if unexpired leases have unusually low (or high) contract rent, this relationship could bias the estimate of the resale price if not properly accounted for when estimating the resale price.

Analysts often estimate the resale price using the concept of a terminal cap rate, which was discussed previously. Although the intention is to capture the details of the leases for the next 10 years of the holding period, getting the resale price involves reverting to the direct capitalization approach. If the holding period is 10 years, the expected NOI in year 11 would be used to estimate the resale price because this is the first-year NOI for the next buyer.

Recall the previous discussion of the terminal cap rate and the relationship among the cap rate, discount rate, and expected future growth in NOI and value. The terminal cap rate will capture how income and value are projected to change for a new investor; that is, the resale price will be the present value of cash flows expected after the holding period. Despite selecting a holding period when the property will be sold, all future cash flows for the property are still implicitly considered. The intent is only to capture the details of the cash flows on an annual basis until the end of the holding period plus one additional year.

Discount Rate

Ultimately, the purpose of DCF analysis is to discount the projected future cash flows, including the resale price, to obtain a present value. This calculation requires selecting an appropriate discount rate to capture the riskiness of the cash flows. Determining what discount rate should be used is challenging because this rate is not directly observable; that is, an analyst does not know what the investor projected as cash flows in the future and what return was expected when the investor originally bought a property. However, an analyst could ask the buyer, which is one way to determine an appropriate discount rate; that is, an analyst could survey buyers of properties to find out what return they expected when they purchased their properties. Some companies and organizations publish the results of investor surveys, such as the PWC Investor Survey (www.pwc.com/us/en/asset-management/real-estate/publications/korpacz-real-estate-investor-survey.jhtml).

The discount rate should be higher than what the mortgage rate would be for a loan on the property—independent of whether the investor plans to finance the purchase with a loan. The rationale is that investing in the property is usually considered riskier than making a loan on the property. The lender gets repaid before the investor receives any cash flows, and thus the lender has less risk than the investor. Thus, the discount rate should have a risk premium beyond that reflected in the mortgage rate.

More than one discount rate may be applicable because some cash flows expected from a property are riskier than others. For example, an analyst might use a lower discount rate to find the present value of the income from existing leases but a higher discount rate for the income from lease renewals and resale. Even if an analyst uses a single discount rate, the rate can be thought of as an average of the different rates that might be applied to different components of the cash flow. So, the analyst should use a discount rate that reflects, on average, how risky the investment is compared to alternatives. The estimated cash flows should be based on what is likely and/or reasonable to expect based on the information available. The risk of the cash flows should only be accounted for by selecting the discount rate.

Although spreadsheets can be used for DCF analysis, they can become tedious and error-prone when many leases exist. Furthermore, lenders and investors often want to receive reports in a more standardized format, and they may even want to conduct some of their own sensitivity analysis of the projections to see how value is impacted. For these reasons, analysts often use software such as ARGUS Valuation DCF or ARGUS Enterprise for this type of analysis. ARGUS Valuation DCF (hereafter ARGUS), which is one of the tools from ARGUS Software, is one of the most commonly used programs for DCF analysis and is available in numerous languages. Many lenders and institutional investors require their appraisers to use ARGUS. Exhibit 10.1 shows the summary screen from ARGUS for a DCF analysis of an office building with five tenants. In this case, the proposed purchase price is $15 million, but this only results in an unleveraged IRR of 8.23 percent and a leveraged IRR of 4.45 percent, suggesting negative leverage at that purchase price. Exhibit 10.2 shows a summary of the cash flows that are being discounted. The exhibit indicates that the estimated value is only slightly over $12 million based on a 13.5 percent discount rate, so that is all that someone should pay for the property.

ARGUS also produces several graphs, as illustrated in Exhibit 10.3. These graphs are helpful in visualizing the NOI each year as well as cash flows and when leases are expiring. Exhibit 10.4 shows the details of the annual cash flows.

Advantages and Disadvantages of the Income Approach

The income approach can be applied in a number of ways, ranging from a relatively simple use of a cap rate with direct capitalization to the more advanced DCF analysis that involves projecting cash flows over a specified holding period and

Summary Cash Flow (Year 1)	$ Amount	$ /SqFt
Potential Gross Revenue	$2,113,491	$26.58
Effective Gross Revenue	2,113,491	26.58
Operating Expenses	(677,218)	(8.52)
Net Operating Income	1,436,273	18.07
Leasing & Capital Costs	(344,925)	(4.34)
Cash Flow Before Debt	1,091,348	13.73
Debt Service	(1,291,991)	(16.25)
Cash Flow After Debt	($200,643)	($2.52)

Property Resale	
Resale Method	Capitalize Net Operating Income
Cash Flow for Resale Amount	$1,502,335
Terminal Cap Rate	9.50%
Gross Proceeds from Resale	15,814,053
Resale Adjustments	(474,422)
Net Proceeds from Sale	15,339,631
Debt Retirement	(10,544,747)
Net Resale Proceeds After Debt	$4,794,884
Implied PV to Gross Resale Growth	0.05%

Cap Rate Matrix - Unleveraged			
Cap Rates	PV @13.00%	PV @13.50%	PV @14.00%
8.00%	$14,010,718	$13,743,696	$13,483,323
10.00%	12,033,355	11,809,506	11,591,178
12.00%	10,715,114	10,520,045	10,329,749

Cap Rate Matrix - Leveraged			
Cap Rates	PV @13.00%	PV @13.50%	PV @14.00%
8.00%	$4,039,354%	$3,947,843	$3,858,742
10.00%	2,061,991	2,013,653	1,966,597
12.00%	743,749	724,192	705,168

Property Information	
Property Name	Day 1 Review
Address	1000 Review Road
City	Houston
State	Texas
Zip	77056
Country	
Portfolio	ARGUS Training
Property Type	Office & Retail
Property Size	79,500 SqFt
Average Occupancy	98.43%
Analysis Start	January 2012
Reporting Start	January 2012
End Date	December 2016
General Inflation	2.50%
Expense Inflation	2.50%
CPI Inflation	2.50%
Market Rent Inflation	3.00%
General Vacancy Rate	0.00%
Credit & Collection Loss	0.00%

Top 5 Tenants	Term	Eff. Rent	Mkt. Rent
The Dot.Net	6/14	$22.73	$20.00
Europa Incorporated	1/17	$23.54	$24.00
Focus Web Group	8/15	$33.01	$29.00
Global Outlook	9/18	$18.05	$24.00
Loud Noises Co.	6/13	$29.64	$29.00

Cash Flow & Returns	
Initial Purchase Price	$15,000,000
Total Purchase Price	$15,000,000
Net Operating Income	$1,436,273
Derived Cap Rate	9.58%
Cash Flow Before Debt Service	$1,091,348
Cash to Purchase Price	7.28%
Debt Funding	$11,250,000
Loan to Purchase Price	75.00%
Initial Equity Contribution	$3,750,000
Cash Flow Distribution	($200,643)
Cash to Initial Equity	(5.35%)
Unleveraged IRR	8.23%
Leveraged IRR	4.45%

Unleveraged Present Value Analysis

Exhibit 10.1 ARGUS Summary Output

This exhibit shows the main output screen from ARGUS Valuation DCF (included here with permission of ARGUS Software, Inc). It includes a summary of the key inputs and outputs for a typical discounted cash flow (DCF) analysis. The IRR is shown on both an unleveraged (as if no debt) and leveraged basis, assuming the property is acquired at the purchase price. In this case, the proposed purchase price is $15 million, but this only results in an unleveraged IRR of 8.23 percent and a leveraged IRR of 4.45 percent, suggesting negative leverage at that purchase price. As Exhibit 10.2 shows, the estimated value is only slightly over $12 million based on a 13.5 percent discount rate, so that is all that should be paid for the property.

Unleveraged Present Value Analysis			
Analysis Period	For the Year End	Annual Cash Flow	PV of CF @ 13.50%
Year 1	12/2012	1,091,348	961,540
Year 2	12/2013	1,309,579	1,016,576
Year 3	12/2014	938,431	641,823
Year 4	12/2015	1,140,479	687,232
Year 5	12/2016	1,142,002	765,573
Total Cash Flow		5,921,839	4,072,744
Resale @ 9.50%		15,339,631	8,143,959
Total Present Value			$12,216,703
Per SqFt			153.67
Percentage Value Distribution			
Assured Invome			24.70%
Prospective Income			8.64%
Prospective Property Resale			66.66%
Total			100.00%

Exhibit 10.2 ARGUS Cash Flow Summary

This exhibit shows the resulting cash flows for each of the five years the property is held and the cash flows from sale at the end of the five-year holding period. It also shows the present value of the cash flows discounted at 13.5 percent, which is the estimated value using the DCF methodology. This value is parsed into components to indicate how much of the present value came from different types of cash flow (assured income from existing leases, prospective income from new leases, and resale of the property). This allocation of value is often used as a risk measure. Assured income is less risky than prospective income from new leases, and cash flow from resale is more risky because it depends on income the buyer expects in the future when the property is to be sold.

capturing the details of the leases each year of the holding period. The advantage of the more complex DCF approach is that it captures the cash flows investors view as important and explicitly addresses the various components of the cash flow and the inherent growth. This approach does not depend on current transactions from comparable sales as long as the analyst can select an appropriate discount rate. The disadvantage is the amount of detailed information required and the need to forecast what will happen in the future even if just forecasting a growth rate for the NOI and not conducting a detailed lease-by-lease analysis. Selecting an appropriate discount rate and terminal cap rate are both critical. Small variations in assumptions can have a substantial impact on valuation.

Because capturing all the details of existing leases can be tedious, appraisers often use specialized software such as ARGUS or ARGUS Enterprise to perform DCF analysis. These programs allow for modeling of complex lease structures and provide a standardized output for lenders and investors.

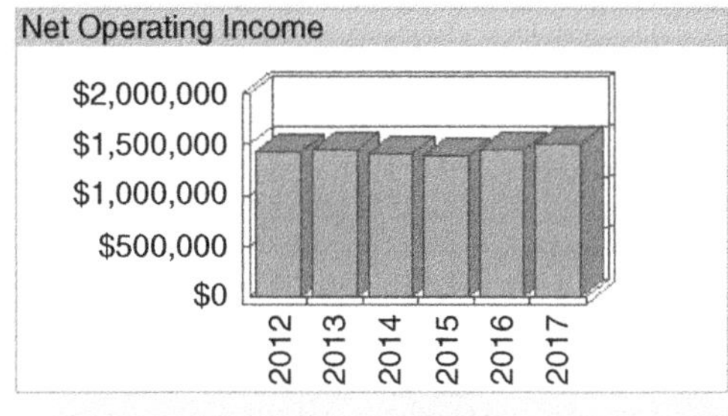

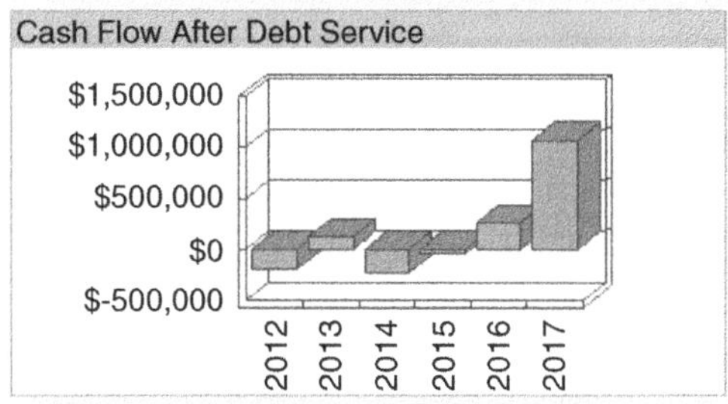

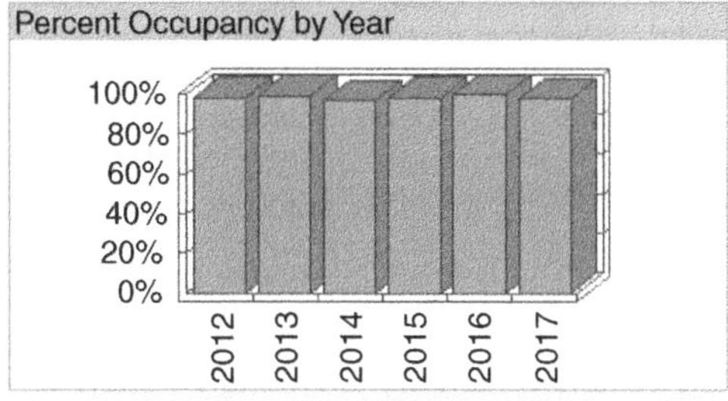

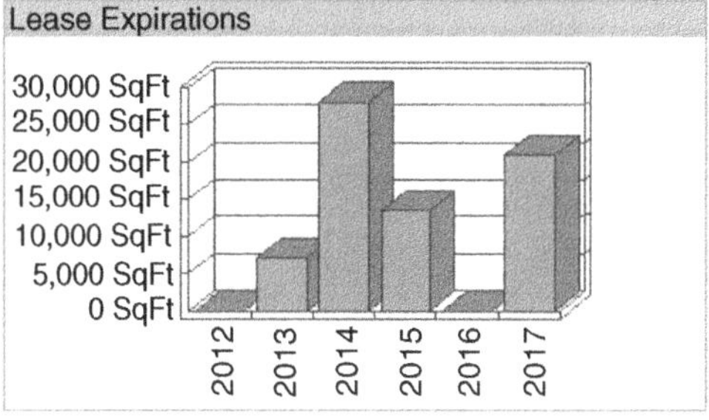

Exhibit 10.3 Selected ARGUS Graphs

This exhibit shows an example of the graphs produced by the ARGUS Valuation DCF software. The first graph is the net operating income (NOI); the second graph is the cash flow (NOI less debt service); and the third graph shows when existing leases expire. In general, all the leases should not expire at the same time.

Common Errors in DCF Analysis

DCF analysis requires many assumptions, and analysts may knowingly make assumptions that are inconsistent with reality. The following are some of the more common erroneous assumptions:

Schedule of Prospective Cash Flow In Inflated Dollars for the Fiscal Year Beginning 1/1/2012						
For the Years Ending	Year 1 Dec-2012	Year 2 Dec-2013	Year 3 Dec-2014	Year 4 Dec-2015	Year 5 Dec-2016	Year 6 Dec-2017
Potential Gross Revenue						
Base Rental Revenue	$1,980,434	$2,021,930	$2,031,152	$2,038,827	$2,064,328	$2,190,271
Absorption & Turnover Vacancy		(17,424)	(51,896)	(37,289)		(51,587)
Scheduled Base Rental Revenue	1,980,434	2,004,506	1,979,256	2,001,538	2,064,328	2,138,684
Expense Reimbursement Revenue	80,857	90,563	81,751	70,873	84,725	78,293
Parking & Other Income	52,200	53,505	54,976	56,626	58,324	60,074
Total Potential Gross Revenue	2,113,491	2,148,574	2,115,983	2,129,037	2,207,377	2,277,051
Effective Gross Revenue	2,113,491	2,148,574	2,115,983	2,129,037	2,207,377	2,277,051
Operting Expenses						
Repair & Maintenance	258,478	264,940	272,226	280,393	288,804	297,468
Real Estate Tax	115,000	117,875	121,117	124,750	128,493	132,347
Utilities	95,486	97,873	100,565	103,582	106,689	109,890
Property Insurance	65,849	67,495	69,351	71,432	73,575	75,782
General & Administrative	55,000	56,375	57,925	59,663	61,453	63,297
Advertising & Promotion	24,000	24,600	25,277	26,035	26,816	27,620
Management Fee	63,405	64,457	63,479	63,871	66,221	68,312
Total Operting Expenses	677,218	693,615	709,940	729,726	752,051	774,716
Net Operting Income	1,436,273	1,454,959	1,406,043	1,399,311	1,455,326	1,502,335
Debt Service						
Interest Payments	1,063,799	1,052,316	1,039,695	1,025,820	1,010,569	
Principal Payments	115,692	127,174	139,796	153,670	168,921	
Origination Points & Fees	112,500					
Total Debt Service	1,291,991	1,179,490	1,179,491	1,179,490	1,179,490	
Leasing & Capital Costs						
Tenant Improvements	225,000	51,660	212,323	105,441		174,008
Leasing Commissions	108,000	81,497	242,730	140,455		241,289
Structural Reserves	11,925	12,223	12,559	12,936	13,324	13,724
Total Leasing & Capital Costs	344,925	145,380	467,612	258,832	13,324	429,021
Cash Flow After Debt Service But Before Taxes	($200,643)	$130,089	($241,060)	($39,011)	$262,512	$1,073,314

Exhibit 10.4 ARGUS Projected Cash Flows

This exhibit shows more detail of the calculation of cash flows in a typical DCF analysis, including the rental income, expenses, and debt service. The CPI adjustment is from a lease term that allows the rent to increase with any increase in the CPI. Expense reimbursements come from another lease clause that allows increases in operating expenses to be charged to the tenant.

A discount rate that does not adequately reflect the risk.
An income growth rate that is substantially greater than an expense growth rate.
A terminal cap rate that differs markedly from the implied going-in cap rate.
A terminal cap rate that is applied to income that is atypical.
Market rents that always increase even though real estate tends to be cyclical.

THE COST APPROACH

The cost approach involves estimating the value of the building(s) based on an adjusted replacement cost. The estimated value of the land (usually from a sales comparison approach) is added to the estimated value of the building to arrive at the estimated value of the property. To determine the value of the building, the replacement cost is first estimated using current construction costs and standards.

Sometimes a distinction is made between replacement cost and reproduction cost. *Replacement cost* refers to creating a building that provides the same utility to users but is constructed with modern building materials. In contrast, *reproduction cost* refers to the cost of creating an exact replica of the building using the original building materials. Reproduction cost may be higher than replacement cost because constructing the building using the original materials is uneconomical. Thus, replacement cost is more relevant as a starting point to estimate value using the cost approach. The replacement cost is adjusted for different types of depreciation (loss in value) to arrive at a *depreciated replacement cost*. The depreciation estimated for the cost approach may have little relationship to the depreciation that would be used on financial statements using a historical cost approach to accounting.

The first type of depreciation is for *physical deterioration*, which is generally related to the age of the property as components of the property wear out over time. The two types of physical deterioration are curable and incurable. *Curable* means that fixing the problem will add value that is at least as great as the cost of the cure. For example, replacing a roof might increase the value of the property by at least as much as its cost and therefore is curable deterioration. Fixing a structural problem with the foundation of the building may cost more to cure than the amount it would increase the value of the property if cured and would be considered incurable deterioration.

The replacement cost estimate for the property assumes that the building is new and has no obsolescence; that is, the property value assumes nothing needs to be cured. Thus, the cost of fixing any curable items would have to be deducted from the replacement cost. A prospective purchaser would not pay as much for a property that had items that needed to be fixed and would likely deduct the cost of fixing them from the purchase price.

After deducting the cost of fixing curable items from the replacement cost of the property, a deduction still has to be made for incurable depreciation. A buyer would pay less for a building that is older and exhibits wear and tear. Because incurable depreciation by definition would be infeasible to fix because it does not affect value as much as the cost to fix, the cost of fixing it is deducted from the replacement cost. Appraisers try to estimate how the age of a property is likely to affect its value. A simple way that analysts often use to estimate this depreciation is based on the effective age of the property relative to its economic life. The effective age can differ from the actual age if it has more or less than the normal amount of wear and tear. For example, if the property has an effective age of 10 years and its economic life is usually 50 years, then the physical depreciation is assumed to be 10/50, or 20 percent. This ratio is applied to the value calculated above after subtracting the curable depreciation from the replacement cost so as to not double count; that is, the analyst has already taken into account the loss in value due to curable depreciation.

The second type of depreciation is referred to as *functional obsolescence.* This is a loss in value due to a design that is not what would be found with a new building constructed with an appropriate design for the intended use of the property. Functional obsolescence could result from changes in design standards since the building was constructed or because the building had a poor design to start, even if the building was relatively new. Functional obsolescence usually results in the building generating less NOI than if it did not have functional obsolescence because the building may be less efficient and may have higher operating expenses or may not command as much rent as a building with the proper design.

Appraisers often estimate the amount of functional obsolescence by the present value of the income loss due to the obsolescence. For example, suppose an office has a poorly designed elevator system that results in unusually long waiting times for tenants and visitors to use them. This affects the types of tenants who are willing to rent space in the building and the rent is less than if the elevators had greater capacity. The appraiser determines that this likely reduces the NOI by about $25,000 per year. An 8 percent cap rate is considered appropriate to estimate the value of the property. This cap rate can be applied to the $25,000 loss in the NOI due to the poor elevator design to arrive at a $312,500 loss in value due to functional obsolescence. This amount is deducted from the replacement cost.

Finally, depreciation may be external to the property. *External obsolescence* is due to either the location of the property or economic conditions. *Locational obsolescence* results when the location is not optimal for the property. Locational obsolescence usually occurs because something happens after the building was constructed that changes the desirability of the location for the existing use; the existing use may no longer be the highest and best use of the site.

For example, say that an apartment building is on a site where the highest and best use was to construct a luxury apartment when it was first developed. However, after the apartment was constructed a landfill was developed on a nearby site that was allowed by the zoning, making the location for the apartments much less desirable. The result is that less rent can be collected than necessary to support the original investment in the apartments, resulting in locational obsolescence.

Economic obsolescence results when new construction is infeasible under current economic conditions. This is usually because rent levels are insufficiently high to generate a value for a newly constructed property that is at least equal to the development costs, including a profit to the developer. Thus, the replacement cost of the new property exceeds what it would really be worth if it were developed. In this situation, even a new building would have a loss in value. This type of obsolescence is often commonly found in down markets and most easily identified when comparing the result of sales transactions on a per unit basis to the replacement cost per unit of a similar property. Typically, the sale price per unit will be less than the replacement cost per unit.

THE SALES COMPARISON APPROACH

The sales comparison approach implicitly assumes that the value of a property depends on the selling prices for comparable properties in the current market. Ideally, the comparables would be exactly the same as the subject property in terms of size, age, location, quality of construction, amenities, view, and so on, and sold on the same date as the date of the appraised value. Obviously, this situation is impossible, so adjustments have to be made to each of the comparables for differences from the "subject" property due to these factors. The idea is to determine what the comparables would have sold for if they were like the subject property.

Exhibit 10.5 shows the sales comparison approach applied to a subject property. Five comparable properties have sold within the last year. They are similar to the subject property but all have some difference(s) that need to be taken into account. The idea is to determine how much each of the comparables would have sold for if they were exactly the same as the subject property. Calculating the price per square foot (or square meter) is often a good way to account for differences in size, although other measures of size may be appropriate in some cases, such as cubic feet (cubic meters) for a warehouse, number of units in an apartment building, or number of rooms for a hotel.

Next, the price per square foot is adjusted for each of the comparables. For example, comparable 1 is in good condition. The subject property is only in average condition. Thus, the price per square foot of the comparable is lowered to determine what it would have sold for if it were only in average condition like the subject property. Each comparable is adjusted to what it would sell for if its location, condition, age and time of sale were the same as the subject property. Notice that after these adjustments the range in price per square foot is tighter across the five comparables.

In this example, the price per square foot is averaged for each of the comparables. In many cases, appraisers may give more weight to comparables that they consider more similar to the subject property or when they are more confident in the adjustments. This price per square foot is multiplied by the square feet of the subject property to arrive at an estimate of value using the sales comparison approach.

Some appraisers have taken a different approach over the past 10 to 20 years to the sales comparison approach in recognition of the fact that investors buy investment properties because of the properties' ability to generate cash flow. Some appraisers forgo the adjustment process outlined above and use regression analysis instead. A common way of performing this analysis is to regress the price per square foot against NOI per square foot for each of the comps. The theory behind this process is that making adjustments for various physical aspects of a property, particularly large, institutional quality assets, can be difficult. A property may have too many characteristics that require adjustments, and credibly quantifying all of those adjustments could be difficult.

Exhibit 10.5 The Sales Comparison Approach

		Comparables				
Variable	**Subject Property**	**1**	**2**	**3**	**4**	**5**
Size (square feet)	30,000	50,000	40,000	20,000	32,000	25,000
Age (years)	10	1	5	10	15	20
Condition	Average	Good	Good	Good	Average	Poor
Location	Prime	Prime	Secondary	Secondary	Secondary	Prime
Date of Sale (months ago)		3	9	6	7	12
Sale Price		$11,000,000	$6,000,000	$2,600,000	$3,500,000	$2,600,000
Sale Price per Square Foot		$220	$150	$130	$109	$104
Adjustments						
Age (years)		−22.5%	−12.5%	0.0%	12.5%	25.0%
Condition		−10.0%	−10.0%	−10.0%	0.0%	10.0%
Location		0.0%	20.0%	20.0%	20.0%	0.0%
Date of Sale (months ago)		1.5%	4.5%	3.0%	3.5%	6.0%
Adjusted Price per Square Foot		$151.80	$153.00	$146.90	$148.24	$146.64
Average Price per Square Foot	$149.30					
Appraised Value	**$4,479,000**					

The following indicates how the adjustments were made to the comparables to reflect the characteristics of the subject property. The adjustments to comparable 1 are discussed to help clarify the process.

Depreciation is 2.5 percent per year. Because the subject property is 9 years older, a depreciation adjustment of −22.5 percent (= 9 × 2.5 percent) reduces the value of comparable 1.Condition adjustment after average depreciation is taken into account: Good—none; Average—10 percent; Poor—20 percent. Because comparable 1 is in good condition and the subject property is only in average condition, a condition adjustment of −10 percent reduces the value of comparable 1.

Location adjustment: Prime—none; secondary—20 percent. Comparable 1 and the subject property are both in prime locations, so no location adjustment is made.

The market has been rising by 0.5 percent per month. Thus, an adjustment of 1.5 percent is made to the sale price of comparable 1 because the sale occurred 3 months ago.

This exhibit shows an example of the sales comparison approach to estimate value. It shows how the prices from the comparable sales are adjusted to arrive at an estimate of the value of the subject property. Each of the comparable sales (comps) is adjusted to indicate what it would sell for if it were the same as the subject property. This results in an adjusted price per square foot for each comp. These may be averaged or some comps may be considered more reliable and given more weight to arrive at an adjusted price per square foot that is used to estimate the value of the subject property.

The idea behind regressing, for example, price per square foot against NOI per square foot is that the revenue-producing capability of a property will reflect its physical attributes. For example, a building in an inferior location will likely have a lower rent and/or a higher vacancy. The relationship between price per square foot and NOI from the regression is applied to the subject property to estimate its value based on its NOI.

Advantages and Disadvantages of Cost and Sales Comparison Approaches

The cost approach to valuation is sometimes said to set an upper limit on the value. An assumption is that an investor would never pay more than the cost to buy land and develop a comparable building. This assumption may be an overstatement, because it can take time and effort to develop another building and find tenants. Furthermore, the demand for another building in the market of the same type may not exist. That said, one would question a value that is much higher than implied by the cost approach. The main disadvantage of the cost approach is the difficulty in estimating the depreciation for a property that is older and/or has much obsolescence. So the cost approach will be most reliable on newer properties that have a relatively modern design in a stable market.

The sales comparison approach relies on a reasonable number of comparable sales to be able to gauge what investors expect to pay for the subject property. When the market is active, the sales comparison approach can be reliable. But when the market is weak, fewer transactions increase the difficulty of finding comparable properties in a similar location to the subject property. Even in an active market, limited comparable sales for some properties may exist, such as regional malls or special-purpose properties.

Finally, the sales comparison approach assumes the investors who are buying properties are behaving rationally; that is, it assumes that the prices investors pay in the current market are representative of market values. But investors are not always rational, and "bubbles" often occur in real estate markets where prices increase at a faster pace than supported by the underlying economic fundamentals. Such market conditions are often hard to know until it is too late and prices have dropped substantially, often overshooting what might be a rational price in the opposite direction.

RECONCILIATION

So far, the chapter has discussed three different approaches to valuation: the income, cost, and sales comparison approaches. Obtaining the same answer from all three approaches would be highly unusual because each method relies on different sources of data and different assumptions. Furthermore, imperfections in the data and inefficiencies in the market are also present. Thus, the appraiser needs to reconcile the differences and reach a final value conclusion.

Some approaches may be more applicable than others depending on the property types and market conditions. The purpose of *reconciliation* is to decide in which approach or approaches the appraiser has the most confidence and to develop a final estimate of value. In an active market with many transactions, the appraiser may have more confidence in the sales comparison approach. This may be the case for apartment buildings in many markets. When fewer transactions exist as might be the case during weak markets or for property types that do not transact as frequently, the appraiser may have more confidence in the income approach. For example, a small town may have only one large regional mall, so no comparable sales of regional malls are available for the appraiser to use. However, the appraiser may have all the details of the existing leases and be fairly confident

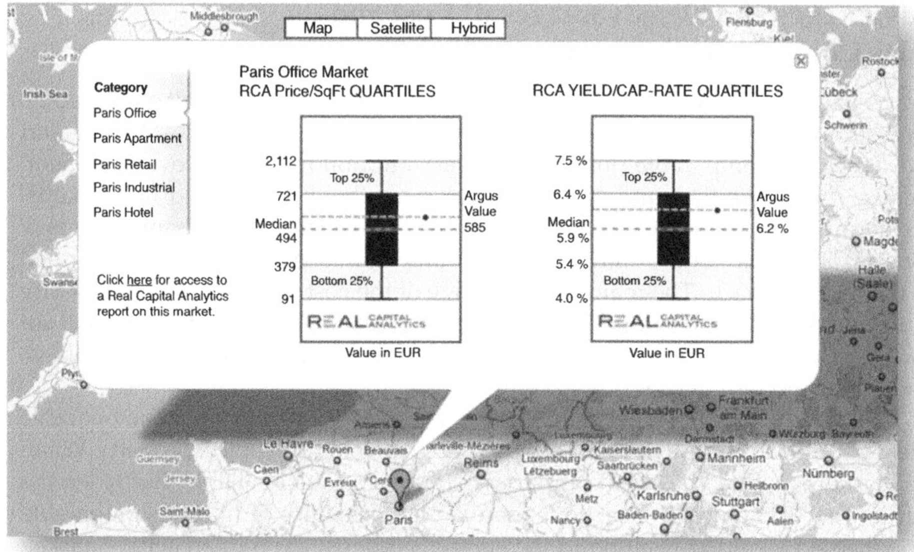

Exhibit 10.6 Benchmarks Using RCA Data

This exhibit illustrates how benchmarks on cap rates and price per square foot are incorporated into ARGUS Valuation DCF based on data from properties in the area near the subject property. Based on the property address, the database is searched for nearby comparable sales, and a quartile distribution of cap rates and price per square foot is generated within the ARGUS software.

in what investors want as a rate of return for regional malls around the country because they have similar kinds of tenants.

In recent years the availability of data to verify assumptions and conclusions for an appraisal has increased significantly. For example, Real Capital Analytics (www.RCAnalytics.com) tracks all transactions of commercial real estate exceeding $2.5 million in the United States and reports cap rates, price per square foot, and other information about each transaction. This provides benchmarks that can be used to verify that the results for a particular appraisal are in line with transactions of the same property type in the same market. These benchmarks can be seamlessly incorporated into programs such as ARGUS Valuation DCF for side-by-side comparisons with the results for the subject property being appraised as long as the user has an Internet connection. The property address is automatically geocoded, and the RCA database is queried to obtain benchmarks in the same geographic area, such as a quartile distribution of cap rates and price per square foot. This is illustrated in Exhibit 10.6 for a property being appraised in Paris, France. RCA tracks transactions in 88 different countries.

VALUATION OF CONSTRUCTION PROJECTS

Thus far, the focus of this chapter has been on analyzing a property that is already developed as opposed to a project that will be developed. Existing projects usually require only a single estimate of value at the time of the appraisal.

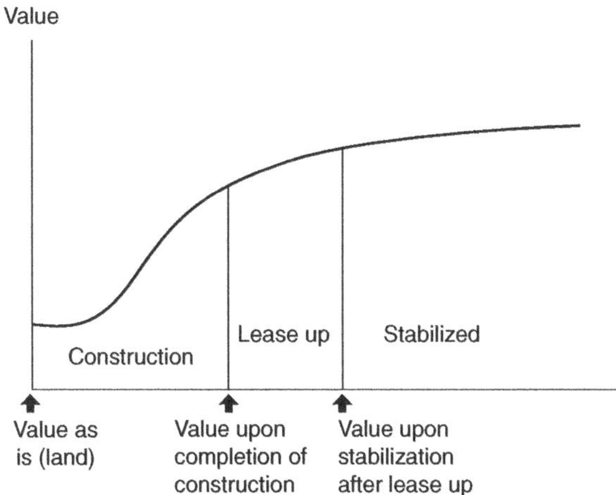

Exhibit 10.7 Prospective Values
This exhibit illustrates how value increases during the development stage of a project and the three points at which value is typically estimated. Initially, land value is all that exists. As development progresses, the value should increase until the project is complete. It then increases due to leasing up the space.

Proposed construction projects require estimates of three different values, as outlined below:

- Value "As Is"—An estimate of the as-is value is based only on the land if development has not started. If construction has already begun, the value includes the contributing value of any improvements.
- Prospective Value on Completion but before Lease Up—This value is based on what the property will be worth after the construction is complete but before it has been leased up to a stabilized level of occupancy. This is an estimate of value at a future date when construction is expected to be complete.
- Prospective Value on Reaching Stabilized Occupancy—The value upon reaching stabilized occupancy is the expected or prospective value of the property at the time when the building is forecast to be occupied at a stabilized level of occupancy. *Stabilized occupancy* is what is normal in the market under the current market conditions. This measure is seldom 100 percent accurate because of the difficulty in accurately predicting construction completion and the time to lease a property to a stabilized level. The effective date of this value estimate falls at the end of the typical construction period plus the estimated time to rent the property. Exhibit 10.7 illustrates the timing for when each of these values would be estimated.

Value should increase as funds are spent on construction that will lead to a building that tenants can lease. As the building is leased up, the value should continue to increase as tenants are in place paying rent and the risk is decreasing. Exhibit 10.8 illustrates this point.

Developers should earn a profit for their entrepreneurial efforts in developing the project. This value is captured by the property being worth more upon completion of development and lease up compared to the construction costs, including

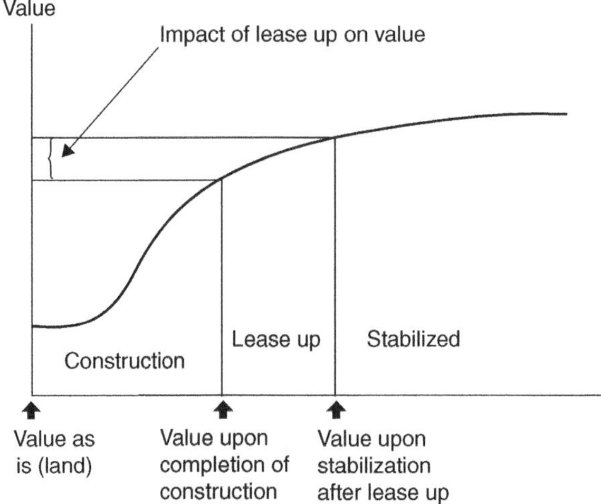

Exhibit 10.8 Lease-up Value Creation
This exhibit illustrates the portion of value created by lease up of the property after construction is complete.

purchase of land and both hard and soft costs associated with development. *Hard costs* are the actual construction costs, and *soft costs* are fees such as architect, engineering, appraisal, and legal. Exhibit 10.9 illustrates a developer's profit.

Risk Factors for Development Projects

Many risks are associated with development projects. Some are unique to development projects, whereas others also apply to completed projects. The following summarizes key risk factors:

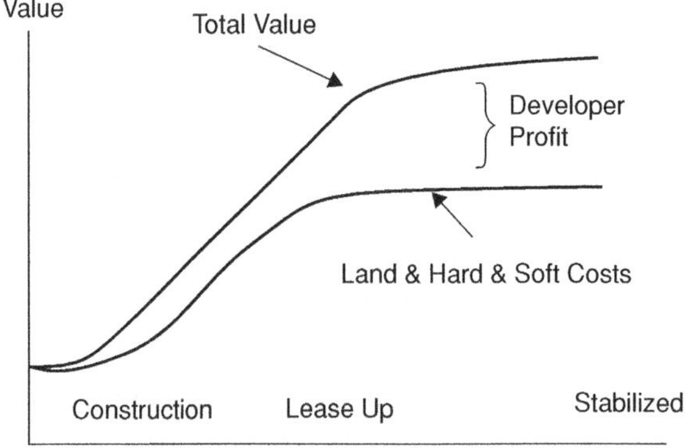

Exhibit 10.9 Developer's Profit
This exhibit illustrates how the developer earns a profit during the development of a project as value is created above the development cost. Most of the developer's profit is earned once the project is complete and lease up is in progress. This is also when the risk is starting to decrease after having risen during development.

- *Entitlement risk.* Risk of obtaining appropriate land entitlements, construction permits, and possibly zoning variances.
- *Construction risk.* Risk that the cost of materials may change substantially from the original construction budget or that planned construction completion could be prolonged due to weather delays, labor disputes, and material delivery delays.
- *Leasing/sales risk.* Risk that forecasted absorption (leasing or unit sales) volume will not be realized.
- *Operating expense risk.* Risk of a substantial change in one or more fixed or variable expense categories, such as insurance, electricity, or real estate taxes.
- *Credit risk.* Risk that prelease tenants and/or the tenants' industry segment is negatively affected during development.
- *Capital market risk.* Risk of a substantial change in interest rates during the development period. This could affect the cost of construction or, in the case of a condominium project, the buyer's ability to obtain suitable purchase price financing or that rates of return for alternative investments will change, resulting in shifts in capitalization and discount rates.
- *Pricing risk.* Risk that unanticipated competitive supply will enter the market before lease-up or sellout is achieved, resulting in short-, mid-, or long-term concessions, less absorption, and lower pricing, and that changes in market supply/demand dynamics may negatively affect rental rates.
- *Event risk.* Risk of a material physical, economic, or other event occurring that substantially affects asset operations and value. Weather, discovery of previously unknown environmental contamination, exodus of major employment providers, and terrorism comprise a sampling of such events.

Exhibit 10.10 illustrates risk changes over the development cycle. The cycle begins slowly because the property is just land value and the developer has not committed funds. At this point, the developer had many options available, including doing nothing. As the developer puts funds into the project, the risk increases, because changing plans and developing something else becomes more difficult. As the end of construction nears, especially if the market still looks favorable for the project, risk should begin to decrease. At this point, income will be generated from leasing space. As the space is leased, risk declines even further, assuming the property is leasing up at a reasonable rate as originally anticipated. Once lease-up is complete, the risk is generally at its lowest level. In fact, this is often a point at which the developer will want to sell the completed and leased-up property to a more passive investor, such as a pension fund, that does not want to incur the development risk and prefers to purchase completed projects.

SUMMARY AND CONCLUSIONS

This chapter has shown the importance of appraisals for real estate investors and developers and how to estimate the value using three traditional approaches to value. Because each approach has both advantages and disadvantages, the appraiser needs to reconcile the results into a single estimate of value for the property. Investors should also be aware of the risks associated with the investment and realize that the actual value may differ from what was estimated due to these risk factors and the lack of perfect data to estimate value. The chapter also examined

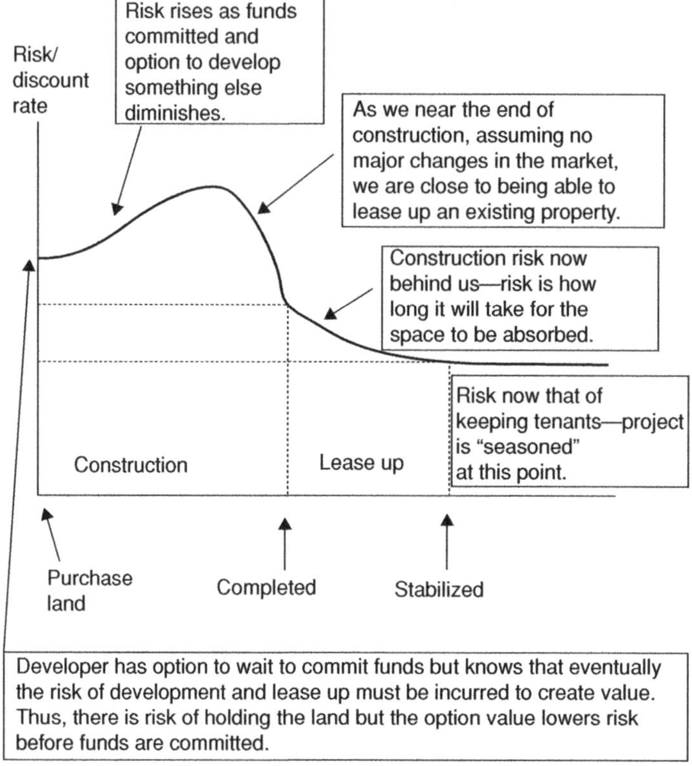

Exhibit 10.10 Risk Profile during Development
This exhibit illustrates how the risk changes from the time that development starts until the project is completed and then leased up.

how the value of construction and land development projects can be estimated. The nature of the risks and cash flow patterns may differ for construction and development projects but the same basic concepts apply as for existing properties. Fisher and Martin (2007) and Chapter 9 in Brueggeman and Fisher (2011) provide a more in-depth discussion of real estate appraisal.

DISCUSSION QUESTIONS

1. What type of value is usually estimated for the purpose of a real estate loan? Why?
2. What is the relationship between a capitalization rate and a discount rate?
3. What assumptions in a DCF analysis could lead to overestimating the property value?
4. What might cause the sales comparison approach to result in a poor estimate of value?
5. Identify and explain the three types of value typically estimated for a development project.
6. When is risk the highest for a development project? Why?

REFERENCES

Brueggeman, William B., and Jeffrey D. Fisher. 2011. *Real Estate Finance and Investments*, 14th ed. New York: McGraw-Hill Irwin.

Fisher, Jeffrey D., and Robert S. Martin. 2007. *Income Property Valuation*, 3rd ed. Chicago: Dearborn Real Estate Education.

Hodges Jr., McCloud B. 1993. "Three Approaches." *Appraisal Journal* 61:1, 553–564.

Lennhoff, David C. 2011. "Direct Capitalization: It May Be Simple but It Isn't Easy." *Appraisal Journal* 79:1, 66–73.

Parli, Richard L., and Jeffrey D. Fisher. 2010. "Risk and Reasonableness for Non-Market Occupancy—A Second Look during a Recession." *Appraisal Journal* 78:1, 94–103.

Wincott, D. Richard. 2012. "Daily Pricing: An Appraiser's Dream." *Appraisal Journal* 80:2, 130–139.

ABOUT THE AUTHORS

Jeffrey D. Fisher is Co-President of the Homer Hoyt Institute and Professor Emeritus of Real Estate at the Indiana University Kelley School of Business. He is also Senior Global Consultant to ARGUS Software and Real Capital Analytics and Senior Consultant to the National Council of Real Estate Investment Fiduciaries (NCREIF) and an advisor to Sterling Valuation. Dr. Fisher was a founding trustee of The Appraisal Foundation and served as President of the American Real Estate and Urban Economics Association (AREUEA). He has published several textbooks including *Real Estate Finance and Investments*, 14th edition, and *Income Property Valuation*, as well as numerous articles in journals dealing with real estate valuation and other topics. He has a PhD in Real Estate from Ohio State University.

Demetrios Louziotis, Jr. is Senior Vice President, Global Real Estate Solutions Group for ARGUS Software and has over 25 years of real estate and finance experience. Before joining ARGUS, he was a Director with Credit Suisse in New York and Tokyo and an adjunct faculty member in New York University's real estate masters program. In New York he established the firm's International Real Estate Pricing and Global Private Equity Pricing Groups, managed the Domestic Real Estate Pricing Group, and was a global member of the bank's real estate investment. In Tokyo he was involved in the origination, underwriting, and distribution of real estate loans and the management of assets in the Asia-Pacific region. Mr. Louziotis joined Credit Suisse from Price Waterhouse's Valuation and Advisory Services Group, where he was a manager and involved in various consulting, transaction support, and corporate real estate engagements. He holds a BS in finance from the University of Connecticut, an MS in real estate from Penn State University, and the CRE, FRICS, and MAI designations.

CHAPTER 11

Performance of Real Estate Portfolios

DAVID GELTNER
Professor of Real Estate Finance, Massachusetts Institute of Technology

INTRODUCTION

This chapter focuses on the measurement of the investment returns to portfolios of commercial properties. Nothing is more fundamental and important to investors than measuring how the value of the investment changes over time. Closely related to this issue is the question of measuring the performance of real estate as an investment asset class for purposes of portfolio analysis and benchmarking. Although current income, such as dividends or rents, can be a very important component of investment performance, measurement of income is usually relatively straightforward. Income also tends to be relatively stable over time. Thus, the main focus and major challenge in measuring investment performance is in tracking asset values. Yet, the measurement of investment value is particularly challenging for many forms of alternative investments. This is because the underlying assets generally trade privately (if at all), and because the individual assets are heterogeneous and traded infrequently.

Among alternative investments, commercial real estate has some advantages for measuring and tracking its value changes. Real estate assets are generally simpler, more transparent, and more homogeneous than other forms of private equity investments. Real estate assets also trade in a generally very active and well-functioning private asset market, the property market. This provides direct empirical evidence about the current market values of property assets. Furthermore, commercial property also trades indirectly in the stock market by the trading of real estate investment trust (REIT) shares of common stock.

As a result, three major ways are available to measure or track commercial property values, each corresponding to a different type or source of information about asset values: (1) professional appraisals of individual properties, (2) property market transaction prices summarized directly by econometric-based price indices, and (3) stock market–based indices derived from REIT share prices. This chapter provides a review of all three of these approaches, with a view toward the general methodological considerations, strengths, and weaknesses of each approach, and also toward what each approach says about the recent history and nature of commercial property price and investment performance. The chapter concludes with the suggestion that each approach to measuring commercial real estate returns has different strengths and weaknesses. Therefore, a "triangulation" approach, blending and applying all three perspectives to the extent possible, will often give the most insight and understanding about price changes and performance.

PROFESSIONAL APPRAISALS OF INDIVIDUAL PROPERTIES

Private property markets are ancient, certainly predating even the earliest stock and bond exchanges. As a result, procedures and institutions for trading and valuing property assets have been highly developed for a long time. These institutions include a highly developed property appraisal profession, which is discussed in depth in the preceding chapter. Thus, the most traditional way to measure the investment performance of portfolios of commercial properties is to have the properties professionally appraised on a frequent and regular basis. This process generally involves hiring an appraisal firm to estimate the current market value of each property in the subject portfolio. The individual property appraisals are then aggregated across the entire portfolio. To obtain a measure of capital return or appreciation of asset value, the end-of-period aggregate valuation of the portfolio is compared to the beginning-of-period aggregate valuation for the same properties, namely, the properties in the portfolio at the beginning of the period. Properties sold during the period can be valued at their actual sales prices. To gross the resulting capital return up to a total investment return involves adding the aggregate net cash flow produced during the period by the (same) properties as a fraction of the beginning-of-period aggregate value. Net cash flow consists of the net operating income (NOI) of the properties, minus any capital improvement expenditures (*capex*) made during the period.

The Employee Retirement Income Security Act of 1973 (ERISA) mandates that pension plans be funded with investments that are prudently diversified and that real estate assets in such funds should be valued by professional appraisals at least once every three years (Iezman, 2011). The modern institutional commercial property investment industry in the United States was born from that act and mandate. Starting in the 1970s and 1980s, a great flowering of institutional real estate investment management funds and services catering to pension funds and other tax-exempt institutions took place. These funds represented the most sophisticated and quantitative commercial real estate investors of that time, and they generally reappraised most of their properties annually (with more done in the fourth calendar quarter of the year).

In this environment, the National Council of Real Estate Investment Fiduciaries (NCREIF) was established in 1982 in order to collect all of the institutional real estate valuations under one umbrella to produce a nationwide index of commercial property investment performance. The NCREIF Property Index (NPI) was launched with an inception date of fourth quarter 1977, reporting quarterly appreciation, income, and total returns. The NPI rapidly became "the standard," the most widely cited and used benchmark and representation of commercial property asset values and total returns in the United States. Growing from 233 properties worth

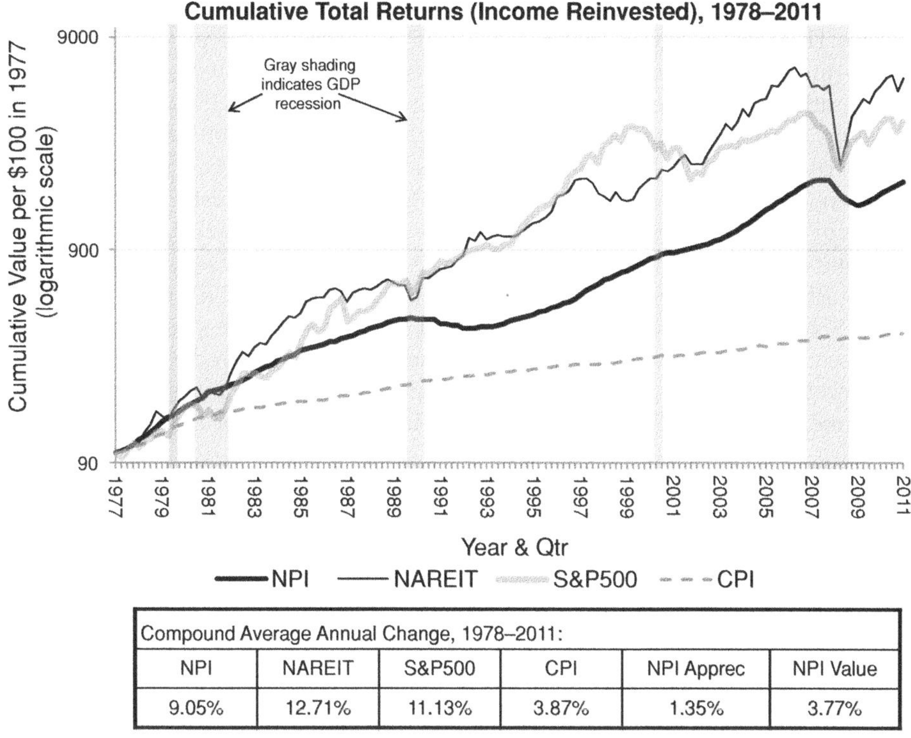

Compound Average Annual Change, 1978–2011:					
NPI	NAREIT	S&P500	CPI	NPI Apprec	NPI Value
9.05%	12.71%	11.13%	3.87%	1.35%	3.77%

Exhibit 11.1 Cumulative Total Returns (income reinvested), 1978–2011
This exhibit shows the NPI total return cumulative value index with income reinvested since its inception in 1977 through 2011, along with the NAREIT Equity REIT total return index, the S&P 500 index, and the Consumer Price Index (CPI) tracking inflation, juxtaposed on periods of national recession. Data sources: NCREIF, NAREIT, Ibbotson Associates, and NBER.

in aggregate $581 million in 1977, the NPI tracked over 7,000 individual properties owned by over 70 data-contributing member firms, worth in aggregate about $300 billion as of early 2012.

Exhibit 11.1 shows the NPI total return cumulative value index (with income reinvested) since its inception in 1977 through 2011, along with the NAREIT Equity REIT total return index, the S&P 500 large-cap stock total return index, and the Consumer Price Index (CPI) tracking inflation. During this 34-year period, which included four major recessionary periods (indicated by the gray-shaded vertical bands) and two full commercial property market cycles (one peaking in the late 1980s and another in 2007), the NPI produced an average annual total return of just over 9 percent. During the same period, inflation averaged just under 4 percent, implying an annual real total return of over 5 percent.

The NPI total return is broken into additive capital and income components. Exhibit 11.1 shows that the NPI averaged 1.35 percent annual appreciation, less than inflation. However, NCREIF defines the appreciation component net of capex. If the capex is subtracted from the income rather than the capital growth component of the total return (leaving the total return unchanged), the NCREIF same-property valuation growth rate was 3.77 percent per year, almost equal to inflation. This also suggests that the NCREIF average annual property income yield during 1978–2011 measured on a cash basis was about 9.05 – 3.77 = 5.28 percent, rather than the earnings or net income based 9.05 – 1.35 = 7.70 percent, which was more reflective of historical *cap rates* (defined as net income divided by property value). NCREIF members probably spend a larger proportion of property net operating income on capex, over 30 percent in the historical database, than is typical of other segments of the commercial property market.

Exhibit 11.1 also shows that the National Association of REITs (NAREIT) index of equity REITs and the S&P 500 index both outperformed the NPI in total return during 1978–2011 (12.7 percent a year and 11.1 percent a year, respectively, versus 9.05 percent). But these stock market–based indices also displayed greater volatility and cycle amplitude. Note that the vertical axis in the exhibit is presented in logarithmic scale, and all indices are set to an inception value of 100 as of the end of 1977.

Appraisal-based indices of commercial real estate values and investment performance are very useful, and the NPI remains a widely respected gauge. The NPI is particularly appropriate as a benchmark for evaluating the performance, at the property level, of specialized institutional real estate investment managers who are members of NCREIF. The NPI essentially represents the universe of such managers, and the property-level performance of these managers is reported to their investors based on the appraised values of the properties held, exactly the same type of data on which the NPI is based. Appraisal-based indices similar to the NPI are produced in a number of countries around the world for tracking commercial properties held by investment institutions. Most notable internationally are the indices produced and published by a private U.K.–based company, the Investment Property Databank (IPD, purchased in late 2012 by MSCI).

Problems with Appraisal-Based Indices

As important as indices such as the NPI are, some issues need to be considered (Geltner, MacGregor, and Schwann, 2003). For example, the NPI is based on the self-reported property valuations of the investment managers who are members of NCREIF. These valuations are not generally based on a new, independent appraisal of each property each quarter. Though adjustments in value have been more frequent in recent years than they were through the 1990s (and this has largely eliminated the strong seasonality in the NPI that was caused by the bunching of reappraisals in the fourth quarters), many properties' reported valuations in the NPI are left standing for two or more consecutive quarters at their previously reported values. This results in some stale valuations in the index, which can make the index sluggish or lagged.

Another issue is the possibility of subjective valuation or valuation by other than an independent professional appraiser, however well intentioned. For example, during the worst of the financial crisis for real estate (2008–2009), transactions were very scarce and professional appraisers had difficulty justifying sharp reductions in valuations based on market evidence and traditional appraisal procedures. As a result, some NCREIF managers or auditors simply determined their own markdowns and reported these into the index. In that historical instance, these actions caused the index to move more quickly than one based on traditional appraisals would have done. But more generally, even apart from stale valuation reports in the index, the professional appraisal process can result in a temporal lag bias and a smoothing of market value volatility, particularly when the same appraisal firm reappraises the same properties repeatedly.

The result is that while appraisal-based indices such as the NPI are very thoroughly documented, they tend to display a smoothing and lagging bias compared to contemporaneous asset market values as reflected by current transaction prices directly. This presents problems for some applications of commercial property price indices, such as identifying exact turning points in the market or comparing real estate with other asset classes in terms of volatility or covariance, as is useful in classical portfolio optimization and other investment analysis applications.

Another problem with appraisal-based indices is that hiring appraisers to value each property very frequently in a large portfolio is expensive. As a result, the vast majority of commercial properties in the United States are not regularly or frequently appraised. An appraisal-based index such as the NPI can only be constructed in the United States for a relatively small and specialized population of properties, those held by or for pension funds and other such entities that are required to "mark to market" frequently. In contrast to the situation in most other countries, operating under so-called "fair value" accounting standards, generally accepted accounting principles (GAAP) typically do not require REITs and other real estate investment entities in the United States to mark properties to market. Although this may change in the future, for now assets are generally still carried on firms' accounting books at historical cost.

As noted earlier, the NPI tracks 7,000 properties worth $300 billion, for an average value of $42,000,000 per property. But a study by CoStar suggests that the total value of U.S. commercial real estate is at least $9 trillion in over three million properties, for an average value of $3,000,000 (Florance, Miller, Spivey, and Peng, 2010). About half of the total commercial stock by value consists of several hundred thousands of "larger" properties that are actively traded or financed by institutional and professional investors such as banks, insurance companies, REITs, commercial mortgage backed securities (CMBS), major private investors, pension and other investment funds, and foreign investors. U.S. REITs alone hold well over $700 billion of property, and there are more than $3 trillion of commercial mortgages outstanding. Thus, the NPI represents only a small fraction of the effective investable commercial property population. While NCREIF is an important segment, it is not representative of commercial property in some ways. For example, $42 million properties can experience very different price dynamics than $3 million properties. Thus, a need exists for other sources and perspectives on commercial property price change and performance in the United States.

TRANSACTION-BASED PRICE INDICES

Transaction-based price indices have been the major innovation in the past decade for tracking U.S. commercial real estate performance. The idea of transaction-based price indices is to base the estimate of price change more directly and purely on the fundamental empirical evidence about the market value of properties, their transaction prices. Of course, appraisers make heavy use of transaction price evidence. But they filter that evidence through a somewhat subjective process of judgment that is more oriented toward accurately estimating the value of individual properties than toward the up-to-date tracking of contemporaneous movements in market-wide central tendencies. Until the 1990s, there was a lack of accessible and comprehensive commercial property transactions data. But more recently, firms such as CoStar, Real Capital Analytics (RCA), and others have developed very large and sophisticated databases of commercial property transaction prices in the United States.

Once a good database of commercial property transaction prices is available, various methods can be used to construct an index to track price changes over time. For example, a simple method is to compute the average or median price per square foot (SF) of all the properties sold in each period. But commercial properties are very heterogeneous. The simple techniques do not always work. For instance, during the downturn in the commercial property market some indicators of average or median price/SF at first increased. This occurred not because prices were rising, but because of a "flight to quality": The only deals that could get done were on "trophy" assets (i.e., properties of particularly high quality in prime locations).

A key challenge in constructing good commercial property transaction price indices is to control for the variation in the "quality" (broadly speaking, including the size) of the properties that are transacting between different periods of time. This challenge heads a list of several important considerations in designing commercial property transaction-based price indices.

Another consideration is using good statistical techniques that are designed to make as efficient use as possible of the data. This means filtering out as much noise as possible, without inducing a problematical temporal lag bias, as can occur with appraisal-based indices. Fortunately, many advancements in the field of econometrics have occurred in recent decades, including the development of techniques for estimating real estate price indices. Large data sets of transaction prices lend themselves to modern econometric techniques.

Transaction-based price indices can make an important contribution by providing more objective and replicable information as compared to appraisal-based or other more subjective or "notional value" indices. Thus, reasons exist to employ econometrically rigorous techniques that are transparent and vetted in the academic community.

Finally, commercial properties are not only heterogeneous at the individual property level, but asset markets also tend to cleave and segment, often in dynamic ways. As noted previously, a flight to quality can affect different types of assets at various points in the cycle. Different price dynamics often apply in various types of locations, such as central business districts versus suburbs or at different scales of property (large or small). These dynamics can reflect differences in capital sources as well as differences in physical supply and demand. So when constructing transaction price indices, one should think carefully about the segmenting and the structuring of a *suite of indices*, a system of composite indices representing aggregates of property markets or submarkets.

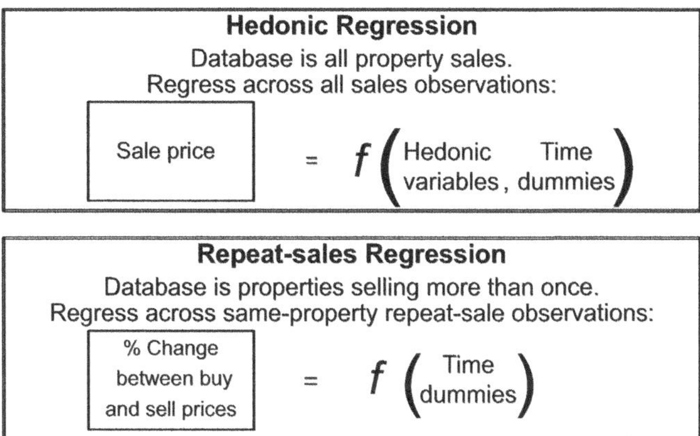

Exhibit 11.2 Two Types of Econometric Transaction-Based Indices
This exhibit shows two major approaches used to deal with the variation-in-quality problem relating to a real estate price index: hedonic modeling and repeat-sales regression.

Two Ways to Control for Quality

In the real estate price index econometric literature, two major approaches are widely accepted to deal with the variation in quality problem. One approach is called *hedonic modeling*, and the other is *repeat-sales regression*. Exhibit 11.2 summarizes these two approaches.

Hedonic indices use all available transaction price observations. They control for quality differences between properties transacting in different time periods by building a *hedonic valuation model*, that is, a model that estimates the values of the various possible attributes of commercial property (what causes one property to be worth more than another as of the same point in time) (Court, 1939; Adelman and Griliches, 1961; Rosen, 1974). Typical hedonic attributes might include factors such as the size, age, and type of property; attributes of its location, such as how close it is to downtown or to an airport; perhaps even aspects of its lease structure. The modeler (index builder) regresses sale prices onto measurements of all of these hedonic attributes, plus a set of time-dummy variables corresponding to the historical periods of the price index. This process is called a *panel regression*. The regression's estimated time-dummies coefficients capture the change in "average" pricing over time, and the index is constructed from these coefficients. However, this approach is susceptible to omitted variables. If the hedonic attributes are changing systematically over time in ways not captured in the hedonic metrics, then changes in quality can be erroneously imputed to changes in pricing. For example, suppose office buildings with atriums sell at a premium compared to those with old-fashioned lobbies, and over time proportionately more and more buildings with atriums are produced and sold, yet this variable is not captured or not well measured in the database. The increase in pricing due to the propagation of atriums would be erroneously imputed in the price index to an increase in the general market price of all buildings. Such error would be particularly problematic for using the index to help track investment performance. An investor is stuck with whatever building she has bought. If the building does not have an atrium, its price will not reflect the value of having an atrium.

This panel regression hedonic approach seems to work quite well in the special circumstance when a good appraisal of the transacting properties' values is available not long before each transaction has occurred. Then this appraisal can serve as a catch-all "hedonic" variable. To continue the previous example, the appraiser presumably notes whether the building has an atrium or not and understands the value of atriums. Regressing transaction prices onto recent appraised values plus time-dummy variables can result in a good "hedonic-type" transaction-based price index. The procedure involves combining the regression results with an index of changes in the appraised values, using the time-dummy coefficients from the regression to represent the average difference each period between the transaction prices and the appraisals and the appraisal-based index to represent the change in appraised values over time.

This process is how the MIT Center for Real Estate developed the first regularly produced and published regression-based commercial property transaction-based price index, the so-called "transaction-based index" (TBI) based on the properties sold from the NCREIF Index population. The TBI was launched at MIT in 2006 with the support of NCREIF, and in 2011 was taken over by NCREIF and is now known as the NTBI. Although essentially a hedonic type of index and based on a regression model, this type of index can be produced in a simplified manner without using formal regression modeling. As such, it may be referred to as a sales price/appraisal ratio (SPAR) index, calculated by computing the average ratio of sales prices to recently appraised values among all the properties sold each period and then multiplying this ratio by the corresponding appraisal-based index value level each period. NCREIF uses this methodology to produce the NTBI, although the earlier index produced at MIT was regression based. By 2012 IPD had begun producing SPAR-type transaction-based indices in some other countries, labeling them as "transaction-linked indices" (TLIs) (Cullen, Clacy-Jones, and Devaney, 2012).

TBI- or TLI-type appraisal-based hedonic or SPAR indices of transaction prices can only be applied in the limited context where good, consistent, regularly updated appraisal information for the sold properties is available. In the United States, this is presently limited more or less to the NCREIF and IPD populations of properties. But where TBI- or TLI-type indices can be produced, they provide a particularly meaningful comparison between appraisal-based and transaction-based price indices (for the relevant population of properties). IPD has found that the difference between their traditional appraisal-based indices and their new TLIs varies across countries. For example, relatively little difference exists in Britain. Apparently, commercial property markets function very differently in different cultures even among institutional investors, and it is also clear that the appraisal profession and practices differ.

Exhibit 11.3 presents the traditional appraisal-based NPI in comparison with the transaction-based NTBI capital value (asset price change) indices over the period 2000–2011. Although the two indices track each other closely overall, the transaction-based NTBI appears to lead the appraisal-based index in terms of the timing of the major turning points. The 2000s decade peak occurred about three quarters earlier in the NTBI than in the NPI, and the trough occurred one quarter

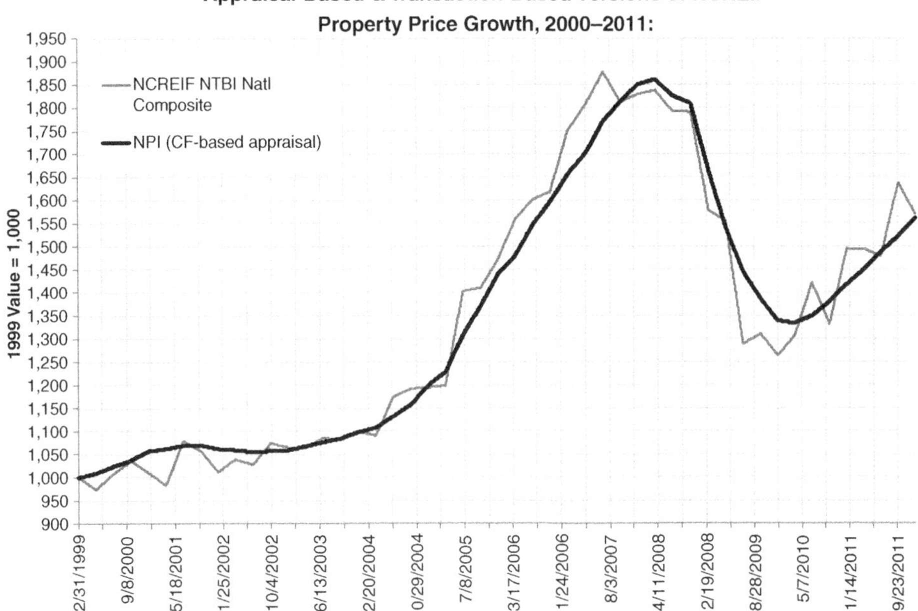

Exhibit 11.3 Appraisal and Transaction-Based Versions of NCREIF Property Price Growth, 2000–2011

This exhibit presents the traditional appraisal-based NPI in comparison with the transaction-based NTBI capital value (asset price change) indices over the period 2000–2011.

Data source: NCREIF.

earlier. Also the transaction-based index compared to the appraisal-based index is a bit more volatile (5.7 percent versus 2.9 percent quarterly volatility, though the difference is much less at the annual frequency), and the TBI displays somewhat greater cycle amplitude (34 percent peak-trough drop versus 29 percent).

Repeat-Sales Indices

The other major approach to building a transaction-based price index is the repeat-sales method (Bailey, Muth, and Nourse, 1963; Case and Shiller, 1987). As Exhibit 11.2 indicates, in the repeat-sales approach quality differences are controlled for by basing the index only on properties that have sold at least twice. The index is constructed using the changes in price within the same properties between their consecutive sales, rather than the price levels of all the sales. The observations are generally screened insofar as possible to filter out properties that underwent major physical rehabilitation or renovation and improvement between the consecutive sales. The repeat-sales model regresses the percentage changes in price between the "buy" and the "sell" of each property onto time-dummy variables representing the periods of historical time tracked by the price index. The time-dummies variables equal one if they correspond to a time period between the buy and the sell dates in the given observation, and zero otherwise.

The repeat-sales method has the disadvantage of only being able to use transactions of properties that have sold at least twice within the database. But it has the advantage of not needing hedonic data about the properties, and this can make the method more robust. The repeat-sales method also has the advantage of being a very simple and transparent model that investors can readily understand. After all, this model is based purely on the actual roundtrip price-change experiences of actual investors. Investors must sell the same property that they have previously bought. With its parsimonious data requirements, the repeat-sales approach can be applied very broadly to any population of properties that is actively traded and for which price data can be compiled. Thus, the repeat-sales approach has great appeal in practice and may be becoming a sort of industry standard in the United States.

The first regularly produced and published commercial property repeat-sales index was developed at the MIT Center for Real Estate in cooperation with Real Capital Analytics (using RCA data) and launched in late 2006. In 2007, the index was transferred to Moody's Investors Service and was subsequently produced and published by Moody's for five years as the Moody's/REAL Commercial Property Price Index (CPPI). Moody's discontinued this index in late 2011 and replaced it in early 2012 with an enhanced version under the name Moody's/RCA Commercial Property Price Index (still referred to as the CPPI). In 2009, Green Street Advisors began publishing an index of REIT-held property values, which it also labeled "CPPI." However, the GSA-CPPI is neither based solely on closed transaction price data nor on an econometrically rigorous repeat-sales model. It therefore does not track actual investment cash experiences. In some ways, the GSA-CPPI is more like an appraisal-based index, although it does not appear to suffer from the lagging and smoothing apparent in the NPI. In 2010 CoStar launched its own repeat-sales index, the CoStar Commercial Repeat-Sales Index (CCRSI), based on the same general type of econometrically rigorous regression model as the Moody's/REAL CPPI, but using CoStar's more extensive database of property transactions. In 2012 the "RCA CPPI" index suite was launched, based on data and methodology the same as the Moody's/RCA CPPI only including more than 180 granular repeat-sales indices tracking metro-level markets and sub-markets or property niches at a more micro level.

The Moody's and RCA CPPI suites are based on the RCA database that seeks to capture all commercial property sales above $2,500,000, a cutoff roughly distinguishing between professional investment properties and smaller properties, many of which are owner-occupied. This sales value also roughly corresponds to a cutoff below which nonbank sources of debt or equity financing, such as life insurance companies, REITs, private equity, foreign investors, and CMBS, have generally been unavailable. As of 2012, RCA had more than 100,000 transactions in its database, yielding more than 23,000 repeat-sales pairs that pass the filters for use in the CPPI, which begins in 2001. The CCRSI is based on the CoStar database, which attempts to track virtually all commercial properties regardless of size (at least down to around $150,000). As of 2012, CoStar had well over one million properties in its database, yielding more than 90,000 postfilter repeat-sales observations for the CCRSI, which is published going back through 1998.

A relevant feature of the CCRSI is that CoStar breaks out the index into two major market segments (mutually exclusive and exhaustive), which it labels

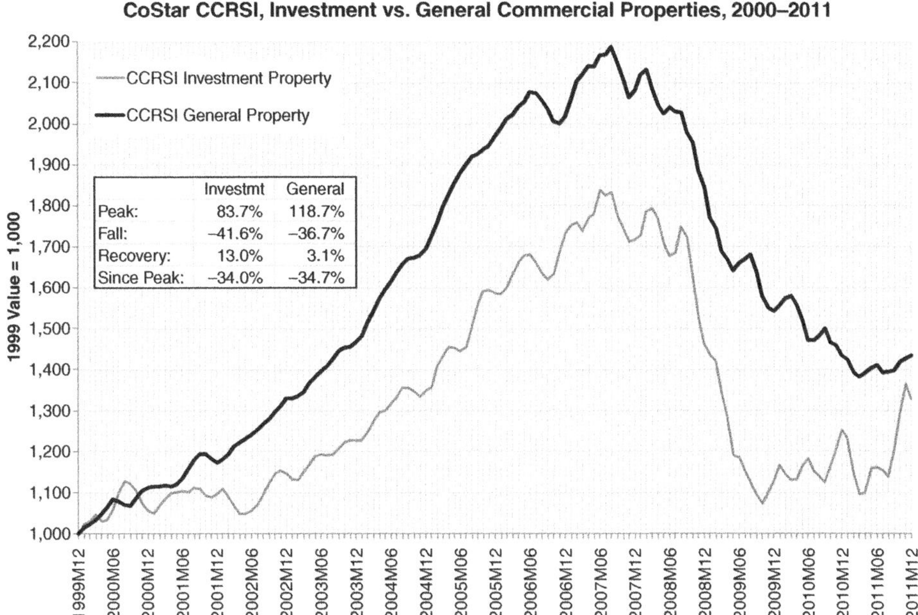

Exhibit 11.4 CoStar Repeat-Sales Price Indices, Investment vs. General Properties
This exhibit compares the CCRSI Investment and General price indices over the periods 2000–2011. Investment properties are larger, corresponding generally to institutional or professional investment assets. General properties are smaller and often user-owned.
Data source: CoStar Group, Inc.

"Investment" property and "General" property. Investment property roughly corresponds to the $2.5 million lower-bound cutoff similar to the CPPI population, although CoStar uses physical criteria rather than a value-based cutoff. As of 2012, the CCRSI General index is based on over 76,000 repeat-sales observations, whereas the Investment index is based on approximately 16,000 observations, in both cases underlying 14 years of published index results. Thus, the CCRSI Investment index and the RCA-based CPPI both track similar (though not identical) populations, probably amounting to about half by value of the total $9 trillion commercial property stock, and reflecting most of the actively traded professional investment properties owned or financed by major institutions and large- to medium-scale investors. By way of comparison, the approximately 23,000 repeat-sales observations on which the CPPI is based underlie only 12 years of published index results, giving it a greater temporal density of estimation sample size for the larger properties. In contrast, the CCRSI General index is a unique source for tracking the rest of the U.S. commercial property population, the smaller properties accounting for the vast majority of the properties but perhaps only about half of the value of the stock and less than half the dollar volume of trading.

Exhibit 11.4 compares the CCRSI Investment and General price indices starting in 2000. Note how different the price dynamics have been between the major properties in the Investment index versus the smaller properties in the General index.

Apparently, the smaller properties increased more in price during the bull market of the 2000s, and then fell less far during the financial crisis. However, in the subsequent recovery, the smaller properties had not yet rebounded through 2011, whereas the Investment properties climbed over 10 percent in 2011 after a rocky period. The result is that both segments as of 2011 were about equally far below their respective peaks in relative terms.

The two indices are not totally comparable. For example, they reflect different mixes of property types and locations, so one must be cautious about drawing comparative conclusions. It is important to note that these are indices only of same-property price change, not total investment return, so they do not necessarily imply superior or inferior investment performance. The differential price performance since the peak probably substantially reflects the different types of financing sources available to the two different market segments. During the worst of the financial crisis, nonbank sources of capital virtually completely froze up, causing Investment property to plummet in value. The more locally based relationship lending of small-scale bank financing for the General properties did not dry up as completely. But after 2009, nonbank financing sources bounced back strongly, whereas banks, especially small- to medium-sized local and regional banks, remained saddled and constrained, in no small part due to excessive commercial mortgage lending during the peak. This dynamic demonstrates the importance of market segmentation for tracking commercial property prices.

Exhibit 11.5 adds the Moody's/RCA CPPI National Composite repeat-sales index to the previous comparison of the appraisal-based and transaction-based versions of the NCREIF same-property price-change indices. The CPPI tracks a much broader population of properties than the NCREIF indices, with a much smaller average price point. The CPPI is also based on the different methodology of repeat-sales rather than SPAR or appraisal-based estimation. Nevertheless, the CPPI National Composite Index describes a similar path of price change in the big picture. The biggest difference at this broad-brush level is that the CPPI fell farther during the financial crisis, losing 39 percent of its peak value (42 percent in the CCRSI Investment index), compared to 34 percent and 29 percent for the NTBI and NPI, respectively.

Market Segmentation in the CPPI

Segmentation exists not only between General and Investment properties, but also within the Investment property market. Structuring a system of indices that appropriately reflects this phenomenon requires some art. Although no single or permanent solution exists to this challenge, the new second-generation CPPI offers one approach.

Exhibit 11.6 displays the structure of the Moody's/RCA CPPI suite of indices. The basis of the system is a set of 10 monthly updated "building-block" indices that are directly estimated by regression modeling of the RCA repeat-sales database. These indices are equally weighted across repeat-sale observations, because equal weighting is generally most efficient from a statistical perspective, being less susceptible to being thrown off by a few large individual property deals. However, the underlying assumption in any regression model is that the sample is drawn from a single population. Thus, the 10 building-block indices represent 10 market

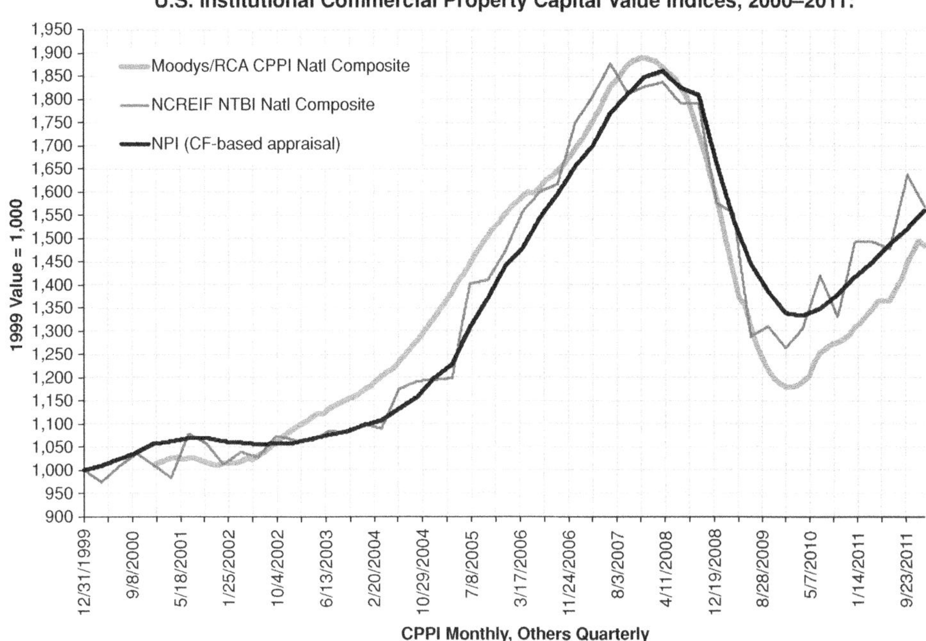

Exhibit 11.5 Adding the Moody's/RCA CPPI Repeat-Sales Index Perspective on U.S. Private Property Market Same-Property Price Growth

This exhibit adds the Moody's/RCA CPPI National Composite repeat-sales index to the previous comparison of the appraisal-based and transaction-based versions of the NCREIF same-property price-change indices shown in Exhibit 11.3. The CPPI begins in 2001.

Data sources: Moody's Investors Service and NCREIF.

segments that attempt to reflect better than traditional breakouts the more abiding differentials in asset-pricing behavior such that within each segment the price behavior is more homogeneous. These underlying segments reflect several dimensions: traditional property sectors (apartment, industrial, office, retail); CBD versus suburban locations; and the "market tier" of the metropolitan location. For example, CBD office properties tend to be larger and more expensive than suburban offices, so the two types are not mixed within the same underlying directly estimated index.

The market tier dimension of the system represents a new way to define geographical groupings not based on the traditional contiguous multistate regions such as East, Midwest, South, and West (as in the NPI). Instead, "Major Markets" are identified as the metro areas of Boston, New York, Washington DC, Chicago, San Francisco Bay, and Los Angeles. These six metros account for nearly half of all of the CPPI trading by dollar volume and have consistently attracted capital from major domestic and foreign institutions much more strongly than other locations. They also tend to be somewhat supply constrained in terms of new property development due to physical or political factors. As a result, the CPPI Major Markets exhibit a tendency toward different price dynamics than the Non-Major Markets, both in the short and the long run.

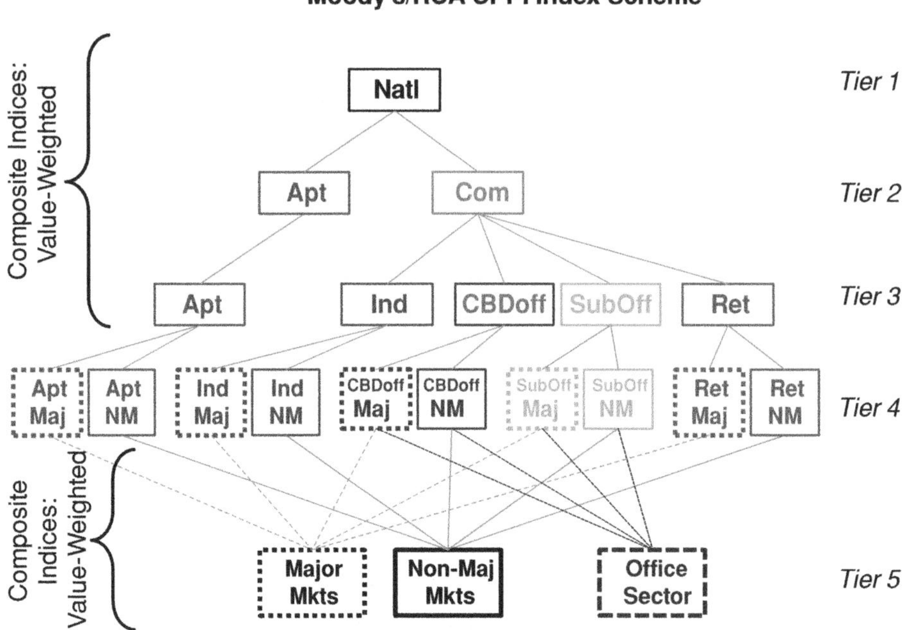

Exhibit 11.6 Moody's/RCA CPPI Index Scheme

This exhibit displays the structure of the Moody's/RCA CPPI suite of indices. An index suite is a system of underlying directly estimated market segments articulated in a value-weighted hierarchy of composite indices.

Separately differentiating along all three of these dimensions comprehensively, which would require 16 segments (four sectors × two intra-metropolitan locations × two market tiers) is presently impossible due to data limitations. But the 10 underlying segments in the CPPI system distinguish between the most important of these differences. Five sectors (apartment, industrial, retail, CBD-office, and suburban-office) are tracked separately for the Major Markets and the Non-Major Markets (NMM), resulting in the 10 building-block indices labeled "Tier 4" in Exhibit 11.6.

This system of market segmentation captures a wide range of different pricing behaviors across different points in the asset market cycle, as displayed in Exhibits 11.7 and 11.8. Exhibit 11.7 shows the difference between the Major Markets and the Non-Major Markets composite indices. Exhibit 11.8 shows all 10 underlying building-block indices separately for the Major Markets (Panel A) and the Non-Major Markets (Panel B). The exhibits are all presented with the same vertical scale and range, for easy direct visual comparison. Across the 10 building-block indices, little redundancy and good spread exists among the long-run trend rates of price growth as well as in the shorter-term behavior. For example, CBD office properties are more cyclical, but after the financial crisis they recovered strongly in the Major Markets while they languished for several years in the Non-Major

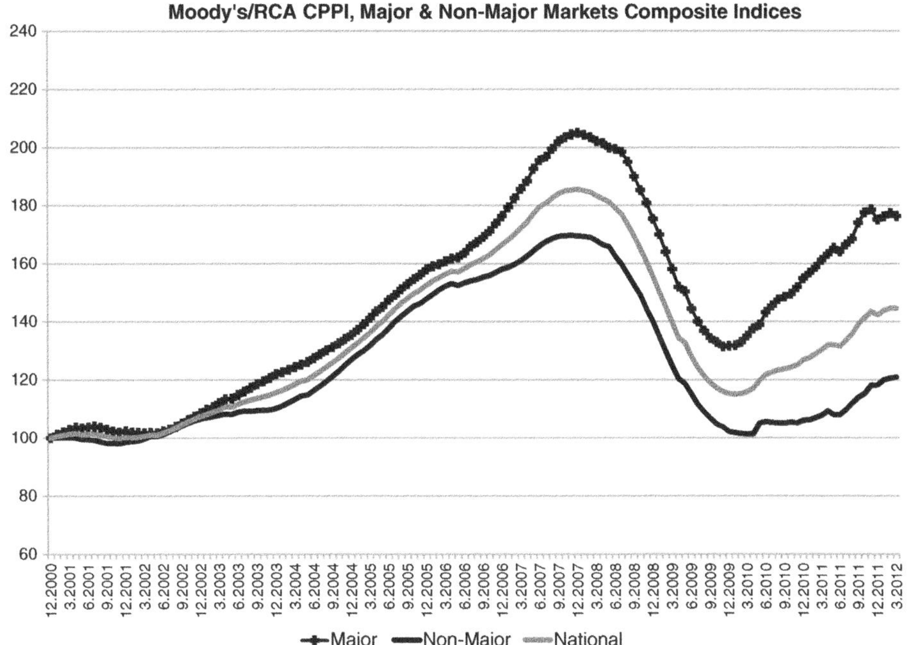

Exhibit 11.7 Moody's/RCA CPPI, Major and Non-Major Markets Composite Indices
This exhibit shows the difference between the Major Markets and the Non-Major Markets composite indices. Major Markets are Boston, New York, Washington DC, Chicago, San Francisco Bay, and Los Angeles metro areas. Non-Major Markets are all other locations. The National Index is value-weighted composite (based on trading volume).
Data source: Moody's Investors Service.

Markets. In general, the Major Markets recovered strongly after the financial crisis, as nonbank financing sources entrepreneurially sought out "safe harbors." By contrast, the Non-Major Markets, which had been more dependent on bank and CMBS financing or which were viewed as more risky, continued to suffer pricing doldrums for several years.

The 11 other higher-level, more aggregate indices in the CPPI system, labeled in the other index tiers in Exhibit 11.6, are all constructed directly or indirectly from the 10 building-block indices by value-weighting the building blocks based on the dollar volume of trading in the RCA database. This enables the composite indices to better reflect the economic impact or importance of the property market price movements. For example, the average weighting within the Tier 3 composite CBD-office index is 76 percent on Major Markets and 24 percent on Non-Major Markets. In the composite apartment index of Tiers 2 and 3, the Non-Major Markets outweigh the Major Markets by an average of 63 percent to 37 percent. At the top level, the Tier 1 National Composite ("headline") index has a 73 percent weight on the Tier 2 composite commercial index and a 27 percent weight on the apartment composite.

In summary, the advent of large and sophisticated databases of commercial property transactions information, combined with advances in econometric procedures, has allowed the development of a whole new class of commercial property

Panel A. Major markets

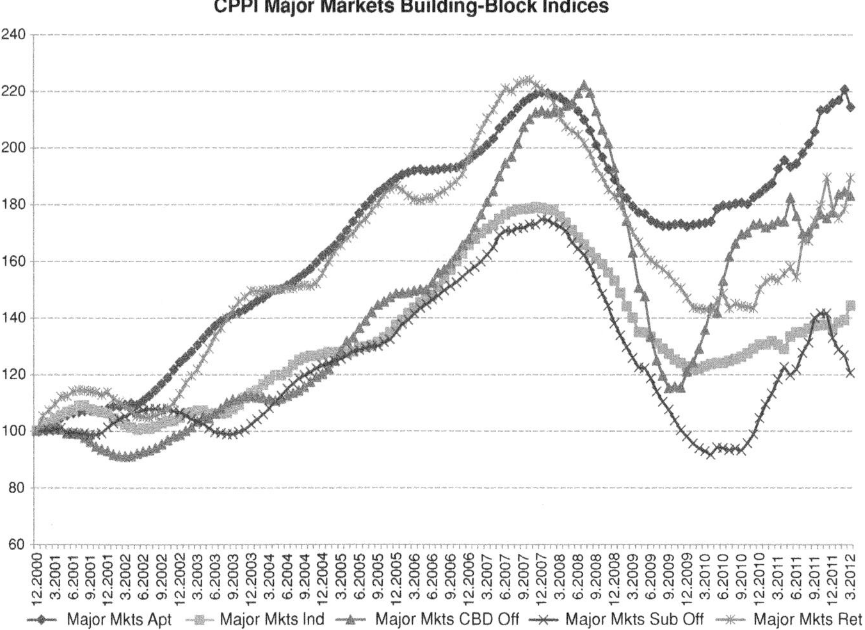

Panel B. Non-major markets

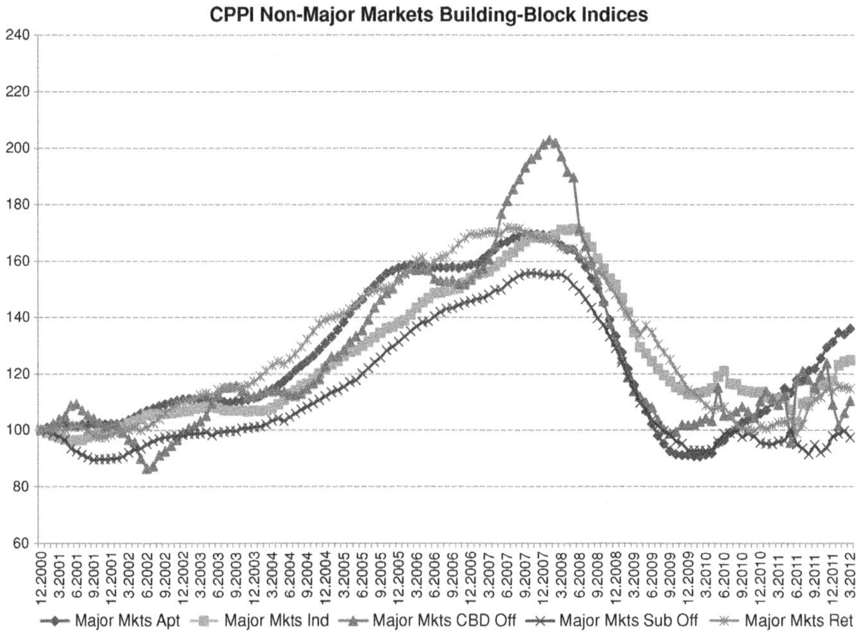

Exhibit 11.8 Moody's CPPI Building-Block Indices

This exhibit shows all 10 underlying building-block indices separately for the Major Markets (Panel A) and the Non-Major Markets (Panel B). The 10 underlying directly-estimated repeat-sales indices reflect mutually exclusive and exhaustive market segments for each market tier: apartments, industrial, retail, CBD-office, and suburban-office.

Data source: Moody's Investors Service.

price indices in the United States since 2005 based more directly and purely on transaction prices. These new indices are still in a rapid state of development and will no doubt continue to evolve. They afford a new perspective on commercial real estate asset price performance, a perspective that is most fundamental, because it is based on actual investor experiences and on actual transactions in the asset marketplace.

STOCK MARKET–BASED INDICES

If transaction-based indices were the major commercial property performance measurement innovation of the first decade of the twenty-first century, then perhaps stock market–based indices will play that role in the second decade. Stock market–based indices are made possible by the existence of a large and mature REIT sector within the stock market. REITs are publicly traded firms that are essentially "pure-plays" in commercial property investment; that is, they are largely confined in their activities to doing nothing except owning and operating commercial investment property. REITS also must pay out most of their earnings as dividends, and they are constrained in the extent to which they can engage in development or construction activity. Thus, REITs are vehicles for investment in largely stabilized, operational commercial properties. As such, REIT equity share prices provide a direct indication of the value of such property (as levered by the REITs), and in particular how this value changes over time (Geltner and Kluger, 1998; Horrigan, Case, Geltner, and Pollakowski, 2009)

Of course, the property valuation in stock market–based indices is made by the stock market, not the private property market in which the commercial property assets actually trade directly. The private property market and the public stock market do not always agree about the value of commercial property. But when such "disagreement" exists, which market is "more correct"? In favor of the private property market is the fact that the assets trade directly in that market. Additionally, a much greater number and aggregate value of property assets are owned privately outside of REITs, and the property market has a long history and is specialized in such assets. But in favor of the stock market is the fact that it is extremely efficient at information aggregation and price discovery. The stock market is also more liquid than the private asset market, with a much greater velocity of trading volume (turnover ratio) and highly developed and rapid public information and publication processes.

Evidence suggests that, when the REIT and private market valuations of commercial property differ in the aggregate, that difference tends to be mean-reverting (i.e., it tends to average toward zero), and the stock market valuation tends to lead in time the private market valuation (Gyourko and Keim, 1992; Barkham and Geltner, 1995; Ang, Nabar and Wald, 2012); that is, major turning points often occur first in the REIT valuations. REITs now are major players in the property market in the United States. By the early twenty-first century, there were more than 100 actively traded public equity REITs (i.e., REITs primarily investing in property equity as opposed to mortgages), with a total aggregate stock market capitalization over $400 billion, holding over $700 billion worth of property assets, more than twice the value of assets in the NCREIF Index. With REITs being pure-plays, stockholders investing in and trading REITs can be under no illusions that commercial property assets are fundamentally determining the value of their shares. In short, saying that both the stock market and the private property market have something important to say about the value of commercial property seems appropriate. Stock market–based indices are a way to distill and focus that market's information and news about commercial property values in a way that is practical and useful to the investment industry.

The launching of the first stock market–based index of commercial property prices occurred in June 2012 in the form of the FTSE NAREIT PureProperty™ Index Series, updated and published daily by FTSE. This index product was developed initially in a sponsored research project between NAREIT and the MIT Center for Real Estate and was subsequently refined and commercialized by a joint venture between NAREIT and FTSE. The PureProperty indices represent a third major source of information and perspective on commercial property price performance in the United States, after appraisal-based and direct transaction-based price indices, as discussed previously. The over 25,000 properties held by the 109 actively traded REITs on which the PureProperty indices were initially launched are generally large, institutional-quality investment properties comparable to the type tracked by NCREIF, the CCRSI Investment Index, and the CPPI. Thus, the PureProperty Indices are directly comparable to these other types of indices. Furthermore, stock market based–indices can provide not just price-change or capital returns, but total investment returns, including current income.

How Stock Market–Based Indices Work

The construction of a stock market–based property return index (SMPRI) involves two major steps: de-levering the REIT equity returns, and constructing a targeted long/short portfolio of REIT holdings. In the PureProperty indices, de-levering is accomplished at the level of each individual REIT, based on its capital structure and a (generic) cost of debt. For example, suppose REIT X has a share price total return on a given day of 10 percent, consisting of a 3 percent dividend payment (ex dividend after that date) plus another 7 percent gain in share price even after subtracting the dividend. For example, assume the share price excluding the dividend at the beginning of the day is \$50; the dividend is \$1.50; and the closing price ex dividend at the end of the day is 1.07(\$50) = \$53.50. Also suppose REIT X has a capital structure that is 60 percent equity and 40 percent debt, with these percentages based on the market value of the equity and the book value of the debt. Thus, for this REIT, at the beginning of the day total asset value per share ex dividend is \$83.33, including \$50 equity and \$33.33 debt. Finally, suppose the debt is interest only at 5 percent annually [which is 0.05(\$33.33)/250 trading days per year = \$0.0067 per day, or 0.05/250 = 0.02 percent of the debt per day]. Then the de-levered return on assets (ROA) of REIT X for that day is, for the income return:

$$
\begin{aligned}
\text{(Dividends + Interest)/Assets} &= [0.03(0.60) + 0.0002(0.40)]/(0.60 + 0.40) \\
&= (1.50 + 0.0067)/83.33 = 1.81 \text{ percent}
\end{aligned}
$$

for the capital return:

$$\begin{aligned}\text{Share gain/Assets} &= 0.07(0.60)/(0.60 + 0.40) = (\$53.50 - 50.00)/83.33 \\ &= 4.20 \text{ percent}\end{aligned}$$

and the total return:

$$\begin{aligned}[0.10(0.60) + 0.0002(0.40)]/(0.60 + 0.40) &= (1.5067 + 3.50)/83.33 \\ &= 1.81 \text{ percent} + 4.20 \text{ percent} \\ &= 6.01 \text{ percent}\end{aligned}$$

Unless explicitly adjusted, the capital return on assets in the SMPRI will not exactly be a same-property asset price change like that in the private market indices presented in previous sections. This is because it will reflect asset turnover and renewal within the REIT property portfolio and will also include the effect of REIT scale expansion due to retained earnings not paid out to stakeholders. This consideration is minor, however, given that REITs pay out most of their earnings.

Once the daily de-levered ROAs are computed for each REIT at the close of each trading day, these ROAs are regressed across all REITs onto the REITs' holdings percentages of their property assets broken out by the target segments. For example, suppose investors are interested in computing SMPPIs for mutually exclusive and exhaustive geographic regions: East, South, Midwest, and West. The next step is to determine the percentage of each REIT's property assets that is in each of those four regions. The ROAs are regressed onto those percentages. The resulting regression estimated coefficient on each region's holdings shares represents the stock market's implied ROA for that region for that day, according to the basic REIT linear return model (akin to a weighted average cost of capital, or WACC) shown in Equation 11.1:

$$\mathrm{ROA}_{i,t} = b_{E,t}X_{i,E,t} + b_{S,t}X_{i,S,t} + b_{M,t}X_{i,M,t} + b_{W,t}X_{i,W,t} \tag{11.1}$$

where the X_i values are REIT i's shares of its property assets in each of the four regions ($\Sigma X = 1$), and the b values are the estimated coefficients representing the estimated ROAs to the four regions (e.g., $b_{E,t}$ is the estimated ROA to the East Region in day t).

The mathematics of this regression are such that in the process of estimating the REIT holdings coefficients (the b values), the regression actually produces a specification of the "pure-play portfolios." These are combinations of long and short positions in the REITs such that the portfolio has complete 100 percent exposure to the target segment and zero net exposure to any other segment, under the linear return model of Equation 11.1. Indeed, the regression procedure produces the most "efficient" such portfolio, the one that minimizes the idiosyncratic volatility in the portfolio.

As a simple example of such a pure-play portfolio, consider Exhibit 11.9. Suppose REIT X has property assets consisting of 75 percent office properties and 25 percent industrial properties, by value. Such data are now compiled and available from several sources in the industry. Suppose another REIT, labeled Y, has property holdings that are 25 percent office and 75 percent industrial. For simplicity, assume neither REIT has any debt. As the calculations in Exhibit 11.9 show, a

Example of Pure-PlayTarget Portfolio

- Two target segments: Office & Industrial; Returns = RO, RI.
- Two firms: **REIT X** & **REIT Y**; Returns = RX, RY.
- Both firms with no debt and no investment other than in properties.

Suppose: **REIT X**: 75% Office, 25% Industrial: $RX = (3/4)RO + (1/4)RI$

REIT Y: 25% Office, 75% Industrial: $RY = (1/4)RO + (3/4)RI$

Construct two portfolios:

- **Office** Portfolio: \$150 Long **REIT X** + (–\$50) Short **REIT Y**.
- **Industrial** Portfolio: (–\$50) Short **REIT X** + \$150 Long **REIT Y**.

Office Portfolio Return:

$$= \left(\tfrac{150}{100}\right)RX - \left(\tfrac{50}{100}\right)RY = \left(\tfrac{150}{100}\right)\left(\tfrac{3}{4}RO + \tfrac{1}{4}RI\right) - \left(\tfrac{50}{100}\right)\left(\tfrac{1}{4}RO + \tfrac{3}{4}RI\right)$$

$$= \left(\left(\tfrac{150}{100}\right)\left(\tfrac{3}{4}\right) - \left(\tfrac{50}{100}\right)\left(\tfrac{1}{4}\right)\right)RO + \left(\left(\tfrac{150}{100}\right)\left(\tfrac{1}{4}\right) - \left(\tfrac{50}{100}\right)\left(\tfrac{3}{4}\right)\right)RI$$

$$= \left(\left(\tfrac{9}{8}\right) - \left(\tfrac{1}{8}\right)\right)RO + \left(\left(\tfrac{3}{8}\right) - \left(\tfrac{3}{8}\right)\right)RI = (1)RO + (0)RI = RO. \leftarrow \text{Pure Office}$$

Industrial Portfolio Return:

$$= -\left(\tfrac{50}{100}\right)RX + \left(\tfrac{150}{100}\right)RY = -\left(\tfrac{50}{100}\right)\left(\tfrac{3}{4}RO + \tfrac{1}{4}RI\right) + \left(\tfrac{150}{100}\right)\left(\tfrac{1}{4}RO + \tfrac{3}{4}RI\right)$$

$$= \left(-\left(\tfrac{3}{8}\right) + \left(\tfrac{3}{8}\right)\right)RO + \left(-\left(\tfrac{1}{8}\right) + \left(\tfrac{9}{8}\right)\right)RI = (0)RO + (1)RI = RI. \leftarrow \text{Pure Indust}$$

Exhibit 11.9 Example of a Pure-Play Target Portfolio
This exhibit provides a simple example of a pure-play portfolio.

portfolio consisting of a 150 percent (long) position in REIT X and a negative 50 percent (short) position in REIT Y will have complete exposure to the office segment and zero net exposure to the industrial segment. In other words, per dollar of the portfolio investment, one sells short \$0.50 worth of REIT Y and uses the proceeds from that short sale combined with the portfolio net investment to buy (long) \$1.50 worth of REIT X. This long and short combined position is the office pure-play portfolio. The return to this portfolio will track the return to the office segment, as evaluated by the stock market's pricing of REIT X and REIT Y shares. Therefore, the return to this pure play portfolio represents the SMPRI index for the office sector. This is the essence of how pure-play target portfolios and SMPRI indices are constructed. As noted, the pure-play portfolio weights are actually derived from the regression noted previously, based on the model in Equation 11.1.

Stock Market–Based Indices as Information Products

The most basic use of SMPRI returns is as information products that provide an important third perspective about commercial property price evolution, on top of appraisal-based and transaction-based indices from the private property market. Exhibit 11.10 compares the FTSE NAREIT PureProperty composite capital return index with the three indices previously described in earlier sections. The PureProperty Index describes the same general price history at the big picture level as the other three indices. But the stock market–based PureProperty Index tends to lead the private market based indices in the timing of the major turning points in the cycle. The PureProperty Index is updated daily, whereas the private market–based indices are updated monthly or quarterly. The PureProperty Index also appears to show greater short-run volatility and to exhibit some transient price movements

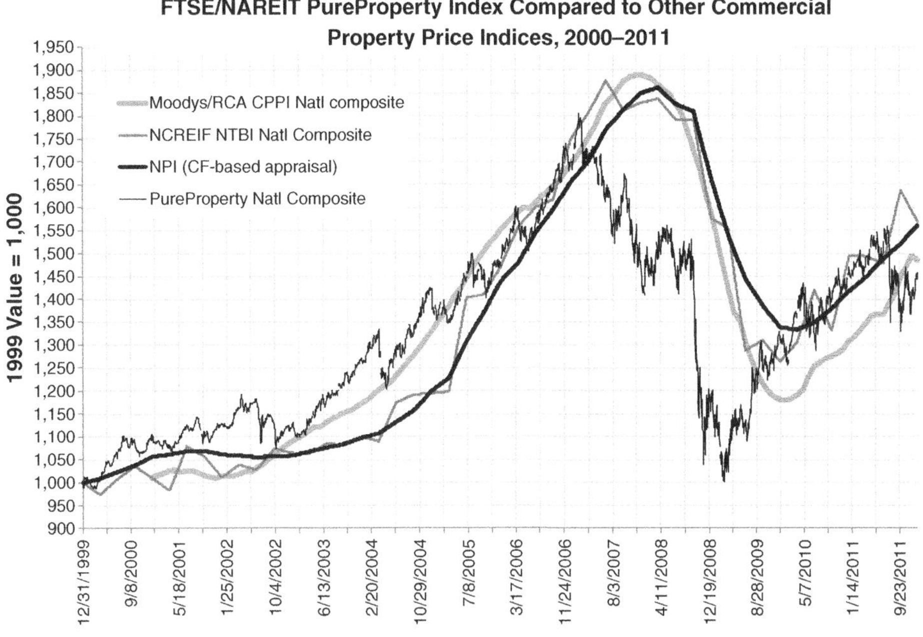

Exhibit 11.10 Adding the Stock Market Perspective, the FTSE/NAREIT PureProperty Index

This exhibit compares the FTSE NAREIT PureProperty composite capital return index with other commercial property prices indices.
Data sources: Moody's Investors Service, NCREIF, FTSE.

that are not echoed in the private market–based indices. However, by controlling for frequency of information updating (e.g., by reporting the PureProperty Index only at the end of every quarter or year), then the PureProperty index would have about the same volatility as the transaction-based private market indices over the 2000–2011 period examined.

As noted previously, another advantage of SMPRIs is that they can measure total investment return as well as capital returns. Exhibit 11.11 shows this relationship for four major geographic regional indices, comparing the cumulative total return of the PureProperty Index with that of the corresponding transaction-based NTBI. All the charts use the same scale, which facilitates seeing how the stock market–based and NCREIF-based indices trace the same long-run result. For example, the East and West regions had higher overall return trends than the South and Midwest regions during the 2000–2012 period, in both the NCREIF-based and the stock market–based indices. Yet, the stock market based index leads and provides much more frequent information updating.

Stock Market–Based Indices as Trading Products

A final point worth noting about SMPRIs is that, in addition to being information products, they may serve more readily as trading and investment products.

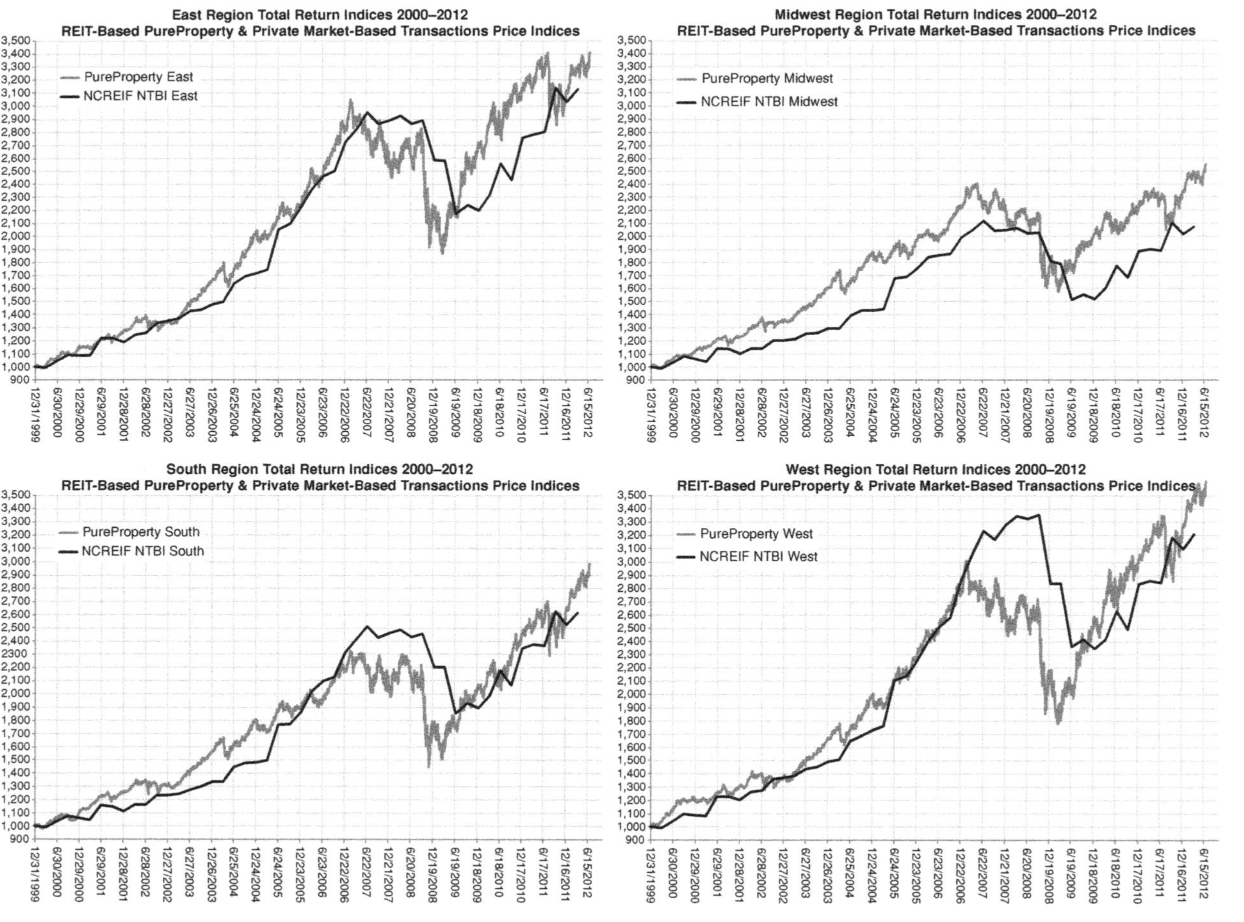

Exhibit 11.11 Cumulative Total Returns of FTSE NAREIT PureProperty Indices Compared to NCREIF NTBI for Four Regional Target Segments, 2000–2012

This exhibit shows this relationship for four major geographic regional indices, comparing the cumulative total return of the PureProperty Index with that of the corresponding transaction-based NTBI. Data sources: FTSE and NCREIF.

This is because SMPRIs are based on the aforementioned pure-play portfolios of actively traded REIT stocks. Thus, in principle, the indices can be replicated by cash-funded portfolios such as exchange traded funds (ETFs). The private property market–based indices presented earlier cannot be so exactly duplicated by any directly investable product. Of course, in principle, contracts can be written and traded based on any information product, including private market–based indices, thus allowing purely synthetic trading of commercial property. But such purely synthetic trading presents greater challenges because synthetic contracts usually must be traded over the counter, with all positions exactly matched by offsetting opposite-party positions. This may involve matching difficulties, high trading costs, and possibly counterparty credit risk. Even in the synthetic arena, SMPRIs have advantages, because daily updating reduces the magnitude of margin requirements for traders and the stock market–based pricing of the underlying index facilitates accurate pricing (or "marking to market") of the derivative products.

Using commercial property price or return indices as tradable or investment products could theoretically benefit commercial property investors and improve the efficiency of the entire commercial property asset market in the process. Such trading could allow short sales of real estate, hedging of unwanted "beta" (market risk) exposure, as well as facilitating rapid and efficient portfolio adjustment and rebalancing. In general, investors would be presented with the possibility of investing effectively in commercial property at lower transaction and management cost than through traditional direct private market mechanisms, with greater liquidity, and based on daily pricing derived from the generally more informationally efficient stock market. Yet, the investment is freed from REIT financing and leverage policies and can be more precisely targeted at commercial property sectors or regions.

SUMMARY AND CONCLUSIONS

The previous sections have presented and reviewed three different types and sources of commercial property price or return indices, which address the key challenge in real estate investment performance measurement. The three types of indices included: (1) the traditional appraisal-based indices, (2) the new and still rapidly developing transaction-based indices, and (3) the even newer stock market–based indices that may offer exciting opportunities for the investment industry in this decade. Each of these types of indices has different strengths and weaknesses. Although in some uses a single index or type of index may suffice, employing at least two, if not all three, of the types of indices could be desirable. Not unlike a surveyor "triangulating" on a location to be fixed on a map or plan, each of the three indices can present a useful perspective about commercial property price dynamics and investment performance.

DISCUSSION QUESTIONS

1. Identify the three major types of commercial property price or return indices and their basic sources of asset price data or information.

2. Suppose news relevant to property value arrives at a certain point in time. Identify and explain the order in time that news is likely to be reflected in the three types of indices.
3. Explain how the meaning of "capital return" differs in the traditional official NCREIF Property Index, repeat-sales transaction-based indices, and stock market–based indices.
4. How can tradability or investability in a price or return index be useful for the real estate investment industry? Why are stock market–based indices advantageous in theory for serving such a role?

REFERENCES

Adelman, Irma, and Zvi Griliches. 1961. "On an Index of Quality Change." *Journal of the American Statistical Association* 56:295, 535–548.

Ang, Andrew, Neil Nabar and Samuel Wald. 2012. "Searching for a Common Factor in Public and Private Real Estate Returns." Working Paper, Columbia Business School, New York.

Bailey, Martin, Richard Muth, and Hugh Nourse. 1963. "A Regression Method for Real Estate Price Index Construction." *Journal of the American Statistical Association* 58:304, 933–942.

Barkham, Richard, and David Geltner. 1995. "Price Discovery in American and British Property Markets." *Real Estate Economics* 23:1, 21–44.

Case, Karl, and Robert Shiller. 1987. "Prices of Single Family Homes since 1970: New Indexes for Four Cities." *New England Economic Review*, September/October, 45–56.

Court, Andrew T. 1939. "Hedonic Price Indices with Automotive Examples." In *The Dynamics of Automobile Demand*, 99–117. New York: General Motors Corporation.

Cullen, Ian, Mark Clacy-Jones, and Steven Devaney. 2012. "The Use of Valuations and Transactions in Measuring Commercial Property Market Cycles." Presentation to the Eurostat/ECB International Conference on Commercial Property Price Indicators, Frankfurt, Germany, May, 2012.

Florance, Andrew, Norman Miller, Jay Spivey, and Ruijue Peng. 2010. "Slicing, Dicing, and Scoping the Size of the U.S. Real Estate Market." *Journal of Real Estate Portfolio Management* 16:2, 111–128.

Geltner, David, and Brian Kluger. 1998. "REIT-Based Pure-Play Portfolios: The Case of Property Types." *Real Estate Economics* 26:4, 581–612.

Geltner, David, Bryan MacGregor, and Greg Schwann. 2003. "Appraisal Smoothing & Price Discovery in Real Estate Markets." *Urban Studies* 40:5–6, 1047–1064.

Gyourko, Joe, and Donald Keim. 1992. "What Does the Stock Market Tell Us about Real Estate Returns?" *Real Estate Economics* 20:3, 457–486.

Horrigan, Holly, Bradford Case, David Geltner, and Henry Pollakowski. 2009. "REIT-Based Property Return Indices: A New Way to Track & Trade Commercial Real Estate." *Journal of Portfolio Management* 35:5, 80–91.

Iezman, Stanley. 2011. "Complying with ERISA: A Primer for Pension Plan Trustees." Available at *QPAM.com* American Realty Advisors.

Rosen, Sherwin. 1974. "Hedonic Prices and Implicit Markets: Product Differentiation in Pure Competition." *Journal of Political Economy* 82:1, 34–55.

ABOUT THE AUTHOR

David Geltner is Professor of Real Estate Finance in the Department of Urban Studies and Planning, School of Architecture & Planning at the Massachusetts

Institute of Technology. He has been teaching real estate investments for over 20 years and is the lead author of a major graduate text in the subject, *Commercial Real Estate Analysis & Investments* (OnCourse). He is a winner of the PREA Graaskamp Award and the ARES Ricardo Medal, for research excellence and influence, and currently chairs MIT's Master of Science in Real Estate Development program. He received his PhD in Civil Engineering from MIT in 1989.

PART III

Private Equity

CHAPTER 12

Venture Capital

TOM VANACKER
Assistant Professor, Department of Accountancy and Corporate Finance, Ghent University

SOPHIE MANIGART
Professor, Department of Accountancy and Corporate Finance, Ghent University; Vlerick Business School

INTRODUCTION

Although private equity currently represents a major component of the alternative investment universe (European Venture Capital and Private Equity Association, 2004; Metrick and Yasuda, 2011), its function is not always well understood. *Private equity* refers to unregistered equity and equity-linked securities sold by private and sometimes public companies or partnerships to financial buyers. It encompasses an array of investment activities, including venture capital, buyout financing, or restructuring capital. *Venture capital* is hence a subset of private equity and specifically refers to equity or equity-linked investments made for the launch, early growth, or expansion of companies. It is distinctive from *buyout*, which refers to investments in more mature companies with established business plans to acquire equity stakes from existing shareholders such as families or corporations (European Venture Capital and Private Equity Association, 2004). This chapter exclusively deals with venture capital, thereby leaving the discussion of buyout investments for Chapter 14.

Driven by technological developments in information and communication technology (ICT), the Internet, and biotechnology, the venture capital industry experienced extraordinary growth over the last two decades and is now broadly accepted as an established asset class within many institutional portfolios worldwide (European Venture Capital and Private Equity Association, 2004). Funds committed to venture capital in the United States increased dramatically from $2.3 billion in 1990 to a record of $104.8 billion in 2000. While the burst of the Internet bubble halted this phenomenal development, funds committed to venture capital still equaled $12.3 billion in 2010 (National Venture Capital Association, 2011). Similar trends are observed in Europe and Australasia, where venture capital markets have grown substantially. For instance, Ahlstrom, Bruton, and Yeh (2007) point out that China represents one of the fastest growing venture capital markets in the world. Additionally, while the venture capital industry had long been a local industry, the last decade has witnessed a remarkable growth in the flows of venture capital worldwide (Alhorr, Moore, and Payne, 2008; Manigart, De Prijcker, and Bose, 2010; Meuleman and Wright, 2011). As local markets become increasingly competitive, venture capital investors have broadened their geographic investment criteria to include overseas companies to increase their portfolio diversification and to search for higher returns. In Europe, for instance, the share of inflows of venture capital from nondomestic sources was just over 50 percent of the market between 2005 and 2009, and the share of total outflows accounted for by cross-border investments equaled close to 35 percent of the market over the same time period (European Venture Capital and Private Equity Association, 2010).

This chapter provides a review of the academic literature on venture capital. Although it does not minimize the importance of the numerous research papers that have studied various aspects of venture capital, the chapter emphasizes the following key questions:

- Why do venture capital markets exist?
- What are the different venture capital models?
- What do venture capital investors do?
- How do venture capital–backed companies perform?
- How does venture capital as an asset class create value for investors?

Sahlman (1990), Barry (1994), Berger and Udell (1998), Wright and Robbie (1998), and Metrick and Yasuda (2011) provide some excellent surveys on venture capital. This review of the literature is distinctive from these previous studies in that it combines insights from the largely fragmented finance, entrepreneurship, and management literatures.

WHY DO VENTURE CAPITAL MARKETS EXIST?

Evidence on the financing of entrepreneurial companies indicates that most of their financing needs are addressed by traditional sources of financing, such as internal finance (including retained profits and owner funds) and bank finance (e.g., Berger and Udell, 1998; Ou and Haynes, 2006; Brav, 2009; Cosh, Cumming, and Hughes, 2009; Vanacker and Manigart, 2010). One of the most fundamental questions to ask is why entrepreneurial companies need a specialized set of investors such as venture capital firms. Put differently, why do venture capital firms exist as separate financial intermediaries? Venture capital investors have a comparative advantage over traditional financing sources, such as banks and public equity investors, in working in environments characterized by high information asymmetry and high uncertainty (Chan, 1983; Amit, Brander, and Zott, 1998). The main reason venture capital firms exist is their superior ability both to reduce the cost of informational asymmetry related to investing in entrepreneurial companies and to display investment strategies that allow them to cope with high uncertainty.

Two types of informational asymmetry may arise in an entrepreneur–investor relationship: hidden information and hidden action (Amit et al., 1998). *Hidden information* refers to the fact that parties hold different information. A classic example of hidden information is the lemons problem (Akerlof, 1970). In the market of used cars, for instance, well-informed sellers generally have more information on the quality of their cars compared to less-informed buyers, who can only assess the average quality of cars on the market. Given the information disadvantage of buyers, they are only willing to pay the price charged for average-quality cars. But sellers of above-average quality cars have no incentive to sell at average prices and withdraw from the market, thereby lowering the average quality of the cars still offered for sale. *Hidden action* refers to the fact that parties cannot fully observe each other's behavior. A classic example of hidden action is the behavior of car insurance buyers (Pauly, 1968). Insurance companies cannot force owners to be careful because car owners' actions are largely unobservable. Insurance buyers, however, will act in their own self-interest and probably neglect the interest of insurance sellers, for example, by not caring about their cars as much as they would in the case they were not insured.

Outside financiers are also confronted with problems originating from hidden information or hidden action when they invest in young, entrepreneurial companies. In the venture capital context, adverse selection pertains to the risk that outside investors select low-quality projects, which have been presented to them as high-quality projects (Amit et al., 1998). Entrepreneurs, by virtue of being intimately involved in their companies, are likely to possess superior information about the prospects of their companies (hidden information). Entrepreneurs generally have an incentive to misrepresent any superior information they possess to their advantage when searching for financing. To decrease the risk of adverse selection, venture capital investors engage in extensive information collection in a preinvestment due diligence process. The processes and instruments to reduce information asymmetries used by more traditional investors, such as banks, are insufficient to overcome hidden information problems in the context of investing in young companies. The screening process of banks, for instance, focuses mainly on historical financial information, but such information is not always available, let alone positive, for young companies (Rosman and O'Neill, 1993; Berger and Udell, 1998). Furthermore, banks typically use collateral to deal with information problems (Berger and Udell, 1998), but young companies with high potential often lack assets that may serve as collateral because their investments are often in research and development (R&D), and hence intangible in nature (Carpenter and Petersen, 2002). In contrast, venture capital investors perform extensive due diligence before investing in order to reduce hidden information problems, focusing on the entrepreneurial team, the technology, and product-market characteristics. Companies raising venture capital consequently have little collateral, are characterized by high growth but high risk, and have high prospects of profitability (Ueda, 2004; Heughebaert, Vanacker, and Manigart, 2012).

Besides adverse-selection problems, outside investors are confronted with hidden action problems because they cannot perfectly observe the effort and actions of entrepreneurs. This situation may lead to moral-hazard problems, especially if the goals of entrepreneurs and investors are not perfectly aligned. After the investment, for instance, entrepreneurs may shirk effort or invest in their favorite or pet projects in order to achieve private, nonmonetary benefits at the expense of outside investors. Venture capital investors have a comparative advantage over banks to reduce moral-hazard problems. Banks provide debt finance that involves a fixed claim, which is restricted to interest and principal payments. This relationship gives banks limited incentives to monitor their creditors (Winton and Yerramilli, 2008).

Venture capital investors, however, typically provide equity and equity-linked securities that entail a claim on the company's residual wealth creation. Consequently, venture capital investors have more powerful incentives to tightly monitor their portfolio companies than banks, thereby reducing the risk of hidden action because their return potential depends on company value creation. Taking the above differences between venture capital investors and banks into account, Winton and Yerramilli (2008) contend that raising venture capital finance rather than bank debt is optimal for companies facing high risk and positively skewed cash flows and those with a low probability of success and low liquidation value. Finally, venture capital investors write complex contracts that mainly serve to align the goals of entrepreneurs and investors, thereby further reducing agency risks (Kaplan and Strömberg, 2004; Cumming, 2008; Cumming and Johan, 2008).

Overall, venture capital investors fill an important void in the financing of young, entrepreneurial companies. Their comparative advantage over other investors, such as banks, relates to their relative efficiency in selecting and monitoring investments characterized by high informational asymmetries and high uncertainty and in writing adequate contracts.

THE DIFFERENT VENTURE CAPITAL MODELS

Exhibit 12.1 shows the typical players and their interactions in the most common dual-structure venture capital firms. Limited partnerships (LPs) contribute funds to a venture capital fund, and general partners (GPs) may also provide a small

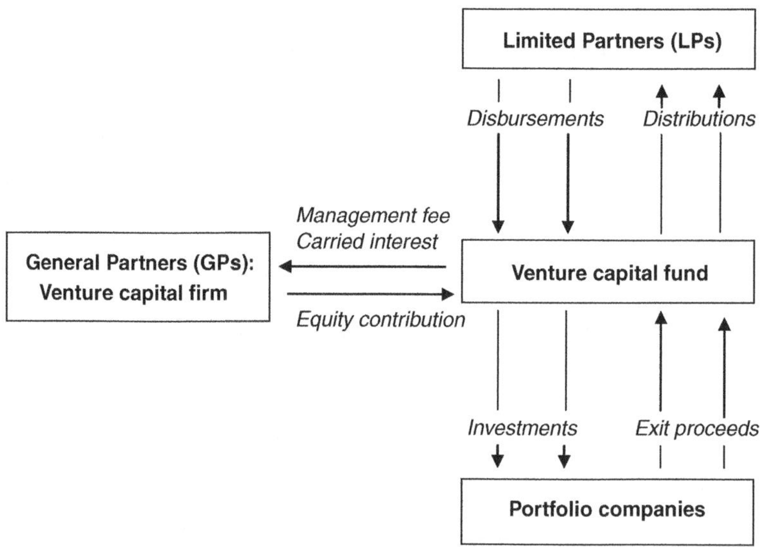

Exhibit 12.1 The Dual-Structure Venture Capital Model

This exhibit depicts the typical venture capital model. A venture capital firm is usually organized in a dual model as a limited partnership managing legally independent venture capital funds (Sahlman, 1990; Sammut, 2011), with venture capitalists serving as general partners (GPs) and their investors as limited partners (LPs).

Source: Based on Ooghe, Deloof, and Manigart (2003) and Sammut (2011).

equity contribution. These funds are subsequently invested in entrepreneurial companies. When exits are realized in the portfolio companies of a venture capital fund, the proceeds are distributed to the LPs. GPs generally manage several funds for which they obtain management fees and potentially a carried interest on realized capital gains.

LPs typically include institutional investors, such as banks, insurance companies, and pension funds, but also governments, sovereign wealth funds, corporations, family offices (which manage funds of wealthy families), and private individuals (European Venture Capital and Private Equity Association, 2004, 2007). Importantly, LPs cannot participate in the active management of venture capital funds if their liability is to be limited to the amount of their commitments. From an investor's perspective, two main alternatives are available for investing in venture capital besides investing in venture capital funds (European Venture Capital and Private Equity Association, 2004): (1) direct investments in private companies and (2) outsourcing the selection of venture capital funds through investing in funds of funds. Direct investments in private companies require more capital to achieve similar diversification as investing in venture capital funds. Additionally, direct investments in venture capital require a different skill set, which LPs in venture capital funds typically lack. Investors in funds of funds further need to realize that another layer of management fees and expenses is involved, but institutional investors thereby reduce their cost of selecting and managing their investments in different venture capital funds.

Most venture capital firms are organized as management companies responsible for managing several pools of capital, each representing a legally separate limited partnership. The economic life of most funds is 10 years, although provisions are often included to extend the life of the funds by 2 years (Sahlman, 1990; Sammut, 2011). As Sammut notes, each new fund typically moves through various stages. In the investment period stage, usually from year one to year four, the investment portfolio is formed. First-round investments are made in entrepreneurial companies, and intense value-adding activities are provided. Second-round investments to the earliest deals in the portfolio may also occur during this stage. In the fund maturity stage, normally from year three to year seven, follow-on financing rounds are provided to the portfolio companies in order to further support their growth. Some exits may already occur at this stage. Finally, in the harvest or liquidation stage, generally from year five to the end of a fund's life, fund managers are fully focused on exiting their investments.

The most likely exit routes include the sale of investments to other companies in the industry or to the company's own management team in a buyout structure. Another exit mechanism, typically reserved for the most successful portfolio companies, is an initial public offering (IPO). Failures also remain very common. As Puri and Zarutskie (2012) show, almost 40 percent of U.S. venture capital–backed companies created between 1981 and 2005 failed, some 34 percent were acquired, and 16 percent went public. The remaining companies were "living death" companies whose equity stakes were difficult to sell.

The compensation of venture capitalists plays a critical role in aligning their interests with those of the LPs (Sahlman, 1990). A rather homogenous compensation system has emerged within the venture capital industry, including management fees and carried interest (European Venture Capital and Private

Equity Association, 2004; Sammut, 2011). GPs receive an annual management fee of approximately 1.5 to 2.5 percent of total capital committed or total amount invested. These fees serve to pay salaries and to cover due diligence and other costs incurred to manage the fund. Such fees often decrease over a fund's lifetime as the efforts devoted to managing a fund and its portfolio companies decrease over time. Successful venture capital investors are expected to raise follow-on funds with new fee streams every three to five years. In order to align the interests of LPs and GPs, GPs typically have a carried interest of 20 percent. This implies that GPs obtain 20 percent of the capital gains realized by the fund. The carried interest is often only applicable if the LPs realize a minimum return, or *hurdle*. For successful funds, the carried interest outweighs the management fees.

Although the LP organizational form, as previously described, dominates the venture capital industry, other important venture capital models exist that have received comparatively little scrutiny from scholars (Manigart and Wright, 2012). First, listed investment firms obtain most of their capital from the stock exchange. An increasing number of private equity firms (e.g., 3i in the United Kingdom and Gimv in Belgium), partnerships, and funds are quoted on stock exchanges. Because some investors cannot invest in unquoted securities, quoted funds are a good option to invest in this asset class. An important distinction between quoted funds and the more common privately held funds is the limited ability of quoted funds to return cash to investors. More specifically, when cash is realized from exiting portfolio companies, the cash typically remains inside the quoted fund and hence dilutes its return until the cash can be reinvested (European Venture Capital and Private Equity Association, 2004). This arrangement is distinctive from privately held funds, where investors allocate cash as needed to make new investments. Further, as portfolio companies mature and privately held funds realize exits, they immediately distribute the exit proceeds to the LPs. Such distinctions are important when considering the return realized by public versus privately held funds. Another distinction is that many quoted private equity or venture capital firms are *evergreen firms*; that is, they have no explicit liquidation date, in contrast with the typical 10-year lifespan of unquoted venture capital firms.

Second, in captive funds one shareholder (e.g., a bank, an insurance company, an industrial company, or a family office) contributes most of the capital. A parent organization allocates money to the fund from its own internal sources. Banks often seek complementarities between their venture capital and their lending activities. For example, Hellmann, Lindsey, and Puri (2008) show that when banks have a prior relationship with a company in the venture capital market, this increases their likelihood of subsequently granting a loan to that company at more favorable prices. In a similar vein, corporate venture capital funds are not only interested in financial returns, but also in getting a "window on technology." Hence, they search investments in sectors relevant to their core activities in order to identify new technologies (Dushnitsky and Lenox, 2005).

WHAT DO VENTURE CAPITAL INVESTORS DO?

The previous section provided a brief overview of how venture capital firms are typically structured. This section elaborates on what venture capitalists do and

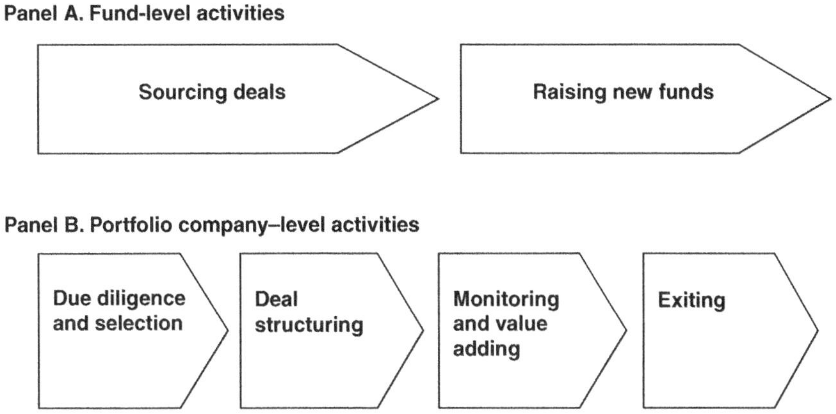

Panel A. Fund-level activities

Sourcing deals

Raising new funds

Panel B. Portfolio company–level activities

Due diligence and selection

Deal structuring

Monitoring and value adding

Exiting

Exhibit 12.2 The Venture Capital Firm Value Chain

The most common dual structure in which venture capital firms engage comprises two broad categories of activities. Panel A shows fund-level activities, including fundraising and deal sourcing. Panel B portrays portfolio company–level activities, including due diligence and selection, deal structuring, monitoring and value adding, and exiting.

Source: Based on Fried and Hisrich (1994) and Sammut (2011).

how they claim to create value for their portfolio companies and their investors. Exhibit 12.2 summarizes the venture capital firm value chain.

This section focuses on the most common dual-structure venture capital firms. Two categories of activities are distinguished: (1) fund-level activities, including fundraising and deal sourcing; and (2) portfolio company–level activities, including due diligence and selection, deal structuring, monitoring and value adding, and exiting.

Fundraising

Fundraising is the first activity that all new venture capital firms perform. Successful venture capital investors typically do not manage a single venture capital fund, but they engage in fundraising activities to establish a new venture capital fund some three to five years after the start of their previous fund (Sahlman, 1990). What determines fundraising activities at the venture capital industry level? Gompers and Lerner (1998) study industry-aggregate, state-level, and firm-specific fundraising to determine if macroeconomic, regulatory, or performance factors affect venture capital activity in the United States. Supply-side effects, such as the easing of pension investment restrictions or the overall performance of the venture capital industry, and shifts in demand for venture capital, for example originating from technological breakthroughs or R&D investments, have a positive impact on fundraising levels. Interestingly, commitments by taxable and tax-exempt investors seem equally sensitive to changes in capital gains tax rates, which is consistent with the notion that decreases in capital gain taxes increase the demand for venture capital, as more people are incentivized to become entrepreneurs. Finally, as Gompers and Lerner note, venture capital firm characteristics, such as their reputation, also lead to more fundraising.

Differences across countries in venture capital fundraising have traditionally largely been attributed to the development of their stock markets. Black and Gilson (1998) maintain that venture capital flourishes especially and perhaps only when venture capitalists can exit from successful portfolio companies through IPOs, which, in turn, requires an active stock market. Jeng and Wells (2000), who analyze the determinants of venture capital investments using a sample of 21 countries, also find that IPOs are the strongest driver of venture capital investing. However, different types of venture capital are affected differently. In particular, early stage venture capital investing is negatively affected by labor market rigidities, whereas later-stage venture capital investing is not. IPOs have no effect on early stage venture capital investing but are a major determinant of later-stage venture capital investing across countries. More recently, Groh, von Liechtenstein, and Lieser (2010) show that although investor protection and capital markets are important determinants in explaining the attractiveness of 27 European countries for institutional investments in the venture capital and private equity asset class, numerous other criteria exist. Survey evidence by Groh and von Liechtenstein (2011), for instance, indicates that the protection of property rights is a dominant concern of institutional investors, followed by the need to find local quality GPs and the quality of management and skills of local entrepreneurs. Interestingly, IPO activity and the size of local public equity markets are not as relevant as proposed by early scholars.

Deal Sourcing

Once a venture capital fund is established, a second challenge is to secure an adequate flow of high-quality business proposals to evaluate. Nevertheless, relatively little academic research focuses on this aspect of the venture capital investment cycle. Matching venture capital investors with entrepreneurs is difficult because the venture capital market is not transparent. From a venture capital fund's perspective, having access to the best propositions is essential. This access may be problematic for newly established venture capital firms given that entrepreneurs prefer to team up with investors with a strong reputation (Hsu, 2004). From an entrepreneur's perspective, Kirsch, Goldfarb, and Gera (2006) clearly demonstrate the importance of referrals. In a sample of 1,063 business plans submitted to a single venture capital investor, 277 business plans were unsolicited, but none of these unsolicited proposals received funding.

Rather than generating their own deal flow, funds may attract investment proposals through their network of coinvestors or syndicate partners. Given the dominance of syndication in the venture capital market (Lerner, 1994; Wright and Lockett, 2003), obtaining a high-quality level of deal flow may depend on being able to enter syndication networks (Yung, 2012). Prior research contends that venture capital investors are more likely to collaborate with other venture capital investors they know from prior investments, as this provides information about their specific capabilities and reliability (Hallen, 2008; Meuleman, Lockett, Manigart, and Wright, 2010). Experienced investors, by virtue of being actively involved in the venture capital industry, have more ties to other venture capital investors and have more legitimacy, allowing them to enter more syndicate relationships (Hopp, 2010). Less clear is how new venture capital investors obtain central positions in syndication networks and thereby secure access to adequate deal flow.

Selection and Due Diligence

Venture capital investors are extremely selective. Although large venture capital funds may receive hundreds of investment proposals annually, they eventually invest in a portfolio of only 15 to 25 companies over a five-year period. Many investment proposals do not receive more than a few minutes of attention from venture capital investors. A quick screening ascertains whether an investment proposal fits with the general investment criteria of the venture capital fund (Fried and Hisrich, 1994). Some venture capital investors, for instance, specialize in certain investment stages (e.g., seed, early stage, or development), certain industries (e.g., biotechnology, ICT, or retail), or certain geographic regions. Others, however, prefer a more generalist approach (Norton and Tenenbaum, 1993). As an entrepreneur, understanding the basic investment criteria of the targeted venture capital investors is important in order to increase the odds of successfully moving beyond their early selection filter. For example, targeting a venture capital investor with a stated preference for later-stage deals by an entrepreneur of a young company is pointless.

Proposals that pass the initial screening are subjected to in-depth due diligence before an investment decision is made. How venture capital investors decide on which investment proposals they will invest has been a major research topic since the emergence of academic research on venture capital. Based on questionnaire evidence, MacMillan, Siegel, and Subba Narasimha (1985, p. 119) state that "irrespective of the horse (product), horse race (market), or odds (financial criteria), it is the jockey (entrepreneur) who fundamentally determines whether the venture capitalist will place a bet at all." Venture capital investors are not always successful in selecting the best entrepreneurial companies. Extant research shows that venture capital investors are overconfident in selecting the "right" investment (Zacharakis and Meyer, 2000; Zacharakis and Shepherd, 2001). Venture capital investors are further known to exhibit a local bias. They mostly prefer to invest in companies within their home market, because this arrangement eases information transfer, which benefits identifying investment targets, evaluating these ventures, and postinvestment monitoring and value adding (Cumming and Dai, 2010).

Nevertheless, multiple scholars contend that no single hierarchy of decision criteria exists across all venture capital investors (Muzyka, Birley, and Leleux, 1996). Rather, venture capital investors differ on the selection criteria that matter most to them. Knockaert, Clarysse, and Wright (2010), for instance, identify differences in importance attached to selection criteria in a sample of early stage high-tech venture capital investors. Specifically, whereas some venture capital investors are more likely to focus on management team characteristics, others primarily focus on technological criteria, and still others focus mainly on financial criteria when evaluating investment proposals.

Kaplan, Sensoy, and Strömberg (2009) study 50 venture capital–backed companies that eventually went public and hence could be described as successful investments. They show that while business lines remain relatively stable from early business plan to IPO, changes to the management team occur frequently. According to the authors, this finding suggests that the business or technology, rather than the management team, should be the key criterion used by venture capital investors on which to base their investment decisions.

In studies on the selection behavior of venture capital investors, a typical assumption is that venture capital investors are the most powerful actors, while entrepreneurs are more or less passive. However, more recently, scholars contend and show that venture capital investing is a multistage investment process where entrepreneurs may also play a key role in determining the identity of their investors. Eckhardt, Shane, and Delmar (2006), for instance, maintain that entrepreneurs must first be willing to raise outside financing before venture capital investors can select from the pool of entrepreneurial companies that are willing to raise outside financing. Further, entrepreneurs receiving multiple financing offers from venture capital investors select among competing investors based upon their reputation rather than relying on purely financial criteria (Hsu, 2004).

Recently, Hallen and Eisenhardt (2012) identify two equifinal paths for how entrepreneurs are able to raise venture capital finance. One path relies on existing strong direct ties, but this path is only available to privileged companies founded by well-networked entrepreneurs or to companies with a venture capital fund in its institutional environment, such as university spin-off funds (Vanacker, Manigart, and Meuleman, forthcoming). The other path relies on using catalyzing strategies (i.e., a means by which entrepreneurs advantageously shape opportunities and inducements to form ties).

Valuation and Contracting

A key challenge for venture capital investors is to determine the value of entrepreneurial companies or, alternatively, the percentage of equity capital they want in return for their investment (Heughebaert and Manigart, 2012). The valuation of an entrepreneurial company is in essence the same as the valuation of any other economic good: It is the sum of the present value of all future cash flows that will be generated for the investor. Nevertheless, high levels of uncertainty and the optionlike character of many entrepreneurial opportunities make the valuation of entrepreneurial companies especially challenging. This chapter, however, does not provide detailed insights into how investors value entrepreneurial companies. Readers interested in this specialized literature should consult Damodaran (2010).

The required return of venture capital investors is high compared to that of public investors. Venture capital investors want to be compensated not only for the systematic risk of their investment, but also for the illiquidity of their investment and for their active involvement in portfolio companies. For early stage deals, the average required return will be between 30 and 50 percent, while for expansion capital the average required return will be between 20 and 30 percent (Manigart, Wright, Robbie, Desbrières, and De Waele, 1997; Sammut, 2011). These return characteristics have important implications for the types of companies for which venture capital is a suitable source of financing. A required return of 50 percent entails that company value should be multiplied 7-fold five years after the investment and 17-fold seven years after the investment. This relationship suggests that venture capital is only a realistic and suitable financing option for entrepreneurial companies with high growth ambitions and potential. Puri and Zarutskie (2012), who find that venture capital–backed companies tend to be faster growing than peers that are not backed by venture capital, confirm this finding. However, the high ex-ante expected returns by venture capital investors are not necessarily realized ex-post. Rather, a few high-growth companies will have to compensate for the many failures in the portfolios of venture capital investors (Sahlman, 1990).

In addition to conducting valuation at the time of investment, venture capital investors write complex contracts that optimize both their cash flow rights and their control rights, thereby shifting risk to the entrepreneurs. An extensive literature is emerging on the contracts between venture capitalists and their portfolio companies. Two particular features of this contract, namely the use of convertible securities and staged financing, have drawn much attention. Using data on 213 venture capital investments in 119 portfolio companies by 14 U.S. venture capital firms, Kaplan and Strömberg (2003) show that convertible preferred stock is the most commonly used security, appearing in some 95 percent of finance rounds. Convertible preferred stock optimizes an entrepreneur's effort incentives (Schmidt, 2003). Cumming (2005a, 2005b) and Bottazzi, Rin, and Hellmann (2008), however, show that Canadian and European venture capital investors use a variety of securities. Bottazzi et al., for instance, show that instruments used for initial financing include common equity and warrants in 51 percent of portfolio companies. In other cases, straight debt, convertible debt, or preferred equity is used.

Staging implies that venture capital investors commit themselves to further invest if predefined milestones, which may be financial or nonfinancial (e.g., technical milestones), are met. Staging gives venture capitalists an option to abandon companies if they do not perform as expected. Staging is one of the strongest control mechanisms used by venture capitalists because it provides a powerful incentive for entrepreneurs to perform well (Sahlman, 1990). Using a sample including 2,143 equity finance rounds in 794 venture capital–backed companies for the period 1961 through 1992, Gompers (1995) shows that decreases in industry ratios of tangible assets to total assets, higher market-to-book ratios, and greater R&D intensities are associated with shorter funding durations and hence tighter control.

Monitoring and Value Adding

In order to reduce hidden action problems after the investment, venture capital investors are strongly engaged in their portfolio companies. The literature identifies three broad postinvestment activities: (1) monitoring, (2) assisting, and (3) certifying their portfolio companies. Gorman and Sahlman (1989) show that, on average, venture capital investors spend over half their time monitoring and assisting portfolio companies. Next to decreasing hidden action problems, their involvement is expected to further increase the return potential of their portfolio companies for several reasons.

First, venture capital investors actively monitor the progress of their portfolio companies. Such investors often require board seats, linked to veto rights and other contractual provisions, which allow them to influence the behavior of the entrepreneurs. Boards of directors in venture capital–backed companies are smaller and more involved in both strategy formation and evaluation than are boards where members do not have large ownership stakes (Fried, Bruton, and Hisrich, 1998). Lerner (1995) examines the representation of venture capitalists, as intensive monitors of managers, on the boards in their portfolio companies. He shows that venture capitalists' representation on the board increases around the time of chief executive officer (CEO) turnover. Moreover, the distance to the company is an important determinant of the board membership of venture capital investors.

Second, venture capital investors professionalize their portfolio companies and influence how their portfolio companies are run. Venture capital–backed companies are better able to add structure and experience to the management team compared to those not backed by venture capital (Beckman and Burton, 2008), including the development of human resource policies, the adoption of stock option plans (Hellmann and Puri, 2002) or the adoption of management accounting systems (Davila and Foster, 2005). As Hellman and Puri note, venture capital–backed companies are also more likely and faster to replace the founder with a professional CEO. Venture capital investors further bring valuable networks of contacts with suppliers, customers, financiers, and other stakeholders (Sapienza, Manigart, and Vermeir, 1996; Hochberg, Ljungqvist, and Lu, 2007).

Finally, even without being actively involved in their portfolio companies, the mere fact that a company can raise financing from venture capital investors may certify its quality to outsiders. For example, venture capital–backed companies can attract more employees compared to non-venture capital–backed companies in the Silicon Valley area (Davila, Foster, and Gupta, 2003). After controlling for portfolio company quality, Vanacker and Forbes (2012) show that Belgian companies backed by venture capital investors with more industry-specific experience can raise more follow-on (debt and equity) financing. Additionally, portfolio companies backed by venture capital investors with more media citations can attract more employees over time. Further, Megginson and Weiss (1991) find early support for the certification role of venture capitalists in IPOs: Venture capital backing resulted in significantly lower underpricing and gross spreads in the 1980s in the United States. Interestingly, this effect seems to have disappeared recently (Lee and Wahal, 2004), and is not found in IPOs in other parts of the world (e.g., da Silva Rosa, Velayuthen, and Walter, 2003, for Australia; Bruton, Chahine, and Filatotchev, 2009, for the United Kingdom; Elston and Yang, 2010, for Germany).

Since Gorman and Sahlman (1989), many studies have contributed to understanding the conditions under which venture capital investors engage in monitoring and value-adding activities. Prior research demonstrates that the involvement of venture capitalists in their portfolio companies depends upon a range of factors, including company characteristics such as agency risk (Sapienza 1992; Sapienza et al. 1996; Fredriksen, Olofsson, and Wahlbin, 1997), entrepreneurial characteristics (Sapienza 1992; Sapienza et al., 1996), investment manager characteristics (Sapienza et al., 1996; Dimov and Shepherd 2005; Bottazzi et al., 2008), venture capital fund and firm characteristics (Sorensen, 2007; Bottazzi et al. 2008), external conditions (Sapienza et al., 1996; Bruton, Fried, and Manigart, 2005), syndication (Brander, Amit, and Antweiler, 2002; De Clercq, Sapienza, and Zaheer, 2008), and the selection behavior of venture capital investors (Knockaert and Vanacker, 2012). Manigart and Wright (2012) provide a detailed review of this literature.

While the previous discussion highlights many positive aspects of venture capital investor involvement for portfolio companies, this should not necessarily be the case. Steier and Greenwood (1995), for instance, point toward some dark sides of venture capital involvement. By establishing milestones with tight time lines, venture capital investors themselves may paradoxically contribute to many of the delays experienced by startup companies. Moreover, Steier and Greenwood note that the operating logic of venture capital investors may be incompatible with the needs of startup companies. Further, venture capital investors or entrepreneurs may engage in unethical behavior, leading to the emergence of conflict in their relationship (Collewaert and Fassin, 2012).

Exit

The primary goal of venture capital investors is to generate returns from their investments by realizing an exit some three to seven years after the initial investment, thereby turning their illiquid stakes in private companies into realized returns (Gompers and Lerner, 2001). While scholars often use exit rates as a proxy for venture capital fund returns (discussed in more detail later in this section), care is needed. Hochberg et al. (2007), for instance, show that the correlation between exit rates and internal rates of return (IRRs) is only 0.42, thereby suggesting that exit rates are a useful but noisy proxy for IRRs. Consistent with the idea that venture capital investors operate in environments characterized by high informational asymmetries, exits are most likely to occur through sales to informed investors, including other companies in the industry or the company's own management team (Amit et al., 1998). Unfortunately, failures and liquidations also remain an important exit route. Puri and Zarutskie (2012) present evidence suggesting that venture capital investors heavily invest in all their portfolio companies for an initial period until they have a better sense of which ones will be the successes. Venture capital investors allow their portfolio companies to grow over a window, but once this period is over venture capital investors are just as likely to shut their firms down.

IPOs represent another less frequent but typically successful exit option for venture capitalists. IPOs are more likely in countries with a higher legality index (Cumming, Fleming, and Schwienbacher, 2006). Especially in Continental Europe, but more recently also in the United States, venture capital–backed IPOs are relatively rare events (La Porta, Lopez-De-Silanes, Shleifer, and Vishny, 1997; Ritter, Gao, and Zhu, 2012). Scholars contend, however, that, on average, IPOs provide the highest return to investors. Trade sales may include very successful exits, but typically also include less successful exits. Yet, Puri and Zarutskie (2012) find no evidence that venture capital investors would camouflage failures through acquisitions.

Scholars also point towards dynamics of exit options for venture capital funds. Giot and Schwienbacher (2007), for instance, show that as time passes venture capital–backed companies first exhibit an increased likelihood of exiting through an IPO. However, after reaching a plateau, nonexited investments have fewer possibilities of IPO exits over longer holding periods. This situation sharply contrasts with trade sale exits, where the hazard rate is less time-varying.

The contracting behavior of venture capital investors may also influence the exit options they are likely to pursue. When venture capital investors plan to exit through acquisitions, they obtain stronger control rights and are more likely to use convertible preferred stock (Cumming, 2008; Cumming and Johan, 2008). The identity of venture capital investors may further influence the exit options for their portfolio companies. For example, pre-IPO ownership by foreign venture capital investors is positively related to IPOs on foreign exchanges (Hursti and Maula, 2007).

PERFORMANCE

The previous section highlighted the key activities performed by venture capital investors. The question remains, however, whether venture capital investors actually create value. This section first provides a discussion of the role of venture capital investors in the performance of their portfolio companies. Next, it discusses whether venture capital investors create value for their investors.

Performance of Venture Capital–Backed Companies

How venture capital influences portfolio company–level outcomes, such as performance, survival, or growth, has attracted much attention from scholars. With few exceptions, research reveals a positive association between venture capital and company success. Venture capital–backed IPO companies, for instance, exhibit relatively superior post-issue operating performance compared to their non-venture capital–backed peers (Jain and Kini, 1995). Moreover, the involvement of venture capitalists improves the survival profile of IPO companies (Jain and Kini, 2000). Yet, Manigart, Baeyens, and Van Hyfte (2002), who do not limit their sample to IPO companies, find that European venture capital–backed companies do not have a higher probability of surviving than comparable non-venture capital–backed companies. More recently, Puri and Zarutskie (2012) show that U.S. venture capital–backed companies have a lower cumulative failure rate, which is especially driven by a much lower likelihood of failing in the first few years after initially receiving venture capital. The difference in the failure rate subsequently tapers off. Venture capital is also associated with a sizeable reduction in the time to bring a product to the market (Hellmann and Puri, 2000), higher employment growth (Davila et al., 2003), and an increased investment rate (Bertoni, Colombo, and Grilli, 2010).

Yet, venture capital investors are not homogenous, and scholars demonstrate how different venture capital investors have a different impact on company-level outcomes. For example, the general human capital of top management teams in venture capital firms is positively associated with the proportion of portfolio companies that go public, while their specific human capital is negatively associated with the proportion of portfolio companies that went bankrupt (Dimov and Shepherd, 2005). Research also shows that companies perceived as being more uncertain and disclosing the presence of more experienced venture capital investors are better able to attract subsequent financing (Janney and Folta, 2006). Companies backed by more experienced investors in their first financing round are more likely to conduct an IPO (Sorensen, 2007). Further, portfolio companies of better-networked venture capital investors are more likely to survive to subsequent financing and eventual exit (Hochberg et al., 2007). As a final example, Bertoni et al. (2010) show that the investments of firms backed by corporate venture capital investors remain sensitive to shocks in cash flows, whereas firms backed by independent venture capital investors exhibit an insignificant investment to cash flow sensitivity, suggesting the removal of financial constraints for these companies.

Do venture capitalists merely select the "best" entrepreneurial companies or do they build the "best" companies through active involvement in their portfolio companies? Baum and Silverman's (2004) findings point to a joint logic that combines the selection and value-adding roles of venture capital investors. Specifically, venture capital investors finance startups that have strong technology but are at risk of failure in the short run, and thus are in need of management expertise. Sorensen (2007) also finds that both effects are important to understand why more experienced venture capital investors invest in companies that are more likely to conduct an IPO. Bertoni, Colombo, and Grilli (2011) find that the value-adding effect of venture capital investors is of large economic magnitude in their sample of Italian companies. Most of this effect is obtained immediately after the first round of venture capital finance. The selection effect of venture capital investors appears to be negligible in the Italian context.

Value Creation for Investors in Venture Capital

Analyzing the performance of venture capital funds is a daunting task, as this information is private. Ljungqvist and Richardson (2003), who use a data set derived from the records of one of the largest institutional investors in private equity in the United States, provide an early empirical study in this domain. Between 1981 and 1993, this LP invested in 73 funds, including both venture capital and private equity funds. Private equity investments generated excess returns of 5 to 8 percent annually relative to the aggregate public equity market.

Kaplan and Schoar (2005) investigate the performance of a broader sample of venture capital and private equity partnerships. Their evidence for venture capital funds indicates returns are lower than the S&P 500 Index on an equal-weighted basis, but higher than the S&P 500 Index on a capital-weighted basis. Yet, Phalippou and Gottschalg (2009) find an average net-of-fees fund performance of 3 percent per year below that of the S&P 500 Index. Adjusting for risk brings the underperformance to 6 percent per year. Nevertheless, as Phalippou and Gottschalg note, substantial heterogeneity exists across funds: Top quartile funds outperform the S&P 500 Index. Interestingly, both of these studies show that returns persist strongly across subsequent funds of a partnership, with the best partnerships having a higher probability to continue to outperform.

Findings overall indicate that venture capital might create value for investors, especially when investors develop capabilities to select the "best" venture capital partnerships. Access to these top funds is challenging because they can choose between numerous eager investors. Therefore, this asset class is sometimes referred to as an *access class*. Moreover, as Ljungqvist and Richardson (2003) indicate, the objective of venture capital investors to invest may include other factors besides maximizing financial returns. Investors, for instance, may have twin investment objectives in which they not only want to obtain the highest risk-adjusted return, but also want to increase the likelihood that venture capital funds will purchase services from the limited partner. Banks, for instance, are strategic investors in the venture capital market because they use their venture capital investments to build relations for their lending activities (Hellmann et al., 2008).

SUMMARY AND CONCLUSIONS

This chapter begins by providing an overview of why venture capital markets exist. Venture capital investors have a comparative advantage over other traditional investors, such as banks, in reducing informational asymmetries and operating in environments characterized by high uncertainty. Next, the chapter discusses the different venture capital models. A discussion of the limited partnership structure follows, with venture capitalists serving as GPs and their investors as LPs. While this is the most common venture capital model worldwide, the chapter also discusses other models, including listed investment firms and captive funds. Then, the chapter describes what venture capital investors do. Venture capital investors engage in multiple activities, including fundraising, selecting portfolio companies, structuring their investments in portfolio companies, monitoring their investments, providing value-adding services, and arranging an exit from the portfolio company. Finally, the chapter provides some initial insights into the role of venture capital for portfolio company development and how venture capital may create value for investors. Scholars generally find positive effects of venture capital on the performance, survival, and growth of portfolio companies. Not all venture capital is the same. More experienced or better-networked venture capital investors may contribute more to the development of portfolio companies compared to less sophisticated venture capital investors. From the perspective of investors in venture capital, some disagreement exists about whether venture capital investors outperform the market. Nevertheless, scholars demonstrate that substantial variation exists in the return generated by venture capital investors. Moreover, scholars show the existence of performance persistence across funds of a partnership.

DISCUSSION QUESTIONS

1. Why do banks and venture capital investors coexist within an economy?
2. Comment on the follow-on quote: "Given the pressure of running out of cash for most young, innovative entrepreneurial companies and the unavailability of more traditional sources of financing, raising venture capital is a key milestone."
3. What are the implications of the traditional venture capital model for entrepreneurs who want to raise venture capital financing?
4. How can venture capital investors increase the probability of realizing a successful exit?
5. How can investors in venture capital increase the return potential of their investments? Discuss whether investors should contribute funds to relatively inexperienced partnerships.

REFERENCES

Ahlstrom, David, Garry D. Bruton, and Kuang S. Yeh. 2007. "Venture Capital in China: Past, Present, and Future." *Asia Pacific Journal of Management* 24:3, 247–268.

Akerlof, George A. 1970. "The Market for 'Lemons': Quality Uncertainty and the Market Mechanism." *Quarterly Journal of Economics* 84:3, 488–500.

Alhorr, Hadi S., Curt B. Moore, and Tyge G. Payne. 2008. "The Impact of Economic Integration on Cross-Border Venture Capital Investments: Evidence from the European Union." *Entrepreneurship Theory and Practice* 32:5, 897–917.

Amit, Raphael, James Brander, and Christoph Zott. 1998. "Why Do Venture Capital Firms Exist? Theory and Canadian Evidence." *Journal of Business Venturing* 13:6, 441–466.

Barry, Christopher. 1994. "New Directions in Research on Venture Capital Finance." *Financial Management* 23:3, 3–15.

Baum, Joel A. C., and Brian S. Silverman. 2004. "Picking Winners or Building Them? Alliance, Intellectual, and Human Capital as Selection Criteria in Venture Financing and Performance of Biotechnology Startups." *Journal of Business Venturing* 19:3, 411–436.

Beckman, Christine, and Diane Burton. 2008. "Founding the Future: Path Dependence in the Evolution of Top Management Teams from Founding to IPO." *Organization Science* 19:1, 3–25.

Berger, Allen N., and Gregory F. Udell. 1998. "The Economics of Small Business Finance: The Roles of Private Equity and Debt Markets in the Financial Growth Cycle." *Journal of Banking and Finance* 22:6–8, 613–673.

Bertoni, Fabio, Massimo G. Colombo, and Annalisa Croce. 2010. "The Effect of Venture Capital Financing on the Sensitivity to Cash Flow of Firm's Investments." *European Financial Management* 16:4, 528–551.

Bertoni, Fabio, Massimo G. Colombo, and Luca Grilli. 2011. "Venture Capital Financing and the Growth of High Tech Start-ups: Disentangling Selection from Treatment Effects." *Research Policy* 40:7, 1028–1043.

Black, Bernard S., and Ronald J. Gilson. 1998. "Venture Capital and the Structure of Capital Markets: Banks versus Stock Markets." *Journal of Financial Economics* 47:3, 243–277.

Bottazzi, Laura, Marco Da Rin, and Thomas Hellmann, T. 2008. "Who Are the Active Investors?: Evidence from Venture Capital." *Journal of Financial Economics* 89:3, 488–512.

Brander, James, Raphael R. Amit, and Werner Antweiler. 2002. "Venture-Capital Syndication: Improved Venture Selection vs. the Value Added Hypothesis." *Journal of Economics and Management Strategy* 11:3, 423–452.

Brav, Omer. 2009. "Access to Capital, Capital Structure, and the Funding of the Firm." *Journal of Finance* 64:1, 263–308.

Bruton, Gary D., Vance H. Fried, and Sophie Manigart. 2005. "Institutional Influences on the Worldwide Expansion of Venture Capital." *Entrepreneurship Theory and Practice* 29:6, 737–760.

Bruton, Gary D., Salim Chahine, and Igor Filatotchev. 2009. "Founders, Private Equity Investors and Underpricing in Entrepreneurial IPOs." *Entrepreneurship Theory and Practice* 33:4, 909–928.

Carpenter, Robert E., and Bruce C. Petersen. 2002. "Capital Market Imperfections, High-Tech Investment, and New Equity Financing." *Economic Journal* 112:477, F54–F72.

Chan, Yuk-Shee. 1983. "On the Positive Role of Financial Intermediation in Allocation of Venture Capital in a Market with Imperfect Information." *Journal of Finance* 38:5, 1543–1568.

Collewaert, Veroniek, and Yves Fassin. 2012. "Conflicts between Entrepreneurs, Venture Capitalists and Angel Investors: The Impact of Unethical Practices." *Small Business Economics*, forthcoming.

Cosh, Andy, Douglas Cumming, and Alan Hughes. 2009. "Outside Entrepreneurial Capital." *Economic Journal* 119:540, 1494–1533.

Cumming, Douglas. 2005a. "Agency Costs, Institutions, Learning, and Taxation in Venture Capital Contracting." *Journal of Business Venturing* 20:5, 573–622.

Cumming, Douglas. 2005b. "Capital Structure in Venture Finance." *Journal of Corporate Finance* 11:3, 550–585.

Cumming, Douglas. 2008. "Contracts and Exits in Venture Capital Finance." *Review of Financial Studies* 21:5, 1947–1982.

Cumming, Douglas, and Na Dai. 2010. "Local Bias in Venture Capital Investments." *Journal of Empirical Finance* 17:3, 362–380.

Cumming, Douglas, Grant Fleming, and Armin Schwienbacher. 2006. "Legality and Venture Capital Exits." *Journal of Corporate Finance* 12:2, 214–245.

Cumming, Douglas, and Sofia Johan. 2008. "Preplanned Exit Strategies in Venture Capital." *European Economic Review* 52:7, 1209–1241.

Damodaran, Aswath. 2010. *The Dark Side of Valuation: Valuing Young, Distressed and Complex Businesses*. Upper Saddle River, NJ: Pearson Education, Inc.

da Silva Rosa, Raymond, Gerard Velayuthen, and Terry Walter. 2003. "The Sharemarket Performance of Australian Venture Capital-Backed and Non-venture Capital-Backed IPOs." *Pacific Basin Finance Journal* 11:2, 197–218.

Davila, Antonio, and George Foster. 2005. "Management Accounting Systems Adoption Decisions: Evidence and Performance Implications from Early-Stage/Startup Companies." *Accounting Review* 80:4, 1039–1068.

Davila, Antonio, George Foster, and Mahendra Gupta. 2003. "Venture Capital Financing and the Growth of Startup Firms." *Journal of Business Venturing* 18:6, 689–708.

De Clercq, Dirk, Harry Sapienza, and Akbar Zaheer. 2008. "Firm and Group Influences on Venture Capital Firms' Involvement in New Ventures." *Journal of Management Studies* 45:7, 1169–1194.

Dimov, Dimo P., and Dean A. Shepherd. 2005. "Human Capital Theory and Venture Capital Firms: Exploring 'Home Runs' and 'Strike Outs'." *Journal of Business Venturing* 20:1, 1–21.

Dushnitsky, Gary, and Michael M. Lenox. 2005. "When Do Incumbents Learn from Entrepreneurial Ventures?: Corporate Venture Capital and Investing Firm Innovation Rates." *Research Policy* 34:5, 615–639.

Eckhardt, Jonathan T., Scott Shane, and Frédéric Delmar. 2006. "Multistage Selection and the Financing of New Ventures." *Management Science* 52:2, 220–232.

Elston, Julie A., and Jimmy J. Yang. 2010. "Venture Capital, Ownership Structure, Accounting Standards and IPO Underpricing: Evidence from Germany." *Journal of Economics and Business* 62:6, 517–536.

European Venture Capital and Private Equity Association. 2004. "Why and How to Invest in Private Equity." An EVCA Investor Relations Committee Paper. Brussels: EVCA.

European Venture Capital and Private Equity Association. 2007. "Guide on Private Equity and Venture Capital for Entrepreneurs." An EVCA Special Paper. Brussels: EVCA.

European Venture Capital and Private Equity Association. 2010. *2010 EVCA Yearbook, Pan-European Private Equity & Venture Capital Activity Report*. Brussels: EVCA.

Fredriksen, Öystein, Christer Olofsson, and Clas Wahlbin. 1997. "Are Venture Capitalists Firefighters? A Study of the Influence and Impact of Venture Capital Firms." *Technovation* 17:9, 503–511.

Fried, Vance H., and Robert D. Hisrich. 1994. "Towards a Model of Venture Capital Investment Decision Making." *Financial Management* 23:3, 28–37.

Fried, Vance H., Gary D. Bruton, and Robert D. Hisrich. 1998. "Strategy and the Board of Directors in Venture Capital-backed Firms." *Journal of Business Venturing* 13:6, 493–503.

Giot, Pierre, and Armin Schwienbacher. 2007. "IPOs, Trade Sales and Liquidations: Modelling Venture Capital Exits Using Survival Analysis." *Journal of Banking and Finance* 31:3, 679–702.

Gompers, Paul A. 1995. "Optimal Investment, Monitoring, and the Staging of Venture Capital." *Journal of Finance* 50:5, 1461–1490.

Gompers, Paul, and Josh Lerner. 1998. "What Drives Venture Capital Fundraising?" *Brookings Papers on Economic Activity: Macroeconomics*, 149–192.

Gompers, Paul, and Josh Lerner. 2001. "The Venture Capital Revolution." *Journal of Economic Perspectives* 15:2, 145–168.

Gorman, Michael, and William A. Sahlman. 1989. "What Do Venture Capitalists Do?" *Journal of Business Venturing* 4:4, 231–248.

Groh, Alexander P., and Heinrich von Liechtenstein. 2011. "International Allocation Determinants for Institutional Investments in Venture Capital and Private Equity Limited Partnerships." *International Journal of Banking, Accounting and Finance* 3:2–3, 176–206.

Groh, Alexander P., Heinrich von Liechtenstein, and Karsten Lieser. 2010. "The European Venture Capital and Private Equity Country Attractiveness Indices." *Journal of Corporate Finance* 16:2, 205–224.

Hallen, Benjamin L. 2008. "The Causes and Consequences of the Initial Network Positions of New Organizations: From Whom Do Entrepreneurs Receive Investments?" *Administrative Science Quarterly* 53:4, 685–718.

Hallen, Benjamin L., and Kathleen M. Eisenhardt. 2012. "Catalyzing Strategies and Efficient Tie Formation: How Entrepreneurial Firms Obtain Investment Ties." *Academy of Management Journal* 55:1, 35–70.

Hellmann, Thomas, Laura Lindsey, and Manju Puri. 2008. "Building Relationships Early: Banks in Venture Capital." *Review of Financial Studies* 21:2, 513–541.

Hellmann, Thomas, and Manju Puri. 2000. "The Interaction between Product Market and Financing Strategy: The Role of Venture Capital." *Review of Financial Studies* 13:4, 959–984.

Hellmann, Thomas, and Manju Puri. 2002. "Venture Capital and the Professionalization of Start-up Firms: Empirical Evidence." *Journal of Finance* 57:1, 169–197.

Heughebaert, Andy, and Sophie Manigart. 2012. "Firm Valuation in Venture Capital Financing Rounds: The Role of Investor Bargaining Power." *Journal of Business Finance and Accounting* 39:3–4, 500–530.

Heughebaert, Andy, Tom Vanacker, and Sophie Manigart. 2012. "The Role of Venture Capital in Company Financial Decision Making and Capital Structure." Working Paper, Ghent University.

Hochberg, Yael V., Alexander Ljungqvist, and Yang Lu. 2007. "Whom You Know Matters: Venture Capital Networks and Investment Performance." *Journal of Finance* 62:1, 251–301.

Hopp, Christian. 2010. "When Do Venture Capitalists Collaborate? Evidence on the Driving Forces of Venture Capital Syndication." *Small Business Economics* 35:4, 417–431.

Hsu, David H. 2004. "What Do Entrepreneurs Pay for Venture Capital Affiliation?" *Journal of Finance* 59:4, 1805–1844.

Hursti, Jani, and Markku M. V. J. Maula. 2007. "Acquiring Financial Resources from Foreign Equity Capital Markets: An Examination of Factors Influencing Foreign Initial Public Offerings." *Journal of Business Venturing* 22:6, 833–851.

Jain, Bharat A., and Omesh Kini. 1995. "Venture Capital Participation and the Post-Issue Operation Performance of IPO Firms." *Managerial and Decision Economics* 16:6, 593–606.

Jain, Bharat A., and Omesh Kini. 2000. "Does the Presence of Venture Capitalists Improve the Survival Profile of IPO Firms?" *Journal of Business Finance & Accounting* 27:9–10, 1139–1183.

Janney, Jay J., and Timothy B. Folta. 2006. "Moderating Effects of Investor Experience on the Signaling Value of Private Equity Placements." *Journal of Business Venturing* 21:1, 27–44.

Jeng, Leslie A., and Philippe C. Wells. 2000. "The Determinants of Venture Capital Funding: Evidence across Countries." *Journal of Corporate Finance* 6:3, 241–289.

Kaplan, Steven N., and Antoinette Schoar. 2005. "Private Equity Performance: Returns, Persistence, and Capital Flows." *Journal of Finance* 60:4, 1791–1823.

Kaplan, Steven N., Berk A. Sensoy, and Per Strömberg. 2009. "Should Investors Bet on the Jockey or the Horse? Evidence from the Evolution of Firms from Early Business Plans to Public Companies." *Journal of Finance* 64:1, 75–115.

Kaplan, Steven N., and Per Strömberg. 2003. "Financial Contracting Theory Meets the Real World: An Empirical Analysis of Venture Capital Contracts." *Review of Economic Studies* 70:2, 281–315.

Kaplan, Steven N., and Per Strömberg. 2004. "Characteristics, Contracts, and Actions: Evidence from Venture Capitalist Analyses." *Journal of Finance* 59:5, 2177–2210.
Kirsch, David, Brent Goldfarb, and Azi Gera. 2006. "Do Business Plans Predict Venture Funding?" Working Paper, University of Maryland.
Knockaert, Mirjam, Bart Clarysse, and Mike Wright. 2010. "The Extent and Nature of Heterogeneity of Venture Capital Selection Behaviour in New Technology-Based Firms." *R&D Management* 40:4, 357–371.
Knockaert, Mirjam, and Tom Vanacker. 2012. "The Association between Venture Capital Selection and Value Adding Behavior: Evidence from Early Stage High Tech Venture Capital Investors." *Small Business Economics*, forthcoming.
La Porta, Raphael, Florencio Lopez-De-Silanes, Andrei Shleifer, and Robert W. *Vishny.* 1997. "Legal Determinants of External Finance." *Journal of Finance* 52:3, 1131–1150.
Lee, Peggy M., and Sunil Wahal. 2004. "Grandstanding, Certification and the Underpricing of Venture Capital Backed IPOs." *Journal of Financial Economics* 73:2, 375–407.
Lerner, Josh. 1994. "The Syndication of Venture Capital Investments." *Financial Management* 23:3, 16–27.
Lerner, Josh. 1995. "Venture Capitalists and the Oversight of Private Firms." *Journal of Finance* 50:1, 301–318.
Ljungqvist, Alexander, and Matthew Richardson. 2003. "The Cash Flow, Return and Risk Characteristics of Private Equity." NBER Working Paper No. 9454.
MacMillan, Ian C., Siegel, Robin, and P.N.S. Subba Narasimha. 1985. "Criteria Used by Venture Capitalists to Evaluate New Venture Proposals." *Journal of Business Venturing* 1:1, 119–128.
Manigart, Sophie, Katleen Baeyens, and Wim Van Hyfte. 2002. "The Survival of Venture Capital Backed Companies." *Venture Capital: An International Journal of Entrepreneurial Finance* 4:2, 103–124.
Manigart, Sophie, Sofie De Prijcker, and Bivas Bose. 2010. "International Private Equity Flows." In Douglas Cumming, ed., *Private Equity—Fund Types, Risks and Returns and Regulation*, 395–418. Hoboken, NJ: John Wiley & Sons, Inc.
Manigart, Sophie, and Mike Wright. 2012. "Reassessing the Relationships between Private Equity Investors and Their Portfolio Companies." *Small Business Economics*, forthcoming.
Manigart, Sophie, Mike Wright, Ken Robbie, Philippe Desbrières, and Koen De Waele. 1997. "Venture Capitalists' Appraisal of Investment Projects: An Empirical European Study." *Entrepreneurship Theory and Practice* 21:4, 29–43.
Megginson, William L., and Kathleen A. Weiss. 1991. "Venture Capitalist Certification in Initial Public Offerings." *Journal of Finance* 46:3, 879–903.
Metrick, Andrew, and Ayako Yasuda. 2011. "Venture Capital and Other Private Equity: A Survey." *European Financial Management* 17:4, 619–654.
Meuleman, Miguel, Andy Lockett, Sophie Manigart, and Mike Wright. 2010. "Partner Selection Decisions in Interfirm Collaborations: The Paradox of Relational Embeddedness." *Journal of Management Studies* 47:6, 995–1019.
Meuleman, Miguel, and Mike Wright. 2011. "Cross-Border Private Equity Syndication: Institutional Context and Learning." *Journal of Business Venturing* 26:1, 35–48.
Muzyka, Dan, Sue Birley, and Benoit Leleux. 1996. "Trade-offs in the Investment Decisions of European Venture Capitalists." *Journal of Business Venturing* 11:4, 273–287.
National Venture Capital Association. 2011. *Yearbook 2011*. New York, NY: Thomson Reuters.
Norton, Edgar, and Bernard H. Tenenbaum. 1993. "Specialization versus Diversification as a Venture Capital Investment Strategy." *Journal of Business Venturing* 8:5, 431–442.
Ooghe Hubert, Marc Deloof, and Sophie Manigart. 2003. *Handboek Bedrijfsfinanciering*, Second edition. Antwerp: Intersentia.
Ou, Charles, and George W. Haynes. 2006. "Acquisition of Additional Equity Capital by Small Firms—Findings from the National Survey of Small Business Finances." *Small Business Economics* 27:2–3, 157–168.

Pauly, Mark V. 1968. "The Economics of Moral Hazard: Comment." *American Economic Review* 58:3, 531–537.

Phalippou, Ludovic, and Oliver Gottschalg. 2009. "The Performance of Private Equity Funds." *Review of Financial Studies* 22:4, 1747–1776.

Puri, Manju, and Rebecca Zarutskie. 2012. "On the Lifecycle Dynamics of Venture Capital and Non-venture Capital Financed Firms." *Journal of Finance*, forthcoming.

Ritter, Jay, Xiaohui Gao, and Zhongyan. 2012. "Where Have All the IPOs Gone?" Working Paper, University of Florida.

Rosman, Andrew J., and Hugh M. O'Neill. 1993. "Comparing the Information Acquisition Strategies of Venture Capital and Commercial Lenders: A Computer-Based Experiment." *Journal of Business Venturing* 8:5, 443–460.

Sahlman, William A. 1990. "The Structure and Governance of Venture-Capital Organizations." *Journal of Financial Economics* 27:2, 473–521.

Sammut, Stephen. 2011. "Venture Capital and Entrepreneurial Management." Lecture Notes, The Wharton School.

Sapienza, Harry J. 1992. "When Do Venture Capitalists Add Value?" *Journal of Business Venturing* 7:1, 9–27.

Sapienza, Harry J., Sophie Manigart, and W. Vermeir. 1996. "Venture Capitalist Governance and Value Added in Four Countries." *Journal of Business Venturing* 11:6, 439–469.

Schmidt, Klaus M. 2003. "Convertible Securities and Venture Capital Finance." *Journal of Finance* 58:3, 1139–1166.

Sorensen, Morton. 2007. "How Smart Is Smart Money? A Two-Sided Matching Model of Venture Capital." *Journal of Finance* 62:6, 2725–2762.

Steier, Lloyd, and Royston Greenwood. 1995. "Venture Capital Relationships in the Deal Structuring and Post-Investment Stages of New Firm Creation." *Journal of Management Studies* 32:3, 337–357.

Ueda, Masako. 2004. "Banks versus Venture Capital: Project Evaluation, Screening and Expropriation." *Journal of Finance* 59:2, 601–621.

Vanacker, Tom, and Daniel Forbes. 2012. "How Do Different Resource-Providers Respond to Affiliation-Based Signaling? Evidence from Venture Capital-backed Firms." Working Paper, Ghent University.

Vanacker, Tom, and Sophie Manigart. 2010. "Pecking Order and Debt Capacity Considerations for High-Growth Companies Seeking Financing." *Small Business Economics* 35:1, 53–69.

Vanacker, Tom, Sophie Manigart, and Miguel Meuleman. Forthcoming. "Path-Dependent Evolution versus Intentional Management of Investment Ties in Science-Based Entrepreneurial Firms." *Entrepreneurship Theory and Practice*.

Winton, Andrew, and Vijay Yerramilli. 2008. "Entrepreneurial Finance: Banks versus Venture Capital." *Journal of Financial Economics* 88:1, 51–79.

Wright, Mike, and Andy Lockett. 2003. "The Structure and Management of Alliances: Syndication in the Venture Capital Industry." *Journal of Management Studies* 40:8, 2073–2102.

Wright, Mike, and Ken Robbie. 1998. "Venture Capital and Private Equity: A Review and Synthesis." *Journal of Business Finance and Accounting* 25:5–6, 521–570.

Yung, Chris. 2012. "Venture Capital before the First Dollar: Deal Origination, Screening, and Evaluation." In Douglas Cumming, ed., *The Oxford Handbook of Venture Capital*, 303–327. Oxford: Oxford University Press.

Zacharakis, Andrew L., and G. Dale Meyer. 2000. "The Potential of Actuarial Decision Models: Can They Improve the Venture Capital Investment Decision?" *Journal of Business Venturing* 15:4, 323–346.

Zacharakis, Andrew L., and Dean Shepherd. 2001. "The Nature of Information and Overconfidence on Venture Capitalists' Decision Making." *Journal of Business Venturing* 16:4, 311–332.

ABOUT THE AUTHORS

Tom Vanacker is an Assistant Professor at Ghent University. He was visiting scholar at the Carlson School of Management (University of Minnesota) and The Wharton School (University of Pennsylvania). His research interests focus on the financing of entrepreneurial companies, comprising the behavior of venture capital investors, and the impact of financing decisions on company growth and performance. He has published (or work forthcoming) on these topics in *Entrepreneurship Theory and Practice, Small Business Economics, Journal of Small Business Management,* and *Entrepreneurship & Regional Development.* He obtained his Ph.D. in Business Administration from Ghent University.

Sophie Manigart is a Full Professor at Ghent University and partner at the Vlerick Business School (Belgium), where she holds the Gimv Private Equity Chair. Her research interests focus on financing entrepreneurial companies, comprising the behavior of intermediaries (business angel and venture capital investors) and the interaction between financing choices and entrepreneurial company development. She has published on these topics in the *Journal of Management Studies, Journal of Business Venturing,* and *Journal of Business Finance & Accounting,* among other journals. She holds a degree in Civil Engineering, an MBA, and is Doctor in Management (Ghent University).

ACKNOWLEDGMENTS

We are grateful to H. Kent Baker and Greg Filbeck (the editors) for feedback on this chapter. Tom Vanacker acknowledges the financial support of the Research Foundation Flanders (Grant FWO11/PDO/076).

CHAPTER 13

Mezzanine Capital

SAMEER JAIN
Managing Director, American Realty Capital

PHILLIP MYBURGH
Chief Executive Officer, STANLIB Credit Partners

INTRODUCTION

The last decade witnessed a dramatic increase in the number of private equity funds under management in both the developed and the developing world. This trend of increased strategic asset allocations to private equity was not accompanied by appropriately proportionate increased commitments of capital to mezzanine funds. About $75 billion of mezzanine capital was raised between 2006 and 2011, largely via closed-end blind investment pools. About $400 to $500 billion in equity *dry powder* (i.e., committed but uninvested capital waiting to be deployed as stockholders' equity in buyouts or mergers and acquisitions) is available globally, a substantial portion of which will likely require mezzanine leverage. With less than $50 billion of uninvested mezzanine capital remaining, a sizable opportunity exists for new money to be raised for investment in this subasset class (UBS Alternative Investments, 2011).

The purpose of this chapter is to provide an introductory overview of mezzanine capital as an asset class. The remainder of the chapter has the following structure. The first section attempts to define mezzanine capital. The second section analyzes the return components found in typical mezzanine financing instruments. The third section provides an overview of some of the principal risks associated with investing mezzanine capital, such as credit risk. This section also discusses factors that determine the likelihood of borrower default, probable default scenarios, and recovery rates. The fourth section compares the key differences between mezzanine financing in the United States and Europe. The fifth section explores the interaction between the mezzanine capital and high-yield bond markets. The sixth section reviews the supply and demand drivers in the mezzanine capital market. The seventh section considers mezzanine as an asset class from a prospective investor's perspective. The final section offers a summary and conclusions.

DEFINITION AND FORMS OF MEZZANINE CAPITAL

Although mezzanine capital may take on many forms, including preferred stock, it most typically takes on the form of a debt instrument, and then as a privately negotiated subordinated debt instrument with some form of equity participation. The word *mezzanine* is derived from the Latin *medianus*, which means "in the middle."

As Exhibit 13.1 shows, mezzanine financing is most commonly used to refer to the layer of capital that is located between a company's senior debt and its equity from both a priority of claims and risk-return trade-off perspective. The typical range of the relative sizes of each layer in a company's capital stack is expressed as percentages.

Mezzanine capital is either structurally or contractually subordinate in priority of payment to senior debt, but it ranks senior to the borrower's equity or common stock. *Structural subordination* is attributable to the borrower group's corporate structure, which means lenders to the operating company are structurally senior, and lenders to the parent company can only be repaid from the operating assets after the operating company lenders have been repaid. *Contractual subordination* is achieved through the registration of first-priority liens, mortgages, or pledges of security over the borrower's real assets in favor of the senior lenders. An intercreditor deed typically governs the interaction of the rights of mezzanine and senior lenders.

These combined characteristics have led to mezzanine capital being called *middle-risk, middle-return financing*, or *intermediate capital*. The likely timing for the investment of mezzanine capital, such as a preinitial public offer (IPO), middle-stage leveraged buyout (LBO), or expansion capital, is also sometimes given as a reason for calling this type of capital *mezzanine* (Gompers and Lerner, 2001). Exhibit 13.2 stylistically illustrates mezzanine capital's risk-reward characteristics within a borrower's capital stack.

Mezzanine capital can adopt various forms, many of which are hybrid instruments that combine the features of senior subordinated debt with some sort of equity "kicker" or "sweetener," typically in the form of warrants, options,

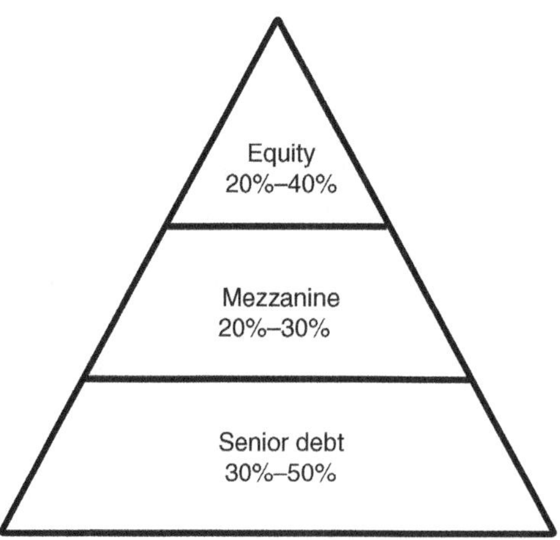

Exhibit 13.1 A Diagrammatic Illustration Showing the Relative Positioning and Size of the Key Layers in a Company's Capital Stack

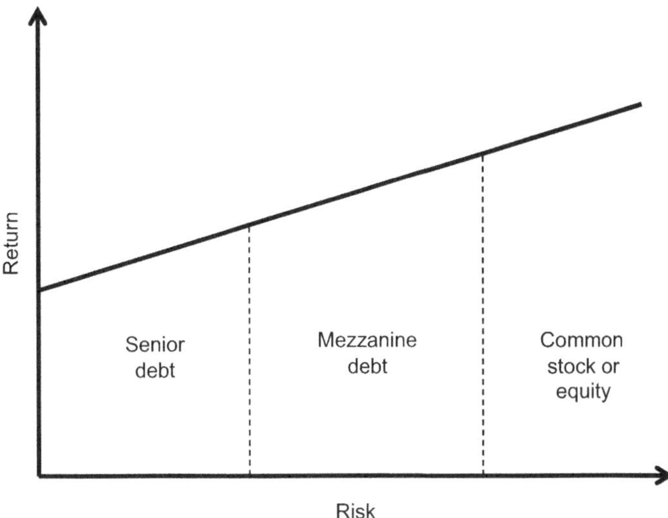

Exhibit 13.2 The Relative Risk and Reward Characteristics of the Key Layers in a Company's Capital Stack

This exhibit illustrates that from a risk-return trade-off perspective, mezzanine debt is positioned between a company's capital layers composed of common stock or equity and senior debt.

or conversion rights. The debt component of mezzanine funding instruments can also take on numerous forms, including zero coupon bonds or so-called payment-in-kind (PIK) notes; original issue discount coupon-bearing notes/loans; notes with toggle options, which allow the borrower to elect whether it wants to service its contracted interest rate or capitalize the accrued interest; notes with ratchet margins, which change the interest margin accruing with reference to agreed covenants (e.g., agreed leverage thresholds and total debt service cover ratios); and preferred stock, which is typically cumulative and redeemable in nature. Exhibit 13.3 contrasts mezzanine capital's distinctive characteristics with those of typical leveraged loans, high-yield bonds, and common equity.

To the extent that mezzanine investors are secured lenders, they typically have the benefit of second-ranking security interests over the assets of the borrower. This priority ranking order essentially means that mezzanine capital ranks junior to the first-priority collateral rights granted on a senior-ranking basis to senior secured lenders, but ranks ahead of the borrower's unsecured creditors (e.g., trade creditors or stockholders' loans). Mezzanine lenders may also enjoy the benefit of the protections afforded by various contracted maintenance-based financial and operating covenants. This protection would typically be derived indirectly by the operation of cross-default and cross-acceleration provisions contained in the mezzanine instrument terms.

RETURN COMPONENTS

Mezzanine investors normally contract to receive both interest coupon returns and equity upside participation returns. The two distinct interest service and equity-participatory return components of mezzanine capital are intended to compensate a mezzanine capital provider for its subordinated ranking relative

	Mezzanine	Leveraged loans	High yield	Public equity
Security/collateral	Unsecured	First lien	Unsecured	None
Priority/relative ranking	Contractual/ structural subordination	Senior	Contractual/structural subordination	Junior
Contractual/ indenture covenants	Less restrictive, mostly financial; maintenance-based	Comprehensive	Incurrence based	None
Term/maturity	8 years	5 years	10 years	Open-ended
Interest coupon	Cash pay/PIK – variable or fixed	Cash pay –variable	Cash pay –fixed	Dividends
Warrants/options/ conversion rights	Almost always	None	Generally not	Not applicable
Prepayment penalties	Moderate via prepayment premium, usually after a year	Minimal	No-call periods, penalties/call protection premiums	Not applicable
Capital providers	Private capital, nonbank institutions	Banks, nonbank institutions	Public offering	Public/ private
Recovery (%)	20	80	40	0
Liquidity	None/low	Medium	High/medium	High
CRA rating requirements	None	Required/none	Required	None
Capital providers	Institutional investors, mezzanine funds/ private equity funds/credit funds	Collateralized loan obligations/ institutional Investors	Institutional investors/high net worths/ collateralized bond obligations/credit funds	General public, institutional investors

Exhibit 13.3 A Comparison of Mezzanine's Characteristics with Other Key Layers of Capital

This exhibit contrasts mezzanine capital's distinctive characteristics with those of typical leveraged loans, high-yield bonds, and common equity.

to senior lenders, as well as its capped or limited upside participation relative to ordinary stockholders.

Interest Returns

Interest coupon payments on mezzanine capital could incorporate either or both a current cash-pay interest component and a PIK component. The cash interest component of a mezzanine instrument provides the investor with a contracted minimum return. The timing of the payment of the interest coupons can be tailored to suit the free cash flow constraints of the borrower. For example, interest payments could either be paid in arrears on a quarterly or semiannual basis, or the borrower could be afforded a so-called toggle option (sometimes for a limited part of the loan term, such as the first eight quarters in a loan with a five-year term), which allows the borrower to elect whether it wants to pay or capitalize its accrued interest obligation with respect to a particular interest period. An election to capitalize the accrued interest could result in either (1) triggering a margin ratchet, which effectively increases the borrower's contracted interest rate until such time as the accrued interest is actually paid, or (2) the borrower's interest obligation could be accrued for the full loan term (a so-called PIK note) or a predetermined portion of the loan term (a so-called interest payment "holiday" period).

Equity Returns

The balance of the mezzanine provider's all-in return is normally provided by the equity-linked component of these bifurcated instruments, most commonly adopting the form of so-called "penny warrants" that enable the grantee of the warrant to subscribe for common stock to be issued by the borrower at a predetermined nominal price. The mezzanine borrower is valued at the inception of the transaction, and the warrant strike price is determined with reference to this initial valuation. The equity-linked portion of the mezzanine lender's total return is realized when the investor exercises the warrants and disposes of the underlying stock, usually upon either of the following: (1) the occurrence of a so-called exit event (e.g., a sale of the borrower's business, a change in control of the borrower, or a recapitalization of the borrower) or (2) the exercise of a put option back on the issuer or its key sponsors at some pre-agreed price and date.

The warrants granted to the mezzanine provider are usually to acquire stock that ranks *pari passu* (equally) with the sponsors' ordinary shares, and therefore potentially affords the mezzanine provider an uncapped upside with respect to this component of its return. The mezzanine provider's potential future stockholding in the borrower requires it (1) to perform a careful review of the investment opportunity from a prospective stockholder's perspective (e.g., possible exit strategies) and (2) to perhaps become involved in negotiating the terms and conditions of the borrower's constitutional documents and of any agreements between the borrower's stockholders (common in many LBOs) relating to minority stockholder protections.

Exhibit 13.4 illustrates mezzanine capital's participation in a typical LBO and the various component parts used to generate its returns, which might be comprised of fees, cash and PIK interest, as well as some form of equity participation, or equity kicker.

For downside protection, mezzanine providers are dependent on negotiating the following: contractual rights, cash sweep arrangements, seller undertakings, representations and warranties, loan covenants, events of default, access to information covenants, and so-called second-bite-at-the-cherry provisions, which are aimed at increasing the PIK interest return component of a mezzanine loan or the lender's warrant allocation in the event of a borrower default.

Expected Returns

The combination of high contracted interest yields, with the potential upside offered by equity participation through warrants, options, and conversion rights, have historically combined to produce high returns with lower volatility relative to many private equity returns. Depending on the prevailing market conditions in which pure mezzanine funds invest, they tend to target a gross internal rate of return (IRR) of between 13 and 18 percent per annum. This return might be broken down as follows:

- *Cash interest.* Mezzanine investments carry a high annual so-called "cash pay" interest rate, normally yielding around 4 to 7 percent per year over the London Interbank Offered Rate (LIBOR).

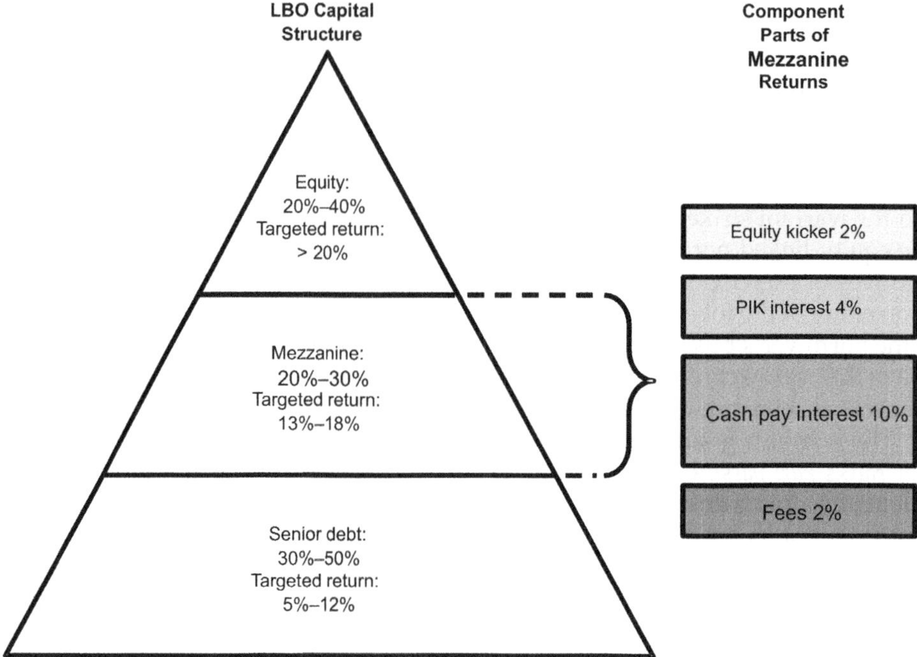

Exhibit 13.4 The Relative Returns of the Various Layers in a Company's Capital Stack, Combined with a Breakdown of the Key Component Parts of a Typical Mezzanine Return

- *PIK interest.* Mezzanine instruments may yield a further 3 to 5 percent per year in the form of capitalized interest. This PIK interest component typically compounds quarterly, semiannually, or annually, and the accrued amount is due in full upon the final capital redemption date.
- *Equity participation.* The balance of the annualized return is back-ended and realized through the exercise of the relevant warrants, options, or conversion rights.

In order to attempt to protect the mezzanine provider's returns, mezzanine instruments normally include both call-protection and anti-dilution provisions. Call-protection provisions include combinations of no call periods, no call penalties, and make-whole provisions. *No call periods* refer to times during which the borrower is not permitted to prepay any principal before scheduled redemption dates. *No call penalties* are contracted penalties payable on any principal amounts prepaid before scheduled redemption dates. For example, for a five-year instrument these penalties typically are 3 percent for amounts prepaid in year 3, 2 percent in year 3, and 1 percent for amounts prepaid in year 4. *Make-whole provisions* oblige the borrower to pay the mezzanine provider the present value of any interest foregone by the latter as a consequence of any principal being repaid before scheduled redemption dates. Anti-dilution provisions require the borrower to issue more warrants, options, or conversion rights in favor of the mezzanine provider in the event that the borrower has a rights issue subsequent to raising the mezzanine loan.

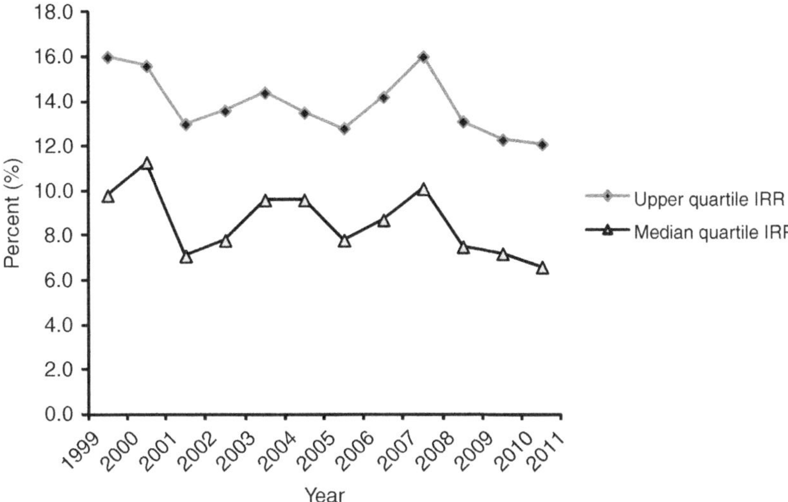

Exhibit 13.5 Annualized Mezzanine Fund Internal Rates of Return by Quartile
This exhibit graphs the upper and median quartile IRRs of mezzanine fund returns during the period 1999 to 2011.
Source: Thomson One.

The addition of modest leverage applied to a diversified portfolio of mezzanine investments has the potential of increasing the gross IRR of fund investors. In the past, lightly levered mezzanine capital deals grossed returns in the high teens—typically around 10 percent cash interest, 4 percent PIK interest, 2 percent arrangement fees/prepayment penalties, and about 2 percent equity participation. Exhibit 13.5 graphs the upper and median quartile IRRs of mezzanine fund returns during the period 1999 to 2011.

Historically, there has been moderate return performance dispersion across fund sizes. Exhibit 13.6 shows that larger funds have, in general, underperformed

Fund size in USD Millions	Upper Quartile (%)	Median (%)
0–30	14.89	12.04
30–50	6.12	3.43
50–100	15.80	11.66
100–300	12.52	7.07
300–500	10.25	3.90
500–1,000	7.04	5.34
1,000+	8.14	4.62

Exhibit 13.6 Comparison of Annualized Upper- and Median-Quartile Performances of Different Sizes of Mezzanine Funds
This exhibit shows that larger funds have in general underperformed smaller and medium-sized funds. For instance, the median performance of the largest funds has historically been about one-third that of the smallest funds.
Source: Thomson One.

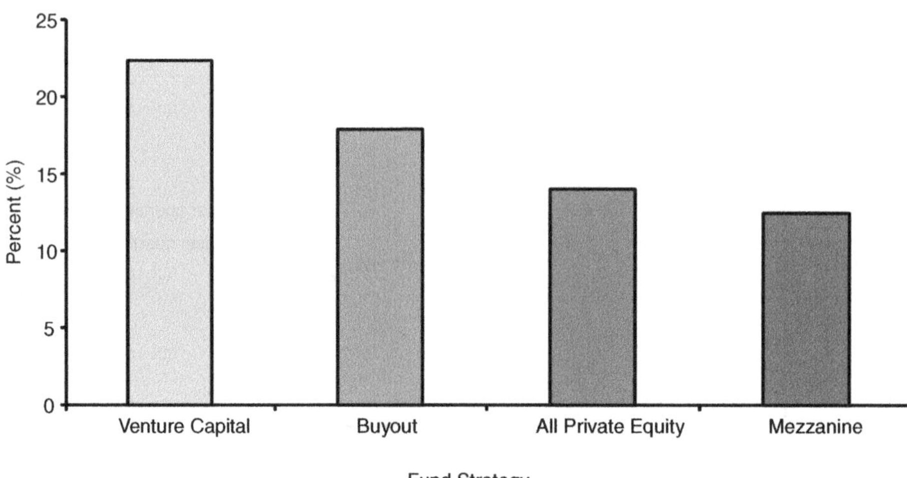

Exhibit 13.7 Average Annual Volatility of Various Private Equity Investment Strategies from 1991 to 2010

This exhibit shows that the average long-term volatility of mezzanine over the period 1991 to 2010 was 12.5 percent while the long-term volatilities for venture capital and buyout capital over this period were 22.4 percent and 17.9 percent, respectively.
Source: Thomson One.

smaller and medium-sized funds. For instance, the median performance of the largest funds has historically been about one-third that of the smallest funds. This performance differential may be attributable to the average deal size of these funds because small cap transactions, though riskier, often generate higher returns.

From a portfolio management perspective, a noteworthy fact is that the contracted interest rate and equity components of mezzanine funding instruments act as natural hedges; that is, in general, when interest rates go up, equity valuations decrease and vice versa. This characteristic, combined with the fact that contracted returns make up a substantial component of mezzanine investors' returns means that mezzanine funds have historically delivered much less volatile returns than other private equity investment strategies. Exhibit 13.7 shows that the average long-term volatility of mezzanine capital over the period 1991 to 2010 was 13.5 percent, while the long-term volatilities for venture capital and buyout capital over this period were 22.4 percent and 17.9 percent, respectively.

ANALYZING AND MITIGATING MEZZANINE CAPITAL INVESTMENT RISKS

Mezzanine capital is basically a form of debt capital that is advanced to the borrower with an obligation, at a minimum, to pay the lender a contracted (interest rate) return and to repay/redeem the principal by the contracted maturity date. Any analysis of a mezzanine capital investment opportunity entails a two-step credit evaluation process (McGirt and Pitre, 2003). The first step is aimed at establishing the probability of borrower default (i.e., the likelihood of the borrower being unable to meet all of its contracted financial obligations in respect of its various debt obligations). The second step is to estimate the expected level of recovery (or loss severity) in the event of a borrower default, which is sometimes called the projected loss given default.

In determining the likelihood of borrower default, mezzanine providers typically take into account the borrower's:

- Projected sustainable free cash flow generating capability.
- Projected degree of financial leverage.
- Projected total debt-service coverage.
- Business and operating risks.
- Exposure to financial risks, including among other things exposure to interest rate risks, currency exchange rate risks, and exposure to capital structure related risks, having regard to the various funding layers and the relevant intercreditor relationships and exposure to various capital markets.
- Industry fundamentals.
- Stability and consistency of historical financial results, including, among other things, earnings growth, margin sustainability, working capital utilization, and capital expenditure requirements.
- Quality, depth, and experience of the management team.
- Stockholders of reference and their background and experience.
- Accounting quality and corporate governance.
- Sensitivity to macroeconomic considerations and exogenous exposures.

Because some mezzanine borrowers are relatively small, any credit review needs to focus on analyzing the impact that the borrower's lack of scale might have on the defensibility of its business position. Others are large market-leading businesses, with clearly identifiable competitive advantages or critical success factors making their business models somewhat more robust and resilient.

The prospective mezzanine provider's credit analysis process should ensure that the provider develops a clear understanding of the borrower's major growth opportunities, as well as the economic factors that underpin the markets in which it operates, its profitability, and its financial results.

The level of leverage acceptable to a prospective mezzanine financier is a function of the company's historic financial performance, the financial performance of the sector(s) in which the company operates, and the prevailing economic conditions as a whole. The stronger the borrower's overall position, the higher is the likely permitted level of leverage, while weaker positions and economic uncertainty will likely result in lower levels of leverage.

In attempting to determine the likely loss given default, mezzanine providers take into account several factors. For example, mezzanine capital is usually subordinated to all existing and future senior indebtedness of the borrower. The value of its second-ranking collateral rights over the borrower's assets are dependent on a combination of senior debt amortization and sustained growth in free cash flow that results in an effective deleveraging of the principal obligations that enjoy first-priority collateral rights. Second, mezzanine instruments are often held by either a

Current EBITDA $m	50
Discount %	40
Distressed EBITDA $m	30
Transaction Multiples	4X
Valuation ($30m × 4) $m	120

	Amount $	Recovery $	Recovery %
Total debt	280	120	43
Senior secured debt	150	106	71
Mezzanine debt (Operating Co.)	70	14	20
PIK preferred mezzanine (Holding Co.)	20	0	0

Exhibit 13.8 Dispersion of Postbankruptcy Recoveries
This exhibit provides a hypothetical example that illustrates that a distressed firm might be valued at a 40 percent discount to its trailing EBITDA.

single creditor or a club consisting of a few creditors with closely aligned interests. This arrangement increases the likelihood of the business being restructured and reorganized in the event of the borrower experiencing financial distress.

The increased likelihood of an ordered capital structure reorganization being promoted by the borrower's mezzanine providers means that when evaluating an investment opportunity investors need to pay greater attention to determining whether the borrower is a viable going concern and to place less emphasis on the value of the borrower's real assets. These going-concern valuations entail stress-testing the borrower's cash flow projections to reflect a probable default scenario. This often involves applying a "haircut" to the business' earnings before interest, tax, depreciation, and amortization (EBITDA) and margin forecasts.

Exhibit 13.8 provides a hypothetical example illustrating that a distressed firm might be valued at a 40 percent discount to its trailing EBITDA. If the firm's trailing EBITDA is $50 million, its distressed EBITDA would be valued at $30 million. Further, if a comparable transaction multiple of four is applied to the distressed EBITDA, the firm would be valued at $120 million. Exhibit 13.8 also provides a hypothetical example of the recovery rate for each tranche of the capital structure. It illustrates that a 43 percent overall assumed recovery rate for all lenders could result in only a 20 percent recovery for the mezzanine tranche. In this example, mezzanine debt valued at $70 million with a 20 percent recovery rate implies a recovery amount of $14 million. The majority of the recovery amount would be returned to the senior secured debt holders.

The dispersion of forecast recoveries forms the basis of any attempt to calculate the likely loss given default. Investors also need to account for other factors in predicting the loss recovery of mezzanine providers. One factor is the probability of mezzanine creditors achieving recoveries in excess of their expectations due to their flexibility in the event of reorganization. For example, creditors could arrange a debt-for-equity swap and then secure the necessary expertise or other resources to turn the borrower's business around over time. Another factor is that higher levels of senior secured debt in the overall capital structure will probably lower recoveries on the borrower's subordinated borrowings. Finally, investors should consider that the cash-on-cash (cash received/initial cash outlay) return yielded by a mezzanine investment could be conceptually construed as a component of the mezzanine provider's recovery of its principal.

Warrantless Mezzanine Capital

Warrantless mezzanine capital is financing advanced without any requirement that the borrower issues warrants, options, or conversion rights to the mezzanine provider. Usually these instruments carry a reduced cash interest coupon and a much higher PIK component. The market for warrantless mezzanine capital has grown substantially, especially due to the growing search for yield by credit investors during the credit-fueled run-up to the onset of the global financial crisis at the end of 2008. However, in the aftermath of the global financial crisis of 2007–2008, a much more limited appetite exists for mezzanine capital structured in this manner.

Historically, several factors attracted investors favoring warrantless mezzanine investments. First, the higher contracted PIK return provided them with superior risk-adjusted returns. Second, their entire mezzanine return is prioritized before stockholders' returns. Notwithstanding its current drop in popularity with investors, sponsors and issuers are likely to be attracted to offering investors warrantless mezzanine capital once again during a more favorable economic cycle. This is due to various factors. For example, warrantless mezzanine capital leaves the equity interests of stockholders undiluted and offers a lower all-in effective cost of capital than traditional mezzanine funding (i.e., mezzanine instruments with warrants or some other form of equity kicker). Also, warrantless mezzanine provides the benefits of prepayment flexibility normally associated with the contracted return component of mezzanine funding (subject of course to the protection mechanisms discussed earlier). Finally, it makes the entire debt service cost of the mezzanine funding deductible for income tax purposes because both the cash interest and PIK expense are deductible. In contrast, the costs associated with issuing warrants are generally not deductible for income tax purposes.

COMPARISON OF U.S. AND EUROPEAN MEZZANINE CAPITAL TERMS

Analyzing how mezzanine capital differs within the context of both the U.S. and European markets can be useful because the comparison provides further insights into some of the unique characteristics of mezzanine capital as a distinct sub-asset class and its particular attraction for prospective investors in these two regions.

Exhibit 13.9 compares aggregate capital raised by dedicated mezzanine funds in the United States to that raised by counterparts in Europe. The aggregate amount raised by managers operating out of the United States has consistently exceeded that raised by European-based managers.

Mezzanine capital fulfills the same function in both the U.S. and European markets by effectively filling the funding gap between senior debt and equity in a borrower's capital structure. However, distinct differences exist in the likely attributes

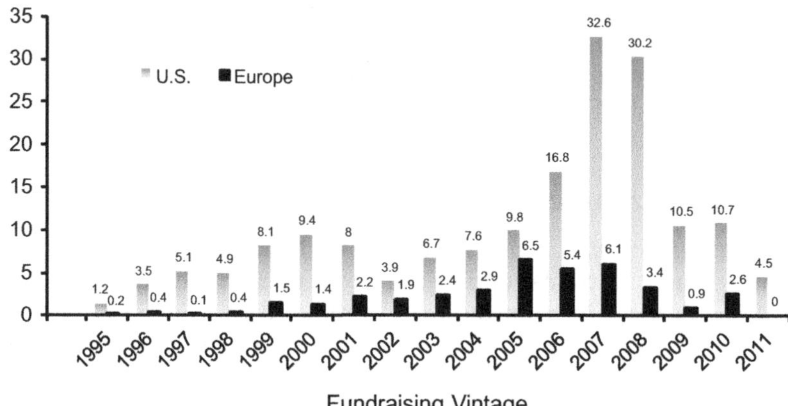

Exhibit 13.9 Mezzanine Fundraising in the United States versus Europe
This exhibit compares the aggregate capital raised by dedicated mezzanine funds in the United States to that raised by their counterparts in Europe; the aggregate amount raised by managers operating out of the United States has consistently exceeded that raised by European-based managers.
Source: Thomson One.

of a typical mezzanine instrument on the two sides of the Atlantic. The primary difference relates to the priority of the mezzanine providers' claims and their associated collateral rights. In the United States, mezzanine investments are usually comprised of subordinated notes, which rank junior to the borrower's senior debt. This subordination is mostly contractual, but in some instances it may also be structural. In Europe, conversely, mezzanine capital typically enjoys a second-priority lien over the collateral, immediately behind the first-priority claims of senior lenders.

This evidence suggests that mezzanine capital fills slightly different gaps in companies' capital structures in the United States and Europe. U.S. mezzanine capital is similar to European high-yield bonds because both carry fixed coupons, may be structurally subordinated, and may be totally unsecured and subordinated to all other indebtedness of the borrower. Conversely, European mezzanine capital more typically carries a floating-rate coupon, is contractually subordinated, and its second-secured ranking makes it more akin to U.S. second-lien loans.

Exhibit 13.10 provides a comparison of the ranking of various categories of debt instruments in the United States and Europe (Hardee, Mazzini, and Stringer, 2003). Collectively, total mezzanine capital in the United States and Europe accounts for 93 percent of the global mezzanine capital market. The United States remains the dominant player in mezzanine financing, accounting for 73 percent, compared to Europe at 20 percent.

MEZZANINE FUNDING AS AN ALTERNATIVE TO HIGH-YIELD BONDS

As previously discussed, subtle differences exist in debt capital market conventions that make clear and generally applicable distinctions between mezzanine and high-yield bond funding difficult. Nonetheless, these are two sources of intermediate capital that frequently compete with each other to finance the same (or

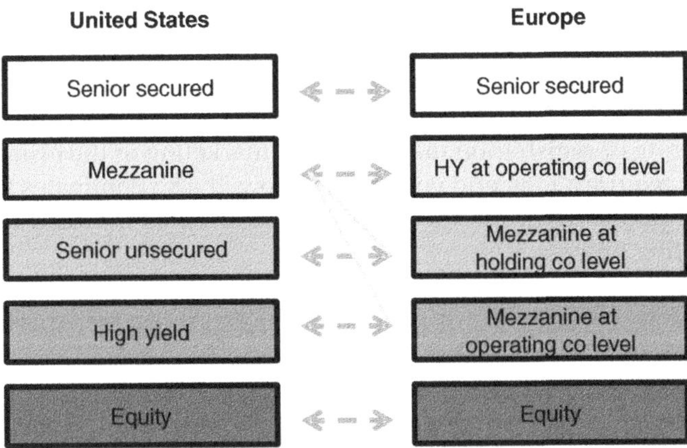

Exhibit 13.10 Comparative Ranking of Various Capital Types in the United States and Europe

an overlapping) part of a borrower's capital structure. Depending on the state of global liquidity and strategic asset allocations, one or the other of these potential sources of funding may be in ascendancy in the intermediate capital space from time to time.

Various reasons explain why many private equity sponsors tend to favor mezzanine financing over high-yield funding:

- *Relative certainty of funds and financing terms.* Unlike high-yield bonds, for which execution and terms are only determined after an extensive marketing effort, mezzanine financing is firmly underwritten by arranging banks or underwriters providing the sponsors with relative certainty of terms. High-yield bond issuances may be bridge financed, and oftentimes material changes can arise in the terms at the last minute. If a mandated lead arranger is unable to refinance a bridge loan, it becomes a so-called "hung bridge," and the cost of funding for the borrower can increase materially until such time as debt capital market conditions enable a refinancing of the hung bridge.
- *Flexibility.* Mezzanine finance is typically more flexible, affording sponsors greater flexibility to exit investments opportunistically as IPO markets open or trade buyers emerge. High-yield issuance tends to follow more regimented conventions around no call periods and early repayment penalties. In fact, probably the most important consideration for a borrower in determining whether to raise its intermediate capital needs from the mezzanine or high-yield bond markets is the fact that the high-yield bond markets are far more rigid and prescriptive about the overall structure of their borrowing terms and covenants. Mezzanine lenders, conversely, are more likely to be willing to craft a subordinated funding layer that is tailored to meet an individual borrower's specific requirements. The trade-off is that a mezzanine

lender will more likely want to be more restrictive (e.g., by imposing maintenance-based covenants rather than incurrence based covenants in the funding instrument) and involved in the borrower's business.

- *Private distribution.* Mezzanine finance does not require extensive and expensive offering or registration materials, and marketing in the primary market does not require a long and costly road show. It also eliminates the requirement for public disclosure of information as well as the need for a formal credit rating process.
- *Knowledge of investors.* Mezzanine finance is syndicated among a relatively small number of selected investors with limited secondary-market trading. Mezzanine investors often have a long history of collaboration with financial sponsors, which facilitates the process of consent or amendment requests.
- *Private resolution of credit events and restructurings.* With mezzanine instruments, adverse credit developments are almost always resolved through private negotiation between the borrower, the lenders' club, and the financial sponsors. This process does not attract unwanted attention from other constituencies, such as customers or trade creditors, or participation from unknown bondholders.
- *Volatility.* The higher volatility in the liquidity of global high-yield debt markets, especially since the onset of the global financial crisis, makes mezzanine debt a far less reliable and predictable source of a borrower's intermediate capital needs over time.
- *Volume.* Historically, one of the key differences between the mezzanine and high-yield markets has been the size/volume constraint of each. Given the high cost of conducting road shows and broadly syndicating high-yield debt, raising debt via a high-yield bond issue for amounts less than around $200 to $250 million is generally not considered viable. In fact, the minimum threshold for high-yield bond issues has been increasing steadily, locking many prospective borrowers out of this capital market and causing them instead to turn to the mezzanine capital market for some of their leverage requirements.

MEZZANINE FINANCING DEMAND AND SUPPLY DRIVERS

Demand for mezzanine funding is essentially a function of broader market demand for credit. If no demand exists for wholesale credit, little demand will likely be present for mezzanine funding, which is just a potential layer in a borrower's broader debt capital structure. In this context, growth prospects of businesses and the need to raise capital to fund expansion either organically or by acquisition drive credit and mezzanine-funding demand.

A secondary driver of demand for mezzanine funding is the need for highly leveraged borrowers to refinance their debt obligations. Many borrowers were successful in raising leverage at historically high leverage multiples before the onset of the global financial crisis. Subsequently, they had to refinance their maturing outstanding debt obligations in prevailing market conditions characterized by considerably lower levels of liquidity, higher funding costs, and tighter covenant requirements. These market conditions have already provided and are likely to continue to provide the basis for a steady demand for funding with a flexible mandate, which is capable of bridging the borrower's funding gap.

On the supply side, key drivers are the availability of credit for highly leveraged borrowers from either traditional debt capital markets (and insofar as mezzanine funding is concerned, particularly from the high-yield bond market), or the availability of bank credit. The global financial crisis and the ensuing sovereign debt crisis have had a material effect on global debt capital markets as well as the regulation of key players in those markets. One effect is to constrain borrowers' abilities to tap volatile global high-yield markets in recent years. A second effect involves credit rating agencies' (CRAs) credibility being called into question by some bond investors and CRAs becoming the focus of Financial Stability Board principles specifically adopted to reduce global investor reliance on their ratings. Third, combined with the adoption of the Basel III Accord by the Basel Committee on Banking Supervision (and its effects on bank capital adequacy and liquidity requirements), global banks' capacity and appetite to extend credit, especially in the leveraged loan space, has been substantially curtailed. Finally, investor demand for collateralized loan obligations (CLOs) and collateralized debt obligations (CDOs) has fallen off sharply and, in so doing, has diminished banks' and other intermediary credit asset originators' ability to distribute leveraged loan and intermediate capital credit risks.

INVESTMENT IN MEZZANINE AS AN ASSET CLASS

As a distinct asset class, mezzanine capital has rapidly increased in popularity with investors in alternative assets in the U.S. and European capital markets over the previous 15 years. During this time, a dramatic increase has occurred not only in the aggregate amount of capital committed to the asset class, but also in both the number of investors and the different categories of investors who have committed capital for investment in mezzanine instruments.

On the demand side, LBO sponsors have shown increased interest in incorporating layers of mezzanine funding into their investment capital structures. Traditional bank lending, during the period after the global financial crisis, has been substantially reduced and the amount of senior debt capital available as a component of total acquisition price is scarcer, and junior debt has become more expensive. An increase in equity needed to consummate transactions makes the debt piece more secure than transactions before the global financial crisis.

Future market demand for mezzanine funding may be driven primarily by a pickup in middle-market LBO activities. Despite the difficult global economic environment and the general downturn in merger and acquisition (M&A) activity, LBO activity seems likely to pick up in the medium to long term, with investors still harboring high return expectations for private equity as an asset class and gradually returning to making new commitments to the asset class.

The LBO markets' resilience generally can be attributed to a combination of the large amount of capital raised by private equity sponsors ahead of the global financial crisis, a considerable portion of which remains uninvested. Also, new opportunities are expected to arise on account of refocusing on core activities by major industrial conglomerates as well as the acceleration of asset disposal processes by distressed or semidistressed companies.

The trend of increased strategic asset allocations to private equity ahead of the onset of the global financial crisis was not accompanied by appropriately proportionate increases in commitments of capital to mezzanine funds. Although many reasons account for this skewed relationship, the major reason is the fact that during this period global high-yield bond markets, CDOs and CLOs became the key debt capital market sources of leveraged finance, with demand for mezzanine funding dwindling to a trickle.

Fundraising for Dedicated Mezzanine Funds

Mezzanine funds tend to be structured along the same lines as private equity funds. Typically they have 10-year fund terms, incorporating 3- to 5-year investment periods, 1 to 2 percent management fees, and carried interest of 20 percent payable after (1) a hurdle rate has been met or (2) a preferred return has been provided.

The three years before the onset of the global financial crisis at the end of 2008 witnessed a notable increase in the aggregate amount of capital committed to the mezzanine capital asset class. The onset of this crisis saw a dramatic drop-off in investor commitments to alternative investments generally. The trend of increasing capital commitments to mezzanine financing will likely resume as institutional investors identify the market opportunity in this space due to the enormous undersupply of liquidity, especially for leveraged finance transactions. With the new capital adequacy and liquidity guidelines contained in the Basel III Accord proposed by the Basel Committee on Banking Supervision, many banks will be less inclined to advance illiquid medium- to long-term leveraged and mezzanine loans. Thus, much of the supply of this type of funding is likely to come in from independent specialized mezzanine funds or credit funds.

A secular increase has occurred in the amount of mezzanine capital that has been raised as a percentage of the total private equity that has been raised. This trend is likely to continue as mezzanine capital is now more widely established with institutional investors as a discrete asset class subcomponent of private equity. Raising mezzanine capital is marginally correlated to the amount of capital raised for primary buyout activity. This relationship makes sense intuitively since mezzanine capital is a complement to traditional forms of debt and equity financing used to finance LBOs. Historically, global buyout funds have raised, at times, in excess of 10 times the capital raised by mezzanine funds.

The tightening in credit market conditions following the global financial crisis and the ensuing sovereign debt crisis, suggest that LBO sponsors have had access to lower leverage multiples at higher interest margins and on more restrictive terms. This dynamic has also resulted in the equity layer of some LBO capital structures increasing by as much as two-thirds, with some LBOs now having an equity layer comprising up to 50 percent of the overall capital structure. The increased equity component naturally provides an additional buffer for subordinated creditors, including the mezzanine funders, which, when combined with reduced overall leverage and tighter maintenance-based covenants, provide mezzanine financiers with enhanced risk-adjusted returns.

The broadening universe of institutional investors interested in the mezzanine capital asset class will be underpinned by the superior risk-adjusted returns that it offers. Additionally, mezzanine capital's investment performance has historically displayed a low correlation with traditional asset classes, and it therefore offers investors the opportunity to reduce their risk through portfolio diversification. Also, the running/current yield that a typical mezzanine investment portfolio offers helps to mitigate the J-curve effect associated with commitments of principal to closed-end blind pool funds (i.e., the *J-curve effect* describes the negative impact on closed-end fund investors' returns, caused by the fact that they are charged management fees on their full capital commitments, even though this capital is only drawdown and invested over time). Next, the fact that most mezzanine assets (particularly in Europe and emerging markets) have a variable interest rate component means that investors are not required to take a view on inflation and rising interest rates.

Finally, the fact that stocks' values have a negative correlation to interest rates limits the variability in the all-in-yield of a portfolio of hybrid mezzanine assets over the long term. This relationship makes them useful investments to reduce the interest rate risk in a debt portfolio or to reduce the volatility in a private equity investment portfolio. Mezzanine capital now accounts for about 6.3 percent of all private equity funds raised in both the United States and Europe.

SUMMARY AND CONCLUSIONS

Mezzanine capital's unique hybrid characteristics are precisely what enable it to bridge the funding gap between the senior debt and equity in a borrower's capital structure. The flexibility of the mezzanine investor to tailor the bifurcated nature of a particular mezzanine instrument to suit the requirements of a particular situation ensures the sustained relevance of this asset class through the peaks and troughs of credit liquidity. However, the bespoke nature of mezzanine instruments combined with their term structure mean that mezzanine capital is an illiquid asset class. For this reason, mezzanine debt is an asset class best invested in by using either a dedicated closed-end blind pool fund or a specialist credit fund. Seasoned investors in alternative assets have come to realize its resilience as an asset class capable of generating stable noncorrelated returns across a wide variety of prevailing market conditions.

DISCUSSION QUESTIONS

1. Define *mezzanine securities*.
2. What is the risk profile and return potential of making investments in mezzanine securities?
3. What is the opportunity set for investing in mezzanine debt securities?
4. What are the supply and demand drivers of the mezzanine capital market?

REFERENCES

Gompers, Paul, and Josh Lerner. 2001. *The Money of Invention: How Venture Capital Creates New Wealth.* Boston: Harvard University Press.

Hardee, Rachel, Pablo Mazzini, and Tony Stringer. 2003. *European Mezzanine Reconsidered: European Leveraged Finance Specialist Report.* New York: Fitch Ratings Limited.

McGirt, Derek, and Christine Pitre. 2003. *Mezzanine Debt Another Level to Consider*. New York: Fitch Ratings Limited.

UBS Alternative Investments. 2011. *Investing in Credit Series—Mezzanine Debt*. New York: UBS Financial Services, Inc.

ABOUT THE AUTHORS

Sameer Jain is based in New York and is a Managing Director at American Realty Capital. Prior to this he headed investment content and strategy at UBS Alternative Investments. He has 18 years of experience across a broad array of alternative investment activities, including product development, research, asset allocation, and private investments oversight. Mr. Jain is a graduate of MIT and Harvard University and has his Series 7 and 66 licences.

Phillip Myburgh is based in Johannesburg, South Africa, where he is the Chief Executive Officer of STANLIB Credit Partners, a specialist corporate and high-yield credit asset management subsidiary of STANLIB Asset Management, one of Africa's largest asset management companies. He has over 20 years' experience in structured and leveraged finance in the investment banking and asset management industry. Before founding STANLIB Credit Partners (originally as Mezzanine Partners), he worked at Standard Merchant Bank, Rand Merchant Bank, and Brait. Mr. Myburgh is a graduate of Stellenbosch University and Harvard University.

CHAPTER 14

Buyout Funds

CHRISTIAN RAUCH
Assistant Professor, Goethe University

MARK WAHRENBURG
Professor of Finance, Goethe University

INTRODUCTION

Although the first private equity investments date back to the Industrial Revolution era and the merchant banking business in the United States in the 1900s fronted by J. Pierpont Morgan, the modern-day buyout business did not start to develop until the early 1980s. Blossoming capital markets, the creation of junk bonds as a financing tool by Michael Milken and Drexel Burnham Lambert, and the formation of large and inefficient conglomerates during the third mergers and acquisitions (M&As) wave during the 1960s are largely credited as the main triggers for the development of the buyout industry as it is known today. Corporate raiders, such as Carl Icahn, Kirk Kerkorian, and T. Boone Pickens, and financiers, such as Jerome Kohlberg Jr., Henry Kravis, and George Roberts of private equity powerhouse KKR, were among the first to apply the tools of so called "classic" leveraged buyouts (LBOs). The buyout industry has since established itself as a centerpiece of modern-day corporate finance, both as an asset class for investors as well as a funding source for companies.

A modern-day *buyout fund* is an investment vehicle set up and run by managers of a private equity firm and funded by outside investors' money. The primary goal of the fund is to generate returns for its investors by acquiring companies, restructuring them, and selling the restructured companies at a premium to the original purchase price, usually within a period of five to seven years. The fund is set up as a partnership between the outside investors as limited partners (LPs) and the fund managers as general partners (GPs). The GPs run the fund and have unlimited liability, whereas the LPs provide the capital, have no say in the management of the fund, and are liable only up to the amount of capital they provide to the fund. The terms by which the fund and the investment process are governed are set in a predetermined partnership agreement between the GPs and LPs. For running and managing the fund, the GPs are compensated with a management fee (usually 1 to 3 percent of the total fund volume) and a performance-based pay called the *carried interest* (usually 20 to 30 percent of the returns distributed to investors). A fund is usually composed of several different investors, whose money is invested

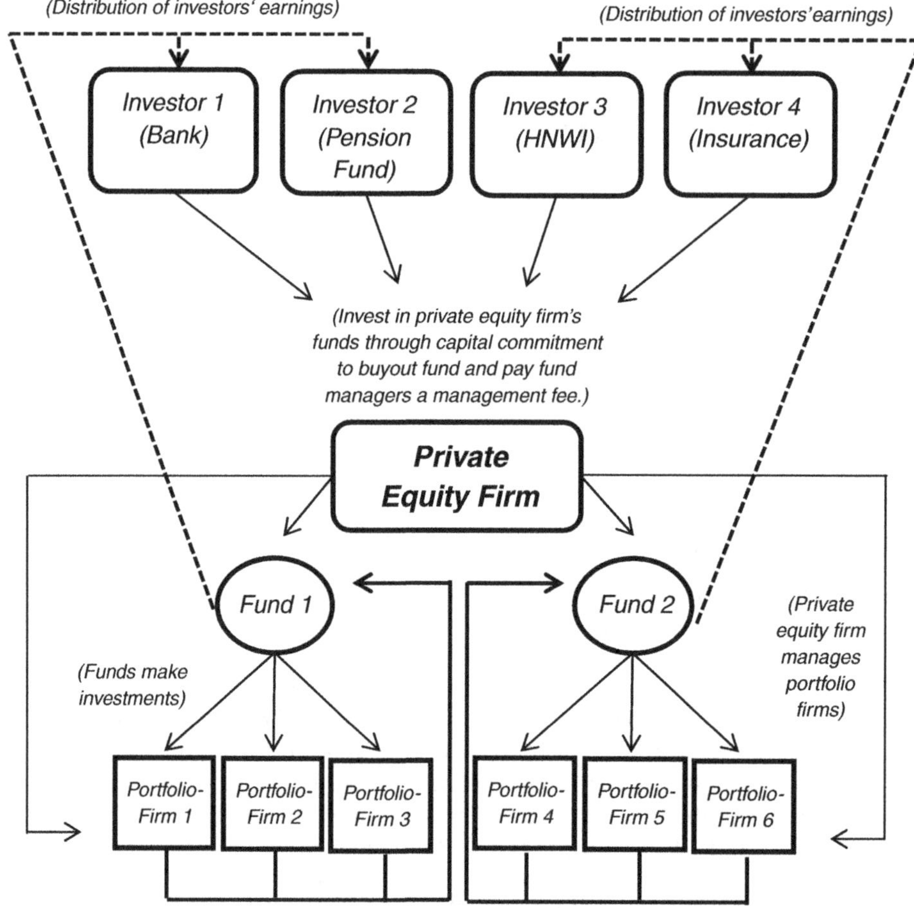

Exhibit 14.1 Private Equity Investment Structure
The exhibit shows a typical organizational structure of a buyout fund.

in various companies, called *portfolio companies*. Figure 14.1 shows a typical fund structure.

Every buyout fund has three typical features. First, and arguably the most typical feature, is the use of leverage in the investment process. Large amounts of debt are not only used to purchase the portfolio companies but also to create value for the fund investors. The term *buyout* is therefore frequently used in conjunction with the term *leverage*, to create the term *leveraged buyout*, or *LBO*. Second, buyout investors usually pursue an aggressive restructuring of their portfolio companies. The major goal of the restructuring processes is to create free cash flows from the portfolio companies' operations that can be used to pay down the enormous amounts of debt used by the portfolio companies. Third, and the prerequisite to allow for the leveraging and aggressive restructuring of the portfolio companies, is that the funds purchase large controlling stakes in their portfolio companies,

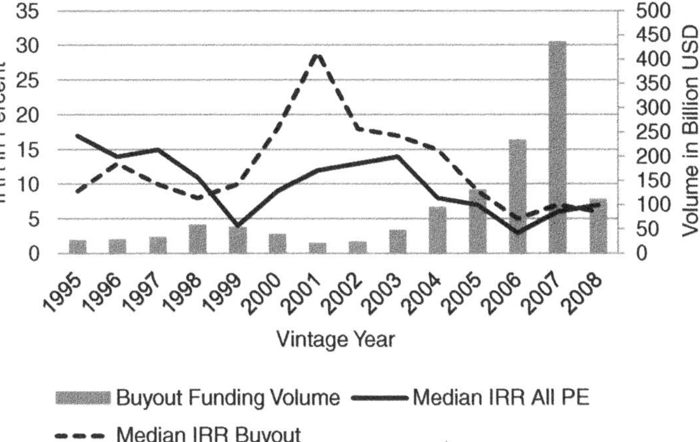

Exhibit 14.2 Buyout Industry Development
This exhibit shows the development of the buyout fund industry in the United States over the period 1995 to 2008. Displayed are the median internal rate of return (IRR) numbers for all private equity sectors (mezzanine, venture, and buyout) and for the buyout segment. The secondary y-axis displays the total equity and debt funding volumes of all U.S. buyout deals annually. All IRR numbers are shown for the funds, with the vintage years (i.e., the years in which the respective buyout funds were launched) displayed on the x-axis.
Source: Performance numbers are taken from the Preqin Special Report: US Private Equity, 2011. The S&P LCD database is the source of the buyout funding volume.

frequently reaching close to 100 percent. This control is necessary because fund managers need to adopt measures to restructure the portfolio companies in the desired way. It is also necessary because buyout funds invest in both private and publicly listed corporations. To exercise full control and apply all restructuring measures, fund managers purchase all shares of these corporations (sometimes in hostile takeover battles), take them private, and then take the company public again after the successful restructuring. This is called a *reverse LBO*.

These three features are also among the main value drivers of buyout funds. Using these value drivers, fund managers have created tremendous value for investors over time, as Exhibit 14.2 shows. Thus, the buyout industry has constantly grown both in terms of number of funds and total deal volumes, as Exhibit 14.2 also shows. However, the financial crisis of 2007–2008 had strong adverse effects on the buyout fund industry. The reason was that the main features of the crisis, such as the capital market turmoil and the distress of the banking sector, severely crippled many of the buyout managers' main value drivers. Besides these economic effects, the buyout sector has more recently become subject to stronger regulatory scrutiny of policy makers, especially in Europe and the United States. Taken together, these events raise many questions about the future of the buyout industry and the LBO business model. To understand the current state of the buyout sector and its future development, this chapter explains the buyout funds' business model and its value drivers. The chapter also discusses possible developments within the industry by explaining the effects the recent crisis-related events had on the buyout industry and how these effects might change the LBO investment approach and the buyout sector as a whole.

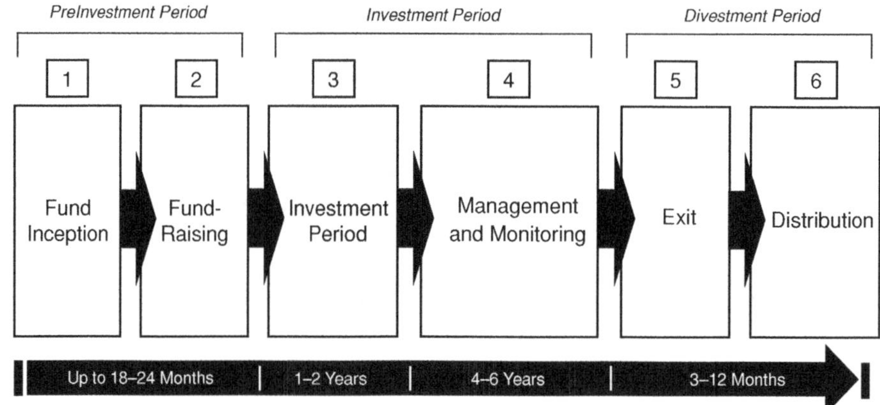

Exhibit 14.3 Private Equity Investment Process
The exhibit shows the typical six-stage investment process of a buyout fund.

VALUE DRIVERS IN THE BUYOUT INVESTMENT PROCESS

The buyout fund investment process can be separated into three consecutive phases: (1) preinvestment, (2) investment, and (3) divestment. Each phase consists of one or more stages. Specifically, the preinvestment phase comprises the fund inception and the fundraising; the investment phase consists of the investment period and the management and monitoring period; and the divestment phase contains the exit and distribution of returns. Exhibit 14.3 displays a graph of the different process stages.

Each stage of the investment process contains one or more crucial value drivers for the buyout fund managers and their investors. Subsequently, each stage's value drivers are explained in detail to provide an understanding of the way buyout funds conduct their investments to create economic value.

Preinvestment Phase: Fund Inception and Fundraising

The first two periods of the preinvestment phase are the inception of the fund period and planning and conducting the fundraising period. The two crucial value drivers in this phase are the choice for the type of fund to be pursued (i.e., the focus of the fund) and the magnitude of the fundraising. Generally, two different types of funds can be distinguished: (1) macro funds and (2) industry funds. Macro funds focus on certain geographic or economic regions, such as the BRIC (Brazil, Russia, India, and China) countries or emerging markets. The main goal is to participate in the economic growth of these markets as broadly as possible and regardless of the industry.

Industry funds focus on a certain industry, mostly without a geographic focus. The reasoning for constructing a fund solely out of companies from a certain industry is similar to the reasoning for focusing a fund on a certain economic region: economic growth. A buyout fund might believe that a certain industry will exhibit

Exhibit 14.4 Private Equity Investor Groups

	Texas Pacific Group %	Goldman Sachs %	Kohlberg, Kravis, Roberts %	The Carlyle Group %	The Blackstone Group %
Public pension funds	51	8	53	41	59
Private pension funds	6	8	5	10	6
Banks	0	8	14	12	8
Insurance	10	0	5	20	14
Government funds	0	0	0	0	0
Endowment funds	5	8	1	3	6
Funds-of-funds	5	0	14	0	0
High-net-worth individuals	4	38	8	14	9
Financial sponsors	0	31	0	0	0
Other	19	0	0	0	0

The exhibit shows the typical funding sources for some of the largest buyout firms worldwide. The numbers are based on historical values over several funds.

strong growth in the near future. The goal is thus to build up exposure to that industry to participate in its growth, and, more important, to pick the respective champions in the industry. Some buyout funds recruit managers from a certain industry that can help to make investment decisions for the industry funds, which is why they are sometimes also called *industry-specialist funds*. This industry knowledge is the reason many buyout funds tend to make investments in their domestic markets. The choice for the kind of market or industry on which a fund focuses is the first step in the value-creation process. The fund managers' economic assumptions about a certain industry or market must be correct to increase the fund's chances of generating returns for its investors.

A broad body of literature shows that some managers persistently perform better in setting up funds and allocating capital than other managers (e.g., Raschle and Ender, 2004; Kaplan and Schoar, 2005, with a broad overview given by Meyer and Mathonet, 2005, and Fraser-Sampson, 2007, especially regarding the returns). Therefore, the value driver at this stage is the fund's management team.

The fundraising process usually starts with the buyout fund managers approaching potential future investors either directly or through placement agents, who are consultants to the GPs and advise them on the general strategic approach to the fundraising process. Kaplan and Schoar (2005) and Kaplan and Strömberg (2008) provide a more detailed analysis of buyout fundraising.

Exhibit 14.4 provides a typical investor structure for buyout funds. The most prominent investor groups of the listed buyout firms are public and private pension funds, banks, insurance companies, government funds, private endowment funds, funds-of-funds, high-net-worth individuals, and other buyout firms (financial sponsors). The volume of the raised funds is the most important value driver in the fundraising process. Typically, buyout firm managers have a certain target amount of funds they want to raise for a given fund, based on the estimated number and volume of investments they plan to make over the fund lifecycle. If the

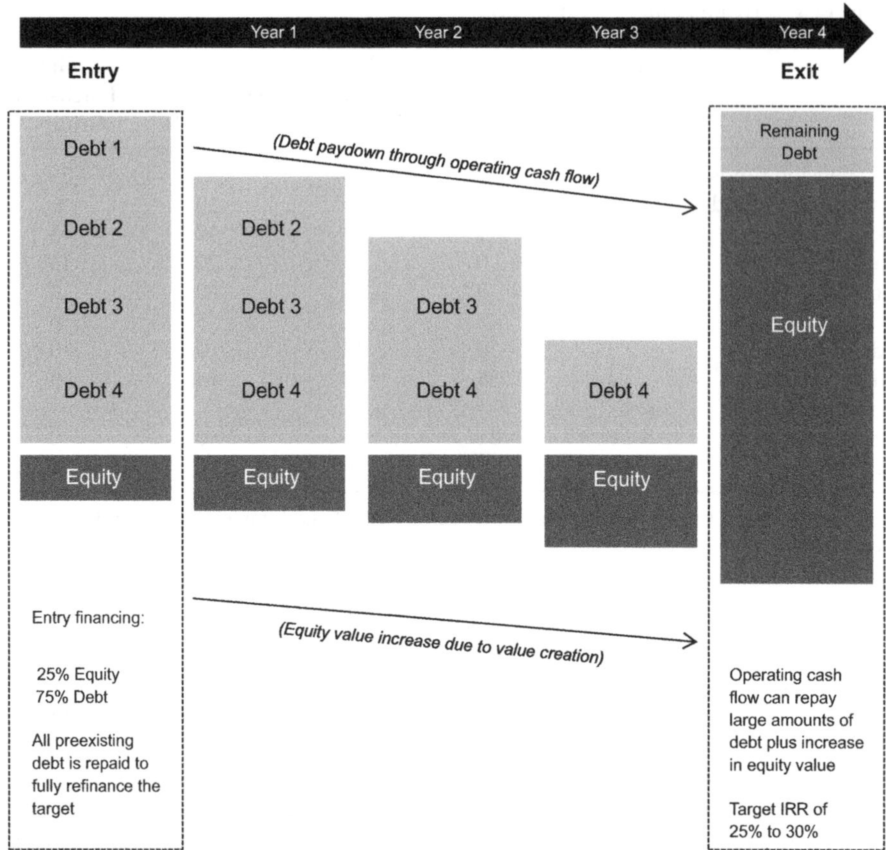

Exhibit 14.5 Buyout Financing Structure
The exhibit shows a typical leveraged buyout investment structure over time.

fundraising volume drastically exceeds or falls below the desired target volume, the value-creation potential of the fund is hampered. If the fundraising volume is too low, the fund managers might lack the financial firepower to invest in the deals they desire or might not be able to raise sufficient debt because their equity participation in the deals' funding structures is too low. However, if a buyout fund is endowed with too much capital, fund managers might be unable to invest all provided capital within the fund lifecycle or they may engage in subpar investments in order to fully invest the committed capital. Either way, the funds' value creation could be decreased. To obtain the desired funding structure, buyout firms usually raise funds until the desired funding volume is reached, upon which the process is closed immediately.

Investment Phase: Investing and Management and Monitoring

The investment phase is the second phase of the buyout investment process. Fund managers screen the market for potential portfolio companies, acquire the ownership stakes, and subsequently restructure the companies. The main value drivers in this phase are the choice of a portfolio company and the successful restructuring.

The most important task in scanning the market for potential takeover candidates is to find a company to apply the leveraged buyout model. The underlying notion of leveraging a private equity investment in a company is simple to grasp: Using a small portion of equity along with a large portion of debt to finance the acquisition allows for an attractive equity return at the end of the investment period. The success of this model depends on two pivotal factors that have to be met by potential portfolio companies. First, the portfolio company's operating business has to create enough cash to service the debt interest rate payments and additionally repay a substantial portion of the debt over the investment horizon. Second, the debt repayments and restructurings have to create an exit value for the portfolio company that allows the buyout fund to reach a given target return at the end of the expected investment phase. Exhibit 13.5 shows a typical leverage structure over the period of the buyout investment.

The two critical value drivers in this phase are obtaining sufficient and cheap debt funding for the deal and creating large free cash flows to service the debt. The debt used for the leverage structure comprises three different layers, as presented in Exhibit 14.6, with each layer having different characteristics and costs. Cotter and Peck (2001) provide an overview of how buyout funds structure their portfolio companies' debt and equity financing.

The management and monitoring stage of the buyout investment phase occurs as fund managers create economic value from the portfolio companies. The general perception today is that modern-day buyout funds create value

Exhibit 14.6 Debt Used in Buyout Financing Structures

Debt Features	Bank Loans	Senior Debt	Subordinated Debt
Maturity	5+ years	5–10 years	6–10 years
Lender	Commercial banks	Commercial banks, investment banks, and mutual funds	Pension funds, investment banks, and hedge funds
Interest	LIBOR + 2/2.5 percent	LIBOR + 3/4 percent	LIBOR + 5–7 percent
Seniority	Senior claim, secured, collateral is the target company's assets	Most senior, secured, collateral is the target company's assets	Lowest seniority, partly secured
Structure	Flexible; varying deal specifics (e.g., covenants and repayments)	Flexible; varying deal specifics (e.g., covenants and repayments)	Flexible structure, more flexible than other loan categories
Part of total debt	About 5–15 percent	About 25–50 percent	About 20–40 percent

The exhibit shows the typical debt instruments used for a leveraged buyout financing.

in portfolio companies through three different factors, besides the financial engineering process as previously described: (1) management monitoring, (2) operational engineering, and (3) governance intervention (Kaplan and Strömberg, 2008; Acharya, Gottschalg, Hahn, and Kehoe, 2013).

Management monitoring describes the process by which buyout funds can create value in their portfolio firms through managerial oversight and incentive creation by aligning the managements' interests with the (buyout fund) owners' interests. Monitoring dates back to the original idea of the separation of ownership and control by Jensen and Meckling (1976) and Shleifer and Vishny (1986), who show that external institutional shareholders can solve agency conflicts or free rider problems and thereby improve company performance. Close monitoring allows the buyout fund owners to alleviate managerial inefficiency caused by insufficient efforts, entrenchment or self-dealing of the incumbent managers (Tirole, 2006). The buyout managers usually establish reporting schemes under which the portfolio companies' managers have to report profit/loss and certain balance sheet measures on a regular (sometimes monthly) basis to the buyout fund.

Operational engineering is a value-creation strategy that can either be directed at the operations of a portfolio company or at its general business strategy. The operations side of the strategy focuses on enhancing a company's efficiency along the supply chain. Most actions aim at cost reductions through process optimization, supply chain management, overhead spending, or stoppage of production of deficient products. Operational engineering can also be directed at the general business strategy of a company, such as by engaging in M&As or joint ventures to use or create synergies, or the spin-offs/carve-outs of departments or subsidiaries. The main goal here can be twofold: (1) to create abundant cash that can be used for debt reduction in the company and (2) to reduce costs and make the company more efficient. The latter will especially increase the economic value of the portfolio company and allow for a higher exit valuation of the buyout funds' stakes in the company.

Governance intervention describes the strategy that aims at improving a portfolio company's management quality by making direct changes in the management (Kaplan, 2010). A frequently used action by fund managers upon purchasing a portfolio company is to replace the existing top-level management through new and allegedly better management (Acharya, Gottschalg, Hahn, and Kehoe, 2013). However, the actions to improve management quality can also be directed at certain governance structures, such as board composition, or the introduction of committees to improve management oversight, such as audit or compensation committees (Gertner and Kaplan, 1996; Cornelli and Karakas, 2008).

The major value driver is thus the increase in operational efficiency of the portfolio companies through these strategies. A broad body of literature confirms that private equity firms (in general) and buyout funds (in particular) create economic value for their portfolio firms by applying these measures successfully. Kaplan (1989), Smith (1990), Muscarella and Vetsuypens (1990), Holthausen and Larcker (1996), Bruton, Keels, and Scifres (2002), and Murray, Niu, and Harris (2006) show this value creation in terms of the operating performance of portfolio companies.

Divestment Phase: Exit and Distribution

The divestment, or exit, phase is the phase in which the buyout fund exits the portfolio companies by selling off its shareholdings. Fund managers leave the portfolio company's board of directors during this stage. The exit of the portfolio firms is among the most crucial stages in the investment process. The created value in the portfolio companies can only be realized if the fund manages to sell its stakes at a premium to the original purchase price.

Disregarding bankruptcies, two major ways are available by which the buyout fund can exit portfolio companies: (1) trade sales and (2) initial public offerings (IPO) (Kaplan and Strömberg, 2008). A *trade sale* is the sale of the company to another financial or strategic investor through a merger or acquisition transaction. The IPO process is regarded as being the most profitable and challenging exit scenario. IPOs provide the most profitable scenario because share valuations are usually higher than trade sale scenarios. Further, if the portfolio company can be taken public, this means that it underwent successful restructuring and became a highly profitable company (Schmidt, Steffen, and Szabó, 2010).

The IPO process is the most challenging exit scenario for two reasons. First, taking a company public is a difficult, costly, and time-consuming process in which many rules and regulations have to be followed and a broad variety of future investors have to be convinced of purchasing the portfolio company's shares. Also, the buyout fund usually has to obey share-lockup rules, which prevent pre-IPO investors from selling their shares in the open market before the end of a 180-day period, starting on the day of the IPO (Field and Hanka, 2001). This means that investors face the risk of adverse market reactions that could possibly diminish the value of the shares before they can be sold.

Second, the actual sale of the shares presents a challenge. The buyout owner faces a trade-off in disposing of its shares. Because the internal rate of return (IRR) is the main performance measure for a buyout fund, and its value depends on the return over time, the buyout fund should dispose of its shares as quickly as possible. However, selling off all shares at once might drive down the price of the stock and therefore hurt the return of the fund. The fund managers therefore have to find the optimal trade-off between selling the shares quickly without hurting the stock price too much. Buyout funds tend to distribute the shares to their fund investors instead of selling them to the market directly.

Gompers and Lerner (1998) provide an overview of this process for venture capital firms. Exhibit 14.7 provides empirical evidence of the IPO market for buyout investments. The graph shows the increasing importance of IPOs for buyout exits. Both the relative number of all buyout-backed IPOs in comparison to all IPOs and their size (as expressed by market capitalization at the IPO) has continuously increased over time.

The last part of the buyout investment phase is distributing capital and returns to the fund investors. In a procedure called the *distribution waterfall*, the proceedings from the portfolio companies' sales are divided to the fund investors on a pro rata basis after a complicated procedure of deducting costs and the carried interest. A detailed discussion of the distribution waterfall is beyond the scope of the chapter. However, Metrick and Yasuda (2010) provide a comprehensive description of buyout funds' fee structures and carried interest payments.

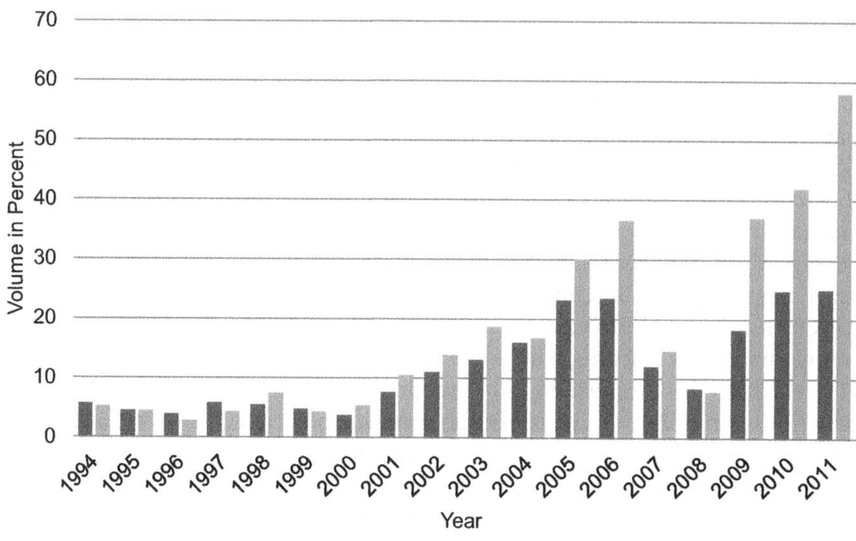

Exhibit 14.7 IPOs as Buyout Exits 1994–2011

The exhibit displays frequencies and volumes of buyout-backed initial public offerings (IPOs) over the period 1994 to 2011 in the United States. Shown are two indicators: (1) the ratio of the number of buyout-backed IPOs to the total number of IPOs taking place in the United States in each calendar year ("% of IPOs") and (2) the ratio of the market capitalization of all buyout-backed IPOs to the market capitalization of all IPOs in the United States in each calendar year ("% of Market Cap"). Buyout-backed IPOs are defined as all companies that went public in an IPO and had a buyout fund as an investor before and at the time of the IPO.

Source: The graph is based on information drawn from the Thomson SDC database on IPOs and the S-1 and 424B filings of the IPO companies.

PAST, PRESENT, AND FUTURE: OPPORTUNITIES AND RISK

The buyout industry experienced some of the most difficult times in its history during the financial crisis of 2007–2008. As later described in greater detail, the economic effects of the crisis as well as subsequent regulatory scrutiny affected many of the key value drivers of buyout funds.

Economic Effects of the Financial Crisis of 2007–2008

The financial crisis posed many difficult challenges for the private equity industry in general. For various reasons, the buyout segment was hit especially hard and continues to struggle even after the worst of the crisis ended. Before examining the specific reasons, the chapter elaborates on how the buyout segment has performed over the course of the financial crisis, both in terms of fundraising, investing, and returns. Exhibit 14.8 presents the PrEQIn Private Equity Index for the period 2000 to 2011. The index is a combination of several buyout fund performance indicators and provides a good overview of the performance of the buyout industry.

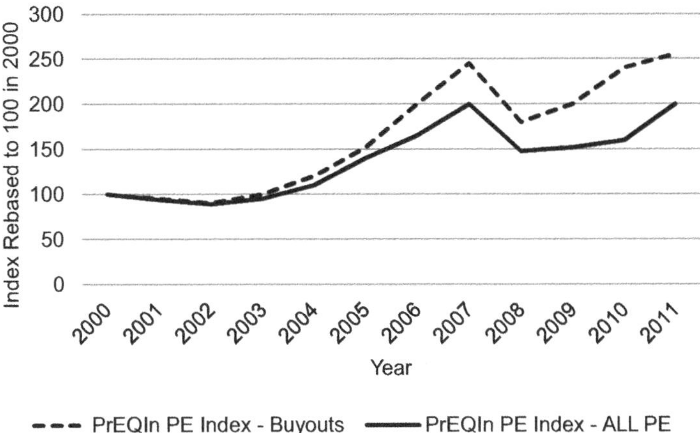

Exhibit 14.8 Private Equity Index Development
The exhibit displays the PrEQIn Private Equity Quarterly Index for the period 2000 to 2011. The index is a money-weighted index that uses fund-level cash flow transactions as well as net asset values (NAVs) for more than 3,900 private equity funds with a total volume of 2.7 trillion USD. The index began in 2000 with a value of 100. Its calculation is based on the quarterly change in fund-level NAVs and investor distributions. The current and historical values are reported in quarterly reports published by the data provider Preqin.
Source: Adapted from Preqin Private Equity Quarterly Index Report, March 2012.

The index progressively increases in the period leading up to the escalation of the financial crisis, indicating a healthy and well-performing buyout industry, reaching its high point in early 2007. The initial drop in the index over the 2007–2008 period was then followed by a period of stagnation throughout 2008, only picking up speed again in 2009 and 2010. The index shows the huge impact the financial crisis had on the buyout industry.

Exhibit 14.9 shows the effects of the financial crisis on the market capitalization of four of the largest private equity investors: 3i, KKR, Blackstone, and Apollo. All stock prices show a steep decline in late 2008 and early 2009, from which none of the firms has fully recovered as of late 2011. The charts also show the market turmoil in terms of intraday trading volatility, which reached peak levels in the same period.

What adversities did the industry face during the crisis? Generally speaking, three major problems affected the buyout industry throughout the crisis: (1) the distress of the banking system and the resulting credit crunch, (2) the economic downturn, and (3) the turmoil in capital markets. At the height of the financial crisis in the fall of 2008, banking systems around the world were in distress. One of the effects of the banks' distress, especially in the United States, was that banks reduced lending to customers. This reduction in lending also included buyout funds, which struggled to obtain sufficient debt funding to pursue their business model and to make investments. The economic downturn negatively affected both the portfolio companies and potential investors. The crisis also affected typical fund investors, such as banks, insurance companies, and large endowment funds; that is, investors reduced their potential capital commitments to buyout funds. Many potential target firms struggled as a result of the economic downturn.

Buyout funds, therefore, witnessed a strong decrease in the number of possible portfolio companies that could stem the financial pressure from an LBO given the adverse economic conditions. The capital market downturn affected both bond and equity markets. Low equity market valuations did not allow funds to execute successful IPO exits of their portfolio companies. Plus, (junk) bond markets came under severe pressure, meaning that buyout funds could not easily find buyers for their issued debt. Taken together, these problems affected the buyout industry and its value drivers in the worst possible way.

The first adversely affected value driver was fundraising volume. Exhibit 14.10 shows that the total fundraising volume of U.S. buyout funds decreased dramatically at the height of the crisis period in 2008 and 2009. The same pattern occurred for the deal and exit volumes of U.S. buyout deals; that is, a strong

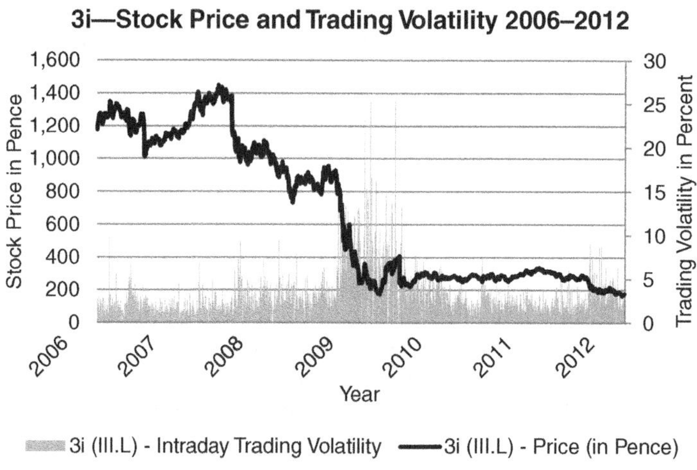

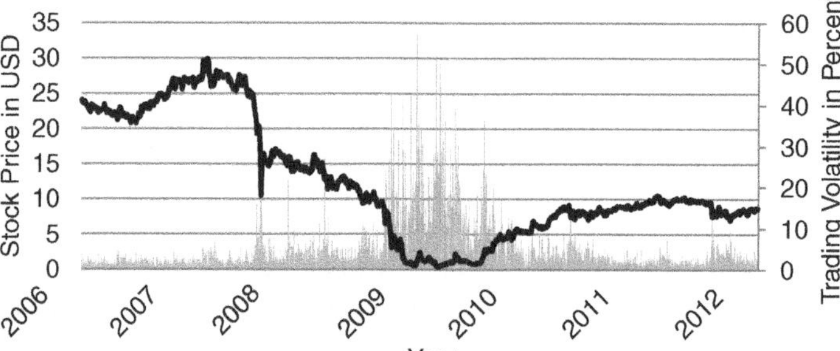

Exhibit 14.9 Stock Valuations of Private Equity Firms during the Financial Crisis

The exhibit shows the stock price and intraday trading volatility development of four of the major buyout/private equity firms—3i; Kohlberg, Kravis, and Roberts (KKR); Blackstone; and Apollo Capital Management—over the financial crisis period.

Source: Stock data are obtained from CRSP Database and Thomson Datastream.

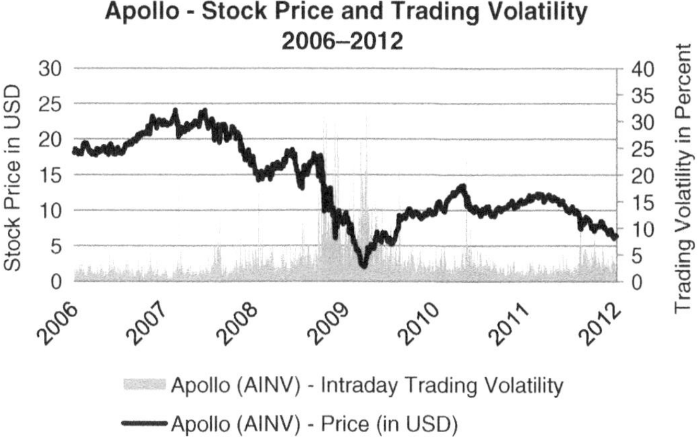

Exhibit 14.9 Stock Valuations of Private Equity Firms during the Financial Crisis (*Continued*)

decline in volume took place at the escalation of the financial crisis in 2007 and 2008 that could not be recovered in the following years.

Exhibit 14.11 presents some anecdotal evidence on the problems in buyout fundraising and of the wariness of possible investors that has been raised after the escalation of the financial crisis during 2007 and 2008. Exhibit 14.11 reports information about the EQT Partners EQT IV fund, BC Partners BCEC IX fund, Cinven Fifth Fund, Apax Partners Apax VIII fund, and Blackstone Capital Partners VI fund. The information about the process, raised funds, duration, and relative size shows the problems the buyout industry still faces in terms of fund setting as a consequence of the crisis. The Apax VIII fund is a fifth smaller than it was before the crisis. The Blackstone Capital Partners VI raised a stunning 16 billion USD but needed almost four full years to do so. The BCEC IX took 18 months to raise only 6.5 billion Euros, and the Cinven Fifth Fund missed its targeted fund volume by 50 percent.

However, as Exhibit 14.10 shows, problems exist in terms of both the funds raised and the entries and exits of deals. Exit volume almost ceased in 2008 and 2009 but picked up again slightly in 2010. These numbers show that even though

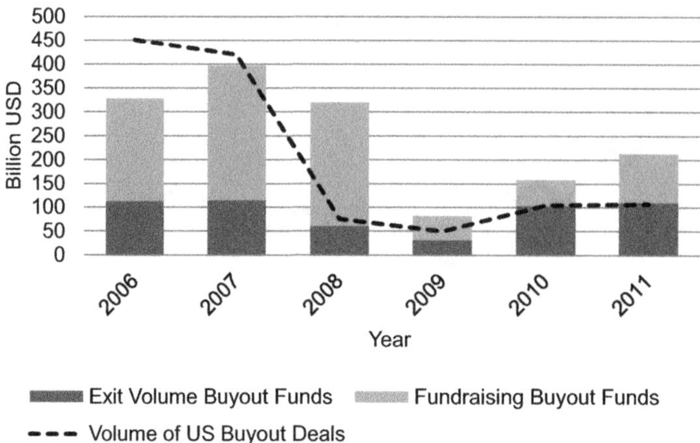

Exhibit 14.10 Buyout Fundraising, Exit Volume, and Deal Volume during the Financial Crisis

The exhibit displays the total fundraising volume, exit volume, and deal volume of the buyout industry in the United States shortly before, during, and after the financial crisis of 2007–2008. The numbers are taken from official PitchBook data compiled and provided by the Private Equity Growth Capital Council (PEGCC) and are based on 315 buyout funds based in the United States. The fundraising volume is the total capital volume of all U.S.-based buyout funds per year. The exit volume is the total volume of all U.S.-based buyout firm exits per year. The deal volume is the total volume of all U.S.-based buyout firm acquisition deals in which U.S.-based buyout funds purchased portfolio companies. All values are in billions of USD.

Source: PitchBook, adapted from Private Equity Growth Capital Council, PEGCC, 2012.

Exhibit 14.11 Examples of Private Equity Fundraising after the Crisis

Firm	Fund Name	Location	Notes
EQT Partners	EQT IV	Sweden and Europe	4.75 billion EUR raised in 9 months. Fund closed in 2011.
BC Partners	BCEC IX	United Kingdom and Europe	6.5 billion EUR in 18 months. Fund closed in 2012.
Cinven	Cinven Fifth Fund	United Kingdom and Europe	2.5 billion EUR (5 billion target). Fund closed in 2011.
Apax Partners	Apax VIII	United Kingdom and Europe	9 billion EUR in 10 months. Fundraising down by a fifth as compared to prior fund.
Blackstone	Blackstone Capital Partners VI	United States	16 billion USD in 4 years. Fund closed in 2012.

The exhibit displays information about selected buyout fundraising since the start of the financial crisis in fall 2007. Listed are five distinct funds by five different buyout firms, along with information about the volume, time, and closing of the fundraising process.

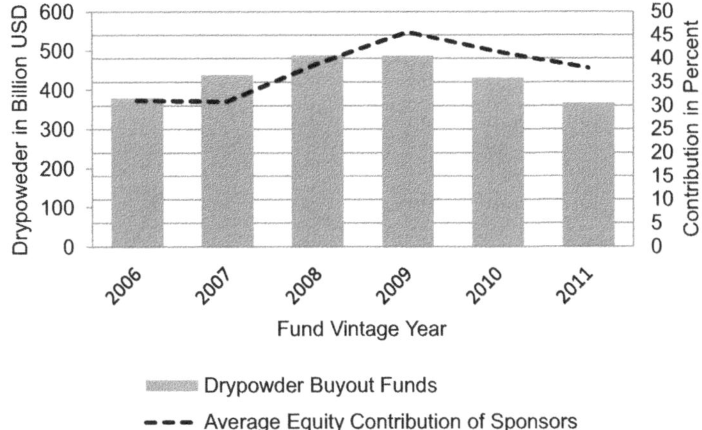

Exhibit 14.12 Buyout Fund Dry Powder and Equity Contribution during the Financial Crisis

The exhibit shows the remaining capital in U.S.-based buyout funds (i.e., dry powder) as well as the average equity contribution of buyout firms to their own funds shortly before, during, and after the financial crisis. The numbers are taken from official data provided by the Private Equity Growth Capital Council (PEGCC) and are based on 315 buyout funds based in the United States. The dry powder numbers are reported in billion USD; the average equity contribution is reported on the secondary *y*-axis in percent of the total fund volume. All numbers are listed over time by vintage fund year (i.e., the year in which the each fund was launched).

Source: Adapted from Preqin (Dry Powder) and S&P LCD (Equity Contribution), as compiled by Private Equity Growth Capital Council, PEGCC, 2012.

buyout funds raised tremendous amounts of capital before the escalation of the crisis, they could not unload the companies they purchased during this period. The capital market turmoil and the economic downturn were responsible for this situation. Low stock market valuations and the unwillingness of market participants to invest in newly issued companies denied the buyout funds the exit via the IPO route. Also, trade sales to strategic buyers became tremendously difficult to execute due to the economic struggles many companies faced during the crisis period.

Exhibit 14.12 shows two further aspects of the financial crisis that are directly related to the lack of deal making and fundraising: (1) the remaining capital in the vintage funds (the uninvested capital, or *dry powder*) and (2) the average equity contribution to the funds by the buyout firms themselves. A steady increase in dry powder occurred until 2009, with values falling again in 2010. The sponsor equity contribution follows a very similar path by increasing until 2009 and then dropping during the 2010–2011 period. This dynamic shows that buyout funds strongly reduced the amount of invested capital in portfolio firms. Additionally, the funds had to chip in by providing equity, as banks did not lend sufficient debt and capital commitments from the fund investors were too low.

Fund performance also reflects the lack of deal flow and profitable exit opportunities. Exhibits 14.13 and 14.14 contain information on private equity and buyout fund performances in the period leading up to and during the financial crisis period. Exhibit 14.13 shows average IRRs of all investments made in private equity

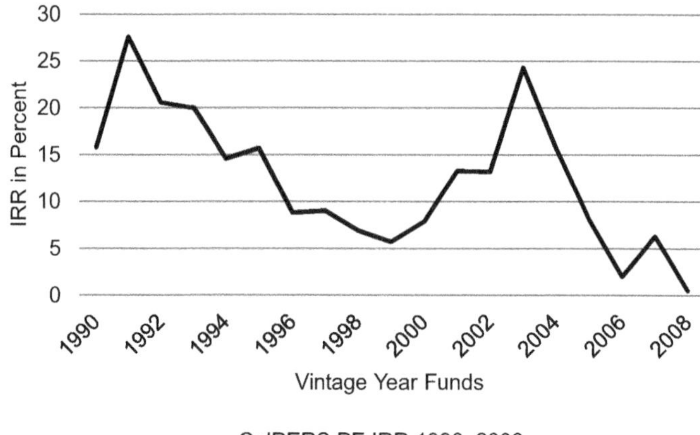

Exhibit 14.13 Private Equity Performance Development

The exhibit shows the historical internal rate of return (IRR) numbers of all private equity investments made by the California Public Employees' Retirement System (CalPERS) agency over the period 1990 to 2008. The IRR numbers are the averages across all invested funds in each respective (vintage) year (i.e., the year in which each funds was launched).

Source: CalPERS Private Equity Performance Numbers as of September 30, 2011, as reported in the CalPERS Alternative Investment Management (AIM) Program.

vehicles by the California pension fund CalPERS. A sharp drop in IRRs occurred between 2003 and 2005, which represent years when the funds would most likely try and unload their investments during the financial crisis period. The low average IRR figures reflect the adverse capital market environment. Apparently, the buyout funds could not obtain fair exit prices for their investments, resulting in lower returns for the investors.

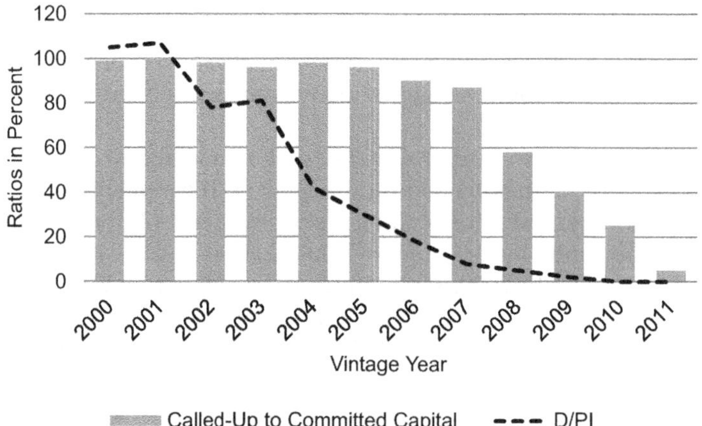

Exhibit 14.14 Buyout Fund Performance Development

The exhibit shows two buyout fund performance indicators over the period 2000 to 2011. Reported are two ratios (both displayed in percent): the ratio of called-up to committed capital and the ratio of distributed to paid-in capital (D/PI). The numbers are based on a total of 3,600 buyout funds, including 2,314 U.S.-focused, 828 Europe-focused, and 468 Asia Pacific–focused funds.

Source: Adapted from the Preqin Special Report: U.S. Private Equity, 2012.

Exhibit 14.14 shows similar information. The chart indicates that the D/PI multiple, which is calculated as the ratio of distributed capital to paid-in capital, strongly declined for all funds beginning in 2003. Overall, the buyout industry was affected in almost every aspect of the business model, and therefore also in every major value driver: funding, acquiring companies, and successfully selling companies. Thus, investor returns suffered tremendously.

Regulatory Challenges

In the wake of the financial crisis, public demand pressured policy makers into designing and passing laws to regulate the financial services industry. Although commercial and investment banks are most affected, rules and regulations included alternative investment funds such as buyouts. One of those regulations is the Private Fund Investment Advisers Registration Act (PFIARA), which was signed into law in the United States in 2010 as part of the Dodd-Frank Wall Street Reform and Consumer Protection Act (Dodd-Frank Act). Although PFIARA is only directed at the registration and transparency of private equity funds and does not directly address their business model or investment procedures, it is the first U.S. law specifically designed to place private equity funds under regulatory scrutiny. The act requires private equity advisers to register with the Securities and Exchange Commission (SEC) and to disclose a specific set of information, such as the volume under management, the use of leverage, and each single investment position. A similar law was introduced in Europe in 2010. The Alternative Investment Fund Manager Directive (AIFM) also calls for higher transparency of alternative investment funds and more prudence in their business procedures. Even the taxation of carried interest payments has been subject to a heated discussion, with many politicians in the United States demanding a tax rate at 39 percent, as on ordinary income, instead of the current 15 percent tax rate on capital gains. Jenkinson (2010) provides a detailed discussion of the regulatory scrutiny.

A more prominent and harsher regulation, which triggered immediate reactions of the financial services sector directly affecting the buyout industry shortly after its introduction, is the so-called Volcker Rule. Paul Volcker, the former Chairman of the Federal Reserve and economic advisor to President Obama, first suggested the Volcker Rule in 2009, which was signed into law as Section 619 of the Dodd-Frank Act. The act was the result of the financial crisis and subsequent recession in the United States in the late 2000s. Its rules, including Section 619, must be implemented by all U.S. financial institutions by July 2014 (exemptions are available until July 2017). The Volcker Rule argues along the lines of the Glass-Steagall–induced separation of securities and retail banking. It prevents financial institutions from proprietary trading in virtually all securities, and from investing in hedge funds or private equity–type investment structures. Skadden, Slate, Meagher, and Flom LLP and Affiliates (2011) and Sullivan and Cromwell LLP (2011) provide for a detailed description of the Volcker Rule. Essentially, banks are not allowed to use their own money (as opposed to clients' money) to take one-sided bets on any kind of security or derivatives thereof, neither directly by purchasing or trading them, nor by owning, managing or sponsoring investment vehicles that engage in proprietary trading. The act defines investment vehicles as all investment funds covered by the Investment Company Act of 1940. The act thereby directly aims at banks' hedge fund and private equity businesses. As will be discussed in more detail, the act is believed to have a major impact on the buyout industry as first reactions of banks to comply with the act have already begun to affect buyout funds.

A SEC informal inquiry into the industries' business models and practices might pose another regulatory postcrisis challenge for the buyout industry. In late 2011, the SEC sent a letter to several undisclosed buyout funds, informing them of a planned "informal inquiry" into the industry. Among other things, the inquiry will strongly focus on the funds' valuation techniques. The main reasoning behind this investigation, according to the SEC, was the protection of pension assets that are given to buyout funds. The private equity industry already agreed on uniform accounting and valuation practices in the mid-2000s through the International Private Equity and Venture Capital Valuation (IPEV) Guidelines. The IPEV board developed these sets of rules to provide fund managers with a "best practice" case of how to measure and present fair valuations of their investments. Mathonet and Monjanel (2006) provide further information on this subject. The SEC might either question the IPEV rules itself or their prudential application. The SEC's fear is that fund managers might report false or incorrect investment values to investors in order to use these flawed numbers for fee calculation or fund-level performances to attract new investors. The investigation comes at a time at which most buyout funds are expected to have marked down the value of their investments, in line with the general economic conditions (as Exhibits 14.13 and 14.14 also suggest). The SEC investigation is only in an informal stage, which means that only minor inquiries and interviews are being conducted with buyout fund managers. How the industry will react to that and whether the SEC expands the scope of the investigation remains to be seen. However, given the strong scrutiny under which hedge funds and banks have been placed in the recent regulations, by, for example, the prohibitions on naked short-selling or the prohibition of proprietary trading, a similar regulation for private equity firms cannot be fully ruled out.

Reactions of the Buyout Industry

How did the buyout industry react to these numerous challenges? First, fund managers reacted swiftly and decisively by adopting several measures to deal with the immediate economic adversities during the crisis such as job cuts. Most of these measures will presumably only persist until financial markets and the general economy fully recover from the crisis. To cope with the difficulties in the fundraising process, many buyout firms, such as Cinven in the Cinven Fifth Fund, started to adopt so-called early bird clauses, which allow investors a discount of up to 15 percent on their fees if they commit capital to the fund in the early fundraising stages. Additionally, as Exhibit 14.12 also shows, fund managers contributed more of their own equity to their funds. To deal with the lower overall funding levels, buyout funds turned to smaller target companies, thereby abandoning the classic mega-buyout investment model in which they purchased only large stock-listed conglomerates. Additionally, some buyout funds started to invest in foreign markets, such as pan-Asia, that are less affected by the financial crisis and therefore provide a better investment environment. Examples include Providence Equity Partner's 1 billion USD investment in Indian telecom powerhouse Idea Cellular in 2008 and Blackstone's 2011 Renminbi Fund for Chinese growth investments.

Fund managers are looking at alternative exit routes such as special-purpose acquisition corporations (SPACs). First introduced in the mid-2000s, SPACs closely resemble regular private equity funds; that is, they are blank-check investment vehicles that are endowed with investor money with the primary goal of using this money to make equity investments in private companies. Lewellen (2009), Jenkinson and Sousa (2010), and Ince (2012) provide a detailed overview of SPACs.

SPACs are publicly listed corporations making a singular investment that has to be preapproved by the SPAC investors. Next to generating returns for their investors, the primary economic goal of SPACs is to take a private company public without having to go through the lengthy and expensive stock-listing process with the SEC. Thus, some initially regarded SPACs as competitors to "classic" private equity funds. However, SPACs might establish themselves as reliable buyers of buyouts' portfolio companies and thereby offer fund managers an attractive additional exit route. These examples show that the buyout industry is willing and able to react to adverse market environments by adjusting the business models to stay competitive and to generate returns for their investors.

What effects did the regulatory scrutiny have on the buyout industry, and how did fund managers react to such scrutiny? Some regulatory actions, such as the PFIARA or AIFM regulations, are not believed to have had any major impact on the buyout industry. Although the wording of both acts is quite harsh, they only aim at the transparency and reporting guidelines of buyout funds. Thus, the effects are likely to be minor. So far, other regulatory discussions have not had any impact on the buyout industry, such as a possible new taxation of carried interest payments. If a new taxation method of this kind is implemented, buyout funds would most likely react with a relocation to avoid higher taxes. However, the exact effects remain to be seen, especially since the political discussion about this topic is ongoing.

The Volcker Rule is expected to have the biggest impact on the buyout industry. As a result of the act, many large banking institutions are selling and/or closing their hedge fund and private equity operations, along with selling stakes they held in third-party managed funds. Most notably, Citigroup and Bank of America sold their respective 1.7 and 1.9 billion USD private equity portfolios to AXA Private Equity in 2011. However, the Volcker Rule also seems to affect banks outside of its regulatory scope. Other banks exiting the buyout market by selling their stakes in portfolios are Europe-based Barclays (valued at 740 million USD), Crédit Agricole (sold for 700 million USD) and West-LB (sold for 270 million USD).

These transactions will likely have two effects on the buyout industry. First, buyout funds will lose some of their financially most potent and important investor groups. As Exhibit 14.4 shows, banks provide up to 15 percent of the funding for some buyout firms. Such funding will be unavailable for future buyout funds. Buyout firms will, therefore, have to find additional funding sources or cut back on their fund volumes. Second, banks' abandoning of the private equity market might also have a beneficial effect for buyout funds. As some banks not only sold their stakes in third-party funds but also closed their in-house private equity divisions, competition for both top-notch investments and fund investors will likely decline in the future.

SUMMARY AND CONCLUSIONS

This chapter provides an overview of private equity buyout investments, explains the current state of the industry, and discusses the most recent obstacles and possible future developments. Over the past 40 years, buyout investments have become one of the major alternative investment vehicles for institutional investors and high-net-worth individuals. Buyout funds have established themselves as an important funding source for large public and private companies, and their managers' leverage-driven high-risk investment approaches have become both notorious for their rigorous corporate restructuring methods but also celebrated for their frequently high investor returns. However, despite their successful business model and their value creation for portfolio companies and investors, buyout funds overcame numerous obstacles in the late 2000s. The subprime-related financial crisis of 2007–2008 and its aftermath caused dwindling debt and equity funding, fewer investment opportunities and exit possibilities, and consequently lower fund returns. Additionally, private equity firms came under regulatory scrutiny, and the buyout market was reshaped by the prohibition of banks' investments in buyout funds through the Volcker Rule in the Dodd-Frank Act. How these factors will affect the buyout industry remains to be seen. Nonetheless, buyout funds have proven their resilience to adverse economic environments in the past and, as the latest evidence suggests, have already started to adapt their business model to overcome these obstacles and to make use of the presented opportunities.

DISCUSSION QUESTIONS

1. Identify and discuss the three major value-creation measures used by buyout funds other than the financial-engineering process.
2. List and explain the three major obstacles buyout funds faced during the financial crisis of 2007–2008.
3. Discuss why one of the corporate restructuring activities used by buyout fund managers in their portfolio companies aims at increasing a company's free cash flow.
4. What is the Volcker Rule, and how could it affect the buyout industry in the United States?

REFERENCES

Acharya, Viral V., Oliver Gottschalg, Moritz Hahn, and Conor Kehoe. 2013. "Corporate Governance and Value Creation: Evidence from Private Equity." *Review of Financial Studies* 26:2, 368–402.

Bruton, Garry D., J. Kay Keels, and Elton L. Scifres. 2002. "Corporate Restructuring and Performance: An Agency Perspective on the Complete Buyout Cycle." *Journal of Business Research* 55:9, 704–724.

Cornelli, Francesca, and Oguzhan Karakas. 2008. "Private Equity and Corporate Governance: Do LBOs Have More Effective Boards?" Working Paper, European Corporate Governance Institute (ECGI).

Cotter, James F., and Sarah W. Peck. 2001. "The Structure of Debt and Active Equity Investors: The Case of Buyout Specialists." *Journal of Financial Economics* 59:1, 101–147.

Field, Laura Casares, and Gordon Hanka. 2001. "The Expiration of IPO Share Lockups." *Journal of Finance* 56:2, 471–500.
Fraser-Sampson, Guy. 2007. *Private Equity as an Asset Class.* Chichester, UK: John Wiley & Sons, Ltd.
Gertner, Robert, and Steven N. Kaplan. 1996. "The Value-Maximizing Board." Working Paper, National Bureau of Economic Research (NBER).
Gompers, Paul, and Josh Lerner. 1998. "Venture Capital Distributions: Short-Run and Long-Run Reactions." *Journal of Finance* 53:6, 2161–2183.
Holthausen, Robert W., and David F. Larcker. 1996. "The Financial Performance of Reverse Leverage Buyouts." *Journal of Financial Economics* 42:3, 293–332.
Ince, Ufuk. 2012. "Going Public through the Back Door: A Comparative Analysis of SPACs and IPOs." Working Paper, Pacific Lutheran University.
Jenkinson, Tim. 2010. "Private Equity Faces the Future: Candid Views from the Market." New York: BNY Mellon and PEI Research Publication.
Jenkinson, Tim, and Miguel Sousa. 2010. "Why SPAC Investors Should Listen to the Market." Working Paper, University of Oxford.
Jensen, Michael J., and William H. Meckling. 1976. "A Theory of the Firm—Managerial Behavior, Agency Costs and Ownership Structure." *Journal of Financial Economics* 3:4, 305–360.
Kaplan, Steven N. 1989. "The Effects of Management Buyouts on Operating Performance and Value." *Journal of Financial Economics* 24:2, 217–254.
Kaplan, Steven N. 2010. "Method over Magic: The Drivers behind Private-Equity Performance." In Robert A. Finkel and David Greising, ed., *The Masters of Private Equity and Venture Capital*, 17–31. New York: McGraw Hill.
Kaplan, Steven N., and Annette Schoar. 2005. "Private Equity Performance: Returns, Persistence, and Capital Flows." *Journal of Finance* 60:4, 1791–1823.
Kaplan, Steven N., and Per Strömberg, 2008. "Leveraged Buyouts and Private Equity." Working Paper, NBER Working Paper Series, Paper #14207.
Lewellen, Stefan M. 2009. "SPACs as an Asset Class." Working Paper, Yale University.
Mathonet, Pierre-Yves, and Gauthier Monjanel. 2006. "New International Valuation Guidelines – A Private Equity Homerun." Luxembourg: European Investment Fund.
Metrick, Andrew, and Ayako Yasuda, 2010. "The Economics of Private Equity Funds." *Review of Financial Studies* 23:6, 2303–2341.
Meyer, Thomas, and Pierre-Yves Mathonet. 2005. *Beyond the J-Curve—Managing a Portfolio of Venture Capital and Private Equity Funds.* Chichester, UK: John Wiley & Sons, Ltd.
Murray, Gordon, Dongmei Niu, and Richard D. F. Harris. 2006. "The Operating Performance of Buyout IPOs in the UK and the Influence of Private Equity Financing." Working Paper 06/10, University of Exeter.
Muscarella, Chris J., and Michael R. Vetsuypens. 1990. "Efficiency and Organizational Structure: A Study of Reverse LBOs." *Journal of Finance* 45:5, 1398–1413.
Raschle, Bruno E., and Rainer Ender. 2004. "Absolute Returns or Private Equity Asset Allocation?" Zurich: Adveq Management.
Schmidt, Daniel, Sascha Steffen, and Franziska Szabó. 2010. "Exit Strategies of Buyout Investments: An Empirical Analysis." *Journal of Alternative Investments* 12:4, 58–84.
Shleifer, Andrei, and Robert W. Vishny. 1986. "Large Shareholders and Corporate Control." *Journal of Political Economy* 94:3, 461–488.
Skadden, Arps, Slate, Meagher, and Flom LLP and Affiliates. 2011. "Dodd-Frank Rulemaking: Volcker Rule and SIFI Proposals—Commentary and Insights." New York.
Smith, Abbie J. 1990. "Corporate Ownership Structure and Performance—The Case of Management Buyouts." *Journal of Financial Economics* 27:1, 143–164.
Sullivan & Cromwell LLP. 2011. "Volcker Rule." New York.
Tirole, Jean. 2006. *The Theory of Corporate Finance.* Princeton, NJ: Princeton University Press.

ABOUT THE AUTHORS

Christian Rauch is an Assistant Professor at the Finance Department of Goethe University in Frankfurt, Germany. He researches and teaches in the fields of banking regulation and corporate finance, especially alternative investments. His work has been presented at international conferences and published in such journals as the *Journal of Banking and Finance, European Journal of Finance,* and the *International Finance Review.* Besides his work at Goethe University, Professor Rauch holds positions as guest lecturer at the Frankfurt School of Finance and Management and several associate research positions. He graduated with degrees in Business Administration and Corporate Law from European Business School and New York University, and earned his Ph.D. in finance from Goethe University, Frankfurt.

Mark Wahrenburg is a tenured Professor of Finance at Goethe University in Frankfurt, Germany. Besides his extensive research and teaching at Goethe University, he serves as Associate Dean for Goethe University's Business School. Professor Wahrenburg is also President of the Goethe Finance Association and a founding member of research institute E-Finance Lab. Before coming to Frankfurt in 1999, he was a tenured Professor at the University of Witten-Herdecke, Germany and worked as consultant for McKinsey & Co. His research in the fields of banking, risk management, and mergers and acquisitions has been published in leading international journals such as the *Journal of Banking and Finance, European Financial Management,* and *Empirical Economics.* Professor Wahrenburg also serves as board member and external consultant to industrial and financial companies in Germany.

CHAPTER 15

Distressed Debt Investing

MICHELLE M. HARNER
Professor of Law and Associate Dean for Academic Programs, Francis King Carey School of Law, University of Maryland

PAUL E. HARNER[1]
Partner, Finance Department, Latham & Watkins LLP, New York, New York

CATHERINE M. MARTIN
Associate, Finance Department, Latham & Watkins LLP, New York, New York

AARON M. SINGER[2]
Associate, Finance Department, Latham & Watkins LLP, New York, New York

INTRODUCTION

Investors want healthy returns on investments. They employ a variety of strategies to achieve this objective and extract value from cash-strapped, underperforming, undervalued, or mismanaged companies. Historically, investors' strategies generally focused on gaining control of these companies through the acquisition of substantial equity positions. More recently, investors have diversified their approaches by incorporating the acquisition of debt securities of troubled companies into their overall investment strategies. In the distressed-company context, investors often seek to maximize their returns through acquisitions, spin-offs, liquidations, and other means.

An investor who strategically acquires the debt securities of a troubled company is commonly referred to as a *distressed debt investor*. Distressed debt investors

[1] This chapter includes a summary of certain aspects of the Premier International Holdings Inc. (a.k.a. Six Flags, Inc.) bankruptcy. Mr. Harner, previously of Paul, Hastings, Janofsky & Walker LLP, formerly represented Premier International Holdings Inc., and its debtor subsidiaries and affiliates, in their bankruptcy cases before the Bankruptcy Court for the District of Delaware. Notwithstanding Mr. Harner's involvement in those cases, this chapter only presents and discusses information that is publicly available.

[2] This chapter includes a summary of certain aspects of the Washington Mutual, Inc. (a.k.a. WaMu) bankruptcy. Mr. Singer represented an interested party in those bankruptcy cases. Notwithstanding Mr. Singer's involvement in those cases, this chapter only presents and discusses information that is publicly available.

generally are financial institutions or other nonindividual entities, such as investment banks and hedge funds, but they may also be individuals (Altman, 2006; Harner, 2008a).

Distressed debt investors are faced with a unique set of strategic considerations based on the financial condition of the companies in which they invest. Besides common investment considerations such as the stability of a company's industry, economic indicators, and the financial condition of the company itself, distressed debt investors need to understand the rights and obligations related to the debt they purchase and the potential implications of a prospective bankruptcy on those rights and obligations. Additionally, as distressed debt investors make investment decisions, they may consider the extent to which they want to be involved in the prospective bankruptcy cases of the companies in which they invest. These complexities differentiate distressed debt investing from other investment strategies.

This chapter provides an introduction to distressed debt investing, including a summary of the risks faced by distressed debt investors and certain investment strategies they implement when purchasing distressed debt. In examining these strategies, this chapter also discusses various roles and issues faced by distressed debt investors when the underlying company is in bankruptcy. Finally, this chapter will consider the positive and negative implications of distressed debt investing on actual Chapter 11 reorganization cases.

WHAT IS DISTRESSED DEBT?

Distressed debt is the outstanding debt of a company that is or is perceived to be experiencing financial distress and that, as a result, impairs the prospects for a full and timely repayment, whether or not the company is actually insolvent or has filed for bankruptcy. The outstanding debt of the distressed company may include term loans, revolving loans, bonds, investment notes or trade claims, and the debt may or may not be secured by the company's assets. The distressed company may be a solitary entity or part of a complex structure. In the latter case, the distressed debt of the company may reside at one or more subsidiaries or affiliates in the corporate structure.

Several factors may affect whether debt is classified as distressed. Relevant factors include whether the party with the direct repayment obligation on the debt (referred to herein as the *company*, *borrower*, or *debtor*) or any other obligor on the debt, such as a guarantor, is in bankruptcy; is engaged in an out-of-court restructuring; has experienced a credit rating downgrade; faces litigation liability or public relations concerns; or faces industry-wide issues (Loan Syndications and Trading Association, 2007).

WHAT IS DISTRESSED DEBT INVESTING?

Distressed debt investing is the process through which an entity purchases or sells (collectively referred to as *trades* or *trading*) the debt of a financially troubled company, usually by paying an amount to the seller that is less than the amount the seller is owed on the debt (commonly referred to as the *face amount of the debt*) (Lhabitant, 2002). The investor may purchase debt before the company files for bankruptcy relief or, as is common, after the company has already entered bankruptcy. The distressed debt investor receives a discount for purchasing distressed debt securities because whether the obligor will be able to meet its obligations under the relevant debt instrument or contract is unclear. Although a distressed debt investor typically purchases distressed debt at a discount, the investor generally acquires all of the seller's rights under the debt, including the right to a full repayment of the debt on the terms provided in the debt instrument.

Discounts applied in distressed debt trades are often based upon available information about the company's business plan, financial statements, and potential for bankruptcy (assuming the company has not already filed), but can also be affected by industry-specific and macroeconomic trends. As investors absorb information related to the company, its industry, and the economy, the discount rate for a particular type of debt can change materially.

Distressed debt investors purchase the debt of financially troubled companies for several reasons. Certain distressed debt investors believe they can realize a gain by selling the debt in the future at a higher price (Altman and Swanson, 2007). Others, including Rosenberg (2000) as well as Altman and Swanson, believe distressed debt investors can realize a gain by holding the debt until repayment by the company at maturity or through redemption or until a distribution is made in the bankruptcy of the distressed company pursuant to a Chapter 11 plan of reorganization. As Rosenberg notes, such distribution may be in the form of cash or new debt or equity issued by the reorganized company as it emerges from bankruptcy. In all cases, the distressed debt investor elects to purchase the debt at the agreed discount because the investor believes that its recovery will be greater over time than the amount it initially paid to purchase the debt.

Distressed debt investing is an industry with well-established markets. For example, a market exists for trading in distressed bank loans, which is facilitated by the Loan Syndications and Trading Association. A market for trading in swaps and derivatives involving distressed debt also exists and is facilitated by the International Swaps and Derivatives Association. Moreover, a burgeoning market is available for trading claims against companies in bankruptcy as more investors are willing to purchase bankruptcy claims at a portion of their face value from creditors that are willing to take an early cash payment to eliminate the possibility of limited or no recovery.

CERTAIN RISKS ASSOCIATED WITH DISTRESSED DEBT INVESTING

Distressed debt investing is inherently speculative and risky. Although the investor may acquire all the rights established under the debt instruments or contracts, including the potential to recover the full face amount of the debt at a discount, the investor may be limited in its ability to analyze the financial condition of the underlying obligor. The distressed debt investor, for example, may have access only to publicly available information. Similarly, if the seller is an institution that has a longstanding relationship with the company, such as a lender, the distressed debt investor may be at an information disadvantage. The distressed debt investor may have insufficient time to perform diligence on the company as, for example, a lender would ordinarily do in a similar scenario.

Distressed debt investors risk purchasing debt that cannot be repaid by the borrower or that ranks too low in priority to recover meaningfully in a Chapter 11 bankruptcy. This risk is heightened when an investor purchases unsecured debt. Investors buying secured debt risk having the value of the collateral being insufficient to repay the debt. In such a case, the investor is left with a claim that is partially secured by the value of the collateral, and partially unsecured, which is referred to as the *deficiency claim*. An investor may also run the risk that the seller's rights under the debt it is selling are subject to contractual offset. For example, if a distressed debt investor purchases a distressed secured bank loan from a seller that breached its lender covenants under the applicable credit agreement, the seller's liability for the breach could possibly be transferred to the investor, leaving the investor with a claim against the seller. Similarly, an investor may risk that the claim it purchases will be disallowed or otherwise subject to avoidance actions under certain provisions of the Bankruptcy Code (See *In re KB Toys, Inc.*, No. 04–10120, 2012 Bankr. LEXIS 1958, at ∗35 (Bankr. D. Del. May 4, 2012) (explaining that "[a] purchaser of claims in a bankruptcy is well aware (or should be aware) that it is entering an arena in which claims are allowed and disallowed in accordance with the provisions of the Bankruptcy Code . . ."). Finally, and as will be discussed in the next section, a distressed debt investor seeking to purchase debt in the hope that it will be exchanged for equity at a later date risks that the company does not exchange that particular debt for equity.

DISTRESSED DEBT INVESTING STRATEGIES

The basic strategy for distressed debt investors is to purchase debt on the secondary market at a discount in an attempt to realize a gain on the investment when the debt issuer achieves, or the market anticipates, a successful turnaround (Lhabitant, 2002). Investors with long-term investment strategies, typically more than one year, often seek to realize gains by holding the debt until maturity or redemption or by acquiring equity through a debt-for-equity exchange in the company's financial restructuring (Rosenberg, 2000; Altman and Swanson, 2007). According to Rosenberg, investors with short-term investment strategies often seek to flip the debt quickly to realize profits resulting from small movements in the market. Alternatively, some distressed debt investors, such as hedge funds, engage in a value-creation investment strategy (Rosenberg, 2000; Lhabitant, 2002). As Altman and Swanson note, these investors may try to purchase a controlling position in the company's distressed debt and then use this control to help turn the company around. Regardless of strategy, distressed debt investors must understand the bankruptcy laws that drive the market valuation for distressed debt (Harner, 2008a).

This section discusses passive and active investing strategies, factors that may be assessed in determining which debt securities to buy, and certain case studies exemplifying these strategies.

Passive vs. Active Investing

Each distressed debt investor has its own strategy and valuation models for identifying the companies in which to invest, which type of debt to purchase, when to buy the debt, and at what price it is willing to pay for that debt. In fact, investors that engage in trading distressed debt generally maintain that the timing of and price paid for their investments is proprietary information (Fisher and Morgenstern, 2007). Although each distressed debt investor may have its own strategy, distressed debt investors can generally be separated into two camps: passive investors and active investors.

Passive Investing

Many distressed debt investors follow a "passive" investing strategy, trading in and out of debt positions with some frequency and at varying purchase rates as new information becomes available in the market. Such passive investors use complex and proprietary models to determine which debt to buy, when to buy, and how much to pay for it. These investors minimize the risks associated with investing in distressed debt by diversifying their debt holdings. Such an investment strategy can foster gains if, among other things, the investor resells the debt to another investor at a price higher than it paid for the debt or the company makes payment on the debt in an amount greater than the investor paid.

Other passive investors purchase distressed debt with the intention of holding it until a distribution is made in the company's bankruptcy. These investors may acquire a company's debt before a bankruptcy or purchase an existing creditor's claim after the company files for bankruptcy relief (Rosenberg, 2000; Lhabitant, 2002; Altman and Swanson, 2007). Once in bankruptcy, investors can purchase claims at a discount from creditors who are unwilling or unable to await repayment or receive other distributions through the claims resolution process. Alternatively, a creditor may sell its claim, subject to any limitations on the sale of such claims in the relevant bankruptcy case, to a distressed debt investor because the creditor believes the investor is offering a better price than will be achieved through any distribution at the end of the case. In either event, investors that intend to hold the debt claims through the company's bankruptcy bet that their recoveries in the case will be in amounts greater than what the investor paid to acquire the claims (Lhabitant, 2002). Moreover, the investor likely calculates achieving a solid return on its investment without having to broker a deal with the debtor or other creditors, take an active role in Chapter 11 plan negotiations, or appear in the bankruptcy case (Harner, 2008b).

Active Investing

An increasingly common phenomenon in Chapter 11 bankruptcy cases is the presence of "activist" distressed debt investors. Activist investors often seek to influence or assume control of the troubled company or its bankruptcy case through the purchase of the company's debt (Rosenberg, 2000; Lhabitant, 2002; Altman and Swanson, 2007). Activist distressed debt investors often believe they can unlock value through their involvement in the restructuring of the company and, unlike passive distressed debt investors, may try to leverage their position as large debt holders to achieve their goals. Activist distressed debt investors generally can be broken into two camps: those seeking to maximize their distributions under a Chapter 11 plan and those seeking to gain control of the company upon emergence from bankruptcy.

Whether the investor seeks a distribution of cash, new debt, or equity in the reorganized company, the activist investor likely has a specific plan for the company's restructuring that will create a return on its investment. In a Chapter 11 bankruptcy, however, management for the debtor has a statutory right to maintain control or "possession" of its business and restructuring activities. Under this statutory arrangement, the debtor company is referred to as the *debtor-in-possession*. Under section 1121 of the Bankruptcy Code, the debtor-in-possession is granted the exclusive right to file a Chapter 11 plan of reorganization within the first 120 days after the debtor files for bankruptcy and to solicit acceptances of such a plan within the first 180 days of the bankruptcy filing. These exclusivity periods may be extended with bankruptcy court approval up to a maximum of 18 months to file a Chapter 11 plan and 20 months to solicit acceptances of such plan. The debtor's Chapter 11 plan of reorganization (the Chapter 11 plan) classifies all of the claims against and interests in the debtor and describes the type of distributions each class will receive, if any, and sets forth specifically how the company will reorganize and emerge from bankruptcy. The *exclusivity periods* for filing and soliciting acceptances of the Chapter 11 plan are intended to give debtors a reasonable time to negotiate a plan without the threat of a competing plan being filed, and also serve to limit a debtor's ability to unreasonably delay the reorganization process to the detriment of its creditors by setting deadlines.

The activist investor needs to determine how best to advance its interests in the restructuring process during the debtor's exclusivity periods. For example, the activist investor may seek to work with the debtor during its exclusivity periods to develop a consensual Chapter 11 plan. If a consensual plan is not achievable, an activist investor may seek to shorten or terminate the debtor's exclusivity periods for cause shown.

Other activist investors purchase distressed debt securities with the objective of controlling and owning the reorganized company upon the debtor's emergence from bankruptcy. As will be discussed next, these investors purchase particular debt that they expect will receive the equity of the reorganized company in satisfaction of their claims under the Chapter 11 plan. The purchase of debt for the purpose of becoming a substantial or controlling equity holder in the reorganized company is one type of loan-to-own strategy (Ayotte and Morrison, 2009). In such case, these distressed debt investors likely believe that control of the debtor's business is more valuable than a distribution under the Chapter 11 plan.

Although federal securities laws generally regulate acquiring a company through the purchase of a controlling interest in the company's stock, purchasing debt under a loan-to-own strategy is largely unregulated. Indeed, apart from mandatory disclosures under Rule 2019 of the Federal Rules of Bankruptcy Procedure (discussed in the next section), activist investors rarely disclose their investment strategies or the targets of their investments, and are not required to disclose debt purchases under the federal securities laws (Harner, 2011). Consequently, management of the debtor rarely knows the extent to which distressed debt investors have acquired controlling shares of classes of creditors, and thereby control the restructuring process until such distressed debt investors assert their claims in the bankruptcy (Harner, 2008b).

DETERMINING WHICH DISTRESSED DEBT SECURITY TO BUY

When a distressed debt investor decides to invest in a company, the investor generally has a choice of debt to purchase. The investor will consider the purchase price and expected rate of recovery for each type of debt under a Chapter 11 plan and whether the claims associated with any particular debt will likely receive a distribution of cash, new debt or equity in the emerging company, or some combination of the foregoing.

Priority of the Debt Securities

In the context of Chapter 11 bankruptcies, the priority of the debt informs the investor's analysis of the expected rates of recovery for each type of debt in the company's capital structure. The debt's priority dictates the order in which claims will be satisfied in a liquidation or under a Chapter 11 bankruptcy plan. Under the priority rules, unless a creditor agrees to different treatment of its claim through a contractual subordination agreement or otherwise, if the debtor liquidates, secured claims must be paid in full before any junior or unsecured claims can receive a distribution. Moreover, all creditors must be paid in full before any equity interest holders can receive a distribution.

Generally, if an investor purchases secured debt, its claim in bankruptcy will rank highest in the priority scheme. *Secured debt* refers to debt that is backed by assets of the borrower (i.e., collateral) to reduce the risk associated with lending to the borrower. If the borrower defaults on its secured debt, a secured creditor generally forecloses upon the collateral by either taking possession of the collateral itself or taking the value of the collateral in cash. If the collateral securing the debt is worth less than the outstanding amount of the debt, then the claim of the investor that purchased the secured debt will be bifurcated into a secured portion covered by the collateral and an unsecured deficiency claim for the residual amount not covered by the value of the collateral. The deficiency claim is entitled to receive a *pro rata* share of any distributions to general unsecured creditors.

Unsecured creditors generally follow secured creditors in the priority scheme. *Unsecured debt* refers to debt obligations that are not supported by anything other than the debtor's promise to repay the debt. Certain types of unsecured claims are given priority status over other types of unsecured claims, and those priority unsecured claims must be paid in full before junior unsecured claims can receive a distribution. The order of priority among various classes of unsecured creditors is set forth in section 507 of the Bankruptcy Code. For example, claims for administrative expenses, which are the actual and necessary costs of preserving the debtor's bankruptcy estate, are near the top of the list of priority unsecured claims. Administrative expense claims may include essential trade vendor claims and the claims for fees and expenses of professionals providing services to the debtor and its bankruptcy estate. Thus, to ensure that a debtor can function in bankruptcy and that the key service providers will continue to provide services to the debtor, administrative claims are given high priority with respect to distributions of the debtor's assets. Generally, administrative expenses and other priority unsecured claims must be paid in full before the debtor company can exit bankruptcy, while all other unsecured claims will recover only if the debtor company has enough value left over after its secured claims, administrative claims and other priority claims are satisfied.

Administrative expense claims are followed by certain tax claims and employee wage and benefit claims, among others. Unsecured claims that are not granted specific priority under section 507 of the Bankruptcy Code are classified as general unsecured claims and rank near the bottom of the priority list established under section 507. Once all general unsecured claims are satisfied, distributions may be made to any junior unsecured creditors, such as those unsecured creditors that have contractually subordinated their claims pursuant to a subordination (or intercreditor) agreement. Absent extraordinary circumstances, equity interest holders will be entitled to a distribution only after all creditor claims are satisfied in full, with interest.

At times, understanding the priority structure of debt securities in a bankruptcy case will require consideration of applicable subordination agreements, such as an intercreditor agreement. Pursuant to section 510(a) of the Bankruptcy Code, subordination provisions are generally enforceable in bankruptcy. Nonetheless, the extent of enforceability has been increasingly litigated as the use of intercreditor agreements has proliferated and the terms of the agreements have expanded beyond mere lien or claim subordination. At a minimum, a distressed debt investor should be aware before investing that the holders of contractually subordinated claims or liens pursuant to an intercreditor agreement may litigate over the enforceability of their agreements to impact claim recoveries.

The priority rule in bankruptcy helps determine how the various classes of creditors will be treated under a Chapter 11 plan, whether that plan contemplates liquidation or reorganization. A distressed debt investor armed with a general understanding of the distributable value of the debtor's estate and the aggregate claim amount in each class of claims can estimate such treatment and, therefore, the recoveries of the various classes of claims. With these estimations, the investor can decide which debt to buy and the price it is willing to pay in order to realize a gain on its investment. Thus, debt priority is integral to distressed debt investing decisions, especially where an investor seeks to receive a distribution in bankruptcy.

The Fulcrum Security

Although some investors seek a return on their investments through distributions of cash or new debt under a Chapter 11 plan, other investors seek to identify and purchase the fulcrum security (Smythe, 2009). As Smythe notes, the *fulcrum security* is the debt obligation in the debtor's capital structure that is anticipated to be exchanged for equity in the reorganized company upon emergence from bankruptcy and will result in equity control. The fulcrum security is the point in the capital structure where the enterprise value no longer fully covers the claim, such that equity in the emerging company must be distributed to satisfy the claims in bankruptcy. Distressed debt investors seeking to own the debtor's business upon emergence from bankruptcy must estimate where, among the classes of claims, the enterprise value will no longer cover the claim, and then purchase a sufficient amount of such claims to ensure that a sufficient amount of equity will be exchanged to provide control of the emerging company.

In conducting this analysis, investors must be aware that, in today's world of complex capital and organizational structures, the fulcrum security could reside at an operating subsidiary, an intermediate holding company, or at the parent company. Well-documented instances are available of distressed debt investors speculating as to the identity of the fulcrum security in bankruptcy cases. An illustration is the Chapter 11 bankruptcy case of the theme park Six Flags, Inc. in 2009 ("Six Flags"). In *Six Flags*, as discussed more fully in the next section, distressed debt investors successfully calculated that purchasing the unsecured debt of Six Flag's holding company would entitle them to receive equity in the reorganized company. Other investors previously had miscalculated that purchasing debt at more senior levels in the capital structure would provide a means of equity control of the reorganized debtor.

Distressed debt investors are not limited to purchasing one particular type of debt. To manage its exposure in pursuit of the fulcrum security, investors can buy various types of debt. Such a strategy may create internal conflicts of interest as the various claims acquired all draw from the same assets in the bankruptcy (Harner, 2008b). Nonetheless, where determining what debt obligation will prove to be the fulcrum security is difficult, this approach may provide investors with a better opportunity ultimately to acquire the emerging company.

CASE STUDIES

The bankruptcies of Allied Holdings, Inc. and Six Flags provide examples of distressed debt investors using different strategies to achieve various investment goals. The following sections highlight relevant developments in those cases.

Allied Holdings

The bankruptcy of Allied is a commonly cited case that provides an example of how institutional investors have used distressed debt and the Chapter 11 process to influence the restructuring of a troubled company. Allied, the largest vehicle transporter in North America, was experiencing financial distress due to a declining demand for new cars, rising fuel costs, and increased labor expenses. In response to these pressures, Allied sought to restructure its balance sheet and renegotiate its labor contract with its union, the International Brotherhood of Teamsters. After Allied filed for bankruptcy in 2005, two funds owned by the Yucaipa Companies, a distressed debt investor, purchased 66 percent of Allied's unsecured debt to take control of the reorganization process (Allied Disclosure Statement at 21–23, 2007).

Yucaipa first attempted to broker a deal with both Allied and the Teamsters, but negotiations stalled, and Allied sought bankruptcy court approval to terminate its labor contract. Yucaipa then entered into direct negotiations with the Teamsters, eventually reaching an agreement that included a 15 percent wage cut. Subsequently, Yucaipa and the Teamsters made a joint proposal to Allied regarding a Chapter 11 plan. The plan involved a debt-for-equity exchange where

Yucaipa acquired a majority equity position in the reorganized entity, Allied Systems Holding, Inc., and it ultimately garnered support from Allied, Yucaipa, the Teamsters, and Allied's unsecured creditors' committee (Allied Systems Holdings, Inc., 2007). Yucaipa obtained substantial control over the company's affairs via its investment, including the right to appoint four of the company's five board members including the chief executive officer (CEO) and the discretion to direct a sale of the company's Canadian assets (Allied Disclosure Statement at 18, 34–35, 49, 2007).

Although Allied emerged from bankruptcy in 2007, three of Allied's lenders—each of which is a distressed debt investor—filed involuntary Chapter 11 petitions against Allied in the United States Bankruptcy Court for the District of Delaware on May 17, 2012. On June 10, 2012, Allied consented to the involuntary petitions and, on the same day, filed voluntary petitions for Chapter 11 relief.

Six Flags

A more recent example of how investors use distressed debt to gain control of a company is the bankruptcy of Six Flags in 2009. The Six Flags corporate enterprise had a three-tiered structure: Six Flags, Inc. (SFI), SFI's wholly owned subsidiary, Six Flags Operations, Inc. (SFO), and SFO's wholly owned subsidiary, Six Flags Theme Parks, Inc. (SFTP) (collectively, the Six Flags Debtors). In 2007, SFTP entered into a credit agreement for an $850 million term loan due in April 2015 and a revolving credit facility totaling $275 million. SFO and its subsidiaries acted as guarantors of the loan, which was secured by substantially all of SFO's and SFTP's assets. Besides the secured loan, Six Flags had unsecured debt obligations at all three levels of the corporate enterprise. The unsecured debt was structurally and contractually subordinated up the ownership ladder; that is, any distributable value in a bankruptcy would first be used to satisfy the unsecured SFTP debt, followed by the unsecured SFO debt and, finally, the unsecured SFI debt. Besides the secured and unsecured debt, in 2001, SFI issued preferred income equity redeemable shares (PIERS) redeemable for cash at 100 percent of the liquidation preference in August 2009 (approximately $275 million) (Six Flags Disclosure Statement at 44, 45, 46, 47–48, 2009).

Due to the economic downturn in 2008, coupled with a highly leveraged balance sheet, SFI was prospectively unable to satisfy its PIERS obligations. Failure to satisfy these obligations would lead to an event of default under its secured debt agreements, which would allow those lenders to accelerate the obligations owed thereunder. If the secured lenders accelerated their loans, Six Flags would be unable to pay, and the unsecured lenders could then accelerate their debt as well. Thus, failure to pay the PIERS notes would result in most, if not all, of the Six Flags Debtors' long-term debt becoming due and payable immediately (Six Flags Disclosure Statement at 50, 2009).

To avoid accelerating all of their obligations, the Six Flags Debtors entered into negotiations with their unsecured lenders and preferred equity holders to exchange their debt holdings for common stock. The Six Flags Debtors also entered into independent negotiations with SFO's largest unsecured note holder, Avenue Capital Management, to exchange its debt holdings into a majority equity position in the restructured company. These negotiations, however, failed, and the Six Flags

Debtors filed Chapter 11 bankruptcy petitions in June 2009. In bankruptcy, the Six Flags Debtors' proposed a Chapter 11 plan that provided for, among other things: (1) SFTP's secured creditors to receive a 92 percent equity share in the reorganized company; (2) SFTP's unsecured creditors to be paid in full or have their claims reinstated; (3) SFO's unsecured creditors to receive a 7 percent equity share; (4) SFI's unsecured creditors to receive a 1 percent equity share; and (5) a new $600 million term loan to finance the company at exit (Six Flags Disclosure Statement at 3–4, 51–52, 2009).

Avenue was a distressed debt investor that purchased debt at various levels of the Six Flags corporate structure. At the time of the bankruptcy filing, Avenue held portions of both secured and unsecured debt and was the largest holder of the SFO unsecured debt (Six Flags Disclosure Statement at 2, 2009). Avenue used its position to propose a Chapter 11 plan that provided for the following: (1) a $650 million term loan and a $450 million rights offering to repay secured creditors; (2) a 22.89 percent equity share in the reorganized company for SFO's unsecured creditors; and (3) a 7.34 percent equity share in the reorganized company for SFI's unsecured creditors (Six Flags Disclosure Statement at 5–6, 2009). Also, the proposed Chapter 11 plan gave each SFO unsecured creditor the option to purchase its *pro rata* share of the $450 million rights offering (Six Flags Disclosure Statement at 6, 2009). In essence, Avenue used its position as the largest holder of unsecured SFO debt to transform what would have been a small distribution of equity into a more substantial share in the reorganized company. This chapter will discuss some of the tools Avenue utilized to achieve this remarkable turnaround.

DISTRESSED DEBT INVESTORS AND CHAPTER 11 BANKRUPTCIES

According to Harner (2008a, p. 126), "[t]he extent of a distressed debt investor's influence in the Chapter 11 proceedings of the underlying company will depend largely on three factors: the characteristics of its debt holdings, its statutory rights, and its contractual rights." Others discussing this issue are Carruthers and Halliday (1998) and Fletcher (2005).

Debt Characteristics

A creditor's influence depends largely on the amount and type of debt it holds. For example, a senior secured creditor typically has more bargaining power than an unsecured creditor, and a creditor with a controlling or majority position in the debt has more bargaining power than a minority holder (Carruthers and Halliday, 1998; Harner, 2008b). In the *Allied* case discussed previously, Yucaipa was able to use its majority position in Allied's unsecured debt to influence the restructuring and facilitate a debt-for-equity exchange (Harner, 2008a). Yucaipa's holdings also gave it a blocking position in any vote on a Chapter 11 plan, which enhanced its leverage at the negotiating table and ensured it would receive a substantial equity stake in the reorganized company.

Rights of the Distressed Debt Investor under the Bankruptcy Code

Distressed debt investors may also utilize their statutory rights under the Bankruptcy Code to influence a debtor's conduct and decisions during the bankruptcy case. For example, a distressed debt investor can threaten to file an involuntary petition, threaten to seek relief from the automatic stay to foreclose on collateral, or threaten to seek the appointment of a bankruptcy trustee to replace the debtor's management and oversee all restructuring activity (11 U.S.C. §§ 303(b), 362(d), 1104(a)). Distressed debt investors can also use the Chapter 11 bankruptcy plan process to exert influence over how the company reconfigures its capital and operational structure (Harner, 2008a). Creditors holding substantial positions in a debtor's secured debt or unsecured debt will likely be invited to the negotiating table by the debtor to discuss treatment of claims and the reorganization process (Rosenberg, 2000). Alternatively, a creditor can become involved in the bankruptcy process by essentially being a thorn in the debtor's side; that is, the distressed debt investor can file various motions or objections until the debtor opens a dialogue with the investor to discuss the structure and terms of the plan (Harner, 2008a).

The Bankruptcy Code may also provide a creditor that provides the debtor with liquidity support during the bankruptcy case with superpriority status for its claim. Superpriority gives the postpetition lender the right to be paid before other administrative expense creditors, and, in some instances, a debtor may grant a priming first lien on assets encumbered by prepetition security interests, which entitles the secured postpetition lenders to be paid before the prepetition secured lenders (11 U.S.C. § 364(c)(1)-(3); 11 U.S.C. § 364(d)(1)).

A postpetition lender and the debtor may document their agreement for postpetition financing pursuant to what is called a *debtor-in-possession financing agreement*, or *DIP financing agreement*. In negotiating a DIP financing agreement, Harner (2008a, p. 112) notes that postpetition lenders may bargain for "financial and operational covenants that, among other things, allow the lender to foreclose on its collateral package or otherwise exercise control over the debtor's assets upon a default." A DIP financing agreement may also require the debtor to operate in accordance with a set budget, deliver periodic financial reports and pay the professional fees of the postpetition lenders incurred during the bankruptcy case. Because the DIP financing agreement is subject to the approval of the bankruptcy court, once approved, a postpetition lender can usually exercise its rights under the DIP financing agreement without further bankruptcy court approval or relief from the automatic stay (Kuney, 2004; Baird and Rasmussen, 2004; Harner, 2008a).

The Bankruptcy Code Governs a Creditor's Right to Vote

To confirm a Chapter 11 bankruptcy plan, each class of impaired creditors (i.e., creditors that are not repaid in full) and shareholders must vote in favor of the plan (11 U.S.C. § 1129(a)(8), 2006). Absent this unanimous vote, the plan may still be confirmed under the *cramdown provisions* of the Bankruptcy Code (11 U.S.C. § 1129(b)). The cramdown provisions require at least one class of impaired creditors to vote in favor of the plan, and the debtor must show that the plan is fair and equitable and satisfies the absolute priority rule (11 U.S.C. § 1129(b), 2006). A class votes to accept or reject a plan based on an *adjusted majority rule* in which a controlling vote requires at least half in number and two-thirds in amount of claims in the class (11 U.S.C. § 1126, 2006). Accordingly, a distressed debt investor can hold a blocking position in its own class if it has a large enough share (both in number and amount) of claims in its class or if it has a large enough coalition with other creditors in its class.

Limitations on a Creditor's Right to Vote

The ability of a distressed debt investor to utilize a blocking position within an impaired class to control a vote on a proposed Chapter 11 bankruptcy plan may not be without limits. Section 1126(e) of the Bankruptcy Code allows the court to designate a vote on a plan that was not made in good faith (11 U.S.C. § 1126(e), 2006). When a bankruptcy court designates a vote, it effectively disregards that vote when determining if a Chapter 11 bankruptcy plan received the requisite votes necessary for confirmation. The potential to have one's vote designated may be especially relevant to a distressed debt investor seeking to influence the plan process.

The Bankruptcy Code does not provide any guidance regarding what constitutes a vote not made in good faith; however, a recent Second Circuit decision, *In re DBSD N. Am., Inc.* (2011), illustrates the types of considerations a court may make when examining a creditor's motive in the Chapter 11 bankruptcy plan process (634 F.3d 79 (2d Cir. 2011)). DBSD was a development stage mobile communications company that generated little income to service its large debt load. As a result, it sought Chapter 11 protection in May 2009, and shortly thereafter, DISH Network Corporation, a large investor in DBSD's competitor, purchased all of DBSD's first lien debt and certain second lien claims. The first lien debt was separately classified under DBSD's proposed plan, which meant that DISH controlled an entire impaired class and voted against the plan. In response, DBSD moved to designate DISH's vote. The bankruptcy court found sufficient evidence that DISH voted in bad faith to designate its vote and the district court affirmed (*In re DBSD*, 634 F.3d at 87; *Sprint Nextel Corp. v. DBSD North Am., Inc.*, 2010 U.S. Dist. LEXIS 33253 (S.D.N.Y. Mar. 24, 2010)).

In reviewing the lower courts' decisions in *DBSD*, the United States Court of Appeals for the Second Circuit explained that merely purchasing claims in bankruptcy for the purpose of securing the approval or rejection of a plan does not of itself amount to bad faith. The Second Circuit, however, found that particular facts weighed in favor of finding that DISH did not cast its vote in good faith. Specifically, DISH was a large investor in one of the debtor's competitors and purchased first lien debt at par rather than at a discount. Further, DISH's own internal documentation revealed that its intent in acquiring the claims was to further a strategic business objective that was not focused on maximizing a return on its claims. Thus, the Second Circuit's decision in *DBSD* is a reminder that a creditor's motives in purchasing distressed debt is subject to scrutiny in the Chapter 11 bankruptcy process and that the bankruptcy courts have the power to penalize creditors for overreaching in the plan process (*In re DBSD*, 634 F.3d at 101–05).

DISTRESSED DEBT INVESTORS AND THE CREDITORS' COMMITTEE

Unsecured creditors can influence Chapter 11 bankruptcy plan negotiations by seeking appointment to the official committee of unsecured creditors (the creditors' committee) (Rosenberg, 2000; 11 U.S.C. § 1102(a), 2006; Harner, 2008a). The *creditors' committee* is generally composed of certain of the debtor's largest unsecured creditors appointed by the U.S. Trustee. The creditors' committee is established to represent the interests of all unsecured creditors and to maximize recoveries on unsecured claims through negotiations with the debtor, the secured creditors and other parties in the case. In theory, the members of the creditors' committee act as fiduciaries to all other unsecured creditors in the bankruptcy case and have the authority to, among other things, monitor the debtor's conduct, investigate the assets, liabilities, and financial condition of the debtor and challenge claims asserted in the bankruptcy case.

The members of the creditors' committee are often forced to balance the potential conflict between their interests as independent creditors and their fiduciary duty to other unsecured creditors. Although members of the creditors' committee act as fiduciaries, Harner (2008b, p. 99) notes they also "obtain valuable information regarding the debtor and its restructuring process and a useful platform to further their own investment agendas" (see also Eklund and Roberts, 1997). The potential misuse of confidential information by members of the creditors' committee is often minimized by restricting the members' trading in the debtor's securities or by requiring that trading walls be established at each member's business that effectively separate a member's traders from its representatives on the creditors' committee.

DISTRESSED DEBT INVESTORS AND MEMBERS ON AD HOC COMMITTEES

Collective participation by creditors in a Chapter 11 bankruptcy case extends beyond membership on official committees sanctioned by the Bankruptcy Code. Unofficial, or *ad hoc,* committees, which may be composed of secured or unsecured creditors or equity interest holders, may also play a prominent role in bankruptcy cases.

WHAT IS AN AD HOC COMMITTEE?

Unlike official committees, ad hoc committees are largely unregulated and membership on one is a useful way for a distressed debt investor to join with other investors with a similar agenda to influence the restructuring process without being subject to statutory duties. Although some view ad hoc committees as owing no fiduciary duties to other creditors, that view is not free from debate. For example, in the Chapter 11 bankruptcy case of Washington Mutual Inc. (WaMu) in the United States Bankruptcy Court for the District of Delaware, an opinion by Judge Walrath included *dicta* suggesting that the ad hoc committee of note holders in the case may have owed "some obligation" of a fiduciary nature to other members of the same class of creditors even though the group was not purporting to represent other creditors in its class (*In re Washington Mutual. Inc,* et al., 419 B.R. 271, 279 (Bankr. D. Del. 2009). The bankruptcy court never determined what, if any, duties of a fiduciary nature that the ad hoc committee actually owed to the other creditors in the class, but the opinion has brought the issue to light. Thus, ad hoc committee members should be mindful of conduct that may work to the detriment of nonmembers in their class.

What Are the Potential Consequences of Ad Hoc Committee Membership?

There are potential disadvantages to an investor if it joins an ad hoc committee. For example, members of an ad hoc committee may be subject to the same disclosure requirements as official committee members under the recently amended Rule 2019 of the Federal Rules of Bankruptcy Procedure. Under Rule 2019, "every group or committee that consists of or represents . . . multiple creditors," must file a disclosure statement when the creditors are "(A) acting in concert to advance their common interests, and (B) not composed entirely of affiliates or insiders of one another" (Fed R. Bankr. P. 2019(b)(1), 2011).

Rule 2019 requires, among other things, disclosure of the nature and amount of the investor's interest in the debtor and could be problematic for distressed debt investors. Indeed, many investors assert that information about their investment strategies is proprietary information. Distressed debt investors could be concerned that other investors may be able to reverse-engineer investing strategies based on the publicly disclosed information, particularly the size of their position in the debt. Moreover, although Rule 2019 does not require a disclosing party to submit the price it paid for the debt, it may be discoverable to particular parties upon order from the bankruptcy court.

If a member of an ad hoc committee fails to file a required Rule 2019 disclosure, the consequences can be harsh. A bankruptcy court may prevent any noncomplying party from taking certain actions during the bankruptcy proceeding or bar it completely from participating in the case (Harner, Reilly, Schwartz, and Singer, 2011). In the *WaMu* case, mentioned previously, the official committee of equity interest holders in the case asserted that members of an ad hoc creditors' committee had improperly traded in WaMu's securities during the company's bankruptcy while in possession of material nonpublic information received in private negotiations with the company (*Washington Mutual,* 461 B.R. at 262–66). The bankruptcy court granted standing to the equity committee to pursue insider trading claims against the ad hoc committee members (*Washington Mutual,* 461 B.R. at 262–66). Ultimately, the parties settled before any trial occurred and the issue of insider trading was never decided. Moreover, as part of the settlement, the bankruptcy court agreed to vacate that portion of its prior opinion that referred to insider trading allegations against the ad hoc committee members.

Following *WaMu,* liability for insider trading among members of an ad hoc committee remains an unresolved issue. Therefore, distressed debt investors need to consider the costs of restricting their trading in the debtor's securities if, by joining an ad hoc committee or otherwise, they become privy to material nonpublic information about the debtor.

SUMMARY AND CONCLUSIONS

Distressed debt investing has drawn both criticism and approval from within and outside the corporate sector. Although some regard distressed debt investing as disruptive to the out-of-court restructuring and formal Chapter 11 bankruptcy processes, others view it as beneficial to the distressed debt market and in furtherance of traditional policy goals of a Chapter 11 bankruptcy: the reorganization of viable companies and the repayment of creditors (Harner, 2008b).

Distressed debt investors may be willing to supply additional liquidity to a distressed company because, as investors, they have a stake in the company's rehabilitation. This additional liquidity may be instrumental in reducing a company's debt, retaining employees, and helping the company emerge from bankruptcy as a viable going concern. Distressed debt investors may also be able to steer the restructuring process in a positive direction and offer creative solutions based on prior experience in other distressed situations. Conversely, where a distressed debt investor gains considerable leverage in a case and aggressively pursues its own interests, it may disadvantage other creditors and even a bankruptcy court that is trying to guide an outcome that is in the best interests of the bankruptcy estate and stakeholders generally. Additionally, distressed debt investors may disrupt the bankruptcy case by prolonging negotiations in the Chapter 11 bankruptcy plan process and aggressively pursuing litigation for potentially small rewards.

Going forward, the impact and future implications of distressed debt investing, particularly on Chapter 11 bankruptcy cases, are difficult to determine because the market remains largely unregulated. The potentially competing interests of the debtor, which is charged with maximizing value for its stakeholders, and the distressed debt investor, which generally has no duty to act on behalf of the debtor's other stakeholders, presents an ongoing challenge: maintaining a balanced playing field that fosters investment and investor involvement, but also protects the interests of the debtor and its stakeholders.

DISCUSSION QUESTIONS

1. What is a distressed security?
2. What factors may motivate a distressed investor?
3. If the company ultimately files a Chapter 11 bankruptcy case, what considerations might come into play for an investor?
4. Do distressed investors face regulatory concerns?

REFERENCES

11 U.S.C. § 303(b). 2006.
11 U.S.C. § 362(d). 2006.
11 U.S.C. § 364(c)(1) (3). 2006.
11 U.S.C. § 364(d)(1). 2006.

11 U.S.C. § 1102(a) 2006.
11 U.S.C. § 1104(a). 2006.
11 U.S.C. § 1126. 2006.
11 U.S.C. § 1129(a)(b). 2006.
Allied Systems Holdings, Inc. 2007. *Current Report* (Form 8-K), item 5.01, June 4.
Altman, Edward I. 2006. "Are Historically Based Default and Recovery Models in the High-Yield and Distressed Debt Markets Still Relevant in Today's Credit Environment?" New York University Salomon Center. Available at http://pages.stern.nyu.edu/~ealtman/Are-Historical-Models-Still-Relevant1.pdf.
Altman, Edward I., and Jeffrey Swanson. 2007. *The Investment Performance and Market Size of Defaulted Bonds and Bank Loans: 2006 Review and 2007 Outlook*. New York: New York University Salomon Center. Available at http://pages.stern.nyu.edu/~ealtman/2006%20InvestPerf.pdf.
Ayotte, Kenneth M., and Edward R. Morrison. 2009. "Creditor Control and Conflict in Chapter 11." *Journal of Legal Analysis* 1:2, 511–551.
Baird, Douglas G., and Robert K. Rasmussen. 2004. "Private Debt and the Missing Lever of Corporate Governance." *University of Pennsylvania Law Review* 154:5, 1209–1250.
Carruthers, Bruce G., and Terrence C. Halliday. 1998. *Rescuing Business*. Oxford: Oxford University Press.
Disclosure Statement for Debtors' Fourth Amended Joint Plan of Reorganization under Chapter 11 of the Bankruptcy Code. *In re* Premier Int'l Holdings Inc., et al., No. 09–12019 (Bankr. D. Dela. Dec. 18, 2009) [hereinafter Six Flags Disclosure Statement] (Docket No. 1227).
Disclosure Statement for Joint Plan of Reorganization of Allied Holdings, Inc. and Affiliated Debtors Proposed by the Debtors, Yucaipa and the Teamsters National Automobile Transportation Industry Negotiating Committee. *In re* Allied Holdings, Inc., No. 05–12515 (Bankr. N.D. Ga. Mar. 2, 2007) [hereinafter Allied Disclosure Statement] (Docket No. 2562).
Eklund, Carl A., and Lynn W. Roberts. 1997. "The Problem with Creditors' Committees in Chapter 11: How to Manage the Inherent Conflicts without Loss of Function." *American Bankruptcy Institute Law Review* 5:1, 129–149.
Fed R. Bankr. P. 2019. 2011.
Fisher, Eric B., and Peter D. Morgenstern. 2007. "Hedge Funds in Bankruptcy Court: Rule 2019 and the Disclosure of Sensitive Claim Information." *Finance and Banking Committee, American Bankruptcy Institute* 4:2. Available at www.abiworld.org/committees/newsletters/financebank/vol4num2/2.pdf.
Fletcher, Ian F. 2005. *Insolvency in Private International Law*. Oxford: Oxford University Press.
Harner, Michelle M. 2008a. "The Corporate Governance and Public Policy Implications of Activist Distressed Debt Investing." *Fordham Law Review* 77:2, 703–773.
Harner, Michelle M. 2008b. "Trends in Distressed Debt Investing: An Empirical Study of Investors' Objectives." *ABI Law Review* 16:69, 69–110.
Harner, Michelle M. 2011. "Activist Distressed Debtholders: The New Barbarians at the Gate?" *Washington University Law Review* 89:1, 155–206.
Harner, Paul, Annemarie Reilly, Roger Schwartz, and Aaron Singer. 2011. Client Alert from Latham & Watkins LLP on Amended Bankruptcy Rule 2019.
In re DBSD N. Am., Inc., 634 F.3d 79 (2d Cir. 2011).
In re KB Toys, Inc., No. 04–10120, 2012 Bankr. LEXIS 1958 (Bankr. D. Del. May 4, 2012).
In re Washington Mutual. Inc., et al., 419 B.R. 271, 279 (Bankr. D. Del. 2009).
Kuney, George W. 2004. "Hijacking Chapter 11." *Emory Bankruptcy Developments Journal* 21:1, 19–36.
Lhabitant, François-Serge. 2002. *Hedge Funds: Myths and Limits*. New York: John Wiley & Sons.

Loan Syndications and Trading Association. 2007. *User's Guide for LSTA Distressed Trading Documentation*. Available at www.lsta.org/content.aspx?id=1112.

Memorandum from Latham & Watkins LLP on Insider Trading Issues in Bankruptcy. (May 14, 2012) (on file with author). [hereinafter WaMu Memo].

Rosenberg, Hilary. 2000. *The Vulture Investors*. New York: John Wiley & Sons.

Smythe, Christie. 2009. "'Fulcrum' Deals Rising to Prominence, Experts Say." *LAW360.com*.

ABOUT THE AUTHORS

Michelle Harner is the Associate Dean for Academic Programs and a Professor of Law at the Francis King Carey School of Law, University of Maryland. She is also the Co-Director of the School of Law's business law program. Professor Harner teaches courses in bankruptcy and creditors' rights, business associations, corporate finance, business planning, and professional responsibility. Professor Harner is widely published and lectures frequently on various topics involving corporate governance, financially distressed entities, and related issues. Professor Harner currently is serving as Reporter to the ABI Commission to Study the Reform of Chapter 11. Additionally, in March 2009 and April 2012, Professor Harner received research grants from the American Bankruptcy Institute Endowment Fund to study the role of creditors' committees in Chapter 11 bankruptcies and potential reforms to the Chapter 11 bankruptcy process, respectively. Professor Harner is a member of various professional organizations and, among other honors, is an elected member of the American Law Institute.

Paul Harner is a partner in the New York office of Latham & Watkins LLP and a member of the firm's insolvency practice group. Mr. Harner has played leading roles in a number of major corporate restructurings, including notable Chapter 11 cases such as Six Flags Entertainment, National Century Financial Enterprises, Loewen Group, Laidlaw International, Nextel International, R.H. Macy & Co., Federated Department Stores, and Kmart Corporation. He represents debtors, committees, private equity investors, bank groups, institutional investors, secured lenders, boards of directors, and other parties in bankruptcy cases, out-of-court workouts, and related litigation. He is, among other professional associations, a Fellow of the American College of Bankruptcy. Mr. Harner earned his JD from the Duke University School of Law and earned a BA from Duke University.

Catherine Martin is an associate in the New York office of Latham & Watkins LLP and a member of the firm's insolvency practice group, where she specializes in corporate restructurings and Chapter 11 bankruptcy reorganizations. She represents various creditors, shareholders, and distressed companies in all facets of the restructuring and reorganization process. Ms. Martin was also recently seconded at Citigroup, where her work included coverage of Citi's credit and equity derivatives businesses, including over-the-counter credit default swaps and equity swaps. She also participated in several industry groups and projects dedicated to financial reform. Ms. Martin earned her JD from the Syracuse University College of Law and earned a BA from the University of Arizona.

Aaron Singer is an associate in the New York office of Latham & Watkins LLP and a member of the firm's insolvency practice group. Mr. Singer specializes in restructurings, Chapter 11 bankruptcy reorganizations, distressed debt transactions, and other financial transactions. He represents lenders, creditors, creditors' committees, ad hoc groups, borrowers, and debtors in connection with such transactions and proceedings. Mr. Singer also assists financial institutions with distressed debt trades, both in and out of the secondary market for bank loans, in the purchase and sale of U.S. and non-U.S. bankruptcy claims and provides advice regarding developments in the area of distressed debt. Mr. Singer earned his JD from the Duke University School of Law and earned a BA from the University of Michigan, Ann Arbor.

ACKNOWLEDGMENTS

The authors gratefully acknowledge the extensive research and drafting assistance of Nicholas B. Goss (JD candidate 2013, New York University) and Steven M. Schmulenson (JD candidate 2013, Duke University), both summer associates at Latham & Watkins LLP, New York, New York, in the preparation of this chapter. Any views expressed in this chapter are solely those of the authors, and not of either the University of Maryland Francis King Carey School of Law or Latham & Watkins LLP. Any errors or omissions are the sole responsibility of the authors.

CHAPTER 16

Performance of Private Equity

CHRISTOPH KASERER
Professor of Finance, Head of the Department of Financial Management and Capital Markets, TUM School of Management, Technische Universität München

RÜDIGER STUCKE
Research Fellow in Finance and Economics, Saïd Business School and Oxford-Man Institute of Quantitative Finance, University of Oxford

INTRODUCTION

Measuring the performance of private equity and its various subasset classes is a challenging task. To gain a better understanding of this problem requires examining the typical structure of a private equity fund. In general, private equity funds are established as private limited partnerships and as such are not subject to disclosure requirements. Therefore, the partnership only rarely reports its performance to the general public. The partnership is managed by the fund managers (general partners, or GPs). GPs initially raise capital from institutional investors (i.e., they aim to convince potential investors to commit capital to a fund). These fund investors (limited partners, or LPs) are not allowed by contract to share any information about the private partnership. Typically, 95 to 99 percent of the capital committed to the fund comes from the LPs, while the GPs contribute the remainder.

Once the target amount of money is raised, the fund is closed and the investment period starts, which is usually four to six years. GPs make investment decisions based on the guidelines determined in the partnership agreement, and capital is drawn down from LPs once a new investment has been identified or management fees are due. Generally, a private equity fund invests only in non listed companies. As an exception to this rule, larger buyout funds should be mentioned because they regularly invest in publicly listed firms. However, even these large buyout funds pursue a going-private strategy with their listed targets. Therefore, the portfolio of companies held by a private equity fund eventually consists of non listed companies. As a result, observing the fair market value of this portfolio is impossible. Even though the fund manager reports a book value (net asset value, or NAV) to the LPs, no reliable way exists to infer a true market value from this.

After the investment period expires or the fund is fully drawn down, GPs are not allowed to make any new investments. Instead, the remaining lifetime of the fund, which is about 10 to 12 years, is used to harvest remaining investments made during the investment period.

Due to the construction of private closed-end funds with LPs being locked-in for over 10 years, a public and transparent secondary market in the partnership interests of private equity funds has never evolved, and the fair value of such shares cannot be regularly tracked over regular time intervals (e.g., days or months). Despite a growing number of individual secondary transactions, with specialized secondary investors gaining increased attention and capital, the development of a transparent and liquid secondary market is unlikely for several reasons. First, establishing such a market would conflict with the economic nature of the private equity industry, which is based on capital commitments for a long-term investment in privately held firms. Second, in some markets, such as the United States, certain institutional restrictions exist that avoid regular trading of fund interests. In such a case, a fund would lose its private status with the advantages of limited regulatory and disclosure requirements and instead be recognized as a public fund.

Consequently, no straightforward way is available to calculate time-weighted returns without relying on the quarterly NAVs reported by the funds. In this respect, performance measurement in the private equity arena is completely different from performance measurement in the investment or mutual fund world where regular price information can be observed.

This chapter starts with an overview of how the challenge of calculating time-weighted returns is currently approached in the private equity literature. The chapter focuses only on the performance measurement of unlisted private equity funds, which combine more than 90 percent of capital in the asset class. Measuring the performance of listed private equity funds is comparably straightforward because these vehicles are traded in public markets (Kaserer, Lahr, Liebhardt, and Mettler, 2010). The chapter does not examine the performance at the deal level (i.e., at individual company transactions conducted by a private equity fund), which is available in Graf, Kaserer, and Schmidt (2012). The chapter then introduces the standard cash flow–based performance measures used in private equity and describes the different types of relative performance measures developed by practitioners and academics. After examining the challenges in measuring a reliable performance for private equity, the chapter reviews relevant literature on the performance of private equity and presents recent performance results on selected subasset classes. The final section provides a summary and conclusions.

ASSET VALUE–BASED MEASURES OF PERFORMANCE

A simple way to calculate time-weighted returns for an investment in a private equity fund would be to interpret the quarterly NAVs disclosed by the fund as fair market prices. Equation 16.1 illustrates the return of a fund over a period from $t-1$ to t:

$$R_t = \frac{P_t + D_t - C_t}{P_{t-1}} - 1 \tag{16.1}$$

where P_t is the NAV of a private equity fund at the end of the period $t-1$ to t; D_t is the capital distributions paid by the fund to its LPs, and C_t is the capital contributions (fund drawdowns) made by the LPs during the same period. Given that private equity funds invest in non listed companies, knowing whether the reported NAVs are at least unbiased estimates of the market values of such companies is difficult. Industry valuation guidelines give GPs some flexibility with respect to the valuation of their assets. Achleitner, Kaserer, and Wagner (2005) point out that because of certain accounting and other incentives, skepticism arises, especially during unstable times in equity markets. Moreover, as accounting adjustments take place less frequently than market price adjustments, NAV-based returns will be much less volatile than market returns. This phenomenon is also called the *stale pricing problem* of private equity returns. As a result, any risk-adjusted comparison on the basis of NAVs is likely to be heavily biased.

Getmansky, Lo, and Makarov (2004) propose an econometric approach of how to mitigate the stale pricing problem. While this approach works well with hedge fund returns, where market prices can be observed at some intervals, the effectiveness of this approach is less clear in the private equity context. Therefore, many reservations against using NAV-based performance measures for private equity funds exist.

CASH FLOW–BASED MEASURES OF ABSOLUTE PERFORMANCE

With respect to cash flow–based measures of a private equity fund's absolute performance, the internal rate of return (IRR) and the money multiple are the standard measures used both in practice and in the academic literature. The following sections provide discussions of both measures.

Internal Rate of Return

The IRR, also known as money-weighted rate of return, represents the discount rate that makes the net present value (NPV) of all cash flows between the private equity fund and the LP equal to zero. In other words, the IRR is the effective return on the stream of individual capital contributions from the LP to the fund with respect to the timing and the size of the distributions back to the LP. Mathematically, the IRR can be expressed as the solution to Equation 16.2a:

$$NPV = \sum_{t=0}^{T} \frac{CF_t}{(1+IRR)^t} = 0$$

$$\Leftrightarrow \sum_{t=0}^{T} \frac{D_t - C_t}{(1+IRR)^t} = 0 \Leftrightarrow \frac{\sum_{t=0}^{T} \frac{D_t}{(1+IRR)^t}}{\sum_{t=0}^{T} \frac{C_t}{(1+IRR)^t}} = 1 \qquad (16.2a)$$

In Equation 16.2a, CF_t is the net cash flow generated at time t, defined as the difference between the capital contribution (C_t) made by the LP and the capital distribution (D_t) returned by the fund to the LP.

If a private equity fund is still active and carries a certain residual value, the fund's actual NAV at time T is considered as a terminal value (i.e., a

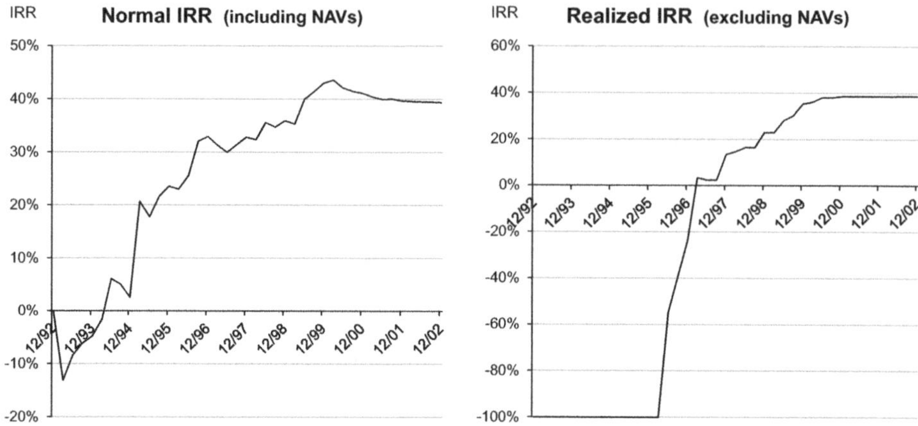

Exhibit 16.1 Development of a Fund's Standard and Realized IRR
The graphs show the time series of interim IRRs for a U.S. venture capital fund from 1992 to 2002. The left graph shows standard IRRs including end-of-quarter NAVs. The right graph shows realized IRRs, which are based only on realized cash flows.

hypothetical, final capital distribution). This adds an additional term shown in Equation 16.2b:

$$NPV = \sum_{t=0}^{T} \frac{CF_t}{(1+IRR)^t} + \frac{NAV_T}{(1+IRR)^T} = 0 \Leftrightarrow \frac{\sum_{t=0}^{T} \frac{D_t}{(1+IRR)^t} + \frac{NAV_T}{(1+IRR)^T}}{\sum_{t=0}^{T} \frac{C_t}{(1+IRR)^t}} = 1 \quad (16.2b)$$

For a still active private equity fund, the IRR calculated based only on realized cash flows (Equation 16.2a) is called *realized IRR*, while distributing the last quarter's NAV (Equation 16.2b) is standard when calculating an interim IRR.

Exhibit 16.1 draws the time series of IRRs for a venture capital fund from 1992 over its entire lifetime. The left graph shows the standard IRRs of the venture capital fund, calculated on a quarterly basis and including the end-of-quarter NAVs as interim terminal values. During the first quarters of a fund's lifetime, management fees and expenses usually drive a negative balance between the overall contributed capital and the NAV of the first investments, which results in a negative IRR. As early investments increase in value and the NAV is written up, the IRR turns increasingly positive. This typical shape of the time series of fund IRRs is commonly referred to as the *J-curve*. The right graph draws the time series of realized IRRs, which are based solely on realized cash flows but not NAVs. Consequently, a fund's realized IRR stays at, or close to, −100 percent in the early years until returns on the first investments are realized and capital flows back to LPs. At the break-even point, capital distributions match previous contributions. Upon a fund's liquidation, the standard and the realized IRR are identical.

Problems associated with the IRR as a return measure have been extensively discussed in the literature (Kaserer and Diller, 2004). For instance, if more than one change occurs in the signs of the time series of net cash flows, the IRR may have more than one (economically meaningful) solution. Also, the IRR depends heavily on the timing of the cash flows. For example, higher distributions in early years of a fund's life can boost the IRR disproportionately higher. Setting these more technical aspects aside, the most important issue associated with the interpretation of the IRR arises when using it as a relative return measure. Comparing the performance of two or more different private equity funds based solely on the IRR can be difficult. Because capital distributions generated by a fund cannot be reinvested at the IRR, but only at the opportunity cost of capital, the present value of a fund with a higher IRR may fall below the terminal wealth of another fund with a lower IRR. Although the rank correlation of the IRR with other performance measures is high, it is clearly below one (Diller and Kaserer, 2009).

An alternative to the standard IRR is the so-called modified IRR (MIRR), which takes the financing costs, as well as the reinvestment returns of the LP into account. Under the MIRR, capital contributions (C_t) into a private equity fund are discounted to their present value by using the LP's financing cost (r_i). Capital distributions (D_t) are reinvested at the reinvestment rate (r_j) to arrive at their future value. As an alternative, the returns of a public equity index, such as the S&P 500 Index or a small-cap index, could be used to calculate the present and the future values. Finally, the ratio of the future value of distributions and the present value of contributions is turned into an annualized rate of return. Equations 16.3a and 16.3b formalize the MIRR:

$$MIRR = \sqrt[T]{\frac{\sum_{t=0}^{T} D_t\left(1+r_j\right)^{T-t}}{\sum_{t=0}^{T} \frac{C_t}{(1+r_i)^t}}} - 1 \qquad (16.3a)$$

$$MIRR = \sqrt[T]{\frac{\sum_{t=0}^{T} D_t\left(1+r_j\right)^{T-t} + NAV_T}{\sum_{t=0}^{T} \frac{C_t}{(1+r_i)^t}}} - 1 \qquad (16.3b)$$

Equation 16.3a calculates the MIRR solely based on realized cash flows; Equation 16.3b accounts for the residual value of the fund in case it has not been liquidated.

Money Multiple

The money multiple, or distributed to paid-in capital (DPI) ratio, is another absolute return measure for private equity funds, commonly presented alongside a fund's IRR. The DPI puts the sum of all capital distributions returned by the fund to the LP in relation to the sum of all capital contributions made by the LP. Mathematically, the DPI can be expressed by Equation 16.4a:

$$DPI = \frac{\sum_{t=0}^{T} D_t}{\sum_{t=0}^{T} C_t} \qquad (16.4a)$$

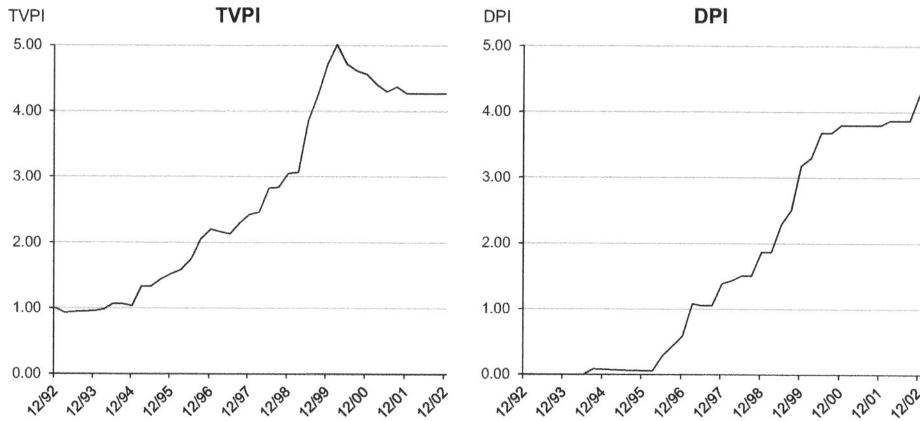

Exhibit 16.2 Development of a Fund's TVPI and DPI
The graphs show the time series of interim TVPIs and DPIs for a U.S. venture capital fund from 1992 to 2002. The left graph shows TVPI ratios including end-of-quarter NAVs. The right graph shows DPI ratios, which are based only on realized cash flows.

In Equation 16.4a, the capital contribution into the fund at time t is C_t, while D_t denominates the capital distribution to the LP at time t. If a private equity fund is still active, Equation 16.4b illustrates the money multiple expressed as the total value to paid-in capital (TVPI) ratio, which includes the fund's actual NAV at time T as a final capital distribution. The TVPI is defined as the sum of the DPI and the residual value to paid-in capital (RVPI) ratio.

$$TVPI = DPI + RVPI, \text{ with } RVPI = \frac{NAV_T}{\sum_{t=0}^{T} C_t} \tag{16.4b}$$

Exhibit 16.2 illustrates the time series of TVPIs and DPIs for the venture capital fund from 1992 over its entire lifetime.

The money multiple has the disadvantage that it does not take the time value of money into account. Therefore, it should be used in combination with the IRR or MIRR, especially when comparing the performance of different private equity funds.

Exhibit 16.3 shows an example for the absolute performance measures in this chapter, based on the cash flows and NAV of an illustrative simple private equity fund.

CASH FLOW–BASED MEASURES OF RELATIVE PERFORMANCE

Sophisticated LPs have been benchmarking the performance of private equity and venture capital funds against public equity since the early 1980s. In contrast to

Exhibit 16.3 IRR, MIRR, and Money Multiple for a Private Equity Fund

Time t	Contributions C_t	Distributions D_t	Net Asset Value NAV_T	Net Cash Flow $-Ct + Dt$	Net Cash Flow +NAV $-C_t + Dt + NAV_T$	PV C_t $r_i = 5\%$	FV D_t $r_j = 8\%$	FV $D_t + NAV_T$ $r_j = 8\%$
0	100	0		−100	−100	100	0	0
1	0	0		0	0	0	0	0
2	150	0		−150	−150	136	0	0
3	50	75		25	25	43	119	119
4	0	0		0	0	0	0	0
5	0	225		225	225	0	306	306
6	0	100		100	100	0	126	126
7	0	0		0	0	0	0	0
8	0	150		150	150	0	162	162
9	0	0	75	0	75	0	0	75
Internal Rate of Return (IRR)					18.0%			
Realized IRR				15.8%				
Modified IRR (MIRR)								12.2%
Realized MIRR							11.0%	
Money Multiple (TVPI)					2.08			
Realized Money Multiple (DPI)				1.83				

The exhibit shows the calculation of the standard (including NAV) and realized (excluding NAV) IRR, modified IRR, and money multiple values for an illustrative private equity fund.

investments in public equity, private equity is a very expensive asset class. Over the lifetime of a fund, the amount of management fees can make up 20 percent of a fund's size (or an LP's commitment). Another 20 percent of the profits, the "carried interest," remain with the GP in case a minimum performance is exceeded. At the same time, due to the illiquid nature of the funds, investors require a premium over public markets. Not surprisingly, some LPs have been keen to determine whether their investee funds delivered excess returns, at least, beyond the major public stock index. For U.S. private equity, the S&P 500 Index has traditionally been used as a benchmark, although it is not directly comparable in terms of size, leverage, and liquidity. Higson and Stucke (2012) propose to further compare against a small-cap equity index, such as the S&P Small-Cap 600 Index. In any event, using a performance, or total return index, where dividends are reinvested seems appropriate.

Long and Nickels (1995) are the first to document a formalized method of how to benchmark private and public equity, the index comparison method (ICM). Venture Economics subsequently implemented this approach into their system and rebranded it the public market equivalent (PME). ICM/PME calculates a spread between the IRR (money multiple) of a private equity fund and the IRR (money multiple) of its "public market equivalent." Under the original approach, every drawdown by a private equity fund (i.e., contribution by an LP) is matched by an equal investment in a public equity index. Similarly, every capital distribution from the fund is matched by an equal sale of the respective index. During any period, currently invested amounts change in value according to the index. The result is an identical series of capital contributions and distributions, but a different residual value of the index investment. Based on this series of cash flows and the derived residual value, the IRR (money multiple) for this public market equivalent can be calculated, which then serves as the basis for deriving the spread with the IRR (money multiple) of the private equity fund.

ICM/PME is a very intuitive approach and fairly simple to implement but it has one obvious drawback. If the private equity fund delivers a higher return than the public equity index, the PME's (interim) residual value will run into a negative position at some point, namely, when a matched distribution by the fund exceeds the residual value. Subsequent distributions from the fund might further increase that short position, which, as the terminal value, has to be offset by a contribution.

A similarly intuitive and widely accepted solution to this drawback has been to stop further distributions when the PME's residual value turns zero (Stucke, 2011; Higson and Stucke, 2012). As a result, further distributions from the private equity fund are no longer matched by the PME. Exhibit 16.4 shows an example for the relative performance measures in this chapter, based on the cash flows and NAV of an illustrative simple private equity fund.

Rouvinez (2003) offers the PME+ approach as another option to avoid the short position. The rationale of PME+ is to downscale all distributions of the PME by multiplying them with a scaling factor lambda ($\lambda < 1$), such that the PME's terminal value is equal to the private equity fund's NAV (or zero in case the fund has been liquidated). Equations 16.5a and 16.5b illustrate the calculation

Exhibit 16.4 Relative Performance Calculation

Time	Contributions	Distributions	Net Asset Value	Index		ICM/PME		ICM/PME (no short)	
t	C_t	D_t	NAV_T	I_t	$R_{t-1..t}$	NAV_t	$CF + NAV_T$	NAV_t	$CF + NAV_T$
0	100	0		100		100	−100	100	−100
1	0	0		95	−5.0%	95	0	95	0
2	150	0		90	−5.3%	240	−150	240	−150
3	50	75		105	16.7%	255	25	255	25
4	0	0		110	4.8%	267	0	267	0
5	0	225		120	9.1%	66	225	66	225
6	0	100		115	−4.2%	−36	100	0	64
7	0	0		125	8.7%	−39	0	0	0
8	0	150		130	4.0%	−191	150	0	0
9	0	0	75	140	7.7%	−206	−206	0	0
Internal Rate of Return			18.0%						
Money Multiple			2.08						
ICM/PME IRR							5.8%		
ICM/PME IRR Spread							12.2%		
ICM/PME Money Multiple							1.10		
ICM/PME Money Multiple Spread							0.99		
ICM/PME (no short) IRR									6.1%
ICM/PME (no short) IRR Spread									11.9%
ICM/PME (no short) Money Multiple									1.25
ICM/PME (no short) Money Multiple Spread									0.83

(Continued)

Exhibit 16.4 *(Continued)*

Time	Contributions	Distributions	Net Asset Value	PME+					"PME"/index-adj. multiple		
t	C_t	D_t	NAV_T	C_t/I_t	D_t/I_t	NAV_T/I_T	New D_t	New CF + NAV_T	PV C_t	PV D_t	PV NAV_T
0	100	0		1.00	0.00		0	−100	100	0	
1	0	0		0.00	0.00		0	0	0	0	
2	150	0		1.67	0.00		0	−150	167	0	
3	50	75		0.48	0.71		42	−8	48	71	
4	0	0		0.00	0.00		0	0	0	0	
5	0	225		0.00	1.88		127	127	0	188	
6	0	100		0.00	0.87		57	57	0	87	
7	0	0		0.00	0.00		0	0	0	0	
8	0	150		0.00	1.15		85	85	0	115	
9	0	0	75	0.00	0.00	0.54	0	75	0	0	54
Internal Rate of Return			18.0%								
Money Multiple			2.08								
PME+ Lambda					0.565						
PME+ IRR								5.4%			
PME+ IRR Spread								12.6%			
PME+ Money Multiple								1.29			
PME+ Money Multiple Spread								0.80			
"PME" / Index-adjusted multiple										1.64	

The exhibit shows the calculation of IRRs and money multiples relative to a public equity index using the original ICM/PME approach, ICM/PME without running into a short position, the PME+ approach, as well as the PME/index-adjusted multiple approach introduced by Kaplan and Schoar (2005).

of lambda:

$$\lambda = \frac{\sum_{t=0}^{T} \frac{C_t}{I_t}}{\sum_{t=0}^{T} \frac{D_t}{I_t}} \Leftrightarrow \lambda = \frac{\sum_{t=0}^{T} \frac{C_t}{(1+r_t)}}{\sum_{t=0}^{T} \frac{D_t}{(1+r_t)}} \tag{16.5a}$$

$$\lambda = \frac{\sum_{t=0}^{T} \frac{C_t}{I_t} - \frac{NAV_T}{I_T}}{\sum_{t=0}^{T} \frac{D_t}{I_t}} \Leftrightarrow \lambda = \frac{\sum_{t=0}^{T} \frac{C_t}{(1+r_t)} - \frac{NAV_T}{(1+r_T)}}{\sum_{t=0}^{T} \frac{D_t}{(1+r_t)}} \tag{16.5b}$$

In Equation 16.5a, I_t is the value of the index at time t; C_t is the contribution and D_t is the distribution at time t. Furthermore, r_t denotes the return on the index for the period from 0 to t. While the left part of Equation 16.5a implicitly adjusts all cash flows for the change in the index, the right part of Equation 16.5a explicitly capitalizes all cash flows to time 0. If a residual value is carried by the fund, Equation 16.5b subtracts the relevant term from the nominators. In a second step, the IRR (money multiple) is calculated for the stream of capital contributions and downscaled distributions, as well as a possible NAV. This PME+ IRR (money multiple) then serves as the basis for the spread with the IRR (money multiple) of the private equity fund. One drawback of the PME+ approach is that it tends to inflate the IRR spread. Because early capital distributions drive the IRR, downscaling such distributions has a dilutive effect on the PME+'s IRR.

The literature contains an additional approach, also branded as a public market equivalent (Kaplan and Schoar, 2005). Similar to PME+, this approach arrives at a scaling factor via the ratio of the present values of distributions and contributions, indicating to what extent contributions invested in the public equity index would have to be increased to meet all subsequent distributions from the private equity fund. Equations 16.6a and 16.6b formalize this factor, with variables being the same as for the PME+:

$$PME = \frac{\sum_{t=0}^{T} \frac{D_t}{(1+r_t)}}{\sum_{t=0}^{T} \frac{C_t}{(1+r_t)}} \tag{16.6a}$$

$$PME = \frac{\sum_{t=0}^{T} \frac{D_t}{(1+r_t)} + \frac{NAV_T}{(1+r_T)}}{\sum_{t=0}^{T} \frac{C_t}{(1+r_t)}} \tag{16.6b}$$

Equation 16.6a calculates this factor for a fully liquidated fund; Equation 16.6b considers a fund's final NAV. These equations are similar to the money multiple of a fund (DPI and TVPI). Therefore, Stucke (2011) characterizes them as an index-adjusted multiple. By definition, a ratio greater than 1.0 indicates that the private equity fund has generated excess returns over the public equity index. A factor less than 1.0 indicates that public equity has generated excess returns (i.e., lower contributions would be sufficient to meet all distributions, given the index returns). The disadvantage of this approach is that it does not generate an annualized measure of relative performance. In line with PME+, one could calculate an IRR (money multiple) over the series of upscaled capital contributions, as well as the distributions and NAV. However, the IRR would be similarly diluted as via the PME+ approach.

CHALLENGES IN MEASURING THE PERFORMANCE OF PRIVATE EQUITY

Various challenges exist when measuring the performance of private equity. This section introduces the main issues.

Incomplete Cash Flow History

All cash flow–based return measures suffer from the drawback that, in principle, they can only be applied once a fund is fully liquidated and its entire cash flow history is known. However, as private equity funds have average maturities of more than 10 years, a long time is needed before a definite, ex-post performance measurement can be applied. Therefore, in most practical applications, as well as in the academic literature, mature but not yet liquidated funds are also involved in performance analyses. Some research studies use a minimum fund age of, for example, 6 to 10 years (Kaplan and Schoar, 2005; Phalippou and Gottschalg, 2009), while others implement more formal age rules (Diller and Kaserer, 2009; Higson and Stucke, 2012).

However, once not yet liquidated funds are involved in the analysis, the question of how to handle residual values arises. One solution to this problem would be to assume that the NAV is an unbiased estimate of the residual fair market value of the fund. In that case, the NAV is interpreted as a final capital distribution, and the performance of the fund is calculated on this basis, as done in the previous sections. As Higson and Stucke (2012) note, an alternative could be to apply a certain discount to the NAV, for example, derived from the secondary market for LP interests. Secondary market intermediaries regularly publish such discounts. Actual work in progress suggests that private equity funds' NAVs tend to understate subsequent distributions during good markets, but overstate NAVs in down markets (i.e., tend to smooth residual values of their investments). This result is consistent with the finding of Stucke (2011) that interim money multiples understate the final money multiples for funds raised between 1980 and 1993.

Risk-Adjusted Performance

All performance measures discussed so far are one-dimensional. That is, they do not take the risk profile of the investment into account, such as exposure to systematic risk. While different risk-adjustment methods in the context of time-weighted returns are available, determining how a risk adjustment should be implemented on the basis of cash flow–based returns is less clear. Achleitner et al. (2005) offer one approach of using NAV-based returns and correcting them for the stale pricing problem. The effectiveness of this approach for private equity funds remains unclear. Buchner, Kaserer, and Wagner (2010) contend that modeling the asset pricing dynamics of illiquid private equity funds on the basis of observed cash flows could be a viable alternative. On the basis of such models, the derivations of well-known risk-adjusted performance measures become possible.

An additional challenge comes from the fact that the exposure to market risk by a private equity fund changes over time. For example, the availability of financial leverage has differed substantially for funds from certain vintage years or investment periods. Funds investing in the mid-1980s often employed more than 90 percent of debt in their transactions; investments in the early 2000s, however, were regularly conducted with less than 60 percent of debt. Also, as the focus of private equity investments has often followed or advanced certain industry trends, the general sensitivity of the underlying companies to market risk has varied in time.

Finally, the exposure to market risk changes during the lifetime of a fund. While in early years of a private equity fund a portfolio of often highly leveraged companies is built, these companies aim to quickly reduce leverage and increase in performance. Consequently, in the middle of a private equity fund's lifetime, a diversified portfolio of less leveraged companies has developed, and certain amounts of capital have already been distributed back to LPs.

Funding and Illiquidity Costs

Additional risks and costs arise at the overall asset allocation level of an institutional investor's portfolio, resulting from the fact that the LP cannot control the cash flows into and out of a private equity fund. As mentioned earlier, LPs commit capital to private equity funds, which the fund manager draws down at his own discretion over a period of four to six years upon short notice. To the extent to which drawdowns from younger funds are not matched by distributions from mature funds (e.g., because the program is still young and has limited vintage year diversification, the program has recently grown considerably in size, or exit markets are closed, such as between mid-2007 to 2009), the LP has to provide capital from selling liquid securities. While this arrangement is very convenient for the GP and the IRR of the fund, it creates certain individual costs for the LP.

In addition to the risks and costs of funding and meeting capital calls, the illiquid nature of the asset class creates additional costs to an institutional investor. Unlike frequently traded asset classes, the absolute and relative exposure to private equity is difficult to estimate when commitments to new funds are given, and cannot easily be rebalanced as the value of an institutional portfolio changes or liquidity is needed. Although today's secondary market for private equity fund interests has reached a mature stage, a sale of a portfolio of funds usually takes several weeks' time and is often associated with meaningful discounts to the NAVs. As a result, investors in private equity require an illiquidity premium, which may differ in size between different types of LPs.

Availability of Performance Information

Early providers of performance information on the venture capital and private equity industry were Venture Economics and Cambridge Associates. Venture Economics operated as a general data provider for the private equity industry. Part of its service was collecting fund performance information from LPs and GPs who were willing to share their data subject to anonymity and confidentiality via data aggregation. Venture Economics was the first official benchmarking partner of the National (United States) and European Venture Capital Associations and was ultimately acquired by Thomson and renamed VentureXpert (TVE). In a recent study, Stucke (2011) identifies unusual patterns in the TVE database, which result from truncated data records that cause a significant downward bias of TVE's private equity performance figures.

Cambridge Associates was one of the first advisory companies to investors in the asset class. In its role as a data custodian and running client portfolios, this firm had direct access to fund performance information. Supplementing these data with performance figures collected from additional GPs and LPs, Cambridge Associates has been publishing its own, proprietary performance benchmark for more than a decade. In a recent study, Higson and Stucke (2012) confirm the representativeness of the Cambridge Associates benchmark for U.S. buyout funds, which had been assumed by practitioners and academics to have a success bias due to its positive difference to the TVE benchmark.

The information environment on private equity performance changed materially with the enacting of the Freedom of Information Act (FOIA) in 2003. Under FOIA, public institutions investing in private equity, such as pension plans and certain endowments, are required to make information on their investment holdings and corresponding returns available. While some larger public institutions provide such information on their websites, the vast majority only responds to individual FOIA requests. Well-known examples are the California Public Employees Retirement System (CalPERS) and the Washington State Investment Board.

Preqin (formerly known as Private Equity Intelligence) is the data provider that built its business model on FOIA. Preqin regularly collects and updates performance numbers on private equity funds from the Internet and via FOIA requests. It has been the first source of non aggregated performance figures at the individual fund level.

In recent years, additional providers of private equity performance benchmarks have emerged. State Street and the Burgiss Group are data custodians and solution providers that offer aggregated performance benchmarks based on the private equity funds in their clients' portfolios. Efront is a software provider for LPs and similarly generates benchmarks based on its clients' data. Pevara is a recent product, also developed by Efront, which is fully Web-based. Pitchbook is a data provider following the Preqin example, collecting performance data from the Internet and via FOIA requests.

Limitations to Existing Benchmarks

Although the information environment on private equity performance improved over the past decade, comprehensive and representative benchmarks for the asset class still do not exist. The universe of private equity funds is not well defined. While TVE, Preqin, and Pitchbook all offer a list of private equity funds currently or previously in the market, their lists differ substantially. The overall number of private equity funds raised worldwide varies between 12,000 and 20,000. For those funds being constituents of two or all three lists, one can regularly observe differences in vintage year or size for the same fund. Moreover, a certain fraction of the funds differ in their investment focus, especially at the threshold between venture capital and buyout.

As Harris, Jenkinson, and Stucke (2010) show, the traditional benchmark providers TVE, Cambridge Associates, and Preqin have only performance information for one-quarter to one-third of these funds by number. In the case of Preqin, many of the funds that are not denominated in U.S. dollars have a currency bias because their performance data, for example for European funds, are often collected from U.S. investors.

Finally, a general issue that still needs to be resolved is a consistent definition of a fund's vintage year. While TVE uses the year of the first fund cash flow as the vintage year, Cambridge Associates refers to the year of a fund's legal inception. Preqin simply keeps the vintage year as defined by the LP or its custodian. At least five different vintage year definitions have been used historically: (1) the year of a fund's legal inception, (2) the year of its first closing, (3) the year of its first capital call, (4) the year of its first investment, or (5) the year of its final close. If a fund had more than one closing, the first capital call or first investment can further differ depending on the closing round.

LITERATURE ON THE PERFORMANCE OF PRIVATE EQUITY FUNDS

Higson and Stucke (2012) provide the most comprehensive evidence on the absolute and relative performance of U.S. private equity funds. The authors use a sample of 1,169 U.S. buyout funds between 1980 and 2008 from Cambridge Associates' fund cash flow database as well as a number of other LPs. With respect to the absolute performance, Higson and Stucke find that buyout returns follow a highly pronounced wave pattern, with higher returns in the first half of each decade and correspondingly lower returns toward the end of each decade (when equity markets used to overheat and eventually drop). At the same time, buyout returns show a strong downward trend with respect to both IRRs and money multiples. The weighted-average IRRs (money multiples) in the 1980s, 1990s, and 2000s were 16.5 percent (2.34), 11.4 percent (1.61), and 7.2 percent (1.28), respectively. Compared to the performance of public equity, measured by the total returns of the S&P 500 Index, quasi-liquidated funds between 1980 and 2000 have generated excess returns of about 450 basis points (bps) annually. Adding partially liquidated funds up to 2005, annual excess returns rise to over 800 bps.

In another study, Harris, Jenkinson, and Kaplan (2012) find similar excess returns for U.S. buyout funds from more recent vintage years based on a sample of 598 U.S. private equity funds from the Burgiss Group. The authors also analyze U.S. venture capital funds and find a constant outperformance for funds between 1987 and 1998 but a constant underperformance thereafter, except in 2005.

These findings on excess returns of U.S. private equity over public equity differ from earlier, influential studies based on fund performance data from Thomson VentureXpert (TVE). Kaplan and Schoar (2005) report an underperformance of 197 U.S. buyout funds between 1980 and 1995 by 2 percent. Phalippou and Gottschalg (2009) find an underperformance of the entire asset class by 3 to 6 percent. However, Stucke (2011) and Higson and Stucke (2012) contend that about half of the TVE funds that these studies used in their working sample had incomplete cash flow data. Moreover, Phalippou and Gottschalg misinterpret the carried-forward and constant NAVs of these funds as "living dead" investments and falsely write them off to zero.

Using a sample of 200 European private equity funds between 1980 and 1993, Diller and Kaserer (2009) find an outperformance of 1.0 percent for private equity over European stock markets. Although their study is also based on fund cash flow data from TVE, the authors limit their working sample to widely liquidated funds and thus mostly avoid incomplete fund data.

PERFORMANCE OF SELECTED SUBASSET CLASSES

Although private equity is regularly characterized as an alternative asset class, returns clearly have equity-like characteristics. Thus, private equity as an asset class is much less "alternative" in a sense, but substantially correlates with returns of general equity markets. Mezzanine or distressed debt funds are an exception to some extent because they contain fixed-income components.

This section reviews the past and current performance in terms of vintage years IRRs and money multiples of the three major subasset classes: (1) venture capital, (2) buyout, and (3) real estate private equity for U.S.-focused funds. A private equity fund's investment period stretches over four to six years following its inception (vintage year), while assets are typically held three to six years. Therefore, funds from the end-1990s are just about to fully liquidate.

Venture Capital Returns

The institutional venture capital industry gained traction in the United States in the mid- to late-1970s. In the early 1980s, the number of venture capital funds reached levels of 50 to 100 new funds per year. Exhibit 16.5 shows the performance of U.S. venture capital funds since 1980. While performance benchmarks regularly report return figures for different investment stages of venture capital funds, such as early, balanced, or later stage, a clear differentiation is difficult in practice. Notably, previous studies find that larger venture capital funds and firms tend to outperform smaller ones (Harris, Jenkinson, and Kaplan, 2012).

In the first half of the 1980s, the median venture capital fund delivered an IRR of about 10 percent per year, while the top-quartile threshold was roughly 5 percentage points higher. These figures are consistent with both the year-over-year return of U.S. small-cap stocks and the yield of 10-year Treasury bonds. By 1987, venture capital funds started to deliver increasingly higher IRRs, with the median fund IRR peaking at about 35 percent in 1993 and a top-quartile threshold

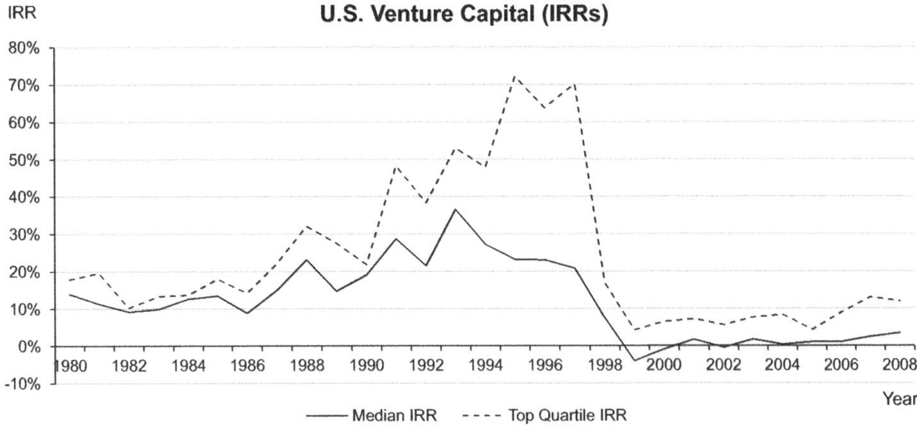

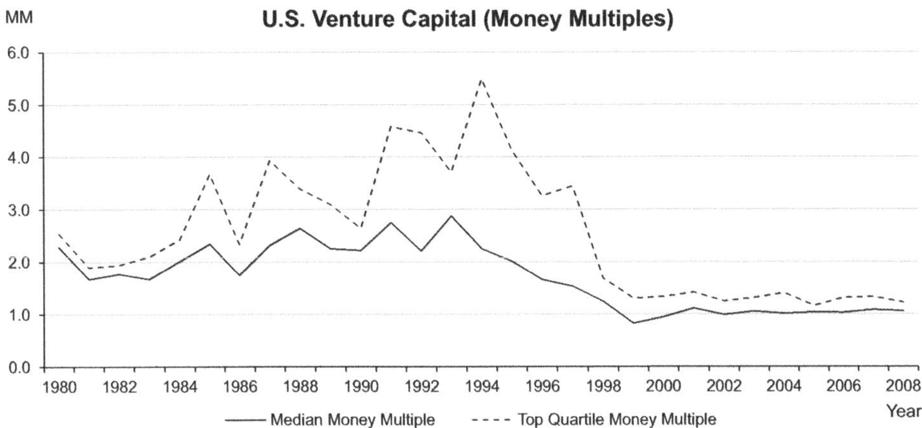

Exhibit 16.5 Performance of U.S. Venture Capital Funds
The graphs show the IRR and money multiple measures from U.S. venture capital funds with vintage years from 1980 to 2008. The graphs are based on the performance of 926 funds from Preqin as of 2011.

of slightly over 70 percent for funds from 1995. These funds were benefitting most from quickly exiting their portfolio companies into the late-1990s' "new economy boom."

By vintage year 1998, returns from venture capital funds dropped substantially and have not recovered. The IRRs of the median funds stayed constantly at about 0 percent. Until 2006, the threshold of the top-quartile (interim) IRR has not exceeded 10 percent.

However, besides the sole financial returns from venture capital funds, the highly innovative character of this industry clearly generates additional value to society and economies as a whole. For example, venture capital–backed companies generate many additional jobs in an economy and are often at the forefront of developing and testing innovations, even if they eventually do not turn into expected, highly profitable businesses or do not sustain in their original form.

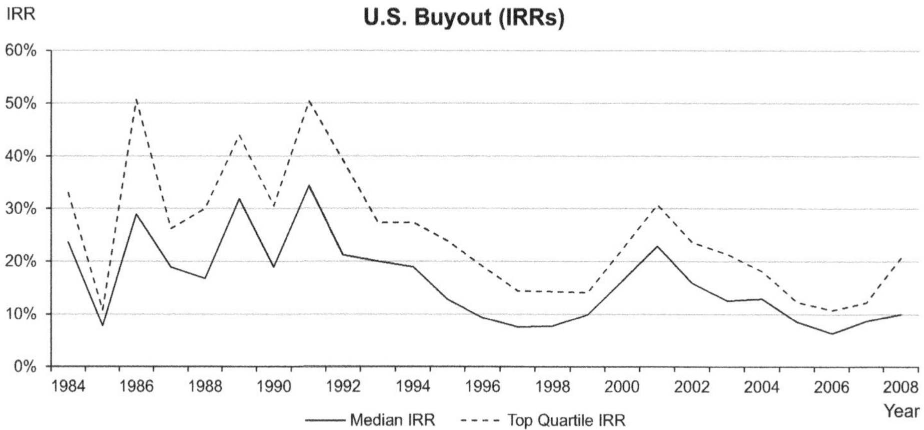

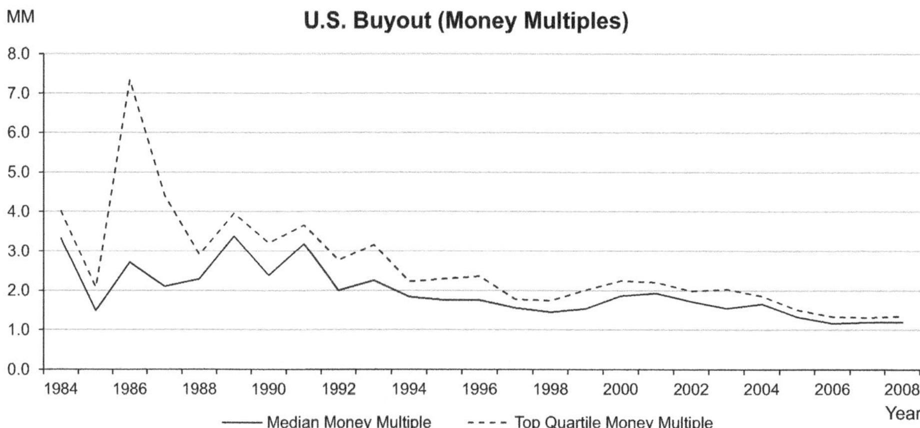

Exhibit 16.6 Performance of U.S. Buyout Funds

The graphs show the IRR and money multiple measures from U.S. buyout funds with vintage years from 1984 to 2008. The graphs are based on the performance of 677 funds from Preqin as of 2011.

Buyout Returns

The institutional leveraged buyout industry started in the United States in the late 1970s but did not reach mainstream status until the mid-1980s. As Exhibit 16.6 shows, median IRRs were regularly above 20 percent per year until the mid-1990s; top-quartile funds regularly achieved IRRs of more than 30 percent.

Vintage year returns from 1997 to 1999 dropped materially. These funds invested most of their capital at peak valuations during the end-1990s and their leveraged companies were hit particularly hard by the economic downturn after 2000–2001.

Median funds with vintage years 2000 to 2004 delivered double-digit IRRs, with a top-quartile threshold of about 20 percent and above. Funds from 2005 to 2008 delivered correspondingly lower returns. However, these funds need additional time to move toward their eventual performance, and many of which are still subject to the J-curve effect. Nonetheless, since buyout funds from 2005 to 2008 attracted roughly 50 percent of capital ever raised into this subasset class, their final performance will be influential to the overall long-term returns of private equity.

In general, buyout returns, due to the high level of financial leverage, follow a pronounced wave pattern. For a widely complete account of U.S. buyout funds since 1980, Higson and Stucke (2012) illustrate this pattern of IRRs and money multiples in greater detail. Furthermore, the authors find that larger buyout funds tend to outperform smaller funds, which is consistent with a world where skilled managers attract larger funds.

Returns from Real Estate Private Equity

Real estate private equity funds gained traction by the mid-1990s and became similarly mainstream as buyout funds in terms of number and size by the early 2000s. Exhibit 16.7 shows that returns of real estate private equity funds were very similar

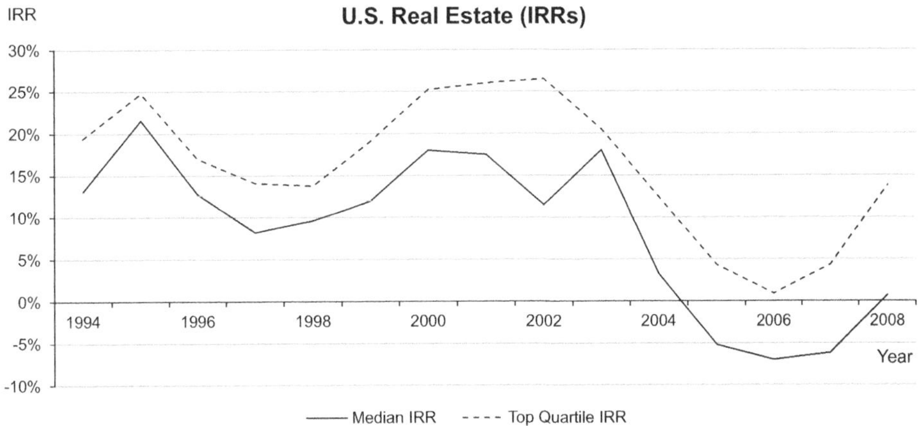

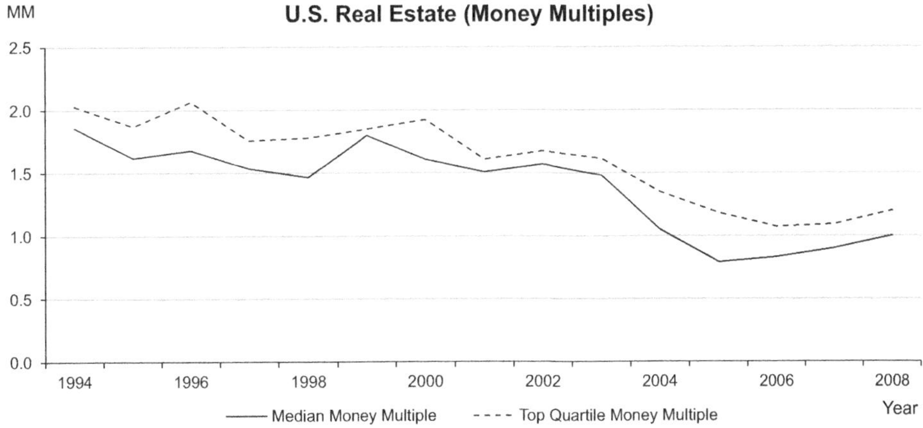

Exhibit 16.7 Performance of U.S. Real Estate Private Equity Funds

The graphs show IRR and money multiple measures from U.S. real estate private equity funds with vintage years from 1994 to 2008. The graphs are based on the performance of 408 funds from Preqin as of 2011.

to those of buyout funds until 2003, with median returns between 8 and 18 percent and a top-quartile threshold ranging from 15 to 25 percent. An attractive feature of this type of funds, however, was a systematically lower intra-year volatility of returns compared to buyout funds. Vintage years between 2004 and 2007 have been hit severely by the financial crisis and the drop in highly inflated real estate markets.

SUMMARY AND CONCLUSIONS

This chapter provides an overview on the performance of private equity by introducing and discussing the different performance measurement methods for private equity funds, reviewing empirical evidence from the literature, and presenting current performance figures from one of the main data providers. The chapter explains that, by construction, the usual calculation of a time-weighted return for mutual funds is extremely difficult or almost impossible for private equity funds. The reason is that neither the fund nor its portfolio companies are traded on an organized market. Consequently, market prices cannot be observed on a regular basis.

Therefore, alternative performance measurement methods have been developed. Some of these methods are based on NAVs reported by the fund. However, because of reporting biases, cash flow–based methods have become much more important. In fact, the cash flow is the only reliable performance indicator that can be observed for a private equity fund. On the basis of this cash flow information, the IRR and the money multiple are widely used as absolute performance measures, whereas the PME is used as a relative performance measure. The methodological as well as operational problems associated with these methods have been discussed. Most important, the chapter emphasizes why these performance measures cannot easily be adjusted for the risk involved with a given investment. Therefore, comparing private equity funds on a risk-adjusted basis is still an unresolved issue.

Despite all these problems, a vast literature on private equity performance measurement has evolved over the last 10 years. Interestingly, no clear results emerge from this literature with respect to the performance of private equity vis-à-vis other asset classes. Part of this problem is the fact that some of the earlier influential studies used partly incorrect data. Therefore, the chapter concludes by presenting some up-to-date absolute performance figures for a sample of venture capital, buyout, and real estate private equity funds.

DISCUSSION QUESTIONS

1. Why is performance measurement so difficult for private equity funds?
2. What different types of performance measures exist, and what are their primary characteristics?
3. Discuss the challenges in measuring the performance of private equity as an asset class.
4. Identify and explain the advantages and disadvantages of different PME methods.
5. What kind of risk-adjustments would be required to better benchmark buyout funds against public equity?

REFERENCES

Achleitner, Ann-Kristin, Christoph Kaserer, and Niklas Wagner. 2005. "Managing Investment Risks of Institutional Private Equity Investors—The Challenge of Illiquidity." In Frenkel, Michael, Ulrich Hommel, and Markus Rudolf, ed., *Risk Management—Challenge and Opportunity*, 259–277. Berlin: Springer.

Buchner, Axel, Christoph Kaserer, and Niklas Wagner. 2010. "Modeling the Cash Flow Dynamics of Private Equity Funds: Theory and Empirical Evidence." *Journal of Alternative Investments* 13:1, 41–54.

Diller, Christian, and Christoph Kaserer. 2009. "What Drives European Private Equity Returns? Fund Inflows, Skilled GPs, and/or Risk?" *European Financial Management* 15:3, 643–675.

Getmansky, Mila, Andrew W. Lo, and Igor Makarov. 2004. "An Econometric Model of Serial Correlation and Illiquidity in Hedge Fund Returns." *Journal of Financial Economics* 74:3, 529–609.

Graf, Christian, Christoph Kaserer, and Daniel Schmidt. 2012. "Private Equity: Value Creation and Performance." In Douglas Cumming, ed., *The Oxford Handbook of Private Equity*, 347–385, Oxford: Oxford University Press.

Harris, Robert, Tim Jenkinson, and Steven N. Kaplan. 2012. "Private Equity Performance: What Do We Know?" Working Paper, University of Virginia.

Harris, Robert, Tim Jenkinson, and Rüdiger Stucke. 2010. "A White Paper on Private Equity Data and Research." Working Paper, University of Virginia.

Higson, Chris, and Rüdiger Stucke. 2012. "The Performance of Private Equity." Working Paper, London Business School.

Kaplan, Steven N., and Antoinette Schoar. 2005. "Private Equity Performance: Returns, Persistence, and Capital Flows." *Journal of Finance* 60:4, 1791–1823.

Kaserer, Christoph, and Christian Diller. 2004. "Beyond IRR Once More." *Private Equity International* 4:6, 30–38.

Kaserer, Christoph, Henry Lahr, Valentin Liebhardt, and Alfred Mettler. 2010. "The Time-Varying Risk of Listed Private Equity." *Journal of Financial Transformation* 28:3, 87–93.

Long, Austin, and Craig Nickels. 1995. "A Method for Comparing Private Market Internal Rates of Return to Public Market Index Returns." Working Paper, University of Texas System.

Phalippou, Ludovic, and Oliver Gottschalg. 2009. "The Performance of Private Equity Funds." *Review of Financial Studies* 22:4, 1747–1776.

Rouvinez, Christophe. 2003. "Private Equity Benchmarking with PME+." *Venture Capital Journal* August, 34–38.

Stucke, Rüdiger. 2011. "Updating History." Working Paper, Oxford University.

ABOUT THE AUTHORS

Christoph Kaserer is a Full Professor of Finance at the TUM School of Management at Technische Universität München (TUM). He heads the Department of Financial Management and Capital Markets and is also a Co-Director of the Center for Entrepreneurial and Financial Studies at TUM. Before joining TUM, Professor Kaserer was a Full Professor of Finance and Accounting at the Université de Fribourg, Switzerland. His research has been published in the *Journal of Business Finance and Accounting, European Financial Management, Journal of Risk, Journal of Alternative Investing*, and *International Review of Finance*, among others. He is among the top 1 percent of downloaded authors on the Social Science Research Network

(SSRN). Professor Kaserer is also active as an advisor for large private companies and associations, private equity funds, and public institutions, including the Swiss and German governments. Professor Kaserer earned a degree in economics from the University of Vienna and a Ph.D. in finance from the University of Würzburg.

Rüdiger Stucke is a Research Fellow in Finance and Economics at the Saïd Business School and the Oxford-Man Institute of Quantitative Finance, University of Oxford. His research interests cover the whole field of private equity with particular focus on the buyout industry. In this area, he has done extensive research on the performance and benchmarking of private equity funds, as well as on structuring and value creation of leveraged buyout transactions.

As a Marie Curie Fellow of the European Commission, he came to the Saïd Business School in 2007 to finish his Ph.D. (summa cum laude), which he had previously started at Paderborn University, Germany. Before this, he studied economics, business administration, and computer science at Paderborn University and graduated with first class honors with distinction. During his studies he worked in several positions in investment banking and management consulting.

CHAPTER 17

Private Equity: Risk and Return Profile

AXEL BUCHNER
Associate Professor of Finance, Passau University

ARIF KHURSHED
Senior Lecturer, Manchester Business School

ABDULKADIR MOHAMED
Assistant Professor, University of Liverpool

INTRODUCTION

This chapter examines the risk and return of private equity investments. Private equity firms provide equity financing to companies that are not yet traded on a stock market. Funding is provided in stages known as financing or investment rounds. Practitioners broadly categorize private equity investments into venture capital and buyout investments. *Venture capital* involves investments in young and risky businesses, whereas *buyout* involves investments in mature companies that require financing to pursue growth opportunities. As a general rule, risk and expected returns are generally considered to be higher in venture capital investments as compared to buyout investments.

The purpose of this chapter is to analyze the abnormal performance and systematic risk of private equity investments using the single-factor market model. An extension of the standard internal rate of return (IRR) approach is used to permit making inferences about the abnormal returns of private equity investments and their exposure to market risk. This methodology is applied to a comprehensive data set of private equity investments from around the world. Its unique feature is that this methodology enables only measuring systematic risk and abnormal returns of pure private equity investments and not that of combined investments into private equity and other asset classes. The MSCI World Index and the S&P 500 Index are used as proxies for the market benchmark.

The results show that the systematic risk (beta) varies between venture capital and buyout investments. Using the MSCI World Index, the beta for venture capital is 2.32, compared to 1.51 for buyout deals. By changing the market benchmark to the S&P 500 Index, the beta becomes 2.39 for venture capital versus 2.00 for buyout investments. Evidence also shows that buyout investments exhibit a lower exposure to market risk compared to venture capital investments, despite their high leverage. This evidence is consistent with the findings of Kaplan and Stein (1990), who document that the effect of an increase in the debt ratio has a small effect on the market beta of private equity investments. The findings indicate that the estimates of market risk for the venture capital and buyout investments are significantly different from the market index beta of 1.0. Hence, the assumption of a beta equal to 1.0 (Kaplan and Schoar, 2005) is likely to understate the true exposure of venture capital or buyout investments to the market risk. Abnormal returns (as measured by alpha) are significantly positive for both segments. By comparison, buyout investments show higher average abnormal returns than venture capital investments. This evidence implies that private equity funds add considerable value to their investments and that the value added is higher for buyout than for venture funds.

The following sections provide an overview of venture capital investments around the globe and review the literature on returns of private equity investments followed by sections discussing performance measurements and the methodology employed and the empirical findings. The final section offers a summary and conclusions.

GLOBAL OVERVIEW OF VENTURE CAPITAL INVESTMENT AND INDUSTRY

Venture capital investment is typically regarded as a form of "risk capital" that is invested in a business where a substantial risk is associated with the creation of future profits and cash flows. The risk capital is invested in the form of equity, rather than as a loan, and venture capital firms require a high return to compensate them for the high risk. Generally, venture capital firms provide long-term investments to unquoted companies as a means of facilitating their growth and success. Obtaining venture capital funding is substantially different from raising public debt or a loan from a lender or bank. Lenders have a legal right to receive interest on a loan and the repayment of the capital, irrespective of the success or failure of the business. Conversely, venture capital firms invest in exchange for an equity stake in the business, and hence their returns depend on the success and growth of that business. These returns are normally realized when venture capital firms exit their investments successfully through initial public offerings (IPOs), trade sales, or public mergers. Venture capital investments are not restricted to small or new businesses, but can also apply to businesses with potential growth opportunity. Generally, venture capital firms are keen to finance companies with high growth potential and are managed by ambitious teams who are capable of turning their business plans into reality (Harrison and Mason, 1996).

Initially, the focus of venture capital firms was to back startup businesses, usually those with technological prospects. However, venture capital industries have developed considerably over the last few decades across the globe, and funding patterns have shifted to include different asset classes (i.e., financing nontechnological companies). Venture capital firms have played an essential role in identifying business opportunities that are vital for economic growth and supporting such business financially and operationally. For instance, in the United States venture capital firms backed Digital Equipment Corporation, Apple Inc., Sun Microsystems, Lotus, Compaq, and Prime Computer during each of their startup phases. Similarly, in Europe venture-backed companies have boosted the economy substantially, with the European Venture Capital Association (EVCA) describing them as the "engine for the economy." Venture capital firms are well known for rescuing small businesses and providing them with capital to finance their potential growth opportunities. The venture capital market has played a major role in financing small entrepreneurial businesses in the United States, Europe, and elsewhere since the late 1980s. Recently, buyout investments have received academic attention as a separate class from venture capital investments, due to their different characteristics relative to other investment stages. Buyout investments involve investing in an established company that requires funding in order to pursue a growth opportunity. As a result, the size of buyout investments is typically larger than venture capital investments.

The institutional settings vary in North America, Europe, and Asia, and hence the practices of venture capital firms differ. For instance, in China private firms have limited discretion to acquire and allocate resources. More often, venture capital firms engage in financing where personal connections are more important than a backed company's capability (Bruton and Ahlstrom, 2003). In the 1990s, banks were the main providers of investment in the expansion and later-stage financing rounds, with local government acting as a guarantor in China and possibly Asia in general.

The environments in North America and Europe differ substantially from those in Asia. As a result, venture capital firms are likely to follow a different model of venture capital practice to reflect the structural differences (Bruton, Dattani, Fung, Chow, and Ahlstrom, 1999). In Canada, government intervention is important and dominates venture capital financings. Government funds tend to invest more than other venture capital funds. The largest single fund in Canada is the Labor Sponsored Venture Capital Corporation (LSVCC) owned by the government of Quebec (MacIntosh, 1997).

Similarly, in Israel, after a stock market crash in 1994, the Tel Aviv Stock Exchange adopted listing rules that limited IPOs for early stage companies. As a result, Israeli venture capital funds have shifted their IPOs from the Tel Aviv Stock Exchange to the NASDAQ market (Black and Gilson, 1998). In Europe and the United States, a large number of pharmaceutical companies began responding to biotechnology entrepreneurship by providing later-stage financing and partnering arrangements, mostly with U.S.-based companies (Lerner, 1994; Hellmann, 1998).

The management styles of venture capital firms differ markedly around the globe. In the United States and the United Kingdom, for instance, venture capital firms are actively involved with their investee companies, whereas in China their involvements with the investee companies are minimal (White, Gao, and Zhang 2005). In Germany and Japan, venture capital firms are not involved with the backed companies, neither in the management nor through board representation (Jeng and Wells, 2000). Variation in venture capital investments differs substantially across the globe. Hurry, Miller, and Bowman (1992) find evidence that Japanese venture capital firms make more investments than U.S. venture capital firms. Nonetheless, the typical size of a single investment is larger for the U.S. venture capital firms than their Japanese counterparts. As Jeng and Wells note, this style of investment allows U.S. venture capital firms to focus more on management and understanding their investee companies, which ultimately leads to a better monitoring system. Managers of backed companies have increased incentives to invest their human capital when a reputable venture capital firm finances their companies. A reputable venture capital firm provides a credible signal to the market about the company's likelihood of success (Black and Gilson, 1998). Further, suppliers tend to extend their trade credit to a company with respected venture capital backers.

LITERATURE REVIEW

Seppä and Laamanen (2001) investigate the risk and return profiles of venture capital investments using a binomial model. Their sample consists of 597 investment rounds for companies that went public on a U.S. stock exchange between 1998 and 1999. The authors find that early stage investments have higher returns and implied volatility than other investment rounds. They conclude that the risk and implied volatility related to venture-backed companies decreases as they reach high stages of development, such as expansion or later-round investments. Hence, a model that assumes a constant volatility may be inappropriate in modeling venture capital investments.

Manigart, Waele, Wright, Robbie, Desbrières, Sapienz, and Beekman (2002) examine the determinants of venture capital returns in five markets: the United States, United Kingdom, Netherlands, Belgium, and France. Their sample consists of 209 venture capital firms between 1994 and 1997. The results show that venture capital firms require higher returns for early stage investments than expansion, buyout, and later-stage financings. They also find evidence that venture capital firms do not view stage diversification as a risk-reduction strategy. Venture capital investors acting as lead investors more often generate low returns for early stage investments, and only a few investments are associated with high returns. Moreover, returns of independent venture capital firms are higher than captive and publicly supported venture capital firms for early and expansion stages. The authors conclude that the required returns vary by the stage of financing, size of investment, and country of a portfolio company.

Chen, Baierl, and Kaplan (2002) examine the long-term risk and return characteristics of venture capital investments and their role in long-term strategic asset allocation. Their sample includes 148 venture capital funds that had been liquidated as of 1999. They report an average arithmetic return of 45 percent with a standard deviation of 115.6 percent. The authors conclude that investors should allocate only between 2 and 9 percent of a portfolio to venture capital for the minimum-variance portfolio, due to high volatility of venture capital returns.

Ljungqvist and Richardson (2003) investigate the cash flow, return, and risk characteristics of private equity investments. Using data from one of the largest institutional private equity investors in the United States from 1981 to 1993, they find that the IRR is 19.8 percent and the beta of private equity funds is greater than 1.0. The authors also find a risk premium of 5 to 6 percent over the public equity returns, which they interpret as compensation for illiquidity of venture capital investments. Ljungqvist and Richardson conclude that the timing of actual cash inflow and outflows is an important factor in understanding the performance of private equity funds.

Woodward (2004) examines the risk and performance of buyout and venture capital investments in the United States. The sample consists of quarterly venture capital and buyout returns reported by the fund from 1990 to 2003. Woodward finds that the risk of buyouts and venture capital investments is higher in terms of beta and standard deviation. The results show that the beta for venture capital investments is 2.00 and for buyout investments is 0.86.

Kerins, Smith, and Smith (2003) examine the opportunity cost of capital for diversified and undiversified portfolios using newly listed high-tech companies on U.S. stock exchanges. Their sample consists of 992 high-technology companies from eight industries that went public during 1995 to 2000. Using the capital asset pricing model (CAPM) to estimate opportunity cost of capital for diversified and undiversified portfolios, they find that the average beta of undiversified portfolio is identical to market beta. Nonetheless, the risk of undiversified portfolios as measured by standard deviation averaged across the eight industries is five times higher than the market total risk. The authors also find that the ratio of total risk to market decreases as the age and size of the company increases. Further, the correlation between high-tech companies' return and the market is only 20 percent.

Cochrane (2005) examines the mean, standard deviation, alpha, and beta of venture capital investments. Using a sample of 16,613 investment rounds between 1987 and 2000, he finds that the expected returns are 71 percent for the first round and 65 percent, 60 percent, and 51 percent for rounds two through four, respectively. The corresponding beta values are 1.1, 0.9, 0.7, and 0.5, respectively.

Kaplan and Schoar (2005) examine the performance of private equity funds and the relationship among fund performance, capital flows, fund size, and private equity survivals. The sample covers the years from 1980 to 2001 and consists of 1,090 funds. The evidence shows that the average fund returns are relatively close to the S&P 500 returns and persist over time. Further, competitive forces do not drive away return persistence. The study also finds that top performing funds grow at a lower rate than underperforming funds.

Weidig, Kemmer, and Born (2005) examine the risk profiles of private equity funds of funds for European and U.S. venture firms. Using the period 1983 to 2003, they collect data consisting of 927 observations of which 282 are European funds and 745 are U.S. funds. The authors find that investments in funds of funds have higher returns and lower risk than individual funds. They also find that European funds of funds provide investors higher returns than their U.S. counterparts. Further, U.S. funds of funds have lower risk than individual funds, but this relationship does not hold in Europe.

Hege, Palomino, and Schwienbacher (2008) compare the performance of venture capital investments between the United States and Europe by evaluating venture-backed companies. The study finds that U.S. venture capital investors generate lower returns than those in Europe during the period 1987 to 2002 using a sample of 234 U.S. firms and 147 European firms. Nonetheless, the U.S. venture capital providers investing in Europe do not outperform their European peers. Additionally, European venture firms exiting their investments via IPOs generate similar returns to their U.S. counterparts, while the returns of trade sale exits are lower than the U.S. returns.

Korteweg and Sorensen (2010) examine the alpha and beta values of venture capital investments in entrepreneurial companies. The authors focus on the U.S. venture capital firms and examine the risk and returns from 1985 to 2005. Correcting for sample selection bias, they find that the monthly alpha values range from 3.3 to 3.5 percent, while the beta values are greater than 1.0 using CAPM and three factor models. Their findings are robust using different specification of pricing models and selection equations.

To summarize, previous studies document the systematic risk for venture capital investments (buyout investments) to be greater than 1.0 (less than 1.0) and provide mixed results for abnormal returns. Further, most of these studies focus on the U.S. market. The study included in this chapter examines systematic risk and abnormal returns of private equity investments from a global perspective.

DATA AND METHODOLOGY

This section presents information on the data and the methodology used to evaluate performance characteristics of private equity investments. An extension of the standard IRR approach is used to infer the abnormal return of the investments and their exposure to market risk.

Data

The Center for PE Research (CEPRES GmbH) provided the data set used for the empirical analysis. CEPRES was established in 2001 based on cooperation between VCM Capital Management (now part of the Deutsche Bank Group) and the University of Frankfurt. Currently, CEPRES is an independent consulting firm focusing on private equity portfolios and risk-management advisory. The unique feature of the data provided by CEPRES is that it contains detailed information on the monthly cash flows generated by private equity investments.

CEPRES obtains data from private equity funds that participate in a service called the "PE Analyzer." Participating private equity funds sign a contract that stipulates that they are giving the correct cash flows generated for each investment they have made in the past. In return, each firm receives aggregate industry statistics, such as risk-adjusted performance measures. These firms then internally use the statistics for various purposes, including bonus payments and strengths/weaknesses analysis. Importantly, and unlike other data collectors, CEPRES does not benchmark private equity firms to peer groups. This difference improves data accuracy and representativeness because it eliminates incentives to manipulate cash flows or "cherry-pick" past investments. This program is well established in the industry. In 2012, it reached coverage of approximately 1,300 private equity funds and 29,000 direct investments from all major segments, including venture capital, buyout, infrastructure, and mezzanine.

Previous studies used earlier versions of these data. For example, Krohmer, Lauterbach, and Calanog (2009) and Cumming, Schmidt, and Walz (2010) used a subset of this database covering mainly venture capital investments. Franzoni,

Nowak, and Phalippou (2011) used buyout investments of the database. Contemporary researchers also use two proprietary databases that are similar to CEPRES. Ljungqvist, Richardson, and Wolfenzon (2007) collect data from a large investor. Lopez-de-Silanes, Phalippou, and Gottschalg (2009) develop a data set with the performance of private equity investments from hand-collected private placement memoranda, but do not have the detailed cash flows generated for each investment. In terms of data coverage and representativeness, Franzoni et al. find that the CEPRES dataset appears to contain firms that are slightly above average performance-wise. However, the data set has very good coverage, with around 85 percent when benchmarked against Standard & Poor's Capital IQ database, which researchers often consider to be the most comprehensive data set at the investment level.

Methodology

Performance characteristics are evaluated based on a panel of cash flow data for N private equity investments. For each investment i ($i = 1, \ldots, N$), a stream of cash flows is observed between the start date of the investment, t_i, and its final liquidation date, T_i. The cash flows consist of investments paid into the portfolio companies and of repayments of dividends and proceeds. In the following, let I_{it} denote the amount invested into portfolio company i at time t. Similarly, let R_{it} denote the repayments of portfolio company i at time t.

The IRR can be applied to evaluate performance characteristics of private equity investments. The IRR is the standard performance measure employed in situations where only a stream of cash flows (but no market valuations) can be observed. Mathematically, the IRR of investment i, IRR_i, can be found in Equation 17.1 as a solution to

$$\sum_{t=t_i}^{T_i} \frac{R_{it} - I_{it}}{(1 + IRR_i)^{t-t_i}} = 0 \tag{17.1}$$

where I_{it} denotes the amount invested at time t and R_{it} denotes the repayments at time t.

Besides the several drawbacks discussed in the literature, this methodology does not allow inferring the abnormal return of the investments and their exposure to market risk. Therefore, the standard IRR approach is extended by using a time-varying discount rate instead of the constant rate employed in Equation 17.1. Similar to Driessen, Lin, and Phalippou (2012), the rate of return Re_{it} of investment i in period t is assumed to be generated by the single-factor market model in Equation 17.2 of the form

$$\mathrm{Re}_{it} = r_f + \alpha_i + \beta_i \cdot R_{Mt} + \varepsilon_{it} \tag{17.2}$$

where r_f is the constant risk-free rate, and R_{Mt} is the period-t return on the market portfolio in excess of the risk-free rate. The terms α_i and β_i are the abnormal return and beta coefficient of investment *i*, respectively. The ε_{it} is an independent and identically distributed (i.i.d.) disturbance term with zero mean that is uncorrelated with the return of the market portfolio for all *t*. Replacing IRR_i by Re_{it} in Equation 17.1 results in Equation 17.3:

$$\sum_{t=t_i}^{T_i} \frac{R_{it} - I_{it}}{\prod_{s=t_i+1}^{t} (1 + r_f + \alpha_i + \beta_i \cdot R_{Ms} + \varepsilon_{is})} = 0 \qquad (17.3)$$

Equation 17.3 cannot be evaluated directly because the error terms ε_{it} are unobservable when market valuations are unavailable. Therefore, expectations on both sides of the equation are taken, which yields Equation 17.4:

$$E\left[\sum_{t=t_i}^{T_i} \frac{R_{it} - I_{it}}{\prod_{s=t_i+1}^{t} (1 + r_f + \alpha_i + \beta_i \cdot R_{Ms})}\right] = 0 \qquad (17.4)$$

Note that the error term ε_{is} no longer needs to appear in the denominator of the expectation on the left-hand side of the equation. This follows as ε_{is} has zero expectation by definition. Additionally, the error term ε_{is} and the market return R_{Mt} are uncorrelated for all *t* and *s*, and the expectation of cross-products of the form $\varepsilon_{is}\varepsilon_{it}$ (as well as higher-order cross-products) are equal to zero for $s \neq t$.

To evaluate Equation 17.4 requires imposing the additional assumption that all sample deals have the same abnormal return and exposure to market risk; that is, $\alpha_i = \alpha$ and $\beta_i = \beta$ for all *i*. For example, Cochrane (2005) and Driessen et al. (2012) use this assumption. The economic rationale behind it is that the performance of a given deal type is subject to the same systematic risk together with an idiosyncratic component. Under this condition, and given that the sample size *N* is sufficiently large, the expectation in Equation 17.4 can be approximated by the simple average across all *N* sample investments in Equation 17.5:

$$\frac{1}{N}\sum_{i=1}^{N}\sum_{t=t_i}^{T_i} \frac{R_{it} - I_{it}}{\prod_{s=t_i+1}^{t} (1 + r_f + \alpha + \beta \cdot R_{Ms})} = 0 \qquad (17.5)$$

Using this result, α and β can be finally estimated by a numerical optimization in Equation 17.6 of

$$\min_{\alpha,\beta}\left(\sum_{i=1}^{N}\sum_{t=t_i}^{T_i} \frac{R_{it} - I_{it}}{\prod_{s=t_i+1}^{t} (1 + r_f + \alpha + \beta \cdot R_{Ms})}\right)^2 \qquad (17.6)$$

One might ask whether optimization in Equation 17.6 leads to a unique solution for α and β. Although a formal proof for uniqueness of the solutions is beyond the scope of this chapter, the results always show unique optima in the examples used and in the empirical application of this chapter. Hence, this approach enables finding abnormal returns and systematic risk of a private equity investment even though periodic investment returns cannot be observed. Furthermore, stressing that the estimation approach does not require any assumption on how intermediate capital outflows are reinvested by the investor is important; that is, the estimation results are unaffected by whether an investor reinvests capital outflows (e.g., in a stock market index or government bonds). This relationship assures that only systematic risk and abnormal returns of a pure private equity investment are measured, and not that of a combined investment into private equity and another asset class.

A Numerical Example

The estimation method is illustrated with a simple example in which the returns of three private equity investments are driven by the single-factor market model given in Equation 17.2 with no idiosyncratic risk and a risk-free rate equal to zero; that is, $R_{it} = \alpha + \beta R_{Mt}$. Exhibit 17.1 shows the market returns and periodic cash flows of the three investments.

The information given in Exhibit 17.1 is a common situation in private equity research. One can only observe a stream of multiple cash inflows and outflows of a private equity investment, whereas market valuations of the assets are unobservable because of the illiquid nature of the asset class. Therefore, standard econometric methods to estimate risk and return fail in this situation because periodic returns cannot be derived. A return could only be computed here if and only if the cash flow stream of each investment consists of a single inflow at the start of the investment and a single outflow at the end. When multiple inflows and outflows occur, returns can only be computed at the cost of making an assumption on how intermediary cash flows are reinvested. An example for this is the IRR approach previously discussed.

Exhibit 17.1 Illustrative Example of the Estimation Methodology

Year	0	1	2	3	4
Market return (%)		10	15	10	20
Investment 1 ($)	−100	−50	252	0	0
Investment 2 ($)	0	−200	50	207	0
Investment 3 ($)	0	0	−100	10	120

The exhibit gives the market returns and cash flows of three sample private equity investments. Negative cash flows are investments and positive cash flows are dividends of the projects. Cash flows of all investments are assumed to occur at the end of each year.

For the situation shown in Exhibit 17.1, α and β can be directly estimated by solving Equation 17.5, resulting in Equation 17.7:

$$\begin{aligned}
&-100+\frac{-50}{(1+\alpha+0.1\beta)}+\frac{252}{(1+\alpha+0.1\beta)(1+\alpha+0.15\beta)}\\
&-200+\frac{50}{(1+\alpha+0.15\beta)}+\frac{207}{(1+\alpha+0.15\beta)(1+\alpha-0.1\beta)}\\
&-100+\frac{10}{(1+\alpha-0.1\beta)}+\frac{120}{(1+\alpha-0.1\beta)(1+\alpha+0.2\beta)}=0
\end{aligned} \tag{17.7}$$

MATLAB is used to numerically solve this equation and to obtain the unique solution $\alpha = 10$ percent and $\beta = 2$. One can verify that this is the correct solution to the problem at stake. For example, for investment 2 the value of the project after one year using these parameters is 200[1 + 10 percent + (2)15 percent] = 280 before the intermediate dividend of 50 and 230 after the dividend. The final liquidating dividend is then equal to the value of the project after two years, which is given by 230[1 + 10 percent − (2)10 percent] = 207. This result matches the final cash flow of investment 2 shown in Exhibit 17.1. Similar calculations can be carried out to show that this is also the correct solution for investments 1 and 3.

The example shown in Exhibit 17.1 assumes no idiosyncratic shocks in investment returns. This estimation methodology still works under a more general specification with idiosyncratic shocks in investment returns. All that is required in this case is a larger number of sample investments. For a sufficiently large number of investments, idiosyncratic shocks will average out across the sample and permit the correct estimation of α and β.

EMPIRICAL ANALYSIS

This section provides detailed information on the CEPRES database and summary statistics of the investments by region of entrepreneurial companies. The section also provides a discussion of the abnormal performance as measured by the alpha value and the systematic risk as measured by the beta value for venture capital and buyout investments.

Descriptive Statistics

For the purpose of this study, CEPRES granted access to all liquidated investments of its database as of September 2009. In total, information is available on 14,224 investments, with a geographical split of 8,379 from North America, 4,862 from Europe, and 983 from the rest of the world. Access to the entire cash flow history generated by each of these investments is also available. This unique feature enables estimating abnormal returns and systematic risk with the methodology previously described.

Exhibit 17.2 presents summary statistics of the investments. The variables are divided by region of the entrepreneurial company. The results indicate that the deal size is larger in Europe than in all other countries, with a mean of $11.94 million

Exhibit 17.2 Descriptive Statistics of Venture Capital Deals

Variables	North America	Europe	Rest of the World
Number of observations	8,379	4,862	983
Deal size ($M)			
Mean	10.82	11.94	7.99
Median	4.41	5.41	2.95
Standard deviation	82.60	34.05	14.82
Investment duration (years)			
Mean	4.18	4.15	3.65
Median	3.75	3.67	3.25
Standard deviation	2.84	2.64	2.65
Exit type (%)			
IPOs	11.93	8.11	14.34
Trade sales	22.04	35.05	23.91
Public mergers	4.55	1.71	0.81
Write offs	18.33	12.84	21.67
Else/Unspecified	32.03	42.42	31.54
Fund age (years)			
Mean	5.07	3.10	2.08
Median	3.00	2.08	1.42
Standard deviation	6.25	3.24	2.59
Managers' age (years)			
Mean	11.81	13.31	7.66
Median	10.00	11.00	5.00
Standard deviation	9.18	11.71	7.86
Syndication (%)			
Yes	33.26	33.50	34.28
No	16.27	15.60	10.07
Unknown	50.47	50.90	55.65
Financing stages (%)			
Venture capital	59.27	27.70	48.83
Buyout	40.73	72.30	51.17
Industry (%)			
Industrials	13.74	24.89	18.11
Consumer goods and services	19.66	42.19	23.30
Financials	2.47	3.53	3.87
Information technology	48.96	16.77	43.03
Biotechnology	14.46	9.76	4.88
Unspecified	0.72	2.85	6.82
Board seats (%)			
Yes	40.66	38.38	43.64
No	18.40	10.80	13.22
Unknown	40.94	50.82	50.94

The exhibit provides descriptive statistics for the variables across all deals. It shows deal size, investment duration, exit type, fund age, managers' age, syndicated versus nonsyndicated deals, financing stages, industry, and board versus nonboard seats. The variables are classified by the regions: North America, Europe, and the Rest of the World. Observations are per entrepreneurial firm and not per investment round.

and a median of $5.41 million. North America is the second largest after Europe, with a mean of $10.82 million and a median of $4.41 million. The average deal size is larger in Europe than in North America, despite the number of deals in North America being more than one and half times the number of deals in Europe. No differences exist in the investment holding period across all countries except for the rest of the world, where investment durations are shorter than North America and Europe by about five months.

Exhibit 17.2 also shows that trade sales is the most common exit route across all regions compared to IPO, public merger, or write-off exits. This finding is consistent with Giot and Schwienbacher (2007). The percentage of IPO exits is high in the rest of the world, followed by North America and Europe. This evidence implies that venture capital firms are cautious in screening deals and keen on the quality of the entrepreneurial company if a company is outside Europe and North America. Another possibility is that entrepreneurial companies in the rest of the world are reluctant to exit through non-IPO routes.

Black and Gilson (1998) point out that if a market is less active then entrepreneurial companies are likely to impair the venture capital industry if exit is less frequent via IPO. On average, funds are young in the rest of the world (2.08 years) and Europe (3.10 years) when compared to North America (5.07 years). In contrast, venture capitalists are more experienced in Europe than in North America and the rest of the world (13.31 years in Europe versus 11.81 years North America and 7.66 years in the rest of the world).

The exhibit shows that syndication is common in all countries, with non-syndicated deals representing only a small fraction. Percentage deals of early stage rounds are high in North America (40.27 percent) and the rest of the world (33.06 percent) and lowest in Europe (17.23 percent). In terms of industry analysis, the data indicate that the percentage of deals in technology companies is large in North America, Europe, and the rest of the world. By contrast, the financial sector attracts minimum deals from North American, European, and the rest of the world deals. Percentages of board seats are relatively low in Europe and consistent with Schwienbacher (2008), who reports similar the percentage of board seats in Europe.

Overall, the summary statistics show that the deal size is the largest in Europe, while the investment holding period is the shortest in the rest of the world. Exits through trade sales are more common across the globe than any other exit route. Nonetheless, the proportion of IPO exits is higher in North America and in the rest of the world than in Europe. Information technology and consumer goods and services are the most targeted sectors by venture capital firms across the globe.

Exhibit 17.3 shows the means, medians, and standard deviations of IRR by exit type and financing round. Panel A shows the returns for North American venture capitalists investing in North America, Europe, and elsewhere. The exhibit indicates that North American venture capitalists make higher returns through the IPO route than through all other routes. Expansion rounds are characterized by higher IRRs than early, later, and buyout rounds. Returns for North American venture capitalists are lower through the IPO route on European deals as compared to North American deals. The difference in the returns is statistically significant at the 0.01 level. They lose 25.28 percent on early stage deals in Europe, compared to a gain of 10.32 percent in North America. Europe does not appear to be a region of interest for North American venture capitalists, especially for early

Exhibit 17.3 IRR Summary Statistics by Country of Funds and Deals

Countries	North American Deals			European Deals			Rest of the World Deals		
Panel A. North American Deals	**Mean (%)**	**Median (%)**	**Standard Deviation (%)**	**Mean (%)**	**Median (%)**	**Standard Deviation (%)**	**Mean (%)**	**Median (%)**	**Standard Deviation (%)**
IPOs	114.94	49.87	256.69	64.00***	27.30	88.71	215.56	48.97	544.70
Trade sales	67.65	22.01	302.23	41.01**	25.19	69.97	85.44	28.92	259.14
Pubic mergers	86.48	24.89	304.97	50.26**	29.25	66.61	26.45***	26.45	58.50
Write-offs	−98.73	−100.00	8.73	−96.12	−100.00	15.33	−100.00	−100.00	0.00
Early	10.32	−41.98	290.01	−25.28***	−45.38	84.30	−57.76***	−100.00	63.02
Expansion	62.97	12.82	312.48	26.32	23.76	78.25	10.05	43.23	184.80
Later	16.28	4.05	132.05	9.10	14.95	59.34	20.51	6.57	124.02
Buyout	42.92	24.70	177.90	33.10	25.17	79.15	102.33	24.15	398.79

stage investors. As for deals outside Europe, they make a higher return than North American deals. This shows that North American venture capitalists have incentives to seek deals in developing countries as opposed to Europe. The gains at the buyout stage (102.33 percent) are higher in the rest of the world than in Europe and North America.

Panel B of Exhibit 17.3 shows the returns for European venture capitalists investing in North America and the rest of the world. IPO returns are persistently higher than those from trade sales and public mergers similar to the North American venture capitalists. European venture capitalists make 14 percent on their buyout deals and make losses twice the size of this gain on expansion deals. Similarly, they incur losses from the expansion stage (−48.60 percent) on the rest of the world deals. The buyout stage appears to be the safest investment choice for European venture capitalists outside their country of domicile. The returns through the IPO route are also high for investments in the rest of the world, but significantly lower than IPO returns in Europe.

Panel C of Exhibit 17.3 shows returns for the rest of the world venture capitalists investing in Europe and North America. The rest of the world funds benefit from exits in trade sales in both North America and their country of domicile. They make higher returns through trade sales in North America and their country of origin than in Europe. In fact, the returns in trade sales are lower in Europe than the returns from public merger exits. Their early expansion and buyout deals are successful, with high returns, while their later-stage deals are less successful. Perhaps venture capitalists in the rest of the world are overly optimistic when investing in Europe or North America at later stages.

This exhibit shows the means, medians, and standard deviations of the IRR by exit type and financing stage. The variables are classified into countries of the venture capitalists and deals. Panel A shows the returns for North American venture capitalists investing in North America, Europe, and the rest of the world. Panel B shows European venture capitalists investing in North America, Europe, and the rest of the world. Panel C shows the results of the rest of the world venture capitalists investing in North America, Europe, and the rest of the world. The t-test is based on an unequal sample and unequal variance. For North American venture capitalists, IPO exits are used as the base for the European and rest of the world deals. For European venture capitalists, IPO exits are used as the base for North American and the rest of the world deals. For the rest of the world venture capitalists, the rest of the world deals are used as the base for European and North American deals. ***,**,* indicate statistical significance at the 0.01, 0.05, and 0.10 levels, respectively.

Estimation Results

Abnormal performance and systematic risk are examined in the context of the single-factor market model previously described in Equation 17.2. Because the sample contains private equity investments from all around the world, the MSCI World Index is used as the appropriate proxy for the market factor. Also examined is the systematic risk with respect to the S&P 500 Index in order to determine the sensitivity of the sample investments to the U.S. market returns. A constant return

Exhibit 17.4 Abnormal Performance and Systematic Risk of Private Equity

	Venture Capital		Buyout	
Full Sample	**(1)**	**(2)**	**(3)**	**(4)**
Alpha (in % per annum)	20.24***	18.02***	28.93***	27.13***
Beta market (MSCI World Index)	2.32***		1.51***	
Beta market (S&P 500 Index)		2.39***		2.00***

The exhibit reports the estimated abnormal performance (alpha, in % per annum) and market risk (beta market), using the one-factor market model. The MSCI World Index (Columns (1) and (3)) and the S&P 500 Index (Columns (2) and (4)) serve as proxies for market returns. The risk-free rate is set to a constant value of 5 percent per annum. *, ** and *** indicate statistical significance at the 0.10, 0.05, and 0.01 levels, respectively.

of 5 percent is employed for the risk-free rate. Driessen et al. (2012) provide a similar assumption.

Exhibit 17.4 summarizes the estimation results. All results shown are derived from cash flows that are gross of fees. The systematic risk estimates for the venture and buyout segment based on the MSCI World Index are 2.32 and 1.51 and based on the S&P 500 Index are 2.39 and 2.00, respectively. Because the largest fraction of the sample investments (around 60 percent) is from the United States, both the sample venture and buyout investments show a higher sensitivity to the S&P 500 Index than to the MSCI World Index. The results also imply that buyout investments generally show a lower exposure to market risk compared to venture investments, despite their high leverage. Albeit puzzling, this is consistent with the findings of Kaplan and Stein (1990) who point out that the effect of an increase in the debt ratio has a small effect on the market beta of leveraged private equity transactions.

Furthermore, the results suggest that private equity investments carry considerable market risk. In an earlier work, Kaplan and Schoar (2005) acknowledge the difficulty in estimating beta because of the lack of true market values for fund investments and assume that market beta is equal to 1.0. Estimation results reported in this chapter suggest that the assumption of a beta value equal to 1.0 is likely to understate the true exposure to market risk of this asset class. The findings indicate that the estimates of market risk for the venture and buyout segment are significantly different from 1.0. Hence, the assumption used by Kaplan and Schoar (2005) appears to be inconsistent with empirical evidence.

SUMMARY AND CONCLUSIONS

This chapter provides estimates of the risk and return characteristics of private equity investments. The methodology used extends the standard IRR approach and allows estimating the systematic risk and abnormal returns from a cross-section of private equity investment cash flows. This methodology is applied to a comprehensive dataset of private equity investments. The results show that private equity investments carry substantial market risk and that private equity funds can generate significant abnormal returns gross of fees. Although the chapter focuses on private equity, the methodology employed can also be used to estimate systematic risk and abnormal returns of other asset classes where only a stream of cash flows but no market valuations are observable, such as real estate or infrastructure investments.

The study adds to the ongoing discussion on whether private equity funds can add value to their investments. The results show that abnormal returns (as measured by alpha) are significantly positive for both segments and that buyout investments show somewhat higher average abnormal returns than venture investments. This evidence implies that private equity funds add considerable value to their investments and that the value added is higher for buyout than for venture funds.

DISCUSSION QUESTIONS

1. Explain why using investment round data to compute the risk and returns is better than using fund-level data.
2. Explain the standard IRR approach to determine the performance of private equity investments.
3. How can the standard IRR approach be extended to enable inference of abnormal returns of private equity investments and exposure to market risk?
4. Summarize the empirical evidence on the systematic risk and abnormal returns of private equity investments.

REFERENCES

Black, Bernard, and Ronald Gilson. 1998. "Venture Capital and the Structure of Capital Markets: Banks versus Stock Markets." *Journal of Financial Economics* 47:3, 243–277.

Bruton, Garry, and David Ahlstrom. 2003. "An Institutional View of China's Venture Capital Industry: Explaining the Differences between China and the West." *Journal of Business Venturing* 18:2, 233–259.

Bruton, Garry, Maneksh Dattani, Michael Fung, Clement Chow, and David Ahlstrom. 1999. "Private Equity in China: Differences and Similarities with the Western Model." *Journal of Private Equity* 2:2, 7–13.

Chen, Peng, Gary Baierl, and Paul Kaplan. 2002. "Venture Capital and Its Role in Strategic Asset Allocation." *Journal of Portfolio Management* 28:2, 83–90.

Cochrane, John H. 2005. "The Risk and Return of Venture Capital." *Journal of Financial Economics* 75:1, 3–52.

Cumming, Douglas, Daniel Schmidt, and Uwe Walz. 2010. "Legality and VC Governance around the World." *Journal of Business Venturing* 25:1, 54–72.

Driessen, Joost, Tse-Chun Lin, and Ludovic Phalippou. 2012. "A New Method to Estimate Risk and Return of Non-traded Assets from Cash Flows: The Case of PE Funds." *Journal of Financial and Quantitative Analysis*, forthcoming.

Franzoni, Francesco, Eric Nowak, and Ludovic Phalippou. 2012. "PE Performance and Liquidity Risk." *Journal of Finance*, forthcoming.

Giot, Pierre, and Armin Schwienbacher. 2007. "IPOs, Trade Sales and Liquidation: Modelling Venture Capital Exits Using Survival Analysis." *Journal of Banking and Finance* 31:3, 697–702.

Harrison, Richard, and Colin Mason. 1996. "Informal Venture Capital: A Study of the Investment Process and Post-Investment Experience." *Entrepreneurship and Regional Development* 8:2, 105–126.

Hege, Ulrich, Frédéric Palomino, and Armin Schwienbacher. 2008. "Venture Capital Performance: The Disparity between Europe and the United States." Working Paper. HEC Paris.
Hellmann, Thomas. 1998. "The Allocation of Control Rights in Venture Capital Contracts." *Rand Journal of Economics* 29:1, 57–76.
Hurry Dileep, Adam Miller, and Edward Bowman. 1992. "Calls on High-Technology: Japanese Exploration of Venture Capital Investments in the United States." *Strategic Management Journal* 13:2, 85–101.
Jeng, Leslie, and Philippe Wells. 2000. "The Determinants of Venture Capital Fundraising: Evidence across Countries." *Journal of Corporate Finance* 6:3, 241–289.
Kaplan, Steven, and Antoinette Schoar. 2005. "Private Equity Performance: Returns, Persistence and Capital Flows." *Journal of Finance* 60:4, 1791–1823.
Kaplan, Steven, and Jeremy Stein. 1990. "How Risky Is the Debt in Highly Leveraged Transactions?" *Journal of Financial Economics* 27:1, 215–245.
Kerins, Francis, Janet Smith, and Richard Smith. 2003. "Opportunity Cost of Capital for Venture Capital Investors and Entrepreneurs." Working Paper, University of California.
Korteweg, Arthur, and Morten Sorensen. 2010. "Risk and Return Characteristics of Venture Capital Backed Entrepreneurial Companies." *Review of Financial Studies* 23:10, 3738–3772.
Krohmer, Philipp, Rainer Lauterbach, and Victor Calanog. 2009. "The Bright and Dark Side of Staging: Investment Performance and the Varying Motivations of PE." *Journal of Banking and Finance* 33:9, 1597–1609.
Lerner, Joshua. 1994. "Venture Capitalists and the Decision to Go Public." *Journal of Financial Economics*. 35:3, 293–316.
Ljungqvist, Alexander, and Matthew Richardson. 2003. "The Cash Flow, Return and Risk Characteristics of PE." Working Paper 9454, New York University.
Ljungqvist, Alexander, Matthew Richardson, and Daniel Wolfenzon. 2007. "The Investment Behavior of Buyout Funds." Working Paper, New York University.
Lopez-de-Silanes, Florencio, Ludovic Phalippou, and Oliver Gottschalg. 2009. "Giants at the Gate: On the Cross-Section of PE Investment Returns." Working Paper, University of Oxford.
MacIntosh, Jeffrey. 1997. "Venture Capital Exits in Canada and the United States." In Paul J. N. Halpern, ed., *Financing Growth in Canada*, 279–356. Calgary: University of Calgary Press.
Manigart, Sophie, Koen Waele, Mike Wright, Ken Robbie, Philippe Desbrières, Harry Sapienz, and Amy Beekman. 2002. "Determinants of Required Return in Venture Capital Investments: A Five-Country Study." *Journal of Business Venturing* 17:4, 291–312.
Schwienbacher, Armin. 2008. "Venture Capital Investment Practices in Europe and the United States." *Financial Markets and Portfolio Management* 22:3 195–217.
Seppä, Tuukka, and Tomi Laamanen. 2001. "Valuation of Venture Capital Investments: Empirical Evidence." *R&D Management* 31:2, 215–231.
Weidig, Tom, Andreas Kemmers, and Bjorn Born. 2005. "The Risk Profiles of PE Funds of Funds." *Journal of Alternative Investments* 7:4, 33–41.
White, Steven, Jian Gao, and Wei Zhang. 2005. "Financing New Ventures in China: Systems Antecedents and Institutionalization." *Research Policy* 34:6, 894–913.
Woodward, Susan. 2004. *Measuring Risk and Performance of Private Equity*. Palo Alto, CA: Sand Hill Econometrics Incorporated. Available at www.sandhillecon.com.

ABOUT THE AUTHORS

Axel Buchner is an Associate Professor of Finance at Passau University. He also teaches risk and investment management at EDHEC Business School. Before joining Passau University, he was a postdoctoral researcher and lecturer at

Technical University of Munich and a consultant at the Center of Private Equity Research (CEPRES). At CEPRES, he specialized on private equity–related consulting projects for national and European organizations, such as the German Federal Ministry of Economics and Innovation and the European Investment Bank (EIB), and for large institutional investors. His research focuses on issues in private equity, venture capital, as well as asset and option pricing. His teaching interests are in derivatives, empirical finance, portfolio theory, and asset pricing. He holds a master's degree in Business Administration from Munich University and a Ph.D. in Finance from Technical University of Munich.

Arif Khurshed is a Senior Lecturer in Finance at the Manchester Business School, University of Manchester. He has taught corporate finance for more than 10 years. His research interests are in the areas of IPOs, venture capital, institutional investments, share repurchase programs, and corporate governance. He has published his research in such finance journals as the *Journal of Corporate Finance, Journal of Banking and Finance, Journal of Financial Intermediation,* and *Journal of Business Finance and Accounting* and has contributed many book chapters. His research has been covered by the *Investors Chronicle*, the U.K. press (*The Times*), and the Thai press (*The Nation*). Dr. Khurshed has been an external consultant to the Financial Services Authority (FSA) and the British Venture Capital Association (BVCA). He holds a Ph.D. in Finance from the University of Reading.

Abdulkadir Mohamed is an Assistant Professor of Finance at Liverpool University Management School. His research focuses on private equity, venture capital, mergers and acquisitions, and IPOs. His teaching interests include financial markets, financial valuation, and corporate finance. Before joining Liverpool University, he was a research associate at the Manchester Business School and worked on a consulting project for British Venture Capital Association (BVCA). Professor Mohamed was also involved in teaching undergraduate microeconomic, macroeconomic, statistics, and math for the School of Economics at the University of Manchester. He holds a master's degree in Finance and a Ph.D. in Finance and from the Manchester Business School.

PART IV

Commodities and Managed Futures

CHAPTER 18

Investing in Commodities

CLAUDIO BOIDO
Professor of Investments, School of Economics University of Siena and University LUISS Rome

INTRODUCTION

From a theoretical view, the common perception is that the popularity of investing in commodities justifies their inclusion as an alternative asset class. Their returns are expected to show low or even negative correlation with the returns of traditional asset classes such as stocks and bonds. Black (2009), Conover, Jensen, Johnson and Mercer (2010), and Daskalaki and Skiadopoulos (2011) examine whether incorporating commodities in the asset menu improves the risk-return profile of investors' portfolios. Commodity futures have increasingly garnered interest as a viable component of individual investors' portfolios. Bodie and Rosansky (1980), Fortenbery and Hauser (1990), and Conover, Jensen, Johnson, and Mercer (2005) find that investors can reduce risk without sacrificing return by switching from a stock portfolio to a portfolio with stocks and commodities over the periods 1950–1976, 1976–1985, and 1970–2007, respectively. Much of the interest is attributable to research espousing the benefits of adding commodity exposure to equity portfolios. Jensen, Johnson, and Mercer (2000, 2002) and Gorton and Rouwenhorst (2006), for example, show that commodity futures returns are comparable to equity returns over long time periods and confirm that they offer considerable diversification benefits due to their low or even negative correlation with equities. Greer (2000) observes that a typical client allocation to commodity futures is approximately 5 percent, but he notes that the case can easily be made for a 15 percent allocation based on desired risk and return parameters.

Various empirical papers examine the performance of commodities before the financial crisis of 2007–2008. Gorton and Rouwenhorst (2006), Kat and Oomen (2007), Büyüksahin, Haigh, and Robe (2010), and Chong and Miffre (2010) find that the diversification benefits of commodities are more pronounced over turbulent periods. Conversely, Büyüksahin et al., Silvennoinen and Thorp (2010), and Tang and Xiong (2010) find that the return correlations between commodities and equities increased substantially during the financial crisis.

The results during the crisis period may be attributed to the fact that correlations between asset classes tend to increase over periods with extreme market conditions and hence diversification benefits vanish. Baur and McDermott (2010) find that the diversification benefits of gold are consistent with the evidence on its "safe haven" role in periods of crisis.

In terms of financial portfolio construction rules, the features of commodities are that they tend to have a low correlation with traditional asset classes but exhibit a high correlation with inflation. The next section examines possible ways to invest in commodities and various studies that highlight the significant returns, low transaction costs, and high capacity to generate alpha.

HOW TO INVEST IN COMMODITIES

Commodities are real assets such as consumption goods. They have an intrinsic value and are used in industrial manufacturing. Their availability varies in different periods of the year, and the supply has a strong seasonal component for certain commodities, such as agricultural.

The quality of commodities is not standardized because each commodity has specific properties. Thus, investors must distinguish between soft and hard commodities. Soft commodities are divided into agricultural (e.g., cocoa, coffee, corn, cotton, oats, soybeans, sugar, and wheat) and livestock (e.g., cattle, hogs, and pork bellies). Their price depends on the weather in different parts of the world at various times. Hard commodities are the products from the energy, precious metals, and industrial metals sectors and react to industrial drivers.

Another important characteristic of commodities is their storability. This characteristic plays a special role in pricing because investors separate storable from nonstorable commodities. Commodities have a high degree of storability if the cost of storage is low with respect to their total value (e.g., industrial metals). Livestock is storable, but it must be fed and housed continuously. It is profitable in a specific phase of its life cycle. Because availability is an important feature that influences the supply, the discovery of new reserves for some commodities, such as metals and crude oil, affects pricing.

Why do investors consider commodities as alternative assets? As physical goods, commodities are valued as asset classes in financial markets if investors value them as financial goods, such as stocks and bonds. Commodities do not generate continuous cash flows, but they have an economic value, and their prices depend on the relationship between supply and demand on specific markets and, to a lesser degree, by interest rates. In the past, investors did not include commodities in their portfolios because they failed to consider their benefits as a source of an alternative return and as a hedge against inflation.

Historically, viewing commodities as a separate asset class was unusual. Retail investors selected commodities as a direct investment only with precious metals in the form of coins or gold bullion. More recently, investors began to consider commodities as an important asset class for portfolio investment because of a strong proliferation of new investment products that facilitated commodity investing to a larger audience. This trend has not only existed for high-net-worth individuals but also for retail investors who can choose commodities from a wide range of financial instruments. Retail investors can gain exposure to commodities indirectly through derivatives that use underlying commodities or investment vehicles such as mutual funds, exchange-traded funds (ETFs), managed futures, or hedge funds that invest in commodities, commodities indices, or in commodity-related equities.

Various ways are available to invest in commodities through different types of financial instruments, including:

1. Direct investments in the physical goods
2. Indirect investment in stocks of natural resource companies
3. Commodities mutual funds, hedge funds, and ETFs
4. Commodity derivatives
5. Structured products on commodities futures indices

Investors should be aware of the advantages and disadvantages of taking positions in commodities to improve the risk-return relationship. When investors decide to buy physical goods, they follow a direct approach. Although this approach seems obvious if they want to invest in commodities, it has some disadvantages. In fact, when investors buy commodities, they need to understand the quality of the goods and the problems that can exist if that quality is lacking. Another problem is the presence of different costs relating to storage, insurance, and cash opportunity costs. These costs affect the management of the physical good. Unlike stocks and bonds, commodities are an asset class without cash flows over time. Because commodities earn no current income, managers can only measure their return if they decide to sell the commodity. The above-mentioned costs reduce an investment's value. In recent years, some investors have bought imperishable commodity assets such as water resources or timber because they were able to manage the ownership and have long-term investment objectives. Selecting such assets is complicated by the difficulty in determining a correct value for them because interim pricing and mark-to-market are not always possible.

If investors use forward contracts to invest in a commodity directly, they must consider all risks associated with an open position in a derivative contract, including the anticipated supply-demand relationship on the delivery date, the current price, the cost of carry, the risk-free rate of return, and all costs associated with the purchase and holding of the commodity. Also, the parties are subject to counterparty credit risk that becomes known at the maturity of the contract.

As a result, investors prefer to indirectly assume a position in commodity markets to avoid the problems linked to the management of physical goods. The most common way to indirectly invest in commodities is to purchase stocks in companies whose core business depends on different commodities and various sector or geographical markets. When investors select equities, they must consider two different kinds of risk: systematic (nondiversifiable) and specific (diversifiable). If they invest in commodity-related equities, their objective is to earn a positive return given an increase in the value of the commodity. In each case, the return depends not only on the commodity but also on the performance of the stock market. Investors must consider which indirect exposure they want to add: a domestic large cap company, a small cap, or a startup company. Their decision adds other components of risk related to the selected company (specific risk) as well as the overall market (systematic risk) that could reduce the earnings linked to the choice of a specific physical commodity on the market.

Today, mutual funds provide not only the simplest and most common way to invest in commodity-linked equities but also a low-cost, convenient vehicle. Mutual funds invest in commodities, and often in sector commodities, so investors can choose on the basis of their forecasts whether adding exposure to a commodity is rational. Investors can observe the same drawbacks as investing in equities, but commodities offer greater levels of diversification because their asset managers select a variety of assets, offering exposure to energy, precious metals, or basic materials. Commodity mutual funds have a risk similar to those related to stock purchases but their choices are provided with more expertise than retail investors, even if managers have constraints in asset management.

Historically, many retail investors preferred vehicles that were created as hedging instruments for institutional investors. Because buying physical commodities directly is costly and cumbersome, investors typically invest through ETFs and exchange-traded notes (ETNs). ETFs seek to track the price of a single commodity, an equity investment related to a commodity, a basket of commodities, or by holding the actual commodity in storage or by purchasing futures contracts. Commodity ETNs are non-interest-paying, debt instruments whose price fluctuates with an underlying commodities index. Because they are debt obligations, ETNs are subject to the solvency of the issuer.

These investment vehicles offer the opportunity to earn the potential appreciation of each segment of the financial markets so that various commodities can be selected without entering directly into the commodities markets. ETFs offer a low-cost structure and diversification benefits, providing the opportunity to gain potential returns for a specific market segment without the risk of a single stock position. Investors can choose between many different instruments in energy, natural resources, precious metals, and agricultural products on the ETF market, avoiding the direct management of physical goods. Commodity index funds are constructed to mimic the performance of a commodity index. Although these instruments were originally introduced as private investment funds for high-net-worth individuals and institutional investors, the market has evolved into one that includes exchange-traded retail products such as commodity index ETFs. One example is the I-shares S&P Goldman Sachs Commodity Index (GSCI) Commodity-Indexed Trust (ticker GSG), which trades as an ETF based on an index of commodity futures. Its performance (before expenses) is designed to correspond with the returns with the S&P GSCI, which consists of 24 different commodity futures contracts. Commodity swaps provide another alternative to commodity exposure. Commodity index swaps pay the return on a specific commodity index and are available in the over-the-counter (OTC) markets. A user of the commodity may agree to pay the financial institution a fixed price for the commodity in exchange for the institution paying the user the spot price for the same commodity. Both ETFs and swaps are created by using fully collateralized futures positions.

Many investors now take a position in commodities by investing in hedge funds. In fact, more hedge funds have added commodities strategies to diversify their portfolios with the aim of improving risk-return relationships. Some failures in the hedge fund sector, such as Amaranth Hedge Fund in September 2006, show the risk of investing in commodities even by experienced asset managers. According to Jeanneret, Monnin, and Scholz (2011), directional hedge funds took a long position on sugar and cocoa and a short position on wheat and natural gas in 2008, which resulted in large gains. Investors could also select specific maturities to implement their views. For instance, investors engage in a commodity futures–based strategy in which they may choose different maturity structures for a futures contract on natural gas and copper futures. Commodity hedge funds are usually active in the oil industry, refineries, utilities, and mining in order to increase both the weight and risk of their funds.

Jeanneret et al. (2011) indicate that three facts emerge from comparing a commodities hedge funds index and long-only indices from August 1998 to December 2009. First, returns for hedge funds are significantly higher (17.03 percent) than those of long-only indices (e.g., 6.11 percent for the GSCI). Second, the volatility of the hedge fund index (10.99 percent) is considerably lower than that of the long-only indices (e.g., 25.18 percent for the GSCI). Consequently, the Sharpe ratio of a hedge fund investment is typically much higher (1.18) than that of a long-only index portfolio (0.23). Finally, investing in hedge funds offers a much better control of the downside risk, as reflected by a lower downside deviation (4.96 percent) and a smaller maximum drawdown (−13.26 percent).

Commodity hedge fund managers can cut their losses during months in which long-only commodity indices experience negative returns, achieving an average return roughly equal to zero. They can also participate in the gains during boom phases. The downside protection offered by hedge funds stems from their ability to switch rapidly from long to short positions and from using option or relative-value trades. By choosing a portfolio of hedge funds, an investor can achieve better downside protection and an actively managed portfolio, which yields higher returns and a better hedge against inflation than what a traditional long-only commodity index would provide.

Direct investment in commodities can create many problems related to the management of the physical asset, so the best solution to avoid the many drawbacks of direct investment is to use commodity futures. According to Basu and Gavin (2011), futures contracts allow investment in a commodity without being forced to deliver and store the commodities. At the maturity of the contract, investors can choose if they want to close the position with an opposite position or to roll the contracts forward (i.e., sell the expiring contract and simultaneously buy the next contract). The management of a futures contract position requires posting margin (an initial deposit in money or securities) to cover any daily fluctuations in the value of the position. Contract values are adjusted daily (called mark-to-market) to account for gains and loss. Alternatively, investors can use option contracts on commodities to protect against adverse price movements or to gain exposure in commodities. The management of these positions is complicated because of both the volatility of commodities and the complexity of option pricing.

A passive investment in a commodities index represents one of the best-known solutions in investing in commodities. These indices offer a large exposure to commodity assets. Further, investors can choose to select different kinds of indices that consist of future contracts in different sectors of commodity markets. The return of the commodity index depends on three factors: (1) changes in spot prices of an underlying commodity; (2) the interest rate gained from a government bond used to collateralize the future contract; and (3) the roll yield, which depends on the extension of the futures contract and the shape of the term-structure curve at the time of the extension. Roll yield reflects the gain from the convergence of the future price to the spot price over time. The rolling of the maturing future contract into the next nearest future contract determines the roll return.

According to Fabozzi, Fuss, and Kaiser (2008), the spot price is determined by the supply and demand of the physical asset, with the variations reflected directly in the commodity futures markets, as illustrated in Equation 18.1:

$$F = Se^{(r+c-y)(T-t)} \tag{18.1}$$

where F = the futures price, S = the current spot/cash price of the underlying commodity, r = the risk-free rate of return, c = the cost of storage, y = the convenience yield, and $T - t$ = the time to maturity of the contract.

A commodity futures index is unleveraged because the exposure underlying the futures contract basket is fully collateralized by the purchase of a short-term government bond. So for each dollar invested in a commodity futures index, the investor receives a dollar of diversified commodity exposure plus interest on a dollar invested in the short-term government bond. This received interest is called *collateral yield.*

Another component of the return on a futures contract is the roll yield, which depends on the shape of the futures term structure. The market may either be in *contango* (i.e., futures prices are above the current spot price) or in *backwardation* (i.e., futures prices are below the current spot price). When the market is in backwardation, investors can earn a positive return from a buy-and-hold strategy because, as the futures contract gets closer to maturity, its price must converge to that of the spot price of the commodity. Because the spot price is greater than the futures price, the futures price must increase in value. The final convergence is known as *rolling up the yield curve* or *roll yield.* This yield is greater the closer the futures contract is to maturity because uncertainty decreases as the futures contract approaches maturity. The roll yield is negative in a contango market when future prices are greater than the spot price. Investors who short the futures contract will collect the futures premium as the futures contract rolls down the term structure.

Many asset managers appreciate commodity future indices because they are transparent and liquid. Also, they can use such indices in two different ways: (1) to speculate on the expected returns from commodities and (2) to provide passive portfolio diversification. Speculators can use a tactical bet on the future performance of a commodity compared to stocks and bonds. Otherwise, they choose commodity futures indices to provide passive portfolio diversification without any view as to the current state of the business cycle. Asset managers can choose many different commodity future indices in terms of their intrinsic composition.

Whereas Irwin, Sanders, and Merrin (2009) note that the overall magnitude of commodity indices' holdings grew rapidly from 2006 to 2008, Irwin and Sanders (2011) point out that commodity indices' holdings decreased in 2009. Commodity index investors hold diversified portfolios of commodities with prescribed index weights. The GSCI is a long-only index of physical commodity futures, with price levels dating back to August 1989. Its weights are determined on the basis of world production of the underlying commodities. Because the index is designed to be "tradable," futures markets representing each particular commodity are deep and liquid. The GSCI assigns a weight to five commodity groups: precious metals, industrial metals, livestock, agricultural, and energy. Precious metals represent the smallest component, while energy is the largest component, at approximately 70 percent of the index.

The Dow Jones-AIG Commodity Index (DJ-AIGCI) consists of 19 futures contracts on physical commodities traded on the U.S. commodities exchange. The weight of each commodity reflects its global economic importance and its market liquidity. Diversification rules also exist for the DJ-AIGCI: (1) The maximum index weight is 33 percent per individual commodity group and (2) no single commodity may constitute less than 2 percent of the index. The DJ-AIGCI index is less volatile than the GSCI.

The Commodity Research Bureau (CRB) Index has existed since 1957, making it the first commodity-based index. In 2005 it was renamed the Reuters/Jeffries, or CRB. The CRB Index currently consists of the prices of 27 futures contracts on 19 commodities quoted on the different U.S. exchanges and in the London Mercantile Exchange (LME). It is divided into a four-tier system, and each tier has a different weight. The largest tier weight is 42 percent (consisting of aluminum, copper, corn, gold, live cattle, natural gas, and soybeans), but the most heavily weighted (23 percent) individual commodity is crude oil (quoted on NYMEX).

As of February 2008, agricultural futures represented 14.89 percent of the GSCI, while energy futures represented 71.69 percent. Thus, the behavior of energy futures heavily influences the GSCI. Bodie and Rosansky (1980) and Gorton and Rouwenhorst (2006) find that agricultural commodity futures returns have a negative correlation with each national stock exchange, so a weight of agricultural commodities at 31.8 percent for the GSCI could deliver a better risk-return relationship.

In recent years, investable commodity indices and commodity-linked assets have increased the number of available direct commodity-based investment products. Despite the nature of the investment, commodity index investors are sometimes called "speculators" because they are not users of the underlying commodity. Speculators normally take positions in individual commodities; indexers hold well-diversified portfolios of commodities. Speculators buy or sell commodities based on a directional view about prices; indexers buy or sell based only on the fact that commodities serve to reduce the risk of their overall investment portfolios. Speculators typically use leverage (i.e., take futures positions depositing only the necessary margin) to magnify their exposure to price movements; indices are fully collateralized. Although index investors are diversified and are not betting on any particular commodity, their actions can affect the prices of all index commodities. Further, increasing evidence suggests that indirect commodity investment, through debt and equity instruments in commodity-linked firms, does not provide direct exposure to commodity price changes.

Commodity exposure is increasing because of the increasing number of investable commodity indices and commodity-linked assets that facilitate direct investment in commodities. These new products are usually similar to a passive, long-only commodity-based portfolio. They allow investors to benefit from the advantages associated with commodities. Erb and Harvey (2006) and Gorton and Rouwenhorst (2006) show that a portfolio of commodities offers returns that are comparable to traditional assets such as stocks. Further, commodities are a useful diversifier to traditional assets. Jensen et al. (2000, 2002) and Georgiev (2001) show that adding commodities to a portfolio of stocks and bonds significantly increases its risk-adjusted return. Gorton and Rouwenhorst (2006) note that the negative correlation with stocks increases when the latter are in a crisis, making diversification benefits from commodities higher when they are the most needed.

Several authors (e.g., Bodie, 1976; Bodie and Rosansky, 1980; Edwards and Park, 1996; Hoevenaars, Molenaar, Schotman, and Steenkamp, 2008) contend that a commodity portfolio constitutes a valuable hedge against inflation. For example, commodity markets have regular downturn phases and can correct sharply, as they did during the second half of 2008. Results based on various risk measures of the performance of efficient portfolios constructed from different combinations of international equity indices and agri-commodity futures benchmarks support the findings that investors can benefit from diversifying into some other agricultural commodity futures markets.

LITERATURE REVIEW ON THE DIVERSIFICATION EFFECT

This section contains a description of some of the most important research findings on diversification effects of commodities without considering the inflation effect. The first part of the section discusses the issues to consider when including commodity exposure in a portfolio, and the second part examines the performance of commodities over the business cycle.

Including Commodities in Portfolios

In their examination of two commodity future indices, namely the GSCI and the Intermarket Management's Investable Commodity Index (ICI), Ankrim and Hensel (1993) show that diversification increases with commodity futures. Compared to equities investments, the authors note that commodities improve diversification during a period of inflation, such as during the 1970s, by reducing portfolio risk. This effect decreases when inflation falls.

According to Satyanarayan and Varangis (1994), an efficient frontier with commodities is always better than an efficient frontier without commodities. Lummer and Siegel (1993) and Kaplan and Lummer (1998) confirm past studies about the presence of commodities in a portfolio and show that compared to stocks and bonds the GSCI allows for superior diversification. Abanomey and Mathur (1999) study two different portfolios with and without commodity futures contracts and conclude that the presence of commodity futures improves overall performance.

Fung and Hsieh (1997), Ackermann, McEnally, and Ravenscraft (1999), and Edwards and Liew (1999) compare hedge funds and commodity funds performance during bull and bear markets to verify the effects of diversification with the presence of commodities. Becker and Finnerty (2000) show that including a commodities index (CRB or GSCI) as part of a traditional portfolio improves the risk-return relationship during the period between 1970 and 1990. This feature was much more evident in the 1970s, a period characterized by high inflation.

In the 1990s, characterized by the high performance of equities indices, the scenario changed because the best asset allocations no longer included the selection of commodities. During the Internet bubble period between 2000 and 2001, including bonds and commodities helped to enhance the return of a portfolio. Edwards and Caglayan (2001) examine the performance of 16 commodity funds between January 1990 and August 1998 on an "equally weighted" and "value-weighted" basis. They calculate average monthly returns and the Sharpe index for each commodity fund and the correlation among these returns and S&P 500, distinguishing between bull and bear markets. During the 104 months of the study, Edwards and Caglayan classify 62 months as "bull-market months," when the S&P 500 increases more than one percentage point compared to previous month and 25 months as "bear-market months," when the S&P 500 decreases by at least one percentage point. Gorton, Hayashi, and Rouwenhorst (2005) analyze the Japanese market and discover results that are quite similar to previous research.

Gorton and Rouwenhorst (2006) compose a commodities futures index of equal weights with the idea of studying the reaction of this index between July 1959 and December 2004. They notice a large difference between commodity spot prices and futures prices. The authors note that the returns are correlated during high volatility periods. However, afterwards, the returns diverge because with the futures price, a risk-free rate and a risk premium (to invest in futures) must be considered. The collateral yield is almost equal to inflation so the futures return is a risk premium earned by investors.

Gorton and Rouwenhorst (2006) also compare the Ibbotson corporate bond total return index (bond index), the S&P 500 total return index (stock index), and their equally weighted commodity index. They observe that their commodity index obtains a yield quite similar to the S&P 500 Index. In fact, the average risk premium on commodity futures (measured as a mathematical average of excess return) was 5.23 percent, comparable to the equity risk premium (5.65 percent), and larger than the bond risk premium (2.22 percent). Commodity futures had the best performance during the 1970s because of the oil crisis, while the stock index increased the most in the 1990s. Overall, the commodity futures return is almost equal to stock returns but with a lower standard deviation. The stock returns exhibit negative skewness, whereas the distribution of commodity futures exhibits positive skewness. All distributions show positive excess kurtosis. Lower standard deviation and positive skewness for commodity futures returns ensure less downside risk than the stock return.

With the objective of judging the presence of commodity futures in a portfolio, Gorton and Rouwenhorst (2006) study the correlations between commodity futures returns and traditional asset class (i.e., stocks and bonds) returns. Except for a short period (one month), the total return of the commodities future index shows a negative correlation with traditional asset class indices, and this feature improves over time.

Jensen et al. (2000) and Erb and Harvey (2006) show that the correlation with S&P 500 returns is low (−0.0206 for gasoline and 0.0948 for timber) and that their average correlation is 0.0139. Extending this research to other stock indices and bond indices confirms the low correlation with commodity derivatives. By analyzing systematic risk, the authors of both studies show that negative correlations differ based on the commodities analyzed. Beta values are lower for precious metals and agricultural commodities, whereas beta values are positive for energy commodities and some agricultural commodities, such as soy, sugar, and wheat.

Financial and commodity markets exhibit a similar price trend during extreme market events. However, Büyüksahin et al. (2010) find that the comovements between equities and commodities have generally not increased from 2006 to 2010, suggesting that commodities still retain their role as a diversification tool.

Stoll and Whaley (2010) estimate that the total amount invested in commodities indices in the United States is about $174 billion, with 24 percent held by mutual funds, 42 percent by institutional operators, 9 percent by sovereign funds, and 25 percent by retail investors.

Büyüksahin et al. (2010) study the correlation between the GSCI and the S&P 500 for periods before November 2008. They divide their analysis from 1992 to 2008 into three periods: (1) June 1992 to May 1997 (preboom investing in commodities futures), (2) June 1997 to May 2003 (the Asian crisis, Russia and Argentina default, and the Internet bubble), and (3) June 2003 to November 2008 (boom investing in commodities and the credit bubble). During the 18 years, the weekly average return for the GSCI (0.0781 percent) was lower than the S&P 500 (0.1127 percent) and the Dow Jones Industrial Average (DJIA) (0.1335 percent). Using a similar time period, Gorton and Rouwenhorst (2006) report that the GSCI index monthly return was equal to 0.14 percent in the first period and 0.078 percent in the second period. In the third period, which includes the subprime crisis, the return collapsed by 350 percent between May and November 2008. In contrast, the S&P 500 reached a high level of performance during the period May to November 2008.

The correlation between equity and commodity indices was weak between 1997 and 2003 and even negative during the period between June 2003 and May 2008. The benefits in selecting commodities in a portfolio decreased from May to November 2008, and the correlation was positive during the financial crisis. This analysis relates to six subindices: agricultural, energy, industrial metals, livestock, nonenergy, and precious metals. The S&P 500 has a positive and low correlation with commodity returns and this result increases between 2003 and 2008. The only exception is the correlation between precious metals and the S&P 500, which is close to zero.

Chong and Miffre (2010) also study the correlation between alternative and traditional asset classes. Their research covers the period between January 1981 and December 2006 and compares 25 commodities and 13 traditional asset classes. As representative of traditional asset classes, the authors select the following indices: the S&P 500 Index, MSCI Europe Index, Russell 200 Index, Russell 1000 Value Index, Russell 1000 Growth Index, MSCI Asia Pacific Index, and MSCI Latin America Index, whereas the J. P. Morgan indices represent the bond sector. Their results show that the correlation between 11 commodity futures in the sample and S&P 500 returns tends to decrease over time, thus ensuring risk reduction within the portfolio.

Chong and Miffre (2010) find similar results in the Asian and European stock exchanges: Conditional correlation tends to decrease when volatility increases, but this situation only occurs for agricultural commodities and precious metals, whereas for energy commodities conditional correlation and volatility exhibit a positive beta. Some investors explain that this situation is justified by researching "flight to quality" during the financial crisis. Apparently, some investors consider energy commodities as a safe haven.

Investors can observe that the correlation between the bond market and the commodities market decreases when short-term interest rates decrease, the price increases yield, and the length of maturity increases. If medium-term interest rates are volatile, the correlation between bonds and commodities increases, and thus the diversification effect decreases. The correlation is particularly low for metals, energy commodities, and some agricultural commodities, such as soy, sugar, and wheat.

Because the correlation between traditional assets and commodities changed during the financial crisis of 2007–2008, recent research about the correlation after 2008 is worthy of examination. Tang and Xiong (2010) believe that the increase in correlations cannot be solely attributed to the financial crisis but is primarily caused by the process of transforming the physical commodity into a financial commodity, which has a significant impact on commodities. From 1986 to 2004, the returns correlation between copper, cotton, and livestock with oil ranged from 0.1 to 0.2, but this value increased to between 0.5 and 0.6 in 2009. Similarly, the correlation between the GSCI returns and nonenergy commodities gradually increased from 0.1 in 2004 to 0.7 in 2009.

Researchers offer several explanations for the increasing correlation between these commodities over time. For example, Tang and Xiong (2010) support the fact that the financialization of commodities has deteriorated the benefits of commodities diversification. With strong growth of investments in commodities indices, the prices of nonenergy commodities have greatly increased the correlation with oil prices. This situation is much more evident for commodities included in the basket of commodity indices. The outcome of this process is that the price of single commodities is not determined by the interaction between supply and demand, but specifically by the behavior of commodity indices.

Smimou (2010) investigates agricultural commodities. This study updates previous research by Feldman and Till (2006) showing that using three commodities futures contracts (i.e., corn, soy, and wheat) in backwardation has an effect on the ex-post returns of long positions. Analyzing the Canadian market (Toronto Stock Exchange and ICE Futures) and international stock and agricultural markets in the United States, the United Kingdom, Germany, France and Japan, Smimou finds that international agricultural commodities futures have a low correlation with the S&P 500. As a result, U.S. investors can improve their performance by selecting Canadian commodities futures or those of other countries.

Silvennoinen and Thorp (2010) extend the studies of Gorton and Rouwenrhost (2006), Büyüksahin et al. (2010), and Chong and Miffre (2010) with the aim of analyzing the benefits of diversification after the financial crisis of 2007–2008 until June 2009. They note that the correlation between S&P 500 and metal and agricultural commodities is positive, while the correlation is small but positive for energy and gold commodities. All correlations increase during the financial crisis. These results are consistent with past studies, with the exception of the financial crisis period of 2007–2008

Asset managers are naturally curious about whether commodity futures are a suitable alternative investment compared to traditional assets during a financial crisis. The magnitude of volatility of a commodity has increased in the previous 10 years with the increased popularity of hedge funds. The increasing presence of commodity futures in a portfolio pushes investors to sell when the market collapses. Thus, the returns of commodity futures follow traditional asset returns.

Silvennoinen and Thorp (2010) extend their research from May 1990 to July 2009 to 24 individual commodity futures returns with major equity indices in the U.S. and Europe. Examples of the European indices include the U.K. index

FTSE100, German index DAX, and French index CAC. They find that the diversification benefits to equity investors smaller in magnitude than findings in other studies (Chong and Miffre 2010; Büyüksahin et al., 2010.) The correlation between S&P 500 returns and the return to the majority commodity futures has increased over the study period. The authors note a stronger integration between equity and metals, while oil futures returns have a higher correlation with stocks during the 2008 to 2009 period. Many of the features of the U.S. stock commodity futures correlations are repeated in the German, French, and U.K. stock markets. The correlation between bond and commodity futures is generally low and negative. The correlation between commodity futures with U.S. stocks from 1990 to 2009 rises from approximately zero to 0.5.

Commodities and the Business Cycle

According to Bjornson and Carter (1997), commodities provide a good hedge against traditional asset performance during a business cycle. They note an inverse relationship between agricultural commodities and the business cycle, with expected returns higher during low points in the business cycle and the opposite findings when the economy improves. An earlier study by Fama and French (1988) reaches similar conclusions. Gorton and Rouwenhorst (2006) analyze seven business cycles starting in 1959. Their evidence shows that stocks and commodities have a high return during phases related to economic expansion, while bonds have superior performance during recessions. They note that energy commodities show excellent yields during the beginning phase of a recession, while as recessions end their yields are negative. At the beginning of a recession, some commodities, such as cocoa, coffee, copper, propane, soy, and sugar, have positive returns, while stocks and bonds have negative returns. In the last phases of a recession, many commodities have negative returns, with the exception of gold, oats, and soy, which exhibit countercyclical trends.

Kat and Oomen (2007) study the returns of 29 commodities during an economic cycle between 1987 and 2005 and subdivide the cycle into four subperiods: (1) the onset of a recession, (2) the end of recession, (3) the beginning of expansion, and (4) the end of the expansion. Energy, livestock, and meat perform especially well during the start of a recession. Agricultural commodities and metals exhibit a lower return in the first subperiod. Energy performs poorly during the end of a recession.

Hess, Huang, and Niessen-Ruenzi (2008) show that during a recession the direction of the price response to macroeconomic announcements is opposite to that of stocks and bonds. Using two commodity indices as their sample, the CRB (New York Board of Trade) and the GSCI (Chicago Mercantile Exchange), they show that adding commodities to a stock and bond portfolio could reduce its volatility to the macroeconomic news during a weak state of economy.

According to Kat and Oomen (2007), the price of commodities is derived from economic power: The spot price is lower during recession and higher at the end of expansion. Their results confirm the previous conclusion reached by Gorton and Rouwenhorst (2006) that commodities futures returns are different in each phase of an economic cycle. Energy commodities have the best return at the beginning of a recession, whereas agricultural commodities and metals have the worst returns. Until the end of recession, all commodities have negative performances, except cocoa and oats.

Filiptchuk and Lindholm (2011) study the relationship among commodity, stock, and bond indices. From January 1973 until April 2011, for each phase of the economic cycle, they use the GSCI, Barclays Capital U.S. Government Bond Index (BarCap USGBI), and the Morgan Stanley Capital International World Index (MSCI World), which does not include stocks from emerging markets. Their results are similar to those of Gorton and Rouwenhorst (2006). The best commodity returns occur in the last phase of expansion, while the worst returns occur during the last phase of recession. Stock returns peak in the first phase of expansion and exhibit the worst performance during a recessionary period. BarCap USGBI does not exhibit peak up and down returns during the different phases.

SUMMARY AND CONCLUSIONS

In the previous decade, investors have seen impressive returns on raw materials, despite the financial crisis of 2007–2008 (Sanders and Irwin, 2011). This crisis has stimulated a debate between practitioners and academics on the strategic role of commodities as an alternative asset class and their appropriate weight within an investment portfolio.

During the period between 2002 and 2008, the volume of commodity contracts grew by more than 170 percent, indicating that the volume is 20 to 30 times more than the physical production of raw materials. Sanders, Irwin, and Merrin (2010) contend that the speculators in agricultural futures markets increased over the sample period between 2006 and 2008. If observers use open interest as an indicator, then their analysis does not show any material change or shifts over the sample period. Two main investor types drove this interest in investing in commodities: (1) pension funds and mutual funds, which use raw material contracts following a "buy and hold" strategy, and (2) hedge funds, which take a long/short position and almost always close their position before the maturity with another contract of an opposite type (cash settlement).

One of the most attractive aspects of commodity investing today is the availability of various passive indices for different asset classes. Commodity indices are generally based on the returns of futures contracts and/or cash markets. Commodity indices attempt to repeat the return available to holding long and short positions in agricultural, energy, livestock, or metals investments.

The period under examination appears to affect the role of commodities in a portfolio. During the pre-2008 era, researchers find tangible diversification benefits of commodities. Yet, more recent studies find that the return correlations between commodities and equities have increased substantially during the financial crisis of 2007–2008, calling into question the benefits of commodities within a portfolio.

The results over the crisis period may be attributed to the fact that correlations tend to increase over periods with extreme market conditions, and hence reduce diversification benefits. The findings on the diversification benefits of gold are consistent with the evidence on its "safe haven" role in periods of crisis.

DISCUSSION QUESTIONS

1. Identify and discuss the advantages and disadvantages of direct versus indirect investments in commodities.
2. Commodities are classified as either soft or hard, with each category being further subdivided. List and discuss the role of each commodity and its future prospects.
3. Asset managers can choose different commodity indices for their portfolios. Discuss why investors must be careful when evaluating these indices by using different constituents and methodologies to change their asset allocation.
4. Discuss the presence of counterparty risk when investing in physical commodities, commodities derivatives, or commodity-based ETFs or ETNs.
5. Diversified commodity futures historically exhibit low correlations with traditional assets, such as stocks and bonds. Identify the different behavior during the financial crisis of 2007–2008 and the best alternatives for asset allocation during that time.

REFERENCES

Abanomey, Walid S., and Ike Mathur. 1999. "The Hedging Benefits of Commodity Futures in International Portfolio Diversification." *Journal of Alternative Investments* 2:3, 51–62.

Ackermann, Carl, Richard McEnally, and David Ravenscraft. 1999. "The Performance of Hedge Funds: Risk, Return and Incentives." *Journal of Finance* 54:3, 833–874.

Ankrim, Ernst M., and Chris R. Hensel. 1993. "Commodities in Asset Allocation: A Real-Asset Alternative to Real Estate." *Financial Analysts Journal* 49:3, 20–29.

Basu, Parantap, and William T. Gavin. 2011. "What Explains the Growth in Commodity Derivatives?" *Federal Reserve Bank of St. Louis Review* 93:1, 37–48.

Baur, Dirk, and Thomas K. McDermott. 2010. "Is Gold a Safe Haven? International Evidence." *Journal of Banking and Finance* 34:8, 1886–1898.

Becker, Kent G., and Joseph E. Finnerty. 2000. "Indexed Commodity Futures and the Risk and Return of Institutional Portfolios." Working Paper, Office of Futures and Options Research 94–02.

Bjornson, Bruce, and Colin A. Carter. 1997. "New Evidence on Agricultural Commodity Return Performance under Time-Varying Risk." *American Journal of Agricultural Economics* 79:3, 918–930.

Black, Keith H. 2009. "The Role of Institutional Investors in Rising Commodity Prices." *Journal of Investing* 18:3, 21–26.

Bodie, Zvi. 1976. "Common Stocks as a Hedge against Inflation." *Journal of Finance* 31:2, 459–470.

Bodie, Zvi, and Victory I. Rosansky. 1980. "Risk and Return in Commodity Futures." *Financial Analysts Journal* 36:3, 27–39.

Büyüksahin, Bahattin, Michael S. Haigh, and Michel A. Robe. 2010. "Commodities and Equities: A Market of One?" *Journal of Alternative Investments* 12:3, 76–95.

Chong, James, and Joelle Miffre. 2010. "Conditional Return Correlations between Commodity Futures and Traditional Assets." *Journal of Alternative Investments* 12:3, 61–75.

Conover, C. Mitchell, Gerald R. Jensen, Robert R. Johnson, and Jeffrey M. Mercer. 2005. "Is Fed Policy Still Relevant for Investors?" *Financial Analysts Journal* 61:1, 70–79.

Conover, C. Mitchell, Gerald R. Jensen, Robert R. Johnson, and Jeffrey M. Mercer. 2010. "Is Now the Time to Add Commodities to Your Portfolio?" *Journal of Investing* 19:3, 10–19.

Daskalaki, Charoula, and George Skiadopoulos. 2011. "Should Investors Include Commodities in Their Portfolios After All? New Evidence." *Journal of Banking & Finance* 35:10, 2606–2626.

Edwards, Franklin R., and Onur M. Caglayan. 2001. "Hedge Fund and Commodity Investments in Bull and Bear Markets." *Journal of Portfolio Management* 27:4, 97–108.

Edwards, Franklin R., and Jimmy Liew. 1999. "Hedge Funds versus Managed Futures as Asset Classes." *Journal of Derivatives* 6:4, 45–64.

Edwards, Franklin R., and James M. Park. 1996. "Do Managed Futures Make Good Investments?" *Journal of Futures Markets* 16:5, 475–517.

Erb, Claude, and R. Harvey Campbell. 2006. "The Strategic and Tactical Value of Commodity Futures." *Financial Analysts Journal* 62:2, 69–97.

Fabozzi, Frank, J., Roland Fuss, and Dieter G. Kaiser. 2008. *The Handbook of Commodity Investing*. Hoboken, NJ: John Wiley & Sons Inc.

Fama, Eugene F., and Kenneth R. French. 1988. "Business Cycles and the Behavior of Metal Prices." *Journal of Finance* 43:5, 1075–1093.

Feldman, Barry E., and Hillary F. Till. 2006. "Backwardation and Commodity Futures Performance: Evidence from Evolving Agricultural Markets." *Journal of Alternative Investments* 9:3, 24–39.

Filiptchuk, Kristina, and Heinrik Lindholm. 2011. "Portfolio Optimization with Commodities – Sub-Sector and Business Cycle Analysis." Working Paper, Handelshögskolan Stockholm.

Fortenbery, Randall T., and Robert J. Hauser. 1990. "Investment Potential of Agricultural Futures Contracts." *American Journal of Agricultural Economics* 72:3, 721–726.

Fung, William, and David A. Hsieh. 1997. "Survivorship Bias and Investment Style in the Returns of CTAs." *Journal of Portfolio Management* 24:1, 30–41.

Georgiev, Georgi. 2001. "Benefits of Commodity Investment." *Journal of Alternative Investments* 4:1, 40–48.

Gorton, Gary B., Fumio Hayashi, and Geert K. Rouwenhorst. 2005. "Commodity Futures: A Japanese Perspective." *Working Paper Yale ICF*, 05–27.

Gorton, Gary B., and Geert K. Rouwenhorst. 2006. "Facts and Fantasies about Commodity Futures." *Financial Analysts Journal* 62:2, 47–68.

Greer, Robert J. 2000. "The Nature of Commodity Index Returns." *Journal of Alternative Investments* 3:1, 45–52.

Hess, Dieter, He Huang, and Alexandra Niessen-Ruenzi. 2008. "How Do Commodity Futures Respond to Macroeconomic News?" *Financial Markets and Portfolio Management* 22:2, 127–146.

Hoevenaars, Roy P.M.M., Roderick D. J. Molenaar, Peter Schotman, and Tom B. M. Steenkamp. 2008. "Strategic Asset Allocation with Liabilities: Beyond Stock and Bonds." *Journal of Economic Dynamics & Control* 32:9, 2939–2970.

Irwin, Scott H., and Dwight R. Sanders. 2011. "Index Funds, Financialization and Commodity Futures Markets." *Applied Economic Perspective & Policy* 33:1, 1–31.

Irwin, Scott H., Dwight R. Sanders, and Robert P. Merrin. 2009. "Devil or Angel: The Role of Speculation in the Recent Commodity Price Boom." Working Paper, Southern Agricultural Economics Association Meetings, Atlanta, Georgia.

Jeanneret, Pierre, Pierre Monnin, and Stefan Scholz. 2011. "Protection Potential of Commodity Hedge Fund." *Journal of Alternative Investments* 13:3, 35–42.

Jensen, Gerald R., Robert R. Johnson, and Jeffrey M. Mercer. 2000. "Efficient Use of Commodity Futures in Diversified Portfolios." *Journal of Futures Markets* 20:5, 489–506.

Jensen, Gerald R., Robert R. Johnson, and Jeffrey M. Mercer. 2002. "Tactical Asset Allocation and Commodity Futures." *Journal of Portfolio Management* 28:4, 100–111.

Kaplan, Paul D., and Scott L. Lummer. 1998. "GSCI Collateralized Futures as a Hedging and Diversification Tool for Institutional Portfolios: An Update." *Journal of Investing* 7:4, 11–17.

Kat, Harry M., and Roel C. Oomen. 2007. "What Every Investor Should Know about Commodities Part I: Univariate Return Analysis." *Journal of Investment Management* 5:1, 40–64.

Lummer, Scott L., and Laurence B. Siegel. 1993. "GSCI Collateralized Futures: A Hedging and Diversification Tool for Institutional Investors." *Journal of Investing* 2:2, 75–82.

Sanders, Dwight R., and Scott H. Irwin. 2011. "The Impact of Index Funds in Commodity Futures Markets: A Systems Approach." *Journal of Alternative Investments* 14:1, 40–49.

Sanders, Dwight R., Scott H. Irwin, and Robert P. Merrin. 2010. "The Adequacy of Speculation in Agricultural Futures Markets: Too Much of a Good Thing?" *Applied Economic Perspectives and Policy* 32:1, 77–94.

Satyanarayan, Sudhakar, and Panos Varangis. 1994. "An Efficient Frontier for International Portfolios with Commodity Assets." Working Paper Policy Research 1266, The World Bank.

Silvennoinen, Annastina, and Susan Thorp. 2010. "Financialization, Crisis and Commodity Correlation Dynamics." Working Paper, Queensland University of Technology, Sydney.

Smimou, Kamal. 2010. "Stock Market and Agricultural Futures Diversification: An International Perspective." *Journal of Alternative Investments* 12:4, 36–57.

Stoll, Hans R., and Robert E. Whaley. 2010. "Commodity Index Investing and Commodity Futures Prices." *Journal of Applied Finance* 20:1, 7–46.

Tang, Ke, and Wei Xiong. 2010. "Index Investment and Financialization of Commodities." Working Paper, Princeton University.

ABOUT THE AUTHOR

Claudio Boido is an Associate Professor of Investments at the School of Economics University of Siena and the coordinator of the Finance Area in Master Economics and Banking. He also teaches at the LUISS School of Economics University in Rome. Professor Boido's research has been published in the *The ICFAI University Journal of Behavioural Finance, The ICFAI University Journal of Derivative Markets,* and *The ICFAI University Journal of Financial Risk Management.* In 2011, McGraw-Hill (Italy) published his book, *Mercati, Strumenti Finanziari, Investimenti Alternativi* (*Financial Markets, Instruments, and Alternative Assets*).

CHAPTER 19

Performance of Commodities

ANDREW CLARK
Manager of Alternative Investments Research, Lipper

INTRODUCTION

Commodities play important roles in our daily lives. Commodities are found all over the world and can be traded in the global marketplace as part of a diversified investment portfolio. Billions of dollars are invested in commodities daily. Commodities can be traded either on the spot (as real-time trades) or as futures, options, or in exchange-traded funds (ETFs). Most individual commodities are traded in the form of futures, where the object being traded is not the commodity itself but rather a contract to buy or sell it for a certain price by a stated date in the future. This practice carries a potential for losses from market fluctuations, but for investors who are willing to ride out possibly substantial market volatility commodity exposure offers the opportunity to reap higher rewards.

As with most investments except short sales, the goal in commodities trading is to buy low and sell high. The difference is that commodities are highly leveraged and are traded in terms of contract sizes instead of in terms of shares such as with stocks. Also, investors can buy and sell positions whenever the markets are open.

The purpose of this chapter is to provide an introduction to commodity trading. The remainder of the chapter consists of four sections. The first section provides a brief review of the history of commodity trading and includes the basics of commodity trading. This section also examines commodity futures, commodity ETFs, and managed futures. The next two sections discuss the performance of commodities and the future of commodity prices. The final section offers a summary and conclusions.

THE HISTORY OF COMMODITY TRADING

Dating from the ancient use of sheep, goats, pigs, cowrie shells, and other items as commodity money, people have sought ways to standardize and trade contracts for the delivery of such items in order to render trade smooth and predictable. The word *commodity* came into use in English in the fifteenth century from the French *commodite*, meaning "to benefit or profit."

Possibly the earliest examples of commodity trading involved the Sumerians, who consolidated prepayments for food into tubs that they later exchanged for food once the food was harvested. These payment systems were standardized when the spice routes opened in the late 1580s. Spain and Portugal, through their sovereigns, reserved specific quantities of spices for future delivery and according to contracted specifications. Prices were fixed in advance of the journey.

The first futures contracts were rice contracts that traded in seventeenth century Japan, and some evidence exists of rice futures traded in China as long as 2,000 to 2,500 years ago. In Japan, merchants stored rice in warehouses for future use. To raise cash, warehouse holders sold receipts against the stored rice. These were known as *rice tickets*. Eventually, rice tickets became accepted as a kind of general commercial currency, and rules developed that standardized the trading of rice tickets. These rules were similar to the current rules of American futures trading.

Commodity trading is a natural outgrowth of the problem of maintaining a year-round supply of seasonal products such as agricultural crops. In the United States, futures trading started in the middle of the nineteenth century in the grain markets at the Chicago Board of Trade (CBOT)—the oldest established commodities house. The driving force behind the creation of the CBOT was the need for manufacturers to obtain future supplies to meet their developing orders. Also, farmers did not want to rely on prices set only during the harvest, when the maximum supply would be on the market. The first contracts, for flour and hay, were called *to arrive* contracts and later came to be known as *forward* contracts. Other commodities were added, including corn in 1850. Over the next several decades, industrialization in the United States and Europe created demand for many other products that could be purchased for future delivery. In the 1870s and 1880s the New York Coffee, Cotton, and Produce Exchanges were established. The Chicago Mercantile Exchange (CME) created futures markets to trade farm produce as well as byproducts such as soy oil. Later, the New York Mercantile Exchange opened to trade oil and energy products; it was the largest trading facility for physical commodities before its merger with the CME.

Commodity regulation by both state and federal governments came into effect in the 1920s. The Commodity Futures Trading Commission (CFTC) codified regulations upon its creation in the mid-1970s. The commission's purpose was to protect markets and the public from fraud and manipulation with respect to futures markets and their derivative products, such as single-stock futures and options on futures. Various sources, such as Ferris (1988), McCafferty and Wasendorf (1992), and Fabozzi (2008), as well as the websites of the different exchanges, provide more about the history of commodity trading.

Today, the United States has 10 commodity exchanges. The five largest exchanges are the CBOT, CME, New York Mercantile Exchange, New York Commodity Exchange, and New York Coffee, Sugar, and Cocoa Exchange. Worldwide, more than 20 countries, including Australia, Canada, France, Japan, New Zealand, Singapore, and the United Kingdom, have major futures trading exchanges. The products traded range from agricultural staples such as corn and wheat to red beans and rubber.

The Basics of Commodity Trading

Successfully trading or investing in commodities requires knowing the basics of commodity trading. Trading commodities is really trading commodity futures.

Commodity futures are an asset class that differs from stocks or bonds. For example, a standard futures contract for corn futures, oil futures, or gold futures is a claim or a promise relating to a standardized quantity of a tangible asset. The claim for delivery or promise to deliver is on the contract expiration date. As a matter of practice, traders seldom hold a contract through to expiration but execute the opposite trade on the same commodity and expiration date in order to exit the trade.

Supply and demand often cause pronounced commodity price shifts. Agricultural commodities are especially prone to large price fluctuations since variations in weather conditions, amounts of crops planted, or numbers of cattle culled from herds affect supply. The basics of commodity trading are that a trader in commodities is not concerned with the competence of management, a margin of safety, or diversifying a stock portfolio into various market sectors. The trader is concerned with drought in Argentina or Russia, the opening of markets in Asia, or, in the case of gold, the valuation of the U.S. dollar or the euro.

Some commodities, such as gold, oil, and corn, can be stored, but commodities such as milk have a short shelf life. Knowing the basics of commodity trading for a given set of commodities is essential for trading them. Traders should also know that the decisions of large producers and buyers of commodities typically drive the markets of the various commodities. Not all the fluctuation in commodity prices is based on the fundamentals of production and demand. Price fluctuations are also based on anticipation of market factors by these large buyers and sellers. Successful commodity trading requires an ability to anticipate the actions of other traders in the commodities market. In other words, the commodities market, as with most markets, tends to follow the famous Keynes (2010, p. 147) "beauty contest" rules:

> It is not a case of choosing those faces which, to the best of one's judgment, are really the prettiest, nor even those which average opinion genuinely thinks the prettiest. We have reached the third degree where we devote our intelligences to anticipating what average opinion expects the average opinion to be.

Commodity Futures

To start trading commodities via futures requires understanding that, unlike stocks and bonds, trading futures does not typically involve buying the actual commodity. However, producers and processors of commodities do buy and sell futures contracts for delivery on a specific future date. Producers and processors typically hedge their investment risk, helping to provide a stable market for the commodity in question.

Speculators can trade the same commodity futures contracts by buying and selling futures, or they can buy and sell options on futures contracts. Typically, speculating in the futures markets means taking a gamble on the future direction of the price of the commodity being traded. Stated differently, speculators are betting that the future price will go either up or down. The impact of such movements depends on the perspective of the buyer or the seller of the commodity futures. Referring again to the purchasers and buyers of the commodity, the large companies that operate in futures markets use futures contracts to lock in their selling prices for the product in advance of delivery of the product. A company that does this is actually hedging.

On the other side of the transaction—dealing with commodity futures—is the trader who speculates on whether the commodity price will change before the contract is due for delivery. In trading commodity futures, no one necessarily has to take or make a delivery of the underlying product that the futures contract represents. Typically, traders will offset their position at some time before the date the contract expires. Offsetting a position involves changing from a long position (buy) in a security to a short position (sell) in the same security or from a short position to a long position.

The commodity futures market includes items such as corn, gold, heating oil, lumber, pork bellies, silver, wheat, and many other commodities. The main commodity-trading groups also include currencies, energies, food and fiber, grains, interest rates, meats, metals, and stock indices. While including currency, interest rate, and stock index futures as commodities may seem unusual, the price trend of currencies, interest rates, and stock index futures can have a strong influence on commodity prices for most investors and traders. Therefore, following these markets can provide valuable insights to the potential direction of commodity prices. Using currency, interest rate, and stock indices futures (or ETFs) as hedges to commodity positions is common.

Energy, another group used for investing in commodities, is the largest physical commodity group in the world in terms of volume. Energy commodities include crude oil, heating oil, and natural gas. The main focuses for speculators trading in metals are copper, gold, and silver. Other metals that have seen a substantial increase in trading volume are platinum and palladium. The popular commodities in the grains and meats group include feeder cattle, live cattle and hogs, and pork bellies. The last popular group is the food and fiber group. These commodity futures markets include cocoa, coffee, cotton, and orange juice. Cotton is probably the best market for long-term trend followers. Traders in commodities familiarize themselves with the Commitments of Traders (COT) report, published by the CFTC. The report contains detailed information for the futures market on positions and volumes of contracts. It lists the conditions in the futures markets about contracts and whether the net contracts are long or short.

In terms of the mechanics of futures trading, a *futures contract* is an agreement to buy or sell an asset for a certain price at a certain time in the future. Once initiated, the contract takes on a life of its own and trades in the market similar to any other security or commodity. When an exchange develops a new contract it specifies the asset, the contract size (how much of the asset is to be delivered under each contract), and the place and time of delivery.

For instance, the 100-ounce gold futures contract trading on the CBOT has the following asset underlying it: refined gold in the form of one 100-troy-ounce bar or three 1-kilo bars, assaying at not less than 99.5 percent fineness. The three 1-kilo bars, representing the gold futures contract, cannot vary from a 100-troy-ounce weight by more than 5 percent. Currency futures contracts trading on the CME merely mention the currency underlying the contract. No need exists to specify the grade of a Japanese yen or a Canadian dollar.

Another example is the CME's index futures contracts (one month, two months, and three months), which can be based on, for example, the S&P 500 Index.

This contract means that the asset underlying the contract is the 500 stocks comprising the index. Unlike commodity futures, where actual delivery could take place at the end of the term specified in the contract, index futures contracts are cash settled. The delivery is actually a cash settlement of the difference between the original transaction price and the final price at the termination of the contract.

The contract size specifies the amount of assets to be delivered for one contract. The size of the contract is an important aspect that can influence the success of the contract in the market. If the size of the contract is too big, investors who would like to hedge away small exposures or take small speculative positions will be unable to use the contract. Conversely, if the contract size is too small, trading may turn out to be expensive because the user would incur transaction costs with each contract traded. The S&P 500 futures contract trading on the CME trades in multiples of 250; that is, the value of the S&P 500 futures contract can be calculated by multiplying the futures index price by $250.

The futures price is based on the cost-of-carry model. The *cost of carry* is the cost of "carrying," or holding, a position. On the long side, the cost of carry is the cost of interest paid on a margin account. On the short side, the cost of carry is the cost of paying dividends, or rather the opportunity cost: the cost of purchasing a particular security rather than an alternative. For most investments the cost of carry generally refers to the risk-free interest rate that could be earned by investing currency in a theoretically safe investment vehicle such as a money market account, minus any future cash flows that are expected from holding an equivalent instrument with the same risk (generally expressed in percentage terms and called the *convenience yield*). Storage costs, which are generally expressed as a percentage of the spot price, should be added to the cost of carry for physical commodities such as corn, gold, or wheat.

To ensure smooth settlement, all index futures contracts are subject to margins by the clearing corporation. With futures contracts, participants normally put up about 5 to 15 percent of the contract value in margin. For example, the margin on buying a wheat futures contract is about $1,700. The total contract is worth about $32,500 ($6.50 × 5,000 bushels). Thus, the futures margin is approximately 5 percent of the contract value.

The margin paid for a futures contract consists of two parts: one up front and one over time. The *initial margin* is the amount that must be deposited with the clearing corporation when the contract is first entered. This serves as a safeguard against potential losses on outstanding positions; hence, the amount of exposure a member can take is based on the initial margin deposited by the member. *Margin maintenance* is the amount of money required to bring the margin back to the initial margin level if a loss occurs on the futures position. For example, suppose the initial margin on a corn futures contract is $1,000 and the maintenance margin is $700. If the price of corn drops 7 cents (per bushel) or $350 (per 5,000 bushels), the holder has violated the maintenance level and needs to add an additional $350 in margin, called *variation margin*, to bring it back to the initial maintenance level. The holder also has the option of closing the position to eliminate the margin call.

Futures margin rates are typically calculated by an exchange, using a program called Standard Portfolio Analysis of Risk (SPAN). This program measures many variables to determine a final figure for the initial and maintenance margins in each futures market. The main variable is the volatility of each futures market.

Exchanges do adjust their margin requirements occasionally based on market conditions. The importance of this margining system cannot be overstressed. The margining system in the futures markets ensures that market participants do not sustain losses because of default. The margining system forms the foundation on which rests the future of sound futures markets around the world. Investors seeking to invest in commodity futures realize it is one area where an individual with limited capital can make a profit in a relatively short period. But, patience and education are essential for investing in the commodities futures market.

Commodity ETFs

Maeda (2009) and Ferri (2009) provide a good source for the following material. Another way of getting exposure to commodities is via ETFs. *Commodity ETFs* are investment vehicles for investors and traders who need to hedge risk or want to gain exposure to physical goods such as agriculture products, energy resources, and precious metals. The makeup of a commodity ETF is a little different than that of a normal ETF.

Most ETFs invest in equities related to a particular market index, sector, or region. A normal ETF invests in a collection of securities determined by the criteria of the fund. However, commodity ETFs invest in futures or asset-backed contracts. These contracts represent the commodity and track the performance of a particular product. The commodity itself is not in the ETF. For example, if investors buy a gold ETF, they are not buying gold bars; they are buying an ETF consisting of assets backed by gold. Those bars of gold are still locked up in Fort Knox or in a bank vault deep under the streets of New York City.

Because commodity ETFs are made up of futures or asset-backed contracts, some investors for reasons of safety prefer that the commodity ETF invests a healthy dose of its original capital in bonds. Their reasoning is that because commodity ETFs consist of futures contracts, a fair degree of leverage is already built into the original investment vehicle. When futures contracts are leveraged through a commodity ETF, the money put into the fund is being leveraged exponentially. Investors often use the amount of leverage a commodity ETF has to account for the volatility seen in the particular commodity ETF. Because of this volatility, potential investors seeking a safer investment do not buy leveraged ETFs. These investors, as previously mentioned, prefer that the ETF puts some of the fund's capital in safe, interest-bearing instruments such as government bonds. This margin of safety effectively negates the leverage involved in futures trading. However, it can cancel out large gains as well. So, a trade-off of safety and gains typically exists in commodity ETFs, based on the amount of leverage investors want in the ETF.

Several ways are available for investors in a commodity ETF to use the ETF vehicle:

- To stabilize gold investments in a portfolio, selling a gold ETF can help reduce downside gold risk.
- If the portfolio contains many energy stocks, selling an energy ETF can hedge downside risk.

- If the portfolio has exposure to foreign investments in a country where coal is a major source of income, a coal ETF hedges against downside risk.
- Purchasing an inverse commodity ETF emulates the price of a commodity index in the opposite direction. Inverse ETFs are useful if investors want to sell a commodity but cannot short ETFs because of margin or account restrictions.
- If investors do not want to close a commodity ETF position but want some short-term exposure or protection, trading ETF options can be a good strategy.

Another benefit of using commodity ETFs is that commodity-linked products using futures to obtain their market exposure receive special tax treatment by the U.S. Internal Revenue Service (IRS). Regardless of the holding period, 60 percent of gains are taxed at the long-term capital gains rate, while the remaining 40 percent of gains are taxed as short-term profits, which are subject to the investor's ordinary income tax rate. For investors in the highest tax bracket, this 60/40 split creates a maximum blended capital gains tax rate of 23 percent. The tax burden is reduced for investors in lower income brackets. While some reasons for investing in commodity ETFs are the same as those for investing in commodities futures (hedging and diversification of holdings), investors who are not as concerned about safety as the investors noted above should bear in mind the following:

- As noted, most commodity ETFs use futures or forward contracts to underpin their pricing characteristics. The price of the ETF cannot directly track the underlying assets more efficiently than the futures contracts themselves. Thus, traders are exposed to corresponding net asset value (NAV) correlation risk.
- ETF holders are also subject to counterparty risk. The invested funds of an ETF are typically entrusted to the sponsor of the ETF and subsequently are applied to a complex system of structuring and over-the-counter (OTC) derivatives. In the event a counterparty of the ETF fails to perform its obligations, the NAV of the ETF could be adversely affected. Although this risk is very minimal, since 2008 investors have seen the most stable institutions become susceptible to default risk. Conversely, the clearing corporations of the exchange guarantee futures contracts, so there is virtually no risk of default.
- Additionally, futures contracts allow for more complex strategies such as intercommodity spreads and calendar spreads. These strategies allow futures traders to take advantage of more complex or interesting pricing relationships. For example, investors can purchase natural gas and short crude oil to take advantage of a changing price relationship between the two energy sources. Traders can also take advantage of seasonal relationships in commodity pricing. Conversely, commodity-based ETFs allow only simplistic long or short commodity trading strategies.
- Finally, futures contracts offer traders more leverage. Most ETF units limit leverage to two to one, but futures contracts offer leverage of 10 to 1, or even 20 to 1 in some cases. Further, the leverage on a futures contract is clear

and exact, but the leverage ratio of an ETF is an estimate that will fluctuate around a target leverage ratio. Leverage magnifies both the risk and the reward of a potential trading strategy.

For investors who are looking to commodities for simple hedging and diversification purposes, a commodity ETF is probably a better vehicle. It is also going to be the better vehicle if the investor is seeking to gain exposure to commodities because of current long-term trends in the market. For traders and those investors who require a smaller margin of safety, futures are probably the better vehicle for the reasons listed above. Futures carry greater volatility and hence greater potential for losses and gains, but disciplined traders or investors can credibly use futures to their benefit.

Managed Futures

Various sources provide material on managed futures. Investopia, Peters and Warwick (1997), and Fabozzi (2002) are very good source material on managed futures. Commodity trading advisers (CTAs) often specialize in trading in the global commodity and financial futures markets. CTAs are required to register with the U.S. government's CFTC before they can offer themselves to the public as money managers. CTAs are required to go through a Federal Bureau of Investigation (FBI) background check and to provide rigorous disclosure documents and independent audits of financial statements every year, which are reviewed by the National Futures Association (NFA)—a self-regulatory watchdog organization.

CTAs generally manage their clients' assets using various active management methods not limited to going long or short in futures contracts in areas such as metals (gold and silver), grains (corn, soybeans, and wheat), equity indices (S&P 500 futures, Dow futures, and NASDAQ 100 futures), soft commodities (cocoa, coffee, cotton, and sugar), foreign currencies, or U.S. government bond futures.

A major argument for diversifying into managed futures is their potential to lower portfolio risk. Many academic studies of the effects of combining investing in traditional asset classes with alternative investments such as managed futures support such an argument. Lintner (1983) indicates that portfolios of managed futures tend to show substantially less risk than stock and bonds alone across a variety of environments.

Managed futures have produced very good returns in the past 30 plus years. The benchmark index for the industry is the Barclay CTA Index, which includes 565 CTAs. The index includes only advisers with at least four years of performance history. New programs from an adviser are not added until their second year.

The Barclay CTA Index had an 11.1 percent compound annual return from 1980 until early March 2012; its worst drawdown was 15.7 percent. A *drawdown* is the peak-to-trough decline during a specific record period of an investment, fund, or commodity. The drawdown is usually quoted as the percentage difference between the peak and the trough. This performance shows fairly steady returns for the industry, but the higher returns occurring in the 1980s augmented the average return. The CTAs seem to perform well in years that are bad for stocks. The index shows only five years of negative returns, with the lowest return of −3.1 percent in

2011. Overall, the performance of managed returns has been impressive, providing a good reason many large investors and institutions commit more money to managed futures.

The Barclay CTA Index is an index of the returns of CTAs. Unless investors have tens of millions of dollars to invest in managed futures, they will likely have to select one or a few CTAs to place their money. Annual returns from individual CTAs are often different from that of the index. However, all CTAs must furnish their performance records to prospective investors, giving a better idea of what to expect from each individual CTA.

An additional benefit of managed futures is risk reduction through portfolio diversification; that is, taking advantage of very small positive or at times negative correlations between asset groups. As an asset class, managed futures programs have little or no correlation with stocks and bonds. For example, over the past 30 plus years the Barclay CTA Index's correlation to the S&P 500 was 0.12, while its correlation to the Barclay Aggregate Bond Index was 0.00.

Portfolio diversification can also take on other forms. For example, during periods of rising inflation investing in managed futures programs that track the metals markets, such as gold and silver, or foreign currency futures can provide a substantial hedge to the damage an inflationary environment can have on equities and bonds. In other words, if stocks and bonds underperform because of rising inflation concerns, certain managed futures programs might outperform in the same market conditions. Hence, combining managed futures with other asset groups may optimize the allocation of investment capital.

Before investing in any asset class or with an individual money manager, investors should make some important assessments. The CTA's disclosure document, which must be provided upon request, contains much of the information investors need. The disclosure document contains vital information about the CTA's trading plan and fees, which can vary substantially between CTAs but generally are 2 percent of assets under management and 20 percent for performance incentives.

The disclosure documents provide information on the type of trading program operated by the CTA. Two types of trading programs generally exist among the CTA community. One group of CTAs can be described as *trend followers*, while the other group consists of *market-neutral traders,* including options writers. Trend followers use proprietary technical or fundamental trading systems or a combination that provide signals of when to go long or short in certain futures markets. Market-neutral traders attempt to profit from spreading different commodity markets or different futures contracts in the same market. *Spreading* is a type of market-neutral strategy that monitors the performance of two correlated commodities. When the correlation between the two securities temporarily weakens (i.e., one commodity moves up while the other moves down), the trade would be to "short" the outperforming commodity and to "long" the underperforming one, betting that the spread between the two will eventually converge. Also, in the market-neutral category in a niche market, options-premium sellers use delta-neutral programs. *Delta-neutral programs* are those that attempt to offset price risk (the delta of the option in play) by building a portfolio consisting of positions with offsetting positive and negative deltas. The deltas balance out to bring the net change of the position or price risk to zero.

CTAs can also use directional trading strategies and market-neutral strategies. Directional, or trend-following, strategies are easy to understand, can be used to trade all commodity instruments, and need less automation and technical skill. These strategies usually follow some widely accepted trading policy, such as taking a net-long position when the market is predicted to go up, taking a net-short position when the market is predicted to fall, and using stop limits and other risk-minimizing tools.

Regardless of the type of CTA chosen, the most important piece of information to obtain in a CTA's disclosure document is the *maximum peak-to-valley drawdown.* This value represents the money manager's largest cumulative decline in a trading account. The worst historical drawdown provides a framework for assessing risk based on performance during a specific period, and it shows the time needed for the CTA to recoup the losses. Obviously, the shorter the time required to recover from a drawdown, the better the performance profile. Regardless of the time required, CTAs are allowed to assess incentive fees only on new net profits; that is, they must clear what is known in the industry as the *previous equity high-water mark* before charging additional incentive fees.

Another factor to investigate is the annualized rate of return, which CTAs must present net of fees and trading costs. The disclosure document provides this performance number, but it may not represent the most recent month of trading. (CTAs must update their disclosure document every nine months.) If the performance is not current in the disclosure document, investors can request the most recent performance, which the CTA should make available. Investors should especially want to know, for example, if any substantial drawdowns that are not shown in the most recent version of the disclosure document have occurred.

After determining the type of trading program (trend-following or market-neutral), the markets in which the CTA trades, and the potential reward given past performance (annualized return and maximum peak-to-valley drawdown), a risk assessment is the next step in the due diligence process. The NFA requires CTAs to use standardized performance capsules (the data used by most of the tracking services) in their disclosure documents, so making comparisons is easy.

The most important measure investors should compare is return on a risk-adjusted basis. For example, a CTA with an annualized rate of return of 30 percent might look better than one with a 10 percent return, but such a comparison may be deceiving if the two CTAs have radically different dispersions of losses. The CTA program with the 30 percent annual return may have average drawdowns of 30 percent per year, while the CTA program with the 10 percent annual return may have average drawdowns of only 2 percent. This means the risk required to obtain the respective returns is quite different: The 10 percent-return program has a return-to-drawdown ratio (also known as the *Calmar ratio*) of 5.0, while the other has a ratio of 1.0. The first program, therefore, has an overall better risk-reward profile.

Dispersion, which is the distance of monthly and annual performance from a mean or average level, is a typical basis for evaluating CTA returns. Many CTA-tracking data services provide these numbers for easy comparison. They also provide other risk-adjusted return data, such as the Sharpe and Calmar ratios. Investors can use alpha coefficients, such as those provided by single-beta calculations, to compare performance in relation to standard benchmarks such as the S&P 500 Index.

PERFORMANCE OF COMMODITIES

This section explores the value-added monthly index (VAMI) of several long-dated monthly commodity indices, certain individual commodities (their physical prices), as well as select futures data such as historical roll yields. VAMI is a method of tracking the return on an investment over a period of time given an initial \$1,000 investment. For example, suppose the yearly return on an investment is 10 percent; the VAMI would then be 1,100. So, VAMI = Previous VAMI for equal period of time × (1 + return rate).

Figure 19.1 shows the cumulative VAMI chart of Physical Commodity Indices. All physical commodity prices are from Thomson Reuters and are available in both its Datastream and Eikon products.

All commodity prices have risen over the past 30 plus years. The greatest increase in the price of physicals has been in the last 11 plus years. The source of this increase is the increased demand for energy, metals, and industrial materials associated with industrialization of countries such as Brazil, China, and India. This industrialization poses a problem for intermediate- and long-term commodity investors. The first 10 years of commodity price movements in Exhibit 19.1 show that the return on commodities follows a see-saw pattern driven by supply and demand forces in the developed world. After 1999, most commodity prices begin to move upward, again under the sway of supply and demand. This time the movement is not just from the developed world but from the developing world as well.

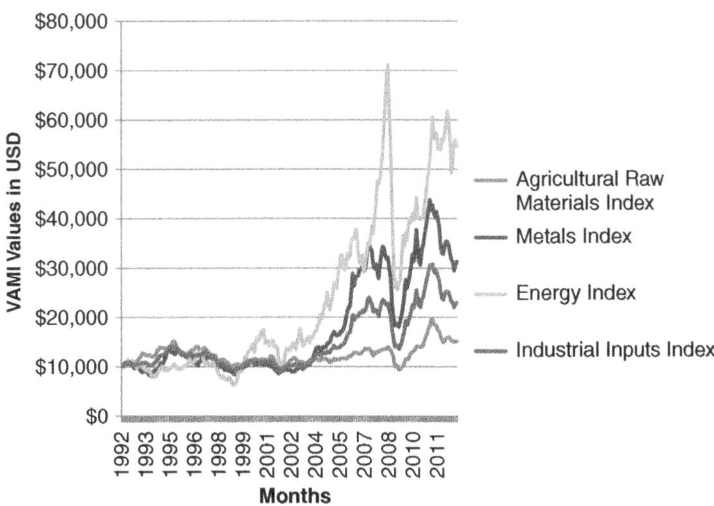

Exhibit 19.1 Cumulative VAMI Chart of Physical Commodity Indices, February 1992 to October 2011

The exhibit shows the increase in commodity prices from 1992 and 2012.
Source: Thomson Reuters.

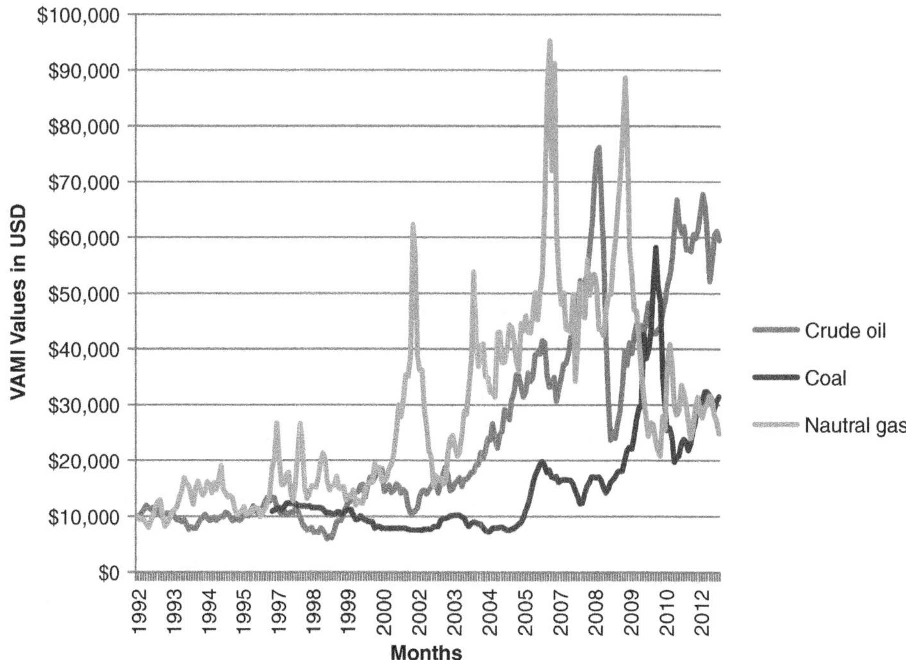

Exhibit 19.2 Cumulative VAMI Chart of Energy Index Components, February 1992 to February 2012

The chart shows that crude oil was the most consistent contributor to the rise in the energy index between 1992 and 2012.

Source: Thomson Reuters.

The question that arises for fundamental investors and traders in the commodities markets and for futures traders is whether the swelling demand for commodities from the developing world will continue for the next 5 to 10 years. If the answer is yes, the potential for commodity returns to exceed those of either developed-country stocks or their bonds could continue. This performance argues well for a separate asset class for commodities, not in the traditional sense of diversification but because commodities have the potential to outperform other asset classes on a regular basis.

Exhibit 19.2 illustrates the performance of some of the individual commodities that comprise each index, beginning with energy. As Exhibit 19.2 shows, coal and oil have been the main reasons the International Monetary Fund (IMF) energy index performed so well, especially over the last 12 years. Again, the industrialization of developing countries plays the largest role, but so does the fear that the world is approaching the limit of its oil reserves. That fear has begun to change, given the growing use of shale oil and the potential for other techniques to extract oil. Because the strongest propulsive force on oil and coal prices has been supply and demand, traders and investors need to be aware that these shifting dominant forces must be watched.

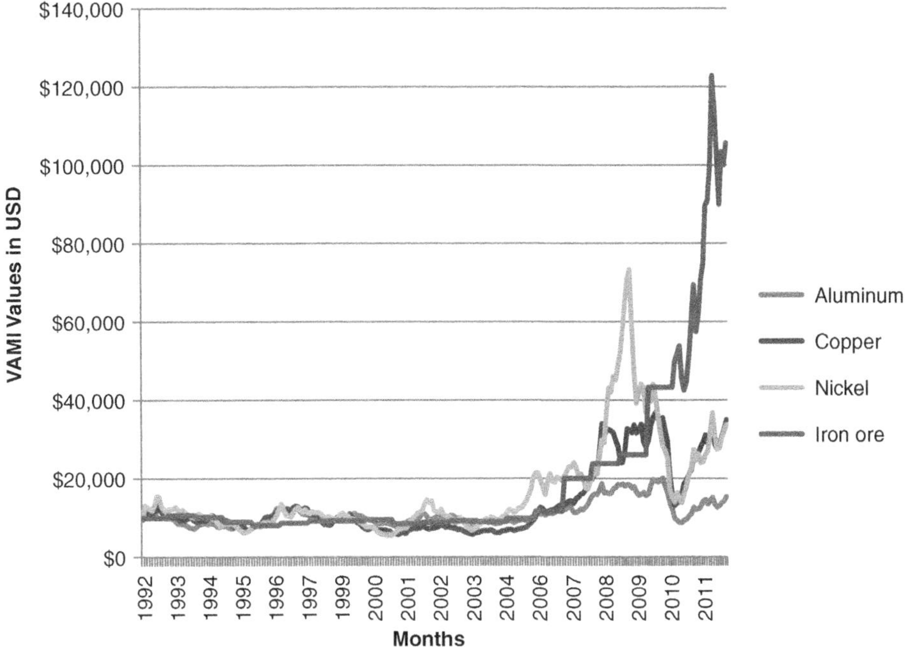

Exhibit 19.3 Cumulative VAMI Chart of IMF Metals Index Components, February 1992 to December 2012

The chart shows that iron ore was the single biggest contributor to the rising metals index between 1992 and 2012.

Source: Thomson Reuters.

As Exhibit 19.3 shows for the metals complex, iron ore imported by China has seen explosive growth, and, relatively speaking, nickel and copper have also done well.

Exhibit 19.4 provides some of the agricultural index components, chosen primarily because of the strength of their price performance over the past 20 plus years.

Commodity futures traders must roll their futures positions into new contracts every month as the old contracts expire. If the commodity futures contracts are more expensive than spot prices, this creates a situation known as *contango*. In this case, the commodity fund's performance is likely to produce negative returns because the rollover replaces expiring contracts with higher-priced contracts. When spot commodity prices are more expensive than futures prices, this is known as *backwardation*. Steep backwardation often indicates the marketplace's perception that an immediate shortage of a particular commodity is at hand.

Roll yield covers both contango and backwardation. Backwardation can add returns to an investor's position, while contango can reduce them. To state this relationship another way, a long-only position in commodity futures is not always expected to provide an excess return above the risk-free rate as is the case with

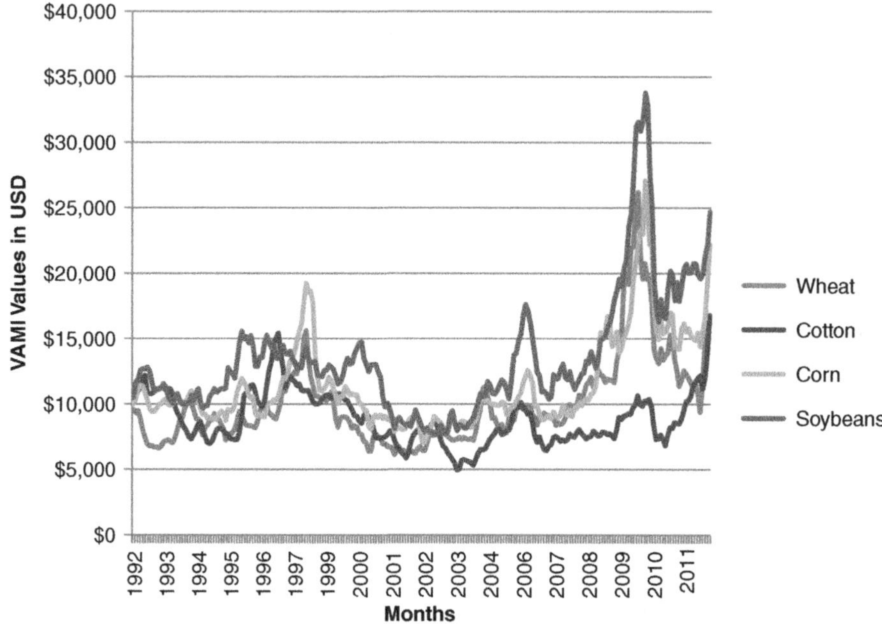

Exhibit 19.4 Cumulative VAMI Chart of Select Agricultural Products, February 1992 to December 2012

The exhibit shows the price performance of some main agricultural index components.
Source: Thomson Reuters.

stocks and bonds. The market always tries to price stocks and bonds such that their expected returns are above that of a cash return. Because the futures market can be considered an insurance market where hedgers and speculators trade risks, no expectation of positive returns exists in the aggregate; that is, someone's gain is exactly offset by someone else's loss, minus frictional costs. Hedgers pay an insurance premium to speculators. They willingly bear a negative expected return in order to shed themselves of risk.

According to Keynes' (2010) theory of normal backwardation, producers are the natural hedgers. They compensate the insurers (the speculators) with a positive roll yield—the profit from rolling over a longer-dated futures contract to a shorter-dated one. This occurs when more distant futures trade at a lower price than the spot price, a condition known as backwardation. In this framework a static long-only futures position should be compensated with positive expected returns.

However, historical data are not very supportive of this story. The average roll yield for the commodities futures in the Thomson Reuters/Jefferies CRB Index from January 1983 to the end of January 2012 was negative. In other words, contango, which is the opposite of backwardation, was the greater force. Something else is happening here.

A different approach accounts for the fact that sometimes long-only futures exposure becomes a negative-return proposition. Two possible complementary approaches are the *hedging pressure hypothesis* and the *theory of storage* (Fabozzi,

2008). The hedging pressure hypothesis is more general than Keynes' theory of normal backwardation. It holds that when producers demand to hedge more, the futures term structure goes into backwardation, rewarding long positions. When consumers demand more hedging, the term structure goes into contango, rewarding short positions. The theory of storage holds that backwardation and contango can be explained largely by physical inventory levels: when inventory is low, markets experience backwardation; when it is high, markets experience contango.

Both theories hold that the rewards for bearing risk accrue to the side, be it long or short, that offers some kind of insurance. In other words, long-only positions will not always possess positive expected returns. A static long-only commodity allocation over the course of a full market cycle will switch between insurance provision (positive expected returns) and insurance consumption (negative expected returns). A static long-only investor is partly betting that the long side of the market will remain mostly in insurance-provision mode over the course of his investment.

Exhibits 19.5 and 19.6 show historical roll yields and should give investors and traders some pause. The source of the graph and table is Hannam and Lejonvarn (2009), who state:

> ... the roll return has an episodic return history, reflecting the changes in the forward curve from the existence of a premium (or backwardation) and the nonexistence of a premium (or contango). This fact combined with the relative short history of the roll return make forecasting its future value difficult.

Clearly, roll yields can markedly reduce the profit of a position or possibly add to it. Various spread methods exist to minimize the impact of roll costs, but these strategies should be limited to professional futures traders because good execution could add to the risk for an inexperienced trader.

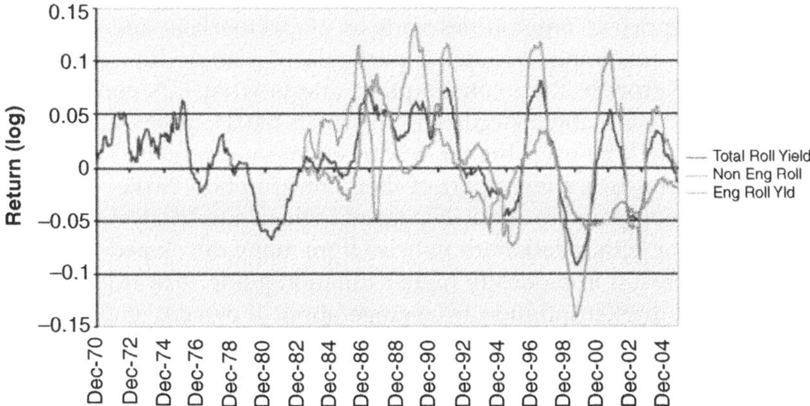

Exhibit 19.5 Historical Roll Yields

The exhibit shows the 12-month moving average of the roll yield for the Total Return GSCI Index from 1970 through 2004 as well as the associated Energy and Non-energy Indices.

Source: Hannam and Lejonvarn (2009).

Exhibit 19.6 Roll Return Estimates

	Annual Return (%)	Method
Total history	1.81	Arithmetic average
Last 3 cycles	0.95	7/88–2/03
Last 4 cycles	2.51	2/84–2/03
Last 5 cycles	0.79	1/84–2/03
Total history	1.02	Exponential smoothing HL = 15 years
Energy history	4.70	Arithmetic average

The exhibit presents various selected empirical values for the roll return. The values are considered real returns because the cash collateral and spot return provide nominal return for the capital invested—equivalent approximately to the rate of inflation, leaving the roll return to represent the real return above inflation.
Source: Hannam and Lejonvarn (2009).

THE OUTLOOK FOR COMMODITY PERFORMANCE

While forecasting any security price is difficult, doing so for commodities is especially complex. This section focuses on expected long-term fundamentals. The forecasts made are aligned with commodities' expected supply and demand.

According to Worah (2011), commodity prices are likely to rise, given the expected global supply and demand imbalances. He notes that commodity prices are volatile and differentiation will occur among commodities. Worah writes that much of the volatility and differentiation among commodities is related to the dynamics in and between developed and emerging economies.

As Exhibit 19.1 shows, the decade of the 1990s was a period of commodity price moderation, when emerging markets (where goods and services could be had at cheaper and cheaper prices) were exporters of disinflation to developed markets. That situation is turning around in various ways, primarily through higher commodity prices. Commodities trade on global markets, and to the extent emerging markets are going through a particularly commodity- and energy-intensive phase of growth, their consumption affects what U.S. consumers, for example, pay at the gas station. According to Worah (2011), inflationary pressure from commodities will be even higher within emerging markets. The reason is that commodities are such a large part of their consumption basket (e.g., nearly 60 percent in India compared to about 25 percent in the United States). Rising commodity prices, along with reflationary policies from many developed-market central banks, should result in modestly higher inflation going forward. The author expects developed-market inflation to average about 3 percent and developing market inflation to average about 5 percent until 2014–2015.

Over the long-run, commodities have given investors a positive real rate of return. The main risk to investors and traders in terms of their expectations of a continuing real rate of return on commodities would be in not understanding that commodities are a volatile asset class. Prices will not go up in a straight line; some periods will have negative returns. Although the IMF Commodities Group (2012) notes that in the short-term commodity prices in general will decline, this does not mean that a basic investment in commodities will not potentially provide a hedge against inflation.

Worah (2011) writes that the commodities with the best opportunities for gain have two characteristics in common: (1) they are geared to global growth and (2) supply constraints exist. Two commodities best fit this bill: crude oil and copper. Both are strongly connected to global growth and emerging-market growth in particular. Both also have substantial supply constraints. Hence, if demand growth continues at the same pace for the next couple of years, substantial supply shortfalls could occur. For example, ore grades in copper are declining, and much of the new production is coming from potentially unstable regions such as central Africa. The issues with oil supply are well known: declining non-OPEC supply, geopolitical uncertainties in most OPEC countries, and increased costs of unconventional sources such as oil sands and deep-sea drilling.

Finally, some commodities are benefitting from the increasing leverage in the financial system and the ongoing presence of low real interest rates. In Worah's (2011) view, avoiding commodities that depend on low real rates and increasing leverage rather than increasing global growth are probably wise. Gold is an example of this relationship.

SUMMARY AND CONCLUSIONS

This chapter presents a brief history of commodities, how they can be traded, their historical performance, and their expected outlook in terms of price. Commodity trading goes back thousands of years, although modern commodity trading is approximately 150 years old. Commodity futures are the most common vehicles used to trade and invest in commodities, but ETFs, which tend to be bundled futures contracts, are starting to be competitors to futures trading. The chapter reviews CTA strategies (directional and market-neutral trading) and provides hints about what to look for and what to review when choosing a CTA. It also presents physical commodity histories, showing the strong growth of commodity prices in the last 10 years or so. Finally, the chapter discusses the future direction of commodity prices with an examination of long-term supply and demand pressures.

In closing, McCafferty and Wassendorf (1992) note that investing in commodities is one area where an individual with limited capital can make great profits in a relatively short period. However, patience and education are needed to be a successful investor in the commodity futures market.

DISCUSSION QUESTIONS

1. Discuss the use of leverage and its tradeoffs in commodities trading.
2. What information should investors obtain before hiring a CTA? In particular, why is obtaining the CTA's disclosure document so important?
3. Describe the cost-of-carry model.
4. Explain the hedging pressure hypothesis and the theory of storage.
5. Discuss the use of margin in futures trading.

REFERENCES

Fabozzi, Frank J. 2002. *The Handbook of Financial Instruments*. Hoboken, NJ: John Wiley & Sons, Inc.

Fabozzi, Frank J. 2008. *Handbook of Commodity Investing*. Hoboken, NJ: John Wiley & Sons, Inc.

Ferri, Rick A. 2009. *The ETF Book, All You Need to Know about ETFs*. Hoboken, NJ: John Wiley & Sons, Inc.

Ferris, William G. 1988. *The Grain Traders, The Story of the Chicago Board of Trade*. East Lansing, MI: Michigan State University Press.

Hannam, Mark, and Jason Lejonvarn. 2009. "The Commodity Risk Premium." Available at www.markhannam.com/essays/essay2a.htm.

Keynes, John Maynard. 2010. *General Theory of Employment, Interest and Money*. Kila, MT: Kessinger Publishing.

Lintner, John. 1983. "The Potential Role of Managed Commodity-Futures Accounts (and or Funds) in Portfolios of Stocks and Bonds." *Annual Conference of the Financial Analyst Federation, Philadelphia, Pennsylvania*.

Maeda, Martha. 2009. *The Complete Guide to Exchange Traded Funds, How to Earn High Rates of Return*. Ocola, FL: Atlantic Publishing Group Inc.

McCafferty, Thomas A., and Russell R. Wasendorf. 1992. *All About Futures: From the Inside Out*. Chicago, IL: Probus Publishing Co.

Peters, Carl C., and Ben Warwick. 1997. *The Handbook of Managed Futures: Performance, Evaluation and Analysis*. New York: McGraw Hill.

Worah, Mihir P. 2011. PIMCO. "Economic Outlook: Higher Commodity Prices and the End of Economic Growth Without Inflation." June. Available at www.pimco.com/EN/Insights/Pages/Higher-Commodity-Prices-and-the-End-of-Economic-Growth-Without-Inflation.aspx.

ABOUT THE AUTHOR

Andrew Clark is Manager of Alternative Investments Research at Lipper. His most recent articles have appeared in *Journal of Indexes*, *Journal of Index Investing*, *Journal of Investing*, *European Physical Journal B*, *Physica A*, and *Quantitative Finance*. He was a plenary speaker at CFE 2010, at the SIAM Conference on Control and Application 2011, and at the World Congress on Engineering and Computer Science 2011, as well as a speaker at Operations Research 2011. He has written book chapters on mathematical and financial topics, most recently on robust optimization, which appeared in *The Handbook of Portfolio Construction*. His recent work on evolutionary algorithms has recently appeared as a book chapter in Springer's LNCS series.

CHAPTER 20

Commodity Futures and Strategic Asset Allocation

YONGYANG SU
Adjunct Lecturer in Economics, Suffolk University

MARCO C. K. LAU
Senior Lecturer of Economics, Newcastle Business School, Northumbria University

FRANKIE CHAU
Lecturer of Finance, Durham Business School, Durham University

INTRODUCTION

The question of whether commodity investment is a distinct asset class has attracted great interest from economists since the 1970s. For example, Greer (1978) shows that a commodity futures contract is a unique and conservative asset, which is as liquid but less risky than common stocks and can be used to hedge inflation risk. Bodie and Rosansky (1980) find that portfolios of commodity futures have similar risk-return characteristics to the S&P 500 Index. During the past century, however, the typical view of strategic asset allocation was to consider allocations based only on three traditional asset classes: stocks, bonds, and cash. Commodities received little attention from investors. To improve the risk-return characteristics of a strategic asset portfolio, institutional investors started to expand the investable asset universe beyond the traditional asset classes, and commodities have, in particular, gained greater prominence in recent years. The World Bank (2012, p. 70) estimates that "Investment fund activity in commodities is currently at 330 US$ billion (as of 2012:Q1)...9 times higher than a decade ago, when this activity started becoming a popular investment vehicle within the financial community."

Despite the growing popularity of commodity investments, little research exists on the potential benefits of including commodities in a portfolio consisting of traditional asset classes in a multiperiod portfolio choice setting. In particular, few studies exist on the subject of dynamic strategic asset allocation across the nontraditional commodities and traditional asset classes. The majority of previous studies investigate the benefits of investing in commodities under a static-asset allocation setting. For instance, Daskalaki and Skiadopoulos (2011) examine the benefits of commodities in portfolio allocation using the mean-variance and non-mean-variance spanning tests. Within an in-sample setting, their results show that commodities are only beneficial to non-mean-variance investors.

You and Daigler (2009) compare the out-of-sample performance of two traditional portfolios with and without including commodities. They find that incorporating commodities into the traditional asset menu may not be optimal for the non-mean-variance investors. However, a few papers try to show that commodities could be an attractive asset class for diversification of traditional portfolios consisting of stocks and bonds. For example, Gorton and Rouwenhorst (2006) create an equally weighted paper portfolio of commodity futures and find that commodity futures returns are negatively correlated with equity and bond returns. However, they study the simple properties of commodity futures as an asset class rather than investigating strategic asset allocation and portfolio choice directly. Jensen, Johnson, and Mercer (2000) perform a similar analysis and find that including commodities in a traditional asset universe improves the risk-return characteristic of efficient portfolios over the period 1973 to 1997. Idzorek (2006) addresses the same issue by investigating the role of commodities within a static, single-period asset allocation setting and reaches similar conclusions.

Estimating the demand for an alternative asset class such as commodities in a multiperiod setting is complicated by the fact that exact analytical solutions are generally unavailable. Finding a closed-form solution is, therefore, essential for discerning the demands for various asset classes. One representative stream of research uses discrete-state approximations to estimate the solutions to multiperiod portfolio choice problems in the Merton (1969) model (e.g., Brennan, Schwartz, and Lagnado, 1997; Barberis, 2000; Lynch, 2001; Lynch and Tan, 2010). The other stream of research uses an analytical approach to solve for multiperiod portfolio choice problems by assuming that long-lived investors have various forms of utility functions (e.g., Campbell and Viceira, 1999, 2001, 2002; Schroder and Skiadas, 1999). Research by Campbell, Chan, and Viceira (2003) combines the analytical method of Campbell and Viceira with a simple numerical method called *vector autoregression* (VAR).

VAR has two important advantages compared to previous methods: (1) VAR can accommodate multiperiod portfolio choice problems with a large number of asset classes and (2) it can decompose intertemporal hedging demands into components associated with individual asset classes. Campbell et al. (2003) use this approach to analyze optimal dynamic asset allocation across U.S. Treasury bills, stocks, and bonds and find significant intertemporal hedging demands for U.S. stocks. Rapach and Wohar (2009) extend their analysis to the G7 countries by allowing domestic investors to access foreign equity markets.

In light of the previously mentioned literature, this chapter takes advantage of the Campbell et al. (2003) approach examining the importance of a commodity asset class in the strategic asset allocation decision. More specifically, the purpose of this chapter is to determine whether commodities should be included in an investors' portfolio under a multiperiod setting. According to the findings of the extant literature, commodity investments and their associated futures markets are particularly effective in providing diversification benefits (i.e., reducing risk for any given level of expected return) for both stock and bond portfolios. Many observers also view the commodity market as an attractive asset class to diversify traditional portfolios of stocks and bonds. For these reasons, obtaining quantitative estimates of the percentage of portfolio allocation across commodities, stocks, and bonds should be useful and important to investors and market practitioners alike.

The chapter has three main objectives: (1) to estimate the demand for and the value of including commodities in a portfolio that consists of traditional asset classes, (2) to gain insights into the reasons commodities are gaining popularity in investors' strategic asset allocation process, and (3) to assess the benefits of commodities by comparing the mean-variance utility functions with and without commodities as an asset class.

Compared to the related literature, the implementation and empirical results of this chapter are atypical in several aspects. First, the results are unique in showing that apart from the mean total demand and hedging demand for stocks, the mean total and hedging demands for commodities are also large in magnitude for U.S. investors. The demands are stable in magnitude, even when investors can gain access to international stocks. Another striking result is that the mean intertemporal hedging demand for commodities is always statistically significant based on a 90 percent confidence interval, despite a magnitude that is generally smaller than those for domestic stocks. Finally, a large and significant mean myopic demand for foreign stocks exists whenever U.S. investors have access to the international stock market. This finding could be attributed to the better risk-return profile of the international stock market compared with the United States.

The remainder of this chapter is organized as follows. The next section describes the research approach and the modeling framework of Campbell et al. (2003). The following two sections present the main findings and discuss the sources of the importance of commodities. Next, an investigation of the utility benefits of including commodities as an asset class follows. The final section summarizes and concludes the chapter.

MODELING FRAMEWORK

The modeling framework in this chapter assumes that the investor in a multi-period asset allocation setting can allocate after-consumption wealth among one benchmark asset and n additional risky asset classes. The expanded investment set includes stocks, bonds, Treasury bills, and commodities. To facilitate the discussion and comparison to the previous literature on asset allocation with commodities, this section summarizes the basic setup of the model using the same notations as Campbell et al. (2003). Defining the real return on a benchmark asset as $R_{1,t+1}$, the investor's real portfolio return, $R_{p,t+1}$, is shown in Equation 20.1:

$$R_{p,t+1} = R_{1,t+1} + \sum_{i=2}^{n} \alpha_{i,t}(R_{i,t+1} - R_{1,t+1}) \tag{20.1}$$

where n is the number of risky asset classes available for investment; $\alpha_{i,t}$ is the portfolio weight on the ith risky asset class; and the benchmark asset is a 3-month

Treasury bill. Equation 20.2 defines the vector of log excess returns for the n risky assets, x_{t+1}, in the following manner:

$$x_{t+1} = \begin{bmatrix} r_{2,t+1} - r_{1,t+1} \\ r_{3,t+1} - r_{1,t+1} \\ r_{4,t+1} - r_{1,t+1} \\ \vdots \\ r_{n,t+1} - r_{1,t+1} \end{bmatrix} \tag{20.2}$$

where $r_{i,t+1} = \log(R_{i,t+1})$ for $i = 1, 2, \ldots, n$. Besides the n risky asset returns, the system includes $k = 3$ instrumental variables (i.e., the nominal Treasury bill yield, log dividend yield, and yield spread). These variables are instrumental as they serve as a proxy for time variation in the distribution of stock and bond returns and are included in the vector s_{t+1}. Equation 20.3 illustrates the whole system of variables that stacked into an $m \times 1$ vector, z_{t+1}:

$$z_{t+1} = \begin{bmatrix} r_{t+1} \\ x_{t+1} \\ s_{t+1} \end{bmatrix} \tag{20.3}$$

where m represents the dimensionality of a single column vector; $r_{1,t+1}$ is the log return for the benchmark asset; x_{t+1} contains the log excess returns for the risky asset classes; and s_{t+1} contains instrumental variables. Campbell et al. (2003) assume that z_{t+1} can be captured in Equation 20.4 by an $m \times 1$ first-order vector autoregressive (VAR) system:

$$z_{t+1} = \Phi_0 + \Phi_{1z_t} + v_{t+1} \tag{20.4}$$

where v_{t+1} is the unexpected shocks to the state variables and is assumed to be homoskedastic and independently distributed with a variance-covariance matrix Σ_v in Equation 20.5:

$$\sum_v = \begin{bmatrix} \sigma_1^2 & \sigma_{1x}' & \sigma_{1s}' \\ \sigma_{1x} & \Sigma_{xx} & \Sigma_{sx} \\ \sigma_{1s} & \Sigma_{xs} & \Sigma_{ss} \end{bmatrix} \tag{20.5}$$

Following Campbell et al. (2003), another assumption is that the investor has a recursive Epstein-Zin utility function that allows each dimension of the investor's preference to be parameterized separately, as in Equation 20.6:

$$U(C_t, E_t(U_{t+1})) = [(1-\delta)C_t^{(1-\gamma)/\theta} + \delta\left(E_t\left(U_{t+1}^{1-\gamma}\right)\right)^{1/\theta}]^{\theta/(1-\gamma)} \tag{20.6}$$

where C_t is the investor's consumption at time t; δ is the time-discount factor; γ is the coefficient of constant relative risk aversion; $\theta = (1-\gamma)/(1-\psi^{-1})$; $\psi > 0$ is the elasticity of intertemporal substitution; and $E_t(.)$ is the expectation operator. The

Epstein-Zin utility function has appealing features for structural modeling frameworks, without compromising the ability of standard models to achieve satisfactory macroeconomic data coherence.

At time t, the investor makes optimal consumption and portfolio decisions by maximizing the Epstein-Zin utility function, subject to the intertemporal budget constraint in Equation 20.7:

$$W_{t+1} = (W_t - C_t)R_{p,t+1} \tag{20.7}$$

where W_t is wealth at time t.

The optimal portfolio and consumption rules are shown in Equations 20.8a and 20.8b:

$$\alpha_t = A_0 + A_1 Z_t \tag{20.8a}$$

$$c_t - \omega_t = b_0 + B_1^{'} Z_t + Z_t^{'} B_2 Z_t \tag{20.8b}$$

where A_0, A_1, b_0, $B_1^{'}$, B_2 are scalar coefficient matrices to be solved. Following Merton (1969), Campbell et al. (2003) solve the portfolio rule and partition the total demand for the assets into myopic and intertemporal hedging demand, as shown in Equations 20.9 and 20.10:

$$A_0 = (1/\gamma)\sum_{xx}^{-1}[H_x\Phi_0 + 0.5\sigma_x^2 + (1-\gamma)\sigma_{1x}] + [1-(1/\gamma)]\sum_{xx}^{-1} - \Lambda_0/(1-\psi)] \tag{20.9}$$

$$A_1 = (1/\gamma)\sum_{xx}^{-1} H_x\Phi_1 + [1-(1/\gamma)]\sum_{xx}^{-1} - \Lambda_1/(1-\psi)] \tag{20.10}$$

where H_x is a selection matrix that selects x_t from z_t. Λ_0 and Λ_1 are coefficient matrices. The first component on the right-hand side of Equations 20.9 and 20.10 represents the myopic demand for assets; the second component on the right-hand side of the two equations represents the intertemporal hedging demand for assets. Then, by solving for the optimal consumption-wealth ratio, Equation 20.11 expresses the value function – the maximized utility function:

$$V_t = exp\left\{-\frac{\psi}{1-\psi}\log(1-\delta) + \frac{b_0}{1-\psi} + \frac{B_1^{'}}{1-\psi}Z_t + Z_t^{'}\frac{B_2}{1-\psi}Z_t\right\} \tag{20.11}$$

The unconditional mean of the value function $E(V_t)$ can be driven and is later used to calculate the utility of long-term investors under combinations of various asset classes.

DATA AND EMPIRICAL RESULTS

Having explained the basic setup of the model, this section presents the data and empirical results for a case where commodities and traditional assets are both available.

Proxies for Commodities

Unlike financial assets such as stocks and bonds, no well-accepted methods are available to measure the direct exposure to commodities. Idzorek (2006) points out that the previous literature on asset allocation with commodities uses three different ways to approximate the exposure to commodities: (1) direct physical investment, (2) a weighted index of commodity-related stocks, and (3) commodity futures. However, a direct physical investment in commodities is not a good measurement of commodity exposure because some commodities are difficult to keep (store) for longer time horizons. The weighted index of commodity-related stocks represents more of the traditional equity, instead of the commodity itself, because it has high positive correlations with other equities. Commodity future contracts, though imperfect, provide better exposure to commodities through their direct connections with spot and expected future spot prices and their relationship with unexpected inflation shocks. This chapter uses the Reuters/Jefferies Commodity Research Bureau (CRB) Index, which is a portfolio of commodity futures contracts, as a proxy for the investor's exposure to commodity markets. Further details on the CRB Index are available on the website of the Commodity Research Bureau (crbtrader.com/crbindex/).

Data Description

The calibration results are based on monthly data for the U.S. market over the period 1956 to 2004. The real return on Treasury bills is defined as the log return on a 3-month Treasury bill minus the log difference of the Consumer Price Index. The log excess stock return is the log return on the S&P 500 Index minus the log return on 3-month Treasury bills. The log excess bond return is the log return on the 10-year government bonds minus the log return on 3-month Treasury bills. The nominal yield on Treasury bills is the log yield on a 3-month Treasury bill and the term spread is the difference between the yields on a 10-year government bond and 3-month Treasury bill. Log excess commodity return is defined as the log difference of the CRB Index and 3-month Treasury bills.

Exhibit 20.1 reports the summary statistics (i.e., mean, standard deviation, and skewness) for Treasury bill, bond, stock, and commodity returns as well as the three instruments. The entries for mean and standard deviations are expressed in percent. The last column also reports the Sharpe ratios for the bond, stock, and commodity returns. As expected, Treasury bills have both low return and low volatility. The mean excess returns for stocks, bonds, and commodities and their standards deviations are 4.62 percent and 14.74 percent, 1.17 percent and 5.87 percent, and 1.98 percent and 10.39 percent, respectively. Both the mean returns and volatility for the stock and commodity returns are higher than for the bond returns. The Sharpe ratios for stocks, bonds, and commodities are 0.31, 0.19, and 0.20, respectively, with stocks having the highest Sharpe ratio. Although the commodity returns have higher volatility than bonds, its Sharpe ratio is almost the same as for bonds.

Exhibit 20.1 Summary Statistics of Asset Returns

Variables	Mean	Standard Deviation	Skewness	Sharpe Ratio
rtb_t	1.391	0.989	−0.185	
xr_t	4.624	14.739	−0.615	0.314
xb_t	1.170	5.873	0.067	0.199
xc_t	1.973	10.394	0.493	0.190
y_t	−0.018	1.072	−0.175	
div_t	1.125	0.385	−0.020	
spr_t	1.424	1.206	−0.870	
xfr_t	7.390	16.921	−0.399	0.437

This exhibit presents the summary statistics for the real Treasury bill return (rtb_t), excess domestic stock return (xr_t), excess bond return (xb_t), excess commodity return (xc_t), nominal Treasury bill yield (y_t), log dividend yield (div_t), yield spread (spr_t), and excess foreign stock return (xfr_t) between October 1956 and May 2004 in the U.S. markets. The last column reports the Sharpe ratios.

VAR Estimation

Exhibit 20.2 reports the estimation results for the VAR system. The top panel of the exhibit reports coefficients estimates and the R^2 statistics (with the p-value in the parentheses) for each equation in the VAR system. The bottom panel presents the cross-correlation matrix of the innovations. The first row corresponds to the real Treasury bill return. The lagged real Treasury bill returns and commodity returns have significant positive and negative coefficients, respectively. The second row corresponds to the equation for the excess stock return. None of the variables is statistically significant. This finding confirms the difficulty of predicting stock returns. The third row corresponds to the equation for the excess bond return. The coefficients for the lagged bond return, excess stock return, commodity return, and yield spread are all significant. The fourth row reports the results for the equation of commodity. None of the coefficients is statistically significant, which indicates that the correlations between commodities and other risky assets are low. This finding implies commodities could be an important component of portfolio choice as a means of reducing the covariance risk.

The bottom section reports the covariance structure of the innovations in the VAR system. The unexpected log excess stock returns have a low correlation with commodity returns, but are statistically significant and negatively correlated with shocks to the log dividend yield, which is consistent with previous empirical evidence (Campbell, 1991; Stambaugh, 1999). The unexpected log excess bond returns are negatively correlated with shocks to the nominal Treasury bill rate, log dividend yield, and commodity returns, but positively correlated with the log excess stock return. Altogether, the correlations between commodity and stock and bond returns suggest that commodities could play an important role in the strategic asset allocation process. The following sections further explore their implications for optimal portfolio choice in a multiperiod setting.

Exhibit 20.2 VAR Estimation Results

Dependent Variables	rtb_{t-1}	xr_{t-1}	xb_{t-1}	xc_{t-1}	y_{t-1}	div_{t-1}	spr_{t-1}	R^2
Panel A. VAR estimation results								
rtb_t	0.379	0.003	0.005	−0.017	0.000	0.000	0.000	0.196
	(7.974)	(1.213)	(0.703)	(−3.342)	(−0.456)	(0.356)	(0.856)	(0.000)
xr_t	0.900	−0.001	0.212	−0.085	−0.004	0.007	0.002	0.043
	(1.458)	(−0.022)	(1.700)	(−1.272)	(−1.693)	(1.276)	(0.816)	(0.001)
xb_t	0.656	−0.063	0.152	−0.070	0.001	0.000	0.002	0.083
	(2.283)	(−3.303)	(2.414)	(−2.153)	(0.974)	(0.106)	(2.825)	(0.000)
xc_t	−0.738	−0.035	−0.039	0.004	0.007	−0.002	0.002	0.013
	(−1.468)	(−1.108)	(−0.371)	(0.068)	(0.378)	(−0.626)	(1.203)	(0.001)
y_t	−9.629	1.481	−5.991	3.857	0.873	−0.016	0.038	0.802
	(−1.020)	(2.587)	(−2.490)	(3.726)	(27.028)	(−0.253)	(1.998)	(0.000)
div_t	−1.038	0.017	−0.231	0.081	0.005	0.994	−0.001	0.987
	(−1.634)	(0.292)	(−1.827)	(1.208)	(2.017)	(175.941)	(−0.408)	(0.000)
spr_t	−2.520	−0.228	2.623	−2.658	−0.006	0.000	0.938	0.889
	(−0.329)	(−0.479)	(1.414)	(−3.420)	(−0.220)	(0.007)	(51.876)	(0.000)

Panel B. Cross-correlation of residuals

	rtb	xr	xb	xc	y	div	spr
rtb	1.000	0.049	−0.035	−0.007	0.112	−0.074	−0.141
xr		1.000	0.138	0.050	−0.038	−0.968	−0.089
xb			1.000	−0.131	−0.652	−0.133	0.024
xc				1.000	0.067	−0.042	0.039
y					1.000	0.027	−0.735
div						1.000	0.100
spr							1.000

Panel A presents the estimation results for a VAR system consisting of the real Treasury bill return (rtb_t), excess domestic stock return (xr_t), excess bond return (xb_t), excess commodity return (xc_t), nominal Treasury bill yield (y_t), log dividend yield (div_t), and yield spread (spr_t). Panel B reports the cross-correlations of residuals.

Demands for Domestic Assets

Exhibit 20.3 reports the mean total, myopic, and intertemporal hedging demands (in percent) for domestic bills, stocks, bonds, and commodities for U.S. investors. The intertemporal elasticity of substitution is $\psi = 1$. The entries in each column are mean asset demands when the coefficient of relative risk aversion, γ, is equal to 4, 7, and 10, respectively. These values represent various levels of risk aversion, with higher values of γ indicating higher levels of risk aversion. Both the total mean demands and the mean myopic demands across the four assets sum to 100, while the mean hedging demands sum to 0. Comparing values within each column enables analyzing how the portfolio is allocated across the four risky assets and how much is the mean total demand, myopic demand, and hedging demand for each of the asset classes. By comparing values within each row, one can examine the incremental effects of relative risk aversion, γ, on asset allocation. The numbers

Exhibit 20.3 Mean Demands for Domestic Asset Classes

CRRA		$\gamma = 4$	$\gamma = 7$	$\gamma = 10$
Stocks	Total demand	**120.889**	**84.224**	**65.284**
		[29.43, 196.24]	[22.74, 153.33]	[10.36, 121.10]
	Myopic demand	**60.339**	**34.333**	**23.930**
		[12.26, 72.41]	[6.30, 40.63]	[4.32, 28.33]
	Hedging demand	60.549	49.891	41.354
		[11.64, 133.75]	[6.15, 112.37]	[8.54, 101.86]
Government bonds	Total demand	70.157	36.890	24.582
		[−70.33, 269.44]	[−39.77, 154.31]	[−29.11, 107.85]
	Myopic demand	98.847	56.787	39.964
		[−76.33, 251.84]	[−43.98, 143.71]	[−30.56, 100.74]
	Hedging demand	−28.690	−19.897	−15.381
		[−48.56, 29.84]	[−32.59, 20.69]	[−28.17, 13.00]
Commodities	Total demand	**80.678**	**49.080**	**35.827**
		[15.41, 159.16]	[9.63, 93.58]	[7.54, 67.27]
	Myopic demand	61.604	35.260	24.723
		[9.04, 140.30]	[5.20, 80.32]	[3.62, 56.33]
	Hedging demand	**19.074**	**13.820**	**11.104**
		[−0.19, 32.81]	[0.44, 22.77]	[1.60, 18.36]
Treasury bills	Total demand	−171.723	−70.194	−25.693
		[−404.42, 38.79]	[−226.65, 42.92]	[−146.17, 53.11]
	Myopic demand	−120.790	−26.380	11.383
		[−305.91, 77.90]	[−132.03, 86.99]	[−70.74, 82.40]
	Hedging demand	−50.933	−43.813	−37.077
		[−161.94, −1.32]	[−140.05, −9.98]	[−108.88, 0.41]

This exhibit reports mean monthly total, myopic, and hedging asset demands in percentage for stocks, 10-year government bonds, commodities, and 3-month Treasury bills (cash) for an investor with a unitary elasticity of intertemporal substitution ($\psi = 1$); a time-discount factor equal to $0.92^{1/12}$; and a coefficient of relative risk aversion (γ) equal to 4, 7, or 10. The numbers in brackets are bootstrapped at a 90 percent confidence interval. A bold entry indicates significance using a 90 percent confidence interval.

in brackets under each entry are the 90 percent confidence intervals for the mean asset demands.

Exhibit 20.3 shows that the total and myopic demand allocation is holding a long position on stocks, bonds, and commodities, while shorting bills. The mean total demand for stocks is about 1.7 and 1.5 times those for bonds and commodities, respectively. The significant mean total and myopic demand for stocks is consistent with the theory that higher demand exists for the asset with the largest Sharpe ratio. Positive mean hedging demands for stocks and commodities are also present. The mean hedging demand for commodities is statistically significant using a 90 percent confidence interval, although the mean hedging demand for stocks is larger in magnitude. Both the mean hedging demands for bonds and bills are negative, which is consistent with the findings in Rapach and Wohar (2009) and Campbell et al. (2003). As expected, by comparing each row, the mean total, myopic,

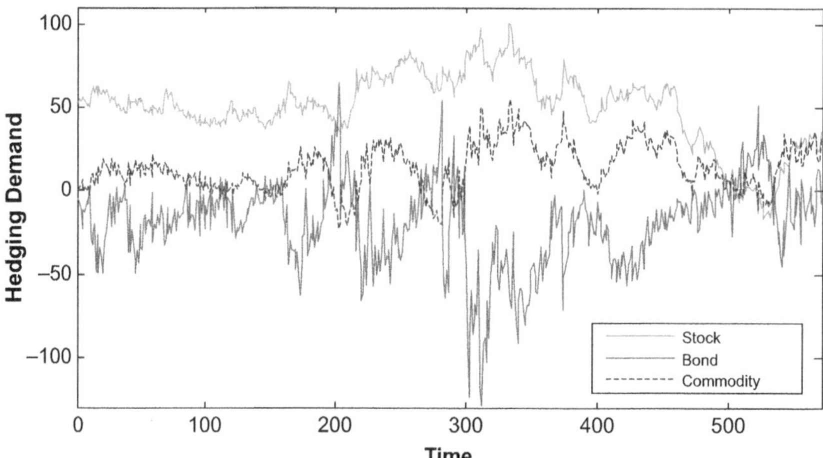

Exhibit 20.4 Historical Intertemporal Hedging Demands for Domestic Stocks, Bonds, and Commodities for U.S. Investors

This exhibit plots the estimated hedging demands for domestic stocks, bonds, and commodities for U.S. investors over the entire sample period.

and hedging demands for all the risky assets decrease as relative risk aversion, γ, increases.

The large mean demands for stocks can be explained by the negative correlation between innovations to log excess stock returns and the log dividend yield. Because the stock returns have large positive Sharpe ratios, investors usually take long positions in stocks. An increase in expected stock returns represents an improvement in the investment opportunity set, while a decrease in expected stock returns represents a worsening of the prospects of the investment set. The VAR estimation results suggest that the lagged dividend yield has a positive effect on the expected stock returns. Given the negative correlation between innovations to excess stock returns and dividend yield, the expectation is that a negative shock to excess stock return next period is accompanied by a positive shock to the dividend yield next period. In turn, a positive shock to the log dividend yield next period can lead to higher expected stock returns in the future. Thus, investors can use stocks to hedge against the negative shocks to futures returns.

Exhibit 20.4 plots the estimated hedging demands for domestic stocks, bonds, and commodities in order to show a more intuitive picture of the intertemporal hedging demands for each of the three asset class. Overall, the hedging demand for commodities appears to be the most stable compared with those for stocks and bonds. The hedging demand for commodities and stocks are well above the hedging demand for bonds over most of the sample period.

A theoretical work by Bhamra and Uppal (2006) suggests that the elasticity of intertemporal substitution, ψ, can affect the magnitude, but not the sign, of the intertemporal hedging demand for the risky asset. As an additional analysis, the mean demands for stocks, bonds, and commodities are computed by setting values of ψ equal to 0.3, 1.0, and 1.5, respectively. Exhibit 20.5 presents the results. The mean total and hedging demands for stocks increase largely as ψ increases

Exhibit 20.5 Mean Demands for Domestic Asset Classes, Assuming Different Values for the Elasticity of Intertemporal Substitution (ψ)

CRRA		$\psi = 0.3$	$\psi = 1.0$	$\psi = 1.5$
Stocks	Total demand	63.833	**84.224**	**108.646**
		[16.28, 152.46]	[22.74, 153.33]	[12.57, 148.42]
	Myopic demand	**34.333**	**34.333**	**34.333**
		[9.16, 42.94]	[6.30, 40.63]	[7.57, 40.84]
	Hedging demand	29.501	49.891	**74.313**
		[8.18, 122.59]	[6.15, 112.37]	[3.94, 115.96]
Government bonds	Total demand	32.525	36.890	42.651
		[−26.86, 160.95]	[−39.77, 154.31]	[−50.72, 138.94]
	Myopic demand	56.788	56.787	56.787
		[−28.19, 147.36]	[−43.98, 143.71]	[−28.73, 148.45]
	Hedging demand	−24.262	−19.897	−14.136
		[−32.29, 20.83]	[−32.59, 20.69]	[−33.56, 20.99]
Commodities	Total demand	**49.256**	**49.080**	**48.703**
		[13.04, 98.45]	[9.63, 93.58]	[0.72, 92.10]
	Myopic demand	35.260	35.260	35.260
		[6.11, 82.90]	[5.20, 80.32]	[2.52, 81.54]
	Hedging demand	**13.995**	**13.820**	**13.443**
		[2.17, 22.86]	[0.44, 22.77]	[0.46, 20.91]
Treasury bills	Total demand	−45.614	−70.194	−100.000
		[−224.27, 41.22]	[−226.65, 42.92]	[−224.86, 45.94]
	Myopic demand	−26.380	−26.380	−26.380
		[−135.99, 65.45]	[−132.03, 86.99]	[−128.46, 85.65]
	Hedging demand	−19.233	−43.813	**−73.620**
		[−131.28, 7.15]	[−140.05, −9.98]	[−133.74, 5.62]

This exhibit reports mean monthly total, myopic, and hedging asset demands in percentage for stocks, 10-year government bonds, commodities, and 3-month Treasury bills (cash) for an investor with an elasticity of intertemporal substitution ($\psi = 0.3, 1.0, 1.5$); a time-discount factor equal to $0.92^{1/12}$; and a coefficient of relative risk aversion (γ) equal to 4. The numbers in brackets are bootstrapped at a 90 percent confidence interval. A bold entry indicates significance using a 90 percent confidence interval.

and gradually becomes positive and statistically significant; that is, investors are becoming more willing to make a trade-off between contemporary and future consumption by taking more long positions in stocks. Both the mean total and hedging demand for commodities do not change very much, but are always positively significant as the value of ψ increases. The stable mean total and hedging demands for commodities over various ψ values provide support for the argument that commodities are an attractive asset class for multiperiod portfolio choice. The results are also consistent with Bhamra and Uppal's theoretical results that ψ only affects the magnitude, but not the sign, of the mean hedging demands for risky assets.

What Explains the Demand for Commodities?

What explains the striking and significant mean total and intertemporal hedging demand for commodities? One explanation might be based on modern portfolio

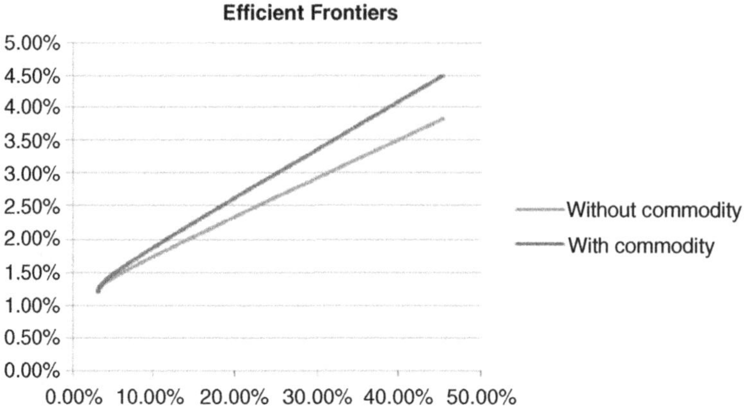

Exhibit 20.6 Efficient Frontiers with and without Commodities as an Asset Class
This exhibit plots the mean-variance efficient frontiers with and without including commodity as an asset class.

theory, which states the interaction of asset classes with each other provides diversification. The commodity future return has a negative correlation of −0.13 with the bond return and a very low positive correlation of 0.05 with the most risky asset, namely, stocks. These findings suggest commodities have the ability to help diversify stock and bond portfolios. Consequently, the large positive intertemporal hedging demand for stocks does not reduce the demand for commodities, which may explain why the positive demand for commodities is significant during the long horizons. The portfolios constructed based on the estimation results provide further evidence to support the explanation. In Exhibit 20.6, the portfolio with commodity futures is more efficient and has a higher ratio of return to risk than the portfolio without commodity futures.

The second tentative explanation involving the demand for commodities relates to the return distributions. Traditional asset returns are usually negatively skewed, while the distribution of commodity returns is positively skewed. The positive skewness of commodity returns together with lower volatility relative to stock returns implies that commodities have lower downward risk compared to equities. In this study, the skewness for monthly average excess stock returns and commodity returns are −0.62 percent and 0.49 percent, respectively, while the corresponding volatilities for each are 14.74 percent and 10.39 percent. If the tail events can happen simultaneously for the two asset classes, commodities as an independent asset class can provide diversification benefits to the portfolio allocation.

Another explanation comes from the correlation between commodity returns and inflation. This explanation is because the ultimate function of portfolios is for consumption. Thus, investors should consider the real purchasing power of their returns (i.e., the asset classes' ability of hedging against inflation). Traditional asset classes such as stocks and bonds are negatively correlated with inflation and are not good asset classes for hedging against inflation. However, commodities represented by commodity futures may be a better hedge against inflation for two reasons: (1) they have a positive correlation with inflation in the long run and (2) commodity prices are directly linked to unexpected inflation shocks, which is an important component of inflation. These explanations taken together may explain why commodities are a better asset class of hedging against inflation risk than stocks and bonds. In summary, the three tentative explanations together with the significant hedging demand for commodities found in this chapter suggest that commodities can be an attractive asset class to diversify a traditional portfolio of stocks and bonds.

CONTROLLING FOR INTERNATIONAL STOCK MARKETS

To check for the robustness and stableness of the estimated hedging demand for commodities, this study expands its analysis by allowing investors to access international equity markets in addition to domestic stocks, bonds, commodities, and Treasury bills. The MSCI World Equity Index excluding the United States is used as a proxy for the foreign stock market, which makes the calibration not too complicated. In this case, investors can make a strategic asset allocation across domestic Treasury bills, bonds, stocks, commodities, and foreign stocks. This study estimates the expanded VAR system and uses the Campbell et al. (2003) methods to approach the mean total, myopic, and hedging demands for each of the asset classes. The VAR estimation results are not reported but are available on request from the authors.

Exhibit 20.7 reports the mean total, myopic, and intertemporal hedging demands (in percent) for domestic stocks, bonds, commodities, Treasury bills, and foreign stocks for a U.S. investor. The results are computed by setting the intertemporal elasticity of substitution $\psi = 1$ and the coefficient of relative risk aversion, γ, equal to 4, 7, and 10, respectively. The demands for various asset classes decrease, as the relative risk aversion increases. The evidence shows that U.S. investors continue to have relative large mean total and intertemporal hedging demands for domestic stocks when they can invest in foreign equity markets, despite these demands being statistically significant using a 90 percent confidence interval. However, the mean myopic demand for domestic stock is essentially low compared to when investors can only allocate across domestic asset classes. The large magnitude in mean total and hedging demands for domestic stocks is consistent with the well-established theoretical and empirical finance literature that U.S. investors have a home bias (Cooper and Kaplanis, 1994; Coval and Moskowitz, 1999; Norman and Xu, 2003; Barron and Ni, 2008).

Although the results also show significant mean total and myopic demand for foreign stocks, the mean total demand is lower relative to the mean total demand for domestic stocks. This phenomenon can be intuitively explained based on some summary statistic characteristics of excess domestic and foreign stock returns. The standard deviations of domestic and foreign stock returns are almost equal, but the log excess foreign stock returns are almost twice that for domestic stock. Thus, the foreign stock returns have a higher Sharpe ratio than domestic stock returns. All else equal, investors should have higher myopic demands for assets with a

Exhibit 20.7 Mean Demands for Domestic and International Asset Classes

CRRA		$\gamma = 4$	$\gamma = 7$	$\gamma = 10$
Domestic stocks	Total demand	77.01	58.37	46.80
		[−52.30, 165.25]	[−33.47, 134.21]	[−22.24, 115.66]
	Myopic demand	8.60	4.69	3.12
		[−45.57, 57.00]	[−26.15, 33.60]	[−21.50, 19.67]
	Hedging demand	68.41	53.69	43.68
		[−17.88, 160.44]	[−13.13, 134.95]	[−6.44, 118.56]
Domestic bonds	Total demand	127.00	69.27	46.96
		[−17.01, 363.00]	[−14.35, 205.01]	[−12.26, 142.90]
	Myopic demand	141.02	81.08	57.10
		[−17.88, 337.15]	[−9.87, 193.28]	[−6.67, 135.73]
	Hedging demand	−14.02	−11.81	−10.14
		[−52.75, 65.19]	[−37.36, 42.45]	[−29.67, 29.65]
Commodities	Total demand	90.24	55.75	**40.99**
		[34.54, 185.67]	[24.52, 113.92]	[16.41, 79.62]
	Myopic demand	63.95	36.62	25.69
		[22.05, 162.01]	[12.79, 92.76]	[8.19, 64.09]
	Hedging demand	**26.29**	**19.13**	**15.29**
		[4.49, 48.52]	[4.82, 34.31]	[3.97, 25.94]
Domestic Treasury bills	Total demand	−262.15	−122.13	−61.86
		[−560.42, −25.35]	[−350.23, −5.78]	[−202.00, 52.93]
	Myopic demand	−179.07	−59.80	−12.09
		[−409.47, −17.48]	[−191.68, 32.76]	[−104.56, 52.86]
	Hedging demand	−83.07	−62.33	−49.77
		[−204.14, 35.68]	[−158.30, −19.19]	[−131.86, 11.81]
Foreign stocks	Total demand	**67.90**	**38.74**	**27.12**
		[−30.03, 115.64]	[−16.55, 67.67]	[−11.67, 47.47]
	Myopic demand	**65.50**	**37.41**	**26.18**
		[−28.58, 122.47]	[−16.24, 69.93]	[−11.31, 48.93]
	Hedging demand	2.39	1.33	0.94
		[−9.56, 18.13]	[−6.72, 12.32]	[−4.20, 10.15]

This exhibit reports mean monthly total, myopic, and hedging asset demands in percentage for stocks, 10-year government bonds, commodities, 3-month Treasury bills (cash), and foreign stocks for an investor with a unitary elasticity of intertemporal substitution ($\psi = 1$); a time-discount factor equal to $0.92^{1/12}$; and a coefficient of relative risk aversion (γ) equal to 4, 7, or 10. The numbers in brackets are bootstrapped to a 90 percent confidence interval. A bold entry indicates significance using a 90 percent confidence interval.

higher Sharpe ratio, which explains why the myopic demand for domestic stocks is lower for U.S. investors.

The most striking result in Exhibit 20.7 is the mean intertemporal hedging demands for commodities. The mean intertemporal hedging as well as the mean total and myopic demand for commodities are fairly stable compared to when investors only have access to domestic asset classes. Furthermore, the intertemporal demand for commodities is still significant, even after investors can access

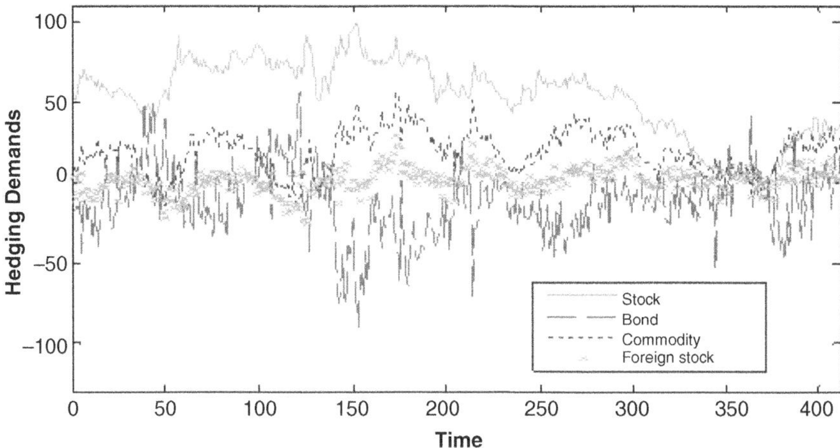

Exhibit 20.8 Historical Intertemporal Hedging Demands for Domestic Stocks, Bonds, Commodities, and Foreign Stocks for U.S. Investors

This exhibit plots the estimated hedging demands for domestic stocks, bonds, commodities, and foreign stocks for U.S. investors between October 1956 and May 2004.

foreign asset classes. This implies the intertemporal hedging demands for commodities are stable and confirm that commodities should be a conservative component in a strategic asset allocation.

Exhibit 20.8 plots the intertemporal hedging demands for domestic stocks, bonds, commodities, and foreign stocks. Overall, the hedging demand for commodities appears to be the most stable compared to those for both domestic and foreign stocks and bonds. Also, the hedging demand for commodities and domestic stocks are well above the hedging demand for bonds and foreign stocks over most of the sample period.

The mean demands for stocks, bonds, and commodities are computed once again by setting values of intertemporal substitution, ψ, equal to 0.3, 1.0, and 1.5, respectively. As Exhibit 20.9 shows, investors become willing to make more tradeoffs between contemporary and future consumption (i.e., the hedging demands for stocks increase substantially and gradually become positively significant, as the intertemporal substitution increases from 0.3 to 1.3). Similarly, when investors can only access domestic asset classes, the mean hedging demand for commodities changes very little and is always positively significant as the value of ψ increases. This evidence reconfirms that commodities are effective in portfolio diversification and are an attractive asset class within the strategic asset allocation process. In summary, U.S. investors have significant intertemporal hedging demands for commodities in addition to domestic stocks. This intertemporal hedging demand remains significant even when investors have opportunities to invest in other asset classes such as foreign stocks.

Overall, the results indicate that commodities are an important determinant in the strategic asset allocation process and multiperiod portfolio choice. A significant and relatively stable intertemporal hedging demand exists for commodities, as well as for domestic stocks for U.S.-based investors.

Exhibit 20.9 Mean Demands for Domestic and International Asset Classes Assuming Different Values for Elasticity of Intertemporal Substitution (ψ)

CRRA		$\psi = 0.3$	$\psi = 1.0$	$\psi = 1.5$
Domestic stocks	Total demand	28.03 [−29.82, 136.66]	58.37 [−33.47, 134.21]	**121.19** [−26.25, 140.56]
	Myopic demand	4.69 [−25.92, 27.65]	4.69 [−26.15, 33.60]	4.69 [−28.15, 33.83]
	Hedging demand	23.35 [−8.10, 135.21]	53.69 [−13.13, 134.95]	**116.51** [−20.32, 125.89]
Domestic bonds	Total demand	63.90 [−11.80, 202.45]	69.27 [−14.35, 205.01]	82.51 [−14.98, 196.10]
	Myopic demand	81.08 [−14.93, 192.35]	81.08 [−9.87, 193.28]	81.08 [0.86, 189.29]
	Hedging demand	−17.18 [−39.66. 39.37]	−11.81 [−37.36, 42.45]	1.44 [37.59, 37.94]
Commodities	Total demand	54.86 [16.98, 112.65]	55.75 [24.52, 113.92]	56.00 [19.77, 112.32]
	Myopic demand	36.62 [5.92, 91.74]	36.62 [12.79, 92.76]	36.62 [8.78, 91.76]
	Hedging demand	**18.24** [1.81, 30.46]	**19.13** [4.82, 34.31]	**19.38** [4.89, 32.74]
Domestic Treasury bills	Total demand	−86.69 [−305.45, 30.41]	−122.13 [−350.23, 5.78]	−196.40 [−293.89, 24.86]
	Myopic demand	−59.90 [−193.18, 41.07]	−59.80 [−191.68, 32.76]	−59.80 [−167.34, 45.80]
	Hedging demand	−26.89 [−175.51, 10.47]	−62.33 [−158.30, 19.19]	−136.61 [−163.24, 20.06]
Foreign stocks	Total demand	**39.90** [−16.95, 69.14]	**38.74** [−16.55, 67.67]	**36.70** [−20.97, 73.35]
	Myopic demand	**37.41** [−21.66, 65.02]	**37.41** [−16.24, 69.93]	**37.41** [−21.79, 74.26]
	Hedging demand	2.49 [−6.76, 12.32]	1.33 [−6.72, 12.32]	0.71 [−7.20, 12.88]

This exhibit reports mean monthly total, myopic, and hedging asset demands in percentage for stocks, 10-year government bonds, commodities, and 3-month Treasury bills (cash) for an investor with elasticity of intertemporal substitution ($\psi = 0.3, 1.0, 1.5$); a time discount factor equals $0.92^{1/12}$; and a coefficient of relative risk aversion (γ) equal to 4. The numbers in brackets are bootstrapped at a 90 percent confidence interval. A bold entry indicates significance using a 90 percent confidence interval.

THE UTILITY BENEFITS FROM INCLUDING COMMODITIES

This section further demonstrates the importance of including commodities in a traditional portfolio by comparing the utility of investors who have access to commodities with those who do not. Exhibit 20.10 reports the mean value function when values of γ are set to 4, 7, 10, and 20. Panel A compares the mean

Exhibit 20.10 Mean Value Function

γ	$E(V_t)$	
Panel A. Domestic assets only		
	Portfolio 1	Portfolio 2
	Bills, Bonds, and Domestic Stocks	Bills, Bonds, Domestic Stocks and Commodities
4	0.035	0.070
7	0.013	0.020
10	0.009	0.012
20	0.005	0.006
Panel B. Domestic and international assets		
	Portfolio 3	Portfolio 4
	Bills, Bonds, Domestic Stocks, and International Stocks	Bills, Bonds, Domestic Stocks, International Stocks, and Commodities
4	0.222	0.490
7	0.036	0.057
10	0.017	0.024
20	0.007	0.008

This exhibit reports the mean value function for investors with a unitary elasticity of intertemporal substitution ($\psi = 1$); a time-discount factor equal to $0.92^{1/12}$; and a coefficient of relative risk aversion (γ) equal to 4, 7, 10 or 20. Portfolio 1 is a benchmark portfolio (traditional portfolio) that allocates across domestic asset classes without including commodities. Portfolio 2 allocates across domestic classes including commodities. Portfolio 3 allocates across both domestic and international asset classes without including commodities. Portfolio 4 allocates across both domestic and international assets.

value function when two investors can only allocate across domestic asset classes. Panel B compares the mean value function when two investors can allocate across domestic as well as international asset classes. The value function is normalized so that a doubling from one portfolio to another implies that an investor would require twice as much wealth to obtain the same utility with the worse portfolio than with the better one.

A comparison of portfolio 1 of Panel A in which commodities are excluded with portfolio 2 shows that commodities generate large welfare gains for all investors. Both aggressive and conservative investors gain by allocating some weight to commodities, which can help hedge against the long positions in domestic stocks and the inflation risk of real interest rates. Comparing portfolio 3 and 4 in Panel B results in drawing the same conclusion. Further, comparing portfolio 1 with portfolio 3 and portfolio 2 with portfolio 4 suggests that adding foreign stocks to an investor's portfolio also creates large gains for all investors.

SUMMARY AND CONCLUSIONS

Using the CRB Index as a proxy for commodities, this chapter documents relatively strong and stable intertemporal hedging demands of U.S.-based investors for commodities. The result is robust when other traditional assets, such as foreign stocks, are included in the portfolio choice. The study also provides evidence that the intertemporal hedging demand for commodities is relatively stable and permanent in magnitude. The results are generally consistent with previous findings showing large mean total and myopic demands for domestic stocks.

Further, this chapter provides some possible explanations as to why U.S.-based investors have a strong intertemporal hedging demand for the commodities using modern portfolio theory, return characteristics, and the ability of commodities to serve as a hedge against inflation. The analysis shows a significant intertemporal hedging demand for commodities. Commodity returns have low and negative correlations with traditional asset classes, while having a lower downside risk because of their higher positive skewness. The significant intertemporal hedging demand for commodities seems to come through its increased ability to hedge against the unexpected future inflation compared to traditional assets.

Institutional investors have been increasingly interested in commodities. Intense debate exists on the role of commodities in strategic asset allocation. This study briefly summarizes the findings of current literature and provides some new empirical evidence for advocating commodities as an asset class in portfolio choice. Further efforts are needed to build a well-accepted theoretical model on commodity pricing and to examine the sources of commodity returns in strategic asset allocation.

DISCUSSION QUESTIONS

1. The question of whether commodities are an investable asset class has been around since the 1970s. What explains the growing demand for commodities?
2. Unlike traditional assets such as stocks and bonds, no well-accepted methods are available to measure the direct exposure to commodities. What proxies can be used to approximate the exposure to commodities?
3. Identify and discuss the biggest challenge facing researchers in estimating the demand for an alternative asset class such as commodities in a multiperiod setting.
4. What are the main advantages of the approach proposed by Campbell et al. (2003) in addressing the practical challenge mentioned in question 3?

REFERENCES

Barberis, Nicholas C. 2000. "Investing for the Long Run When Returns Are Predictable." *Journal of Finance* 55:1, 225–264.

Barron, John M., and Jinlan Ni. 2008. "Endogenous Asymmetric Information and International Equity Home Bias: The Effects of Portfolio Size and Information Costs." *Journal of International Money and Finance* 27:4, 617–635.

Bhamra, Harjoat S., and Raman Uppal. 2006. "The Role of Risk Aversion and Intertemporal Substitution in Dynamic Consumption-Portfolio Choice with Recursive Utility." *Journal of Economic Dynamics and Control* 30:6, 967–991.

Bodie Zvi, and Victor I. Rosansky. 1980. "Risk and Return in Commodity Futures." *Financial Analyst Journal* 36:3, 27–39.

Brennan, Michael J., Eduardo S. Schwartz, and Ronald Lagnado. 1997. "Strategic Asset Allocation." *Journal of Economic Dynamics and Control* 21:8–9, 1377–1403.

Campbell, John Y. 1991. "A Variance Decomposition for Stock Returns." *Economic Journal* 101:405, 157–179.

Campbell, John Y., Yeung L. Chan, and Luis M. Viceira. 2003. "A Multivariate Model of Strategic Asset Allocation." *Journal of Financial Economics* 67:1, 41–80.

Campbell, John Y., and Luis M. Viceira. 1999. "Consumption and Portfolio Decisions When Expected Returns Are Time Varying." *Quarterly Journal of Economics* 114:2, 433–495.

Campbell, John Y., and Luis M. Viceira. 2001. "Who Should Buy Long-term Bonds?" *American Economic Review* 91:1, 99–127.

Campbell, John Y., and Luis M. Viceira. 2002. *Strategic Asset Allocation: Portfolio Choice for Long-Term Investors.* Oxford: Oxford University Press.

Cooper, Lan, and Evi Kaplanis. 1994. "Home Bias in Equity Portfolios, Inflation Hedging, and International Capital Market Equilibrium." *Review of Financial Studies* 7:1, 45–60.

Coval, Joshua D., and Tobais J. Moskowitz. 1999. "Home Bias at Home: Local Equity Preference in Domestic Portfolios." *Journal of Finance* 54:6, 2045–2073.

Daskalaki, Charoula, and George Skiadopoulos. 2011. "Should Investors Include Commodities in Their Portfolio After All? New Evidence." *Journal of Banking and Finance* 35:10, 2606–2626.

Gorton, Gary, and Geert Rouwenhorst. 2006, "Facts and Fantasies about Commodity Futures." *Financial Analysts Journal* 62:2, 47–68.

Greer, Robert J. 1978. "Conservative Commodities: A Key Inflation Hedge." *Journal of Portfolio Management* 4:4, 26–29.

Idzorek, Thomas M. 2006, *Strategic Asset Allocation and Commodities*, Research Reports. Chicago: Ibbotson Associates.

Jensen, Gerald R., Robert R. Johnson, and Jeffrey M. Mercer. 2000. "Efficient Use of Commodity Futures in Diversified Portfolios." *Journal of Futures Markets* 20:5, 489–506.

Lynch, Anthony W. 2001. "Portfolio Choice and Equity Characteristics: Characterizing the Hedging Demands Induced by Return Predictability."*Journal of Financial Economics* 62:1, 67–130.

Lynch, Anthony W., and Sinan Tan. 2010. "Multiple Risky Assets, Transaction Costs and Return Predictability: Allocation Rules and Implications for U.S. Investors." *Journal of Financial and Quantitative Analysis* 45:4, 1015–1053.

Merton, Robert C. 1969. "Lifetime Portfolio Selection under Uncertainty: The Continuous Time Case." *Review of Economics and Statistics* 51:3, 247–257.

Norman, Strong, and Xinzhong Xu. 2003. "Understanding the Equity Home Bias: Evidence from Survey Data." *Review of Economics and Statistics* 85:2, 307–312.

Rapach, David E., and Mark E. Wohar. 2009. "Multi-period Portfolio Choice and Intertemporal Hedging Demands for Stocks and Bonds: International Evidence." *Journal of International Money and Finance* 28:3, 427–453.

Schroder, Mark, and Costis Skiadas. 1999. "Optimal Consumption and Portfolio Selection with Stochastic Differential Utility." *Journal of Economic Theory* 89:1, 68–126.

Stambaugh, Robert F. 1999. "Predictive Regressions." *Journal of Financial Economics* 54:3, 375–421.

The World Bank. 2012. "Prospects for Commodity Markets." *Global Economic Prospects* 4, 1–165.

You, Leyuan, and Robert T. Daigler. 2009. "Optimizing Portfolios with Commodity Futures." Working Paper, Florida International University.

ABOUT THE AUTHORS

Yongyang Su is a Ph.D. student in the Economics Department at Suffolk University. He currently runs a company in the futures industry that focuses on trading platforms. Mr. Su has published in the *Review of Futures Markets*, *Economic Modeling*, and *Emerging Market Finance & Trade*. He has presented his work at such conferences as the 50th CRSP Forum, Southern Finance Association, Asia-Pacific Symposium for Futures Research, and Asia-Pacific Association of Derivatives Conference.

Marco Lau is a Senior Lecturer of Economics at Northumbria University. His research areas are international finance and optimal hedging. Professor Lau's papers appear in such journals as the *China Economic Review*, *Applied Economics*, *Energy Policy*, *Economic Modeling*, *Applied Economics Letters*, and *China and the World Economy*. He currently serves as the Associate Editor for the Eurasian Business Review (EBR). Professor Lau earned his Ph.D. in Economics from Hong Kong Polytechnic University.

Frankie Chau is a Lecturer in Finance at Durham Business School. His main research interests are in behavioral economics and finance, derivative securities, and financial econometrics, specializing in volatility and correlation modeling, hedging effectiveness, and price discovery functions of futures markets. Dr. Chau's research has been published in the *Economic Modeling*, *Journal of Business Finance and Accounting*, and *International Review of Financial Analysis*. He received a Ph.D. in Economics and Finance from Durham University.

CHAPTER 21

Managed Futures: Markets, Investment Characteristics, and Role in a Portfolio

DAVIDE ACCOMAZZO
Adjunct Professor of Finance, Graziadio School of Business and Management, Pepperdine University; Managing Director, Cervino Capital Management CTA; Portfolio Manager, Thalassa Capital Management RIA

INTRODUCTION

The last decade has shattered many traditional investing notions. A climax of instability and uncertainty, which was reached during the financial crisis of 2007–2008, forced investors to reconsider long-lived market beliefs such as buy and hold, strong market efficiency, and blind reliance on constant expected rates of returns for all asset classes. Suddenly, north was south and static portfolios based on traditional asset allocations showed dramatic underperformance. The last 10 years of turbulence have highlighted deficiencies in traditional allocations and have created the need for more sophisticated portfolio repartitions based on a wider range of asset classes and strategies. The era of portfolios driven only by beta has come to a close, ushering in a new, much needed, blend of passive returns (beta) and skill-based performances resulting from active management (alpha).

For many investors, the lack of enough investment capital and/or the lack of analytical resources have precluded some of these avenues to alternative investments and alpha performances. Managed futures can fill the vacuum by providing sophisticated strategies, generally uncorrelated to traditional asset classes; acceptable investment minima; and a much higher level of transparency and liquidity than other alternative solutions, such as hedge funds or private equity vehicles.

The purpose of this chapter is to provide a comprehensive overview of the managed futures industry and a blueprint of how to invest following a methodical approach. The chapter begins with a general explanation of what managed futures are and provides specific insights on the three distinctive characteristics of this investment vehicle. An introduction to the regulatory framework and an analysis of the state of the industry follow. An in-depth look at managed futures' role in a portfolio and how to choose a program or a balanced blend of programs completes the analytical overview. A case study on the MF Global bankruptcy is presented due to its potentially far-reaching consequences on how the industry is likely to operate in the future. The next section introduces the basic concepts of the managed futures industry.

WHAT ARE MANAGED FUTURES?

Managed futures were launched in the early 1970s during the volatility explosion endured by most financial markets as a result of the highly inflationary pressures of those economic times. Managed futures generally rely on futures and options contracts (and occasionally forwards) to gain exposure to commodity, financial, currency, and equity markets. Professional investment managers generally structured as *commodity trading advisers* (CTAs) manage individual client accounts, implementing different strategies that may attempt to profit from long, short, or arbitrage opportunities in many markets around the world. Occasionally, investment managers are organized as commodity pool operators (CPOs) to execute the same strategies in a fund structure, as opposed to the previously described individually managed account solution.

Most CTAs or CPOs are categorized as systematic or discretionary managers. *Systematic managers* implement quantitative strategies based on preset algorithms, therefore removing the emotional involvement that often clouds traders' judgment. *Discretionary managers* leverage their fundamental knowledge or market instinct to produce returns in a flexible manner, shying away from preconceived formulas.

The majority of managers engage in trend-following. *Trend-following programs* benefit from riding long-lasting trends (upward or downward) in different markets. Other managers deploy strategies such as mean-reverting algorithms or different kinds of arbitrage among markets, instruments, and time periods. A substantial component of the CTA universe comprises global macro investing. Managers involved in these programs are an evolution of the original hedge funds strategies, such as those used in George Soros's Quantum Fund. These programs use futures and options to act on macroeconomic views based on a discretionary and fundamentally driven approach. Additional programs include options strategies that may vary from premium capture (i.e., a way to arbitrage the differential between implied volatility and realized volatility) to tail risk trading (essentially betting on outliers) or mixed futures and options strategies (e.g., covered call writing).

The recent increase in money flows to the managed futures space combined with improvements in computing power and technology has also increased the number of peripheral strategies. Shorter-term programs designed to exploit market-flow inefficiencies or intended to work with pattern-recognition techniques based on neural network technology or dictated by more old fashion chart reading have also become increasingly popular (Abrams, Bhaduri, and Flores, 2010). A recent trend is the creation of multistrategy CPOs, which attempt to capture many of the newly available strategic nuances offered by the managed futures spectrum in a single instrument.

Regardless of the strategic blend chosen to gain exposure to managed futures, one element emerges from a time-based analysis: A sufficient time horizon is required to improve the probability of fully capturing that positive and uncorrelated performance indicated by managed futures aggregate indices (Abrams et al., 2010).

A study produced by AlphaMetrix Alternative Investment Advisors (Abrams et al., 2010) analyzes maximum, minimum, and mean rolling returns of the Barclay BTOP 50 Index over various holding periods from January 1987 to December 2008. The results reveal that a holding period of three to five years significantly increases the probability of investors harvesting the benefits of managed futures positive returns. AlphaMetrix research also highlights that an investor should expect to break even, under worst conditions, after two to three years of exposure to managed futures.

In terms of transactional costs, managed futures exhibit low execution costs, with a standard mix of management and incentive fees, which is common practice in the alternative investments universe. Most CTAs charge a fixed fee between 1 and 2 percent of assets under management (AUM) and a 20 percent incentive fee calculated from the net new profits. Industry standard practice is to report performance net of all fees.

DISTINCTIVE CHARACTERISTICS OF MANAGED FUTURES

Managed futures offer three distinctive advantages to investors looking for exposure to alternative investments: (1) liquidity, (2) transparency, and (3) generally uncorrelated returns with traditional investments. Many alternative investment vehicles offer poor liquidity due to long lock-up periods, as is common with most hedge funds, or strategies focused on arbitraging anomalies that arise from the illiquidity of certain markets. By contrast, managed futures often trade in highly liquid contracts (e.g., index futures such as the S&P 500, U.S. Treasury bond futures, or liquid commodities such as gold, silver, or corn). Yet, some programs trade in illiquid markets.

Most managers also trade exchange-listed contracts, which add to the liquidity and transparency of the investment.

The managed account structure provides full transparency to the client. The account is opened and held at a futures commission merchant (FCM), which the client can normally choose. The account holder gives a limited trading authorization to the CTA to enable placing trades for the client. This structure ensures constant and full transparency. It eliminates the problem of *style drift* (i.e., not agreed upon investment style changes from the money manager) and/or unsupervised increases in leverage.

Historically, managed futures, in aggregate, produce returns that are usually uncorrelated to traditional assets. For example, in 2008 when the returns on equities around the world collapsed, the Barclay CTA Index recorded a positive return of about 14 percent. Additionally, commodity futures, as a specific representation of this investment strategy, have also performed well in times of inflation. In a study performed in 1983, Bodie (1992) finds that a buy and hold strategy from 1953 to 1981 with a diversified portfolio of liquid commodity futures produced results highly correlated with the rate of inflation and negatively correlated with stocks and bonds.

Another potential advantage of managed futures is the favorable taxation of capital gains compared to other investment vehicles and strategies. Managed futures gains are treated, as of this writing, at 60 percent long-term rates and 40 percent short-term rates, with a distinctive advantage over speculative short-term equity strategies taxed 100 percent at the short-term capital gains rate. Of course, tax laws can change and apply differently to various investors.

Further, in the case of futures and options, the client initially is required to deposit only a minimum amount of funds to trade, which is usually a small percentage of the total notional value of the position called *initial margin*. The client must maintain a certain equity percentage of total investment value called *maintenance margin*. Should the equity portion drop below the maintenance margin, clients are required to deposit *variation margin* to bring the equity portion of their position back to the initial margin requirement. Such structure allows for high leverage, which is a double-edged sword because the implicit leverage can magnify losses as much as gains. However, such dynamics allow for flexibility, because the investor can decide how much risk to take and how to modify its exposure easily and efficiently. Furthermore, a fully or partially funded position can be collateralized with investments in risk-free instruments earning an additional yield. In other words, a $100,000 position in crude oil may be collateralized by Treasury bills, earning the client an extra yield. In some instances, positions can also be collateralized by gold.

REGULATORY FRAMEWORK

Two main entities largely regulate managed futures: the Commodity Futures Trade Commission (CFTC) and the National Futures Association (NFA). Congress created the CFTC in 1974 as an independent agency invested with the task to protect commodity customers from fraud; market manipulation; and, among other situations, systemic risk (CFTC, 2012). The NFA was established in 1976 as a not-for-profit membership entity (National Futures Association, 2007). Its roles and responsibilities range from auditing of its members to enforcement of customer protection regulations.

One element of the managed futures industry is its inclination towards self-regulation. In addition to self-regulatory bodies such as the NFA, publicly listed organizations, such as the Chicago Mercantile Exchange (CME), also perform self-regulatory functions to police the sector. As part of its mission, the CME: (1) protects market integrity by maintaining fair, efficient, competitive, and transparent markets; (2) issues, monitors, and enforces rules to protect all market participants from fraud, manipulation, and other abusive trading practices; and (3) acts proactively to identify and mitigate potential risks as a means of preventing damage to the marketplace (Chicago Mercantile Exchange, 2012).

One pillar of the managed futures industry and futures in general is the concept of customer-segregated funds. Clients' funds deposited with FCMs are to be kept segregated at all times from the brokers' capital to avoid problematic issues in the unfortunate case of the broker's bankruptcy. Segregation of funds is monitored in different ways by all parties involved, such as the CFTC, and, if the broker is a member, the CME. Unfortunately, as of this writing, the MF Global bankruptcy allegedly broke this cornerstone rule of the futures industry. The case study located at the end of the chapter provides more details and potential future ramifications for the industry. Under CFTC rules, funds deposited with FCMs do not enjoy insurance provided by the Securities Investor Protection Corporation (SIPC); therefore, strict monitoring and enforced segregation are key to the health of the industry.

The increasing integration of the financial services industry over the last few years has opened the door to hybrid structures, such as FCMs, which can be active and also registered as securities brokers/dealers. In this case, regulators/agencies such as the Securities and Exchange Commission (SEC), the Financial Industry Regulatory Authority (FINRA), and SIPC may also get involved.

STATE OF THE INDUSTRY

Exhibit 21.1 illustrates the rapid growth of managed futures in the last few years. AUM has nearly doubled over the last five years, and as of December 2011, stand at roughly $320 billion. This total is still just a fraction of the approximately $1.7 trillion managed by hedge funds. However, an opposite trend occurs for hedge funds, which have suffered net redemptions since 2007 (BarclayHedge, 2012).

The nature of the recent success of managed futures can be explained by their positive aggregate performance during years of disappointing results for traditional assets such as equities. Exhibits 21.2, 21.3, and 21.4 highlight this divergence in performance between the traditional asset classes—bonds and equities—and different categories of CTAs (*Managed Futures Today*, 2010).

Exhibit 21.5 shows a more detailed breakdown of AUM. This exhibit reveals that systematic traders (practically trend-followers) manage the majority of funds, highlighting a potential cluster of similar strategies and trading rules.

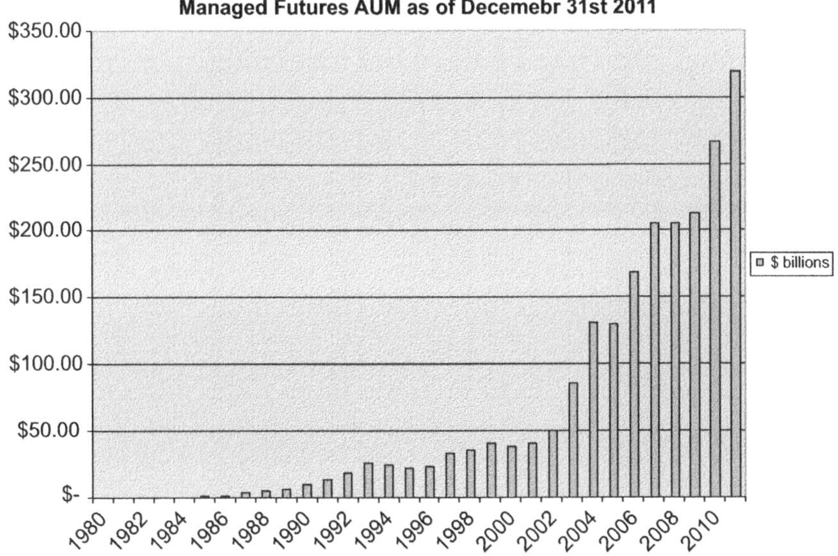

Exhibit 21.1 Assets under Management (AUM) for Managed Futures

This exhibit provides information on AUM for managed futures during the period 1980 through 2011. Source: BarclayHedge, Alternative Investment Database.

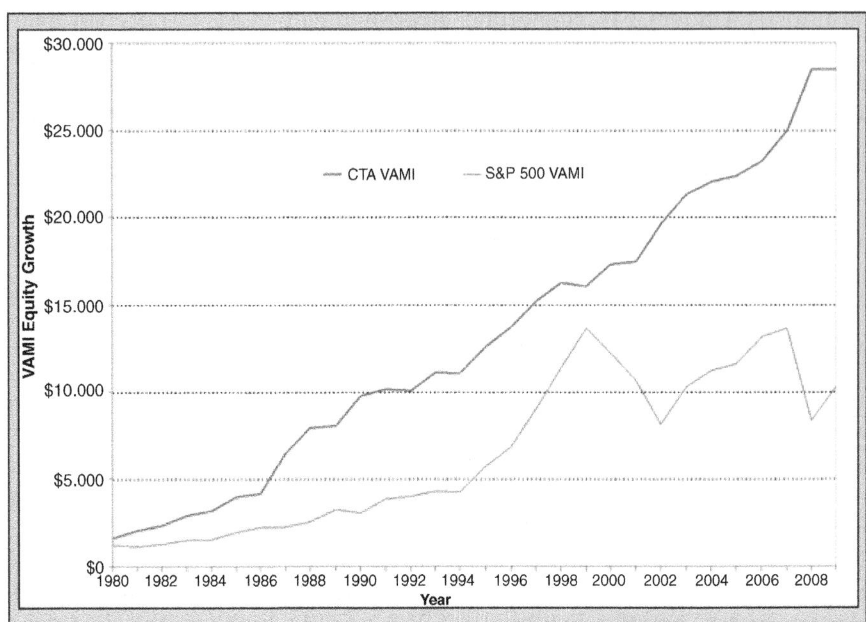

Exhibit 21.2 Performance of the Barclay CTA Index versus the S&P 500 Index
This exhibit shows the divergence in the compounded returns of the Barclay CTA index versus the S&P 500 Index during the last 30 years.
Source: Techinfo (Copyright 2010).

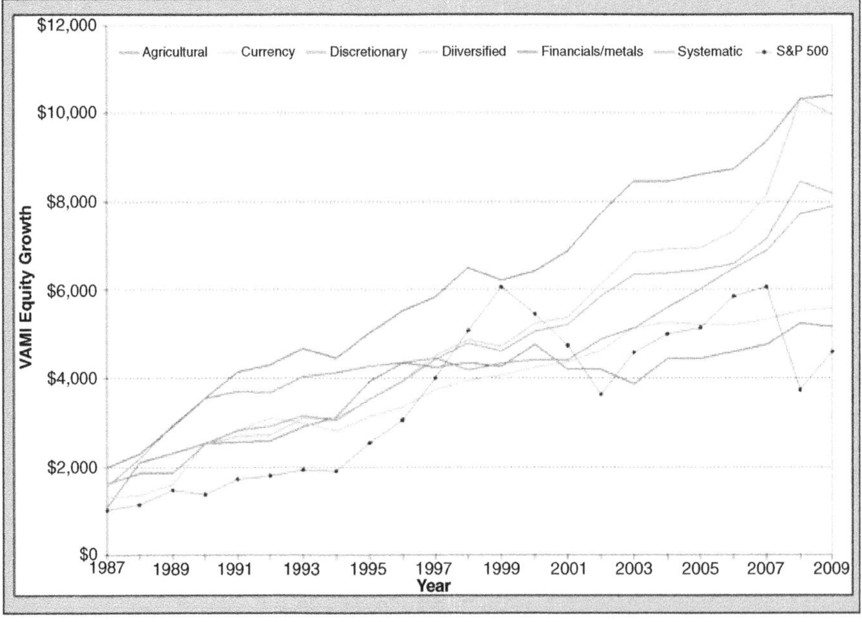

Exhibit 21.3 Performance of Different CTA Categories versus the S&P 500 Index
This exhibit shows the compounded returns of different subcategories of CTAs versus the S&P 500 Index from 1987 to 2009.
Source: Techinfo (Copyright 2010).

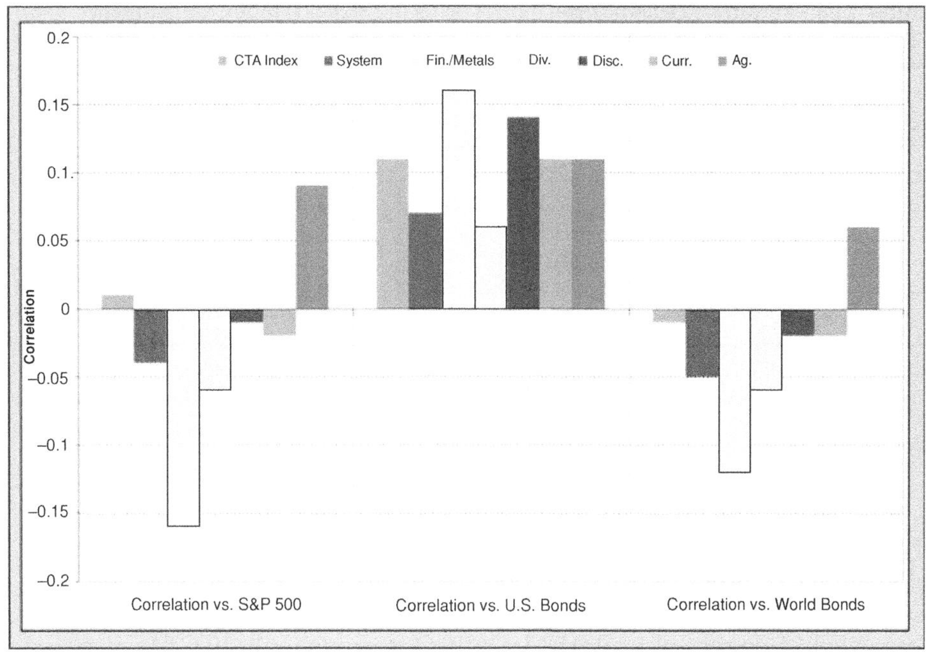

Exhibit 21.4 Correlations between Managed Futures and Traditional Asset Classes
This exhibit shows the correlations of the overall CTA index and CTA subindices with traditional asset classes such as stocks and bonds.
Source: Techinfo (Copyright 2010).

Exhibit 21.6 investigates CTA categories, but from the perspective of risk and return. Although the returns of systematic and discretionary CTAs are practically identical, discretionary traders, in aggregate, achieve such performance with half the maximum drawdown of systematic CTAs.

Frankfurter (2011), Cervino Capital Management LLC, highlights one potentially distorting new trend in fund flows. As part of a presentation given at the

Exhibit 21.5 Assets under Management (AUM) for Different Categories of CTAs

Sectors	AUM as of 3rd Quarter 2011 (in billions $)
Agricultural CTAs	1.38
Currency CTAs	28.09
Diversified CTAs	186.59
Financial/Metals CTAs	86.84
Discretionary CTAs	27.57
Systematic CTAs	269.33

This exhibit shows a detailed breakdown of AUM for various categories of CTAs. The greatest concentration of AUM is with systematic traders (trend-followers).
Source: BarclayHedge, Alternative Investment Database.

Exhibit 21.6 Performance and Correlations versus the S&P 500 Index for Different Categories of CTAs

Sector	Compound Annual Return (%)	Worst Drawdown (%)	Correlation vs. S&P 500 Index
Agricultural CTAs	7.38	19.94	0.10
Currency CTAs	7.37	15.26	−0.01
Diversified CTAs	9.83	17.49	−0.05
Financial/Metals CTAs	10.01	11.14	−0.15
Discretionary CTAs	8.99	10.67	0.01
Systematic CTAs	8.96	22.07	−0.03

This exhibit shows CTA categories from the perspective of risk and return. The evidence shows that discretionary traders achieve their performance with about half of the maximum drawdown of systematic CTAs.
Source: BarclayHedge, Alternative Investment Database.

CTA Expo in New York in 2011, he quoted one of his studies using data provided by Institutional Advisory Services Group (IASG) on AUM in the CTA universe. As of April 2011, the IASG database included 523 CTAs, of which only 15 percent represented 91 percent of total AUM. Of this top group, only 10 CTAs managed 60 percent of assets. These findings reflect a trend also common to hedge funds: Most new money flows seem to migrate toward the largest and most established institutions. This phenomenon, perhaps linked to a perceived inverse relationship between size and risk, overlooks the generally better performance produced by emerging managers (usually defined as having been operational for less than five years and/or with less than $10 million AUM).

ROLE OF MANAGED FUTURES IN A PORTFOLIO

The author disagrees with some of the strictest tenets of modern portfolio theory (MPT), such as the idea that markets are highly efficient or that investment returns should be considered data points independent from each other and distributed normally on a bell curve (Reilly and Brown, 2009). However, proper portfolio diversification carries great benefits. Apparently, one has to go beyond static correlations and incorporate a scenario-dependent approach. Yet, in turbulent times, such as those investors have experienced since 2000, a sophisticated diversification of asset classes and strategies has resulted in optimized performance.

Lintner (1996) promotes the idea of portfolio optimization by including managed futures alongside traditional stock and bond allocations as early as 1983. He finds that including allocations to managed futures in traditional portfolios improves the total risk-adjusted return of the portfolio. This finding is due to the low and often negative correlation between the then-available futures portfolios and stock and bond portfolios. Peters (1992) finds similar results in a study based on monthly data from 1980 to 1988 for the S&P 500 Index, the Salomon Brothers Broad Investment Grade Bond Index, and only one CTA chosen for its conservative institutional orientation with returns similar to the industry benchmarks. Since the 1980s, more managed futures data have become available and more nuanced strategies have come to the market. This enables more detailed analysis than was possible 30 years ago, but it also requires the potential investor/allocator to perform a deeper level of research and due diligence.

If the majority of managed futures programs trade on a trend-following basis, the return-risk characteristics may be similar. This type of approach can be compared to a return-risk profile such as long options. In this situation, the investor should expect positive gamma. In the derivatives universe, positive gamma consists of a rapid increase in the value of the long option during an explosive move in the underlying market. These moves tend to produce large, but infrequent, positive payoffs. Trend-following strategies seem to provide positive gamma exposure that often results in a correlation with large market dislocations, which may explain why managed futures can often perform well when traditional assets are under pressure. A lag may exist between the initial market dislocation and the positive performance of managed futures. If the dislocation is sudden, most managed futures programs will suffer some initial losses as well before their model triggers a reversal of their positions.

Other classic managed futures strategies, such as options arbitrage, provide a different complement to traditional portfolio allocations. Most option strategies tend to be net short gamma exposure by being short-option contracts, in which case they would suffer when explosive moves occur in their underlying markets. These strategies will regularly be net sellers of volatility and therefore will generally suffer when volatility increases suddenly, because their short gamma exposure will work against them. These programs tend to be consistent winners and provide uncorrelated performance in most market scenarios. However, these types of option strategies are highly correlated with large market dislocations, when gamma increases rapidly.

The fact that most managed futures strategies seem to generally provide an expectation for positive returns often uncorrelated to traditional asset classes during times of dislocation makes this strategy a perfect provider of "crisis alpha." Kaminsky and Mende (2011, p. 2) define *crisis alpha* as "the difference between the original Alternative Investment strategy and the strategy without crisis periods where the performance of the strategy is substituted with an investment in the short-term debt rate."

Understanding why managed futures seem to be excellent providers of crisis alpha requires knowledge of market crises and the specific drivers of performance of managed futures as well as what differentiates them from traditional assets and other alternative investments. During a market crisis, two major elements take over trading activity: behavioral inefficiencies (Lo, 2004) and forced liquidation. Other considerations, such as value arbitrage or the dynamic to exploit assets mispricing in relationship to their fundamental fair value, become secondary. Markets exhibit a breakdown in price continuity, and liquidity dries up. Credit risk increases simultaneously. Leveraged players, such as hedge funds, are forced into liquidation of positions, and hedges are closed. Other liquidity providers, such as high-frequency traders who are usually active in normal circumstances, quickly withdraw their bids and offers. This set of dynamics explains why correlations among traditional asset classes increase markedly during market crises. Alternative investments, such as hedge funds, often cannot escape this negative cycle due

Exhibit 21.7 Performance of Managed Futures during Some of the Worst Crises

Time Period	Crisis	S&P 500 Index (%)	BTOP 50 Index (%)	Difference (%)
4th Quarter 1987	Stock market crash	−23.23	16.88	40.11
3rd Quarter 2002	WorldCom bankruptcy	−17.63	9.41	27.05
3rd Quarter 2001	9/11 terrorist attack	−14.99	4.12	19.10
3rd Quarter 1990	Iraqi invasion of Kuwait	−14.52	11.22	25.74
2nd Quarter 2002	Aftermath of technology bubble burst	−13.73	8.52	22.26
1st Quarter 2001	Bear market in U.S. equities	−12.11	5.97	18.01
3rd Quarter 1998	Russia default, Long-Term Capital Management failure	−10.30	10.54	20.84
1st Quarter 2008	Credit crisis	−9.92	5.92	15.84
3rd Quarter 2008	Credit crisis	−8.88	−3.40	5.48
4th Quarter 2000	Dot-com bubble	−8.09	19.78	27.87
3rd Quarter 1999	Y2K worries	−6.56	−0.67	5.89
1st Quarter 1994	Increase in interest rates	−4.43	−2.10	2.33
4th Quarter 2007	Subprime crisis	−3.82	3.02	6.84
1st Quarter 1990	U.S. recession, oil spike	−3.81	1.76	5.57
1st Quarter 2003	Second Gulf War	−3.60	4.68	8.28

This exhibit shows discrepancies in performance between managed futures and the S&P 500 Index as well as the BTOP 50 Index during the worst crises of the previous 25 years.

to their leverage, their tendency to exploit illiquid anomalies, and their increasing dependency on leveraged beta.

When a market crisis strikes, managed futures can quickly exploit dislocations thanks to their utilization of highly liquid instruments and their ability to rapidly switch from long to short exposure. Additionally, the behavioral component that tends to override value considerations during crises contributes to lengthening the time frame of market dislocations, allowing trend followers or volatility arbitrageurs to book a sequence of profitable trades due to price persistence.

Kaminsky and Mende (2011) analyze the performance of managed futures during market crises. They find that the Barclay CTA Index earns a positive crisis alpha as opposed to the BarclayHedge Index, which exhibits a negative crisis alpha. Abrams et al. (2010), who compile a table listing the worst 15 quarters in the S&P 500 since 1987, offer a look at crisis alpha in concrete terms. Furthermore, they identify each geopolitical or economic crisis associated with each quarter and then compare the performance of the market index (S&P 500 Index) versus managed futures via the BTOP 50 Index. Exhibit 21.7 shows such discrepancy in performance between managed futures and the S&P 500 Index during the crises of the last 25 years.

This analysis is subject to a discretionary definition of *market crisis*. More important, it represents only an index response to a price and liquidity breakdown. Understanding this distinction is important when analyzing managed futures as a new positive force in traditional portfolio allocations. Indices generally have flaws, but alternative investment indices are subject more than others to high *survivorship bias* (i.e., the tendency for an index to produce results skewed by the exclusion of failed outfits) and are often not investable. CTA indices can also suffer from backfill bias based on at what point in time managers decide to start reporting their performance to a database. The CTA may decide to start reporting after a number of positive data points, which will then backfill the database, creating a positive bias (Chen, O'Neill, and Zhu, 2005).

Especially for smaller investors, the problem in capturing crisis alpha resides in their ability to choose one or more good CTAs that will deliver that uncorrelated performance. Burghardt and Walls (2012) highlight some of the issues with most common CTA indices. For the purpose of their analysis of CTAs since 1990, they link two different indices: the Newedge CTA Index and the Barclay CTA Index. The Newedge Index consists of 20 of the largest CTAs, making it investable (at least for investors with larger portfolios) and practically untainted by survivorship bias, with only one CTA dropping out since the index's inception. One problem with this benchmark is its relatively short history, given that it started reporting in January 2000. A second problem concerns its concentration with the largest CTAs, such that it may end up suffering from a classic inverse correlation between increases in AUM and positive performance. The Barclay CTA Index has a longer history, but it is not investable, because it reports more than 300 CTAs.

HOW TO CHOOSE A CTA

In light of the information presented in the previous section, the key to a successful investment in managed futures resides in the investor's ability to choose a proper CTA or, more preferably, a proper blend of managers. The manager-selection process should follow two distinct levels of analysis: a quantitative approach and a qualitative screening. Once a trading style (i.e., trend-following versus mean reversion) is chosen, an investor should focus on the size of the CTA. A preferable strategy is to invest in a portfolio that blends an investment in a large and established CTA alongside emerging managers in order to capture the edge often provided by smaller and more agile managers. This approach also mitigates the potential risk associated with younger and potentially flawed smaller outfits. Exposure to larger CTAs should provide performance similar to that reported by the subcategory indices. Once a list of candidates is prepared, a quantitative process should start.

The first quantitative screening should consider a measure called margin-to-equity utilization (M/E), which essentially measures the level of leverage employed by the manager. For example, a manager who returns 20 percent with an M/E of 50 percent is not any better, on a risk-adjusted basis, than a manager who returns 10 percent with an M/E of 25 percent. M/E ratios, however, can be misleading and can vary markedly during different trading periods. A more sophisticated approach to risk-return analysis would require looking at more ratios, such as the manager's standard deviation of returns, Sharpe ratio (risk premium divided by the standard deviation of the manager's portfolio), Sortino ratio (a risk measure similar to the Sharpe ratio that penalizes only for downside volatility), or the omega ratio (the weighted gain/loss ratio relative to a targeted return). Frankfurter (2007a) also indicates rank correlation analysis and Value at Risk (VaR) as useful analytical measures.

The study of monthly returns (institutional investors may want to study daily returns as well when available) gives a better sense of the volatility of the program. Additionally, determining the maximum drawdown (largest loss) and how quickly such loss was recovered is relevant. Technically, a *drawdown* is defined as the decline in the portfolio value from a peak to a subsequent trough. Understanding its future probability of occurring and its probability of exceeding some previous magnitude and by what degree are key elements of CTA analysis. Burghardt and Walls (2011) point to three major determinants of drawdowns: (1) the length of track record, (2) mean return, and (3) volatility of returns. As Burghardt and Walls (p. 199) indicate, although the probability of any given drawdown is independent of the CTA length of trading history, "the likelihood of experiencing a drawdown that is bigger than anything experienced so far increases with every passing day." Empirical observations seem to validate this statement.

Investors should also study the value-added monthly index (VAMI) in order to analyze the value of compounded returns and the effect of volatility on the actual returns. However, a mere quantitative approach may not provide a complete answer. Different studies show that a CTA's past success is not necessarily a strong indication of future performance. For example, Schwager (1996) runs a quintile test on a CTA universe to study correlations between superior past performance of individual CTAs and their future relative returns. His results are not encouraging, because he does not find a significant correlation between these two variables. Schwager tests if CTAs included in the top quintile by performance in a previous period show above-median returns in the following time set. He finds just as many negative correlations between past and future relative return-risk levels as positive correlations. In a different but somewhat related study, Burghardt and Walls (2011) also do not find serial correlation in CTA returns.

Ultimately, a qualitative type of analysis is required. With every investment, the first question prospective investors should ask is: "Where is the edge, and why should I expect positive returns?" Investors often forget this qualitative yet commonsense-driven approach. Frankfurter (2007b) indicates that a priority in the investor's thinking should be the robustness of the underlying strategy as it relates to different market situations. A somewhat clear understanding of the solidity of the strategy in relationship to different market contingencies is paramount when looking at a space such as managed futures, which is marked by a myriad of subspecialties. Frankfurter and Accomazzo (2007, p. 51), in their controversial analysis of the uniquely qualitative aspect of managed futures as an asset class, went as far as defining managed futures as:

> anything but . . . If anything it is the anti-asset class. It is an observable materialization of behavioral finance, where risk, return, leverage and skill operate untethered from the anchor of an accurate representation of beta. In other words, it defies rational expectations equilibrium, the efficient market hypothesis and allied models—the CAPM, arbitrage pricing theory or otherwise—to single-handedly isolate a persistent source of return without that source eventually slipping away.

Another element investors should consider when choosing a CTA is the program's capacity utilization. Some strategies are successful because of the flexibility afforded by a small size, but as the AUM level increases investors may find capacity constraints for their program. A good CTA knows roughly its capacity limitation and communicates well in advance the level at which point the program should be closed to new investors.

Furthermore, investors should investigate the following operational considerations when investing in smaller outfits: the experience of key people and succession/replacement plans, the organizational chart, outfit administration, backup facilities, and risk management procedures. Having a clear understanding of the operational structure of a CTA is a very important yet often overlooked element of analysis. While the operational structure of every CTA is important, it can have even more significance when investigating younger outfits.

One last consideration should be given to the entrepreneurial aspect. Investing in programs where management has a considerable amount of personal funds invested is usually preferable. This element reinforces the alignment of management–client interests.

CASE STUDY: MF GLOBAL

The large increase in AUM for the managed futures universe underscores the success story of this investment vehicle (or asset class, as some would define it) in recent tumultuous years. While other financial entities were fighting to retain control over their business model amid market breakdowns and scandals such as the Madoff affair, managed futures conveyed an image of transparency, aligned the interests of all parties involved, and provided positive and uncorrelated performance to traditional asset classes. This was true until the MF Global bankruptcy.

During the long history of futures and commodity trading, many brokerage houses had to terminate operations as the cumulative impact of their errors became irreversible. However, the system rarely suffered major consequences from such bankruptcies, because customers never lost the funds their brokers had in custody and, generally, trading never suffered dangerous liquidity vacuums. As a result, the regulatory framework increasingly moved toward self-regulation because it seemed to be the most efficient way to manage all the interested parties. The bankruptcy of MF Global may have long-lasting ramifications for the industry, and these potential consequences must be highlighted and analyzed in any serious overview of today's state of the industry.

On October 31, 2011, MF Global filed for bankruptcy (the eighth largest in U.S. history) after a negative earnings surprise and a credit rating downgrade. These events were the epilogue to a failed attempt at restructuring a simple but stale traditional commodity brokerage business by former New Jersey Governor and former Goldman Sachs CEO Jon Corzine.

The traditional brokerage model relies on revenues from commissions for executing trades and interest earned on excess collateral left in custody by the clients. The combination of increased competition among brokerage houses and the near zero interest policy resulting from the financial crisis of 2007–2008 put increased financial pressure on MF Global. When Mr. Corzine was chosen as the new CEO for MF Global in March 2010, he swiftly moved toward implementing a new strategy: move away from traditional brokerage to become more like an investment bank with an aggressive proprietary trading desk. MF Global fired many brokers and replaced them with traders. It also built large positions in European sovereign debt via repo-to-maturity (RTM) transactions, and the Federal Reserve gave it a primary dealer license. Although the market generally accepted this strategy, MF Global's Chief Risk Officer at the time, Michael Roseman, underscored some uneasiness over the level of leverage and the solidity of the underlying financing. MF Global's board of directors subsequently replaced Mr. Roseman with Michael Stockman.

The deepening of the Euro debt crisis in the summer of 2011 increased the volatility levels on the global financial markets and produced increasingly large margin calls for MF Global. As the situation spun out of control in the last week of October, MF Global tried to sell its futures brokerage business to Interactive Brokers. This reaction is a typical dynamic. As a brokerage house careens toward bankruptcy, it will sell its book of clients to a healthy competitor. This strategy is made possible and operationally feasible by the futures industry regulatory requirement of segregating the customers' funds from the firm's capital. Unfortunately, in the case of MF Global, the deal collapsed at the last moment as a substantial shortfall in customers' funds was revealed. An investigation is ongoing, and more will be revealed by the time this book is published. However, the initial handling of this bankruptcy may sow the seeds of a revolution in the way the futures market operates.

Surprisingly, the CFTC did not handle the MF Global bankruptcy. MF Global's dual registration as a FCM and broker/dealer allowed it to sidestep the CFTC in favor of the SIPC to handle the bankruptcy. The SIPC is the agency that handles securities brokers' failures and provides partial insurance to securities accounts. In spite of its dual registration, MF Global had 50,000 futures accounts and about 300 securities accounts. The decision to let the CFTC take a secondary role seriously impaired the ability of customers to regain 100 percent of their funds. If the CFTC had handled the process, the rules of the Commodity Exchange Act would have undeniably given priority to customers, whereas the SIPC-lead process may have turned customers with segregated funds into unsecured creditors.

This situation has important potential consequences for the industry. Segregation of funds is the cornerstone of the futures industry, which does not enjoy any kind of funds insurance in case of malfeasance. Currently, this protection seems certainly weaker at best and may lead to inefficiencies in futures trading. Customers may decide to leave only minimum margin in the accounts and meet margin calls on a constant basis, or different arrangements may be found to avoid leaving excess margin in the form of cash, which may be pooled by the FCM and used for its internal purposes. This dynamic may put even more pressure on the remaining FCMs and their profitability. Another possible consequence is an outright decrease in futures trading, which may increase general market volatility.

The self-regulatory system of the industry may also be at stake. The CME has been implementing regulatory functions of its members based on the belief that the exchange is the ultimate guarantor of all transactions. Thus, the best interests of the CME would be served by policing its members. The size of the MF Global failure may push Congress to strip the CME of its regulatory function, which may now be seen as compromised. In the meantime, the CFTC has already moved to restrict the type of investments allowed to FCMs for the excess customer collateral. Other measures to prevent similar problems that are currently being discussed include the possibility of a third-party custodian for customer funds; a SIPC-type of insurance, at least for smaller accounts; and more intense electronic interfacing between FCMs and regulators.

The MF Global bankruptcy has resulted in a very unique set of contingencies, which are distinctly different from those witnessed in the past. In 2005, the industry suffered another major bankruptcy, Refco (the sixth largest FCM at the time), but with very different dynamics. In the case of the Refco bankruptcy, no shortfall of customer segregated funds existed, and the futures division of the firm continued to work until sold to, ironically, MF Financial (as MF Global was known then). In this case, the clearinghouses were able to protect customers' collateral, prevent customers' funds from being transferred to the bankrupt holding company, and facilitate the exodus of clients, as Refco's segregated funds fell from $6.47 billion at the end of September to $2.53 billion at the end of October (Acworth, 2006).

SUMMARY AND CONCLUSIONS

This chapter highlights the benefits of including a blend of managed futures programs in traditional asset allocations. The most important step in successful investing is a proper asset allocation alongside a rebalancing program. Managed futures, in the aggregate, provide that element of diversification when such diversification is needed.

Such advantage does not come easily, as moving away from theory into implementation carries inevitable issues that need to be carefully considered. Choosing the proper blend of CTAs is the key to a successful plan. A qualitative approach to this dynamic must be carried out in conjunction with the usual quantitative screening. Furthermore, the recent events linked to the MF Global bankruptcy have, at least for now, interjected a new element of counterparty risk that was not perceived to be an issue in the past.

DISCUSSION QUESTIONS

1. Based on a time analysis of managed futures returns, discuss the time frames in which investors can increase their probabilities to break even and experience positive returns.
2. Discuss how managed futures differ from other alternative investments.
3. Discuss the major issues with managed futures indices and why understanding their flaws is critical to investors.
4. Having a proper process to choose a CTA or a blend of CTAs is important to improving portfolio performance. Discuss the three major levels of analysis.
5. In what ways does the MF Global bankruptcy change the future of the industry? Discuss the case and the measures that are being analyzed to improve the industry.

REFERENCES

Acworth, Will. 2006. "Containing a Crisis: How the Clearinghouses Responded to the Collapse of Refco." *Futures Industry*, January–February, 36–42.

Abrams, Ryan, Rnajan Bhaduri, and Elizabeth Flores. 2010. "A Quantitative Analysis of Managed Futures in an Institutional Portfolio." Working Paper, CME Group.

BarclayHedge. 2012. *Alternative Investment Database.* Available at www.barclayhege.com.

Bodie, Zvi, 1992. "Commodity Futures as a Hedge against Inflation." In Carl C. Peters, *Managed Futures: Performance, Evaluation and Analysis of Commodity Funds, Pools and Accounts,* 43–59. Chicago: Probus Publishing Company.

Burghardt, Gale, and Brian Walls. 2011. *Managed Futures for Institutional Investors: Analysis and Portfolio Construction.* Hoboken, NJ: John Wiley & Sons, Inc.

Burghardt, Gale, and Brian Walls. 2012. "Well-Known Managed Futures Researchers Galen Burghradt and Brian Walls Address Hot Topics of Correlation, Volatility and Study Bias." *Futures Intelligence* 37:March, 11–12. Available at www.opalesque.com.

CFTC. 2012. "CFTC Mission and Responsibilities." Available at www.cftc.gov.

Chen, Peng, Christopher O'Neill, and Kevin Zhu. 2005. "Managed Futures and Asset Allocation." Working Paper, Ibbotson Associates.

Chicago Mercantile Exchange. 2012. Available at www.cmegroup.com/market-regulation.

Frankfurter, Michael. 2007a. "Managed Futures: Pitfalls in Performance Evaluation." Working Paper, Managed Account Research Inc.

Frankfurter, Michael. 2007b. "Managed Futures: A Model for Incubating Talent." Working Paper, Managed Account Research Inc.

Frankfurter, Michael, 2011. "Diversity in Danger?" Speech at the CTA Expo, New York City.

Frankfurter, Michael, and Davide Accomazzo. 2007. "Is Managed Futures an Asset Class? The Search for the Beta of Commodity Futures." Working Paper, SSRN. Available at http://papers.ssrn.com/sol3/papers.cfm?abstract˙id=1029243.

Kaminsky, Kathryn M., and Alexander Mende. 2011. "Crisis Alpha and Risk in Alternative Investment Strategies." Working Paper, CME Group.

Lintner, John. 1996. "The Potential Role of Managed Commodity-Financial Futures Accounts (and/or Funds) in Portfolio of Stocks and Bonds." In Carl Peters and Ben Warwick, ed., *The Handbook of Managed Futures: Performance, Evaluation & Analysis*, 99–137. Burr Ridge, IL: McGraw-Hill Professional.

Lo, Andrew W. 2004. "The Adaptive Market Hypothesis." *Journal of Portfolio Management* 30th Anniversary 2004 Issue, 15–29.

Managed Futures Staff. 2010. "30 Years of Managed Futures." *Managed Futures Today* 1:May, 4–6. www.managedfuturestodaymag.com

National Futures Association. 2007. *Manual.* Chicago: Source4, paragraph 1001.1

Peters, Carl C. 1992. *Managed Futures. Performance, Evaluation and Analysis of Commodity Funds, Pools and Accounts.* Chicago: Probus Publishing Company.

Reilly, Frank K., and Keith C. Brown. 2009. *Investment Analysis and Portfolio Management.* Mason, OH: South-Western Cengage.

Schwager, Jack D. 1996. *Managed Trading Myths and Truths.* New York: John Wiley & Sons, Inc.

ABOUT THE AUTHOR

Davide Accomazzo is Adjunct Professor of Finance at the Graziadio School of Business and Management (GSBM) at Pepperdine University. He is also Managing Director at Cervino Capital Management LLC, a CTA specializing in options and futures strategies and Portfolio Manager at Thalassa Capital Management LLC, a Registered Investment Adviser. Mr. Accomazzo writes extensively on markets and portfolio management issues for different specialized publications. He regularly chairs a faculty roundtable at GSBM on macroeconomic topics such as the international monetary system, the future of capitalism, and the global economy. Mr. Accomazzo holds a Laurea degree in International Relations from the University of Genoa, Italy, with a thesis on new dynamics in corporate communication in the postindustrial society, an MA in Journalism from California State University, Northridge, and an MBA in Finance from Pepperdine University.

CHAPTER 22

An Overview of Managed Futures' Performance: 1983 to Post-2008 Credit Crisis

KAI-HONG TEE
Senior Lecturer in Finance, Loughborough University

INTRODUCTION

In the United States, organized futures markets have been in existence since the mid-nineteenth century, following the official opening of the Chicago Board of Trade (CBOT) in 1848, where futures contracts started to trade with grains as the underlying commodity. These futures contracts served a good purpose for grain producers and dealers as a protection against adverse future price movements. The futures markets brought together commercial hedgers and speculators in an open, competitive marketplace to determine an asset's price at a single point in time. As these markets became increasingly complex due to the introduction of new futures contracts, more sophisticated strategies, and international market opportunities, users of the futures markets sought more specialized professional advice in managing their futures market assets. This change is especially noticeable after the substantial growth in futures trading in the early twentieth century when newly established exchanges introduced a variety of commodity contracts. The introduction of the world's first financial futures contracts (foreign currency futures) by the Chicago Mercantile Exchange (CME) in 1972 was also an important landmark in futures trading. Other financial futures contracts (e.g., interest rate and stock index futures) appeared in the late 1970s and 1982, respectively.

The successful introduction of futures contracts to encompass equity indices, interest rates, currencies, options, and conventional commodities, as well as the globalization of futures trading, have expanded the scope of investment possibilities and thus have created new profit opportunities for a new type of market participant—managed futures investors. *Managed futures* refers to the trading of futures and forwards contracts on commodities and financial instruments by either institutions or trading advisers who manage assets in these markets on behalf of their clients. Hence, the managed futures industry consists of professional money managers who manage clients' assets on a systematic or discretionary basis, using global futures and options markets as investment media. Managers who manage clients' assets on a systematic basis use technical trading systems to exploit investment opportunities. In contrast, managers who manage on a discretionary basis use their judgment of market conditions, usually without the use of trading systems, while still relying on some statistical information to make investment decisions.

One major incentive for managed futures investments appears to stem from their ability to offer risk reduction through diversification while still offering returns comparable to other traditional investments (e.g., domestic and international equity indices). Research on traditional security markets shows that market prices react to unexpected changes in micro (e.g., earnings) or macro (e.g., interest rates and gross national product) information. Trading futures contracts based on forecasts of these fundamental variables may likewise result in positive risk-return trade-offs. The importance of this research is that managed futures may allow investors to profit from market trends or unexpected changes in information in ways that are not easily available from other managed assets, such as stock-based mutual funds. The differences occur because the cash market's transaction costs and institutional restrictions on short selling and leverage make engaging in strategies that involve short positions unprofitable for mutual fund managers. Hence, managed futures can, in principle, enable an investor to capture those returns available in the spot market more cheaply (e.g., replicate cash indices with lower transaction costs) and capture opportunities not easily found in spot markets (e.g., the ability to sell short and to alter the degree of leverage in asset positions).

The growth of the managed futures industry increased dramatically in the late 1970s. While less than US$500 million was invested in 1980, the total investment in managed futures exceeded US$120 billion in 2005. Allocation of funds to managed futures increased because of the investors' desire for higher returns and more effectively managed portfolio risk. The Commodity Futures Trading Commission (CFTC) defines a *commodity trading adviser* (CTA) as any person, who, for compensation or profit, directly or indirectly advises others regarding the buying or selling of commodity futures and/or option contracts (Ates and Wang, 2008). It defines a *commodity pool operator* (CPO) as any individual or firm that operates or solicits funds for a commodity pool. Typically, a number of individuals contribute funds to form a commodity pool. In the United States, a commodity pool is usually organized as a limited partnership. Most CPOs hire independent CTAs to make daily trading decisions. The CPO may distribute the investment directly or act as a wholesaler to a broker/dealer.

Investing in managed futures can occur in three ways. First, investors can purchase shares of public commodity funds, which are similar to equity or bond mutual funds except that they invest in futures contracts. Public funds provide a way for small (retail) investors to participate in an investment vehicle usually reserved for large investors because they typically have the lowest minimum investment requirements. Second, investors can place funds with a private CPO who pools all investors' funds together and retains one or more professional traders (i.e., CTAs) to manage the pooled funds. Pools have higher minimum investment requirements than public funds. Third, investors can place their funds directly with one or more CTAs to manage their funds on an individual basis. The minimum investment required by CTAs typically is set higher than public commodity funds and private CPOs.

This chapter discusses the empirical evidence about the performance of managed futures spanning a period of three decades as found in the extant literature. The chapter divides periods of studies into earlier, later, and recent studies. The chapter also discusses and re-evaluates the role of managed futures after the financial crisis of 2007–2008. The final section provides a summary and conclusions.

Performance Assessment of Managed Futures as a Stand-alone Investment

This section discusses the performance of managed futures in the 1980s, 1990s, and 2000s. Each of the periods has some distinctively different approaches for assessing performance. Studies in the 1980s set a benchmark for a performance metric used to assess managed futures. Representative studies in the 1990s used more comprehensive data sets and expanded the scope of research to help gain more insights about the performance of managed futures. Studies in 2000s built on established research in the 1980s and 1990s and focused on additional issues, such as performance persistence and the market-timing ability of managed futures traders.

Earlier Studies in the 1980s

Lintner (1983) is perhaps the first academic to undertake a study on managed futures. He finds that managed futures are an attractive investment vehicle. Yet, later studies, such as Elton, Gruber, and Rentzler (1987, 1990) and Irwin, Krukemyer, and Zulauf (1993), find that managed futures, at least as represented by public commodity funds, did not generate returns above the risk-free rate. Schneeweis, Savanayana, and McCarthy (1992) confirm earlier results relative to public commodity funds but limit the portfolio to 14 CTAs.

Lintner (1983) examines the performance of 15 individual CTAs and 8 public commodity funds for the period July 1979 through December 1982. In computing the returns for the 15 CTAs, Lintner uses their composite performance (trading profits, including interest, net of all fees and commissions) as reported in their disclosure documents (reporting documents required by the CFTC). This composite performance includes results from all accounts traded by the CTA, including public commodity funds, private pools, and individual managed accounts. As such, it offers a weighted return of the three different investment vehicles. Lintner also examines the monthly change in net asset value (NAV) of eight public commodity funds available to investors during the period studied. He shows that the average monthly standard deviation of individual CTAs in his study was 2.72 percent, which was for those of public commodity funds. However, he also shows that diversifying an investment in managed futures by creating portfolios of CTAs lowers the risk of an investment in managed futures because the average correlation among the CTAs was only 0.285.

Besides the stand-alone risk-return characteristics of CTAs, Lintner (1983) also analyzes the potential impact of adding managed futures to a portfolio of stocks (or stocks and bonds). First, he establishes that for the minimum risk portfolio of CTAs the correlation coefficient is –0.07 with stocks and 0.15 with bonds. For the minimum risk portfolio of public commodity funds, the correlation coefficient is 0.23 with stocks and 0.15 with bonds.

Later Studies in the 1990s

The earlier studies focused on correlations between managed futures returns and the returns to stocks and bonds. These earlier studies, however, appear to suffer from insufficient data due to the relatively shorter periods of data availability. The later studies use a relatively larger data set to further verify the findings of the earlier studies in the 1980s.

Edwards and Liew (1999) use a more comprehensive set of data and extend the time of their examination period. They examine the monthly performance of CTAs, private pools, and public funds from 1980 through 1996. Unlike previous studies, their research encompasses a much larger data set. A total of 1,150 CTAs, 439 private commodity pools, and 619 public futures funds combined for 119,481 months of performance data: 60,054 for CTAs, 24,523 for commodity pools, and 34,904 for public funds. The data are from managed account reports (MARs), which receive monthly performance information from participating CTAs, pools, and funds.

Similar to earlier research by Lintner (1983) and Elton et al. (1987, 1990), Edwards and Liew (1999) evaluate the performance of managed futures investments based on three stylized portfolios formed for CTAs, pools, and funds. These portfolios are as follows: (1) portfolios having one CTA, pool, or fund, where a single CTA, pool, or fund is randomly selected; (2) an equally weighted market portfolio (EWMP) of all CTAs, pools, or funds in existence in a particular month, where an identical amount is invested in each CTA, pool, or fund; and (3) value-weighted portfolios (VWMP) of all CTAs, pools, or funds in existence in a particular month, where the weights reflect the proportion of total invested dollars managed by particular CTAs, pools, or funds in the month. Edwards and Liew compute monthly and yearly returns for each of these stylized portfolios.

In assessing the performance of these CTAs, pools, and funds, unlike all other previous studies reviewed, Edwards and Liew (1999) use the Sharpe ratio as a measure of risk-adjusted performance. They analyze returns in two subperiods: 1982 to 1988 and 1989 to 1996.

Their results have five major implications. First, a VWMP of pools stands out as an attractive stand-alone investment, with respect to both alternative nonfutures investments and other managed futures investments, especially during the 1989 to 1996 period. Although a VWMP of pools earned a somewhat lower average annual return than common stock during this period (13.9 percent compared with 16.0 percent), the lower volatility of pool returns resulted in a higher Sharpe ratio of 0.955 for the VWMP of pools. This performance is especially impressive given the extraordinarily high common stock returns during this period. A clear implication of these results is that private pool managers add value: They generate higher returns and Sharpe ratios than do most nonfutures investments and outperform other managed futures returns.

Second, portfolios having a single CTA, pool, or fund or any type of public fund investment do not appear to make an attractive stand-alone investment. The single CTA, pool, or fund portfolios all have high return volatility, and public funds have low returns.

Third, the strong performance of a EWMP of CTAs during the 1982 to 1988 period should be given less credibility for two reasons. According to Edwards and Liew (1999), this period is subject to the greatest survivorship bias, and

CTA-reported returns are highly sensitive to the exclusion rule used to control for self-selection bias.

Fourth, returns on all types of managed futures investments fell substantially from 1989 to 1996, compared to 1982 to 1988, for reasons that remain unclear. A possible "data" explanation, according to Edwards and Liew (1999), is that returns in the 1982 to 1988 period may have been artificially inflated because of an upward survivorship bias, so that the elimination of this bias in the 1989 to 1996 period gives the appearance that returns fell during this latter period. Another possibility is that market conditions from 1989 to 1996 may not have been favorable to commodity traders. In particular, most commodity traders were "trend followers" to a greater or lesser degree. Further, commodity prices appeared to exhibit less trend-following behavior from 1989 to 1996 than in the earlier years, which increased the difficulty for traders to identify price trends and to capitalize on such trends. Finally, increased competition occurred during the 1989 to 1996 period. With more traders and more capital competing for trading profits, commodity markets may have become more efficient, resulting in lower returns.

Fifth, despite the decline in the level of returns between 1989 and 1996, the Sharpe ratio for a VWMP of pools rose significantly from 0.694 during the 1982 to 1988 period to 0.955 during the 1989 to 1996 period. Lower return volatility offset the lower returns. However, this result was not replicated for a EWMP of pools or for either a EWMP or a VWMP of CTAs. Thus, large pools were more successful in managing risk than were either small pools or individual CTAs. Edwards and Liew (1999) also provide an alternative way to view managed commodity funds as a separate asset class in a diversified portfolio. They then determine whether portfolio performance is significantly enhanced by including commodity funds in the portfolio.

Edwards and Liew (1999) show the simple correlation coefficients between managed commodity fund returns and the returns on other asset classes are generally very low (typically below 0.10) and are often not significantly different from zero. Some correlations are even negative. For example, returns on a VWMP of pools are negatively correlated with S&P 500 common stock returns in all time periods, although they are never significantly different from zero. The highest correlation observed for the 1982 to 1996 period is 0.15, which occurs between a VWMP of funds and long-term government bonds. Thus, including managed commodity funds in a diversified asset portfolio should provide diversification benefits.

Recent Studies in the 2000s

The later studies of managed futures performance verified those of the earlier studies. The research conducted by Edwards and Liew (1999) is one of the major studies in the later period. Managed futures returns continue to be low and even more so for the CTA performances. One explanation that Edwards and Liew attribute to the low returns from 1989 to 1996 is a higher supply of CTAs in the market during that period. Research into correlations of managed futures returns with those of stocks and bonds continues to show that they exhibit low correlation with each, further qualifying managed futures as good portfolio diversifiers. Recent studies of managed futures performance have moved into areas that investigate, for example, the performance persistence of CTAs. Gregoriou, Hubner, and Kooli (2010) focus on the issue of performance persistence. Given the inferior performance noted in earlier periods, the study's findings would be of interest particularly if a CTA generates not only low returns but also persistent performance.

Gregoriou et al. (2010) note that the evidence of return persistence for managed futures in the literature is mixed but generally negative. Irwin, Zulauf, and Ward (1992), who examine 363 CTAs during the period of 1979 to 1989, find a lack of performance persistence when using past CTA returns to predict future returns. Irwin et al. (1993) examine commodity pools during the 1979 to 1990 period. Unlike the performance of CTAs investigated in Gregoriou et al., Irwin et al.'s research does not exhibit return persistence, even though they address some issues of market efficiency of the future market. As Gregoriou et al. note, Irwin (1994) focuses on individual CTAs and concurs with the previous finding, but offers little evidence of the predictability in average CTA returns.

In contrast, McCarthy, Schneeweis, and Spurgin (1996) find some evidence of performance persistence. However, their sample size of 56 CTAs is relatively small, and their study only focuses on the 1985 to 1991 time frame. These authors observe that multiadviser managed futures funds display more persistence than single-adviser CTAs (Schneeweis, Spurgin, and McCarthy, 1997). Brorsen (1998) investigates data from private and public funds and CTAs using various statistical methods, such as regression analysis, Monte Carlo methods, and out-of-sample tests. He also finds limited evidence of performance persistence. The main drawback of each of these studies is the short examination period during the bull market, while not encompassing any sustained bear market environment.

According to Gregoriou et al. (2010), only a few attempts to study CTA performance and persistence use parametric models. A possible reason is that regression methods tested so far have hardly produced any satisfactory significance levels. Using the 1990 to 1999 period, Brorsen and Townsend (2002) find limited support for performance persistence using regression analysis.

Gregoriou et al. (2010) reexamine the performance of CTAs and compare their abnormal performances based on various models, as well as a category-specific model introducing asset-, option-, and moments-based factors. Taking more factors into account significantly raises the explanatory power of the model. In fact, 9 out of 12 CTA categories significantly outperform the market. Multifactor models also do a good job of explaining CTA behavior of various categories. The average adjusted R^2 increases from 0.04 for the Carhart four-factor model to 0.31 for more complex multifactor models. The adjusted R^2s of the 12 multifactor models range from 0.02 to 0.51. Although the multifactor models may appear to explain a substantial part of the variation of CTA returns, a key explanatory piece is still missing.

Gregoriou et al. (2010) use monthly data for the 1995 to 2008 sample period for the following variables: *Mkt* (excess return of the market proxy); *SMB* (the factor-mimicking portfolio for size, i.e., small minus big); *HML* (the factor-mimicking portfolio for book-to-market equity); *PRIVR* (the factor-mimicking portfolio for the momentum effect); and *Var, Skew,* and *Kurt* (the factor mimicking portfolios for variance, skewness, and kurtosis, respectively). Furthermore, the study includes option-based factors such as at-the-money (ATM) call and put options, following the work of Fung and Hsieh (2001). These explanatory variables seem to adapt well only to a few CTAs, as revealed by the adjusted R^2 values. For example, adjusted R^2 values for both currency CTA and financial/metal CTA are 0.51, but the value is only 0.40 for systematic CTA. The explanatory variables do not adapt well to discretionary CTAs, with an adjusted R^2 of only 0.02. Liang (2003), who in a similar study reports adjusted R^2s ranging from 0.07 to 0.14, concludes that CTAs are different from hedge funds or fund-of-funds in trading strategies in which those multifactor models have very low explanatory power for CTAs.

Gregoriou et al. (2010) note some unresolved issues. For example, their findings show that CTAs still address challenges to performance measurement and indicate that more needs to be done to identify CTA performance drivers. The return-generating process also shows more than half of total variance is unexplained, possibly indicating a high instability in CTA risk exposures. This finding warrants more research and understanding into what determines and drives CTAs' returns and risk exposures. The authors also examine the performance persistence of CTAs over different time periods. Similar to the work of Brown, Goetzmann, and Ibbotson (1999) and Agarwal and Naik (2002), Gregoriou et al. compare the performance measures in the current period on the performance measures in the previous period. They use alpha (α) as a performance measure, which is defined as the return of a CTA following a particular strategy minus the average return for all CTAs following the same strategy.

Gregoriou et al. (2010) use a nonparametric method to investigate the issue of persistence in two consecutive periods. They construct a contingency table of winners and losers. A CTA is a winner if the α is greater than the median α of all CTAs following the same strategy in that period; otherwise, it is a loser. Persistence refers to the existence of CTAs that are winners in two consecutive periods (1-, 3-, 6-, and 12-month periods), denoted by WW, or losers in two consecutive periods, denoted by LL. Similarly, winners in the first period and losers in the second period are denoted WL, and LW denotes the reverse pattern. The authors define the *cross-product ratio* (CPR) as the product of repeat winners (WW) and repeat losers (LL) divided by the product of winners-losers (WL) and losers-winners (LW); that is, (WW $\times$ LL)/(LW $\times$ WL). A CPR of one would support the hypothesis that the performance in one period is unrelated to that in another. A CPR greater than one indicates persistence; a value below one indicates that reversals in performance dominate the sample. The authors use chi-square statistics similar to Christensen (1990) to detect statistical significance of persistence. They also use the standard error of the natural logarithm of the CPR, as given by Equation 22.1:

$$\sigma_{\ln(CPR)} = \sqrt{\frac{1}{WW} + \frac{1}{WL} + \frac{1}{LW} + \frac{1}{LL}} \tag{22.1}$$

The findings from Gregoriou et al. (2010) show that a CTA displaying persistence over a horizon of at least three months is more likely to exhibit persistence over a longer period. However, most of these results do not stand the "acid test," which aims at assessing the relative performance persistence of a CTA by considering the ability of a CTA to stay in a top quartile rather than the top half of a category. Of all the CTAs assessed by the acid test, the performance persistence of agricultural CTAs appears more robust to a change in testing conditions.

Kazemi and Li (2009) explore the sources of CTA returns. Their study investigates the market and volatility timing ability of CTAs and examines whether discretionary CTAs display different market-timing skills from systematic CTAs.

The goal of their study is to formally test the hypothesis as to whether trend-following CTAs possess timing ability due to the commonly observed similarities between market timers and trend followers. They also explore whether CTAs display market-timing ability in those markets that are the focus of their trading strategy. Their research reports that previous studies such as Fung and Hsieh (2001) show that one important challenge in testing for the presence of market-timing ability is that models employing traditional factors have low explanatory power for CTA returns, and, therefore, may be unable to detect the presence of market-timing skills. Besides, the traditional indices that are based on equity and fixed-income markets may not include important risk factors such as those related to various currencies, commodities, or interest rates that are present in most CTA portfolios. Unlike previous studies, Kazemi and Li use a set of futures-related factors that are based on returns from the most heavily traded futures contracts. They find that these factors possess much higher explanatory power for CTA returns than traditional factors.

Henriksson and Merton (1981) develop a test for market-timing skills and assume that the mutual fund manager allocates capital between risk-free assets and equities based on forecasts of the future excess market returns. Busse (1999) extends the model to detect combined return and volatility timing. Kazemi and Li (2009) also apply this extension to test for CTAs' ability to time the best-performing markets in each category of futures markets, using Equation 22.2 as their model:

$$\begin{aligned} r_{p,i+1} = \alpha_{i+1} + \sum_{j=1}^{k} \beta_j r_{j,t+1} + \sum_{i=1}^{n} D_i \max(max(r_{1,t+1}, r_{2,t+1}, \ldots\ldots, r_{n,t+1}), 0) \\ + \delta r_{m,t+1}(\sigma_{m,t+1} - \bar{\sigma}_m) + \varepsilon_{t+1} \end{aligned} \tag{22.2}$$

where $r_{p,i+1}$ is excess return on a CTA index; $r_{j,t+1}$ represents excess return on a futures contract; and $\sigma_{m,t+1}$ is stock market volatility, measured by end of the month VIX. VIX is the ticker symbol for the Chicago Board Options Exchange Market Volatility Index, which tracks the implied volatility of S&P 500 index options. It represents a measure of the market's expectation of stock market volatility over the next 30-day period. If CTAs have both return- and volatility-timing ability, then this will be shown by a significantly positive coefficient for D and significantly negative coefficients for δ.

The results indicate that the coefficient estimates carry the expected signs for both discretionary and systematic CTA indices. The adjusted R^2s are 0.16 and 0.29, respectively. Both discretionary CTAs and systematic CTAs show ability in timing the best-performing markets among currency futures (represented by Euro, Japanese Yen, and British Pound). Not only are the timing coefficients statistically significant, but their magnitudes are also of economic significance. Due to their ability to time the best-performing markets, on average, CTAs are able to generate an extra return of 0.57 percent when a 1 percent change occurred in any currency futures market. Return timing results of CTAs from other categories and/or models found in Kazemi and Li (2009) show that almost all market-timing regressions have higher explanatory power for systematic CTAs than for discretionary CTAs.

Bhardwaj, Gorton, and Rouwenborst (2008) readdress the moderately low performance of CTAs' returns and explore possibilities that could explain such performance. They analyze the performance of all CTAs that voluntarily report to the Lipper-TASS database. To eliminate the influence of various biases induced by strategic returns reporting and database construction, the authors exclude more than 80 percent of the available observations. Specifically, they exclude 83,201 of the 102,393 available monthly observations on fund performance post-1993 and all returns before 1994. These corrections greatly influence inferences about CTA performance. Bhardwaj et al. estimate that between 1994 and 2007 the average bias-adjusted CTA returns after fees have been statistically indistinguishable from the average return on an investment in U.S. T-bills. Hence, they conclude that the average CTA has not created value for its investors. The authors compare their findings to those by Elton, Gruber, and Rentzler (1987, 1989, 1990), who almost two decades earlier report that publicly traded commodity funds did not create positive returns for investors. Bhardwaj et al. conclude that the combined evidence shows that managed futures have not performed well for the past 20 years.

Other findings from Bhardwaj et al. (2008) include empirical evidence on net returns and the charges of performance-related fees of CTAs. Their methodology follows that of French (2008) in the construction of gross returns for managed futures funds in Lipper-TASS, using the reported net returns. The authors make two assumptions when implementing French's model: (1) fees accrue on a monthly basis and (2) high-water marks, when applicable, increase at the rate of return on T-bills. A *high-water mark* applies when a managed futures manager only receives performance fees on that particular pool of invested money when its ending value is greater than its previous highest value. Should the investment drop in value, then the managers must bring it back above the previous highest value before they become eligible for performance fees again.

Bhardwaj et al. (2008) find that bias-adjusted gross returns of CTAs computed from their database amount to about 5.37 percent and 0.85 percent net of fees. A comparison of fees between hedge funds and CTAs also shows that CTAs appear to have higher management fees and slightly higher incentive fees than hedge funds. Management and incentive fees of CTAs average 2.15 percent and 19.5 percent, respectively, while corresponding fees of hedge funds are only 1.42 percent and 16.33 percent. The authors suggest that the demand for CTAs is possibly less performance-sensitive and more price inelastic. Investors might be investing in CTAs for perceived diversification benefits and mandates for alternative investments (e.g., pension funds) and end up staying invested despite facing poor performance.

The Diversification Benefits of Managed Futures in Times of Market Crisis

Diversification benefits of managed futures in the academic literature are based on the nature of the lack of observed correlation between managed futures returns and those of the traditional investment portfolios composed of bonds and equities. Studies by Lintner (1983) and Edwards and Liew (1999), as well as those by Kat

(2002), Jensen, Johnson, and Mercer (2003), and Cerrahoglu (2005) show the risk-reduction benefits of managed futures. Edwards and Caglayan (2001) examine the performance of various hedge funds and commodity fund investment styles during periods of both rising and falling stock prices. Understanding how different investment styles perform in bear stock markets is important. Research finds that commodity funds offer better downside risk protection than hedge funds.

Oberuc (1992), who focuses on the performance of managed futures outside the United States, provides a case for investors including managed futures in their traditional stock and equity portfolios. According to Oberuc (p. 329),

> ... after the stock market crash of October 1987, investors realized that pinning their hopes of portfolio protection on stock selection methodologies was not successful. Indeed, it was found that diversifying a portfolio across equities from multiple countries provided very little protection since most countries' stock markets crashed at the same time. If stock selection did not provide the key to protection against portfolio drawdowns, then just what is the answer? Investment theory tells us that diversification across multiple investments that are not fundamentally linked with each other is the key. Unfortunately, all stocks are tied together through their linkage to something often referred to as the "market line." This means that as the stock market goes down (as measured by any of a number of market indexes), most individual stocks also tend to go down at the same time. Therefore, stock diversification is of little value against portfolio loss.

Oberuc (1992) analyzes the effect of using managed futures in combination with investment portfolios in four European countries (the United Kingdom, Germany, France, and Switzerland) over the 1979 to 1989 period. His findings reveal that these portfolios, whether or not they use currency-hedged or unhedged managed futures, seem to perform significantly better (i.e., higher return given the same level of risk) than those portfolios that did not include managed futures. The superior performance largely results from the low correlation of managed futures and other stock assets' returns. The low correlation becomes particularly useful in diversifying portfolios during a market crash (i.e., the October 1987 stock market crash). Most existing studies fail to emphasize the benefit of using managed futures during periods of financial crisis as a means of diversifying risk for stock and bond portfolios.

According to the Hedge Funds Review (2011a), a website that surveys hedge fund investment activities, CTAs running managed futures programs experienced record inflows in 2010 based on data from BarclayHedge. Combined assets managed by CTAs reached $267.6 billion at the end of 2010, an increase of more than 25 percent from $213.6 billion in 2009. That increase makes managed futures the single-largest strategy in the hedge fund universe, representing almost 15 percent of industry assets, according to BarclayHedge data. Once again, the focus appears to be on managed futures as a source of uncorrelated returns that can help diversify a broader portfolio. These properties came to the forefront in 2008 when managed futures programs returned more than 14 percent, on average, despite large declines in global markets. In fact, the credit crisis and credit crunch during the financial crisis of 2007–2008 resulted in governments bailing out banks and the collapse of major hedge funds had prompted many to rethink the role of managed futures in a diversified portfolio.

Despite the relatively low returns and higher fees reported in Bhardwaj et al. (2008), Kaminski (2011a) observes that managed futures investments styles have some desirable characteristics not commonly found in the rather aggressive hedge funds trading programs such as the global macro hedge funds. Kaminski comments that managed futures trade exclusively in the most liquid, efficient, and credit-protected markets, and their profitability must rely on those characteristics in order to obtain a competitive edge. Therefore, managed futures will not profit from credit exposures and/or illiquidity, which are commonly cited as risks and opportunities for most hedge fund strategies. Supporting the use of managed futures, Kaminski (2011b, p. 1) contends that:

> Following the onset of a market crisis, managed futures will be one of the few strategies able to adapt to take advantage of the persistent trends across the wide range of asset classes they trade. It is important also to note that managed futures are not about timing equity markets—it profits from a wide range of opportunities during market crises (this includes currencies, bonds, short rates, soft commodities, energies, metals, and equity indices). When equity markets are not in crisis, markets are highly competitive and efficient—especially futures markets. Strategies like hedge funds often provide seductive returns, but many researchers have pointed out that these strategies often contain hidden risks related to liquidity and credit exposures.

Kaminski (2011b) also maintains that managed futures are an offensive investment rather than a defensive investment. The author argues that tail-risk insurance, such as long-dated, out-of-the-money puts on equity indices, with potential for immense payoffs in the event of a crisis, provide little or no return outside the period of the event crisis because they are prohibitively expensive if purchased during a crisis. Therefore, successful implementation of such a strategy is highly dependent on market timing. As market timing tends to be difficult, Kaminski classifies such tail-risk insurance as being defensive. In the case of managed futures, she contends that a managed futures strategy is a highly adaptable, liquid strategy poised to take advantage of predictable trends during market-crisis events but also able to provide modest returns over time and even in the absence of market-timing ability. On that basis, Kaminski describes managed futures as an offensive approach dealing with tail events.

A few points discussed by Kaminski (2011a, 2011b) are important to help investors reconsider using managed futures in the post-2008 crisis period. Conversely, Bhardwaj et al. (2008) contend that managed futures charge such high fees that investors may want to consider investing directly in the futures markets. However, without the expertise of the managed futures traders, investors may be unable to deliver returns comparable to those of managed futures specialists. Therefore, although arguments exist about the fees of managed futures investments, no comparative empirical studies are available concerning the costs of investing in managed futures.

A report from the Hedge Funds Review (2011b) describes the strategy adopted by managed futures as a divergent strategy. The report claims that around

70 percent of CTAs employ trend-following or momentum-based strategies. Trend-following strategies benefit from directional moves that reflect informational gaps, changes in sentiment, and supply and demand imbalances in markets, which partly explain the low correlation of CTA returns with those of the stock market.

The report also claims that investors should not necessarily expect trend-following strategies to generate large profits in every market crisis, although large movement in prices often imply profit opportunities for managed futures. An interview with David Rothberg, from Niagara Capital Partners based in Toronto, reported in the Hedge Funds Review (2011b, p. 1), contains the following comment:

> Trend followers size positions and place stops based on volatility, Rothberg notes. A low volatility environment tilts the odds in favor of trends followers because it allows them to take bigger positions with tight stop losses. But if prices move swiftly in a high volatility regime, trend followers will not be able to take a large enough position to fully benefit from the move, assuming they are not caught on the wrong side of the trend in the first place.

Though the extent of volatility of market environment may affect the profitability of managed futures, appropriate allocation mechanism within equities portfolios are an important determinant. The proportion of managed futures investors committed to their equities portfolios therefore would affect overall portfolio performance. Tee (2009) relates the allocated proportion of managed futures to reflect investors' risk tolerance level and shows that using appropriate models in the asset allocation process can potentially lead to better returns for investors who include some managed futures funds in their equities portfolios.

SUMMARY AND CONCLUSIONS

In the academic literature, managed futures are normally referred to as "trend-followers" because investors use their proprietary trading models to capture trends in futures prices. They also take long or short positions in low transaction–cost investment vehicles, such as in futures contracts, in an attempt to benefit from trends in commodity prices, exchanges rates, interest rates, and equity markets, similar to many other alternative investments such as the hedge funds. As a result, CTAs are also listed as a strategy of hedge funds, with their style named "managed futures." Over the past 20 years, empirical evidence generally shows that the performance of managed futures is, on average, similar to returns on risk-free rates such U.S. Treasury bills. Bhardwaj et al. (2008) find that between 1994 and 2007 managed futures funds average annual returns of 5.37 percent and 0.85 percent net of fees. The authors explain the low returns as resulting from the supply of the inflow of funds to the managed futures sector as one of the reasons. This argument is similar to Edwards and Liew (1999), who observe greater competition in the industry between 1989 and 1996. With more traders and capital competing for trading profits, commodity markets may have become more efficient and resulted in lower returns. Kazemi and Li (2009) provide some evidence of managed futures timing the futures markets, implying that the time-series price movement of futures securities and assets affects the returns of managed futures. This finding, however, does not adequately explain the low returns of managed futures funds.

Chen, Neill, and Zhu (2005) report that the key foundation for futures returns, as posited by some practitioners and academics, is the risk-transfer function of the futures market itself (Kritzman, 1993; Lightner, 2003; Spurgin, 2003). Some commercial market participants, such as hedgers, are willing to pay the equivalent of an insurance premium to noncommercial participants (i.e., investors) for assuming risk. In the aggregate and over the long term, hedgers are willing to act consistently to transfer risk, even if they expect the spot markets to move in their favor and, in doing so, pay a net positive insurance premium. As providers of liquidity, investors receive this premium in the form of net trading profits. Unlike hedgers, investors in the futures markets regard "derivatives" as an asset class. They trade for profit-making purposes instead of hedging exposure of an underlying asset. Thus, the trading strategy should accommodate the trend that hedgers must follow in order to continuously and effectively transfer risk. The futures markets for trading managed futures are regulated, though the disclosures of performance of managed futures traders or CTAs are not as regulated as the markets in which they participate. This trading arena differs from investment trusts or closed-end funds that are listed on a stock exchange. Therefore, information may not be as complete as it should be in order to evaluate whether the performance of managed futures is correlated with future price movements. However, the number and types of the CTAs and hedgers in the future markets may affect the performance of managed futures. This relationship differs from one type of futures instrument to another, as liquidity tends to differ among derivative securities.

The diversification benefits of managed futures are based on the lack of observed correlation between managed futures returns and traditional investment portfolios composed of bonds and equities. Kat (2002), Jensen et al. (2003), and Cerrahoglu (2005) provide evidence of the risk-reduction benefits of managed futures. Interestingly, the diversification benefits of managed futures again attracted huge attention after the financial crisis of 2007–2008. Thus, the fact that managed futures tend to trade in liquid markets becomes a favorable factor. Kaminski (2011a, 2011b) terms managed futures as "crisis alpha," showing how it potentially adds value to a portfolio in market crisis. Researchers find using managed futures in this way is similar to that of the insurance-style strategies, with the latter often being criticized as costly. Others contend that directly investing in futures or commodity markets may be better for investors because it allows them to avoid the higher fee structure of managed futures. However, no empirical comparative studies on the costs of investing in managed futures support the claim. Even so, despite the high fee structure of managed futures, Bhardwaj et al. argue that the demand for CTAs is possibly less performance-sensitive and more price inelastic. Investors might be motivated by the perceived diversification benefits and mandates for alternative investments (e.g., pension funds) and therefore, ending up invested in CTAs despite facing poor performance. Nevertheless, such a decision may be justifiable in the light of the volatility in the financial markets such as the recent 2008 credit crisis, especially due to the low correlations of managed futures' returns with the stock and bonds' assets, and despite relatively low returns, the amount of capital to be invested in managed futures (either as stand-alone or for diversification purpose) remains an important issue, and more so when markets are volatile.

However, the extent of market volatility could affect the profits of managed futures, according to a report in Hedge Funds Review (2011b). A precise study on the performance persistence of managed futures during market crises is therefore an important area for future researchers to investigate. Such research could provide new findings about the performance characteristics of managed futures. Researchers should also investigate the issue involving the extent to which the persistence of performance justifies investing in managed futures during the times of market crisis. This issue is important as can be seen in the academic literatures, which often document the relatively low returns generated by managed futures and that they also appear to be charging higher fees than the hedge funds.

DISCUSSION QUESTIONS

1. Discuss the development of the managed futures industry. What are the various ways to invest in managed futures?
2. Discuss the possible sources of returns of managed futures' investments.
3. Explain the merits of investing in managed futures during times of equity market crisis.
4. What considerations are important when considering whether to include managed futures as part of an equity portfolio?

REFERENCES

Agarwal, Vikas, and Narayan Y. Naik. 2002. "Multi-Period Performance Persistence Analysis of Hedge Funds." *Journal of Financial and Quantitative Analysis* 35:3, 327–342.

Ates, Aysegul, and George H. K. Wang. 2008. "Managed Futures." In Hung-Gay Fung, Xiaoqing Eleanor Xu, and Jot Yau, ed., *Advances in International Investments: Traditional and Alternative Approaches*, 213–214. Singapore: World Scientific Publishing Co. Pte Ltd.

Bhardwaj, Geetesh, Gary B. Gorton, and K. Geert Rouwenhorst. 2008. "Fooling Some of the People All of the Time: The Inefficient Performance and Persistence of Commodity Trading Advisors." Working Paper, Yale International Center for Finance, Yale University.

Brorsen, B. Wade. 1998. "Performance Persistence for Managed Futures." Working Paper, Oklahoma State University.

Brorsen, B. Wade, and John Townsend. 2002. "Performance Persistence for Managed Futures." *Journal of Alternative Investments* 4:4, 57–61.

Brown, Stephen J., William N. Goetzmann, and Roger G. Ibbotson. 1999. "Offshore Hedge Funds Survival and Performance 1989–2005." *Journal of Business* 72:1, 91–117.

Busse, Jeffrey. A. 1999. "Volatility Timing in Mutual Funds: Evidence from Daily Returns." *Review of Financial Studies* 12:5, 1009–1041.

Cerrahoglu, Burak. 2005. "The Benefits of Managed Futures 2005 Update." Working Paper, Center for International Securities and Derivatives Markets, Isenberg School of Management, University of Massachusetts–Amherst.

Chen, Peng, Christopher O'Neill, and Kevin Zhu. 2005. "Managed Futures and Asset Allocation." Working Paper, Ibbotson Associates.

Christensen, Ronald. 1990. *Log-Linear Models*. New York: Springer.

Edwards, Franklin R., and Mustafa O. Caglayan. 2001. "Hedge Fund and Commodity Fund Investments in Bull and Bear Markets." *Journal of Portfolio Management* 24:7, 97–108.

Edwards, Franklin R., and Jimmy Liew. 1999. "Managed Commodity Funds." *Journal of Futures Markets* 19:4, 377–411.

Elton, Edwin J., Martin J. Gruber, and Joel C. Rentzler. 1987. "Professionally Managed Publicly Traded Commodity Funds." *Journal of Business* 60:2, 175–199.

Elton, Edwin J., Martin J. Gruber, and Joel C. Rentzler. 1989. "New Public Offerings, Information, and Investor Rationality: The Case of Publicly Offered Commodity Funds." *Journal of Business* 62:1, 1–15.

Elton, Edwin J., Martin J. Gruber, and Joel C. Rentzler. 1990. "The Performance of Publicly Offered Commodity Funds." *Financial Analysts Journal* 46:4, 23–30.

French, Kenneth R. 2008. "The Cost of Active Investing." Social Science Research Network Working Paper Series. Available at SSRN, http://ssrn.com/abstract=1105775.

Fung, William, and David Hsieh. 2001. "The Risk in Hedge Fund Strategies: Theory and Evidence from Trend-Followers." *Review of Financial Studies* 14:2, 313–341.

Gregoriou, Greg H., Georges Hubner, and Maher Kooli. 2010. "Performance and Persistence of Commodity Trading Advisors." *Journal of Futures Markets* 30:8, 725–252.

Hedge Funds Review. 2011a. "Managed Futures on the Rise as Investors Chase Diversification." Available at www.hedgefundsreview.com/hedge-funds-review/feature/2035509/managed-futures-rise-investors-chase-diversification

Hedge Funds Review. 2011b. "CTA/Managed Futures Hedge Fund Strategies Profit as Volatility Picks Up." Available at www.hedgefundsreview.com/hedge-funds-review/feature/2108244/cta-managed-futures-hedge-fund-strategies-profit-volatility-picks.

Henriksson, Roy D., and Robert G. Merton. 1981. "On Market Timing and Investment Performance II: Statistical Procedures for Evaluating Forecasting Skills." *Journal of Business* 54:4, 513–533.

Irwin, Scott H. 1994. "Further Evidence on the Usefulness of CTA Performance Information in Public Commodity Pool Prospectuses and a Proposal for Reform." In Don M. Chance and Robert R. Trippi, ed., *Advances in Futures and Options Research*, 251–265. Greenwich, CT: JAI Press.

Irwin, Scott H., Terry R. Krukemeyer, and Carl R. Zulauf. 1993. "Investment Performance of Public Commodity Pools: 1979–1990." *Journal of Futures Markets* 13:7, 799–820.

Irwin, Scott H., Carl R. Zulauf, and Barry W. Ward. 1992. "The Predictability of Managed Futures Returns." *Journal of Derivatives* 2:2, 20–27.

Jensen, Gerald R., Robert R. Johnson, and Jeffrey M. Mercer. 2003. "The Time Variation in the Benefits of Managed Futures." *Journal of Alternative Investments* 5:4, 41–50.

Kaminski, Kathryn. 2011a. "In Search of Crisis Alpha: A Short Guide to Investing in Managed Futures." CME Group Education.

Kaminski, Kathryn. 2011b. "Offensive or Defensive? Crisis Alpha vs. Tail Risk Insurance." Working Paper, RPM Risk and Portfolio Management.

Kat, Harry M. 2002. "Managed Futures and Hedge Funds: A Match Made in Heaven." Working Paper, Cass Business School, City University, London.

Kazemi, Hossein, and Ying Li. 2009. "Market Timing of CTAs: An Examination of Systematic CTAs vs. Discretionary CTAs." *Journal of Futures Markets* 29:11, 1067–1099.

Kritzman, Mark. 1993. "The Optimal Currency Hedging Policy with Biased Forward Rates." *Journal of Portfolio Management* 19:4, 94–100.

Liang, Bing. 2003. "The Accuracy of Hedge Fund Returns." *Journal of Portfolio Management* 29:3, 111–121.

Lightner, Charles R. 2003. "A Rationale for Managed Futures." *Technical Analysis of Stocks & Commodities* 17:3, 138–143.

Lintner, John V. 1983. "The Potential Role of Managed Futures Accounts (and/or Funds) in Portfolios of Stocks and Bonds." Presentation to the Annual Conference of the Financial Analysts Federation in Managed Futures, Toronto, Canada.

McCarthy, David, Thomas Schneeweis, and Richard Spurgin. 1996. "Survivor Bias in Commodity Trading Performance." *Journal of Futures Markets* 16:7, 757–772.

Oberuc, Richard E. 1992. "How to Diversify Portfolios of Euro-Stocks and Bonds with Hedged U.S. Managed Futures." Presentation at the First International Conference on Futures Money Management, May, Geneva, Switzerland.

Schneeweis, Thomas, U. Savanayana, and David McCarthy. 1992. "Multi-Manager Commodity Portfolios: A Risk/Return Analysis." In Charles B. Epstein, ed., *Managed Futures in the Institutional Portfolio*, 81–102. New York: John Wiley & Sons, Inc.

Schneeweis, Thomas, Richard Spurgin, and David McCarthy. 1997. "Informational Content in Historical CTA Performance." *Journal of Futures Markets* 17:3, 317–339.

Spurgin, Richard. 2003. "Sources of Return in Managed Futures." Working Paper, Center for International Securities and Derivatives Markets, Isenberg School of Management.

Tee, Kai-Hong. 2009. "The Effect of Downside Risk Reduction on UK Equity Portfolios Included with Managed Futures Funds." *International Review of Financial Analysis* 18:5, 303–310.

ABOUT THE AUTHOR

Kai-Hong Tee is a Senior Lecturer in Finance at Loughborough University Business School, United Kingdom. He worked previously as a Lecturer in Finance at the University of Aberdeen and as a Property Investment Marketing Consultant on both residential and commercial sectors in the international properties markets. His research interests involve the application of asymmetric risks on portfolio optimization, the study of liquidity risks, and efficient performance of managed futures and hedge funds. Other interests include exploring the hedging effectiveness of derivatives and the effectiveness of currency (portfolio) strategy for conditional hedging purposes. Dr. Tee's research has been published in the *European Journal of Operational Research, International Review of Financial Analysis,* and *Applied Financial Economics.* He has a BA in Economics and General Mathematics from the National University of Singapore, an MBA (with distinction) in finance from the Leeds University Business School, and a Ph.D. in Finance from Heriot-Watt University in Edinburgh, Scotland.

PART V

Hedge Funds

CHAPTER 23

Investing in Hedge Funds

HUNTER M. HOLZHAUER
Assistant Professor of Finance, Penn State Erie, The Behrend College

INTRODUCTION

Over the last 60 years, few sectors of the market have seen a similar rise in demand as the hedge fund industry. In fact, hedge funds have grown from a billion dollar industry in the 1970s into an industry currently valued near $2 trillion, which is close to the industry's previous peak established before the financial crisis of 2007–2008 (Strasburg and Eder, 2011). Moreover, the largest 225 American hedge funds added approximately $115 billion in 2010, bringing their total assets under management (AUM) to $1.297 trillion. The largest hedge fund in the world at the time this chapter was written is Bridgewater Associates, with $58.9 billion in AUM (Allen, 2011).

Nevertheless, a broad range of participants exists in the hedge fund market. The market currently contains roughly between 10,000 and 25,000 hedge funds. These funds directly employ between 100,000 and 150,000 professionals and are connected to more than one million other individuals (Wilson, 2010). One positive sign for the future growth of the hedge fund industry is the rise in demand from institutional investors. In 2010, institutional investors accounted for an average of 61 percent of hedge fund AUM, compared to 45 percent in 2008 (Williamson, 2011).

Considering the growing impact of the hedge fund industry, the purpose of this chapter is to provide a clear understanding of both the broader hedge fund industry and its many distinct investment strategies. Therefore, the remainder of the chapter has the following organizational structure. This introductory section defines hedge funds in terms of their investment, legal, and compensation structure, with special attention given to common provisions and incentives in hedge fund contracts. The following section provides context for the growing complexity within the current hedge fund industry by examining the early history of hedge funds. The third section explores the inherent data biases specific to hedge funds and their databases. The fourth section contains a thorough review of the primary investment strategies within hedge fund portfolios. The fifth section includes a brief analysis on the future of hedge funds with regards to current trends and other important issues. The final section concludes with a summary of the chapter.

Structure of Hedge Funds

Various definitions for hedge funds focus on their investment, legal, or compensation structures. From an investment perspective, hedge funds employ a wide array of trading strategies. However, most hedge funds are designed to either generate higher risk-adjusted returns or generate a consistent level of return irrespective of changes in the market. Yet, this is not a completely satisfactory definition of a hedge fund because each hedge fund is unique. In fact, explaining hedge funds may be easier than defining them. For example, even the name *hedge fund* is not truly descriptive. A hedge fund does not necessarily have to employ any hedging strategies. *Hedging* refers to reducing market risk. Some hedge funds actually go a step further than reducing market risk by using sophisticated arbitrage techniques, which focus on eliminating market risk altogether. On the other end of the spectrum, some hedge funds primarily concentrate on *speculating*, which is the process of seeking a higher return by accepting additional market risk. Thus, hedge fund managers can engage in a broad range of investment strategies, from highly conservative (or risk-averse) investing to highly aggressive (or risk-seeking) investing.

From a legal perspective, most hedge funds are lightly regulated, privately managed funds. However, this autonomy legally restricts them to only *accredited investors*. The two most commonly cited qualifications for accrediting investors (listed in Rule 501 of Regulation D of the Securities Act of 1933) are either (1) a net worth exceeding $1 million or (2) an annual income exceeding $200,000 ($300,000 if combined with a spouse) for each of the two most recent years. Although accredited investors are generally more knowledgeable about investments, accreditation serves another vital purpose. Accredited investors can generally tolerate a higher degree of illiquidity. This tolerance is important because many hedge funds are structured with illiquid assets and, consequently, institute substantial withdrawal limits on their investors.

Finally, from a compensation perspective, hedge funds are usually structured to include two types of investor fees: a management fee and a performance fee. This fee structure is representative of both the manager's reputation and the manager's liability. From a reputation perspective, managers with better reputations can require higher performance fees. From a liability perspective, hedge funds are also created as partnerships. Consequently, as the general partner, the fund manager bears unlimited liability, whereas the investors (i.e., limited partners) have only limited liability. Therefore, hedge fund managers require not only a standard management fee, which is usually between 1 and 2 percent of the total AUM, but also a substantial performance fee, which is usually between 10 and 20 percent of a fund's returns.

Provisions and Incentives

Several important variations exist in this dual-fee structure. Two common performance fee provisions structured into many hedge fund contracts are a hurdle rate and a high-water mark (Agarwal, Daniel, and Naik, 2009). The *hurdle rate* is a set performance target that must be achieved before the hedge fund manager can collect any performance fees. This provision effectively endows the manager with an out-of-the-money option at the beginning of each year. The *high-water mark* conditions the payment of the performance fee upon exceeding the previously achieved maximum share value. Consequently, if the fund incurs losses (or insufficient returns to recover past losses), the manager must make up for the losses incurred in the fund and exceed the hurdle rate based on the fund's previously achieved maximum share value before receiving any incentive fees. Essentially, both the hurdle rate and the high-water mark are provisions that protect investors from paying performance fees on poorly performing funds.

Hurdle rate and high-water mark provisions are useful tools for examining management contracts and incentives because they are different than most managerial incentives. Managerial incentives in most corporate finance settings, such as stock options, are not necessarily static and can be subject to change. In contrast, hurdle rate and high-water mark provisions are set at the fund's inception and are not subject to change. For this reason, these provisions, and the high-water mark in particular, have been incorporated into the academic literature. For example, Agarwal et al. (2009) examine the unique characteristics of high-water mark provisions among other incentives and provide evidence that these provisions can lead to superior fund performance. Their finding suggests that high-water mark provisions are highly effective in motivating managerial effort and in alleviating agency problems.

In contrast, Goetzmann, Ingersoll, and Ross (2003) investigate high-water marks included in hedge fund management contracts and provide evidence that these provisions can create agency problems. Specifically, they find that the high-water mark provisions limit the value of the performance fees and create a distinct optionlike feature to the management contracts. In other words, managers have an adverse gambling incentive to increase risk when the fund is not far below the high-water mark. This extreme risk-taking behavior is supported by several earlier studies on portfolio variance and call-like features within incentive contracts (Grinblatt and Titman, 1989; Goetzmann, Ingersoll, and Ross, 1997; Carpenter, 2000).

On the contrary, both Fung and Hsieh (1997) and Brown, Goetzmann, and Park (2001) contend that reputation costs mitigate this potentially extreme risk-taking behavior. Their reasoning is that excess risk and poor performance considerably increase the probability of termination, which creates a reputation cost that effectively offsets the adverse gambling incentive of high-water mark provisions. Brown et al. (2001) also show the importance of reputation by showing that hedge fund managers value relative performance more than absolute performance. In other words, hedge fund managers are more concerned with "beating the pack" than with "beating the benchmark." Thus, the academic evidence suggests that hedge fund managers must weigh their desire for risk-seeking behavior against their desire for reputation-protecting behavior.

Finally, Goetzmann et al. (2003) conclude that the presence of high-water mark contracts may offer some insights into the future of the hedge fund industry in comparison with the mutual fund industry. Hedge funds have several contractual arrangements that contrast with mutual funds. In particular, hedge funds require coinvestment by the manager and longer-term capital commitment by investors. Yet, the most obvious difference is their compensation structure. Mutual fund managers are primarily compensated by growing AUM. However, regulations on the number of investors within hedge funds have essentially capped the growth in

AUM that hedge fund managers might expect. Consequently, hedge fund managers are compensated with contracts that pay a fixed percentage of AUM and a fraction of returns. In other words, hedge fund managers must rely extensively on compensation contracts that provide rewards for positive returns. Further, the managers are often incentivized by high-water mark provisions within these contracts. The authors suggest that the very existence of high-water mark contracts may signal that the hedge fund industry returns are diminishing in scale. These diminishing returns are common in other industries that use optionlike incentive contracts, including real estate and venture capital. Thus, as the hedge fund market continues to grow, future returns may be dependent upon an increasing amount of resources pursuing a limited set of unique opportunities.

HISTORY OF HEDGE FUNDS

Trying to process the current state of the multifaceted hedge fund industry can be a mentally exhaustive task. Since the 1950s, the hedge fund market has grown to include thousands of participants using a vast number of increasingly complex strategies designed to constantly adapt to the ever-changing market. Hence, without historical context, the present makes a convoluted focal point for explaining the hedge fund industry. Thus, to fully understand the magnitude and scope of the current hedge fund industry, this chapter provides an extensive review of the early history of hedge funds.

The evolution of the hedge fund industry began with a mutation from traditional investing in the early to mid-twentieth century. The exact date of the first mutation is debatable. The most credited mutation is the creation of the first public hedge fund by Alfred W. Jones in 1949. Jones has long been considered the founder of the hedge fund industry. Dennistoun (2004, p. 1) writes that Jones' reputation within the hedge fund industry "is unassailable. As a prophet and seer he rests loftily in the hedge fund holy of holies." However, Jaeger (2003) cautions that earlier investors, including Benjamin Graham, may have been engaging in hedging activities such as shorting and arbitrage as early as the 1920s. Moreover, Jaeger argues that Wall Street brokerage and trading firms have long engaged in arbitrage practices, such as buying gold in New York at one price and selling it in London at a higher price. Whether any of these early investors or firms actually implemented hedge fund strategies is debatable. However, documentation of one predecessor to Jones, who is arguably the true founder of the hedge fund industry, exists. Dennistoun (2004, p. 1) writes that "in the background lurks another creator, a writer, academic and investor called Karl Karsten." Although Jones is credited with forming the first public hedge fund, Dennistoun maintains that Karsten should be credited with the earliest known record of hedging activity.

The First Private Hedge Fund

Approximately 18 years before Jones would create the first public hedge fund, Karsten (1931) published a book, *Scientific Forecasting*, which contains the main principles for managing a hedge fund. In Chapter VII, entitled "The Hedge Principle," he explains a hedge as positioning the fund so that general market movements do not have any effects on profits or losses. This positioning is accomplished through "hedge" operations, which entail buying stock in groups predicted to provide the highest positive return and shorting stock in groups predicted to provide the highest negative return (Lhabitant, 2006).

Karsten also founded the Karsten Statistical Laboratory to develop "barometers" that would theoretically forecast future business conditions. These barometers looked at volume of trade, interest rates, price levels, building activities, industry indices, and specific groups of stock. To extrapolate whether the theoretical barometers held up in practice, Karsten Statistical Laboratory established a small private fund on December 17, 1930. The fund proved to be a complete success. By June 3, 1931, the fund had earned an impressive 78 percent return, which equates to a 250 percent compounded annual return. Furthermore, keeping in line with Karsten's hedge principle, the fund's performance seemed to be entirely independent of the direction of the stock market. Thus, Karsten provided the blueprint for many hedge funds today (Dennistoun, 2004).

The First Public Hedge Fund

In 1949, Alfred W. Jones formed the first public for-profit hedge fund. Jones' motivation for the fund came while writing about finance as a member of the editorial staff for *Fortune*. Jones (1949) analyzed the technical methods of market analysis and forecasting. Inspired to design a new investment model, Jones invested $40,000 of his own capital, plus an additional $60,000 in raised capital, to create the equity fund A. W. Jones & Co. He created the fund on the premise that the movements of specific securities were the result of the performance of both the security and the broader market.

In several ways, the fund was extremely innovative. For example, it was the first public fund to use a *long/short strategy* by investing in securities positioned to outperform the market and shorting securities positioned to underperform the market. Consequently, Jones became one of the first conservative investors to leverage his returns by using the proceeds from short sales to finance additional long positions (Wilson, 2010).

The fund was also the first public attempt at creating a *market-neutral strategy* that eliminated market risk by allowing the portfolio to hedge against bearish market movements. Furthermore, the premise of the portfolio was unique in that the fund was expected to sustain steady performance over time. In other words, the fund was structured to perform relatively well during both bull and bear markets and also during markets with high volatility. Jones was essentially attempting to maintain a consistently high alpha and low beta long before the terms alpha and beta were coined (Lhabitant, 2006).

Jones also set the standard for performance fees. To attract investors into the first public hedge fund, the fund decided to charge performance-linked fees, which were 20 percent of realized profits. Jones' performance fee structure has stood the test of time considering that the current industry standard for performance fee is usually between 10 and 20 percent of the overall return. However, Jones did not charge an asset-based management fee, which is now standard in the industry.

Although the performance fees were a novel approach at the time, Jones gave his investors very little reason to object. Like Karsten's private hedge fund, Jones' public hedge fund was an immediate success. In its first year, Jones' fund earned a remarkable 17.3 percent gain. Jones' fund continued to grow and provide satisfactory returns throughout the 1950s and 1960s. During this time, other hedge fund pioneers entered the market (Lhabitant, 2006). Some of the early hedge fund managers included Warren Buffett, Michael Steinhardt, George Soros, and Julian Robertson. By the 1970s, more than 150 hedge funds with approximately $1 billion in AUM started operations (Wilson, 2010). Thus, hedge funds were here to stay.

HEDGE FUND DATA AND BIASES

Unlike mutual funds, which have an industry association to collect and report industry information, obtaining reliable information about hedge funds can be difficult. The main reason is that participating hedge funds provide information to database vendors on a voluntary basis. This process may seem flawed considering that most hedge funds are secretive by nature. However, hedge funds are also actively trying to increase their visibility for marketing reasons. Consequently, hedge funds provide monthly return information to databases, which, in turn, sell the data back to interested buyers, including accredited investors, banks, fund-of-funds managers, consultants, and academic researchers (Lhabitant, 2006). Some of the earliest database vendors include the Center for International Securities and Derivatives Markets (which now owns the popular database Managed Accounts Reports), Hedge Fund Research, and Lipper TASS (Fung and Hsieh, 2006). Lhabitant (2006) lists several other large hedge fund databases: Altvest/InvestorForce, Barclays, Financial Risk Management, Hennessee, Morgan Stanley Capital Indices, Tuna/Hedgefund.net, and Van Hedge Fund Advisors.

Because hedge fund databases do not have a uniform reporting standard, assessing the true impact and scope of the industry is difficult. Each database is uniquely constructed, which makes combining data from different databases an arduous task. Nonetheless, Fung and Hsieh (2006) state that the BNP Paribas Hedge Fund Centre of the London Business School is merging these various databases into one comprehensive database.

Still, two additional complications arise that any comprehensive database will face. First, the merger of hedge fund data causes some firms to report to more than one database, which increases the likelihood that these hedge funds will be counted more than once. Second, each hedge fund database is subject to differing degrees of inaccuracy due to several common biases. Consequently, neither existing hedge fund databases nor a comprehensive hedge fund database is necessarily representative of the entire hedge fund universe (Lhabitant, 2006).

Biases in Hedge Fund Databases

Properly accessing the hedge fund industry requires valid and reliable data. However, several significant biases exist regarding hedge fund databases. Some biases are the result of the database's construction and data-collecting methods. Other biases are the result of the timing and accuracy of the hedge fund's voluntary information. Ackerman, McEnally, and Ravenscraft (1999) identify four specific biases within hedge fund databases: selection bias, survivorship bias, backfill bias, and liquidation bias.

Selection Bias

Selection bias arises when individuals select themselves into a group. As private investment firms, hedge funds are not required to disclose asset or return information to any database. Thus, hedge fund databases create biased samples because inclusion of hedge funds into databases is at the discretion of the hedge fund manager. Moreover, hedge fund managers often decide what information they will provide. Therefore, a strong incentive exits for firms with good track records to report their information to databases because the increased visibility should attract new accredited investors. In contrast, firms with poor track records often opt out of reporting their performance information. Consequently, the hedge fund samples should be biased towards superior performing hedge funds (Fung and Hsieh, 2006).

However, selection bias may also result from the absence of large, high-performing hedge funds that do not need increased visibility. Many large, high-performing funds may already be in high demand and consider the task of reporting performance information as an unnecessary use of resources. Another reason large, high-performing funds may avoid the burden of reporting is that databases often include reporting funds within indices, which abates any performance divergence between those indices and the reporting hedge fund (Lhabitant, 2006).

Thus, neither the magnitude nor the direction of the selection bias within hedge fund databases is clear. Hedge fund databases are biased towards average firms, with several funds displaying either poor performance or superior performance selecting not to report. Regardless of its magnitude or direction, selection bias is evidence that hedge fund database samples are not truly representative of the broader hedge fund market (Fung and Hsieh, 2006).

Survivorship Bias

Survivorship bias occurs whenever funds are excluded from databases, and consequently from research studies, because the funds stop reporting their returns. This bias is severe in the hedge fund industry. Gregoriou (2002) finds that the median life span of a hedge fund from 1990 to 2001 is only 5.5 years. As these funds exit a database, they are usually labeled as either *defunct funds* if they still exist or *dead funds* if they have stopped operations. As the number of defunct or dead funds excluded from a database increases, performance data for the surviving funds becomes further conditioned to overstate returns and understate risk (Lhabitant, 2006). In fact, empirical estimates of annual survivorship bias in hedge funds range from 0.16 to 3.4 percent (Fung and Hsieh 1997, 2000, 2001; Ackerman et al., 1999; Brown, Goetzmann, and Ibbotson, 1999; Brown, Goetzmann, and Park, 1999; Liang, 2000; Bares, Gibson, and Gyger, 2001; Edwards and Caglayan, 2001; Barry, 2003).

Backfill Bias

Backfill bias, or *instant history bias*, arises from the tendency of databases to allow recently listed funds to include their historical returns. Backfill bias provides the recently listed fund with an instant history, even though there was no performance data for the fund in prior years. Lhabitant (2006, p. 485) equates backfill bias to "granting a free option to hedge fund managers, namely, the option to decide when to be included in the database with all or part of the fund's track record." Consequently, this option results in an overstated past performance. Empirical studies approximate annual backfill bias to be around 1.2 to 1.4 percent (Fung and Hsieh, 2000; Edwards and Caglayan, 2001; Barry, 2003).

Liquidation Bias

Liquidation bias results when hedge fund managers stop reporting returns before the final liquidation phase of a fund. One extreme example of liquidation bias took place in August 1998 during the Russian debt crisis. Several funds lost 100 percent of their capital during the crisis, but the fund managers did not report returns of –100 percent in the process of liquidating. In fact, their last reported returns were in July 1998, which created an upward bias in the performance data because the defunct funds were not included (Fung and Hsieh, 2006).

Conversely, the empirical evidence suggests that liquidation bias is rarely extreme. Ackerman et al. (1999) examine defunct and dead fund data from 1988 to 1995 and find that the average loss in fund value beyond the information contained in the database is only 0.7 percent. Their result suggests that liquidation bias has a negligible impact on performance data.

Bias and Serial Correlation in Hedge Fund Returns

Although the previous biases can be attributed to the relationship between hedge funds and databases, two serious issues involve the accuracy of hedge fund returns: illiquidity bias and serial correlation.

Illiquidity Bias

Illiquidity bias, or *infrequent pricing bias*, is the natural inclination for hedge fund managers with illiquid assets to optimize their fund's net asset value in order to smooth returns over time. These managers contend that this smoothing practice is necessary to account for a lack of accurate pricing information for illiquid securities such as small cap stocks, emerging market bonds, over-the-counter securities, and distressed assets. Although managers are ethically bound to assign reasonable market values to the illiquid securities, the bias results when they assign prices simply to smooth returns. This practice is a serious issue because illiquidity bias can lead to wide differences in valuation and transparency (Lhabitant, 2006).

Serial Correlation

The second serious issue with hedge fund returns is serial correlation. *Serial correlation* refers to the relationship between hedge fund returns and those same hedge fund returns from previous time intervals. Serial correlation is often used in investment strategies to determine how well the past price of a security predicts the future price. The evidence suggests a statistically significant, serial correlation in hedge fund returns. Asness, Krail, and Liew (2001) observe serial correlation in hedge fund index returns, while Getmansky, Lo, and Makarov (2004) observe serial correlation in individual hedge fund returns. Both studies attribute the serial correlation to either illiquid securities or return smoothing.

The results of these studies are important because serial correlation can help explain the common characterization that all hedge funds are uncorrelated with market swings, contain relatively low volatility, and yield double-digit returns. For instance, many hedge fund managers explain that the market neutrality, low risk, and high returns within their funds are maintained through both long and short positions in securities (hence the term *hedge fund*), which create relatively small betas while still allowing for gains on both positive and negative information. However, Getmansky et al. (2004) make the case that the standard methods of assessing market neutrality, risks, and returns are misleading due to serial correlation. For example, Asness et al. (2001) show that betas for hedge funds are misleading and that hedge funds may have significantly higher market exposure. Lo (2002) provides the correct method for computing Sharpe ratios for hedge funds and finds evidence that naive Sharpe ratios (based on naive measures of risk and return) can provide risk-adjusted performance measures that differ from the correct method by as much as 70 percent.

HEDGE FUND STRATEGIES

Hedge funds are a broad classification type that includes many different subsets of investment funds loosely tied together based on the following almost universal hedge fund characteristics: privately owned, unregulated, and performance-based fee structures. However, from this loose definition, hedge funds have expanded to encompass other investment strategies. Unfortunately, there is no way to provide an exhaustive list of every hedge fund strategy. Thus, the following section includes a discussion of the most common hedge fund strategies listed in hedge fund databases.

Nondirectional Hedge Funds

Before discussing specific hedge fund strategies, two broader characterizations of hedge fund strategies based on exposure to market risk are discussed: nondirectional hedge funds and directional hedge funds. *Nondirectional hedge funds*, or *absolute-return hedge funds*, seek to provide investors with a consistent return regardless of the performance of the broader market. These hedge funds represent the traditional hedge fund structure that Alfred W. Jones devised with the first public hedge fund in 1949. A more detailed breakdown of nondirectional funds is included within the context of other hedge fund strategies. From a general perspective, these funds are associated with more conservative hedge fund managers who are willing to sacrifice some return in exchange for less risk.

Directional Hedge Funds

Directional hedge funds are simply hedge funds that do not fully hedge. Consequently, one of the main differences between directional and nondirectional hedge funds is that returns for directional hedge funds are usually not as consistent as the returns for nondirectional hedge funds. Conversely, directional hedge funds have the potential to earn relatively higher returns because of their added market risk exposure. The types of directional hedge funds include managed futures, global macro funds, emerging market funds, and dedicated short funds.

Managed Futures

Directional portfolios allow more aggressive hedge fund managers to speculate on the market or provide protection against temporary downturns in the market. Interestingly, many directional hedge funds are more speculative than hedged. One particular hedge fund strategy that attracts both hedgers and speculators is *managed futures*. Hedgers use managed futures to hedge against future price variations in the underlying cash commodities. In contrast, speculators use managed futures to speculate on future price variations in order to realize higher capital gains (Lhabitant, 2006).

Managed futures are managed by *commodity trading advisers* (CTAs), who often incorporate advanced algorithms to trade listed commodity and futures contracts. The Commodity Exchange Act requires nearly all individuals and firms operating in the futures market to register with the Commodity Futures Trading Commission and be members of the National Futures Association. Initially, CTAs were restricted to trading futures contracts for a few traditional commodities. In the 1970s and 1980s, CTAs expanded their trading activities to include listed derivatives on commodities, raw materials, precious metals, equity indices, bonds, interest rates, and currencies (Stefanini, 2006).

In the 1980s, the futures market was dominated by agricultural futures (64 percent) with the remaining market composed of currency and interest rate futures (20 percent) and metals futures (16 percent). However, since then, CTAs have shifted their primary focus to financial futures for currencies, interest rates, and stock indices. With roughly $150 billion in AUM, managed futures currently represent approximately 5 percent of the total hedge fund industry (Lhabitant, 2006).

Global Macro Funds

In the 1980s, some opportunistic hedge fund managers, including several CTAs, migrated to *global macro funds*. Global macro portfolios allowed these managers to make higher leveraged bets in more liquid markets such as global currency, equity, bond, and commodity markets. These managers are only in charge of about 10 percent of the hedge fund AUM. However, in the mid-1990s, global macro managers were major participants in the market and controlled nearly two-thirds of all hedge fund AUM. Several notable global macro success stories include George Soros (Quantum Fund), Julian Robertson (Tiger Fund), Louis Moore Bacon (Moore Global), Paul Tudor Jones (Tudor Investments), and Bruce Kovner (Caxton Associates) (Lhabitant, 2006).

Emerging Market Funds

Directional hedge funds can have varying degrees of market risk exposure, including full market exposure. The two most extreme directional portfolios include long-only and short-only portfolios. Long-only portfolios represent traditional investing and are usually not considered hedge funds. However, about 6 percent of the hedge fund industry is dedicated to *emerging market funds*, which often include long-only positions in securities in emerging countries such as equities, bonds, and sovereign debt (Lhabitant, 2006).

Dedicated Short Funds

Short-only positions in the hedge fund industry are usually reserved for *dedicated short funds*. Dedicated short fund managers borrow shares of overvalued companies and sell them short in anticipation of a price decline. Although dedicated short funds represent only around 1 percent of the total hedge fund market, the demand for dedicated shorts can rise quickly during bear markets. In a similar manner, if any hedge fund manager is bearish on an entire group of stocks, the manager may simply invest in an *inverse fund*. One simple example of an inverse fund is an inverse exchange-traded fund (ETF), which provides returns that are exactly opposite of the underlying index. In other words, if the index drops by 5 percent, the inverse ETF's value increases by 5 percent. Hedge fund managers often use inverse ETFs and other inverse funds as protection against temporary downturns in the market (Strong, 2009).

Long/Short Hedge Funds

Roughly 30 percent of the hedge fund market is structured using *long/short portfolios*. Long/short portfolios involve short selling one set of stocks and using the proceeds to buy another set of stocks. These funds aim to reduce, but not necessarily eliminate, market exposure. Thus, long/short portfolios can technically include either nondirectional or directional hedge fund strategies. For example, with nondirectional strategies, managers make a profit by shorting overvalued securities and investing an equal dollar amount into undervalued securities. In 1990, Yale became the first institutional investor to act on the increased efficiency in long/short portfolios, allocating about 15 percent of its portfolio into a nondirectional strategy. By 2007, more than 40 percent of all hedge funds included some version of a long/short strategy (Strong, 2009). Two specific long/short strategies that are becoming increasingly popular in hedge funds are active-extension funds and market-neutral funds.

Active-Extension Funds

Active-extension funds allow both long and short positions in the portfolio, but they are directional hedge funds because they require the portfolio to maintain a net 100 percent exposure to the market. In 2008, the active-extension market consisted of about 25 active-extension funds, with several of these funds managed by well-known investment firms such as ING Funds, UBS Global Asset Management, Fidelity Investments, and State Street Global Investors (Strong, 2009).

Active-extension funds may employ any proportion of long and short positions as long as the net market exposure is 100 percent (e.g., 110/10, 120/20, 130/30). For example, the 130/30 strategy has 130 percent exposure in long positions and 30 percent exposure in short positions. The empirical evidence suggests that 130/30 strategies, compared to long-only strategies, provide about 40 to 50 percent higher *information ratios*, which measure active return per unit of active risk (Tol and Wanninen, 2009, 2011). The academic literature overwhelmingly suggests that the efficiency gains of 130/30 strategies, compared to long-only strategies, can be largely explained by the removal of the long-only constraint (Jacobs and Levy, 1993, 2006; Brush, 1997; Jacobs, Levy, and Starer, 1998, 1999; Grinold and Kahn, 2000; Johnson, Kahn, and Petrich, 2007, Sorensen, Hua, and Qian, 2007).

Market-Neutral Funds

Market-neutral funds may employ similar shorting techniques as active-extension portfolios, but the two portfolio types have one glaring difference—market participation. Unlike active-extension strategies, market-neutral strategies are insensitive to underlying market movements. Instead, market-neutral strategies are specifically designed to offset the systematic risk of long positions by investing in an equivalent exposure of corresponding short positions within the same market (Jacobs and Levy, 1993). Thus, market-neutral strategies are nondirectional strategies with portfolio betas equal to zero (Badrinath and Gubellini, 2011).

Active-extension strategies also differ from *equitized* market-neutral strategies, which use equity market overlays (e.g., futures contracts or ETFs) to create full market exposure similar to active-extension strategies. The chief difference is that active-extension strategies are actively managed and equity market overlays are passively managed. Consequently, strategies using equity market overlays cannot expect to earn returns in excess of the underlying index (Jacobs and Levy, 2007a). Furthermore, equity market overlays can potentially create *untrim portfolios*, which contain long and short positions in the same security. Conversely, active-extension strategies use individual security positions to create *trim portfolios*, which contain no overlapping long and short positions. Thus, active-extension strategies incorporate leveraged positions more efficiently (Jacobs and Levy, 2007b).

Relative-Value Hedge Funds

Stefanini (2006) defines *relative-value hedge funds* as arbitrage portfolios that seek to profit from the spread between securities rather than from the broader market direction. Using this nondirectional definition, market-neutral strategies could also be included as relative value strategies. However, most relative value funds use sophisticated arbitrage techniques. Two common types of relative value hedge funds include fixed-income arbitrage and convertible arbitrage, which collectively represent around 10 percent of all hedge fund AUM (Lhabitant, 2006).

Fixed-Income Arbitrage Funds

Fixed-income arbitrage funds include a wide range of strategies for pursuing pricing anomalies throughout the global fixed-income markets. Although fixed-income arbitrageurs usually focus on relative value, they can also use market-neutral and directional strategies. Regardless of the strategy, the primary tool of fixed-income arbitrageurs is the *term structure of interest rates*. The term structure of interest rates reflects the pure "price of time" in that it represents the relationship between pure interest rates and their maturity. With coupon-paying bonds, the term structure of interest rates is often referred to as the *yield curve*. Simply stated, the yield curve can be used for not only forecasting forward interest rates, but also for benchmarking and comparing relative values for debt instruments (Lhabitant, 2006).

Convertible Arbitrage Funds

Similar to fixed-income arbitrage funds, *convertible arbitrage funds* seek to exploit pricing anomalies. Yet, convertible arbitrageurs focus on pricing anomalies within a highly specialized fixed-income market—the convertible bond market. *Convertible bonds* are bondlike securities that can be converted into equity at the owner's discretion, which can create a wide array of optionlike features. Not surprisingly, convertible arbitrage funds AUM are only about one-fourth the size of fixed-income arbitrage AUM due to the complexity of these securities (Lhabitant, 2006).

Event-Driven Hedge Funds

Representing nearly a quarter of the hedge fund industry, *event-driven hedge funds* take advantage of opportunities for gains that transpire due to either the ordinary corporate life cycle or extraordinary corporate events (Lhabitant, 2006). The most common event-driven strategies focus on extraordinary events such as mergers, acquisitions, liquidations, and restructuring (Stefanini, 2006). Thus, two common hedge fund strategies for taking advantage of these events include merger arbitrage funds, which specialize in mergers and acquisitions, and distressed securities funds, which specialize in liquidations and restructuring.

Merger Arbitrage Funds

Merger arbitrage funds invest in event-driven situations such as mergers and acquisitions (M&As). Merger arbitrage funds can be viewed as relative value strategies as well as event-driven strategies because they track the relative value in the spread between the offered price and the target share price (Stefanini, 2006). In this manner, merger arbitrageurs essentially take bets on whether a merger or acquisition will be successful. If the merger is successful, the market price of the target shares usually rises and converges towards the offered price. If the merger is unsuccessful, the market price of the target shares usually falls, often dramatically, as it diverges away from the offered price (Lhabitant, 2006).

Merger arbitrage is also known as *risk arbitrage* because it requires extensive knowledge about the inherent risks involved in different types of M&As, including leveraged buyouts and hostile takeovers. Two specific risks include (1) *transaction risk,* which measures the uncertainty of the transaction being completed, and (2) *calendar risk,* which measures this uncertainty relative to the elapsed time between the merger's announcement and its consummation (Lhabitant, 2006).

Distressed Securities Funds

Distressed securities funds are event-driven funds that focus on companies experiencing financial or operational difficulty. These companies may include reorganizations, distressed sales, and other corporate restructurings. However, one obvious sign of a distressed company is if it has filed for either Chapter 7 *bankruptcy,* which indicates that the company is being liquidated with the proceeds going to creditors, or Chapter 11 *bankruptcy,* which offers short-term protection from creditors while a company is undergoing reorganization.

During the bankruptcy process, hedge funds use three main strategies: (1) investing in debt claims, (2) buying equity stakes, and (3) pursuing "loan-to-own" strategies, which acquire debt from distressed borrowers with the intention of converting the debt into equity after the firm completes the Chapter 11 process. Jiang, Li, and Wang (2012) study the role hedge funds play in the Chapter 11 process, including their impact on bankruptcy outcomes. They analyze 474 Chapter 11 cases from 1996 to 2007 and find that about 90 percent of these cases include observable participation by hedge funds. Their results suggest that hedge funds have become the most active investors in the distressed debt market.

Siegel (2006) provides practitioner support for these findings. Specifically, he summarizes a Greenwich Associates study on hedge fund trading volume and finds that hedge fund trading in U.S. fixed-income markets more than doubled from 2005 to 2006. Additionally, hedge fund trading represents nearly half of the annual volume in both emerging bond markets and distressed debt markets. Hedge fund trading also generates close to one-third of the annual volume in leveraged loans and one-fourth of the annual volume in high-yield bonds.

FUTURE OF HEDGE FUNDS

Are hedge fund managers evil geniuses who profit from wreaking havoc in capital markets, or do they represent the quintessence of "smart money," providing risk capital to capital markets unencumbered by securities regulations (Fung and Hsieh, 2006, p. 4)? Answering this proposed question requires examining the future of the hedge industry within the context of two different discussions. The first portion of this section concentrates on the potential impact of hedge funds on the broader market. The second portion of this section focuses on current trends and issues that are shaping the future of the hedge fund industry.

Market Impact of Hedge Funds

Two of the earliest studies on hedge fund returns examine the potential impact of hedge funds on the integrity of the market (Fung and Hsieh, 1997; Eichengreen, Mathieson, Sharma, Chadha, Kodres, and Jansen, 1998). Fung and Hsieh develop a model for hedge fund returns by asking three essential questions: How do hedge funds trade? Where do hedge funds trade? How are hedge fund positions financed? Explaining how and where hedge funds trade can be approached similar to conventional mutual fund models such as Sharpe (1992). The more interesting issue regarding market impact is how the hedge fund positions are financed. Fung and Hsieh (2006) state that when leverage ability is combined with common risk factors hedge fund strategies have the potential to create havoc in capital markets, especially if most hedge fund managers are incorporating the same hedge fund strategies.

Eichengreen et al. (1998) disagree and argue that hedge funds are too small to exert substantial impact on financial markets. They base their conclusion on a series of interviews with hedge fund managers and other market participants about the role of hedge funds during several major market events. These events include the 1992 exchange rate mechanism crisis, the 1994 Mexican peso crisis, and the 1997 Asian currency crisis. Brunnermeier and Nagel (2004) examine the 1999–2000 technology bubble collapse and find little evidence that hedge funds participated in widespread shorting of technology stocks.

However, the assertion that hedge funds are too small to substantially affect the market may no longer hold true. Hedge funds have grown dramatically over the past decade despite some of the most volatile market movement ever recorded. If recent hedge fund growth is any indication of future growth, the future impact of hedge funds on the market seems almost certain. Thus, the real concern is whether that impact will be positive or negative.

Current Hedge Fund Trends and Issues

One way to examine the potential impact of hedge funds on the market is to study the current trends and issues that are shaping the future of the hedge fund industry. Fung and Hsieh (2006) discuss several current trends within the hedge fund industry including increased transparency, advanced risk management tools, enhanced regulations, better organization, and improved diversification methods. For instance, one specific trend that deserves special attention is the rise of fund-of-funds, which offers investors some unique advantages.

Advantages of Fund-of-Funds

Wilson (2010) defines a *fund-of-funds* as an investment fund that allows a single investor broad access to many different hedge funds through one investment. More succinctly, a fund-of-funds is simply a hedge fund that invests in other hedge funds. The main advantage of a fund-of-funds is that it offers diversification within several professionally researched hedge funds without committing considerable resources, such as time to manager selection, portfolio construction, or ongoing risk management and rebalancing (Strong, 2009). Conversely, the main disadvantage of the fund-of-funds is higher expenses. Investors are effectively adding an additional layer of management fees to the underlying investments. Nonetheless, the increasing allocation of capital into fund-of-funds suggests that the benefits outweigh the added management costs.

Besides the obvious diversification and convenience benefits, fund-of-funds investments have two added benefits for smaller investors: affordability and accessibility. The minimum investment for fund-of-funds is usually lower than the minimum investment of its respective component hedge funds. Therefore, the affordability of fund-of-funds may allow a smaller institutional investor access to the skills of the component manager when the smaller investor would otherwise be priced out of the market (Strong, 2009).

Advantages of Larger Hedge Funds

Gaining access to certain larger hedge funds is important because larger firms usually have higher quality operational processes, technology, risk management, trading, and governance features (Wilson, 2010). Consequently, investors increasingly want to work more with *institutional* hedge fund managers compared to *emerging* hedge fund managers. *Emerging hedge funds* are defined by some research organizations as any fund with less than $250 million in AUM. Yet, nearly 80 percent of practitioners consider only those hedge funds with less than $100 million in AUM as emerging hedge funds. Depending on which monetary cutoff is used for emerging hedge funds, *institutional hedge funds* have either over $100 million in AUM or over $250 million in AUM. Regardless, institutional hedge funds clearly have more AUM, which allows them the resources to offer investors more than smaller emerging hedge funds (Wilson, 2010).

Wilson (2010) lists several practices of $1 billion hedge funds that are often not present within smaller emerging funds. For example, larger hedge funds have better research processes in place and can afford to constantly improve their techniques. They also have more stringent compliance, operational, and management processes, which require a higher quality of documentation. For instance, most larger funds have a very detailed due diligence questionnaire (DDQ), which is constantly updated to reflect changes, such as recent operational changes, new AUM, and the number of accounts recently gained/lost. Other examples of documentation include the memorandum and articles of association, which act as the hedge fund's constitution, and the private placement memorandum (PPM), which is designed to provide investors with the key elements needed to make an investment decision. Documentation such as the DDQ and PPM is important because it provides larger funds with more verification points, which allows these larger funds to provide more transparent presentations to future investors (Lhabitant, 2006).

In larger funds, internal marketing and sales teams usually make the presentations to future investors, allowing those employees with financial expertise to focus on the core competencies. This focus on core competencies is very important to larger funds because they can usually afford to retain the most experienced and talented experts. Essentially, larger funds want their expensive financial experts to focus on research, consulting, and management for their hedge funds. Likewise, larger funds can usually raise more capital because they can afford more expensive marketing personnel, including international sales teams. Besides marketing, larger funds also have other additional in-house functions such as their own research, operations, and accounting departments (Wilson, 2010).

Further, larger funds have a more vested interest in human resource strategies for developing long-term talent. Long-term strategies are important to larger firms because these firms usually develop strategic plans for several years into the future, including hiring goals, increased capital projections, and future office locations. The reality of smaller hedge firms is far different, as most of these funds create simpler long-term plans and are focused on the day-to-day or month-to-month operations of the hedge fund (Wilson, 2010).

SUMMARY AND CONCLUSIONS

Initially, Karl Karsten and Alfred W. Jones created hedge funds as simple investments designed so that general market movements did not have any effects on profits or losses. The purpose of the funds was to buy stocks in groups predicted to provide the highest positive return and to short stocks in groups predicted to provide the highest negative return. From this original concept, hedge funds have grown to become a prominent fixture within the financial markets. As the hedge fund industry has matured, it has retained most of the core features outlined by the industry's founding fathers. However, an exact face for the hedge fund industry is difficult to illustrate because the industry has evolved into a multifaceted market with thousands of participants employing an expanding number of increasingly complex strategies.

The complexity of these strategies can create disadvantages. For example, one problem with hedge fund data is the inherent biases within hedge fund databases.

These biases are disadvantageous because properly accessing hedge funds requires valid and reliable data. In fact, in the late 1990s the lack of transparency among hedge funds led many investors to view hedge funds as excessively risky. This view gained credibility in 1997 with the Asian crisis, which actually resulted from the 1994 collapse of the Mexican financial markets. The crisis created sharp declines in the currencies and financial markets in several emerging countries. Hedge funds were blamed for destabilizing the markets during the crisis because of their substantial short positions. The effects of the Asian crisis were compounded in 1998 by the Russian government devaluing the ruble. One of the most alarming effects of the Russian crisis was the shocking bankruptcy of Long Term Capital Management (LTCM). LTCM was expecting the spread between low-quality and high-quality bond yields to shrink. LTCM was wrong. The spread widened, and the excessively leveraged firm lost most of its equity capital. In an effort to suppress fears of a systematic crisis, the New York Fed was forced to issue LTCM a $3.5 billion bailout, which further increased investor skepticism with regard to hedge funds (Lhabitant, 2006).

Despite this incident, hedge funds have flourished over the last several years because they are advantageous to both the investor and manager. Similar to many traditional investors, hedge fund investors seek to decrease risk and increase return. Yet the key advantage for hedge fund investors is that hedge funds are capable of doing what most traditional funds are legally incapable of doing—hedging their investments against risk. Hedge funds also offer advantages to their managers because they require less reporting and provide substantial performance fees. However, these advantages come with an important caveat—hedge fund investors must be accredited. Yet, even with this restriction, the industry has continued to grow, primarily because of the increased participation from one particular type of accredited investor—the institutional investor.

For example, in 2000 the California Public Employees Retirement System (CalPERS) committed to directly invest $1 billion into hedge funds. CalPERS' decision encouraged several other major institutional investors to invest in hedge funds. With institutional investors now representing over 60 percent of hedge fund AUM, the industry's future growth clearly seems dependent on attracting new institutional investors, including pension and benefit plans, endowments and foundations, insurance companies and trust companies, commercial and private banks, brokerage firms and financial advisers, and even corporations (Lhabitant, 2006).

The aggressive pursuit of hedge fund investments by institutional investors suggests that the advantages of hedge funds outweigh their disadvantages. Yet, institutional acceptance is only one reason why the future of hedge funds is very promising. The primary reason for this bullish outlook is that hedge funds are adaptive, by their nature, to market conditions. Hence, hedge fund managers are constantly innovating new trading techniques, restructuring asset classes, incorporating new equity markets, and finding new sources of financing. This innovation will remain the standard within the hedge fund industry as long as the barriers of entry are low and the rewards for success are high. Thus, the hedge fund market is fully incentivized to explore new financial frontiers and evolve with the market hand-in-hand (Wilson, 2010).

DISCUSSION QUESTIONS

1. Discuss the challenges in identifying a satisfactory definition for a hedge fund and list the general hedge fund requirements from investment, legal, and compensation perspectives.
2. Discuss whether provisions in performance fees incentivize hedge fund managers or create agency problems.
3. Discuss three reasons data within hedge fund databases might not be representative of the actual hedge fund market.
4. Hedge fund strategies can broadly be classified as either nondirectional or directional investment strategies. Discuss the primary difference between the two strategies and identify three specific types of hedge funds.

REFERENCES

Ackerman, Carl, Randall McEnally, and David Ravenscraft. 1999. "The Performance of Hedge Funds: Risk, Return, and Incentives." *Journal of Finance* 54:3, 833–874.

Agarwal, Vikas, Naveen D. Daniel, and Narayan Y. Naik. 2009. "Why Is Santa So Kind to Hedge Funds? The December Return Puzzle!" Working Paper, London Business School.

Allen, Katrina Dean. 2011. "Billion Dollar Club." Absolute Return. Available at www.absolutereturn-alpha.com/Article/2775999/Billion-dollar-club.html?ArticleId=2775999.

Asness, Cliford, Robert Krail, and John Liew. 2001. "Do Hedge Funds Hedge?" *Journal of Portfolio Management* 28:1, 6–9.

Badrinath, Swaminathan, and Stefano Gubellini. 2011. "On the Characteristics and Performance of Long-Short, Market-Neutral and Bear Mutual Funds." *Journal of Banking & Finance* 35:7, 1762–1776.

Bares, Pierre-Antoine, Rajna Gibson, and Sebastien Gyger. 2001. "Style Consistency and Survival Probability in the Hedge Funds Industry." Working Paper. University of Geneva.

Barry, Ross. 2003. "Hedge Funds: A Walk Through the Graveyard." Working Paper, Ross Barry Macquarie Applied Finance Centre.

Brown, Stephen J., William N. Goetzmann, and Roger G. Ibbotson. 1999. "Offshore Hedge Funds: Survival and Performance, 1989–95." *Journal of Business* 72:1, 91–117.

Brown, Stephen J., William N. Goetzmann, and James M. Park. 1999. "Hedge Funds and the Asian Currency Crisis of 1997." Working Paper, National Bureau of Economic Research (NBER).

Brown, Stephen J., William N. Goetzmann, and James M. Park. 2001. "Conditions for Survival: Changing Risk and the Performance of Hedge Fund Managers and CTAs." Working Paper, New York University.

Brunnermeier, Markus, and Stefan Nagel. 2004. "Hedge Funds and the Technology Bubble." *Journal of Finance* 59:5, 2013–2040.

Brush, John. S. 1997. "Comparisons and Combinations of Long and Long/Short Strategies." *Financial Analysts Journal* 53:3, 81–89.

Carpenter, Jennifer. 2000. "Does Option Compensation Increase Managerial Risk Appetite?" *Journal of Finance* 55:5, 2311–2331.

Dennistoun, Christopher. 2004. "Karsten, Jones and the Origin of Hedge Funds." Hedge Fund Monthly. Available at www.eurekahedge.com/news/04may˙archive˙origin˙of˙hedge˙funds.asp.

Edwards, Franklin R., and Mustafa Onur Caglayan. 2001. "Hedge Fund Performance and Manager Skill." *Journal of Futures Markets* 21:11, 1003–1028.

Eichengreen, Barry, Donald Mathieson, Sunil Sharma, Bankim Chadha, Laura Kodres, and Anne Jansen. 1998. "Hedge Fund and Financial Market Dynamics." International Monetary Fund Occasional Paper 166, May.

Fung, William, and David A. Hsieh. 1997. "Empirical Characteristics of Dynamic Trading Strategies: The Case of Hedge Funds." *Review of Financial Studies* 10:2, 275–302.

Fung, William, and David A. Hsieh. 2000. "Performance Characteristics of Hedge Funds and Commodity Funds: Natural vs. Spurious Biases." *Journal of Financial and Quantitative Analysis* 35:3, 291–307.

Fung, William, and David A. Hsieh. 2001. "The Risk in Hedge Fund Strategies. Theory and Evidence from Trend Followers." *Review of Financial Studies* 14:2, 313–341.

Fung, William, and David A. Hsieh. 2006. "Hedge Funds: An Industry in Its Adolescence." Federal Reserve Bank of Atlanta *Economic Review* 91:4, 1–33.

Getmansky, Mila, Andrew W. Lo, and Igor Makarov. 2004. "An Econometric Model of Serial Correlation and Liquidity in Hedge Fund Returns." *Journal of Financial Economics* 74:3, 529–609.

Goetzmann, William N., Jonathon E. Ingersoll, and Stephen A. Ross. 1997. "High-Water Marks." Working Paper, Yale University.

Goetzmann, William N., Jonathon E. Ingersoll, and Stephen A. Ross. 2003. "High-Water Marks and Hedge Fund Management Contracts." *Journal of Finance* 58:4, 1685–1718.

Gregoriou, Greg N. 2002. "Hedge Fund Survival Lifetimes." *Journal of Asset Management* 3:3, 237–252.

Grinblatt, Mark, and Sheridan Titman. 1989. "Adverse Risk Incentives and the Design of Performance-Based Contracts." *Management Sciences* 35:7, 807–822.

Grinold, Richard C., and Ronald N. Kahn. 2000. "The Efficiency Gains of Long-Short Investing." *Financial Analysts Journal* 56:6, 40–53.

Jacobs, Bruce I., and Kenneth N. Levy. 1993. "Long/Short Equity Investing." *Journal of Portfolio Management* 20:1, 52–62.

Jacobs, Bruce I., and Kenneth N. Levy. 2006. "Enhanced Active Equity Strategies: Relaxing the Long-Only Constraint in the Pursuit of Active Return." *Journal of Portfolio Management* 32:3, 44–55.

Jacobs, Bruce I., and Kenneth N. Levy. 2007a. "20 Myths About Enhanced Active 120–20 Strategies." *Financial Analysts Journal*, 63:4, 19–26.

Jacobs, Bruce I., and Kenneth N. Levy. 2007b. "Enhanced Active Portfolios Are Trim Equitized Long-Short Portfolios." *Journal of Portfolio Management* 33:4, 19–25.

Jacobs, Bruce I., Kenneth N. Levy, and David Starer. 1998. "On the Optimality of Long-Short Strategies." *Financial Analysts Journal* 54:2, 40–51.

Jacobs, Bruce I., Kenneth N. Levy, and David Starer. 1999. "Long-Short Portfolio Management: An Integrated-Approach." *Journal of Portfolio Management* 25:2, 23–32.

Jaeger, Robert A. 2003. *All About Hedge Funds*. New York: McGraw-Hill.

Jiang, Wei, Kai Li, and Wei Wang. 2012. "Hedge Funds and Chapter 11." *Journal of Finance* 67:2, 513–559.

Johnson, Seanna, Ronald N. Kahn, and Dean Petrich. 2007. "Optimal Gearing: Not All Long-Short Portfolios are Efficient." *Journal of Portfolio Management* 33:4, 10–18.

Jones, Alfred W. 1949. "Fashion in Forecasting." *Fortune* 88:39, 186.

Karsten, Karl. 1931. *Scientific Forecasting: Its Methods and Application to Practical Business and to Stock Market Operations*. New York: Greenberg.

Liang, Bing. 2000. "Hedge Funds: The Living and the Dead." *Journal of Financial and Quantitative Analysis* 35:3, 309–326.

Lhabitant, Francois-Serge. 2006. *Handbook of Hedge Funds*. London: John Wiley & Sons, Inc.

Lo, Andew W. 2002. "The Statistics of Sharpe Ratios." *Financial Analysts Journal* 58:4, 36–52.

Sharpe, William. 1992. "Asset Allocation: Management Style and Performance Measurement." *Journal of Portfolio Management* 18:2, 7–19.

Siegel, Aaron. 2006. "Hedge Funds Turn Up the Volume." Available at www.investmentnews.com/article/20060914/REG/609140707.

Sorensen, Eric H., Ronald Hua, and Edward Qian. 2007. "Aspects of Constrained Long-Short Equity Portfolios." *Journal of Portfolio Management* 33:2, 12, 14, 16–22.

Stefanini, Filippo. 2006. *Investment Strategies of Hedge Funds*. London: John Wiley & Sons, Inc.

Strasburg, Jenny, and Steve Eder. 2011. "Hedge Funds Bounce Back." *Wall Street Journal*. Available at http://online.wsj.com/article/SB10001424052748704204604576269114056530484.html.

Strong, Robert A. 2009. *Portfolio Construction, Management, & Protection*, 5th ed. Mason, OH: South-Western Cengage Learning.

Tol, Ramon, and Christiaan Wanningen. 2009. "On the Performance of Extended Alpha (130/30) Versus Long-Only." *Journal of Portfolio Management* 35:3, 51–60.

Tol, Ramon, and Christiaan Wanningen. 2011. "130/30: By How Much Will the Information Ratio Improve?" *Journal of Portfolio Management* 37:3, 62–69.

Williamson, Christine. 2011. "Institutional Share Growing for Hedge Funds." *Pensions & Investments*. Available at www.pionline.com/article/20110210/DAILYREG/110219980.

Wilson, Richard C. 2010. *The Hedge Fund Book: A Training Manual for Professionals and Capital-Raising Executives*. Hoboken, NJ: John Wiley & Sons, Inc.

ABOUT THE AUTHOR

Hunter M. Holzhauer is an Assistant Professor of Finance at Penn State Erie, the Behrend College, where he teaches both graduate and undergraduate classes in corporate finance and portfolio management. His financial industry experience includes positions as credit analyst with Colonial Bank and financial planner and fixed-income portfolio manager with AmSouth Bank. Besides hedge funds, Professor Holzhauer's research interests are in investments and financial planning. He received his PhD from the University of Alabama, his MBA from Mississippi State University, and his BS in Business Administration and Bio-Psychology from Birmingham-Southern College.

CHAPTER 24

Performance of Hedge Funds

DIANNA PREECE
Professor of Finance, University of Louisville

INTRODUCTION

While many investors have just recently become aware of hedge funds as a viable alternative investment, hedge funds in one form or another have been around for nearly 100 years. Ziemba and Ziemba (2007) trace hedge funds back to the 1920s. John Maynard Keynes ran one of the first precursors to hedge funds at Cambridge University's King's College. The fund was called the Chest Fund and averaged an annual return of 13 percent, even during the Great Depression. The first hedge fund structured as a general partnership can be traced back to 1949. Alfred Winslow Jones, a sociologist and journalist as well as a fund manager, managed this fund. He took long and short positions in an attempt to "hedge" downside risk in bearish markets. Today, a "hedged" fund is less applicable than a leveraged fund. According to Wiethuechter (2010), the ratio of estimated market positions to actual assets was nearly 5 to 1 in 2007. Thus, leverage has become a central theme in modern-day hedge funds.

Ibbotson, Chen, and Zhu (2011) estimate that more than 8,000 hedge funds managed $1.6 trillion in assets in 2011. As of the first quarter of 2012, HFR (2012b) announced that assets under management hit an all-time high of $2.13 trillion. The growth has been astonishing given that only 68 hedge funds existed in the mid-1980s, $11.3 billion was invested in hedge funds in 2000, and $49.5 billion was invested in hedge funds in 2005 (Fung and Hsieh, 2006).

The rapid growth of the hedge fund industry is a function of several factors, including the following: (1) increased interest from investors due to reported high returns; (2) more sophisticated, high-net-worth investors, known as *accredited investors*; (3) greater wealth during the 1990s bull market; and (4) a willingness of institutional investors to consider hedge funds as an appropriate alternative asset class beginning in the late 1990s. Also, in the early 2000s, investors began searching for ways to diversify holdings in the face of falling equity values and lower bond yields (Lhabitant, 2004). The low correlation of asset returns with traditional assets, as reported in several studies discussed in this chapter, is a major draw of hedge funds. Although hedge funds attract the attention of all types of investors, access for individuals without high net worth is limited.

According to the Securities and Exchange Commission (SEC), hedge funds lack a precise definition because they take on such varying strategies. The investment strategies of managers even within a particular style may differ. In general, a *hedge fund* is a loosely regulated, professionally managed pool of capital. Firms are generally structured as limited partnerships or offshore corporations, and thus regulation is minimal. Fund managers can employ various strategies, including leverage, short positions, and derivatives, to achieve a fund's goals. Until recently, neither the SEC nor any other governing body required registration for hedge funds. This exemption allowed funds a wide berth in terms of what they could do. While the push for hedge fund registration increased over time, the financial crisis of 2007–2008 finally made it happen. As of March 30, 2012, funds with more than $100 million in assets under management must register with the SEC as part of the Dodd-Frank Act. Also, the SEC prohibits hedge funds from advertising.

While many investors think hedge funds are riskier versions of mutual funds, Fung and Hsieh (1999) contend that hedge funds exhibit risk characteristics similar to startup companies. The authors suggest that a hedge fund manager is financing a new business. The manager has the skills to earn above-average, risk-adjusted returns in the market but lacks sufficient capital to meet the fixed costs of a trading operation. As such, he must form a fund to attract external capital. According to Fung and Hsieh, approximately 10 percent of hedge funds fail each year, which is similar to the attrition rate of new ventures. Also, hedge fund returns contain substantial idiosyncratic risks, similar to small, undiversified companies.

Because hedge funds are only available to accredited investors (i.e., high-net-worth individuals and institutions) and are allowed to use advanced investment strategies such as short positions to achieve results, fund managers are expected to earn high risk-adjusted returns independent of whether asset values are rising or falling in the overall market. Thus, managers are expected to perform well in both bull and bear markets. This type of return objective is known as an *absolute return strategy* because it does not rely on a market-based benchmark.

Al-Sharkas (2005) examines the difference between absolute return managers and traditional, long-only managers. He describes the differences between the two approaches and examines the development of the absolute return approach to investing. He finds that the major difference between traditional managers and absolute return managers is the way they define their return objectives. Traditional managers typically state return objectives relative to a benchmark while hedge fund managers do not.

According to Waring and Siegel (2006), absolute return investing became a hot topic in the mid-2000s. Pension funds, endowments, foundations, and other institutional investors, feeling pressure to increase returns, looked to absolute return products for a solution. However, the authors contend that such products should not be used because doing so implies a "magic investment approach" that allows managers to earn higher total returns with little or no risk of negative returns simply by eschewing benchmarks. Despite this criticism, many managers still use absolute return as a term to describe the returns earned by their hedge funds.

Hedge fund managers are well compensated as a result of the pressure to perform. Unlike mutual fund managers, who only receive management fees based on assets under management, hedge fund managers receive management fees and performance fees that, if performance is strong, can be much larger than the fees of traditional actively managed funds. Many researchers, including Lhabitant (2007), note that management fees are typically 1 to 1.5 percent of assets under management and performance fees are typically 20 percent of the hedge fund's annual profits.

For example, assume a hedge fund makes a 6 percent net trading profit for the year. The performance fee would be 1.2 percent of assets (0.2 × 6 percent). Assuming a management fee of 1 percent, the total fee to the manager would equal 220 basis points for that year. Incentive fees are usually paid only if the current holding-period fund value exceeds its *high-water mark* (i.e., the highest lifetime value of the fund before the current holding period). This restriction means that fund managers must make up any losses before they can earn performance fees. Investors often expect managers to invest a large proportion of their own investable funds in the hedge fund in order to mitigate agency problems such as excessive risk taking intended to maximize potential performance fees (Anson, 2006).

The purpose of this chapter is to describe hedge fund risks and returns. The remainder of the chapter is organized as follows. The chapter begins with a brief overview of hedge fund investment styles. Hedge fund databases and the biases inherent in databases are critical to any discussion of hedge fund performance and are reviewed in the second section. A discussion of hedge fund risk factors follows. This presentation includes a description of the asset-based style factor model developed by Fung and Hsieh (2004). The relationship between hedge fund performance fees and risks and returns is then discussed, followed by a description of the common models used to capture hedge fund risk-adjusted returns. Alpha is also considered in the context of returns earned by active hedge fund managers. The correlation of hedge fund returns with other asset classes is considered, followed by a discussion of the higher moments of hedge fund return distributions, specifically skewness and kurtosis. The final section provides a summary and conclusions.

HEDGE FUND INVESTMENT STYLES

Risks and returns vary widely across hedge fund strategies. Hedge fund styles range from aggressive and performance-oriented to less aggressive and more diversification-oriented. Lipper Trading Advisor Selection System (TASS) classifies hedge funds into 10 styles. Lhabitant (2004) collapses the categories into five, plus an "other" category that captures multistrategy funds and funds of hedge funds. Basic investment styles include:

- *Tactical trading styles.* Global macro funds, commodity trading advisers (CTAs), and managed futures fall in this category. Global macro fund managers use leverage and make directional bets, taking long and/or short positions in stocks, bonds, currencies, and commodities. The decisions are purely discretionary, so the quality of the fund manager is the most important contributing factor to the performance of the fund. CTAs and managed futures managers trade futures contracts and commodities for clients, again making directional bets on prices. Managed futures use trend-following strategies.

- *Equity long/short funds.* Managers within this group of funds take long and short positions in equities to manage market risk (i.e., to create a market-neutral position). Fund returns tend to be positively correlated with the market because fund managers generally maintain a net long position. Fund managers may focus on specific industries, regions, or sectors and may have a global or emerging market focus. Dedicated short funds focus on short positions and short sell securities that fund managers perceive as being overpriced.
- *Event-driven hedge funds.* Fund managers following event-driven strategies attempt to profit from firm-specific events such as potential mergers, distressed equities or bonds, spin-offs or recapitalizations.
- *Relative-value arbitrage strategies.* Fund managers using relative-value arbitrage strategies attempt to profit from relative price discrepancies between related securities. Trades typically have two sides: a purchase and a sale of two related, but mispriced, securities. In general, the prices of the two securities are expected to converge. Fund managers use equities, debt securities, futures, and options in relative-value strategies. Convertible arbitrage is an example of a relative-valuation strategy.

In addition to these hedge fund strategies, investors may also choose diversified products such as funds of hedge funds (FoFs) and multistrategy hedge funds. FoFs offer investors diversification through a portfolio of hedge funds. Investors may diversify across managers within the same strategy in style specific funds or across strategies in multistrategy funds. Some individual hedge funds have also started combining strategies and creating multistrategy funds in the same organization.

HEDGE FUND DATA

Obtaining data on hedge funds and the hedge fund industry has traditionally been difficult. As unregulated entities, hedge funds are not required to report information on investments, returns, or risks. Any information available on hedge funds has historically been self-reported and/or incomplete.

Hedge Fund Databases

Although several hedge fund databases are available, three have amassed more than 15 years of collected data: the Center for International Securities and Derivatives Markets (CISDM), Hedge Fund Research (HFR), and Lipper TASS (TASS). Some hedge funds report to a single database while others report to multiple databases. To properly measure hedge fund performance, returns must be accurately measured. However, hedge fund databases have several potential biases. Numerous studies note hedge fund database problems (Ackermann, McEnally, and Ravenscraft, 1999; Fung and Hsieh, 2000; Liang, 2000; Fung and Hsieh, 2002b; Malkiel and Saha, 2005). Some biases arise out of the very nature of hedge funds (e.g., unregulated, not required to report performance data to a regulatory body, and high attrition rates), whereas others are spurious and occur because of statistical techniques used by firms to "fix" problems with hedge fund data. In fact, Straumann (2009) finds "man-made" patterns in hedge fund data that he contends are worth examining. These studies identify several potential biases, such as survivorship bias, selection bias, backfill bias, and liquidation bias, which are discussed throughout the remainder of this section.

Survivorship Bias

As previously noted, hedge funds typically experience a 10 percent attrition rate each year. For new funds, managers may be unable to attract sufficient external capital to achieve the economies of scale required to make the fund a viable business. For older funds, performance may be lackluster and investors may choose to redeem their shares.

Survivorship bias implies that reported returns are higher than actual returns because the funds that are still around are likely to have higher returns than defunct funds or funds that quit reporting because of underperformance. Several mutual fund studies, including Brown, Goetzmann, Ibbotson, and Ross (1992) and Malkiel (1995), report this result. As a precursor to research on hedge fund database biases, Malkiel examines mutual fund return data for biases. Malkiel finds that survivorship bias affects hedge fund data during the 1980s and early 1990s. However, Fung and Hsieh (2009) note that the issue may be at least partially offset in the case of hedge funds because some successful funds quit reporting to databases after closing the fund to new investors. In fact, they find that 40 percent of the top 100 hedge funds did not report to the four hedge fund databases examined in their study.

Fung and Hsieh (1997b, 2000, 2002b, 2006, 2009), Brown, Goetzmann, and Ibbotson (1999), Liang (2000, 2001), and Aggarwal and Jorion (2010) investigate hedge fund database biases. Fung and Hsieh (2006) analyze the returns of live hedge funds in the TASS, HFR, and CISDM databases between 1994 and 2004. They estimate survivorship bias to be 2.4 percent (TASS), 1.8 percent (HFR), and 2.4 percent (CISDM). The authors indicate that this rate is consistent with previous research. Malkiel and Saha (2005) also find evidence of survivorship bias in FoFs return data.

Selection Bias

Because hedge funds are largely unregulated, fund managers determine whether to report performance to hedge fund databases. If databases are unrepresentative of the universe of hedge funds, they may suffer from selection bias. *Selection bias* likely results in upwardly biased returns, because only better-performing funds have an incentive to make their performance public. However, as previously discussed, funds that are closed to new investors often choose not to report to a hedge fund database. Thus, researchers do not know if the returns of funds reporting to databases are higher or lower than those funds not reporting. In general, selection bias is impossible to measure and difficult to estimate.

Backfill Bias

Backfill bias, also called *instant history* or *incubation bias*, is the result of the "waiting period" before a new fund can establish a track record to report to a database. If the fund performs well, the manager will report to a database in order to attract outside capital. When the fund enters the database, the prior performance history is "backfilled." This instant history bias causes hedge fund performance to be overestimated.

As noted previously, Fung and Hsieh (2006) analyze the returns of live hedge funds in the TASS, HFR, and CISDM databases between 1994 and 2004. They estimate backfill bias to be 1.5 percent (TASS), 1.4 percent (HFR), and 1.5 percent (CISDM). The authors indicate that this finding is consistent with previous research.

Liquidation Bias

Fund managers of failed funds stop reporting returns to databases before the final liquidation of the fund. This action results in a *liquidation bias*. For example, a fund that fails as a result of a crisis does not report a −100 percent to the database. Some studies, such as Posthuma and van der Sluis (2003), make assumptions about the return in the month of liquidation (e.g., assume −100 percent return for liquidating funds). Others, such as Ackerman et al. (1999), do not include the liquidation month in their calculations.

Hedge fund databases should accurately reflect the return experience of hedge fund investors. The issue of bias is critically important to investors because a key selling point of hedge fund investing is higher risk-adjusted returns. Hedge fund managers seek *alpha*, the return in excess of the compensation for risk. In other words, alpha is the return in excess of what the investor requires for assuming systematic risk (i.e., beta risk). Alpha is the "smart money return," the return for active, aggressive, sophisticated management. If the alpha of a particular strategy is 4 percent but the combined selection and backfill biases are also 4 percent (e.g., 2.5 percent plus 1.5 percent), then the alpha is actually zero. Hedge fund investors must truly understand database biases if they want to understand hedge fund performance.

Avoiding Hedge Fund Bias

Funds of hedge funds are subject to fewer biases than individual hedge funds. Thus, an alternative to hedge fund indices as a basis for hedge fund performance is using the average return of FoFs. Fung and Hsieh (2000) suggest this approach, indicating that FoF returns reflect the actual experience of investors rather than returns that may be artificially high due to selection, survivorship, backfill, and liquidation biases.

Investible Indices

Several investable indices have been created beginning in 2003. The goal of these passive portfolio products is to mimic the performance of hedge fund indices and to allow investors an opportunity to earn hedge fund returns without directly investing in hedge funds. However, the products have largely underperformed the style benchmarks that they are meant to mimic. For example, Fung and Hsieh (2006) report that the HFRX Equity Hedge Investable Index returned 6.6 percent between April 2003 and September 2005, while the corresponding HFRI Equity Hedge Index it was meant to mimic returned 14.1 percent over the same period. The authors report that the reasons for the divergence are varied but conclude that reported index performance may differ from the returns actually experienced by hedge fund investors.

Hiedorn, Kaiser, and Voinea (2010) compare the risk and return of FoFs, investable hedge fund indices (IHFIs), and hedge fund replication strategies (HFRSs) between January 2002 and September 2009. The authors show that IHFIs are highly correlated with noninvestible hedge fund indices. Also, IHFIs outperform both FoFs and HFRSs on a risk-adjusted basis during the study period in a best-case scenario. However, they underperform in a worst-case scenario. Hiedorn et al. contend that averaging the performance of IHFIs provides a sound alternative to using FoFs as a performance benchmark with lower cost, greater liquidity, and more transparency.

HEDGE FUND RISK FACTORS

A substantial body of academic research addresses the issue of biases present in hedge fund databases. While data biases distort hedge fund alphas, they do not represent systematic risk factors. To address the issue of hedge fund risk, many researchers ask the question of whether systematic risk factors are inherent in hedge fund returns. Because hedge fund strategies are both varied and unique, much of the research on hedge fund risk has been strategy or style specific (i.e., a bottom-up approach). Examples of this bottom-up approach include Agarwal and Naik (2004) who examine risk factors in equity-oriented hedge funds. Fung and Hsieh (2004) take a similar approach in an examination of equity long/short funds. Patton (2009) studies equity market–neutral strategies, while Agarwal, Fung, Loon, and Naik (2011) investigate convertible arbitrage risks in a bottom-up approach. Mitchell and Pulvino (2001) analyze merger arbitrage strategy risks. Fung and Hsieh (2004) and Duarte, Longstaff, and Yu (2007) examine the risks and returns of fixed-income arbitrage funds, and Fung and Hsieh (2001) consider managed futures (i.e., trend-following strategies). Finally, Fung and Hsieh (2002a) scrutinize fixed-income hedge funds. Exhibit 24.1 summarizes the results of these studies.

Fung and Hsieh (2006) also examine the risk factors in several niche styles, including emerging market funds, distressed securities funds, and an equity nonhedge fund, which takes long positions and generally does not hedge market risks. They find that emerging market fund returns are highly correlated with the IFC Emerging Market Stock Index, and distressed securities fund returns are highly correlated with the CSFB High-Yield Bond Index. The authors also note that the equity nonhedge fund returns are highly correlated with the Wilshire Small Growth Stock Index.

These results imply that systematic risk factors are inherent in individual hedge fund styles. The returns for many of the individual styles are highly correlated with similar stock and bond market indices. Thus, the "hedge" in hedge fund does not mean that systematic risks are managed. In fact, the name is largely historical. Unlike mutual funds, hedge funds can take short positions because they raise capital from sophisticated investors. Because early hedge funds attempted to hedge against falling prices in market downturns, they became known as *hedge funds*.

To broaden this body of literature from individual strategies to hedge funds in general, Fung and Hsieh (2003, 2004) employ a top-down approach identifying

Exhibit 24.1 Summary of a Sample of Hedge Fund Style Risk Studies

Hedge Fund Style	Year	Authors	Results
Convertible arbitrage strategy	2011	Agarwal, Fung, Loon, and Naik	Examine three common convertible arbitrage strategies and find that convertible arbitrage hedge funds provide liquidity (i.e., act as an intermediary) to the convertible bond market. Much of the return to convertible arbitrage strategies is derived from a liquidity premium paid by convertible bond issuers to hedge funds.
Equity long/ short	2004	Fung and Hsieh	Find positive exposure to stock market returns as well as long exposure to small-cap stocks and short exposure to large-cap stocks. This is similar to the Fama and French (1992) three-factor model that describes stock returns.
Equity market neutral	2009	Patton	Finds that one-quarter of the funds examined are statistically significantly related to equity market factors and more than one-quarter are exposed to other hedge fund styles. The author concludes that the equity market-neutral style is generally not market neutral.
Equity-oriented style	2004	Agarwal and Naik	Show that many equity-oriented strategies have payoffs that resemble a short position in a put option on a market index. This strategy bears substantial left-tail risk, which a mean-variance framework ignores.
Fixed-income arbitrage	2007	Duarte, Longstaff, and Yu	Find significant systematic risk exposure to bond and stock market returns and a strong correlation between the returns of other strategies examined and the returns of fixed-income arbitrage funds.
Fixed-income hedge funds	2002a	Fung and Hsieh	Find that returns are strongly correlated with convertible bond indices and changes in default spreads.
Managed futures (i.e., trend followers)	2001	Fung and Hsieh	Extend Merton's (1981) work on market timers to the hedge fund market, which is similar to a trend follower taking long and short positions to profit from large swings in prices with payoffs similar to a look-back straddle. Market volatility is a key determinant of trend-following returns.
Merger arbitrage strategy (event-driven strategy)	2001	Mitchell and Pulvino	Find merger arbitrage is long "deal" risk. The risk inherent in this strategy is that the merger will fail. Mergers often fail for company specific or idiosyncratic reasons, but in a market downturn mergers are called off, leading to systematic risk related to the overall market.

This exhibit includes a sample of hedge fund studies that examine risk for various hedge fund strategies.

the systematic risks inherent in a diversified portfolio of hedge funds. They use a model similar to those used based on arbitrage pricing theory (APT) but allow the betas to change over time. The authors use risk factors identified in empirical studies of major hedge fund styles, as previously described. Fung and Hsieh (2004) indicate that this is an asset-based style (ABS) factor model because risk factors are based on traded securities and their derivatives. According to the authors, this approach is important because by using easily observable risk factors based on assets that trade in public markets, investors and analysts can avoid some of the nontransparency that shrouds hedge funds. To avoid biases associated with hedge fund databases, the model relies on asset returns rather than hedge fund returns. The seven significant risk factors identified by Fung and Hsieh are:

1. The excess return of the S&P 500 Index (i.e., the S&P 500 Index return minus the risk-free rate).
2. Small cap stock returns minus large cap stock returns. These two equity factors are most important to the long/short equity funds and account for 30 to 40 percent of all hedge funds.
3. The excess return of the 10-year Treasury bond relative to the risk-free rate.
4. The excess return of Baa bonds relative to the 10-year Treasury bond. These two risk factors are most important to fixed-income funds.
5. Call and put options on bonds.
6. Call and put options on currencies.
7. Call and put options on commodities.

According to Fung and Hsieh (2004), the seven-factor model explains 80 percent of the variations in the monthly returns in the HFR Funds of Funds Index. The authors note that while hedge fund indices exhibit alphas of 1.32 percent to 3.24 percent annually, FoFs do not have positive alphas.

According to Fung and Hsieh (2004), this model is useful in identifying common sources of risk. It allows investors to manage hedge fund risks in the framework of the overall portfolio because the risk factors are based on assets (i.e., based on traded securities). They liken this model to the capital asset pricing model (CAPM) based on its simplicity. The CAPM identifies market risk as the only source of risk. The hedge fund model identifies several sources of risk related to the specific hedge fund strategy. The authors also note that Sharpe (1992) applied this type of risk/return model to model mutual fund returns.

Risk, Return, and Performance Incentives

Performance fees can "muddy the waters" with respect to risk and hedge fund performance. Fees are contentious. First, fees can be a drag on performance if they are large in proportion to the size of the fund. For example, Brooks, Clare, and Motson (2008) find that between 1994 and 2006 hedge fund fees averaged 5.15 percent annually. Even more surprising, Goetzmann, Ingersoll, and Ross (2003) estimate that hedge fund performance fees may actually reduce portfolio values by 10 to 20 percent, depending on the variance of returns. Second, the performance fee structure is meant to align the interests of investors with those of fund managers. One question is whether performance fees actually achieve that goal. Anson

(2001) maintains that performance fees have optionlike characteristics that incentivize managers to increase the volatility of returns to maximize the value of their options.

In a study of the Zurich hedge fund universe, Kouwenberg and Ziemba (2007) find that higher incentive fees generally result in higher risk in hedge funds. Loss-averse managers increase the risk of the fund as incentive fees increase. Lower mean returns net of fees and higher downside risk accompany funds with incentive fees. The authors also find that FoFs charging higher incentive fees earn higher returns, albeit with higher risk. Finally, risk is better managed if fund managers have a minimum of 30 percent of their own investable funds in the hedge fund.

According to Clare and Motson (2009), investors want to maximize their risk-adjusted returns while fund managers want to maximize their fees. The authors maintain that the best compensation structure is one that aligns the interests of these two groups. Clare and Motson examine the risk-taking behavior of managers in the context of incentive fees. They consider the risk-taking behavior of managers in response to their high-water mark and also managerial risk taking relative to a peer group of fund managers. In general, Clare and Motson find that incentive fees alter the risk-taking behavior of hedge fund managers. Their evidence shows that managers of high-performing funds tend to reduce risk to lock in high returns and hit performance targets. This behavior may concern investors who want to see consistent risk taking throughout the year.

However, the results are more complex with respect to the "moneyness" of options built into incentive contracts. Clare and Motson (2009) find that if options are well in-the-money (i.e., performance exceeds the high-water mark), managers decrease risk to lock in returns. Yet, they also find that managers do not increase risk substantially to win back losses if the options are well out-of-the-money. This asymmetry is contrary to the authors' expectations. Clare and Motson posit that this is good news for hedge fund investors because managers are likely to decrease risk to protect returns but are unlikely to increase risk to win back losses. The authors indicate that their results might influence how compensation plans are structured, arguing that a rising scale of incentive fees might discourage managers from engaging in "lock in" behavior.

Agarwal, Daniel, and Naik (2009) combine the data of four major hedge fund databases—TASS, HFR, CISDM, and MSCI—to examine 7,535 funds (3,924 live and 3,611 defunct) between January 1994 and December 2002. They find that better incentives are associated with better performance. The authors define "better" incentives as high-water mark provisions, greater managerial ownership, and greater managerial incentives proxied by the delta of the optionlike incentive fee contracts. Agarwal et al. conclude that incentive contracts can alleviate agency costs and can be used effectively to motivate hedge fund managers.

HEDGE FUND RETURNS

Hedge fund managers are charged with earning high risk-adjusted returns to compensate investors for risk. Investors do not typically compare performance to a benchmark, as is the case with mutual funds, because hedge fund strategies are unique. Fund managers must perform well in bear or bull markets and earn an absolute return.

Performance Measures

Many ways are available to measure hedge fund returns. One simple measure of return is the holding period return (HPR). As Equation 24.1 shows, HPR is defined as the ending net asset value (NAV) of the fund minus the beginning NAV divided by the beginning NAV.

$$\text{HPR} = (\text{NAV}_2 - \text{NAV}_1)/\text{NAV}_1 \tag{24.1}$$

HPR is a raw return measure because it is not adjusted for risk. Adding one to the HPR (i.e., 1 + HPR) results in the simple gross return.

Risk-Adjusted Return Measures

Several popular measures of risk-adjusted return are used to describe hedge fund returns. Perhaps the most famous is the Sharpe ratio (Sharpe, 1966). As Equation 24.2 shows, the *Sharpe ratio* measures the return in excess of the risk-free rate relative to the standard deviation of the portfolio's returns.

$$\text{Sharpe ratio} = (R_p - R_f)/\sigma_p \tag{24.2}$$

where R_p is the return on the portfolio; R_f is the risk-free rate of return; and σ_p is the standard deviation of the returns of the portfolio.

Sharpe (1994) revised the Sharpe ratio, which he called the *information ratio*, concluding that the differential return should be relative to an appropriate benchmark return (R_B) rather than to the risk-free rate and that the information ratio is a generalized Sharpe ratio. Volatility is in the denominator, but it is redefined as the tracking error (TE_p). Equation 24.3 shows the information ratio.

$$\text{Information ratio} = (R_p - R_B)/TE_p \tag{24.3}$$

The Treynor ratio, suggested by Treynor (1965), replaces the standard deviation of the portfolio from the Sharpe ratio with the beta of the portfolio (β_p), as shown in Equation 24.4:

$$\text{Treynor ratio} = (R_p - R_f)/\beta_p \tag{24.4}$$

Finally, Jensen's alpha (Jensen, 1968) considers the return of a portfolio relative to the return predicted by the CAPM (Sharpe, 1964). As Equation 24.5 shows, Jensen's alpha measures the difference between the realized risk premium and the expected risk premium. Thus, Jensen's alpha is:

$$\alpha_p = (R_p - R_f) - \beta_p(R_M - R_f) \tag{24.5}$$

where α_p is equal to the portfolio's alpha and R_M is the return on the market portfolio.

In recent years, many researchers have reconsidered and reformulated risk-adjusted return measures. Fung and Hsieh (2000) and Mamoghli and Daboussi

(2009) contend that these traditional measures are inappropriate because of the insufficiency of the mean-variance framework to capture hedge fund risks and returns. Other researchers (Brooks and Kat, 2002; Eling and Schuhmacher, 2007; Kat and Miffre, 2008) show that hedge fund returns are asymmetric. Consequently, others have developed alternative measures to describe the risk-adjusted performance of hedge funds. One of the most popular measures is the Sortino ratio (Sortino and Price, 1994). According to Sortino and van der Meer (1991), calculating the return in excess of a minimum acceptable rate (MAR) would be more meaningful than calculating return in excess of a risk-free rate. They also note that downside risk, not the total variability of returns, matters to investors. Thus, rather than dividing by the standard deviation of returns, the Sortino ratio divides by the downside deviation of returns. Equation 24.6 shows the Sortino ratio:

$$\text{Sortino Ratio} = (R_p - MAR)/DD_p \tag{24.6}$$

where MAR is the minimum acceptable rate and DD_p is the downside deviation of returns of the portfolio.

When comparing various risk-adjusted return measures, Mamoghli and Daboussi (2009) show that these alternative risk-adjusted return measures result in different rankings of hedge funds relative to the Sharpe ratio. Their study uses the Credit Suisse/Tremont Hedge Fund Index during the period January 1995 to December 2004.

Hedge Fund Performance and Alpha

Hedge fund performance is the subject of much debate. First, performance can differ dramatically across hedge fund styles. Thus, in some sense, there is no such thing as "hedge fund performance." Second, the rewards can be difficult to understand. For example, how much of hedge fund returns are due to beta risk(s) exposure and how much are due to alpha generated by the skills of hedge fund managers? Alpha, as noted previously, is the return in excess of the "deserved" return given exposure to beta risk(s). Some authors attribute returns to higher moment risks (i.e., skewness and kurtosis), discussed within this section.

Liang (2001) was one of the first to study hedge fund performance over a longer period of time. He examines the performance of 1,921 hedge funds over the period 1990 to 1999. Liang finds that the S&P 500 Index outperformed hedge funds during the period but with greater volatility of returns. Hedge fund returns averaged 14.2 percent versus 18.8 percent for the S&P 500 Index. Liang also examines hedge fund database biases in the study.

Malkiel and Saha (2005) study various hedge funds strategies represented in the TASS database over the period 1995 to 2003. Average annual returns over the period ranged from −0.01 percent for a dedicated short strategy to 14.19 percent for emerging market strategies. Several strategies earned less than 10 percent over the period including equity market neutral (5.56 percent), event-driven (9.71 percent), fixed-income arbitrage (7.04 percent), global macro (6.79 percent), and managed futures (7.68 percent). FoFs averaged 6.67 percent during the period. For comparison, the Treasury bill yield was 4.2 percent and the S&P 500 Index averaged 12.38 percent over the same period. Malkiel and Saha also report Sharpe ratios that range from −0.18 for the dedicated short bias style to 0.46 for convertible arbitrage strategies. Using the Jarque-Bera statistic, they also report significant negative skewness and positive excess kurtosis for all strategies except global macro and managed futures strategies. The Jarque-Bera statistic is a test of the goodness of fit of the sample data. It measures whether the sample data has skewness and kurtosis that match a normal distribution.

In a more recent study, Ibbotson et al. (2011) update the work of Brown et al. (1999) who find statistically significant alphas in the hedge fund industry using data from 1989 to 1995. Hedge fund data were much more difficult to acquire in the late 1990s than today. Ibbotson et al. use monthly hedge fund return data from the TASS database and have access to data from 1995 to 2009. Their sample includes 2,252 live funds and 3,917 dead funds as of December 2009. They decompose the estimated pre-fee return into alpha, beta, and fees. Noting the concerns of Malkiel and Saha (2005) and others, Ibbotson et al. correct the 15-year data set for survivorship bias by including defunct funds and for backfill bias by excluding backfill data.

The objective of the Ibbotson et al. (1999) study is to determine how much of hedge fund returns are derived from long beta exposures (i.e., stocks, bonds, and cash) and how much are the result of manager skill (i.e., alpha). Additionally, the authors use the Fung and Hsieh (2004) seven-factor model described previously to examine nontraditional betas (i.e., hedge fund betas). The authors note that not everyone agrees on what these nontraditional beta exposures are and that in some sense alpha is simply beta exposure that has yet to be discovered. They contend that because the primary way to gain exposure to these nontraditional betas is via hedge funds, the exposure can be considered part of the value that hedge funds provide. Ibbotson et al. decompose the 11.13 percent pre-fee return over the period into three component parts: (1) fees accounted for 3.43 percent of the return; (2) beta exposure accounted for 4.70 percent of the return, and (3) alpha accounted for 3.00 percent of the return.

Alpha was positive and statistically significant during the entire period. Also, except in 1998, alphas stayed positive in year-to-year tests, implying that hedge fund managers added value in both bull and bear markets occurring during the study period. All hedge fund styles have positive alphas and four are statistically significant. Additionally, when accounting for nontraditional (i.e., hedge fund) beta risks, the R^2 of the model is higher but alpha is still positive and statistically significant.

Can hedge fund managers generate returns that are greater than the required returns given their systematic risk exposures? Fung, Hsieh, Naik, and Ramadorai (2008) use the seven-factor model proposed by Fung and Hsieh (2004) to estimate the alpha of FoFs from the merged TASS, HFR, and CISDM databases. They find that about 22 percent of funds generate positive alphas but that the majority of funds do not. The authors also note that these alpha-generating funds have a steady inflow of capital from investors, ensuring that they will likely remain as positive alpha-generating funds. Fung et al. contrast this behavior with "beta-only" FoFs that exhibit more return-chasing behavior, with investors routinely adding and removing capital from funds.

According to data gathered from the HFR (2012a), hedge fund returns have been quite variable over the recent one-, three-, and five-year windows. For example, over the 12-month period ending April 2012, the Emerging Market Russia/Eastern European Index lost 18.65 percent while the Fixed-Income Asset-Backed Index earned a positive 7.61 percent. In contrast, over the 36-month period ending April 2012, the Short Bias Index lost 14.87 percent on an annualized basis while the Fixed-Income Convertible Arbitrage Index gained 15.49 percent annually. Finally, over the 60-month period ending April 2012, the Emerging Market Russia/Eastern European Index lost 6.58 percent annually while the Fixed-Income Asset-Backed Index gained 8.33 percent annually. Also, of the 29 indices listed, 22 exhibit negative returns over the 12-month period ending April 2012; 1 exhibits negative returns over a corresponding 36-month period; and 9 exhibit negative returns over the corresponding 60-month period. These data indicate that hedge fund returns exhibit considerable variability and may not be the panacea that many investors believe.

Persistence in Hedge Fund Returns

Both mutual fund and hedge fund investors often choose funds based on past performance. Investors hope that strong past performance will repeat in the future. Brown and Goetzmann (1995) examine the issue of mutual fund performance persistence and find that any persistence in mutual fund returns is primarily due to funds that lag the S&P 500 Index. Malkiel and Saha (2005) examine hedge fund performance persistence by asking the question, "Is past performance a good predictor of future performance?" They examine hedge fund returns between 1996 and 2003. The authors test the hypothesis that hedge fund winners will repeat their superior performance in the following year. A "winner" earned a return greater than the median return in the following year, and a "loser" earned a return below the median return for the subsequent year. Malkiel and Saha find that while some winners repeat, others do not, and, statistically speaking, the chance of observing a repeat winner is about 50 percent. This result conflicts with Agarwal and Naik (2000) who find evidence of return persistence in their study of hedge fund returns.

Malkiel and Saha (2005) also conclude that hedge fund returns are lower than commonly supposed after correcting for backfill and survivorship biases. While hedge funds may have desirable risk-reduction benefits in terms of lower correlation with traditional asset classes, they also have much greater cross-sectional variation of returns relative to traditional asset classes, increasing the risk that an investor will choose a poor or failing fund.

CORRELATION WITH OTHER ASSET CLASSES

As various studies report, one of the most important benefits cited for including hedge funds in portfolios of traditional assets is the low correlation with standard asset classes. In one of the earlier hedge fund studies, Fung and Hsieh (1997a) report that hedge fund returns typically have low correlation with traditional asset classes. Schneeweis and Spurgin (1998) document this result in even greater detail. Fung and Hsieh (2000, 2006) continue to consider the issue in later studies.

According to Fung and Hsieh (2000), all subsequent studies on hedge fund returns confirm this finding. They revisit the issue in 2006 examining 2,082 hedge funds in TASS and 14,927 mutual funds from Morningstar and confirm their previous results. Fung and Hsieh (2006) include hedge funds or mutual funds that have at least 36 months of monthly return data. For funds with longer histories, the authors use the last 60 months of return data. Each fund's returns are regressed on eight asset classes comparable to those in Fung and Hsieh (1997a). For each group (i.e., hedge funds and mutual funds), they tabulate the distribution of R^2 values. The distribution of R^2 values reveals that mutual funds have much higher correlation with the returns of the eight asset classes than hedge funds. Liang (2001) reports a low correlation with traditional assets and also between various hedge fund strategies. Brown et al. (1999) find correlation coefficients with the S&P 500 Index ranging from −0.70 for short-focused funds to 0.83 for opportunistic funds.

HIGHER MOMENTS OF THE RETURN DISTRIBUTION

Portfolio construction methods that rely on the Markowitz (1952, 1959) mean-variance framework assume that returns are normally distributed. This assumption means that the distribution of returns is symmetrical. *Skewness* refers to the asymmetry of the return distribution. Skewness is the third moment of the return distribution. Negatively skewed distributions have long left tails. This relationship implies small gains but large losses and is, all else equal, less desirable than a normally distributed or right-skewed distribution. The risk associated with skewness is called *tail risk*.

Kurtosis is the fourth moment of the return distribution and measures the "peakedness" of the distribution. A *leptokurtic distribution* is tall and skinny, whereas a *platykurtic distribution* is short and fat. Kurtosis can be viewed as the "volatility of the volatility." For a normal distribution, skewness is zero, kurtosis equals three (excess kurtosis is zero), and the distribution is fully described by the first two moments of the distribution, the mean and standard deviation of returns. Positive excess kurtosis implies a greater likelihood of extreme positive or negative returns. Scott and Horvath (1980) show that, with respect to investors' utility functions, investors generally prefer high odd number moments (i.e., mean and skewness) and low even number moments (i.e., standard deviation and kurtosis).

Both high-net-worth individuals and institutional investors add hedge funds to portfolios of traditional assets to improve the risk-return profiles of their portfolios. The risk-reducing benefits of hedge funds stem from low correlation with traditional assets. A mean-variance approach to portfolio construction is common, and many studies use the CAPM in the portfolio construction process. Fung and Hsieh (1997a), Lo (2001), Brooks and Kat (2002), Agarwal and Naik (2004), and Malkiel and Saha (2005) show that hedge fund returns are not normally distributed but exhibit persistent negative skewness and positive excess kurtosis.

The level of skewness and kurtosis is dependent on the hedge fund strategy. In the Malkiel and Saha (2005) study of TASS data between 1995 and 2003, they find that all of the most common hedge fund strategies exhibit negative skewness except for managed futures and global macro. This result means that the mean-variance framework used in the CAPM is generally inappropriate for measuring hedge fund risks. Investors must consider the higher moments of the return distribution when constructing portfolios that include hedge funds. The authors also find that with the exception of global macro and managed futures (i.e., trend-following) strategies, hedge fund returns exhibit undesirably high kurtosis. Malkiel and Saha reject the hypothesis of normally distributed hedge fund returns except for managed futures and global macro styles.

Haglund (2010) uses higher moment betas to examine the effect of the inclusion of hedge funds into portfolios of stocks on volatility, skewness, and kurtosis. He finds that hedge funds are useful in improving the risk profile of the portfolio. Specifically, Haglund finds that hedge funds can lower volatility, skewness, and kurtosis, but that the risk-reducing benefits vary across hedge fund strategies. He finds that market macro, merger arbitrage, convertible arbitrage, fixed income arbitrage, and equity market neutral strategies are best for investors who want to limit downside risk and are concerned about higher moment risks.

In an examination of long/short equity funds, event-driven funds, and managed futures, Agarwal, Bakshi, and Huij (2009) find that hedge fund styles are exposed to higher moment risks. Their evidence also shows that the risks are more relevant to funds that apply strategies to equity markets and less important to funds that have a lesser degree of equity market exposure.

Hedge Funds and the Financial Crisis

Wiethuechter (2010) examines the role of hedge funds in financial crises over the last decade, paying particular attention to the financial crisis of 2007–2008. He contends that loose regulation and opportunistic behavior combined with leverage and increasing correlation of asset returns in a highly efficient capital market contribute to the systemic risk in the market. According to Lo (2009), *systemic risk* is the broad-based collapse in the financial system, often resulting from a series of correlated defaults, usually caused by a single major event. Wiethuechter concludes that hedge funds contributed to systemic risk and market instability in the recent financial crisis. He maintains that abuses of the strategies and interactions with macroeconomic factors and not the hedge fund strategies themselves contributed to market instability. Lo concludes that if banks cannot fulfill their roles as prime brokers, a lack of liquidity could lead to panic that could ultimately lead to global economic collapse.

SUMMARY AND CONCLUSIONS

Hedge funds have become extremely popular investment vehicles since the 1990s. While hedge funds have been around for at least 60 years in their current form, growth skyrocketed in the 1990s and 2000s. In 2012, assets under management exceeded $2 trillion. Hedge fund investors have traditionally been an elite group of high-net-worth individuals and institutional investors.

Hedge fund managers use various strategies to earn absolute returns. Investors expect hedge funds to perform well in both bull and bear markets because they are not limited to long-only positions in traditional assets. Hedge fund managers use long and short positions as well as leverage and derivatives to generate high, risk-adjusted returns. Fund managers seek alpha in a multitude of ways. FoFs and investable indices have also become popular in recent years.

Studies find that hedge funds can improve the risk/return profile of a portfolio of traditional assets. Low correlation with traditional asset returns appears to be a key advantage of hedge fund investing. Hedge funds do not come without risks. First, returns are often negatively skewed. This result means a greater likelihood of low returns relative to normally distributed returns or positively skewed returns. Hedge fund returns also exhibit positive excess kurtosis, which implies a greater likelihood of very large or very low returns, relative to normally distributed returns. Both of these factors increase the risk assumed by hedge fund investors.

An issue that has become of interest in recent years is the relationship between hedge fund performance, hedge fund risk, and performance compensation plans. Hedge fund managers receive not only a management fee but also a performance fee. This performance fee is typically a percentage of profits earned above a high-water mark. Fees are meant to align the interests of hedge fund investors and managers but may not serve the intended purpose. Studies such as Agarwal et al. (2009) find that better incentives are associated with better performance and good incentive contracts can alleviate agency costs and be used effectively to motivate hedge fund managers.

DISCUSSION QUESTIONS

1. Discuss why a mean-variance framework used to describe traditional asset returns is unsuitable for explaining hedge fund returns.
2. Identify three reasons for the recent growth in hedge fund investing.
3. List and describe two biases of hedge fund databases.
4. Identify four of the seven asset-based style factors that Fung and Hsieh (2004) maintain can be used to model hedge fund returns.

REFERENCES

Ackermann, Carl, Richard McEnally, and David Ravenscraft. 1999. "The Performance of Hedge Funds: Risk, Return, and Incentive." *Journal of Finance* 54:3, 833–874.

Agarwal, Vikas, Gurdip Bakshi, and Joop Huij. 2009. "Do Higher Moment Equity Risks Explain Hedge Fund Returns?" Working Paper, Robert H. Smith School Research Paper No. RHS 06–153.

Agarwal, Vikas, Naveen D. Daniel, and Narayan Y. Naik. 2009. "Role of Managerial Incentives and Discretion in Hedge Fund Performance." *Journal of Finance* 64:5, 2221–2256.

Agarwal, Vikas, William Fung, Yee Cheng Loon, and Narayan Naik. 2011. "Risk and Return in Convertible Arbitrage: Evidence from the Convertible Bond Market." *Journal of Empirical Finance* 18:2, 175–194.

Agarwal, Vikas, and Narayan Y. Naik. 2000. "On Taking the 'Alternative' Route: The Risks, Rewards, and Performance Persistence of Hedge Funds." *Journal of Alternative Investments* 2:4, 6–23.

Agarwal, Vikas, and Narayan Y. Naik. 2004. "Risk and Portfolio Decisions Involving Hedge Funds." *Review of Financial Studies* 17:1, 63–98.

Aggarwal, Rajesh, and Philippe Jorion. 2010. "Hidden Survivorship in Hedge Fund Returns." *Financial Analysts Journal* 66:2, 69–74.

Al-Sharkas, Adel A. 2005. "The Return in Hedge-Fund Strategies." *International Journal of Business* 10:3, 217–230.

Anson, Mark. 2001. "Hedge Fund Incentive Fees and the 'Free Option'." *Journal of Alternative Investments* 4:2, 43–48.

Anson, Mark. 2006. *The Handbook of Alternative Assets*. Hoboken, NJ: John Wiley & Sons, Inc.

Brooks, Chris, Andrew Clare, and Nick Motson. 2008. "The Gross Truth about Hedge Fund Performance and Risk: The Impact of Incentive Fees." *Journal of Financial Transformation* 24:4, 33–42.

Brooks, Chris, and Harry Kat. 2002. "The Statistical Properties of Hedge Fund Index Returns and Their Implications for Investors." *Journal of Alternative Investments* 5:3, 26–44.

Brown, Stephen J., and William Goetzmann. 1995. "Performance Persistence." *Journal of Finance* 5:2 679–698.

Brown, Stephen J., William Goetzmann, and Roger G. Ibbotson. 1999. "Offshore Hedge Funds: Survival and Performance, 1989–1995." *Journal of Business* 72:1, 91–117.

Brown, Stephen J., Willliam Goetzmann, Roger G. Ibbotson, and Stephen A. Ross. 1992. "Survivorship Bias in Performance Studies." *Review of Financial Studies* 5:4, 553–580.

Clare, Andrew, and Nick Motson. 2009. "Locking in the Profits or Putting It All on Black? An Empirical Investigation into the Risk-Taking Behavior of Hedge Fund Managers." *Journal of Alternative Investments* 12:2, 7–26.

Duarte, Jefferson, Francis Longstaff, and Fan Yu. 2007. "Risk and Return in Fixed Income Arbitrage: Nickels in Front of a Steamroller?" *Review of Financial Studies* 20:3, 769–811.

Eling, Martin, and Frank Schuhmacher. 2007. "Does the Choice of Performance Measure Influence the Evaluation of Hedge Funds?" *Journal of Banking and Finance* 31:9, 2632–2647.

Fama, Eugene F., and Kenneth R. French. 1992. "The Cross-section of Expected Stock Returns." *Journal of Finance* 47:2, 427–465.

Fung, William, and David A. Hsieh. 1997a. "Empirical Characteristics of Dynamic Trading Strategies: The Case of Hedge Funds." *Review of Financial Studies* 10:2, 275–302.

Fung, William, and David A. Hsieh. 1997b. "Survivorship Bias and Investment Style in the Returns of CTAs." *Journal of Portfolio Management* 24:1, 30–41.

Fung, William, and David A. Hsieh. 1999. "A Primer on Hedge Funds." *Journal of Empirical Finance* 6:3, 309–331.

Fung, William, and David A. Hsieh. 2000. "Performance Characteristics of Hedge Funds and Commodity Funds: Natural vs. Spurious Biases." *Journal of Financial and Quantitative Analysis* 35:3, 291–307.

Fung, William, and David A. Hsieh. 2001. "The Risk in Hedge Fund Strategies: Theory and Evidence from Trend Followers." *Review of Financial Studies* 14:2, 313–341.

Fung, William, and David A. Hsieh. 2002a. "Asset-Based Style Factors for Hedge Funds." *Financial Analysts Journal* 58:5, 16–27.

Fung, William, and David A. Hsieh. 2002b. "Hedge-Fund Benchmarks; Information Content and Biases." *Financial Analysts Journal* 58:1, 22–34.

Fung, William, and David A. Hsieh. 2003. "The Risks in Hedge Fund Strategies: Alternative Alphas and Alternative Betas." In Lars Jaeger, ed., *The New Generation of Risk Management for Hedge Funds and Private Equity Funds*, 72–87. London: Euromoney Institutional Investor PLC.

Fung, William, and David A. Hsieh. 2004. "Hedge Fund Benchmarks: A Risk-Based Approach." *Financial Analysts Journal* 60:5, 65–70.

Fung, William, and David A. Hsieh. 2006. "Hedge Funds: An Industry in Its Adolescence." *Economic Review – Federal Reserve Bank of Atlanta* 91:4, 1–33.

Fung, William, and David A. Hsieh. 2009. "Measurement Biases in Hedge Fund Performance Data: An Update." *Financial Analysts Journal* 65:3, 36–40.

Fung, William, David A. Hsieh, Narayan Naik, and Tarun Ramadorai. 2008. "Hedge Funds: Performance, Risk and Capital Formation." *Journal of Finance* 63:4, 1777–1803.

Goetzmann, William N., Jonathan E. Ingersoll, and Stephen A. Ross. 2003. "High Water-marks and Hedge Fund Management Contracts." *Journal of Finance* 58:4, 1685–1718.

Haglund, Michael. 2010. "Higher Moment Diversification Benefits of Hedge Fund Strategy Allocation." *Journal of Derivatives and Hedge Funds* 16:1, 53–69.

HFR. 2012a. "HFR Indices," Available at: www. hedgefundresearch.com.

HFR. 2012b. "Hedge Fund Assets Surge to Record Level on 1Q Gains." Available at www.hedgefundresearch.com/pdf/pr_20120419.pdf.

Hiedorn, Thomas, Dieter G. Kaiser, and Andre Voinea. 2010. "The Value-Added of Investable Hedge Fund Indices." *Journal of Wealth Management* 13:3, 59–81.

Ibbotson, Roger, Peng Chen, and Kevin X. Zhu. 2011. "The ABCs of Hedge Funds: Alphas, Betas, and Costs." *Financial Analysts Journal* 67:1, 15–25.

Jensen, Michael. 1968. "The Performance of Mutual Funds in the Period 1945–1964." *Journal of Finance* 23:2, 389–416.

Kat, Harry M., and Joelle Miffre. 2008. "The Impact of Non-normality Risks and Tactical Trading on Hedge Fund Alphas." *Journal of Alternative Investments* 10:4, 8–22.

Kouwenberg, Roy, and William Ziemba. 2007. "Incentives and Risk Taking in Hedge Funds."*Journal of Banking and Finance* 31:11, 3291–3310.

Lhabitant, Francois-Serge. 2004. *Hedge Funds: Quantitative Insights*. Chichester, UK: John Wiley & Sons, Inc.

Lhabitant, Francois-Serge. 2007. "Delegated Portfolio Management: Are Hedge Fund Fees Too High?" *Journal of Derivatives and Hedge Funds* 13:3, 220–232.

Liang, Bing. 2000. "Hedge Funds: The Living and the Dead." *Journal of Financial and Quantitative Analysis* 35:3, 309–326.

Liang, Bing. 2001. "Hedge Fund Performance: 1990–1999." *Financial Analysts Journal* 57:1, 11–18.

Lo, Andrew. 2001. "Risk Management for Hedge Funds: Introduction and Overview." *Financial Analysts Journal* 57:6, 16–33.

Lo, Andrew. 2009. "Regulatory Reform in the Wake of the Financial Crisis of 2007/2008." *Journal of Financial Economic Policy* 1:1, 4–43.

Malkiel, Burton G. 1995. "Returns from Investing in Equity Mutual Funds 1971–1991." *Journal of Finance* 50:2, 549–572.

Malkiel, Burton G., and Atanu Saha. 2005. "Hedge Fund Risk and Return." *Financial Analysts Journal* 61:6, 80–88.

Mamoghli, Chokri, and Sami Daboussi. 2009. "Performance Measurement of Hedge Funds Portfolios in a Downside Risk Framework." *Journal of Wealth Management* 12:2, 101–112.

Markowitz, Harry. 1952. "Portfolio Selection." *Journal of Finance* 7:1, 77–91.

Markowitz, Harry. 1959. *Portfolio Selection-Efficient Diversification of Investments*. New Haven, CT: Yale University Press.

Merton, Robert C. 1981. "On Market Timing and Investment Performance: An Equilibrium Theory of Value for Market Forecasts." *Journal of Business* 54:3, 363–407.

Mitchell, Mark, and Todd Pulvino. 2001. "Characteristics of Risk in Risk Arbitrage." *Journal of Finance* 56:6, 2135–2176.

Patton, Andrew J. 2009. "Are 'Market Neutral' Hedge Funds Really Market Neutral?" *Review of Financial Studies* 22:7, 2295–2330.

Posthuma, Nolke, and Pieter van der Sluis, 2003. "A Reality Check on Hedge Fund Returns." Working Paper, University of Amsterdam.

Schneeweis, Thomas, and Richard Spurgin. 1998. "Multifactor Analysis of Hedge Fund, Managed Futures, and Mutual Fund Return and Risk Characteristics." *Journal of Alternative Investments* 1:2, 1–24.

Scott, Robert C., and Philip A. Horvath. 1980. "On the Direction of Preference for Moments of Higher Order than the Variance." *Journal of Finance* 50:2, 549–572.

Sharpe, William F. 1964. "Capital Asset Prices: A Theory of Market Equilibrium under Conditions of Risk." *Journal of Finance* 19:3, 425–442.
Sharpe, William F. 1966. "Mutual Fund Performance." *Journal of Business* 39:1, 119–138.
Sharpe, William F. 1992. "Asset Allocation: Management Style and Performance Measurement." *Journal of Portfolio Management* 18:2, 7–19.
Sharpe, William F. 1994. "The Sharpe Ratio." *Journal of Portfolio Management* 21:1, 49–59.
Sortino, Frank, and Lee N. Price. 1994. "Performance Measurement in a Downside Risk Framework." *Journal of Investing* 3:3, 59–64.
Sortino, Frank A., and Robert van der Meer. 1991. "Downside Risk." *Journal of Portfolio Management* 17:4, 27–32.
Straumann, Daniel. 2009. "Measuring the Quality of Hedge Fund Data." *Journal of Alternative Investments* 12:2, 26–41.
Treynor. Jack. 1965. "How to Rate Management of Investment Funds." *Harvard Business Review* 43:1, 63–75.
Waring, M. Burton, and Laurence B. Siegel. 2006. "The Myth of the Absolute-Return Investor." *Financial Analysts Journal* 62:2, 14–22.
Wiethuechter, Martin D. 2010. "The Contribution of Hedge Funds to the Systemic Instability of Financial Markets: Aspects from the Financial Crisis of 2008." *Journal of Wealth Management* 13:3, 80–96.
Ziemba, Rachel E. S., and William T. Ziemba. 2007. "Good and Bad Properties of the Kelly Criterion." *Scenarios for Risk Management and Global Investment Strategies*, 29–31, Chichester, UK: John Wiley and Sons, Inc.

ABOUT THE AUTHOR

Dianna C. Preece is a Professor of Finance at the University of Louisville where she has taught for more than 20 years. She teaches undergraduate classes in corporate finance, investments, and financial markets and institutions and MBA courses in corporate finance and investments. Professor Preece also teaches in several banking schools, including the Kentucky School of Banking and the Iowa School of Banking. She has published articles in investments and banking in such journals as the *Journal of Banking and Finance* and *Journal of Business Finance and Accounting.* Professor Preece received a DBA from the University of Kentucky and also holds the CFA designation.

CHAPTER 25

Hedge Funds and Risk Management

THEODORE SYRIOPOULOS
Associate Professor of Finance, School of Business Studies, University of the Aegean and Audencia Nantes School of Management

INTRODUCTION

Hedge funds have been one of the fastest growing portfolio management sectors during the last two decades (Hedge Fund Research, 2011). As alternative investment vehicles, hedge funds employ a combination of dynamic and sophisticated investment strategies (e.g., long/short equity, fixed income, convertible arbitrage, emerging markets, statistical arbitrage, derivatives, global macro, and fund-of-funds). They target to deliver outsized "absolute" returns (irrespective of underlying market conditions), in contrast to "relative" returns (compared to a benchmark) of traditional assets such as stocks, bonds, money instruments, and mutual funds.

The complex hedge fund strategies and the aggressive investment positions result consistently in excessive risk undertaking. Severe losses and failures during past turbulent market phases and the financial crisis of 2007–2008 have tarnished the previous reputation of hedge funds and have provoked a sectoral restructuring. The resulting failure of hundreds of hedge funds led to investment portfolio liquidations, a subsequent wave of closures, and a prolonged period of sectoral contraction. More than 600 funds liquidated in 2009, which was more than double the 10-year average (Hedge Fund Research, 2011; J. P. Morgan, 2011). This liquidation, in turn, resulted in a reappraisal of hedge fund risk measures and an increased use of the integrated risk management approach. In this new environment, more conscientious managers and investors now attempt to better assess the type and level of risk exposures involved in generating returns (i.e., risk-adjusted performance). Furthermore, regulatory pressures increase for better operational, reporting, and compliance standards, whereas escalating demands for more liquidity, cost-effective policies, further transparency, and disclosure are anticipated to result in increased costs.

The hedge fund industry made its comeback in 2010, exhibiting an impressive expansion. Global hedge fund assets increased 11 percent to USD 2.02 trillion by the end of 2010, up from USD 1.82 trillion in the previous year. This took the industry back up to levels last seen in 2006, although still below the 2007 historic peak of more than USD 2.6 trillion. These capital inflows at a growing rate indicate that

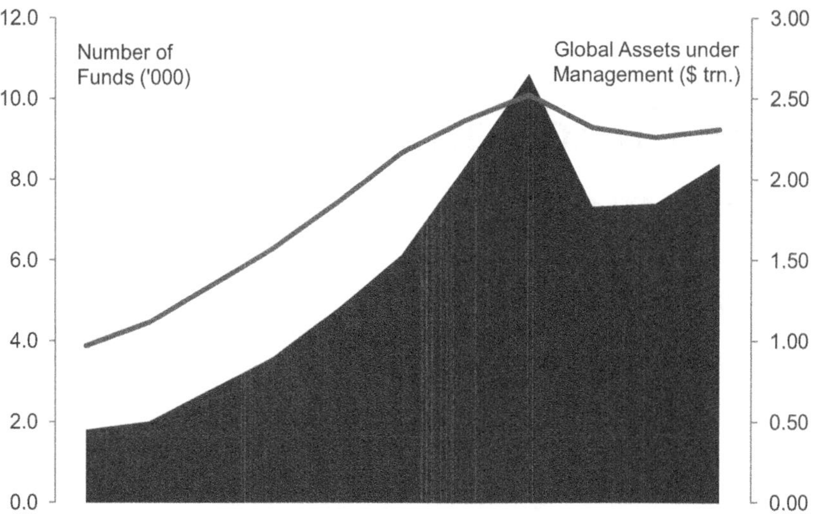

Exhibit 25.1 Hedge Funds: 2000 to 2010

This exhibit depicts the robust and persistent growth in the number of hedge funds as well as in assets under management ($ trn.) over the last decade (2000 to 2010). These figures support the notion that the hedge fund business has been one of the fastest growing segments in dynamic portfolio management. The hedge fund market suffered a serious contraction and adjustment during the financial crisis of 2007–2008.

Source: Data from Hedge Fund Research.

(institutional) investors continue perceiving hedge funds as attractive alternative investment vehicles differing from traditional asset classes (Hedge Fund Research, 2011; J. P. Morgan, 2011). Despite highly volatile and recessionary markets, many hedge fund managers succeeded in delivering robust returns. The concentration of assets with the largest hedge funds has increased substantially, as hedge funds managing more than USD 1.0 billion in assets accounted for 84 percent of the industry's global asset base. Conversely, the financial crisis of 2007–2008 led to a serious hedge fund sectoral restructuring (Exhibit 25.1).

This chapter offers a concise discussion and understanding of recent developments in hedge fund risk management. Alternative risk measures are introduced and subsequently evaluated in the context of hedge funds. Their strengths and weaknesses are assessed and their functionalities are explained. The field of risk management has evolved at a fast pace in recent years, with new, technical, sophisticated, and complex tools coming into use. This chapter explains these concepts and techniques in a meaningful application to hedge funds. However, this is a complex and not straightforward task. The terms *risk* and *risk management* are not uniformly defined but are used under different contexts. Conversely, no risk management tools have been specifically designed for hedge funds. Instead, standard risk measures and tools are taken from traditional assets and are subsequently adjusted to serve hedge funds. This approach should be treated with caution because it is constrained by various limitations that can lead to invalid empirical conclusions about hedge fund risks. Past research indicates that conventional assumptions, such as normally distributed asset returns, linear risk-return relationships, and static correlations of security returns, are inappropriate for hedge fund risks (Jorion, 2009).

The rest of the chapter consists of six sections. The first section critically discusses the distinct properties of hedge funds against traditional assets and relates them to various risk exposures. The inadequacies of conventional risk measures for application to hedge funds are explained. The second section discusses major sources of risk in hedge funds that are associated with complex investment strategies. The third section deals with measuring and managing hedge fund risk and presents widely used methods, including Value at Risk (VaR), expected shortfall, and extreme value theory. An evaluation of hedge fund risk measures and guidelines for efficient risk measurement systems are undertaken in the fourth and fifth sections, respectively. The final section summarizes and concludes.

HEDGE FUND PROPERTIES AND RISK

The distinctive properties of hedge funds as alternative investment vehicles, contrary to traditional asset classes, lead to a unique response in their return-risk profile. This section not only discusses critical hedge fund properties, but also compares and contrasts them with traditional portfolio investments. Furthermore, an initial framework on risk metrics for hedge funds is drawn, taking into account related constraints. The limitations and biases associated with empirical data on hedge funds are also discussed.

Hedge Fund Properties

Hedge funds bear certain unique characteristics and properties that clearly distinguish them from traditional investments, such as mutual funds, equity, or debt instruments. Hedge funds are managed by highly skilled portfolio managers who have considerable flexibility and discretion in pursuing performance. They implement dynamic active and fast-shifting investment strategies and build positions at varying degrees of leverage that are exposed to multiple dynamic risk factors (Eichengreen and Mathieson, 1998; Gregoriou, Hubner, Papageorgiou, and Rouah, 2005). Hedge fund asset allocation is managed by long and short strategies, extensive use of complex derivatives positions and financial engineering techniques, and exploitation of market anomalies and extreme events. According to Eichengreen and Mathieson, no standard method is available to classify hedge funds due to the large variety of hedge fund investment strategies.

Hedge funds usually accept only a limited number of qualified, sophisticated investors; require large initial capital investments, which are subject to lock-up periods; and often exhibit illiquidity due to limited redemptions. Most hedge funds exhibit short life spans of about 3.5 years, on average, with only a few cases of more than 10 years (Lavinio, 2000; Gregoriou et al., 2005). Although the widely used beta coefficient is a conventional risk metric in traditional funds, no specific risk measure exists for hedge funds. The features and properties discussed previously indicate why hedge funds are considered highly risky investment vehicles and justify the need for strict risk management.

Hedge Funds Compared to Traditional Assets

Based on the hedge fund properties discussed previously and compared to traditional mutual funds, hedge funds are typically not as liquid as traditional assets because liquidating their investment positions is sometimes more difficult. Mutual funds have a per-share price, called the net asset value (NAV), which is calculated each day, so investors can sell share units at any time. Most hedge funds, in contrast, seek to generate returns over a specific period of time, called a *lock-up period*, during which investors cannot sell their shares. Furthermore, hedge fund managers are typically compensated differently from mutual fund managers. Mutual fund managers are generally paid management fees based on a percentage of assets under management. In contrast, hedge fund managers receive a percentage of the returns they earn for investors (success or performance fees), in addition to management fees (usually in the range of 1 to 4 percent of the fund's NAV). However, the incentive portion of their compensation structure could lead hedge fund managers to invest aggressively in order to achieve higher returns at the expense of increasing investor risk. Hedge funds customarily set a substantially high threshold as a minimum investment capital requirement and target investors of high-net-worth capacity on a selective basis.

Until recently, hedge funds offered absolute returns that were seemingly uncorrelated with market indices such as the S&P 500 Index, taking advantage of portfolio diversification benefits. Yet, this view was partly obscured by the collapse of the Long Term Capital Management (LTCM) and the negative performance of many hedge funds during major global financial crises, including the 1998 Russian debt crisis and the financial crisis of 2007–2008.

Hedge Funds and Risk Metrics

The complexities in hedge fund strategies and management as well as the recent restructuring seen in the sector have made risk management a priority and a challenging subject in the hedge fund business. The limited progress in tailor-made risk management tools for hedge funds is rather surprising (Lo, 2001; Fung and Hsieh, 2001; Blum, Dacorogna, and Jaeger, 2003; Jorion, 2006). This situation partly relates to the wide variety of hedge fund investment instruments, dynamic trading strategies, and limited reliability of the relevant data. Conversely, certain risk and performance measures, approaches, models, and techniques employed in conventional investments are unsuitable for hedge funds (Lo, 2001, 2002; Blum et al., 2003; Perello, 2007; Jorion, 2009). Conventional metrics and linear factor models such as correlation coefficients, standard deviation, the Sharpe ratio, and the capital asset pricing model (CAPM) are inappropriate for hedge funds. These models assume normally distributed asset returns and fail to capture nonlinearities in hedge funds. The latter are clearly non-Gaussian; exhibit abrupt fluctuations, volatility, and persistent asymmetries in price movements; are highly sensitive to downward markets; and are exposed to nonlinear payoff structures of derivatives trading with pronounced skewness in price distribution (Perello, 2007).

Historically, hedge funds have shown efficient portfolio diversification benefits generating remarkable absolute returns even in turbulent markets. Conversely, some cases show that hedge funds have recorded extensive losses in market crises.

This mixed response has raised concerns as to the flexibility of hedge funds to mitigate various risk exposures and differentiate themselves from traditional asset markets. Two relevant issues are the extreme risks of hedge fund strategies and dependency shifts between hedge fund risks and traditional assets during turbulent periods.

Constraints of Conventional Risk Metrics

The *kurtosis* of (logarithmic) returns with values greater than three is the statistical fourth moment of the distribution that indicates the presence of leptokurtosis or fat tails. For a normal distribution, the kurtosis is three. Kurtosis can be estimated empirically using historical returns measured at different time horizons and comparing the values obtained for the performance of hedge funds with those from the underlying markets traded (Blum et al., 2003). This comparison produces an initial feedback of how heavy tailed the distribution can be and reflects the efficiency of hedge funds to cope with extreme risks. Kurtosis and skewness indicate the degree of asymmetry of the distribution, and the equity indices are known to exhibit a negative skewness. Although some hedge fund indices show considerably higher kurtosis than stock or bond indices, their values for the standard deviations are lower than or equal to the other indices. These statistics also indicate that conventional portfolio optimization techniques for traditional assets are irrelevant for hedge funds (Lhabitant, 2002).

Traditional risk measures (e.g., downside deviation, information ratio, Sortino ratio, M^2, Sharpe ratio, and standard deviation) and management tools (e.g., mean-variance analysis, beta coefficient, and standard VaR models) are based on normal distributions, do not perform adequately, and fail to capture many of the risk exposures of hedge fund investments (Lo, 2001; Jorion, 2009). Appropriate nonlinear risk models should be incorporated in order to take into account the wide spectrum of dynamic hedge fund risk exposures related to the various types of traded securities, such as equities, fixed-income instruments, foreign exchange, commodities, and derivatives, as well as multifaceted factors, including market index returns, business sectors, investment styles, return volatilities, credit and liquidity constraints, and macroeconomic indicators. Exhibit 25.2 summarizes a series of empirical estimates of the first four moments (mean, standard deviation, skewnesss, and kurtosis) of the return distribution of various hedge fund strategies and traditional markets during 1990 to 2011. These key statistics indicate nonlinearities in hedge fund returns and varying risk-return profiles under different hedge fund strategies. Hence, they support the argument that conventional risk management measures are inappropriate for hedge funds.

Data Limitations and Biases

A critical issue in hedge fund analysis and risk management in particular relates to the scarcity of adequate and reliable data input in terms of quality and quantity. A combination of data constraints and biases can lead to distorted empirical conclusions because statistical analysis and modeling of risk exposures in hedge funds cannot be conducted properly.

Exhibit 25.2 Risk and Return Distributions of Hedge Funds

	Mean	Standard Deviation	Skewness	Kurtosis
Hedge Funds				
Directional Strategies				
Macro	0.0116	0.0229	0.4059	3.7246
Emerging markets	0.0121	0.0413	−0.8307	6.7158
Short bias	0.0034	0.0566	0.1462	5.0639
Nondirectional Strategies				
Convertible arbitrage	0.0066	0.0139	−4.1100	35.4353
Distressed securities	0.0106	0.0174	−0.6436	7.8684
Equity hedge	0.0118	0.0256	0.0019	4.5208
Equity market neutral	0.0067	0.0092	−0.1329	4.1892
Event driven	0.0103	0.0191	−1.2340	6.9956
Merger arbitrage	0.0077	0.0124	−2.2549	11.9238
Relative-value arbitrage	0.0087	0.0111	−1.2358	12.4002
Weighted Composite Hedge Fund Index	0.0101	0.0198	−0.6227	5.4513
Traditional Markets				
Stock Market				
S&P500 Index	0.0053	0.0404	−0.6279	4.0500
MSCI World Index	0.0033	0.0411	−0.6767	3.8915
Bond Market				
Barclays Global Aggregate	−0.0000	0.0090	−0.3411	3.2887
CitiGroup Bond Index	0.0058	0.0187	0.1480	2.9467
Interest Rate Market				
3-months LIBOR	−0.0032	0.0677	−0.8104	13.6848
Commodity Markets				
S&P GS Commodity Index	0.0049	0.0571	0.0584	3.4679
Brent Crude Oil Index	0.0070	0.0917	0.1017	4.4543
Gold	0.0032	0.0387	0.4098	3.9983

This exhibit summarizes a series of empirical estimates of the first four moments of the return distribution of various hedge fund strategies and traditional market instruments, between 1990 and 2011. The key statistics indicate nonlinearities in hedge fund returns and varying risk-return profiles under different hedge fund strategies.
Source: Author and data provided by Hedge Fund Research.

First, hedge funds may not have a long active life in markets without an extensive past history. Performance figures are generally reported on a monthly or even a quarterly basis. Further, hedge funds are not subject to frequent (e.g., daily) mark-to-market valuations. In many cases, hedge fund managers do not disclose critical information on investment strategies or risk-return performance. Relevant hedge fund index data suffer from various biases that are difficult to tackle and can distort performance evaluation (Blum et al., 2003). Capocci and Hubner (2004) point out the most frequent biases:

- *Self-selection bias.* Bias from having voluntary reporting to hedge fund databases.

- *Survivorship bias.* Bias from having only surviving funds in the sample, which leads to an upward bias (dead fund databases).
- *Backfill bias.* Bias from backfilling performance when a fund is added to a database, which also gives an upward bias.
- *Stale price bias.* Bias from smoothing returns because investments are in illiquid assets.

A Summary of the Recent Literature

The explosive growth of hedge funds in the last decades resulted in many studies on hedge fund performance and risk analysis, such as Fung and Hsieh (1997, 1999), Ackermann, McEnally, and Ravenscraft (1999), Agarwal and Naik (2004), and Giamouridis and Vrontos (2007). Some past studies apply a linear model on selected risk factors to relate hedge fund returns to risk but manage to explain only 15 to 20 percent of risk in individual hedge fund returns (Fung and Hsieh, 1997, 2001; Lo, 2001; Agarwal and Naik, 2004; Goodworth and Jones, 2004).

Empirical research has also focused on understanding the impact of observable market risk factors on hedge fund returns and exploring different risk management analytics specifically designed for hedge funds (Lo, 2001; Perello, 2007; Cherny, Douady, and Molchanov, 2008; Jorion, 2009). Past research can be distinguished as taking either a "bottom-up" or a "top-down" approach (Fung and Hsieh, 2006). A bottom-up approach is more relevant to the heterogeneity of specific hedge fund styles and corresponding risk factors (Mitchell and Pulvino, 2001; Fung and Hsieh, 2002; Duarte, Francis, and Fan, 2007). From a top-down perspective, the irreducible risk factors are investigated in a diversified portfolio of hedge funds (Fung and Hsieh, 2003, 2006; Agarwal and Naik, 2004). The implications of the dynamic nature of risk exposures are also investigated (Lo, 2002; Chan, Getmansky, Haas, and Low, 2005; Gupta and Liang, 2005; Bali, Gokcan, and Liang, 2007; Boaykye, 2008; Liang and Park, 2008; Khandani and Lo, 2011). Furthermore, the impact of financial crises on hedge funds is examined, whereas liquidity, credit, equity market, and volatility risk factors are studied in various hedge fund strategies (Billio, Getmansky, and Pelizzon, 2009; Bali, Brown, and Caglayan, 2011; Patton and Ramadorai, 2011; Sadka, 2011; Cao, Chen, Liang, and Lo, 2012).

SOURCES OF RISK IN HEDGE FUNDS

The sources of risk in hedge funds are now examined taking into account that financial risk is a broad and multifaceted concept. Different types of risks in hedge funds are discussed. Attention is paid to the fact that the dynamic nature of hedge fund risk is associated with a number of complex investment strategies employed in hedge fund portfolio management.

The Concept of Risk and Risk Management

In financial markets, *risk* refers to the uncertainty of the future outcome of a current decision or situation. A *probability distribution* describes statistically the range of all possible outcomes weighted with their respective probabilities. The uncertain outcome is typically described by some random variable X, the probability distribution of which is specified through its cumulative distribution function $F(x)$, stated as: $F(x) = Pr(X \leq x)$; that is, for each possible outcome x, $F(x)$ refers to the probability of the actual outcome, X, being smaller than or equal to x.

Financial risk management pays attention to the analysis of the probability distribution of the various risk factors on returns. The properties of the distribution function $F(x)$ can be defined by certain statistical measures such as the mean, median, and variance. Standard deviation (i.e., the square root of the variance) is typically used to assess the dispersion of outcomes around the mean and is taken to reflect market volatility or risk. However, the standard deviation assumes that actual returns are symmetrically distributed around the mean. Further, it measures only the average deviation from the mean and fails to capture the extreme risks in the tails of the distribution (i.e., the values of $F(x)$ for values of x that lie far away from the mean).

Risk measures and management approaches in hedge funds should be preferably different from those applied in traditional asset classes. Traditional risk management tools, based on the distribution of realized returns, such as mean-variance analysis, beta, and VaR, do not capture many of the risk exposures of hedge fund investments (Lo, 2001). Standard deviation is a typical measure of dispersion that is also used to compute the Sharpe ratio. In the presence of asymmetric or long-tailed distributions, the standard deviation is an insufficient measure of risk for hedge funds (Jorion, 2007).

Hedge Fund Strategies and Risk

Although *hedging* refers to a risk-reduction technique, in the context of hedge funds it implies a fund that hedges away any risk unrelated to its speculative strategy (Connor and Woo, 2004). Hence, the riskiness of a hedge fund depends upon the investment strategies to which it applies. This relationship constitutes a fundamental distinction relative to a traditional (long-only) active fund, where risk is predominantly related to the benchmark and partly to the active portfolio strategy.

As with traditional investments, a major source of risk for hedge funds is *market risk* (i.e., the risk that the value of a fund's assets declines because of adverse movements in market variables such as interest rates, exchange rates, or security prices). This risk can be increased by leverage or reduced by hedging strategies. Each fund applies its own investment style and *specific risk* (i.e., a risk that is independent of underlying market performance). The reluctance of many hedge funds to disclose information about their operations or risks is an issue of growing concern. The need for disclosure of standardized risk information reporting has become a core issue, especially after the negative performance of many hedge funds during the financial crisis of 2007–2008 (Lhabitant, 2001; U.S. Congress, 2009; Australian Securities and Investments Commission, 2011; Weber and Zimmermann, 2011; Shi, 2012).

Hedge fund strategies can be broadly classified into infrequent and frequent traders. Some strategies invest in illiquid assets (e.g., distressed debt) that do not trade frequently, and this creates risk measurement problems (Jorion, 2007). Hedge funds that trade frequently invest predominantly in liquid assets, and their risk profiles can change rapidly. A relevant concern is whether risk management techniques such as VaR can be applied to measure, control, and manage such dynamic hedge fund risks. This issue is discussed subsequently.

The investment strategy chosen is a key component of the hedge fund risk exposure. Based on estimates by Hedge Fund Intelligence (2011), there are between 10,000 and 15,000 hedge funds globally that implement between 200 to 400 different hedge fund strategies. For major strategies, risks include global macro risks (e.g., interest rates, currency exchange rates, commodity prices, and equity prices); fixed-income arbitrage or distressed securities (e.g., interest rates, including yield, and duration of debt securities, credit risk, probability of default, and liquidity risk); and commodity trading advisers (CTAs) (e.g., commodity risk). Both credit and liquidity crises can affect a hedge fund, especially under extremely adverse market conditions, and under leverage exposure. Although liquidity and credit are separate sources of risk, their combined impact may severely amplify hedge fund risk exposure (Lo, 2001).

Risk preferences and operational risks in hedge funds are also important. Risk preferences play a major role in the risk management of hedge funds from both the manager's and the investors' perspectives. Hedge fund managers are typically compensated with both as a percentage of assets under management and incentive (performance) fees. The asymmetric nature of incentives fees can induce excessive risk-taking behavior. Imposing hurdle rates, high-water marks and other nonlinearities on the manager's compensation creates additional complexities that may affect investment decisions (Lo, 2001). The investors' profile and risk preferences also have an impact because they can affect managers' investment decisions and the types of risk undertaken. Certain constraints on investors' fund allocation decisions, such as the imposition of lock-up periods in the fund and high redemption fees, can further exacerbate investors' risk exposure, particularly during crises. In the context of complex and varying risks to which a hedge fund is exposed, Lo (1999) contends that integrating the three p's of total risk management (i.e., prices, probabilities, and preferences) is important. A broader set of risk factors in hedge funds refers to operational risks and integrates predominantly organizational aspects, such as the reliability of back-office operations, legal infrastructure, accounting and trade reconciliation, personnel issues, and the daily business management. Although these are not strictly financial risks, they can affect a hedge fund's overall risk-return performance.

According to Lhabitant (2001), the combined impact of these risk exposures resulted in the collapse of hedge funds, such as LTCM, Tiger Fund, Niederhoffer Fund, and Granite Fund, and has reinforced the need for efficient risk management. The collapse of these funds revealed that hedge funds are also involved in systemic risk exposures (Chan et al., 2005). Systemic risk is commonly used to describe the possibility of a series of correlated defaults among financial institutions that occur over a short period of time, often caused by a single major event.

Based on historical evidence (Jorion, 2000, 2007, 2009; Lhabitant 2001; Lo, 2001; Blum et al., 2003), an important issue relates to the alternative investment concept. The view that all systematic risks are diversified away is not really applicable in the sense that hedge fund returns represent a combination of superior management of market inefficiencies and conscious exposure to some specific systematic risks. Since only the systematic risks that are undesirable from a strategic viewpoint are diversified away, hedge funds in reality are not fully hedged. The leptokurtosis (fat tails) and negative skewness associated with most classes of hedge funds present a major challenge to risk management.

Different Types of Hedge Fund Risks

The different types of hedge fund risk exposures can be distinguished into two broad categories: (1) risks hedge funds share with other investment classes, and (2) risks more specific to hedge funds (Jaeger, 2005). From a risk management perspective, taking into account the complexity and the implications of the dynamic interactions between different types of risks is important. Major risks that hedge funds share with other investment classes include the following:

- *Market risk.* Risk of loss due to unexpected and adverse price moves or changes of volatility in the broad markets or single sectors.
- *Credit risk.* Risk of counterparties defaulting on their obligations or of changes in the market's sentiment about the probability of their default.
- *Liquidity risk.* Risk of loss due to the (temporary) inability to unwind a position at a normal bid/ask spread or the risk of being unable to fund investment leverage.
- *Common factor risk.* Risk inherent in some, but not all, securities, such as industry-specific risk.
- *Operational risk.* Risk of failure of internal systems, technology, people, external systems, and physical events.
- *Event risk.* Risk of an extraordinary event, such as an unexpected election outcome, military event, or sovereign default.
- *Corporate event risk.* Risk of loss due to an exposure to a particular firm and a specific event affecting its value, including surprise announcements such as earnings revisions, mergers, and changes of management.
- *Model risk.* Risk of a model misspecification.

Major risks that are more specific to hedge funds include:

- *Lack of transparency risk.* Risk due to lack of transparency and disclosure of investment strategies, asset positions, and risk factor exposures.
- *Manager (idiosyncratic) risk.* Risk related to one or a few individual managers having exclusive discretionary decision-making power, such as style drift, with insufficient investor control.
- *Leverage risk.* Risk related to volatility and financing in combination with counterparty risk.
- *Capacity risk.* Risk associated with the potential capacity limits of an investment strategy.
- *Fraud risk.* Risk involving the possibility of a manager defrauding investors.
- *Valuation risk.* Risk occurring when unique standards do not guide the pricing and NAV calculation for investment funds.
- *Concentration risk.* Risk related to high-dependency (large-size) individual investment positions.
- *Regulatory risk.* Risk associated with changing regulatory or tax requirements.

MEASURING AND MANAGING HEDGE FUND RISK

The empirical discussion as to the most appropriate approaches to measuring and managing hedge fund risk has intensified over time (Lo, 2001, 2002; Blum et al.,

2003; Jorion, 2007, 2009). In support of this line of research is the widely accepted notion that standard risk measures and techniques employed in portfolios with traditional assets are inappropriate for hedge funds. Further, hedge funds exhibited volatile risk-return performance during the financial crises. This critical issue raises concerns about the most efficient risk management tools. This section discusses various modern techniques used to measure and manage hedge fund risk, including variance and VaR approaches, expected shortfall, extreme value theory, tail analysis, and generalized Pareto distribution.

Critical Issues

As previously mentioned, growing interest exists among market practitioners, researchers, and academics in implementing an effective risk management framework that is tailor-made to the complexities of hedge fund risk exposures. Lo (2001, 2002) asserts that various critical issues should be considered:

- Traditional risk management tools were originally developed mainly for derivatives portfolios.
- Hedge fund strategies contain risk exposures that can change dramatically in response to market conditions.
- Nonlinearities in hedge fund investment returns can invalidate traditional risk metrics.
- Hedge fund investments are susceptible to complex types of risk that cannot always be measured (e.g., liquidity risk, event risk, operational risk, and political risk).
- Investors should be able to evaluate the fund's risk profile in the context of risk preferences, risk appetite, and tolerance for losses.

Fund managers usually employ two standard approaches to measure portfolio risk: the variance-based approach and the VaR approach (Connor and Woo, 2004). Below is a discussion of each approach.

Variance-Based Approach

The variance of portfolio returns is the expected squared deviation of the returns from their mean. If portfolio returns follow a normal distribution, the variance of returns completely describes the riskiness of returns. This approach is most powerful if returns have a linear factor structure, so that the random return of each asset can be decomposed into linear responses to a small number of market-wide factors plus an asset-specific risk. Although the variance-based approach could be employed for simple stock and bond portfolios, it would be inappropriate for hedge fund portfolios with prevailing non-normalities.

Value-at-Risk Approach

An important issue in hedge fund risk management is assessing the impact of adverse and extreme outcomes. This approach implies a risk management that focuses on the extreme quantiles of the distribution, usually the 1 percent or 0.4 percent quantile, which corresponds to VaR (Blum et al., 2003; Jorion, 2007, 2009). The VaR approach has gained growing popularity to hedge fund risk monitoring, especially in extreme events. The strength of VaR lies in its generality, because it works for portfolios including derivatives and other nonlinear return patterns and does not rely on variance.

A fundamental problem with VaR is that estimating the true probability of low probability events is extremely difficult (Connor and Woo, 2004). Hence, hedge funds require additional risk assessment techniques, such as simulations or stress testing, to monitor the source and severity of low-probability events. Broadly, *simulation* is the imitation of the operation of a real-world process or system over time. It is based on a model that represents the key characteristics or behaviors of the selected process. *Stress testing* is a form of testing that is used to determine the stability of a given system. It involves testing beyond normal operational capacity (often to a breaking point) in order to observe the resulting response. These issues are subsequently discussed in more detail.

VaR assesses the maximum loss that cannot be exceeded in a predefined confidence level and over a certain time horizon (e.g., 99 percent or 99.6 percent, for a 1-day or 5-day horizon, respectively) of all cases. For instance, a hedge fund might have a 5-day, 1 percent VaR of $100,000, meaning that only in one trading week out of 100 the fund will have a loss of $100,000 or more. VaR describes one feature of the return distribution—the length of the lower tail to reach a chosen cumulative probability value.

VaR is widely used in different fields of financial risk management. A key attractive attribute is that it introduces a uniform measuring system for various risks in a global portfolio by providing a method for comparing risk across different instruments and asset classes. Furthermore, VaR is straightforward to understand and evaluate because it translates a function as complex as the probability distribution in value terms.

However, VaR has limitations that are particularly problematic for hedge fund investments (Lo, 2001). First, VaR measures only one specified point on the distribution function, failing to fully capture the spectrum of risks that hedge funds exhibit (Blum et al., 2003). Second, VaR is a purely statistical measure of risk with little or no economic structure underlying its computation. VaR does not capture liquidity risk, event risk, credit risk, factor exposures, or time-varying risks due to dynamic trading strategies (e.g., contrarian, short-volatility, and credit-spread strategies) because it is a static snapshot of the marginal distribution of a portfolio's profit and loss (Lo, 2001).

Third, without additional economic structure, VaR is difficult to estimate. By definition, tail events are events that happen rarely. Hence, historical data contain only a few of these events, often in a sample too small to yield reliable estimates of tail probabilities. Calculating VaR under the assumption of normal distribution is inappropriate because hedge fund returns are known to be asymmetrically distributed, highly skewed, often multimodal, and with fat tails that imply many more rare events than the normal distribution would predict (Lo, 2001). Furthermore, implicit in VaR calculations are assumptions about the correlations between portfolio assets and these correlations are computed unconditionally (Lo, 2001).

Finally, VaR can have inferior aggregation properties with respect to subportfolios, neglecting portfolio diversification benefits. Although VaR does not seem to qualify as a coherent risk measure (Artzner, Delbaen, Eber, and Heath, 1999; Blum et al., 2003), the method has introduced a more disciplined approach to financial risk management. When applied over longer time spans and with more realistic statistical assumptions (e.g., leptokurtic distributions, time-varying risk factors, and event-dependent correlations), VaR can contain some of the earlier concerns (Lo, 2001).

Expected Shortfall Approach

VaR is often criticized for not presenting a full picture of the financial risks under management (Hull, 2006). To overcome certain limitations of VaR, the expected shortfall (ES), also called conditional VaR, average value at risk (AVaR), or expected tail loss (ETL or TailVaR), is employed as an alternative risk measure in hedge funds. ES is a coherent and spectral risk measure, easy to understand, more conservative than VaR, and more sensitive to the shape of the loss distribution in the tail of the distribution (Acerbi and Tasche, 2002). Blum et al. (2003) note that the attractiveness of the ES method is associated with several critical properties, including scalability (twice the risk should give a double measure), correct risk ranking (bigger risks get bigger measures), and accounting for diversification (aggregated risks should have a lower measure).

ES, like VaR, is a function of two parameters: N (the time horizon in days) and x percent (the confidence level). ES is the expected loss during an N-day period, conditional that the loss is greater than the xth percentile of the loss distribution. For example, with $x = 99$ and $N = 10$, ES is the average amount that is lost over a 10-day period, assuming that the loss is greater than the 99th percentile of the loss distribution. More technically, the "expected shortfall at q% level" is the expected return on the portfolio in the worst q% of the cases. ES requires a quantile-level q and is defined to be the expected loss of portfolio value given that a loss is occurring at or below the q quantile. ES evaluates the value or risk of an investment in a conservative way, focusing on the less profitable outcomes. For high values of q, ES ignores the most profitable but unlikely possibilities; for small values of q, ES focuses on the worst losses. A value of q at 5 percent is often used in practice (Acerbi and Tasche, 2002; Yamai and Yoshiba, 2002).

Whereas VaR indicates "how bad things can get," ES investigates "if things do get bad, what the expected loss should be." Hence, the idea with ES is to assess the performance of the assets in the portfolio if certain extreme events occur and to identify the likelihood of experiencing some sort of loss on one or more of those assets. By evaluating the return potential of each asset and paying attention to anticipating the shortfall and the possibility of incurring losses, the fund manager can assess the overall impact on the portfolio and make a decision of whether to hold onto those assets before the expected decrease in value should take place. Because the method is related to potential portfolio restructuring, the fund manager has some idea of how long a given asset is likely to continue dropping in value once the decline begins. This would facilitate portfolio restructuring decisions. Despite the fact that ES has appealing features relative to VaR, it has certain practical drawbacks (Artzner et al., 1999; Christoffersen and Goncalves, 2005; Jorion, 2007).

Extreme Value Theory: Tail Analysis

For risk management purposes, examining the implications of extreme events on hedge fund returns is important. In this case, extreme value theory (EVT) can be useful. The analysis of the tails of the probability distribution (rather than the entire distribution) is more relevant as a means of assessing the probability of large adverse movements (Embrechts, Klüpperberg, and Mikosch, 1999; McNeil, 1999; Embrechts, McNeil, and Straumann, 2002).

A fundamental EVT theorem states that, for a broad class of probability distributions $F(x)$ (with x taking only values greater than some specified, sufficiently high threshold u), the tail behavior above threshold u falls into one of three classes (Blum et al., 2003):

- *Fréchet, or heavy-tailed, class.* The tail of $1 - F(x)$ is essentially proportional to a power function x^{-} for some $\alpha > 0$. This means that the tail decays slowly and the probability of extreme outcomes is relatively high. The parameter α that essentially governs the tail behavior is called the *tail index.* The closer α is to 0, the higher is the tendency for extreme outcomes.
- *Gumbel, or thin-tailed, class.* The tail $1 - F(x)$ is essentially proportional to an exponential function. This means that the tail decays quickly and the probability of extreme outcomes is relatively low but not zero. The thin-tailed case corresponds to the limit of the heavy-tailed case for the tail index α tending to infinity.
- *Weibull, or short-tailed, class.* The tail is zero above some finite end point. When modeling the returns from financial assets, truncated distributions are generally not considered because of the difficulty of defining a reasonable end-point.

According to an important EVT theorem, if a distribution has tail index α, then the nth moment of the distribution is infinite for $n > \alpha$. If a distribution has $\alpha = 3.5$, for instance (often seen in returns distributions of financial assets), then its skewness (third moment) is finite, whereas its kurtosis (fourth moment) does not converge to a finite value. A very high excess kurtosis in a sample of returns can be an indication of a heavy tail.

Generalized Pareto Distribution

Instead of investigating the tail of the return distribution $F(x)$ itself, an alternative approach is to investigate the excess distribution of the return variable X above the threshold u (Blum et al., 2003). Equation 25.1 illustrates this point, which is the conditional distribution of $X - u$ given that X is greater than u.

$$F u(y) = \Pr(X - u = y | X > u) \tag{25.1}$$

The original distribution $F(x)$ shown in Equation 25.2 for $x \geq u$ can then be recovered via:

$$F(x) = (1 - F(u))F_u(x - u) + F(u) \tag{25.2}$$

For some reasonably high threshold, u, an EVT theorem states that $F_u(y)$ can be approximated to deliberate accuracy by the generalized Pareto distribution (GPD), which is defined in Equation 25.3 as:

$$G_{\xi,\beta}(y) = \begin{cases} 1 - (1 + \xi\, y/\beta)^{-1/\xi} & |\xi \# 0 \\ 1 - \exp(-x/\beta) & |\xi = 0 \end{cases} \tag{25.3}$$

where β is a scale parameter ($\beta > 0$); ξ governs the shape of the distribution; and $\xi > 0$ corresponds to the heavy-tailed case, $\xi = 0$ is the thin-tailed case and $\xi < 0$ the short-tailed case. In the first case, the relation $\xi = 1/\alpha$ holds for the shape parameter. In short, tail analysis pays attention to estimating the shape parameter ξ.

The practical application of tail estimation is constrained by certain limitations, including the selection of a reasonable threshold u on which the estimated tail index is often heavily dependent. Further, the availability of sufficient data in the tail is often lacking, leading to broad confidence intervals and only weakly significant estimates. These issues are particularly relevant to hedge funds. If adequately reliable estimated tail models can be defined, the portfolio manager can employ them to estimate tail-related risk measures such as VaR and ES. Apart from the GPD approach, the well-known maximum likelihood technique is another parametric method, whereas the Hill estimator is a popular nonparametric approach to tail-index estimation (Embrechts et al., 1999).

EVALUATION OF HEDGE FIND RISK MEASURES

Despite the conceptual and intuitive simplicity of VaR and ES, the technicalities of their calculation can be complicated, depending on the heterogeneity of the portfolio and the distributional assumptions made. A critical issue is the reliability and the proper interpretation of the data. A brief evaluation overview of the suitability of certain risk measures for hedge funds follows. Artzner et al. (1999) discuss the critical properties that coherent measures of risk should possess including:

- *Monotonicity.* If a portfolio has lower returns than another portfolio for every state of the world, its risk measure should be greater.
- *Translation invariance.* If the portfolio manager adds an amount of cash, k, to a portfolio, its risk measure should decrease by k.
- *Homogeneity.* Changing the size of a portfolio by a factor, λ, while keeping the relative amounts of different items in the portfolio the same, should result in the risk measure being multiplied by λ.
- *Subadditivity.* The risk measure for two portfolios after they are merged should be no greater than the sum of their risk measures before they are merged.

According to Blum et al. (2003), the three main elements of standard risk measure estimation are: (1) mapping the portfolio positions to risk factors, (2) calculating the risk factor covariance matrix based on historical prices, and (3) determining the model for the risk and calculating the risk measures.

In risk-factor mapping, the risk components of individual securities in a portfolio are decomposed into exposures under the control of the fund manager and exogenous factors. A *risk factor* is a variable that directly affects the value of a security, and different risk factors can affect securities. The impact of a specific risk factor on a security (sensitivity) can be modeled by a linear or nonlinear pricing function. Following the identification of portfolio risk factors, estimating the dependence structure between the risk factors is important. Based on the conventional assumption of normally distributed returns, the correlation matrix determines the distribution of portfolio returns, and therefore the portfolio risk measures. A condition for the accurate estimation of the covariance matrix is the sufficiently large data input required in case of large numbers of risk factors. The dependence between risk factors is usually nonlinear and time-varying. The assumption of normally distributed returns is restrictive in the case of hedge funds that often exhibit non-normal, nonlinear behavior and extreme outcomes. According to Blum et al. (2003), most commonly employed models to calculate portfolio variance (volatility) and covariance (correlations) include the following:

- Equally weighted moving average (EWMA) of squared returns and cross products over some specified time horizon.
- Exponential moving average of squared returns and cross products with a specified decay parameter (in practice the decay parameter chosen is 0.94 for daily observations and 0.97 for monthly observations).
- The family of autoregressive conditional heteroskedastic (ARCH) and generalized ARCH (GARCH) models.

The empirical approaches most widely employed to calculate risk measures are parametric models, Monte Carlo simulations, and historical simulations (Blum et al., 2003), as well as scenario analysis, stress tests, and copulas. These approaches differ mainly in the assumptions of security valuation as a function of risk factors and the probability distribution of returns.

Parametric Models

The core principle in parametric models is to approximate the pricing function of every instrument (i.e., the relationship between each instrument and the risk factors) in order to obtain an analytical formula for the risk measures. The simplest parametric approach is variance-covariance VaR (also called RiskMetrics VaR or the delta method).

Monte Carlo Simulations

The *Monte Carlo* (MC) approach is a computerized mathematical stochastic technique, which is based on random numbers and probability statistics to investigate risk management issues. The hedge fund manager can assess a range of possible outcomes generated by MC simulation as well as the respective probabilities for these outcomes to occur. The technique is based on simulating the behavior of the underlying risk factors through a large number of draws produced by a random generator. Using given pricing functions, the values of the portfolio positions are calculated from the simulated values of each risk factor. The method accounts for any nonlinearity of the relationship between instruments and risk factors, as the positions in the portfolio are fully revalued under each of the random scenarios. Every random draw of risk factor values leads to a new portfolio valuation (iteration). Numerous iterations (several thousands) provide a simulated return distribution of the portfolio from which the VaR or the ES values can be determined. The underlying distribution of the randomly generated values of the risk factors can be chosen freely (not constrained to the Gaussian distribution), although some mathematical problems may arise in simulating the dependence structures of the risk factors correctly (Blum et al., 2003).

Historical Simulations

Instead of simulating return distributions, downside risk can be determined by tracing history. The method relies on the (unconditional) historical distribution of returns by applying past asset returns to the present holdings in the portfolio. The values of the portfolio positions are then fully evaluated for each set of historical returns. An advantage of this method is that no explicit assumptions about the underlying return distribution have to be made. However, because the method relies on historical price behavior, this may not be relevant in the current market conditions, or the sample may be too small to assess all possible outcomes, particularly in the tails of the distribution. Moreover, if significant intertemporal dependence is present in the returns, the method may not be sensible (Blum et al., 2003).

Simulation-based risk management systems can offer sufficient flexibility and sophistication and can support portfolio evaluation over a range of possible future states of the markets or scenarios (Burmeister, Mausser, and Rosen, 2003). However, fund managers continue assuming that risk factor returns follow a normal (Gaussian) distribution with the mean and standard deviation observed in the historical data since this remains computationally convenient. This is an unrealistic assumption that leads to underestimation of extreme risks and distortion of the related tail-based risk measures such as VaR. As Blum et al. (2003) point out, comparing VaR estimates obtained from the full distribution of historical returns (empirical) against estimates obtained from the normal distribution (Gaussian) indicates that the Gaussian model systematically underestimates the actual risk and the degree of underestimation becomes higher further out into the tails.

A critical advantage of simulation-based approaches is that they are not conditioned on the restrictive assumption of normally distributed returns and can explicitly price financial instruments in scenario analysis, resulting in a more realistic risk assessment (Burmeister et al., 2003).

Scenario Analysis

This flexible risk management setting can be expanded by using a scenario-based approach to contribute additional benefits in terms of understanding, communicating, and managing the risks faced by hedge funds. A *scenario* is a systematic analysis of risk factor levels at some future time, which represents a consistent evolutionary path of the state of the financial environment. These risk-factor levels can be obtained from historical observations, generated by Monte Carlo methods, or specified subjectively based on the experience of managers. The purpose of scenarios is to span the range of possible future events, rather than to forecast a particular outcome. Accordingly, probabilities can be assigned to scenarios to reflect their relative likelihood of occurrence. A scenario's time horizon and time steps reflect the investment or portfolio strategy horizon and can refer to a short or long time span (Burmeister et al., 2003).

The scenario approach can often be distinguished into scenarios developed for statistical risk measurement, such as computing a portfolio's VaR or ES, and scenarios designed for stress testing. The former case incorporates a large number of scenarios representative of typical market conditions. The latter case develops a selected number of extreme scenarios that shock specific risk factors in a designed manner. In all cases, the financial instruments are priced (i.e., simulated) on the basis of the risk-factor levels in each scenario. A sufficiently large scenario set yields an empirical distribution from which risk measures can be computed (Burmeister et al., 2003).

Stress Tests

The efficiency of the risk management tools discussed earlier can be enhanced with the application of stress tests. Unlike VaR, which attempts to measure the risk of low-probability events in normal markets, stress tests ("what if" extreme stress scenarios) pay attention to the risk of plausible events in highly abnormal markets. Predetermined price shifts to the portfolio positions are introduced in order to assess how the portfolio behaves under extreme but plausible market conditions (Jaeger, 2005).

The following different types of extreme stress scenarios can be distinguished (on underlying assets such as equities, interest rates, yield curve shapes, foreign exchange rates, commodities, stock and bond volatility, and past events): (1) historical scenarios (e.g., the stock market crash of 1987); (2) market scenarios (e.g., a drop of 20 percent in the equity markets); and (3) portfolio specific scenarios (e.g., for credit sensitive portfolios). Systematic stress testing for market risk includes test asymmetries, correlation breakdown, stressing different combinations of asset classes (separately and combined), and appropriate-size shocks.

Dependence and Copulas

Correlation is a statistical measure of linear dependence between returns of different assets. However, it cannot take into account market anomalies and extreme events and is also affected by the assumptions on the distribution of returns. Correlations and dependencies are important quantitative, time-varying inputs for assessing efficient portfolio diversification, especially at volatile market phases (Embrechts et al., 2002; Blum et al., 2003). The hedge fund manager can conveniently combine financial assets that result in reducing diversifiable (asset-specific) risk exposures. The conventional standard tool to investigate the dependence structure of hedge funds on traditional asset classes is to estimate their historical correlation to the returns of the traditional markets.

Copulas represent a general way of modeling dependence between random variables. Copulas have been recently incorporated in financial risk management because they can cater to a wide range of dependence structures, including linear dependence. This attractive property relates to the marginal behavior of the individual risk factors that is separated from its dependence structure. Models for the single risk factors can then be freely combined with those for the dependence structure, without the very restrictive assumptions imposed by linear correlation (i.e., probability distribution being elliptic). This is particularly useful for hedge funds with highly skewed and heavy-tailed returns (Blum et al., 2003).

To briefly discuss copulas, consider an n-dimensional random vector $X = (X_1, \ldots, X_n)$. The information on the distribution of a vector X is fully described by the joint cumulative distribution function in Equation 25.4:

$$F_X(x) = F_X(x_1, \ldots, x_n) = \mathrm{P}(X \leq x) = \mathrm{P}(X_1 \leq x_1, \ldots, X_n \leq x_n) \tag{25.4}$$

where F_{xi} describes the marginal distributions of X_i that is calculated through the joint distribution function. Copulas are multivariate uniform distributions that decompose the above representation of the joint distribution function into two parts—the dependence structure and the marginal distributions. The fact that copula functions apply to uniform distributions over the interval [0, 1] makes essential the extensive use of probability-integral and quantile transformations. Therefore, the initial random vector X with continuous marginal distribution functions $F_1, \ldots, F_n$ is transformed with the method of probability-integral transformation to the uniform marginal distribution $U_i \equiv F_i(X_i)$. A *copula function* is the joint cumulative distribution function of the multivariate vector $U = (U_1, U_2, \ldots, U_n)$, which is denoted by Equation 25.5:

$$C(u_1, \ldots, u_n) = p(U_1 \leq u_1, \ldots, U_n \leq U_n) \tag{25.5}$$

A wide range of copula functions is available in the empirical literature. They can be used to capture different dependency relationships, such as the Gaussian, Clayton, Gumbel, rotated Clayton, and rotated Gumbel copula (McNeil, Frey, and Embrechts, 2005). Some of the most popular copulas are appropriate to capture important symmetric joint extreme events and asymmetric tail dependence and can be convenient for hedge funds. The Gaussian copula, for instance, refers to symmetric joint functional forms of the corresponding elliptical distributions but is quite restrictive because it provides only weak information about tail dependence. Clayton and Gumbel copulas can capture asymmetric dependence, because they assign more probability on single lower or upper tail dependence. In particular, the Clayton copula can model only lower tail dependence, while the Gumbel copula only upper tail dependence. The rotated Gumbel copula (survival copula), similar to Clayton, has stronger lower tail dependence.

ON RISK MEASUREMENT SYSTEMS

The complex trading strategies and diverse financial instruments expose hedge funds to risk factors from different sources, such as market forces, credit conditions, and liquidity constraints. An effective risk management framework should help managers identify the sources of risk in a hedge fund portfolio, assess the impact of potential trades and risk factor shifts, and optimally trade off risk and return. Burmeister et al. (2003) contend that a flexible risk management system should offer the ability to:

- Decompose a portfolio's risk across multiple dimensions (e.g., by asset and/or risk factor).
- Drill down into various levels of the portfolio hierarchy.
- Understand how new trades affect the portfolio risk.
- Generate potential hedges.
- Construct risk-return efficient frontiers.

As discussed previously, simulation techniques can support generic optimization models that extend beyond the traditional mean-variance approach. Blending this output with scenario-based risk management tools can apply not only to variance but also to measures such as VaR and ES. Furthermore, traditional approaches of risk measures have been built from returns-based information. These approaches are easy and cheap to implement and also account for dynamic trading of the portfolio. However, certain drawbacks relate to the fact that they offer no data for new instruments, markets, and managers, are very slow at identifying style drift, and may not reveal hidden risk. Because returns-based risk measures give no insight into the risk drivers of the portfolio, Jorion (2009) contends that an efficient and superior risk measurement system should be preferably position-based.

In broad terms, a modern risk measurement system should incorporate the following main components (Jorion, 2009):

- *Risk factors.* From market data, construct the distribution of risk factors (e.g., normal, empirical, or other).
- *Positions.* Collect the portfolio positions and map them onto the risk factors.
- *Risk engine.* Use the risk engine to construct the distribution of portfolio profit and losses over the selected period. The output can be summarized by a VaR number, which represents the worst loss that will not be exceeded at the prespecified confidence level.

The position-based approach uses the most current position information, which should reveal style drift or hidden risks. It can be applied to new instruments, markets, and managers, whereas most of the return-based drawbacks can be contained. This approach can also be used for forward-looking stress tests. Conversely, position-based risk systems have certain drawbacks because they require more resources and are expensive to implement. Position-based risk measures assume that the portfolio is frozen over the horizon and ignores dynamic trading.

They are susceptible to errors in data and models in that they require modeling all positions from the ground up, repricing instruments as a function of movements in the risk factors.

To better treat hedge fund risks, distinguishing between the management of systematic risk from the management of the manager's specific risk is important. The real risk from hedge funds is related to unwanted and unknown leveraged systematic risk as well as uncontrolled manager-related risk (e.g., style drifts, faulty operations, and fraud). Exposure to systematic risk can be partially assessed through risk-based factor models on the return time series of the fund. Position-based risk management techniques and transparency enables control of manager specific and idiosyncratic risk (Jaeger, 2005; Jorion, 2009).

The implementation of active risk management can play an important role in hedge fund risk dispersion and control. According to Jaeger (2005), the hedge fund manager can discretionally apply a variety of portfolio management techniques, including:

- Limiting portfolio exposure to particular sectors and "risk budgets" (maximally allowed VaR for different risk factors, e.g. specific currencies, equity markets, commodities, or geographic regions); maximizing the risk limit (VaR) for a global portfolio according to the investors' profile.
- Employing tactical allocation shifts based on risk management.
- Using reallocation in case the VaR limit for particular risk factor or the entire portfolio is permanently exceeded.
- Using de-allocation in case of style shifts.
- Using different specific stress test limits depending on current market environment and investors' profile.
- Monitoring and limiting exposure by limiting leverage factor (margin requirements) for each individual manager.

SUMMARY AND CONCLUSIONS

The robust growth of hedge funds and the extreme return performance, on the one hand, but failures and losses during financial crises, on the other, make efficient and integrated risk management a top priority issue for hedge funds. Empirical convergence shows that conventional risk metrics and management tools suffer serious drawbacks that render them inappropriate for application to hedge funds. The dynamic investment strategies and the complex risk exposures of hedge funds require risk management tools that take into account non-normalities in returns; nonlinearities in risk-returns profiles; and time-varying, rather than static, asset correlations.

In order to overcome the limitations of traditional risk tools as well as the lack of tailor-made risk approaches, various modern quantitative risk management techniques have been critically discussed and evaluated in the context of hedge funds. The chapter presents advantages, drawbacks, and functionalities of risk management tools, such as the variance-based approach, VaR method, expected shortfall, extreme value theory, tail analysis, and generalized Pareto distribution.

The chapter also discusses the empirical approaches most widely employed to calculate risk measures, including parametric models, Monte Carlo and historical simulations, scenario analysis, stress tests, and copulas. The chapter concludes with some guidelines on efficient risk measurement systems.

The field of risk management in hedge funds has been growing quickly. Modern, dynamic, and sophisticated quantitative risk tools are now under way (e.g., fuzzy generic algorithms) to enhance the existing armory in hedge fund risk management and to prove that this field remains timely and fascinating.

DISCUSSION QUESTIONS

1. Distinguish between broader and specific hedge fund risk types and briefly explain each risk type.
2. Explain the key points of the expected shortfall (ES) approach employed in hedge fund risk management. Compare the main differences of ES from the VaR approach.
3. Identify and explain the three main elements of standard risk measure estimation.
4. Discuss the concept of copulas and explain their growing attention and flexibility in hedge fund risk management.

REFERENCES

Acerbi, Carlo, and Dirk Tasche. 2002. "On the Coherence of Expected Shortfall." *Journal of Banking & Finance* 26:7, 1487–1503.

Ackermann, Carl, Richard McEnally, and David Ravenscraft. 1999. "The Performance of Hedge Funds: Risk, Return, and Incentives." *Journal of Finance* 54:3, 833–874.

Agarwal, Vikas, and Narayan Naik. 2004. "Risks and Portfolio Decisions Involving Hedge Funds." *Review of Financial Studies* 17:1, 63–98.

Artzner, Philippe, Freddy Delbaen, Jean-Marc Eber, and David Heath. 1999. "Coherent Risk Measures." *Mathematical Finance* 9:3, 203–228.

Australian Securities and Investments Commission. 2011. *Hedge Funds: Improving Disclosure for Retail Investors.* Consultation Paper 147 (February).

Bali, Turan, Stephen Brown, and Mustafa Caglayan. 2011. "Systematic Risk and the Cross-Section of Hedge Fund Returns." Working Paper, Center for Financial Markets and Policy, McDonough School of Business, Georgetown University.

Bali, Turan, Suleiman Gokcan, and Bing Liang. 2007. "Value at Risk and the Cross-Section of Hedge Fund Returns." *Journal of Banking & Finance* 31:4, 1135–1166.

Billio, Monica, Mila Getmansky, and Loriana Pelizzon. 2009. "Non-Parametric Analysis of Hedge Fund Returns: New Insights from High Frequency Data." *Journal of Alternative Investments* 12:1, 21–38.

Blum, Peter, Michael Dacorogna, and Lars Jaeger. 2003. "Performance and Risk Measurement for Hedge Funds: Empirical Considerations." In Lars Jaeger, ed., *The New Generation of Risk Management for Hedge Funds and Private Equity Investments*, 412–433. London: Euromoney Books.

Boakye, Clement. 2008. "Multidimensional Risk/Performance Measurement for Hedge Funds." Working Paper Fin. 5182, Temple University.

Burmeister, Curt, Helmut Mausser, and Dan Rosen. 2003. "Simulation-Based Risk Management Systems for Hedge Funds." In Lars Jaeger, ed., *The New Generation of Risk Management for Hedge Funds and Private Equity Investments*, 347–367. London: Euromoney Books.

Cao, Charles, Yong Chen, Bing Liang, and Andrew Lo. 2012. "Can Hedge Funds Time Market Liquidity?" Available at http://papers.ssrn.com/sol3/papers.cfm?abstract_id=1537925.

Capocci, Daniel, and Georges Hubner. 2004. "Analysis of Hedge Fund Performance." *Journal of Empirical Finance* 11:1, 55–89.

Chan, Nicholas, Mila Getmansky, Shane Haas, and Andrew Lo. 2005. "Systemic Risk and Hedge Funds." Working Paper 11200, National Bureau of Economic Research.

Cherny, Alexander, Raphael Douady, and Stanislav Molchanov. 2008. "On Measuring Hedge Fund Risk." Moscow State University, RiskData, and University of North Carolina at Charlotte.

Christoffersen, Peter, and Silvia Goncalves. 2005. "Estimation of Risk in Financial Risk Management." *Journal of Risk* 7:3, 1–27.

Connor, Gregory, and Mason Woo. 2004. "An Introduction to Hedge Funds." Discussion Paper 477, Financial Markets Group, London School of Economics and Political Science.

Duarte, Jefferson, Longstaff Francis, and Yu Fan. 2007. "Risk and Return in Fixed Income Arbitrage: Nickels in Front of a Steamroller?" *Review of Financial Studies* 20:3, 769–811.

Eichengreen, Barry, and Donald Mathieson. 1998. "Hedge Funds and Financial Markets Dynamics." Occasional Paper 166, International Monetary Fund, Washington, D.C.

Embrechts Paul, Claudia Klüpperberg, and Thomas Mikosch. 1999. *Modelling Extremal Events for Insurance and Finance*, 2nd ed. Berlin: Springer Verlag.

Embrechts Paul, Alexander McNeil, and Daniel Straumann. 2002. "Correlation and Dependence in Risk Management: Properties and Pitfalls." In M.A.H. Dempster, ed., *Risk Management: Value at Risk and Beyond*, 176–223. Cambridge: Cambridge University Press.

Fung, William, and Daniel Hsieh. 1997. "Empirical Characteristics of Dynamic Trading Strategies: The Case of Hedge Funds." *Review of Financial Studies* 10:2, 275–302.

Fung, William, and Daniel Hsieh. 1999. "A Primer on Hedge Funds." *Journal of Empirical Finance* 6:3, 309–331.

Fung, William, and David Hsieh. 2001. "The Risk in Hedge Fund Strategies: Theory and Evidence from Trend Followers." *Review of Financial Studies* 14:2, 313–341.

Fung, William, and David Hsieh. 2002. "The Risk in Fixed-Income Hedge Fund Styles." *Journal of Fixed Income* 12:2, 6–27.

Fung, William, and David Hsieh. 2003. "The Risks in Hedge Fund Strategies: Alternative Alphas and Alternative Betas." In Lars Jaeger, ed., *The New Generation of Risk Management for Hedge Funds and Private Equity Investments*, 72–87. London: Euromoney Books.

Fung, William, and David Hsieh. 2006. "Hedge Funds: An Industry in Its Adolescence." Working Paper, BNP Paribas Hedge Fund Centre, London Business School.

Giamouridis, Daniel, and Ioannis Vrontos. 2007. "Hedge Fund Portfolio Construction: A Comparison of Static and Dynamic Approaches." *Journal of Banking & Finance* 31:1, 199–217.

Goodworth, Tony, and Chris Jones. 2004. "Building a Risk Measurement Framework for Hedge Funds and Funds of Funds." Working Paper 8, Judge Institute of Management, Cambridge Business School, University of Cambridge.

Gregoriou, Greg, Georges Hubner, Nicolas Papageorgiou, and Fabrice Rouah. 2005. *Hedge Funds: Insights in Performance, Measurement, Risk Analysis and Portfolio Allocation.* Hoboken, NJ: Wiley Finance.

Gupta, Anurag, and Bing Liang. 2005. "Do Hedge Funds Have Enough Capital? A Value-at-Risk Approach." *Journal of Financial Economics* 77:1, 219–253.

Hedge Fund Intelligence. 2011. *Global Review* 2011. Available at www.hedgefundintelligence.com/Issue/81983/Global-Review-2011.html.

Hedge Fund Research. 2011. *Global Hedge Fund Industry Report.* Available at www.hedgefundresearch.com/index.php?fuse=products-irglo.

Hull, John. 2006. *Risk Management and Financial Institutions*. Englewood Cliffs, NJ: Prentice Hall.

Jaeger, Lars. 2005. "Risk Management for Hedge Fund Portfolios." Working Paper, ETHZ Conference.

Jorion, Philippe. 2000. "Risk Management Lessons from Long-Term Capital Management." *European Financial Management* 6:3, 277–300.

Jorion, Philippe. 2006. *Value at Risk: The New Benchmark for Controlling Market Risk*, 3rd ed. New York: McGraw-Hill.

Jorion, Philippe. 2007. "Risk Management for Hedge Funds with Position Information." *Journal of Portfolio Management* 34:1, 127–134.

Jorion, Philippe. 2009. "Risk Management Lessons from the Credit Crisis." *European Financial Management* 15:5, 923–933.

J. P. Morgan. 2011. *Regeneration: Entering a Period of Sustainable Growth, Investor Sentiment Report*. J. P. Morgan Prime Brokerage.

Khandani, Amir, and Andrew Lo. 2011. "What Happened to the Quants in August 2007? Evidence from Factors and Transaction Data." *Journal of Financial Markets* 14:1, 1–46.

Lavinio, Stefano. 2000. *The Hedge Fund Handbook A Definite Guide for Analyzing and Evaluating Alternative Investments*. New York: Irwin, McGraw-Hill.

Lhabitant, Francois. 2001. "Assessing Market Risk for Hedge Funds and Hedge Funds Portfolios." Research Paper 24, International Center for Financial Asset Management and Engineering, Geneva.

Lhabitant, Francois. 2002. *Hedge Funds: Myths and Limits*. Chichester: Wiley Finance.

Liang, Bing, and Hyuna Park. 2008. "Risk Measures for Hedge Funds: A Cross-Sectional Approach." *European Financial Management* 13:2, 317–354.

Lo, Andrew. 1999. *A Non-Random Walk Down Wall Street*. Princeton, NJ: Princeton University Press.

Lo, Andrew. 2001. "Risk Management for Hedge Funds: Introduction and Overview." *Financial Analysts Journal* 57:6, 16–33.

Lo, Andrew. 2002. "Risk Management for Hedge Funds." *Canadian Investment Review* 15:1, 29–31.

McNeil, Alexander. 1999. "Extreme Value Theory for Risk Managers." Working Paper, ETH Zentrum, Zurich.

McNeil, Alexander, Rudiger Frey, and Paul Embrechts. 2005. *Quantitative Risk Management: Concepts, Techniques, and Tools*. Princeton, NJ: Princeton University Press.

Mitchell, Mark, and Todd Pulvino. 2001. "Characteristics of Risk in Risk Arbitrage." *Journal of Finance* 56:6, 2135–2175.

Patton, Andrew, and Tarun Ramadorai. 2011. "On the High-Frequency Dynamics of Hedge Fund Risk Exposures." Discussion Paper 8479, CEPR.

Perello, Joseph. 2007. "Downside Risk Analysis Applied to the Hedge Funds Universe." *Physica A* 383:2, 480–496.

Sadka, Ronnie. 2011. "Hedge-Fund Performance and Liquidity Risk." Available at http://papers.ssrn.com/sol3/papers.cfm?abstract_id=1917118.

Shi, Zhen. 2012. "The Impact of Portfolio Disclosure of Hedge Fund Performance, Fees and Flows." Working Paper (June), Georgia State University.

U.S. Congress. 2009. *Hedge Fund Transparency Act*. Bill: S.344, 1/21/2009. 111th US Congress.

Yamai, Yasuhiro, and Toshinao Yoshiba. 2002. "Comparative Analyses of Expected Shortfall and Value-at-Risk: Expected Utility Maximization and Tail Risk." *Monetary and Economic Studies* 20:2, 95–115.

Weber, Peter, and Heinz Zimmermann. 2011. "Hedge Fund Activism and Information Disclosure: The Case of Germany." *European Financial Management* 17:4, DOI: 10.1111/j.1468-036X.2011.00626.x.

ABOUT THE AUTHOR

Dr. Theodore Syriopoulos is Associate Professor of Finance at the School of Business Studies, University of the Aegean, Greece. He also holds regular visiting posts at Audencia Nantes School of Management (France), Newcastle University (United Kingdom), Shanghai Maritime University (China), International Hellenic University (Greece), and Athens University of Economics and Business (Greece). Before joining academia, he served as a top management executive in banking, investments, fund management, and consulting. Professor Syriopoulos has published in the *Journal of International Financial Markets, Institutions & Money*, *Journal of Multinational Financial Management*, *Applied Financial Economics*, and *International Review of Financial Analysis*, among others. He holds a BA in Economics from the University of Piraeus, Greece, and a MA and Ph.D. in Applied Economics from the University of Kent at Canterbury, United Kingdom.

CHAPTER 26

Hedge Funds and the Financial Crisis

JING-ZHI HUANG
McKinley Professor of Business and Associate Professor of Finance, Smeal College of Business, Penn State University

YING WANG
Assistant Professor of Finance, School of Business and Center for Institutional Investment Management, University at Albany, State University of New York

INTRODUCTION

One of the most important developments in the financial markets over the past decade has been the phenomenal growth of the hedge fund industry. Not surprisingly, one main reason for this growth has been the superior performance of hedge funds over the same course of time. However, the hedge fund industry suffered a severe setback in 2008, during the peak of the recent financial crisis. According to Hedge Fund Research (2009), its Global Hedge Fund Composite Index and Equity Hedge Index dropped 18.3 percent and 26 percent in 2008, respectively. Assets under management (AUM) with hedge funds also declined from a peak of $1.93 trillion at mid-year 2008 to $1.4 trillion at year end. Nonetheless, hedge funds made headline news during and after the financial crisis on other fronts, such as the astronomical amounts of money made by top hedge fund managers and the perceived role of the hedge fund industry in the crisis. For instance, John Paulson, the founder and President of Paulson & Co., a New York-based event-driven hedge fund company, became one of the most well-known people in the United States, if not in the world, after he reportedly made a record of $3.5 billion for himself in 2007 by betting against the U.S. housing market.

Some also blamed hedge funds for causing sharp declines in the stock prices of many companies, especially financial companies, during the crisis. Partially due to complaints from banks, including Morgan Stanley and Goldman Sachs, the Securities and Exchange Commission (SEC) issued a ban on short-selling 799 financial stocks on September 19, 2008, a few days after the collapse of Lehman Brothers. Subsequently, the SEC extended the list to 976 stocks between September 22 and October 7 but lifted the ban on October 8, 2008. On November 13, a congressional committee conducted a hearing on the crisis and had five well-known hedge fund managers testify on the role of hedge funds in financial markets.

This chapter provides a synthesis of recent studies on hedge funds and the recent financial crisis. It focuses on three important issues: (1) whether hedge funds played any role in the financial crisis, (2) whether hedge funds pose any systemic risk, and (3) the impact of the crisis on regulations of hedge funds. The rest of the chapter consists of four sections. The first section briefly reviews hedge fund performance during the crisis. The second section surveys some recent academic studies on trading activities of hedge funds during the financial crisis and also discusses the potential link between hedge funds and systemic risk. The third section focuses on regulations of hedge funds and, in particular, the Dodd-Frank Act. The last section provides a summary and conclusion.

PERFORMANCE OF HEDGE FUNDS IN THE FINANCIAL CRISIS

The hedge fund industry has witnessed tremendous growth over the past two decades. For instance, the total AUM by hedge funds has increased dramatically, from about $50 billion in 1990 to $2.01 trillion in 2011 (Hedge Fund Research, 2012). The increasing popularity of hedge funds can be at least partially attributed to their superior performance, particularly in a down market. Exhibit 26.1 plots the performance of the Dow Jones Credit Suisse (DJCS) Hedge Fund Index versus the S&P 500 Index from 1994 to 2011. The figure shows that hedge funds have largely outperformed the S&P 500 Index in down markets, especially during the 2000–2002 Internet bubble and the 2007–2008 financial crisis. For instance, the returns in 2008 of the DJCS Hedge Fund Index and the S&P 500 Index are −19.1 percent and −38.5 percent, respectively. Nevertheless, with record losses and massive redemptions, the overall hedge fund industry suffered its worst year ever in 2008.

Some hedge funds, however, delivered stellar performance in 2008 and/or over the longer financial crisis period. For instance, Renaissance Technologies' Medallion Fund reportedly had a return of 80 percent in 2008. Paulson & Co. (John

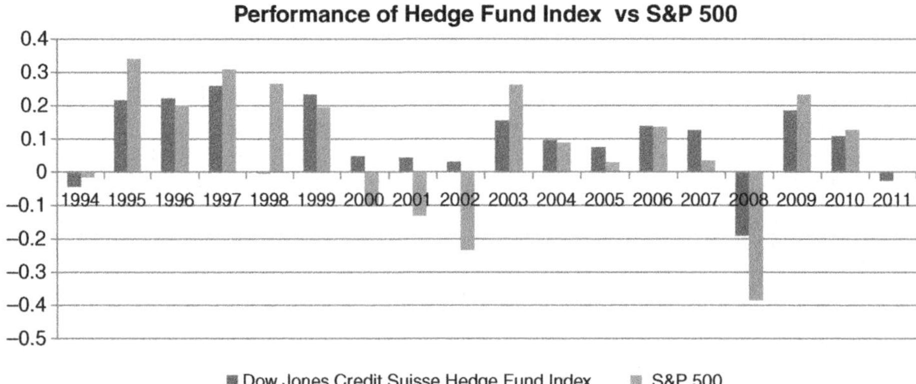

Exhibit 26.1 The Performance of Hedge Funds versus the S&P 500 Index
This exhibit plots the annualized returns of the Dow Jones Credit Suisse Hedge Fund Index versus the S&P 500 Index from 1994 to 2011. The data used to generate the plot are obtained from the Lipper/TASS hedge fund database.

Paulson's firm) had two funds ranked in the top five on the 2009 Barron's Annual Hedge Fund 100 list, which is based on the three-year annualized returns over the 2006 to 2008 period (Willoughby, 2009). The Paulson Advantage Plus Fund (an event-driven fund) ranked number one during the same period, with a three-year annualized return of 62.7 percent, and Paulson Enhanced (a merger arbitrage fund) ranked number four, with a three-year annualized return of 46.8 percent. Not surprisingly, Paulson's company collectively had $30 billion in AUM as of February 2009. In the second, third, and fifth places on the Barron's list are Balestra Capital Partner (a global macro fund), Vision Opportunity Capital (a merger arbitrage fund), and Quality Capital Management—Global Diversified (a global diversified fund), respectively. The strong performance of these top hedge funds in a weak market justifies to some extent the most basic appeal of hedge funds.

Besides their performance, the compensation of top hedge fund managers caught the attention of the media, because some hedge fund managers earned record-high pay during the financial crisis. According to Institutional Investor's *Alpha* magazine (Taub, 2008, 2009), the top 25 managers earned a total of $22.3 billion and $11.6 billion in 2007 and 2008, respectively. Names making the 2008 top four list with more than $1 billion in earnings include James Simons, founder and CEO of Renaissance Technology; John Paulson, founder of Paulson & Co.; John D. Arnold, manager of Centaurus Energy; and George Soros, founder and chairman of Soros Fund Management (Story, 2009). Paulson, who rode to fame by betting against the subprime market, reportedly made $2 billion in 2008 in addition to his $3.5 billion income in 2007. These headline news events attracted much attention from various market participants and regulators. A question remains: Should hedge funds be blamed for causing the financial crisis? The next section reviews the role of hedge funds in the financial crisis.

ROLE OF HEDGE FUNDS IN THE FINANCIAL CRISIS

A widely held belief is that a major event that preceded the financial crisis of 2007–2008 was the collapse in July 2007 of two hedge funds—the High-Grade Structured Credit Fund and the High-Grade Structured Credit Enhanced Leveraged Funds, run by Bear Stearns. Many people ask whether hedge funds should share the blame for causing the financial crisis. Various sources cite mortgage lenders, underwriters of mortgage-backed securities, banks, rating agencies, and regulatory agencies as being culpable. However, very little evidence exists suggesting that hedge funds caused the financial crisis. Brown, Kacperczyk, Ljungqvist, Lynch, Pedersen, and Richardson (2009) point out that hedge funds did not cause the growth in the subprime mortgage market, make housing prices drop substantially, or influence banks to take risks in those subprime mortgage-backed collateralized debt obligations. Some studies, such as Shadab (2009), contend that hedge funds actually helped reduce the impact of the crisis.

In particular, Shadab (2009) clarifies several myths and realities about hedge funds echoed by many people, including both academics and practitioners. For instance, he points out that unlike their mutual fund counterparts, hedge fund managers usually own shares of the funds they manage and, as a result, tend to be more prudent in taking risk. The author also notes that, on average, hedge funds use less leverage than banks, based on a study by Blundell-Wignall (2007), who estimates that average hedge fund leverage is about 3.9 to 1, a level substantially lower than the average leverage of banks. The analysis in this study also suggests that hedge funds play a very positive role in financial markets and engage in certain types of activity that reduce volatility.

In his testimony before the U.S. House of Representatives Committee on Oversight and Government Reform on November 13, 2008, James Simon, Chairman and CEO of the well-known hedge fund Renaissance Technologies, states that "contrary to what one might think, hedge funds are not a particularly volatile asset class" (Simon, 2008, p. 7). He cites evidence that while the volatility of the S&P 500 Index was 15.4 percent over the prior 10 years, the volatility of the standard hedge fund index HFI was only 7.2 percent.

On a related point, although they suffered significant losses during the recent crisis, Shadab (2009) notes that, on average, hedge funds still outperformed mutual funds. As documented in Huang and Wang (2012), the average alternative equity mutual fund, which is a hedge fund–like mutual fund that mimics certain hedge fund strategies, outperformed the standard S&P 500 Index fund, a widely used mutual fund performance benchmark.

As Brown et al. point out (2009), hedge funds add value to the financial system at least in the following four aspects: (1) providing liquidity to the market, (2) helping correct mispricing in the market, (3) increasing price discovery, and (4) allowing investors to have access to sophisticated investment strategies.

Recent Empirical Evidence on the Role of Hedge Funds in the Crisis

Ben-David, Franzoni, and Moussawi (2012) examine stock trading activities of hedge funds during the financial crisis. The conventional wisdom is that hedge funds are liquidity providers, presumably because they are more sophisticated than typical investors. For instance, when investors want to sell, especially during a market crisis, hedge funds typically step in and become a buyer. However, this study finds evidence suggesting otherwise. The authors examine the holdings of U.S. stocks by both hedge funds and mutual funds over the period from the third quarter of 2007 until the first quarter of 2009. They find that hedge funds actually sold 10 times more U.S. stocks than mutual funds did during that period. For instance, Ben-David et al. find that hedge funds reduced their holdings of U.S. stocks by about 10 percent and 30 percent in the second half of 2007 and the first half of 2008, respectively. The authors also find that hedge funds sold these stocks earlier than mutual funds did during the crisis. This implies that hedge funds may have suffered less than mutual funds during the period. Ben-David et al. also find that the average return of hedge funds is much less negative than that of mutual funds over the crisis.

Aragon and Strahan (2012), examine the supposed role of hedge funds as a provider of liquidity from a different angle. The authors investigate the impact of Lehman's collapse on certain hedge funds' ability to trade their positions. Lehman was one of the major prime brokers before its collapse in September 2008. *Prime brokers* are the investment banks and securities firms that provide hedge funds with services such as custody, securities lending, financing, and operational support. When Lehman went bankrupt, its hedge fund clients were unable to access the assets in their accounts, which considerably affected them in a negative way. For instance, the authors document that the relative hazard rate of these Lehman-connected hedge funds more than doubled after Lehman's collapse. Interestingly, this collapse also affected those stocks held by the Lehman-connected hedge funds. Specifically, the authors focus on the impact of the Lehman bankruptcy on the liquidity of these stocks using the Amihud (2002) illiquidity measure. A key finding of this study is that the higher the portion of the stocks owned by Lehman-connected hedge funds, the higher the percentage increase in the Amihud illiquidity measure of the stocks. The authors also provide evidence that, due to this exogenous shock (the Lehman collapse), Lehman-connected hedge funds could not trade their positions, and thus were unable to supply liquidity even if they had wanted.

Carney (2012) contends that hedge funds may have played a bigger role in triggering the crises than previously understood, based on the implications of a study by Gorton and Ordonez (2012). In this paper, the authors develop a theory of the financial crisis that is based on the role played by short-term debt markets in the financial markets and shed some new light on the potential role of hedge funds in the crisis. The purpose of the study is to understand the link between small shocks (e.g., the problem in subprime mortgages) and a larger crisis (e.g., the financial crisis of 2007–2008).

Gorton and Pennacchi (1990) and Dang, Gorton, and Holmström (2011) maintain that short-term debt, in the form of bank liabilities or money market instruments, is designed to be "information insensitive." One way to achieve the information insensitivity is to make the collateral of debt more complex. However, short-term debt becomes information sensitive in a financial crisis due to a sudden loss of confidence in such debt. As a result, a small negative surprise can have a substantial impact (due to the sensitivity) and thus can lead to financial fragility.

How is this connected to hedge funds? Carney (2012) observes that the argument of Gorton and Ordonez (2012) extends to collateralized debt obligations (CDOs). CDOs are complex instruments, and therefore information insensitive until a big negative shock occurs. In this sense, CDOs provide a link between small shocks and a financial crisis. As such, hedge funds might have played a role in the crisis.

Due to the limited space, this subsection covers only a few recent studies concerning the role of hedge funds in the financial crisis. Eventually, more studies will examine this issue given its importance.

Hedge Funds and Systemic Risk

In the aftermath of the financial crisis, one issue of particular concern for investors, and especially regulators, is whether and how hedge funds pose systemic risk. This section examines a basic and yet important question in risk management, namely, the meaning of systemic risk. It then briefly reviews several approaches to measuring systemic risk. Finally, this section focuses on the potential link between hedge funds and systemic risk. The balance of the section, especially in subsections one and three, draws heavily on Lo (2009, 2010). The former provides a comprehensive discussion of potential regulatory reform after the financial crisis, which is based on Lo's written testimony submitted to the U.S. House of Representatives Committee on Oversight and Government Reform for its November 13, 2008, hearing on hedge funds and systemic risk.

What Is Systemic Risk?

Although systemic risk has no formal definition and quantification, Lo (2009, p. 9) points out that systemic risk usually refers to "the risk of broad-based break down in the financial system." A classic example of this is the massive number of bank failures during 1930–1933 in the United States (Mishkin, 1997). In a report based on its Hedge Fund Survey and Hedge Fund as Counterparty Survey, the Financial Services Authority (2011, p. 1), the regulator of the financial services industry in the United Kingdom, defines systemic risk as "a risk which, if it crystallized without any form of intervention by the authorities, would mean a high likelihood of major and rapid disruption to the effective operation of a core function of the financial system (and so leading to a wider economic impact)."

Lo (2009) suggests that a formal definition of systemic risk should capture the interactions and risks of the entire financial system, including not only traditional commercial banks but also "shadow banks," such as investment banks, hedge funds, and mutual funds. Furthermore, he contends that a collection of risk measures rather than a single measure would be necessary in order to quantify systemic risk. Specifically, Lo mentions measures of systemic risk should capture six characteristics of the financial system: leverage, liquidity, correlation, concentration, sensitivities, and connectedness. The subsection entitled "How to Measure Systemic Risk?" will discuss how to estimate those characteristics and systemic risk in general.

Do Hedge Funds Cause Systemic Risk?

In his testimony before the U.S. Congress, Simon (2008, p. 5) states that he does not believe that the hedge fund sector contributed to the recent crisis and that hedge funds "are unlikely as a single class to be a substantial contributor to systemic risk." The latter claim is based on the argument that hedge funds adopt a diverse set of strategies and therefore are sufficiently different from each other. Shadab (2009) also believes that hedge funds are unlikely to severely undermine the stability of the entire financial system. Among the arguments he uses to support that claim is that hedge funds and their trading partners and lenders generally have adequate risk management mechanisms in place that would prevent hedge fund collapses from destabilizing the financial system.

Conversely, as some researchers maintain, little evidence suggests that hedge funds caused the crisis but as "shadow banks" hedge funds can contribute to systemic risk. One often-cited example is the collapse of Long Term Capital Management (LTCM) in September 1998. Triggered by the default of Russian government bonds in August 1997, the fund lost a huge amount of money over a short course of a few weeks, eventually resulting in a bail out by a consortium of 13 banks. The Federal Reserve Bank of New York organized the rescue for fear that liquidity of LTCM would cause chain reactions in financial markets and then a breakdown in the financial system. Indeed, Brown et al. (2009) note that a sufficiently large and leveraged hedge fund, such as LTCM in 1998, could potentially generate systemic risk. Similarly, as mentioned previously, Lo (2009) believes that including hedge funds and other parts of the shadow banking system in the estimation of systemic risk is important. He further contends that hedge funds can serve as a valuable source of "early warning signals" due to their connection to systemic risk. Chan, Getmansky, Haas, and Lo (2004, 2006) present indirect evidence that the level of the systemic risk in hedge funds had increased at that time (as discussed in the next subsection) and thus provide support for the idea of extracting early warning signals from hedge funds.

The issue of hedge funds and systemic risk is extremely important for lawmakers and regulators. In the hearing conducted by the U.S. House of Representatives Committee on Oversight and Government Reform on November 13, 2008, one major question from the Committee was whether hedge funds can be a source of systemic risk. Some of the new regulations passed recently in the United States result specifically from this concern. In particular, research along this line of inquiry will help the market understand better the potential link between hedge funds and systemic risk. The issue of transparency from a regulatory point of view has an important impact on that endeavor.

How to Measure Systemic Risk?

The extant literature offers various methods to measure systemic risk. One way to measure collectively those aforementioned six aspects of the global financial system is to treat this system as a single portfolio and then analyze it using standard portfolio theory. For example, using the framework of contingent-claims analysis originated from Black and Scholes (1973) and Merton (1973, 1974, 1992), Gray, Merton, and Bodie (2007) and Gray and Malone (2008) propose a new approach to analyzing and managing financial risks of a national economy. These studies show that the proposed approach can help generate early warning signals of systemic risk.

A fast-growing literature focuses on the connectedness aspect of systemic risk. For instance, many studies examine contagion in the corporate bond market or correlated corporate defaults, such as Giesecke (2004), Das, Duffie, Kapadia, and Saita (2007), Collin-Dufresne, Goldstein, and Helwege (2009), Duffie, Eckner, Horel, and Saita (2009), and Lando and Nielsen (2010). Studies analyzing counterparty risk or contagion through counterparties include Jarrow and Yu (2001), Hertzel, Li, Officer, and Rodgers (2008), Jorion and Zhang (2007, 2009), Duffie and Zhu (2012), and Helwege and Zhang (2012). Finally, numerous authors, including Eisenberg and Noe (2001), Huang, Zhou, and Zhu (2009), Acharya, Brownlees, Engle, Farazmand, and Richardson (2010), Acharya, Pedersen, Phillipon, and Richardson (2010), Helwege (2010), and Billio, Getmansky, Lo, and Pelizzon (2011), examine the interconnectedness among financial firms.

Lo (2009, 2010) discusses how to extract the information about the aforementioned six aspects of systemic measure from the hedge fund market. Relative to some other measures, such as liquidity, leverage is easier to estimate if the relevant information is available. However, implementing the leverage measure for hedge funds is an issue due to data limitation. Nonetheless, Blundell-Wignall (2007) proposes an indirect way to estimate the implied leverage of hedge funds. The

Financial Services Authority (FSA) directly obtains a snapshot of leverage of hedge funds by conducting a voluntary survey among selected FSA-authorized hedge funds that are believed to capture about 20 percent of the global hedge fund industry in 2010. This survey uses two measures of leverage: (1) the ratio of a fund's gross exposures to its net asset value (NAV) and (2) a fund's total borrowings as a multiple of NAV.

One way to measure the liquidity aspect of systemic risk is to use the illiquidity measure of hedge funds proposed in Getmansky, Lo, and Makarov (2004). The authors develop an econometric model of smoothed hedge fund returns that takes into account both illiquidity exposure and performance smoothing. They find evidence that the amount of smoothing is associated with the illiquidity of funds. For instance, their results show that emerging market debt and fixed-income arbitrage funds engage in a more significant amount of smoothing than other types of funds.

As Lo (2009) notes, however, for the purpose of developing an aggregate measure of hedge fund illiquidity, a related but simpler approach is to construct a cross-sectional weighted average of the first-order autocorrelations of hedge fund returns. A time series of this illiquidity measure can then be obtained from estimates of rolling correlations. Based on a time series plot of this illiquidity measure over the period January 1980 to August 2007, Lo finds evidence that hedge funds' illiquidity exposure is on the rise over the recent past, which indicates indirectly a rise in systemic risk due to hedge funds.

Getmansky, Lo, and Mei (2004) contend that hedge fund liquidations can be a source of systemic risk, as indicated by the collapse and rescue of LTCM in 1998. They propose a logit model of hedge fund liquidations and then estimate the model using a sample of hedge funds over the period January 1994 to August 2004. Their estimation results indicate the average liquidation probability for their sample funds in 2004 is markedly higher than the historical attrition rate. The authors also interpret this finding to indicate indirectly a rise in systemic risk from hedge funds. On a related note, Brown, Goetzmann, Liang, and Schwarz (2008) propose a model of hedge funds' operational risk using an approach in the spirit of Altman (1968).

Chan et al. (2006, 2007) and Lo (2010) also discuss several risk analytics that may be used to measure correlations, sensitivities, and investment concentrations. The connectedness in the financial network potentially can be measured using ideas and tools based on the theory of networks (Soramäki, Bech, Arnold, Glass, and Beyeler, 2007).

Finally, Lo (2010) proposes a hedge fund–based measure of systemic risk using a regime-switching model, where hedge fund indices can switch from a normal to a distressed regime. The probability of being in a distressed regime serves as an indirect indicator of systemic risk due to hedge funds.

Nonetheless, Lo (2009) observes, one major obstacle of quantifying systemic risk is that transparency of the financial system, especially the shadow banking system, including hedge funds, is currently not sufficient enough for direct implementation of many proposed measures of systemic risk. As such, a better understanding of the potential link between hedge funds and systemic risk is a very important issue not only for academics but also for regulators and practitioners. The FSA survey previously mentioned is a good step in this direction.

HEDGE FUNDS AFTER THE FINANCIAL CRISIS

The financial crisis of 2007–2008 reignited the regulatory debate on hedge funds and called for stricter regulation of these largely unregulated privately managed investment vehicles. Historically, hedge funds qualify for exemption from certain securities laws and regulations, including the requirement to register as an investment company, and thus are subject to much less regulatory scrutiny than registered investment companies such as mutual funds. In response to the financial crisis and the worst recession since the Great Depression of the 1930s, President Barack Obama signed into law the Dodd-Frank Wall Street Reform and Consumer Protection Act (the "Dodd-Frank Act") in July 2010, aiming to provide more rigorous regulatory standards and heightened supervision of financial service companies, including hedge funds.

Hedge Fund Regulation before the Dodd-Frank Act

Unlike mutual funds, which are subject to rigorous regulatory oversight under four federal securities laws (i.e., the Securities Act of 1933, Securities Exchange Act of 1934, Investment Company Act of 1940, and Investment Advisers Act of 1940), hedge funds are known to operate in an unregulated, opaque territory. Until the passage of the Dodd-Frank Act, hedge funds typically relied on the exclusions from registration under the federal securities laws that applied to hedge funds and their securities offerings to avoid regulation. The exclusions included the investment strategies allowed by hedge funds, the types of potential hedge fund investors, and how hedge funds could raise capital. More specifically, hedge funds could circumvent regulation by "meeting criteria that are laid out in four general exclusions or exceptions" (Donaldson, 2003):

1. *The registration exclusion of the fund under the Investment Company Act of 1940.* Hedge funds typically rely on Sections 3(c)(1) and 3(c)(7) of the 1940 Investment Company Act to avoid being required to register with the SEC as an investment company. Section 3(c)(1) restricts hedge funds to 100 or fewer investors, while Section 3(c)(7) requires all investors to meet a "qualified purchaser" criterion. In order to qualify as qualified purchasers, an individual must have at least $5 million in investment assets, and companies, including institutional investors, must have at least $25 million in investment assets. Although Section 3(c)(7) in theory imposes no limit on the number of investors, most hedge funds have no more than 499 investors given that any issuer with 500 or more investors and $10 million of assets must register with the SEC under the Securities Exchange Act of 1934.
2. *The registration exemption of the fund's securities under the Securities Act of 1933.* Both of the exclusions under the Investment Company Act of 1940 and the Securities Act of 1933 prohibit hedge funds from making public offerings. As a result, hedge funds typically raise capital via private placement, which means that they cannot solicit or advertise, and thus must comply with the private placement rules under Regulation D of the Securities Act of 1933. Under Regulation D, hedge fund investors must be *accredited investors.* To qualify as accredited investors, an individual must have net

worth exceeding $1 million, or a minimum annual personal (household) income of $200,000 ($300,000) in the past two years and expect to reasonably remain the same level, and banks and corporate entities must have minimum net worth of $5 million.

3. *The registration exemption of the hedge fund manager under the Investment Advisers Act of 1940.* Under Section 203(b)(3) of this act, an investment adviser is not required to register with the SEC if he has 14 or fewer clients and does not publicize himself generally as an investment adviser. Hedge fund managers meet the definition of "investment adviser" under this Act, but they typically satisfy the "private adviser exemption" from registration because each hedge fund, rather than each investor in the hedge fund, is counted as one client of the manager. Despite the registration exemption, hedge fund managers are fully subject to federal prohibitions on fraud, insider trading, and price manipulation under the antifraud provisions of the Investment Advisers Act. Some hedge fund managers voluntarily register with the SEC either because their investors prefer registered investment advisers or they also advise registered investment companies. Funds doing so include well-known ones such as Paulson & Co. Inc. and Renaissance Technologies LLC.
4. *The exception from reporting requirements under the Securities Exchange Act of 1934.* Hedge funds generally have private securities and thus are not subject to the reporting requirements of the Securities Exchange Act. However, like any other large institutional manager, managers of hedge funds that have a minimum $100 million in AUM or hold more than 5 percent of a class of equity securities of a publicly traded company are required to file form 13F to disclose their quarterly equity positions at the management company level.

A long-standing regulatory debate exists on hedge fund regulation. Previously, the primary issue was whether hedge fund managers should be required to register under the 1940 Investment Advisers Act. In December 2004, the SEC proposed an amendment to Section 203(b)(3) of the Investment Advisors Act. Under this proposed rule, a hedge fund manager could no longer rely on the so-called "private adviser exemption" of Section 203(b)(3) of the Advisers Act and would be required to register with the SEC as investment advisers by February 1, 2006, if the fund or funds advised by the manager have more than 14 investors. This proposed new rule was controversial and was later challenged in court by a hedge fund manager. In June 2006, the D.C. Circuit court overturned the SEC's rulemaking in the court's *Goldstein* decision. In response to the court's ruling, the SEC adopted Rule 206(4)-8 in 2007, which does not impose additional filing, reporting, and disclosure obligations or additional fiduciary duties on advisers as the previously challenged rule did, but potentially "increases the risk of enforcement action for negligent conduct in connection with a finding of fraudulent activity" (Adelfio and Griffin, 2007).

The Dodd-Frank Act

On July 21, 2010, President Obama signed the Dodd-Frank Act with the aim of providing more stringent regulatory oversight of the financial service industry, including hedge funds. In a speech at the symposium on "Hedge Fund Regulation and Current Developments" in June 2011, SEC commissioner Troy A. Paredes discussed the various effects that the Dodd-Frank Act might have on hedge funds, either directly or indirectly.

According to Paredes (2011), the Dodd-Frank Act subjects hedge funds to increased regulatory and compliance requirements in several ways. First, the Dodd-Frank Act requires managers of hedge funds with more than $150 million in AUM to register with the SEC as investment advisers. Under the act, most hedge fund advisers can no longer rely on the "private adviser exemption" from registration provided in Section 203(b)(3) of the Investment Advisers Act of 1940. Second, the Dodd-Frank Act requires hedge fund advisers to report a substantial amount of information to the SEC on Form PF to assist the regulators, including the newly created Financial Stability Oversight Council (FSOC), in monitoring and regulating systemic risk. In particular, the SEC requires large hedge funds with $1 billion or higher in assets to provide quarterly detailed reports on their performance, trading positions, and counterparties. For smaller hedge funds, these reports would be less detailed and required only annually. Finally, the SEC, in accordance with the Dodd-Frank Act, has proposed rules to require hedge fund advisers with assets of $1 billion or more to report incentive-based compensation arrangements and prohibit those arrangements that could result in excessive compensation or inappropriate risk.

Other than those that directly impact hedge funds, certain provisions of the Dodd-Frank Act might indirectly "impact the hedge fund industry by influencing, in one way or another, the market activities and strategies of hedge funds" (Paredes, 2011). Here are some examples.

- *Derivatives.* Pursuant to Title VII of the Dodd-Frank Act, the SEC has proposed rules to restructure and oversee the over-the-counter (OTC) derivatives market (e.g., equity-based swaps). The act requires that the OTC-traded swaps be cleared through exchanges or central clearinghouses. As one of the most important players in the OTC derivatives market, hedge funds may be deemed as "major equity-based swap participants," and thus be subject to additional regulation set forth in the derivates section of the act and incur additional costs associated with trading these complex derivatives securities.
- *Short-selling.* The Dodd-Frank Act has called upon the SEC to study (1) the benefits and costs of requiring the real-time reporting of short-sale positions, either publicly or confidentially to the SEC and (2) the prospect of a pilot program that would require that trades be marked as long, short, market-maker short, buy, or buy-to-cover in real time on the Consolidated Tape. Because hedge funds use short sales to a great extent, these rules concerning short-sale disclosure would undoubtedly have a substantial impact on hedge funds.

Hedge Funds after Dodd-Frank

The Dodd-Frank Act represents the most important and controversial overhaul of the U.S. financial regulatory system since the Great Depression. The act has broad implications for the hedge fund industry in the near future. Most importantly, hedge funds will no doubt be subject to increased regulation under the Dodd-Frank Act, but considerable uncertainty remains over the exact scope of future regulatory landscape as many regulatory decisions are up to the regulators to make later. Additionally, the act will have an important impact on the growth and profitability of the hedge fund industry.

Increased Regulation and Uncertainty

As discussed in the previous section, hedge funds will be subject to more rigorous regulatory oversight under the Dodd-Frank Act, including mandatory registration of large hedge funds and disclosure of material information. The new rules on derivatives and short sales might also affect the trading strategies of hedge funds. However, the exact scope and nature of the new rules remains uncertain, because the act leaves up to the regulators, including the SEC, to decide how to implement these rules. For instance, the SEC is given considerable power to expand its own authority in the future, including, but not limited to, requesting any additional necessary information at its discretion, defining and requiring "mid-sized" private funds to register as well, and imposing separate recordkeeping and reporting requirements on all other hedge funds (Brown, Lynch, and Petajisto, 2010). Furthermore, pursuant to Title I of Dodd-Frank, also referred to as the Financial Stability Act of 2010, regulators have the authority to call upon expanded governmental oversight and regulation of nonbank financial companies that the FSOC deems to be "systemically important." How the FSOC and the Federal Reserve Board will choose to exercise their considerable power under this provision is still uncertain. Overall, the Dodd-Frank Act has brought considerable regulatory uncertainty to the hedge fund industry.

In order to use the regulatory power cautiously, regulators need to carefully evaluate the intended benefits as well as the potential undesirable effects of their regulatory decisions (Paredes, 2011). The fundamental trade-off is "between the government's desire to learn more about hedge funds, both to assess systemic risk and to protect investors, and the compliance costs this imposes on funds and investors" (Brown et al., 2010).

The main arguments for hedge fund regulation are for reasons involving investor protection and systemic risk. However, Danielsson, Taylor, and Zigrand (2005) and Brown et al. (2010) maintain that the consumer protection argument is unconvincing, because hedge fund investors are restricted to accredited investors instead of small retail investors. Stulz (2007) also shows that aggregate losses from hedge fund fraud are relatively small. Conversely, the systemic concerns might be sufficiently serious to warrant hedge fund regulation (Danielsson et al., 2005). As Stulz notes regarding the LTCM debacle, hedge funds might create systemic risk by generating counterparty exposure when they use leverage and suddenly collapse due to lack of liquidity. However, Brown et al. (2010) contend that hedge funds do not create sufficient systemic risk in the financial crisis. As a result, the Dodd-Frank Act is more about preventing potential problems from arising in the future than fixing newly revealed problems during the financial crisis.

The primary arguments against hedge fund regulation arise from the potential costs regulation would impose on hedge funds and investors as well as the economy as a whole (Paredes, 2011). Hedge funds play an important and positive role in the financial markets in that they could provide liquidity and contribute to price discovery and the efficient allocation of resources throughout the economy by engaging in diverse investment strategies and trading activities. Hedge funds also benefit the companies in which they invest by providing sound corporate governance and offering valuable opportunities for investors to diversify their portfolios while enjoying higher returns. A regulatory regime that unduly burdens hedge fund activities could dissipate these economy-wide benefits. For instance, problems would occur if providing liquidity becomes more costly for hedge funds under the new legislation. Furthermore, complying with the regulatory obligations is not costless for hedge funds. Compliance costs include both out-of-pocket compliance expenditures and opportunity costs in terms of the time and effort that could have been directed toward other productive activities.

Ultimately, regulators are responsible for balancing the costs and benefits of heightened hedge fund regulation and striking a happy medium so that the new regulation does not diminish incentives and opportunities while fulfilling its mission to protect investors and to reduce systemic risk. Given the considerable leeway the Dodd-Frank Act has left for regulators, the hedge fund industry faces an uncertain regulatory future. As Brown et al. (2010) point out, "the sensibility and impact of the new hedge fund legislation will almost entirely depend on the specific rules that will be written later by the regulators."

Growth and Profitability

Despite the many challenges, including stricter and uncertain government regulation, the hedge fund industry also faces a growth opportunity after Dodd-Frank. In particular, the Volcker Rule of the Dodd-Frank Act mandates banks to end proprietary trading. As a result, many banks have spun off their proprietary trading desks and their internal asset management divisions into independent hedge funds. Thus, hedge funds have become arguably the only outlet for the so-called sophisticated investors. The hedge fund industry remains the industry where managers are most free to develop and employ trading strategies. The continued popularity and size of hedge funds means they remain as a huge source for liquidity to a variety of markets. Still, whether hedge funds would be willing or able to provide liquidity if it becomes too costly to do so remains unclear. Moreover, the Volcker Rule requires banks to cap their investment in both private equity and hedge funds at 3 percent of the assets of any single fund. To comply with the Volcker Rule, banks have taken steps to unwind their investments in hedge funds, which could result in reduced capital for hedge funds. Overall, the Volcker Rule has major implications for the growth of the hedge fund industry.

The Dodd-Frank Act might also affect the future profitability of hedge funds. First, as more money flows into hedge funds, funds have more difficulty generating the same superior returns as they used to due to liquidity and organizational diseconomies (Chen, Hong, Huang, and Kubik, 2004). Second, hedge funds would incur considerable costs in the process of complying with the new legislation, which would put a further drag on their performance. Finally, the act would subject hedge funds to mandatory disclosure of material information about their trades and portfolio, which might reveal the funds' proprietary trading strategies and also raise front-running costs by other investors, such as mutual funds, and thus reduce the profitability of hedge funds.

Shi (2011) evaluates the effects of mandatory disclosure of hedge fund investment companies' aggregate equity positions when their assets exceed $100 million through form 13F on hedge fund performance. The author shows that fund performance drops by around 4 percent annually after a fund firm begins filing form 13F to disclosure the aggregate equity positions at the investment company level alone. The exact effect that the mandatory detailed disclosure of hedge fund trade portfolios under the Dodd-Frank Act might have on hedge fund performance is still to be determined. Nevertheless, the study indicates that hedge fund profitability might dissipate due to the mandatory disclosure of their "trading secrets."

Implications for Academic Research

As Paredes (2011) notes, "regulatory decision making should be supported by data, to the extent available, and economic analysis." Despite the importance of the hedge fund industry, the limited availability of high-quality hedge fund data has constrained academic research on hedge funds. Before the Dodd-Frank Act becomes effective, hedge funds can rely on exemptions from certain securities laws and regulations to avoid registration, and thus are not subject to the report requirements by the SEC. Hedge fund databases commonly used in academic studies, such as Hedge Fund Research, TASS, and CISDM, are based on the information provided by hedge funds on a voluntary basis and thus susceptible to two types of biases: survivorship bias and backfilling bias. *Survivorship bias* occurs when poorly performing funds stop reporting results. By contrast, *backfill bias* occurs when funds do not report returns until they reach acceptable levels. Thus, the databases omit poor results from a startup period. Both biases would artificially inflate the reported results of the remaining universe. Additionally, each of those databases covers only one part of the entire hedge fund universe (Agarwal, Daniel, and Naik, 2009).

Patton, Ramadorai, and Streafield (2011) show voluntary disclosures by hedge funds about their monthly investment performance are unreliable. The researchers track changes to statements of historical performance of more than 18,000 hedge funds recorded in publicly available hedge fund databases at different points in time between 2007 and 2011. The authors find that as many as 40 percent of funds revise their previously reported performance, sometimes many years later, with more than 20 percent of funds later changing a previous monthly return by at least 0.5 percent. They also show that, on average, funds that revise their histories subsequently underperform significantly when compared with funds that have never revised their reported performance.

Another frequently used database in hedge fund research is 13F, which reports the quarterly holdings information of large institutions (Ben-David et al., 2012). As discussed previously, hedge fund firms are also subject to the mandatory disclosure of their portfolios if they have a minimum $100 million in assets under management or hold more than 5 percent of a class of equity securities of a publicly traded company. This disclosure, however, does not necessarily provide relevant insights into any particular hedge fund's portfolios or strategies because the holdings information is aggregated at the investment company level. Further, disclosure is not required of short, debt, and derivatives positions.

As the Dodd-Frank Act subjects hedge funds to more rigorous reporting standards, the mandatory information reported to the SEC, once available, would have important implications for academic research. These data would be free of potential survivorship and backfilling biases and would thus provide a more complete, unbiased picture of hedge fund performance. The detailed complete holdings data would also provide additional insights into the trading activities of hedge funds.

SUMMARY AND CONCLUSIONS

Hedge funds play a very important role in financial markets. If the financial crisis of 2007–2008 has any positive effects, it provides an opportunity for people to see, examine, and understand better what hedge funds have, could have, and should have done during the crisis. Indeed, a new and fast-growing literature has emerged on hedge funds and the financial crisis. This chapter is among the first attempts to summarize some recent developments in this very important area of research. It also hopes to draw attention to two potentially fruitful lines of inquiry: hedge funds and systemic risk as well as the impact of new regulations on hedge funds.

DISCUSSION QUESTIONS

1. Discuss the role of hedge funds in the financial crisis. Should hedge funds be blamed for causing the recent crisis?
2. What is systemic risk and how is it measured? Discuss whether hedge funds pose systemic risk.
3. Compare the financial regulations of mutual funds and hedge funds before the Dodd-Frank Act. Discuss whether hedge funds require more or less regulation.
4. Discuss the implications of the Dodd-Frank Act for hedge fund performance.

REFERENCES

Acharya, Viral, Christian Brownlees, Robert Engle, Farhang Farazmand, and Matthew Richardson. 2010. "Measuring Systemic Risk." In Viral Acharya, Thomas Cooley, Matthew Richardson, and Ingo Walter, ed., *Regulating Wall Street: The Dodd-Frank Act and the New Architecture of Global Finance*, 87–120. Hoboken, NJ: John Wiley & Sons, Inc.

Acharya, Viral, Lasse Pedersen, Thomas Phillipon, and Matthew Richardson. 2010. "Taxing Systemic Risk." In Viral Acharya, Thomas Cooley, Matthew Richardson, and Ingo Walter, ed., *Regulating Wall Street: The Dodd-Frank Act and the New Architecture of Global Finance*, 121–142. Hoboken, NJ: John Wiley & Sons, Inc.

Adelfio, Marco E., and Nicole Griffin. 2007. "United States: SEC Affirms Its Enforcement Authority with New Anti-Fraud Rule under the Advisers Act." Available at www.mondaq.com/unitedstates/article.asp?articleid=51202.

Agarwal, Vikas, Naveen D. Daniel, and Narayan Y. Naik. 2009. "Role of Managerial Incentives and Discretion in Hedge Fund Performance." *Journal of Finance* 64:5, 2221–2256.

Altman, Edward. 1968. "Financial Ratios, Discriminate Analysis and the Prediction of Corporate Bankruptcy." *Journal of Finance* 23:4, 589–609.

Amihud, Yakov. 2002. "Illiquidity and Stock Returns: Cross-section and Time Series Effects." *Journal of Financial Markets* 5:1, 31–56.

Aragon, George, and Philip Strahan. 2012. "Hedge Funds as Liquidity Providers: Evidence from the Lehman Bankruptcy." *Journal of Financial Economics* 103:3, 570–587.

Ben-David, Itzhak, Francesco A. Franzoni, and Rabih Moussawi. 2012. "Hedge Fund Stock Trading in the Financial Crisis of 2007–2009." *Review of Financial Studies* 25:1, 1–54.

Billio, Monica, Mila Getmansky, Andrew Lo, and Loriana Pelizzon. 2011. "Measuring Systemic Risk in the Finance and Insurance Sectors." Working Paper, MIT.

Black, Fischer, and Myron Scholes. 1973. "The Pricing of Options and Corporate Liabilities." *Journal of Political Economy* 81:3, 637–654.

Blundell-Wignall, Adrian. 2007. "An Overview of Hedge Funds and Structured Products: Issues in Leverage and Risk." Working Paper, Organization for Economic Cooperation and Development (OECD).

Brown, Stephen, William Goetzmann, Bing Liang, and Christopher Schwarz. 2008. "Optimal Disclosure and Operational Risk: Evidence from Hedge Fund Registration." *Journal of Finance* 63:6, 2785–2815.

Brown, Stephen, Marcin Kacperczyk, Alexander Ljungqvist, Anthony Lynch, Lasse Pedersen, and Matthew Richardson. 2009. "Hedge Funds in the Aftermath of the Financial Crisis." In Viral Acharya, and Matthew Richardson, ed., *Restoring Financial Stability: How to Repair a Failed System*, 157–178. Hoboken, NJ: John Wiley & Sons, Inc.

Brown, Stephen, Anthony Lynch, and Antti Petajisto. 2010. "Hedge Funds after Dodd-Frank." Available at http://w4.stern.nyu.edu/blogs/regulatingwallstreet/2010/07/hedge-funds-after-doddfrank.html.

Carney, John. 2012. "Did Hedge Funds Trigger the Financial Crisis?" Available at www.cnbc.com/id/46191784.

Chan, Nicholas, Mila Getmansky, Shane Haas, and Andrew Lo. 2004. "Systemic Risk and Hedge Funds." Paper presented at the NBER Conference on the Risks of Financial Institutions, October 22–23, Woodstock, VT.

Chan, Nicholas, Mila Getmansky, Shane Haas, and Andrew Lo. 2006. "Do Hedge Funds Increase Systemic Risk?" *Federal Reserve Bank of Atlanta Economic Review* Q4, 49–80.

Chan, Nicholas, Mila Getmansky, Shane Haas, and Andrew Lo. 2007. "Systemic Risk and Hedge Funds." In Mark Carey and René Stulz, ed., *The Risks of Financial Institutions*, 235–290. Chicago: University of Chicago Press.

Chen Joseph, Harrison G. Hong, Ming Huang, and Jeffrey D. Kubik. 2004. "Does Fund Size Erode Mutual Fund Performance? The Role of Liquidity and Organization." *American Economic Review* 94:5, 1276–1302.

Collin-Dufresne, Pierre, Robert Goldstein, and Jean Helwege. 2009. "Are Jumps in Corporate Bond Yields Priced? Modeling Contagion via the Updating of Beliefs." Working Paper, Columbia University.

Dang, Tri Vi, Gary Gorton, and Bengt Holmström. 2011. "Ignorance and the Optimality of Debt for Liquidity Provision." Working Paper, Yale University.

Danielsson, Jon, Ashley D. Taylor, and Jean-Pierre Zigrand. 2005. "Highwaymen or Heroes: Should Hedge Funds Be Regulated?: A Survey." *Journal of Financial Stability* 1:4, 522–543.

Das, Sanjiv, Darrell Duffie, Nikunj Kapadia, and Leandro Saita. 2007. "Common Failings: How Corporate Defaults Are Correlated." *Journal of Finance* 62:1, 93–117.

Donaldson, William H. 2003. Testimony Concerning Investor Protection Implications of Hedge Funds before the Senate Committee on Banking, Housing and Urban Affairs, April 10. Available at www.sec.gov/news/testimony/041003tswhd.htm.

Duffie, Darrell, Andreas Eckner, Guillaume Horel, and Leandro Saita. 2009. "Frailty Correlated Default." *Journal of Finance* 64:5. 2089–2124.

Duffie, Darrell, and Haoxiang Zhu. 2012. "Does a Central Clearing Counterparty Reduce Counterparty Risk?" *Review of Asset Pricing Studies* 1:1, 74–95.

Eisenberg, Larry, and Thomas H. Noe. 2001. "Systemic Risk in Financial Systems." *Management Science* 47:2, 236–249.

Financial Services Authority. 2011. "Assessing the Possible Sources of Systemic Risk from Hedge Funds." February. Available at www.fsa.gov.uk/pubs/other/hedge_funds.pdf.

Getmansky, Mila, Andrew Lo, and Igor Makarov. 2004. "An Econometric Analysis of Serial Correlation and Illiquidity in Hedge-Fund Returns." *Journal of Financial Economics* 74:3, 529–609.

Getmansky, Mila, Andrew Lo, and Shauna Mei. 2004. "Sifting through the Wreckage: Lessons from Recent Hedge-Fund Liquidations." *Journal of Investment Management* 2:4, 6–38.

Giesecke, Kay. 2004. "Correlated Default Interbank Exposures: Quantifying the Risk of Contagion." *Journal of Money, Credit and Banking* 35:1, 111–128.

Gorton, Gary, and Guillermo Ordonez. 2012. "Collateral Crises." Working Paper, Yale University.

Gorton, Gary, and George Pennacchi. 1990. "Financial Intermediaries and Liquidity Creation." *Journal of Finance* 45:1, 49–72.

Gray, Dale, and Samuel Malone. 2008. *Macro Financial Risk Analysis*. Hoboken, NJ: John Wiley & Sons, Inc.

Gray, Dale, Robert C. Merton, and Zvi Bodie. 2007. "New Framework for Measuring and Managing Macro Financial Risk and Financial Stability." NBER Working Paper No. 13607.

Hedge Fund Research. 2009. "Investors Withdraw Record Capital from Hedge Funds as Industry Concludes Worst Performance Year in History." Press Release, January 21. Available at www.hedgefundresearch.com/pdf/pr_01212009.pdf.

Hedge Fund Research. 2012. "Hedge Fund Investors Rotate into Macro, Arbitrage Strategies for 2012." Press Release, January 19. Available at www.hedgefundresearch.com/pdf/pr_20120119.pdf.

Helwege, Jean. 2010. "Financial Firm Bankruptcy and Systemic Risk." *Journal of International Financial Markets, Institutions, and Money* 20:1, 1–12.

Helwege, Jean, and Gaiyan Zhang. 2012. "Financial Firm Bankruptcy and Contagion." Working Paper, University of South Caroline and University of Missouri-St. Louis.

Hertzel, Michael, Zhi Li, Micah Officer, and Kimberly Rodgers. 2008. "Inter-firm Linkages and the Wealth Effects of Financial Distress along the Supply Chain." *Journal of Financial Economics* 87:2, 374–387.

Huang, Jing-Zhi, and Ying Wang. 2012. "Should Investors Invest in Hedge Fund–Like Mutual Funds? Evidence from the 2007 Financial Crisis." *Journal of Financial Intermediation*, forthcoming.

Huang, Xin, Hao Zhou, and Haibin Zhu. 2009. "A Framework for Assessing the Systemic Risk of Major Financial Institutions." *Journal of Banking and Finance* 33:11, 2036–2049.

Jarrow, Robert, and Fan Yu. 2001. "Counterparty Risk and the Pricing of Defaultable Securities." *Journal of Finance* 56:5, 1765–1799.

Jorion, Philippe, and Gaiyan Zhang. 2007. "Good and Bad Credit Contagion: Evidence from Credit Default Swaps." *Journal of Financial Economics* 84:3, 860–883.

Jorion, Philippe, and Gaiyan Zhang. 2009. "Counterparty Risk." *Journal of Financial Economics* 64:5, 2053–2087.

Lando, David, and Mads S. Nielsen. 2010. "Correlation in Corporate Defaults: Contagion or Conditional Independence?" *Journal of Financial Intermediation* 19:3, 355–372.

Lo, Andrew. 2009. "Regulatory Reform in the Wake of the Financial Crisis of 2007–2008." *Journal of Financial Economic Policy* 1:1, 4–43.

Lo, Andrew. 2010. *Hedge Funds: An Analytic Perspective*, Revised Ed. Princeton, NJ: Princeton University Press.

Merton, Robert C. 1973. "Theory of Rational Option Pricing." *Bell Journal of Economics and Management Science* 4:1, 141–183.

Merton, Robert C. 1974. "On the Pricing of Corporate Debt: The Risk Structure of Interest Rates." *Journal of Finance* 29:2, 449–470.

Merton, Robert C. 1992. *Continuous–Time Finance*, Revised Edition. Oxford: Basil Blackwell.

Mishkin, Frederic. 1997. *The Economics of Money, Banking, and Financial Markets*, 5th ed. Reading, MA: Addison–Wesley.

Paredes, Troy A. 2011. "Remarks at the Symposium on 'Hedge Fund Regulation and Current Developments'." Available at www.sec.gov/news/speech/2011/spch060811tap.htm.

Patton, Andrew J., Tarun Ramadorai, and Michael Streatfield. 2011. "The Reliability of Voluntary Disclosures: Evidence from Hedge Funds." Working Paper, Duke University and Daid Business School.

Shadab, Houman. 2009. "Hedge Funds and the Financial Crisis." Working Paper, New York Law School.

Shi, Zhen. 2011. "The Impact of Portfolio Disclosure on Hedge Fund Performance, Fees, and Flows." Working Paper, Georgia State University.

Simon, James H. 2008. Testimony before the U.S. House of Representatives Committee on Oversight and Government Reform, November 13. Available at http://oversight-archive. waxman.house.gov/documents/20081113120509.pdf.

Soramäki, Kimmo, Morten Bech, Jeffery Arnold, Robert Glass, and Walter Beyeler. 2007. "The Topology of Interbank Payment Flows." *Physica A* 379:1, 317–333.

Story, Louise. 2009. "Top Hedge Fund Managers Do Well in a Down Year" *The New York Times*, March 24. Available at www.nytimes.com/2009/03/25/business/25hedge.html.

Stulz, René M. 2007. "Hedge Funds: Past, Present, and Future." *Journal of Economic Perspectives* 21:2, 175–194.

Taub, Stephen. 2008. "Best-Paid Hedge Fund Managers." April 15. Available at www.absolutereturn-alpha.com/Article/1914753/Search/Best-Paid-Hedge-Fund-Managers.html.

Taub, Stephen. 2009. "Brother, Can You Spare a Billion." March 23. Available at www.absolutereturn-alpha.com/Article/2165684/Search/Brother-Can-You-Spare-a-Billion.html.

Willoughby, Jack. 2009. "The Hedge Fund 100: Acing a Stress Test." *Barron's*, May 11. Available at http://online.barrons.com/article/SB124182239611202181.html.

ABOUT THE AUTHORS

Jing-Zhi Huang is a McKinley Professor of Business and Associate Professor of Finance at the Smeal College of Business, Penn State University. His research interests include derivatives markets, credit risk, fixed-income markets, mutual funds, and hedge funds. Professor Huang's papers have been published in such journals as the *Journal of Finance, Review of Asset Pricing Studies, Review of Financial Studies, Journal of Economic Dynamics and Control, Journal of Financial Intermediation, Journal of Derivatives, Journal of Fixed-Income, Review of Derivatives Research, Economic Theory,* and *Journal of Real Estate Finance and Economics.* His work has also been mentioned in the *Wall Street Journal, Financial Times, CFA Magazine, Forbes,* and *SmartMoney Magazine.* He has won the best paper awards at the Financial Management Association and the Eastern Finance Association Meetings. He also received the NYU Stern School Club 6 Teaching Award. He received a BS in Theoretical Physics from the University of Science and Technology of China, a Ph.D. in Physics from Auburn University, and a Ph.D. in Finance from New York University.

Ying Wang is an Assistant Professor of Finance at the School of Business and Center for Institutional Investment Management at the University at Albany, State University of New York. Her research interests include mutual funds and hedge funds. Professor Wang has published in the *Journal of Banking and Finance*, *Journal of Financial Intermediation*, and *Journal of Financial Markets*. Major business magazines such as *Forbes*, *Smart Money*, and the *Wall Street Journal* have cited her research. She has won the best paper award at the Midwest Finance Association meeting. Professor Wang received her Ph.D. in Finance from Penn State University and is a CFA charterholder.

ACKNOWLEDGMENTS

We would like to thank Greg Filbeck and H. Kent Baker, the editors, for extensive and detailed comments and suggestions that have helped improve this review significantly.

CHAPTER 27

Hedge Funds: Replication and Nonlinearities

MIKHAIL TUPITSYN
Ph.D. Student, Department of Accounting and Finance, Monash University

PAUL LAJBCYGIER
Associate Professor, Department of Accounting and Finance and the Department of Econometrics and Business Statistics, Monash University

INTRODUCTION

Two ways of earning returns are available for investors in financial markets. The first way is to take on systematic risk for which investors will be compensated (Sharpe, 1964). This type of risk, known as *beta*, can be measured in a linear regression of return on risk. *Systematic risk* is a risk inherent to the entire market that cannot be avoided by diversification. However, different financial markets may have different sources of systematic risk, called *risk factors* (Ross, 1976). For the most part, taking on systematic risk by buying or selling securities is easy and inexpensive. Thus, savvy investors should be unwilling to pay additional fees to asset managers who can generate a systematic risk premium for them.

The second way for investors to earn returns is capitalizing on security mispricing. The return generated from such strategies is called *alpha*, which represents an abnormal return that cannot be attributed to systematic risk or beta (Jensen, 1968). Alpha is a zero-sum game: Every alpha trade results in both a winner and a loser (Sharpe, 1991; Fama and French, 2010). Consistently generating alpha is extremely difficult, if not impossible, because an individual manager has to be consistently more profitable than the entire market in contradiction to the efficient market hypothesis (EMH). The EMH is a pillar of financial theory that asserts that one cannot consistently achieve returns in excess of average market return on a risk-adjusted basis. Examples of alpha-generating strategies include market timing and active security selection. Such skill, which some hedge fund managers may have, is rare. Therefore, the fees associated with alpha generation are reasonably high. In view of the fundamental difference between the nature of alpha- and beta-driven returns, as well as associated levels of fees, an important goal of any rational investor should be to distinguish between the two.

Hedge funds were once thought to attract the most talented managers with superior knowledge, expertise, and skill, allowing them to generate high absolute returns uncorrelated with the broad financial market. However, recent evidence challenges this view. First, academics have revealed that hedge funds derive a large part of their returns from risk premiums (i.e., beta) (Fung and Hsieh, 2004b; Hasanhodzic and Lo, 2007), rather than from the unique skill of their managers (i.e., alpha). Second, a lack of empirical evidence of absolute returns and persistence in performance results further confuses the true sources of a fund's returns.

From 1980 to 2008, the dollar-weighted net-of-fees return of a value-weighted portfolio of hedge funds was lower than the return on the S&P 500 Index and only marginally higher than the risk-free rate of return (Dichev and Yu, 2011). Furthermore, a fund manager's outperformance relative to peers does not persist over long horizons (longer than a year) (Brown, Goetzmann, and Ibbotson, 1999; Amenc, El Bied, and Martellini, 2003; Barès, Gibson, and Gyger, 2003; Capocci and Hubner, 2004; Malkiel and Saha, 2005). Therefore, when selecting a fund manager, investors cannot rely on a manager's past performance track record as a proxy for future returns. Additionally, due to the lock-up periods preventing a quick withdrawal of money from a fund, investors are unlikely to benefit from superior short-term returns.

These striking results lay the foundation for academic studies and practical experiments on passive replication of hedge fund returns. In essence, the idea is to create passive investable strategies that investors can cheaply execute with liquid financial instruments, such as futures and exchange-traded funds (ETFs), and provide returns similar to the returns of individual hedge funds or aggregate hedge fund–style indices. Moreover, replication techniques not only eliminate the hefty 20 percent incentive fee, but also save another layer of fees related to investments into fund-of-funds (FoFs) (Jaeger, 2008). For the purpose of diversification, investors often invest in multiple funds through a FoFs rather than taking a risk of relying on a single fund manager. When investing in a FoFs, the performance of underlying funds is not netted before performance fees are paid. In other words, investors may still pay incentive fees to individual managers while experiencing a loss on the overall portfolio. Hedge fund clones prevent these asymmetric incentive fees.

Apart from being cost-efficient, replication strategies possess at least three other attractive features relative to conventional funds. First, hedge fund clones, by design, represent liquid investments, allowing withdrawal of funds at any time based on the market value of highly liquid underlying securities. In contrast, hedge fund investors are usually constrained by often arbitrary redemption rules of the funds. Second, clones are transparent to investors. The precise composition of replicating portfolios is known all the time. This knowledge has important implications allowing investors to accurately assess and manage risks. Lack of transparency is one of the main criticisms of the hedge fund industry, preventing some tightly regulated institutional bodies, such as pension funds, from investing in hedge funds. Third, hedge fund strategies may not be scalable and may face capacity constraints (i.e., the return generating ability of funds deteriorates with the capital inflow) (Naik, Ramadorai, and Stromqvist, 2007). Unlike hedge funds, clones have few capacity constraints as long as they use highly liquid instruments. The arguments for replication, such as reduction of costs, liquidity, transparency, and scalability are standard in the hedge fund replication literature. However, several important clarifications should be made before proceeding with the approaches to the replication.

Academic studies suggest that hedge fund alpha is diminishing (Fung and Hsieh, 2007b; Naik et al., 2007). Moreover, Fung, Hsieh, Naik, and Ramadorai (2008) find that FoFs did not deliver alpha between 2000 and 2004. This begs the question of why investors should try to replicate hedge funds if there is no alpha. Although some researchers contend that hedge funds might be useful for portfolio diversification, the majority of investors are hoping to attain alpha when allocating their wealth into hedge funds. Otherwise, investors could equally consider making bets in casinos as the potential source of return uncorrelated with the market.

Perhaps the answer is that hedge fund alpha is not zero or negative before fees (Fung and Hsieh, 2007a). In other words, hedge fund managers can find alpha, but alpha is consumed by fees. This view is consistent with the recent rational model of active portfolio management introduced by Berk and Green (2004). Empirical studies estimating alpha before fees as much as twice higher than alpha net of fees across all hedge fund styles also provide support to this view (Brooks, Clare, and Motson, 2007).

Furthermore, even if alpha before fees is positive, replication strategies only make sense if they are capable of capturing alpha. Indeed, since clones aim to replicate only beta exposures of hedge funds, instead of inferring and cloning the composition of betas in hedge funds, investors could use asset allocation models to combine and package the betas. However, hedge funds do not maintain a constant beta value (i.e., managers actively employ dynamic trading strategies and adjust portfolio weights). Time-varying betas, in turn, might result in positive alpha, if a manager has market-timing skill. Therefore, an accurate replication strategy can benefit from following and imitating market-timing decisions of fund managers and capture a fraction of their alpha.

The rest of the chapter is organized as follows. The first section introduces linear factor–based replication, which is the most dominant approach to replication in the hedge fund literature. This approach best suits the majority of investors who are interested in replicating alphas and betas of hedge funds. The section also provides the results of empirical tests of replication of hedge fund strategies. The findings suggest that standard linear factor models fall short of conventional funds in producing comparable returns for the majority of the styles. The reason is partly because linear clones do not take into account nonlinear features of hedge fund risk exposures. Therefore, the second section introduces a nonlinear model of hedge fund returns. The model captures the nonlinear exposures but requires more work to be converted into an investable product. The chapter ends with a summary and conclusions.

LINEAR FACTOR–BASED REPLICATION

The linear factor–based replication approach originates from classical asset pricing models such as the capital asset pricing model (CAPM) (Sharpe, 1964) and the arbitrage pricing theory (APT) (Ross, 1976). The CAPM states that in equilibrium the expected excess return from holding an asset is proportional to the covariance of its return with the market portfolio. The market portfolio cannot be observed in reality. Theoretically, the market portfolio consists of all available risky assets including financial assets, real assets, and even human capital. Hence, a suitable proxy has to be selected. For example, market returns that are proxied by returns on the S&P 500 Index explain up to 30 percent of variation of returns of hedge fund style indices, with the exception of dedicated short bias style, for which the S&P 500 Index accounts for 60 percent of returns variation (Lhabitant, 2004). Conversely, a model with another proxy, a portfolio consisting of 70 percent investments in the Russell 3000 Index and 30 percent in the Lehman U.S. Bond Aggregate Index, accounts for up to 60 percent of the return variation across styles (Ranaldo and Favre, 2005).

The APT generalizes a single-factor CAPM and asserts that all assets' returns linearly depend on various risk factors. It leads to a standard linear multifactor model, which can be estimated as a linear regression of hedge fund returns on underlying risk factor structure, as shown in Equation 27.1:

$$R_t^{HF_i} = \sum_{j=1}^{J} \beta_{ij} F_{jt} + \varepsilon_{it} \tag{27.1}$$

where $R_t^{HF_i}$ is the return at time t on the individual hedge fund (or hedge fund style); β_{ij} is the estimated exposure of hedge fund i to factor j; F_{jt} is the return on factor j at time t; and $\varepsilon_{it} \sim N(0, \sigma_i^2)$ is the estimated idiosyncratic random fluctuation of hedge fund i returns at time t.

The initial application of the linear multifactor model in the fund industry involved analyzing mutual funds' performance. Twelve risk factors could successfully explain the performance of an extensive universe of U.S. mutual funds (Sharpe, 1992). If the regression coefficients β_{ij} in the model are constrained, such that Equation 27.2:

$$\sum_{j=1}^{J} \beta_{ij} = 1 \tag{27.2}$$

can be interpreted as portfolio weights, and a replicating portfolio as shown in Equation 27.3 can be constructed:

$$R_t^{Clone_i} = \sum_{j=1}^{J} \beta_{ij} F_{jt} \tag{27.3}$$

where $R_t^{Cline_i}$ is the return of the clone of the fund i.

Since hedge funds might be leveraged, some researchers propose an additional renormalization that equalizes the volatilities of original funds and their clones as shown in Equations 27.4, 27.5, and 27.6 (Hasanhodzic and Lo, 2007):

$$\hat{R}_t^{Clone_i} = \gamma_i R_t^{Clone_i} = \sum_{j=1}^{J} \hat{\beta}_{ij} F_{jt} = \sum_{j=1}^{J} (\gamma_i \beta_{ij}) F_{jt} \tag{27.4}$$

$$\gamma_i = \frac{\sqrt{\sum_{t=t}^{T} \frac{(R_t^{HF_i} - \bar{R}_i^{HF})^2}{T-1}}}{\sqrt{\sum_{t=t}^{T} \frac{(R_t^{Clone_i} - \bar{R}^{Clone_i})^2}{T-1}}} \tag{27.5}$$

$$\bar{R}^{HF_i} = \frac{1}{T} \sum_{t=1}^{T} R_t^{HF_i}, \quad \bar{R}^{Clone_i} = \frac{1}{T} \sum_{t=1}^{T} R_t^{Clone_i} \tag{27.6}$$

The renormalization equation (Equation 27.4) is equivalent to changing the leverage of the clone portfolio because the sum of the renormalized betas $\hat{\beta}_{ij}$ will equal the renormalization factor γ_i, not one. An important issue is associated with the estimation of a linear multifactor model, making hedge fund replication a challenging task: the selection of risk factors.

Identifying Hedge Funds' Risk Exposures

Due to the flexibility granted to hedge funds to invest in almost any asset class or market, hedge fund managers may actually create a myriad of market and trading strategy combinations. Therefore, the true set of risks to which hedge funds have exposure is virtually unknown (Agarwal and Naik, 2004; Vrontos, Vrontos, and Giamouridis, 2008). The lack of transparency of the industry further exacerbates the issue. To uncover risk factors, researchers either have to resort to statistical procedures or rely on their own economic judgment.

Statistical Methods

Statistical methods of variable selection may help in revealing the systematic risks to which hedge funds are exposed. Two groups of statistical methods have been applied in the hedge fund literature. The first group assumes that researchers can identify a set of potential risk factors directly observable in the market, but does not know which of them is actually important. For example, a stepwise regression procedure selects a subset of variables with high explanatory power by iteratively including and dropping variables to achieve a reasonable trade-off between keeping the number of factors small and the accuracy of the fit. Forward stepwise regression starts with no factor, and at each step the most statistically significant term is added to the model. Backward stepwise regression starts with all the factors and removes the least significant factor at each step. Stepwise selection procedures are common in the hedge fund literature (Liang, 1999; Agarwal and Naik, 2004; Fung and Hsieh, 2004a; Wegener, von Nitzsch, and Cengiz, 2010). Although such procedures usually allow deriving an interpretable set of factors, stepwise regression models often are not robust to changes in the data (Giamouridis and Paterlini, 2010). Accordingly, replicating strategies employing stepwise regression tend to fit data well in-sample but produce inferior risk-adjusted returns than conventional funds out-of-sample.

The second group of methods does not require knowledge of the explicit set of potential risk factors. Instead, the factors are implied from hedge fund returns data using a completely different statistical technique called principal component analysis (PCA). The goal of PCA is to explain the behavior of correlated time series of returns using a smaller number of uncorrelated and unobserved variables. Implied variables are defined as linear combinations of the original variables (i.e., the returns of different hedge funds or strategies) and can be extracted from the covariance matrix. PCA has an advantage of being free of the problems of including spurious factors and omitting true factors. Conversely, implicit factors or principal components usually do not have a direct economic interpretation. Also, PCA does not solve the problem of determining the number of relevant factors, which is left to a researcher's discretion.

Fung and Hsieh (1997) perform PCA on 409 hedge funds and commodity trading advisers (CTAs). They find that the first five principal components, which they call return-based style (RBS) factors, jointly explain about 43 percent of the cross-sectional variation of hedge fund returns. However, using RBS factors for hedge fund pricing and replication requires linking them to the market or asset-based style (ABS) factors. In other words, researchers still must identify at least a broad set of potential systematic risk exposures.

In subsequent studies, Fung and Hsieh (2002, 2004b) relate five RBS factors to seven ABS factors. The seven ABS factors are: (1) the S&P 500 Index return, (2) the spread between small-cap returns and large-cap stock returns, (3) the change in 10-year Treasury yields, (4) the change in the yield spread between 10-year Treasury-bonds and Moody's Baa bonds, and (5) the returns on three portfolios of lookback straddles on bonds, (6) currencies, and (7) commodities. A *lookback straddle* pays the difference between the highest and lowest prices of the reference asset during the lookback period. The latter three factors are identified as potential proxies for trend-following investment strategies (Fung and Hsieh, 2001). The authors do not present an out-of-sample test of the model with ABS factors, but compare the actual and forecasted return for one year for composite hedge fund style indices from four different data providers. The four predicted values of return are very close to the actual returns (Fung and Hsieh, 2004b).

Economic Selection

Systematic risk factors can also be identified based on theoretical and/or economic reasoning. The most popular hedge fund pricing model of this sort is a six-factor model proposed by Hasanhodzic and Lo (2007). The model does not have a strong theoretical motivation, but rather attempts to provide a reasonably broad cross-section of risk exposures for a typical hedge fund: stocks, bonds, currencies, commodities, credit, and volatility. Accordingly, the researchers use the following factors: (1) USD—the U.S. Dollar Index return; (2) BOND—the return on the Lehman Corporate AA Intermediate Bond Index; (3) CREDIT—the spread between the Lehman BAA Corporate Bond Index and the Lehman Treasury Index; (4) SP500—the S&P 500 Index total return; (5) CMDTY—the Goldman Sachs Commodity Index (GSCI) total return; and (6) DVIX—the first difference of the end-of-month value of the CBOE Volatility Index (VIX). Hasanhodzic and Lo implement the replication procedure and test the model using 1,610 hedge funds from 11 strategies for the period from February 1985 to September 2005. In terms of the risk-adjusted returns, equal-weighted portfolios of rolling-window clones underperform equal-weighted portfolios of their respective funds in nine strategies, outperform them in one and have comparable returns in one.

Empirical Results

This section presents the empirical results of factor-based replication of 12 hedge fund indices from the TASS database. Indices represent asset-weighted portfolios of hedge funds grouped by the strategy: Emerging Markets, Dedicated Short Bias,

Equity Market Neutral, Multi Strategy, Convertible Arbitrage, Global Macro, Event Driven, Long-Short Equity, Fixed Income Arbitrage, Managed Futures, and Fund of Funds. Also, the analysis includes a composite index consisting of all hedge funds (Hedge Funds Composite Index). Monthly returns data span the period from January 1994 to September 2010.

The potential set of risk factors extends the six factors of Hasanhodzic and Lo (2007) with the other eight variables identified in the literature to have predictive power for hedge fund returns. The full list of variables includes: (1) the return on the Russell 3000 Index (R3000); (2) the return on the MSCI World Index excluding the United States (MSWRLD); (3) the return on the MSCI Emerging Markets Index (MSCIEM); (4) the Fama-French's size (SMB) and (5) book-to-market (HML) factors; (6) Carhart's momentum factor (UMD); (7) the first difference of the end-of-month value of the CBOE Volatility Index (DVIX); (8) the return on the Barclays Capital US Corporate AA Intermediate Bond Index (BOND); (9) the return on the Barclays Capital US High Yield Index (LHYIELD); (10) default spread as proxied by the return differential between the Barclays Capital US Aggregate Intermediate Credit BAA and the Barclays Capital US Aggregate Intermediate AAA indices (CREDIT); (11) the return on the Citigroup World Government Bond Index excluding the United States (WGBINOUS); (12) the return on the Merrill Lynch All Convertible Bond Index (MLALLCNV); (13) the return on the U.S. Dollar Index (USD); and (14) the return on the Goldman Sachs Commodity Index (GSCI). All factor returns except SMB, HML, UMD, DVIX, and CREDIT factors are defined as returns in excess of the risk-free rate as proxied by the U.S. Government three-month Treasury bill (T-bill) rate.

Furthermore, the set of risk factors is customized for each hedge fund style by exhaustively searching for the best combination of factors minimizing the Akaike Information Criteria (AIC). AIC describes the trade-off between accuracy and complexity of the model. Smaller values for AIC indicate more preferable models. To keep the model reasonably small and to limit the time needed for the estimation, the maximum number of variables in the model is set to 10.

Exhibit 27.1 shows the selected variables across the styles. For example, Fama and French's (1992) book-to-market factor (HML) is significant in all the styles except Long-Short Equity and Managed Futures styles. The emerging market equity index is included not only in the model for Emerging Market funds, but also for Multi-Strategy, Global-Macro, Event Driven, Managed Futures, and Funds of Funds, suggesting that funds from these categories also have an exposure to emerging markets. All funds together as proxied by the Hedge Fund Composite Index are exposed to a broad range of systematic factors including emerging market specific risk, book-to-market, momentum premiums, equity volatility risk, U.S. and non-U.S. interest rate risk, and commodity price risk.

Exhibit 27.2 presents the results of a linear regression of hedge fund style returns on risk factors. The values of alpha (i.e., superior return due to manager skill as opposed to systematic risk exposure) are positive and statistically significant for 5 of 11 strategies. The Global Macro style shows the highest alpha value of 4.82 percent. Funds from the Event Driven style generate almost the same alpha value of 4.79 percent. Multi-Strategy funds rank third with alpha value of around 3.78 percent. The Convertible Arbitrage strategy displays an alpha value

Exhibit 27.1 Significant Risk Factors in a Linear Factor Model for Hedge Fund Styles from January 1994 to September 2010

Style	Factors
Emerging Markets	R3000 MSCIEM UMD DVIX MLALLCNV USD
Dedicated Short Bias	R3000 SMB HML DVIX BOND WGBINOUS USD
Equity Market Neutral	R3000 HML DVIX BOND LHYIELD GSCI
Multi-Strategy	R3000 MSWRLD MSCIEM HML DVIX CREDIT MLALLCNV GSCI
Convertible Arbitrage	R3000 SMB HML BOND CREDIT WGBINOUS MLALLCNV GSCI
Global Macro	MSCIEM HML UMD DVIX BOND CREDIT WGBINOUS MLALLCNV
Event Driven	MSCIEM HML UMD CREDIT MLALLCNV USD GSCI
Long-Short Equity	MSWRLD MSCIEM SMB UMD DVIX BOND LHYIELD MLALLCNV
Fixed Income Arbitrage	R3000 SMB HML DVIX BOND LHYIELD WGBINOUS MLALLCNV USD GSCI
Managed Futures	MSCIEM DVIX BOND LHYIELD WGBINOUS GSCI
Fund of Funds	R3000 MSCIEM HML UMD DVIX BOND MLALLCNV USD GSCI
Hedge Fund Composite	MSCIEM HML UMD DVIX BOND WGBINOUS MLALLCNV GSCI

This exhibit contains significant variables selected by an exhaustive search stepwise procedure from an original set of 14 variables: (1) the return on the Russell 3000 Index (R3000); (2) the return on the MSCI World Index excluding the United States (MSWRLD); (3) the return on the MSCI Emerging Markets Index (MSCIEM); (4) the Fama-French's size (SMB) and (5) book-to-market (HML) factors; (6) Carhart's momentum factor (UMD); (7) the first-difference of the end-of-month value of the CBOE Volatility Index (DVIX); (8) the return on the Barclays Capital US Corporate AA Intermediate Bond Index (BOND); (9) the return on the Barclays Capital US High Yield Index (LHYIELD); (10) default spread as proxied by the return differential between the Barclays Capital US Aggregate Intermediate Credit BAA and the Barclays Capital US Aggregate Intermediate AAA indices (CREDIT); (11) the return on the Citigroup World Government Bond Index excluding the United States (WGBINOUS); (12) the return on the Merrill Lynch All Convertible Bond Index (MLALLCNV); (13) the return on the U.S. Dollar Index (USD); and (14) the return on the Goldman Sachs Commodity Index (GSCI). All factor returns except SMB, HML, UMD, DVIX, and CREDIT factors are defined as returns in excess of the risk-free rate as proxied by the U.S. Government three-month Treasury bill rate. A stepwise procedure with an exhaustive search algorithm limits the maximum number of variables in the model to 10 factors.

of 2.78 percent, followed by Long-Short funds at around 2.25 percent. Emerging Markets, Dedicated Short Bias, Equity Market Neutral, Fixed Income Arbitrage, Managed Futures, and Funds of Funds do not produce any statistically significant alpha values. The whole universe of hedge funds, as measured by the Hedge Funds Composite Index, generates an alpha value of around 2.15 percent, which is significant at the 0.06 level.

The quality of the model fit varies markedly across the strategies. The linear factor model explains up to 85 percent of the variation in returns for the Long-Short Equity style, 76 percent of Funds of Funds, 74 percent of Dedicated Short

Exhibit 27.2 In-Sample Performance of a Linear Factor Model for Hedge Funds from January 1994 to September 2010

Style	Adjusted R^2	Alpha (%)	Alpha p-value
Emerging Markets	0.72	1.74	0.40
Dedicated Short Bias	0.74	−1.42	0.53
Equity Market Neutral	0.27	0.27	0.91
Multi-Strategy	0.49	3.78	0.00
Convertible Arbitrage	0.62	2.78	0.01
Global Macro	0.30	4.82	0.03
Event Driven	0.64	4.79	0.00
Long-Short Equity	0.85	2.25	0.02
Fixed Income Arbitrage	0.55	−0.66	0.53
Managed Futures	0.16	1.70	0.54
Fund of Funds	0.76	−0.15	0.84
Hedge Fund Composite	0.68	2.15	0.06

Bias, 72 percent of Emerging Markets, 64 percent of Event Driven, 62 percent of Convertible Arbitrage, 55 percent of Fixed Income Arbitrage, and 49 percent of the Multi-Strategy styles. In contrast, the model performs poorly for the Global Macro, Equity Market Neutral, and Managed Futures styles. In terms of the first two styles, poor performance is expected because these styles employ strategies that are not highly correlated with the markets. The Managed Futures style, in turn, engages in quantitative, high frequency trading strategies, such as momentum or trend following. A static linear factor model cannot capture these strategies because dynamic trading induces nonlinear patterns in risk exposures that lie outside the capability of a linear model. This issue will be addressed later in the chapter. Overall, the model explains about 76 percent of the variation of hedge fund returns.

These results are striking when compared with the similar study of Hasanhodzic and Lo (2007). All alpha estimates are consistently lower than those reported by Hasanhodzic and Lo. Emerging Markets, Equity Market Neutral, Fixed Income Arbitrage, Managed Futures, and Funds of Funds have insignificant alpha values as compared to statistically significant alphas of 18.3 percent, 7.31 percent, 7.19 percent, 5.16 percent, and 5.28 percent, respectively, in the study by Hasanhodzic and Lo. For the Multi-Strategy style, alpha values are 3.78 percent and 8.86 percent, respectively; for Convertible Arbitrage 2.78 percent and 5.28 percent; for Global Macro 4.82 percent and 7.31 percent; for Event Driven 4.79 percent and 11.75 percent; and for Long-Short Equity 2.25 percent and 11.22 percent. Conversely, the model fit is significantly better for all the styles. For example, the adjusted R^2 for Long-Short Equity is 0.85 against 0.22 for the model of Hasanhodzic and Lo; for Funds of Funds 0.76 against 0.22; for Dedicated Short Bias 0.74 against 0.40; and for Emerging Markets 0.72 against 0.19.

Two explanations for this remarkable difference follow. First, Hasanhodzic and Lo (2007) analyze hedge funds during the period that precedes the period used in this study by about 10 years. Therefore, lower values of alpha are consistent with the previously discussed academic evidence that hedge fund alpha is diminishing. Second, the proposed model more accurately fits the data and captures beta exposures that the simpler model of Hasanhodzic and Lo attributes to alpha.

Overall, the results confirm prior findings in the literature that a large part of hedge fund returns is due to various risk premiums and not purely due to skill. Also, the findings emphasize the fact that alpha is a product of the model and its estimates will be reliable only if the underlying hedge fund pricing model adequately captures systematic risk of hedge funds.

Clones' Performance

Good in-sample fit of a linear multi-factor model suggests that linear clones may be able to replicate at least a fraction of the returns of the hedge fund strategies out-of-sample. The clones are constructed in three steps using a rolling-window procedure. The first step is to estimate the linear regression in Equation 27.1 setting the intercept to zero and constraining the betas to add up to unity (Equation 27.2). Because variables are selected automatically from an original set of 14 risk factors, the size of the rolling window should be sufficient to reliably estimate the model. Accordingly, 60 monthly observations are included into each rolling window (five observations per variable). Second, the in-sample volatilities of the original styles and clones are equalized (Equation 27.4). Third, estimated (leveraged) betas are used as clone portfolio weights. The return of the clone is then forecasted for one month. Out-of-sample styles and clones may not have the same volatility because equalization is performed only in-sample. Exhibit 27.3 contains key performance characteristics of original hedge fund styles and their out-of-sample linear clones.

First, the correlation coefficients between style indices and their clones are relatively high. The correlation coefficient exceeds 0.7 for 6 out of 12 styles including the composite index (Long-Short Equity, Emerging Markets, Funds of Funds, Hedge Fund Composite, Event Driven, and Convertible Arbitrage), reaching the level of about 0.9 for Long-Short Equity and Emerging Markets. Correlation of Multi-Strategy and Fixed Income Arbitrage styles and clones is also quite high and above 0.5. As expected from poor in-sample performance, clones of Equity Market Neutral (in-sample adjusted $R^2 = 0.27$), Global Macro (0.30), and Managed Futures (0.16) styles exhibit low correlation with the original styles: 0.13, 0.38, and 0.22, respectively. Unexpectedly, the correlation coefficient of the Dedicated Short Bias style and its clone is low (0.35) despite the good in-sample fit (adjusted $R^2 = 0.74$). This result may be due to the influence of outliers.

A second observation is related to the poor performance of clones. Notwithstanding high correlations, clones' returns and, most importantly, risk-adjusted performance measured by the Sharpe ratio are lower compared to the hedge fund styles for all the styles except the Dedicated Short Bias style, which has a negative annual return of −6.01 percent, while the clone delivered positive return of 6.56 percent, resulting in a Sharpe ratio of −0.37 and 0.33, respectively.

The Global Macro and Event Driven styles have the highest absolute returns (8.65 percent and 6.91 percent) and Sharpe ratios (1.29 and 1.27), respectively. Conversely, the Global Macro clone delivers a return of only 5 percent with twice the volatility (the standard deviation is 6.71 percent for the style and 12.15 percent for

Exhibit 27.3 Performance Comparison of Original Hedge Fund Styles and Their Linear Out-of-Sample Clones from January 1994 to September 2010

	Annual Mean Return (%)		Annual Standard Deviation (%)		Annual Sharpe Ratio		
Style	**Style**	**Clone**	**Style**	**Clone**	**Style**	**Clone**	***Cor***
Emerging Markets	9.32	7.16	11.96	12.64	0.78	0.57	0.87
Dedicated Short Bias	−6.01	6.56	16.32	19.78	−0.37	0.33	0.35
Equity Market Neutral	0.23	0.15	12.44	3.50	0.02	0.04	0.13
Multi-Strategy	4.40	0.31	5.43	5.02	0.81	0.06	0.69
Convertible Arbitrage	5.29	1.11	7.77	7.32	0.68	0.15	0.73
Global Macro	8.65	5.00	6.71	12.15	1.29	0.41	0.38
Event Driven	6.91	2.03	5.45	5.66	1.27	0.36	0.76
Long-Short Equity	5.36	2.33	9.78	11.63	0.55	0.20	0.92
Fixed Income Arbitrage	2.13	1.51	6.37	5.38	0.33	0.28	0.57
Managed Futures	3.40	−1.91	11.71	16.30	0.29	−0.12	0.22
Fund of Funds	2.53	2.79	5.52	7.23	0.46	0.39	0.84
Hedge Fund Composite	5.17	4.18	6.58	8.72	0.79	0.48	0.83

This exhibit compares the performance characteristics of the original hedge fund styles from the TASS database with the out-of-sample performance of their rolling window linear clones. In-sample model estimation uses 60 monthly observations and 1 month for prediction. The factors are selected individually for each style and rolling window via a stepwise procedure from the original set of 14 factors. The Sharpe ratio is calculated using the total return rather than the excess return. *Cor* is the coefficient of correlation between the clone returns and original style returns.

the clone), producing a Sharpe ratio of a mere 0.41. The Event Driven clone return (2.03 percent) is three times less than the corresponding style return (6.91 percent), with comparable volatilities (5.45 percent and 5.66 percent). The Multi-Strategy clone return is nearly zero (0.31 percent) compared to the corresponding style return of 4.4 percent. The Equity Market Neutral and Fixed Income Arbitrage clones display lower returns, which are compensated by lower volatilities, making the clones' and styles' Sharpe ratios almost equal. The Managed Futures replication strategy generates a negative return of −1.91 percent against a positive 3.40 percent of the corresponding style. The risk-adjusted performance of the Long-Short Equity, Convertible Arbitrage, and Emerging Markets clones is also lower than the original styles. With the exception of the Dedicated Short Bias style, the Funds of Funds style is the only one for which the clone's return is above the style return (2.53 percent and 2.79 percent, respectively). However, higher return is offset by higher volatility (7.23 percent against 5.52 percent). Overall, the clone of the aggregate hedge fund index produces a Sharpe ratio of 0.48 compared with the corresponding style's Sharpe ratio of 0.79. The performance of the clones is worse than the performance of replication strategies reported by Hasanhodzic and Lo (2007). The reason may partly be attributed to including the highly volatile period during the financial crisis of 2007–2008 in the current empirical test.

Exhibits 27.4 and 27.5 further shed light on the differences between the clones' performance and their corresponding styles' performance. Exhibit 27.4 illustrates the time series of returns of hedge fund styles and their clones. Consistent with

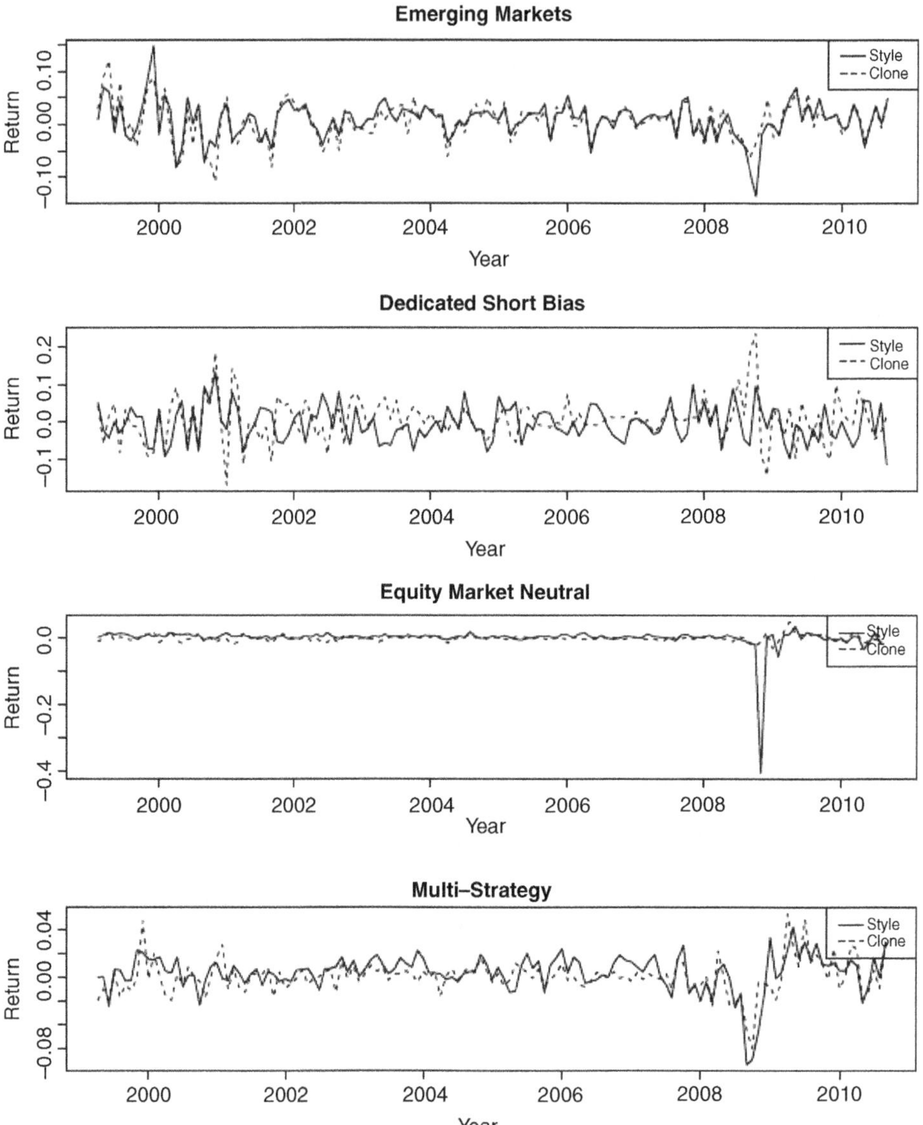

Exhibit 27.4 Time Series of Returns of Original Hedge Fund Styles and Their Linear Out-of-Sample Clones from January 1999 to September 2010

This exhibit demonstrates the time series of performance of the original hedge fund style indices and out-of-sample performance of their rolling window linear clones from January 1999 to September 2010. In-sample model estimation uses 60 monthly observations and 1 month for prediction. The factors are selected individually for each style and rolling window via a stepwise procedure from the original set of 14 factors.

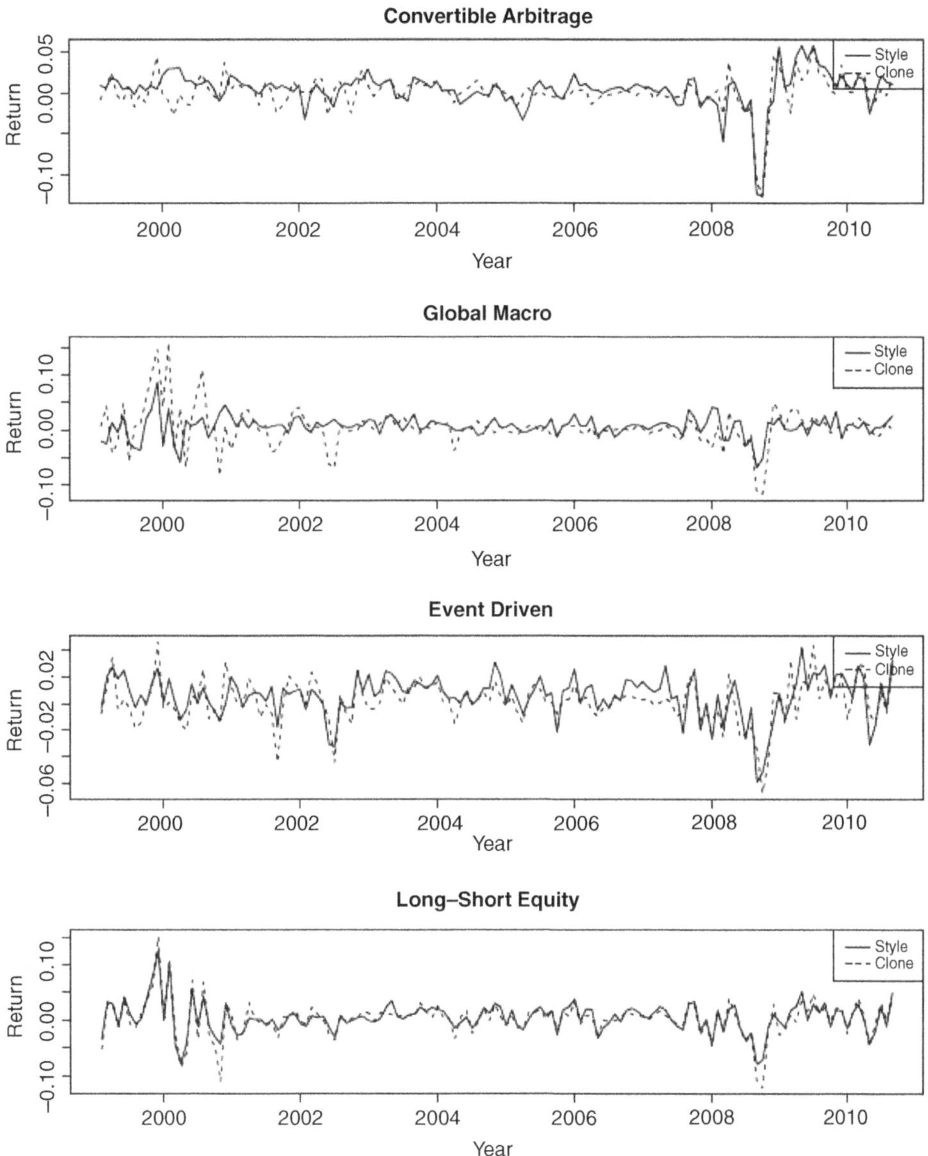

Exhibit 27.4 Time Series of Returns of Original Hedge Fund Styles and Their Linear Out-of-Sample Clones from January 1999 to September 2010 (*Continued*)

the high values of correlation coefficients, the exhibit demonstrates good tracking abilities of hedge fund clones for at least nine styles including the composite index. Also, in accordance with the poor clones' performance, the time series of clones' returns either lies below the time series of styles' returns on the graphs (e.g., the Multi-Strategy and Event Driven styles), resulting in the clones' lower returns, or exhibit higher volatility (e.g., Global Macro, Funds of Funds, and Hedge Fund Composite).

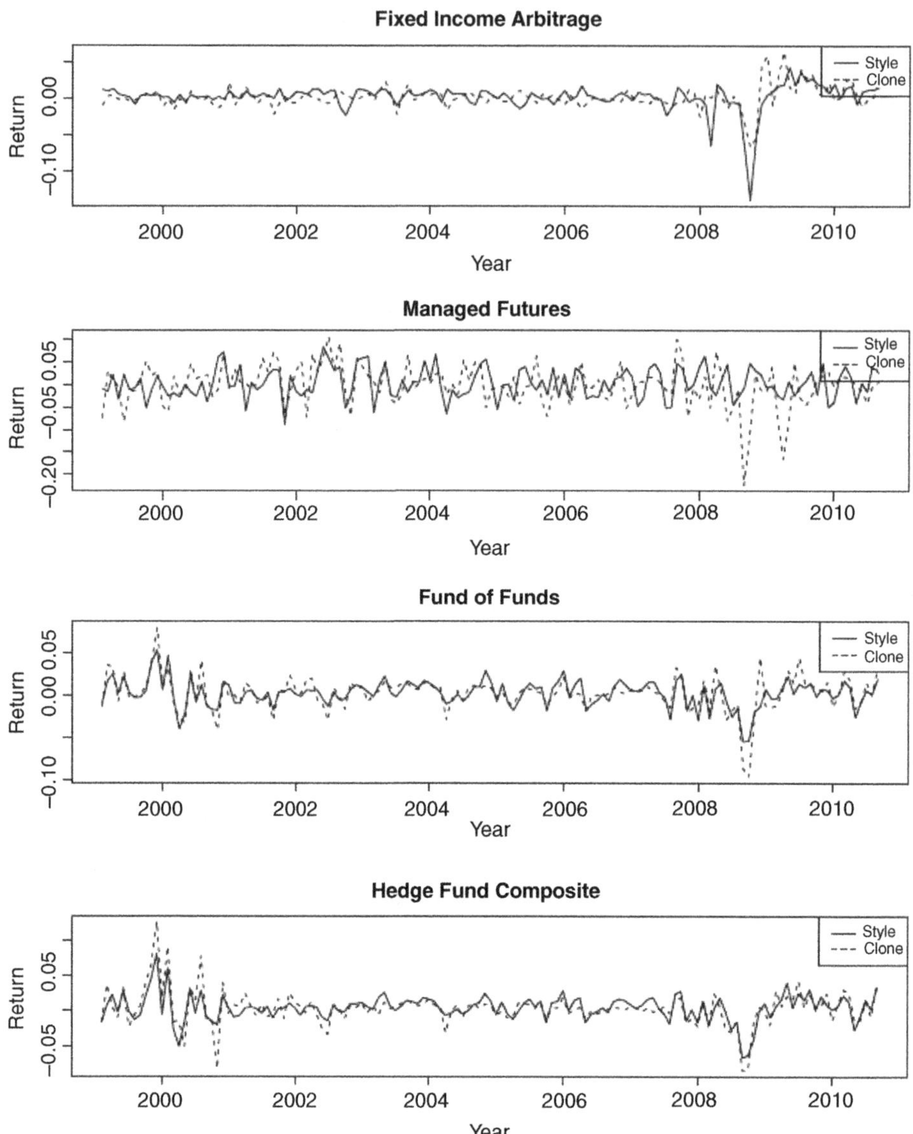

Exhibit 27.4 Time Series of Returns of Original Hedge Fund Styles and Their Linear Out-of-Sample Clones from January 1999 to September 2010 (*Continued*)

Exhibit 27.5 contains the plots of the cumulative returns of hedge fund styles and their linear clones. During the bull market period before the financial crisis of 2007–2008, the Emerging Markets, Equity Market Neutral, Multi-Strategy, Convertible Arbitrage, Event Driven, Long-Short Equity, and Fixed Income Arbitrage styles clearly outperformed the clones. However, during the crisis, styles suffered larger losses, so that clones of several styles, such as Equity Market Neutral and Fixed Income Arbitrage, regained their positions and demonstrated similar cumulative returns over the 11-year period. In contrast, the Global Macro and Managed

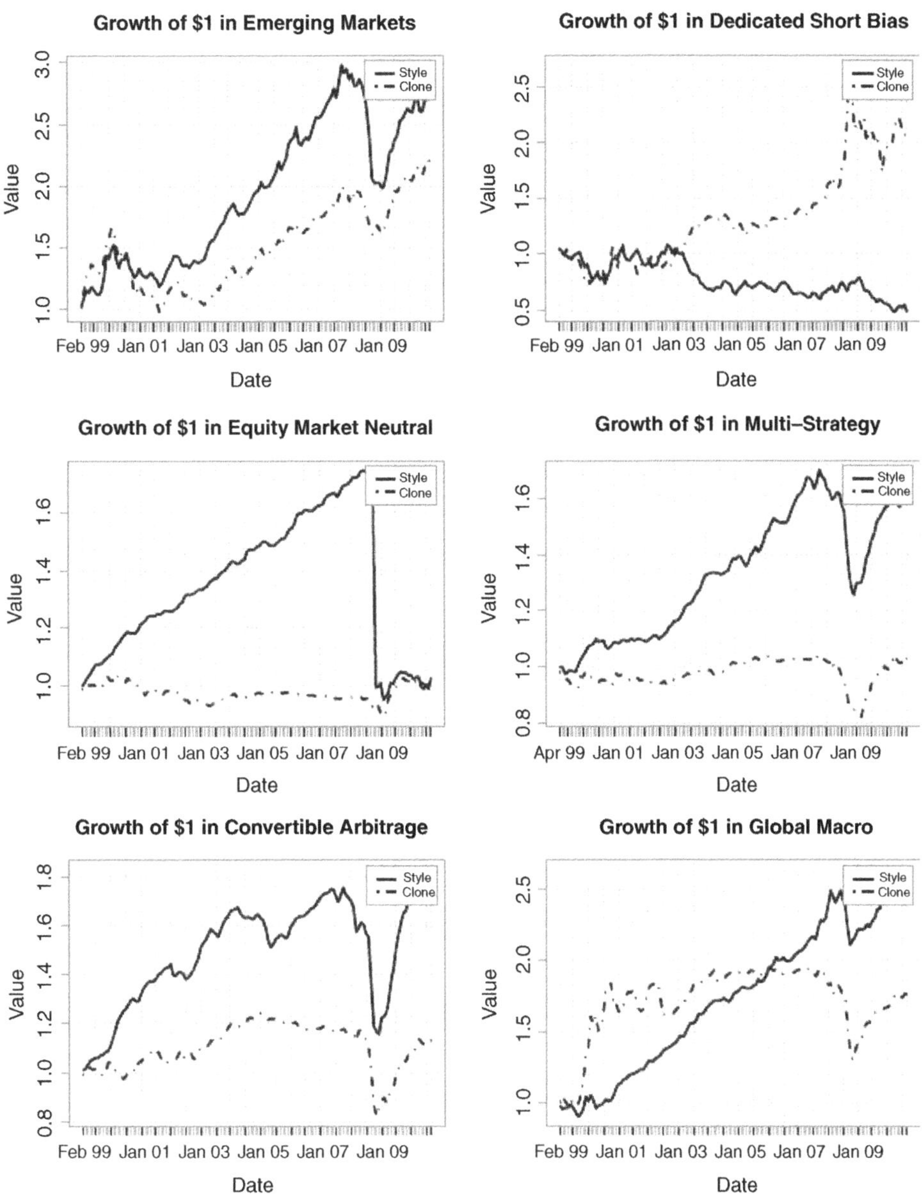

Exhibit 27.5 Cumulative Return of Hedge Fund Styles and Their Linear Out-of-Sample Clones from January 1999 to September 2010

This exhibit showcases the cumulative returns of the original hedge fund style indices and cumulative returns of their out-of-sample rolling window linear clones from January 1999 to September 2010.

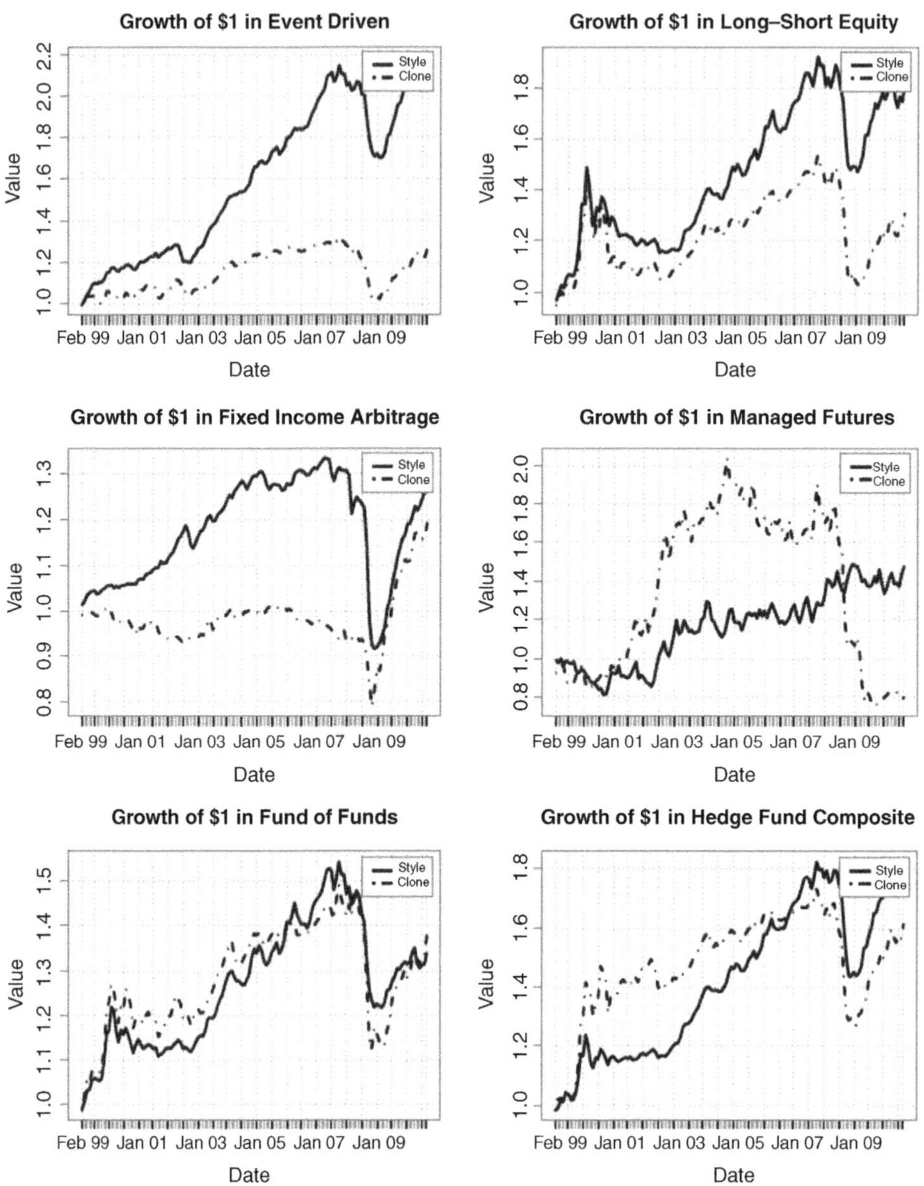

Exhibit 27.5 Cumulative Return of Hedge Fund Styles and Their Linear Out-of-Sample Clones from January 1999 to September 2010 (*Continued*)

Futures clones performed better than conventional hedge fund strategies during the period of expansion, but experienced larger losses during the crisis period.

Next, this chapter analyzes the performance of the Fund of Funds clone. Overall, the cumulative historical returns of the Fund of Funds clone almost exactly replicate the original Fund of Funds style cumulative returns. The result is consistent with the earlier finding (Fung et al., 2008) that this strategy did not deliver positive alpha net of fees during 2000 to 2004 with the largest portion of returns generated by risk premiums and funds' fees consumed the small alpha. Furthermore, the Dedicated Short Bias clone outperformed the style benchmark with the cumulative return of 109 percent for the clone compared with −51 percent for the style.

Several concluding remarks pertain to the factor-based linear replication. First, styles that do not generate significant positive alpha (e.g., Fund of Funds, Dedicated Short Bias, and Fixed Income Arbitrage) can be replicated with a linear model. However, styles that deliver positive alpha, such as Multi-Strategy, Event Driven, and Global Macro, are unlikely to be successfully cloned with a linear model. Positive alpha suggests that managers engage in more complex strategies than buying and holding securities and collecting risk premiums. Therefore, a linear model is unsuitable for such styles.

Nevertheless, a positive result exists even for the styles that linear clones fail to replicate. The correlation between the majority of the styles and their clones is quite high. Thus, clones can accurately track the dynamics of aggregate hedge fund strategies returns. This result has an important practical implication. Because clones are constructed using liquid tradable instruments, an investor can sell short a clone portfolio while investing in a hedge fund strategy that delivers alpha and lock in positive abnormal return due to manager skill (i.e., investors might use clones to hedge the systematic part of hedge fund returns). So far no research exists on this topic.

TOWARD NONLINEAR FACTOR–BASED REPLICATION

The previous section illustrates that a linear factor model fails to replicate hedge fund style returns if it contains a significant alpha component. Perhaps, this limitation could be attributed not only to a linear model but also to any replication model because ideally the superior skill of individual managers drives alpha. However, this is unlikely to be completely true. Understanding the issue involves determining the main sources of alpha. Three sources exist: (1) security selection, (2) market timing, and (3) premiums for systematic risk exposures not captured by a given hedge fund replication model.

Security selection cannot be replicated by any model. *Security selection* refers to picking specific securities within one asset class. For example, finding undervalued individual stocks involves "microforecasting" ability (Merton, 1981). By definition, replication strategies do not attempt to capture idiosyncratic exposures of individual fund managers and consequently are not amenable to reproducing the exact portfolio holdings and individual security choices.

Whether the latter two components of alpha can be replicated depends on the adequacy and accuracy of the replication model. *Market timing* refers to the selection of right entry or exit points for an investment in a particular market rather than any particular security. Merton (1981) refers to this as "macroforecasting" ability. In this seminal paper, Merton demonstrates that the market-timing strategy of selecting equities and bonds is equivalent to a long-only investment in the broad equity index (e.g., the S&P 500 Index), plus a put option on the equity index with a strike price equal to the bond market return (e.g., Treasury bill). In other words, market-timing strategies generate nonlinear optionlike patterns in risk exposures. Moreover, other factors besides market-timing strategies induce nonlinearities in exposures. Hedge funds may physically hold options and other complex derivatives for speculative or hedging purposes. All these instruments might result in even more complex nonlinear patterns.

To clone the part of alpha due to the market-timing skill and reduce the impact of systematic risk premium wrongly attributed to alpha, a replication model must capture nonlinearities. Unfortunately, a linear factor model inherits the restriction of linear factor exposures from classical asset pricing models such as the APT (Ross, 1976) and is thus unsuitable for this reason.

Existing Nonlinear Approaches

Although a consensus exists among academics about the presence of nonlinear features in hedge fund risk exposures, a truly nonlinear hedge fund pricing model is yet to emerge. Instead, three different approaches might capture nonlinear patterns to a certain extent: (1) augmenting a hedge fund pricing model with portfolios of options on some underlying risk factors, (2) using piecewise regression models, and (3) using conditional models.

From an economic perspective, correspondence exists between options and hedge fund returns. Hedge fund managers receive incentive fees if a hedge fund's net asset value (NAV) exceeds the high-water mark (i.e., highest previous NAV), but they do not participate in sharing losses. Such an asymmetric incentive payoff may be viewed as a free call option on the percentage of the performance of the fund granted by the investor to the fund manager (Anson, 2001). The incentive option encourages the manager to actively manage a fund's volatility and its risk exposures. If the fund is considerably below its high-water mark, the manager might be tempted to increase bet size in the hope of recovering and obtaining an incentive fee. On the contrary, if the fund is considerably above its high-water mark, the manager might try to reduce risk exposures and minimize the fund's volatility (Kahn, Scanlan, and Siegel, 2006). Accordingly, the optionlike nature of incentive fees could induce optionlike patterns in hedge fund returns (Brooks et al., 2007). Also, as previously discussed, Merton (1981) suggests using options to explain the performance of managed portfolios. Therefore, attempting to use options in a hedge fund pricing model is natural. Glosten and Jagannathan (1994) are the first to explicitly include the returns on selected option-based strategies as risk factors for an analysis of the performance of mutual fund managers.

Following the suggestions of Glosten and Jagannathan (1994), various authors augment their hedge fund models with factors representing returns on various option portfolios. Fung and Hsieh (2001) use portfolios of lookback straddles (i.e., a lookback call plus a lookback put) on 26 different markets (encompassing world equities, bonds, commodities, and currencies) to explain the returns of CTAs using trend-following strategy. When adding option terms into the model, the new challenge is to determine how many options and which strike prices should be considered. Agarwal and Naik (2004) employ stepwise regression and an F-test to identify the set of relevant options underlying assets, while exogenously determining options moneyness. In contrast, other studies rely on economic judgment to select the underlying options, but estimate strike prices via statistical procedures (Amenc, Martellini, Meyfredi, and Ziemann, 2010; Diez De Los Rios, and Garcia, 2011).

In general, all option augmented models are based on the idea that option payoffs represent an approximation of the true nonlinear function of hedge fund exposures. Since the option payoff function has only one kink, replacing options with linear functions that permit multiple kinks is natural. This leads to an estimation of a piecewise (threshold) regression. Giannikis and Vrontos (2011) develop a threshold regression model for hedge fund pricing and use a Bayesian approach to select both relevant risk factors and the number and position of the kinks.

The hedge fund literature also proposes a completely different approach to address the issue of nonlinearity of the exposures, namely, conditional models. Given a profound correspondence between financial instruments (e.g., derivatives) and strategies (e.g., market timing) with nonlinear payoff profiles and dynamic trading (Merton, 1981), one can try to recreate nonlinear features by substituting fixed beta coefficients in a standard factor model with time-varying coefficients. For example, Amenc et al. (2010) and Diez De Los Rios and Garcia (2011) develop a Markov regime switching (MRS) model for hedge fund returns.

In summary, researchers propose alternative approaches to account for nonlinearities in risk exposures. The important question then is: Do such approaches permit accurately modeling hedge fund returns? Recent empirical analysis of option augmented, conditional, and linear models demonstrates that going beyond the linear case does not necessarily lead to better replication results (Amenc et al., 2010). The finding is striking because it shows that either the significance of nonlinear risk exposures of hedge funds is overstated or these quasi nonlinear models are inappropriate.

Generalized Additive Model

This section introduces a novel nonlinear model of hedge fund returns. Although its practical implementation as a technique for replication is still a work-in-progress, the model illustrates and provides insights on hedge funds' nonlinear exposures.

A traditional linear multifactor hedge fund return model postulates a linear relationship between the return and underlying risk factors, as shown in Equation 27.7:

$$R_t^{HR_i} = \alpha_i^{LM} + \sum_{j=1}^{J} \beta_{ij} F_{jt} + \varepsilon_{it} \tag{27.7}$$

where $R_t^{HF_i}$ is the return at time t on individual hedge fund (or hedge fund style); α_i^{LM} is the abnormal manager-specific return (where LM denotes a linear model); β_{ij} is the estimated exposure of hedge fund i to factor j; F_{jt} is the return on factor j at time t; and $\varepsilon_{it} \sim N(0, \sigma_i^2)$ is the estimated idiosyncratic random fluctuation of hedge fund i returns at time t.

Since the assumption of linearity is likely to be violated, Hastie and Tibshirani (1990) propose an alternative model, called a generalized additive model (GAM). A GAM allows the data to suggest an appropriate functional form. In other words, coefficients β_{ij} are replaced with variable-specific smoothing functions $f_{ij}(.)$, which can take any linear or nonlinear form as shown in Equation 27.8:

$$R_t^{HF_i} = \alpha_i^{GAM} + \sum_{j=1}^{J} f_{ij}(F_{jt}) + \xi_{it} \tag{27.8}$$

A GAM model does not assume a rigid form for the dependence of hedge fund returns on risk factors. Also, the model contains an embedded feature of automatic variable selection. For that, a term that penalizes the model for the lack of smoothness and complexity (number of variables) is added into the optimization procedure (Marra and Wood, 2011). To test nonlinear exposures in hedge funds, a GAM is fitted to the residuals of a linear model. The idea is that if hedge funds have nonlinear exposures for which a linear model fails to consider, then a nonlinear model should be able to identify them, improve the model fit, and capture the part of alpha due to the nonlinear exposures. Exhibit 27.6 contains the list of variables to which hedge funds have significant nonlinear exposure as determined by the GAM.

Exhibit 27.6 Significant Risk Factors in a Generalized Additive Model (GAM) for Hedge Fund Styles from January 1994 to September 2010

Style	**Factors**
Emerging Markets	DVIX
Dedicated Short Bias	R3000 MSWRLD SMB LHYIELD MLALLCNV USD
Equity Market Neutral	R3000 MSWRLD HML DVIX BOND CREDIT LHYIELD MLALLCNV USD
Multi-Strategy	DVIX BOND LHYIELD USD
Convertible Arbitrage	MSWRLD SMB UMD DVIX MLALLCNV GSCI
Global Macro	SMB HML USD
Event Driven	R3000 MSWRLD MSCIEM UMD DVIX CREDIT LHYIELD MLALLCNV
Long-Short Equity	CREDIT
Fixed Income Arbitrage	DVIX WGBINOUS USD GSCI
Managed Futures	R3000 WGBINOUS GSCI
Fund of Funds	MSWRLD HML UMD CREDIT
Hedge Fund Composite	HML USD

This exhibit reflects nonlinear exposures of hedge fund styles not captured by a linear factor model (i.e., the GAM is fitted to the residuals of the linear model and significant variables are selected). The set of factors includes: (1) the return on the Russell 3000 Index (R3000); (2) the return on the MSCI World Index excluding the United States (MSWRLD); (3) the return on the MSCI Emerging Markets Index (MSCIEM); (4) the Fama-French's size (SMB) and (5) book-to-market (HML) factors; (6) Carhart's momentum factor (UMD); (7) the first difference of the end-of-month value of the CBOE Volatility Index (DVIX); (8) the return on the Barclays Capital US Corporate AA Intermediate Bond Index (BOND); (9) the return on the Barclays Capital US High Yield Index (LHYIELD); (10) default spread as proxied by the return differential between the Barclays Capital US Aggregate Intermediate Credit BAA and the Barclays Capital US Aggregate Intermediate AAA indices (CREDIT); (11) the return on the Citigroup World Government Bond Index excluding the United States (WGBINOUS); (12) the return on the Merrill Lynch All Convertible Bond Index (MLALLCNV); (13) the return on the U.S. Dollar Index (USD); and (14) the return on the Goldman Sachs Commodity Index (GSCI). All factor returns except SMB, HML, UMD, DVIX, and CREDIT factors are defined as returns in excess of the risk-free rate as proxied by the U.S. Government three-month Treasury bill rate.

Exhibit 27.7 In-Sample Performance of a Generalized Additive Model (GAM) of Hedge Fund Style Returns from January 1994 to September 2010

Style	Adjusted R^2	Alpha (%)	Alpha p-value
Emerging Markets	0.76	0.14	0.37
Dedicated Short Bias	0.84	−0.11	0.46
Equity Market Neutral	0.69	0.02	0.88
Multi-Strategy	0.63	0.25	0.00
Convertible Arbitrage	0.82	0.21	0.00
Global Macro	0.42	0.36	0.02
Event Driven	0.82	0.32	0.00
Long-Short Equity	0.90	0.17	0.01
Fixed Income Arbitrage	0.77	−0.05	0.44
Managed Futures	0.37	0.13	0.50
Fund of Funds	0.84	−0.01	0.82
Hedge Fund Composite	0.76	0.16	0.04

This exhibit shows the results of the in-sample fit of a GAM of hedge fund style returns from the TASS database on factors selected individually for each style from the original set of 14 factors. Variable selection and identification of the appropriate functional form of the model are a part of the estimation procedure of the GAM.

All the styles have nonlinear relations to at least one systematic risk factor. Some of the most frequent factors to which funds have nonlinear exposures are the MSCI World Index excluding the United States (significant in five styles out of 12), the U.S. Dollar Index (six styles), the Russell 3000 Index (four styles), the book-to-market factor (four styles), and the change in the S&P 500 Volatility Index.

Since the GAM has identified the asymmetric exposures, the fit of the nested linear and generalized additive model is better than the fit of a linear model for all the styles. Exhibit 27.7 provides the estimates of the model fit (adjusted R^2), corrected alpha values, and corresponding p-values.

The Equity Market Neutral style demonstrates the best improvement in terms of the model fit: the R^2 increases almost threefold from 0.26 to 0.68. The Managed Futures style follows next with the R^2 improving from 0.16 to 0.36. For other styles, the R^2 increase ranges from 0.05 (Emerging Markets and Long-Short Equity) to 0.20 (Convertible Arbitrage, Fixed Income Arbitrage, and Event Driven). In line with the improved quality of fit, the values of alpha decrease for all the styles that exhibit statistically significant alpha in a linear model.

Another advantage of a GAM over other nonlinear models is that a GAM allows visualizing and investigating each individual risk exposure. Exhibit 27.8 provides examples of GAM plots for three factors from three styles: Equity Market Neutral, Multi Strategy, and Dedicated Short Bias.

The Equity Market Neutral style is considered to be uncorrelated with global markets. Poor performance of a linear model and low beta estimates partly confirm this statement. For example, the beta value of R3000 is 0.19 and the beta value of HML is 0.10. However, a standard correlation coefficient measures only the degree of the linear relationship between the two variables. If this hedge fund style has nonlinear exposures to the markets, they will not be identified correctly by correlation. Therefore, a nonlinear model allows looking deeper into the issue.

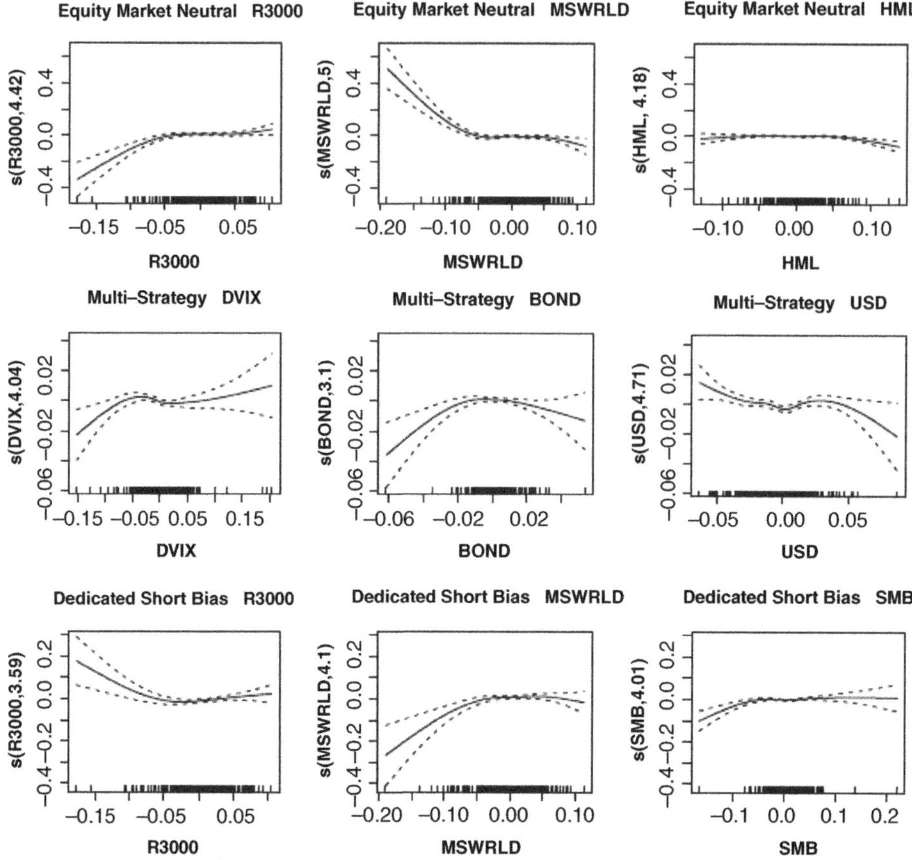

Exhibit 27.8 Nonlinear Risk Factor Exposures of Hedge Fund Styles from January 1994 to September 2010

This exhibit shows the nonlinear exposures of hedge fund styles not captured by a linear factor model (i.e., the GAM is fitted to the residuals of the linear model and significant variables are selected). The solid line on the graphs is a nonlinear exposure of a hedge fund style to a risk factor, the upper and lower dashed lines are drawn two standard errors above and below the estimate of the smooth. The set of factors includes: (1) the return on the Russell 3000 Index (R3000); (2) the return on the MSCI World Index excluding the United States (MSWRLD); (3) the Fama-French's size (SMB) and (4) book-to-market (HML) factors; (5) the first difference of the end-of-month value of the CBOE Volatility Index (DVIX); (6) the return on the Barclays Capital US Corporate AA Intermediate Bond Index (BOND); and (7) the return on the U.S. Dollar Index (USD). All factor returns except SMB, HML, and DVIX are defined as returns in excess of the risk-free rate as proxied by the U.S. Government three-month Treasury bill rate.

The analysis of three nonlinear exposures reveals an interesting picture. The style has strong, nonlinear exposures to equity markets. Exposure to the Russell 3000 Index resembles the payoff of a short position in a put option. This finding means that funds in this style class enhance their returns during bull markets with an option premium, but suffer losses during bear markets. The strike of the option equals the index return of around 5 percent. The style also has an asymmetric exposure to the MSCI World Index excluding the Unites States, but in contrast to short put-like exposure to the Russell 3000 Index, the MSCI World Index excluding the

United States exposure resembles a long position in a put option with the same strike of 5 percent. Therefore, large losses from long spot market and short put option positions during bear markets in the United States might be offset by the gain on a long option on world equity, given that world equity markets will move in the same direction during deep recessions in the United States.

Multi-Strategy fund managers who dynamically allocate capital among strategies falling within several traditional hedge-fund disciplines also exhibit nonlinear exposures to various factors, such as the Barclays Capital US Corporate AA Intermediate Bond Index, the return on the U.S. Dollar Index, and the first difference of the end-of-month value of the CBOE Volatility Index. The dynamic nature of the trading strategies results in nonlinear patterns and the inability of a linear model to accurately explain the returns of this style.

Overall, the results confirm the findings of the Giannikis and Vrontos (2011) threshold regression model that all the styles have nonlinear exposures. Nevertheless, the proposed GAM is more flexible and consequently better suited for hedge fund returns modeling.

SUMMARY AND CONCLUSIONS

This chapter provides a brief introduction into a nascent field of research on passive replication of hedge fund strategies. The main focus is on the most dominant approach in the literature, a linear, factor-based replication. The results of empirical tests demonstrate several interesting findings. The linear replication strategies perform reasonably well in terms of tracking the dynamics of hedge fund returns. However, the actual, risk-adjusted performance of hedge funds is superior to the performance of their synthetic counterparts for the majority of the styles. Nevertheless, for several styles that do not demonstrate significant positive manager skill, clones provide comparable performance.

The chapter also discusses the hotly debated topic of the presence of nonlinearities in systematic risk exposures of hedge funds. The issue is very important from a practical perspective because of the inability of a linear model to capture a large part of hedge fund returns might be attributed to its failure to account for asymmetric risk relations. A brief overview outlines the existing approaches to capture nonlinearities. Furthermore, a new approach, free of a linear specification assumption is introduced. It allows getting insights on asymmetric nature of risk exposures and confirms the presence of nonlinearities across all the styles. Practical implementation of the proposed nonlinear model for the purpose of hedge fund replication is a topic for further research.

DISCUSSION QUESTIONS

1. Academic research suggests that hedge fund alpha is diminishing and that alpha does not exist for certain hedge fund styles. Explain why replication of hedge fund returns may still makes sense.
2. Identify and discuss at least three advantages of hedge fund clones over direct hedge fund investing other than reducing costs.
3. Explain why nonlinearities in hedge funds' risk exposures should be expected.

4. Discuss why classical asset pricing models such as the APT are theoretically unsuitable for modeling hedge fund returns.
5. Hedge fund alpha is an abnormal return due to the superior skill of an individual hedge fund manager and cannot be cloned. Give arguments for and against this proposition.

REFERENCES

Agarwal, Vikas, and Narayan Y. Naik. 2004. "Risks and Portfolio Decisions Involving Hedge Funds." *Review of Financial Studies* 17:1, 63–98.

Amenc, Noël, Sina El Bied, and Lionel Martellini. 2003. "Predictability in Hedge Fund Returns." *Financial Analysts Journal* 59:5, 32–46.

Amenc, Noël, Lionel Martellini, Jean-Christophe Meyfredi, and Volker Ziemann. 2010. "Passive Hedge Fund Replication–Beyond the Linear Case." *European Financial Management* 16:2, 191–210.

Anson, Mark J. P. 2001. "Hedge Fund Incentive Fees and the 'Free Option'." *Journal of Alternative Investments* 4:2, 43–48.

Barès, Pierre-Antoine, Rajna Gibson, and Sebastien Gyger. 2003. "Performance in the Hedge Funds Industry." *Journal of Alternative Investments* 6:3, 25–41.

Berk, Jonathan B., and Richard C. Green. 2004. "Mutual Fund Flows and Performance in Rational Markets." *Journal of Political Economy* 112:6, 1269–1295.

Brooks, Chris, Andrew Clare, and Nick Motson. 2007. "The Gross Truth about Hedge Fund Performance and Risk: The Impact of Incentive Fees." *Journal of Financial Transformation* 24, 33–42.

Brown, Stephen J., William N. Goetzmann, and Roger G. Ibbotson. 1999. "Offshore Hedge Funds: Survival and Performance 1989–95." *Journal of Business* 72:1, 91–117.

Capocci, Daniel, and Georges Hübner. 2004. "Analysis of Hedge Fund Performance." *Journal of Empirical Finance* 11:1, 55–89.

Dichev, Ilia D., and Gwen Yu. 2011. "Higher Risk, Lower Returns: What Hedge Fund Investors Really Earn." *Journal of Financial Economics* 100:2, 248–263.

Diez De Los Rios, Antonio, and René Garcia. 2011. "Assessing and Valuing the Nonlinear Structure of Hedge Fund Returns." *Journal of Applied Econometrics* 26:2, 193–212.

Fama, Eugene F., and Kenneth R. French. 1992. "The Cross-section of Expected Stock Returns." *Journal of Finance* 47:2, 427–465.

Fama, Eugene F., and Kenneth R. French. 2010. "Luck versus Skill in the Cross-section of Mutual Fund Returns." *Journal of Finance* 65:5, 1915–1947.

Fung, William, and David A. Hsieh. 1997. "The Risk in Hedge Fund Strategies: Theory and Evidence from Trend Followers." *Review of Financial Studies* 10:2, 275–302.

Fung, William, and David A. Hsieh. 2001. "The Risk in Hedge Fund Strategies: Theory and Evidence from Trend Followers." *Review of Financial Studies* 14:2, 313–341.

Fung, William, and David A. Hsieh. 2002. "Asset-Based Style Factors for Hedge Funds." *Financial Analysts Journal* 58:5, 16–27.

Fung, William, and David A. Hsieh. 2004a. "Extracting Portable Alphas from Equity Long-Short Hedge Funds." *Journal of Investment Management* 2:4, 1–19.

Fung, William, and David A. Hsieh. 2004b. "Hedge Fund Benchmarks: A Risk-based Approach." *Financial Analysts Journal* 60:5, 65–80.

Fung, William, and David A. Hsieh. 2007a. "Hedge Fund Replication Strategies: Implications for Investors and Regulators." Banque de France, *Financial Stability Review—Special Issue on Hedge Funds* 10, 55–66.

Fung, William, and David A. Hsieh. 2007b. "Will Hedge Funds Regress Towards Index-like Products?" *Journal of Investment Management* 5:2, 46–65.

Fung, William, David A. Hsieh, Narayan Y. Naik, and Tarun Ramadorai. 2008. "Hedge Funds: Performance, Risk, and Capital Formation." *Journal of Finance* 63:4, 1777–1803.

Giamouridis, Daniel, and Sandra Paterlini. 2010. "Regular(ized) Hedge Fund Clones." *Journal of Financial Research* 33:3, 223–247.

Giannikis, Dimitrios, and Ioannis D. Vrontos. 2011. "A Bayesian Approach to Detecting Nonlinear Risk Exposures in Hedge Fund Strategies." *Journal of Banking & Finance* 35:6, 1399–1414.

Glosten, Lawrence R., and Ravi Jagannathan. 1994. "A Contingent Claim Approach to Performance Evaluation." *Journal of Empirical Finance* 1:2, 133–160.

Hasanhodzic, Jasmina, and Andrew W. Lo. 2007. "Can Hedge-Fund Returns be Replicated?: The Linear Case." *Journal of Investment Management* 5:2, 5–45.

Hastie, Trevor J., and Robert J. Tibshirani. 1990. *Generalized Additive Models*. London: Chapman and Hall.

Jaeger, Lars, 2008. *Alternative Beta Strategies and Hedge Fund Replication*. London: John Wiley & Sons, Inc.

Jensen, Michael C. 1968. "The Performance of Mutual Funds in the Period 1945–1964." *Journal of Finance* 23:2, 389–416.

Kahn, Ronald N., Matthew H. Scanlan, and Laurence B. Siegel. 2006. "Five Myths about Fees." *Journal of Portfolio Management* 32:3, 56–64.

Lhabitant, François-Serge. 2004. *Hedge Funds: Quantitative Insights*. London: John Wiley & Sons, Inc.

Liang, Bing. 1999. "On the Performance of Hedge Funds." *Financial Analysts Journal* 55:4, 72–85.

Malkiel, Burton G., and Atanu Saha. 2005. "Hedge Funds: Risk and Return." *Financial Analysts Journal* 61:6, 80–88.

Marra, Giampiero, and Simon N. Wood. 2011. "Practical Variable Selection for Generalized Additive Models." *Computational Statistics & Data Analysis* 55:7, 2372–2387.

Merton, Robert C. 1981. "On Market Timing and Investment Performance: An Equilibrium Theory of Value for Market Forecasts." *Journal of Business* 54:3, 363–406.

Naik, Narayan Y., Tarun Ramadorai, and Maria Stromqvist. 2007. "Capacity Constraints and Hedge Fund Strategy Returns." *European Financial Management* 13:2, 239–256.

Ranaldo, Angelo, and Laurent Favre. 2005. "Hedge Fund Performance and Higher-Moment Market Models." *Journal of Alternative Investments* 8:3, 37–51.

Ross, Stephen A. 1976. "The Arbitrage Theory of Capital Asset Pricing." *Journal of Economic Theory* 13:3, 341–360.

Sharpe, William F. 1964. "Capital Asset Prices: A Theory of Market Equilibrium under Conditions of Risk." *Journal of Finance* 19:3, 425–442.

Sharpe, William F. 1991. "The Arithmetic of Active Management." *Financial Analysts Journal* 47:1, 7–9.

Sharpe. William F. 1992. "Asset Allocation." *Journal of Portfolio Management* 18:2, 7–19.

Vrontos, Spyridon D., Ioannis D. Vrontos, and Daniel Giamouridis. 2008. "Hedge Fund Pricing and Model Uncertainty." *Journal of Banking & Finance* 32:5, 741–753.

Wegener, Christian, Rüdiger von Nitzsch, and Cetin Cengiz. 2010. "An Advanced Perspective on the Predictability in Hedge Fund Returns." *Journal of Banking & Finance* 34:11, 2694–2708.

ABOUT THE AUTHORS

Mikhail Tupitsyn is a PhD student in the Department of Accounting and Finance, Monash University in Clayton, Australia. He is a recipient of the Donald Cochrane

Postgraduate Research Scholarship for outstanding PhD students. Mr. Tupitsyn's current research area is asset pricing with a special interest in nonlinear asset pricing models for hedge funds. He has published and presented in conferences on statistics and probability theory. He also has industry experience in financial modelling and forecasting. Mr. Tupitsyn earned a BS and MS in Applied Mathematics from Peoples' Friendship University of Russia in Moscow.

Paul Lajbcygier holds a joint appointment as Associate Professor in the Department of Accounting and Finance and the Department of Econometrics and Business Statistics, Monash University in Clayton, Australia. Since 1995, Professor Lajbcygier has authored more than 80 academic papers and generated more than $3.1 million in government grants, industry linkage grants, and corporate payments in-kind. He has been a member of more than 10 journal editorial boards and conference program committees and supervised more than 20 Honors, Masters, and PhD students. He has won awards both for his research and teaching. Professor Lajbcygier combines extensive industry and academic experience in investments and has provided investment advice to various funds managers, banks, and hedge funds. Professor Lajbcygier earned a BS in Physics and Computer Science from the University of Melbourne, an MS in Finance from the Royal Melbourne Institute of Technology, and a PhD in Computational Finance from Monash University in Melbourne.

ACKNOWLEDGMENTS

The authors would like to acknowledge an Australian Centre for Financial Studies Grant.

CHAPTER 28

Fund-of-Funds: A Tale of Two Fees

KARTIK PATEL, CFA*
Vice President, Risk and Technology, Prisma Capital Partners LP

INTRODUCTION

Pension plans and other institutional investors typically have the majority of their investments in traditional stock and bond holdings. Alternative asset programs may include investments such as commodities, private equity, venture capital, hedge funds, and others. Institutional investors can gain exposure to hedge funds by direct investing or by investing through a fund-of-funds (FoFs). FoFs invest in a portfolio of hedge funds and diversify the risks associated with a single hedge fund. A FoFs portfolio can broadly allocate to different hedge fund strategies or can be concentrated in one or more strategies. A multistrategy FoFs can take a view on hedge fund strategies that will perform well in a given economic environment and may choose to overweight them relative to those that they forecast will underperform. FoFs select managers whom they think will outperform their respective peer group within a strategy. FoFs are also responsible for conducting operational due-diligence on hedge funds before including them in a portfolio. FoFs charge fees for their services. Management and performance fees are typically 0.5 to 1 percent and 5 to 10 percent, respectively. These fees are in addition to what underlying hedge funds charge.

In the past decade, investments in hedge funds have increased dramatically. The increased popularity of hedge funds, especially among institutional investors, is due to their ability to generate high risk-adjusted returns while at the same time having a low correlation to traditional asset classes such as stocks and bonds.

According to Hedge Fund Research's (2011) year-end report, total assets now represent more than $2 trillion. Assets managed by hedge funds were around $490 billion in 2000, but had grown fourfold by the end of 2011. Over the same time period, assets managed by FoFs increased from $83 billion in 2000 to $629 billion in 2011, a sevenfold increase. During the liquidity crisis in 2008, assets

* The views and opinions expressed are solely those of Mr. Patel and in no way reflect the views of Prisma Capital Partners LP, its affiliates, or representatives. This material is not intended to provide, and should not be relied upon for, investment advice or recommendations. Readers are urged to seek professional advice before making any investments.

under management (AUM) decreased for both hedge funds and FoFs. Post-crisis, hedge fund assets reached historical highs due to an increase in inflows. For the FoFs industry, however, the inflows have not been as strong and the total assets as of 2012 are below the peak reached in 2007 ($798 billion). FoFs now account for 31 percent of the total assets managed by hedge funds, lower than their 42 percent representation in 2006. This trend indicates that investors in the past few years have preferred to invest directly in hedge funds.

Investing via FoFs gives investors exposure to a diversified set of hedge fund managers following different strategies, such as long/short equity and, convertible arbitrage, etc. A majority of FoFs have a diversified approach, whereby investors invest in multiple hedge fund strategies. Yet, some FoFs are strategy specific.

The remainder of the chapter includes an introduction to hedge funds, including a discussion on investment styles and strategies. The subsequent section illustrates how portfolios of hedge funds are synthetically created using hedge fund performance data. The impact of the number of hedge funds on portfolio risk and return is analyzed in a simulation study. The next to last section discusses peer-group analysis of actual FoFs performance data. The final section offers a summary and conclusions.

Hedge Fund Asset Class

This section introduces the hedge fund asset class with a focus on its investment style and trading strategies. Because hedge fund managers are not tied to market-based benchmarks, they are attractive alternatives for institutional investors who are seeking an opportunity to incorporate strategy allocation in their investment selections.

Investment Style

Hedge funds invest in a combination of asset classes, including traditional asset classes such as stocks and bonds and alternative investments such as commodities and distressed bonds. Even if a hedge fund invests only in traditional asset classes, its investment style may include the use of leverage, options, and shorting in which long-only managers do not engage. Using leverage, options, and shorting can make the strategy more risky but it can also offer the potential of better performance.

Hedge fund managers generate higher returns using three major investment skills:

- *Security selection.* Security selection refers to the manager's ability to identify overvalued and undervalued securities and to take long positions in the former and short positions in the latter.
- *Variable risk.* Variable risk concerns the manager's ability to increase exposure (hence risk) ahead of rising markets and reduce exposure ahead of falling markets.
- *Use of leverage.* The manager creates leverage by using margins, futures, and options to magnify the fund's gains based on expressed strategies.

Exhibit 28.1 DJCS Long/Short Index Rolling Beta to the S&P 500 Index
The exhibit shows the rolling monthly beta of the DJCS Long/Short Hedge Fund Index against the S&P 500 Index using a window length of 18 months based on a monthly time series from January 1994 to December 2011. The variability of beta reflects the risk management and market-timing skills of hedge funds.

Exhibit 28.1 shows the rolling beta exposure to the S&P 500 Index (computed over an 18-month window) of the Dow Jones Credit Suisse Long/Short Hedge Fund Index. As the exhibit shows, long/short managers vary their beta over different market conditions. For example, following the initial shocks of financial crisis of 2007–2008, hedge fund managers reduced their beta exposure and kept it low for a considerable period. To understand the risk-return characteristics of hedge fund returns as a function of market factors (e.g., equity and credit indices), Agrawal and Naik (2004) demonstrate the use of linear multifactor regression models.

Hedge Fund Strategies

The following are different investment strategies that hedge funds employ to exploit market inefficiencies. This strategy classification is later used in a simulation case study.

- *Convertible arbitrage.* These funds aim to make profit via the purchase of convertible bonds with simultaneous shorting of equity when a pricing error exists in the conversion factor (i.e., the number of shares for which each convertible bond can be converted.)
- *Credit distressed.* The investment process of these funds focuses on credit instruments of companies that are trading at discounts as a result of financial or operational distress.

- *Event-multistrategy.* These funds invest in credit and/or equity of companies involved in various transactions, including mergers, restructuring, and distress.
- *Equity market neutral.* These funds take equity positions on both long and short positions while keeping the overall market-neutral exposure.
- *Fixed-income arbitrage.* These funds tend to exploit the pricing inefficiencies in related fixed-income instruments.
- *Global macro.* Managers apply a global, top-down approach to identify how macroeconomic events may affect equities, currencies, commodities, and fixed income.
- *Long/short equity.* These funds invest in both long and short positions in equities. Strategies may be focused on specific sectors or regions.
- *Managed futures.* These funds use systematic programs that rely on historical price data to identify market trends.
- *Multistrategy.* These funds allocate capital to different hedge fund strategies based on perceived opportunities.
- *Short bias.* These funds are equity focused and mainly short companies with weak fundamentals.

Manager Selection versus Strategy Allocation

Long-only managers invest in traditional asset classes either actively or passively. In both cases, their benchmark is typically an asset class index, such as the S&P 500 Index. As a result of being tied to a benchmark, long-only managers' performance is tied to the index performance, and returns exhibit little dispersion among managers using the same strategy. Conversely, hedge fund managers typically are not tied to an asset class–dependent market index because they pursue an absolute returns strategy in an attempt to generate returns in a variety of market conditions. Most hedge fund strategies use multiple asset classes (e.g., a global macro strategy invests in equities, bonds, and commodities), and even the ones that are asset-class focused, such as long/short equity strategies, maintain a variable exposure (which may become negative) to equity markets. As a result, a market neutral index or a risk-free rate is typically used as a benchmark. As a result of not being tied to any specific asset class, hedge fund managers experience higher dispersion even when using the same strategy (Reddy, Brady, and Patel, 2007). The authors point out that strategy allocation dominates manager selection in traditional asset classes whereas the opposite is true for hedge funds.

Role of Hedge Funds in Strategy Allocation for Institutional Investors

To compare the performance of traditional asset classes versus hedge funds, the S&P 500 Index is used as a proxy for the long-only, equity investment and the Barclays Aggregate Index is used as a proxy for the fixed-income investment. The DJCS Hedge Fund Index serves as a proxy for the hedge fund asset class. The DJCS Hedge Fund Index is a noninvestable index consisting of an asset-weighted composition of several hundred hedge funds using different strategies.

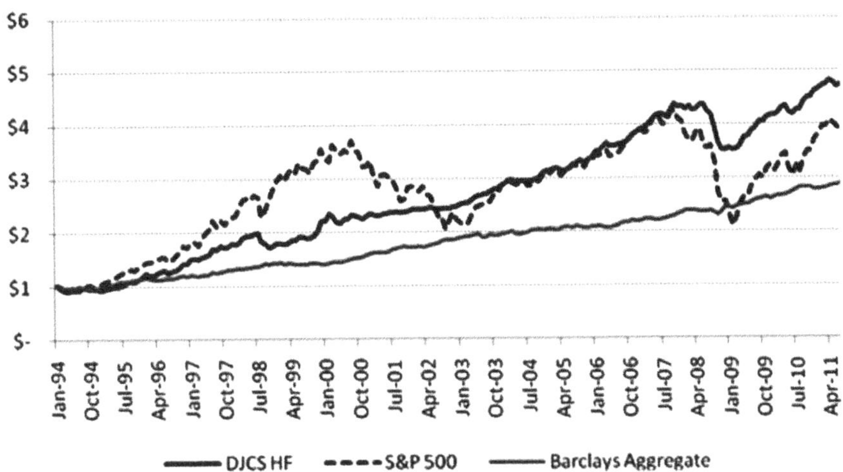

Exhibit 28.2 Growth of $1 Invested in Different Asset Classes
This exhibit shows the growth of $1 invested in the DJCS Hedge Fund Index, S&P 500 Index, and Barclays Aggregate Index. For the period ending December 2011, the initial investment earned the highest amount from hedge funds.

Exhibit 28.2 shows the growth of $1 invested in the DJCS Hedge Fund Index versus the S&P 500 Index (for equity) and the Barclays Aggregate Index (for fixed income). The hedge fund index performance is superior to the traditional asset classes since the inception of the DJCS index in January 1994.

Exhibit 28.3 shows the annualized statistics of the asset classes. The hedge fund asset class provides equity-like returns with about half the volatility of equities. Allocating to hedge funds in addition to equity and bonds reduces the overall risk of the portfolio with the upside of increasing the overall performance.

NUMBER OF FUNDS REQUIRED IN A HEDGE FUND PORTFOLIO

Selecting the funds to include in the portfolio is obviously very critical to the portfolio's performance, as is deciding on the number of funds needed in the portfolio. Since Markowitz (1952), portfolio diversification has been a traditional way of

Exhibit 28.3 Annualized Performance Statistics since 1994

	DJCS Hedge Fund Index (%)	S&P 500 Total Return Index (%)	Barclays Aggregate Index (%)
Returns	9	8	6
Volatility	8	16	4

The exhibit provides the annualized returns and volatility of hedge fund, equity, and bond indices. Hedge funds are capable of generating high risk-adjusted returns similar to equity-like returns, with about half the volatility as measured by annualizing monthly performance data.

reducing risk. In particular, Statman (1987) explores the optimal number of securities in a portfolio for equity portfolios. Lhabitant and Learned (2002) and Amo, Hardasty, and Hillion (2007) perform a similar analysis for hedge funds. Increasing the number of securities in a portfolio results in lower volatility if the securities have low correlation with each other, but the price of lower volatility is usually lower return. This chapter investigates the appropriate number of hedge funds in a portfolio from the perspective of an institutional diversified FoFs investment management mandate. A FoFs typically has a hurdle rate (which is usually a risk-free benchmark such as a 3-month Treasury bill, or T-bill) over which its portfolios have to perform before collecting a performance fee. With the objective of maximizing the excess performance, the chapter examines the impact of portfolio size (*M*) on portfolio performance and presents the results of an empirical study between 2007 and 2011. Although the performance in this period (especially 2008) may not be representative of future performance, the simulation analysis aims to study the impact of the number of funds on a portfolio's performance. As shown later, as *M* increases, the probability of outperforming the benchmark increases, while, at the same time, the probability of generating higher returns decreases.

Universe

Managers in the DJCS Hedge Fund Index comprise the universe under consideration in this study. The reason for selecting the DJCS index is that it has strict inclusion requirements that are similar to the requirements of a typical institutional investor. For example, to be considered for inclusion in the DJCS index requires the following: (1) a fund must have AUM of at least $50 million, (2) a fund must have at least a one-year track record, and (3) firms must have year-end, audited financial statements.

The universe is created by identifying the funds in the DJCS Hedge Fund Index from the Lipper Trading Advisor Selection System (TASS) and Hedge Fund Research (HFR) hedge fund databases. Only funds with full five-year track records from 2007 to 2011 in the index (totaling 213) are considered in the universe. Both survivorship bias and backfill bias exist in the composition of the universe. *Survivorship bias* arises due to exclusion of funds that fail during the sample period and are no longer part of the index. *Backfill bias* arises when funds report historical returns (before entry data) when they start reporting to a database. Estimates of survivorship biases in hedge fund performance range from 2 to 3 percent on an annualized basis, while estimates of backfill biases range from 1.4 to 1.9 percent on an annualized basis (Brown, Goetzman, and Ibbotson, 1999; Park, Brown, and Goetzman, 1999; Fung and Hseih, 2000). The analysis using the constructed universe is not adjusted for any of the biases. Exhibit 28.4 shows the strategy constitution of the universe, which indicates that the universe is skewed by the number of long/short managers, who represent 42 percent of the universe.

Exhibit 28.5 tabulates the average returns of the strategy by investing equally among managers within each strategy. If an investment occurs in all 213 funds equally, the resulting return is identified as "All Funds." Diversifying across different strategies by investing equally in all funds within each strategy and then investing equal dollar amounts per strategy, the resulting returns appear as "All Strategies." The "All Strategies" return for the year 2008 is 0 percent while the DJCS Hedge Fund Index return is −19 percent. One reason for the disparity is that

Exhibit 28.4 The Strategy Constitution of the Universe

	Strategy	Number of Funds	Percent
1	Convertible Arbitrage	11	5
2	Event–Credit/Distressed	12	6
3	Event–Multi Strategy	22	10
4	Equity Market Neutral	12	6
5	Fixed Income	10	5
6	Global Macro	19	9
7	Long Short	89	42
8	Managed Futures	19	9
9	Multi Strategy	15	7
10	Short Bias	4	2
	Total	213	100

The exhibit shows the composition of the universe of hedge funds used in the simulation study. The universe consists of constituent funds of the DJCS Hedge Fund Index (as of December 2011) whose performance data are available in the TASS database.

"All Strategies" is generated by equally weighting all strategies, while the hedging strategies (managed futures and short bias), which performed very well in 2008, are over weighted compared to the actual index. Another reason for the disparity could be because of survivorship bias reflected in the way the universe is constructed in that only the current set of managers in the index is considered.

Instead of investing in all funds, the question is whether portfolios of smaller sizes can be constructed that could potentially yield better performance. This question is addressed by randomly creating portfolios of different sizes. The following section presents the methodology and results.

Exhibit 28.5 Strategy Returns

Strategy	2007	2008	2009	2010	2011	2007–11
Convertible Arbitrage	10	−18	60	10	0	10
Event—Credit/Distressed	15	−21	23	9	−3	4
Event—Multi Strategy	46	−20	34	15	−6	11
Equity Market Neutral	8	3	10	2	4	5
Fixed Income	15	8	42	15	4	16
Global Macro	24	8	8	8	4	10
Long Short	16	−17	26	12	−9	4
Managed Futures	20	30	−5	12	−4	10
Multi Strategy	14	−18	29	13	−5	5
Short Bias	8	45	−30	−22	−2	−4
All Strategies	18	0	20	7	−2	7
All funds	19	−8	23	11	−4	7

The exhibit shows the yearly performance of the funds in the universe (in Exhibit 28.4) by strategy. The funds are equally weighted within their respective strategies. "All Strategies" performance is computed by equally weighting the performance of all strategies. "All Funds" performance is computed by equally weighting the performance of all funds (regardless of their strategies).

Simulation Methodology

Patel (2008) illustrates the use of simple random sampling as well as stratified sampling to simulate portfolios of hedge funds. Stratified sampling is used to simulate performance of a typical FoFs portfolio that is diversified across different strategies. Using stratified sampling, the same number of funds is randomly drawn from each strategy. A naive strategy allocation is assumed that would invest equally in all strategies.

Although one can select M-fund portfolios from a population of size N in N-choose-M possible ways ($^{N}C_{M}$), the sample size is restricted to 1,000. The construction algorithm proceeds for each year between 2007 and 2011 as follows:

1. For a given M, draw M/10 ($M = 10$) funds from each strategy within the universe and equally weight them to create a portfolio. Create 1,000 such randomly generated portfolios.
2. Select the year 2007.
3. Calculate the annualized returns.
4. Determine the average and the 5th and 95th percentiles of 1,000 portfolio returns.
5. Repeat steps 3 and 4 for each of the remaining years from 2008 to 2011.
6. Repeat steps 1 to 5 for different values of M.

Simulation Results

Exhibit 28.6 shows the 95th percentile (5 percent probability) and the 5th percentile (95 percent probability) of performance of portfolios of different sizes. For a given year, as M increases, the 95th percentile decreases. Conversely, as M increases, the 5th percentile point increases. The implication is that the higher the value of M, the higher the minimum returns (with 95 percent probability) that can be guaranteed. At the same time, the higher the value of M, the lower the range of returns that can be achieved.

Exhibit 28.7 presents the same information graphically. Observing that midpoint returns for different portfolio sizes are the same for a given year, which, in turn, corresponds to the "All Strategies" returns in Exhibit 28.5, is not surprising. This relationship is a consequence of the central limit theorem. According to the *central limit theorem*, if S_M is an average of M mutually independent random variables drawn from a parent population, then the distribution function of S_M is approximated by a normal distribution function whose mean converges to the parent population mean. What this implies is that the mean returns of all randomly generated portfolios of different sizes (M) is the same and is equal to the hedge fund universe's "All Strategies" average.

The benchmark for a typical FoFs portfolio ranges from Treasury bill to Treasury bill + 5 percent. A spread (up to 5 percent) is typically applied to the Treasury bill rate because the Treasury bill rate can fluctuate through different years, and the extra spread allows holding the benchmark at a certain level when the Treasury bill rate is very low. Exhibit 28.8 shows three different benchmarks and their annual performance. Consider a hypothetical benchmark of Treasury

Exhibit 28.6 The 95th and 5th percentile Returns of Portfolios of Size M

Panel A. The 95th Percentile Returns of Portfolios of Size M

M	2007 (%)	2008 (%)	2009 (%)	2010 (%)	2011 (%)
10	43	9	33	12	4
20	39	7	28	11	2
30	34	5	27	10	1
40	30	4	25	10	1

Panel B. The 5th Percentile Returns of Portfolios of Size M

M	2007 (%)	2008 (%)	2009 (%)	2010 (%)	2011 (%)
10	7	−10	10	3	−7
20	9	−6	12	4	−5
30	10	−5	14	5	−4
40	11	−4	15	5	−4

Panel A shows the 95th return percentile (equivalent to 0.05 probability) of 1,000 simulated portfolios for different years. For each portfolio size (M) and year, 1,000 of portfolios are randomly generated. Each portfolio, in turn, is generated by randomly selecting an equal number of funds from 10 strategies. For example for $M = 20$, two funds are randomly picked from each strategy that are equally weighted to form a single portfolio, and, in a similar fashion, 1,000 portfolios are simulated. For a given year, with a decrease in M, the 95th percentile increases, implying a lower-sized portfolio offers high return potential at the 0.05 probability.
Panel B shows the 5th return percentile (equivalent to 0.95 probability) of 1,000 simulated portfolios for different years. For a given year, with an increase in M, the 5th percentile increases, implying that a larger-sized portfolio offers a higher return as compared to a smaller-sized portfolio with 0.95 probability.

bill + 2.5 percent and assume the FoFs manager puts more emphasis on meeting the benchmark rather than exceeding the benchmark by a huge amount.

Exhibit 28.7 shows the performance of portfolios of different sizes together with the hypothetical benchmark:

- In 2007, portfolios of all sizes are able to outperform the benchmark with 95 percent probability.
- In 2008, portfolios with 10, 20, and 30 funds are able to outperform the benchmark with more than 5 percent probability, with the highest probability achieved by portfolios of 10 funds (20 percent probability).
- In 2009, portfolios of all sizes are able to outperform the benchmark.
- In 2010, portfolios of all sizes are able to outperform the benchmark with 95 percent probability.
- In 2011, only portfolios consisting of 10 holdings are able to outperform the benchmark with more than 5 percent probability

Selecting a portfolio of 10 funds would outperform the benchmark but with a low probability in 2008 and 2011, and with higher probability for the remaining years. Also a portfolio of size 10 would potentially result in lower performance

Panel A. Portfolio Performance of Varying Size for 2007

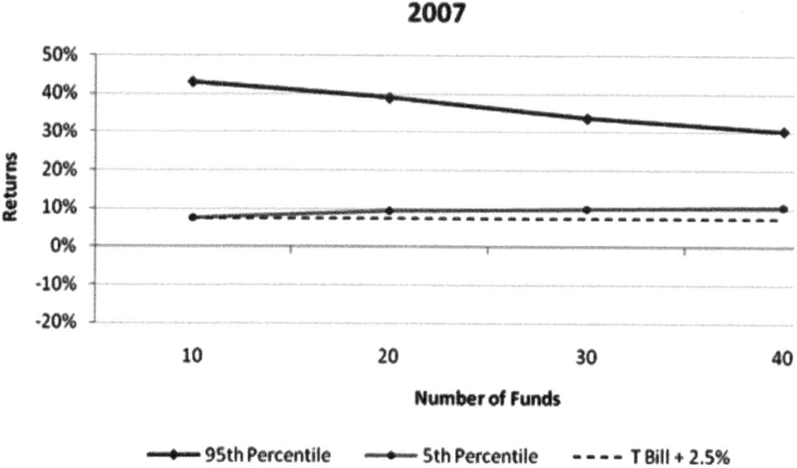

Panel B. Portfolio Performance of Varying Size for 2008

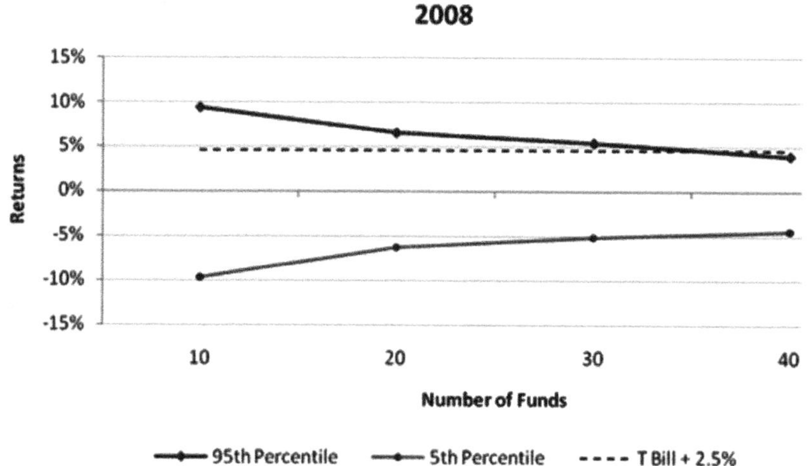

Exhibit 28.7 Portfolio Performance of Varying Size for 2007 through 2011
Panels A through E show the 95th and 5th percentile portfolio performance as a function of the number of managers. The annual performance of the benchmark (T-bill + 2.5%) is shown as a dashed line.

than what is guaranteed by portfolios of higher size (for example, 7 percent for a portfolio of 10 funds compared to 11 percent for a portfolio of 40 funds with 95 percent probability in the year 2007). A FoFs manager may choose to invest in a higher number of funds by forgoing a performance fee for 2008 and 2011, but with a guarantee of a higher performance fee for the rest of the years. Considering a benchmark with lower returns such as Treasury bill returns would result in a higher number of managers which would outperform the benchmark.

Exhibit 28.9 shows the average correlation among funds within a strategy and among all funds year by year. An increase in correlation above 0.2 exists among

Panel C. Portfolio Performance of Varying Size for 2009

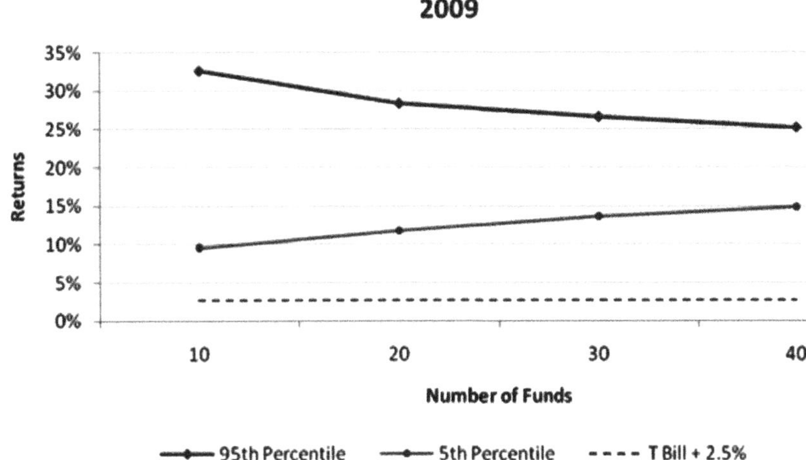

Panel D. Portfolio Performance of Varying Size for 2010

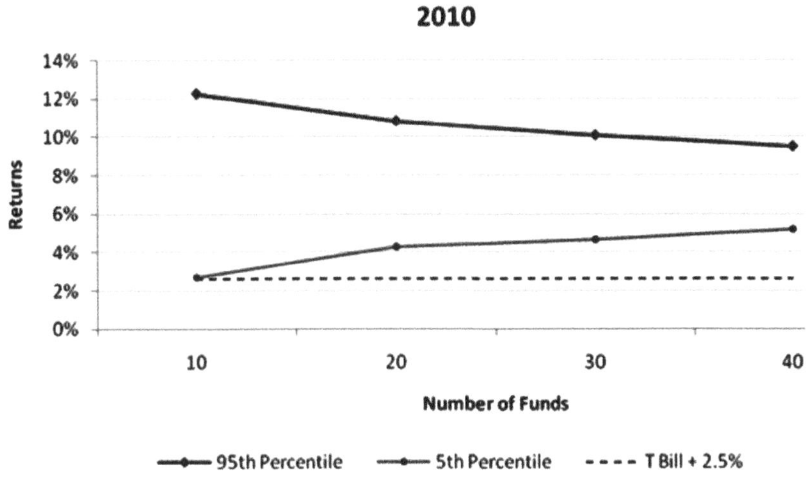

Exhibit 28.7 *(Continued)*

funds in 2008, 2010, and 2011 corresponds to the decrease in range of returns between the 95th percentile and 5th percentile performance for those years.

Zero-Turnover Portfolios

Due to *lock-up* (i.e., the initial time frame in which investors are not allowed to redeem) and liquidity restrictions in hedge fund investments (lock-up periods can vary from 1 to 3 years; liquidity can be monthly, quarterly or on an annual basis), low turnover of funds may exist in a given portfolio. Thus, results should not be analyzed each year on a stand-alone basis but instead should consider portfolio performance in subsequent years. To keep the analysis simple, the same funds are

Panel E. Portfolio Performance of Varying Size for 2011

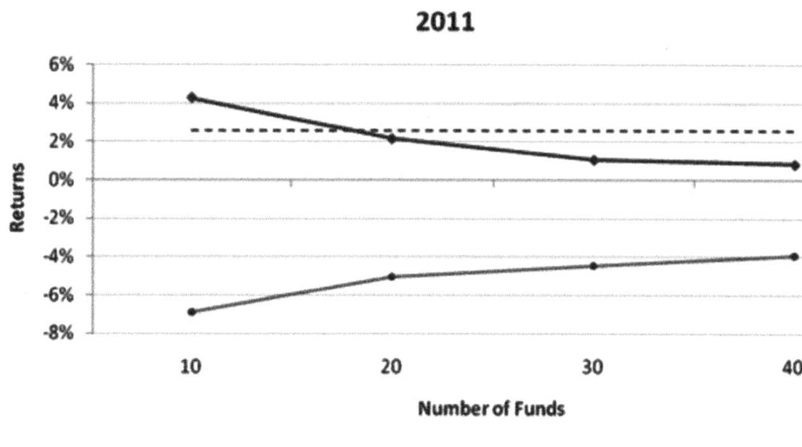

Exhibit 28.7 *(Continued)*

held in the portfolios for all five years. At the beginning of each year, the allocations in the funds are adjusted to keep them equally weighted.

For example, if a fund consisting of 10 funds can achieve a performance of 33 percent in 2009 (being above 95th percentile or equivalently a 5 percent probability event), it may not end up in the top 95th percentile in 2010. In fact, considering that the performance of a hedge fund is independent from one year to the next (i.e., if no persistency in performance is evident from year to year), the probability of a portfolio being in 95th percentile for two consecutive years reduces to 0.25 percent (5 percent squared).

The performance of the 1,000 portfolios can be considered for all the five years combined. Exhibit 28.10 shows the annualized performance of portfolios of different sizes for the five years. Portfolios of 40 funds perform better than portfolios of 10 funds at the 95 percent probability (5th percentile) as well as the 50 percent probability.

As Panel A of Exhibit 28.11 shows, portfolios consisting of 40 funds can guarantee returns in excess of 200 basis points per year compared to portfolios of 10 funds at a 95 percent confidence level. Having guaranteed the minimum return, upward potential exists for generating higher return at lower probability. As

Exhibit 28.8 Benchmarks using the 3-Month Treasury Bill

Benchmarks	2007 (%)	2008 (%)	2009 (%)	2010 (%)	2011 (%)
Treasury bill	5.0	2.1	0.2	0.1	0.1
Treasury bill + 2.5%	7.5	4.6	2.7	2.6	2.6
Treasury bill + 5.0%	10.0	7.1	5.2	5.1	5.1

The exhibit shows three different benchmarks starting with a 3-month Treasury bill as the base rate and then adding 250 bps.

Exhibit 28.9 Average Correlation

Strategy	2007	2008	2009	2010	2011
Convertible Arbitrage	**0.6**	**0.7**	**0.5**	**0.6**	**0.5**
Event–Credit/Distressed	0.2	0.3	0.4	**0.5**	**0.6**
Event–Multi Strategy	0.4	0.4	0.3	**0.5**	**0.7**
Equity Market Neutral	0.0	0.1	0.0	0.1	0.0
Fixed Income	0.1	0.2	0.0	0.2	0.1
Global Macro	0.1	0.2	0.1	0.1	0.1
Long Short	0.3	0.4	0.3	**0.5**	0.4
Managed Futures	0.3	0.4	0.4	**0.5**	0.4
Multi Strategy	0.2	0.4	0.2	0.3	0.4
Short Bias	**0.8**	**0.9**	**0.8**	**0.9**	**0.8**
All Funds	0.18	0.21	0.15	0.26	0.22

This exhibit shows the average monthly cross-sectional correlation within a strategy. For each year, a pair-wise correlation is computed between funds. For 2010 and 2011, the correlation coefficient was high. The "All Funds" correlation coefficient is the average cross-sectional correlation across all funds. Correlation values greater than or equal to 0.5 are indicated in bold.

discussed earlier, the upward potential is lower for portfolios of 40 funds than portfolios of 10 funds.

For a FoFs, the benchmark also serves as a hurdle rate that must be cleared before a performance fee is applied. The concept of a *high-water mark* is also used when the performance fee is applied only if the year-end value of the portfolio is higher than the historical high achieved in prior years. Considering an AUM fee of 1 percent and a 10 percent performance fee charged by a FoFs manager, Panel B of Exhibit 28.11 shows the total fees charged by a FoFs for an investment of $100 over the five-year period for portfolios of 10 funds and 40 funds.

Panel A shows the total return of portfolios of 10 funds and 40 funds at different probability levels. Portfolios of size 10 fare lower than portfolios of size 40 at higher probability, but perform better with lower probability. The graph shows the total fees earned by a FoFs for a $100 initial investment over a period of five years, from 2007 to 2011.

Whether an investment in hedge funds is made directly or indirectly via a FoFs, the graphs in Exhibit 28.11 follow the same trend as far as portfolio size is concerned. Selecting a smaller number of funds (e.g., 10 funds), offers a higher return potential with a lower probability (25 percent). Selecting a higher number of funds

Exhibit 28.10 Portfolio Performance for Five Years

Percentile	10 (%)	20 (%)	30 (%)	40 (%)
95	14.4	12.9	11.4	10.9
75	9.3	9.3	9.0	9.0
50	7.6	7.8	7.9	7.9
25	6.0	6.6	7.0	7.2
5	4.0	5.1	5.9	6.1

This exhibit shows the annualized performance of portfolios of different sizes at different percentiles.

Panel A. Comparing Portfolio Performance of 10 Funds and 40 Funds

Returns

16%
14%
12%
10%
8%
6%
4%
2%
0%

95% 75% 50% 25% 5%

Probability

- - - M = 10 ——— M = 40

Panel B. Comparing Fees Earned for Portfolios of Size 10 and 40

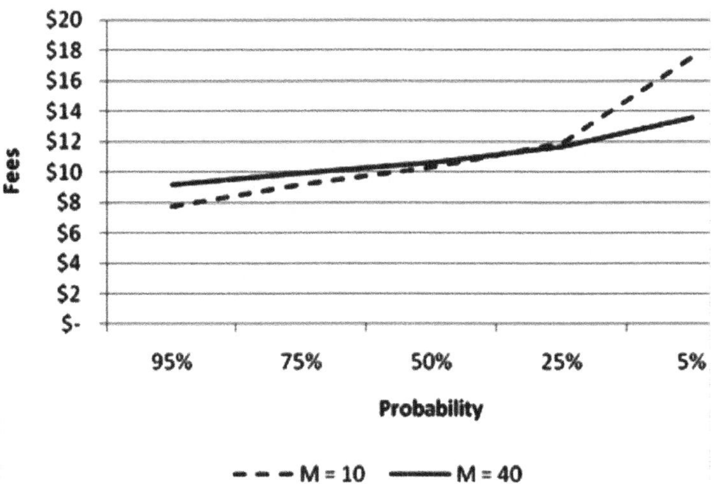

Exhibit 28.11 Comparing Portfolio Performance and Fees of 10 Funds and 40 Funds

(e.g., 40 funds) guarantees a higher return at a higher probability (50 percent to 95 percent) but the return potential (at lower probability of 25 percent) is limited. A similar trend is observed for earning fees by a FoFs manager: choosing a higher number of funds guarantees higher fees earned at a high probability, at the same time a smaller number of funds offer higher fee potential.

Other Portfolio Considerations

Although portfolio construction is not typically based on random selection of funds, the empirical study of randomly generated portfolios illustrates the range of possible returns as a function of the number of managers. The following factors influence the number of managers in a portfolio:

1. *Utility function of the FoFs manager.* An increase in the number of funds increases the returns that can be achieved with a higher probability (95 percent). At the same time, increasing the number of funds restricts the higher end of returns that a manager can achieve with a smaller set of funds. In a difficult year such as 2008, only portfolios with a small number of funds beat the benchmark (that, too, with a low probability). A FoFs manager may be willing to forgo earning a performance fee in a difficult year but with a guarantee of earning performance fees in a normal year by selecting a higher number of managers.
2. *Strategy allocation.* The empirical study assumes a naive strategy allocation. A strategy allocation based on correctly forecasting underperforming/outperforming strategies and allocating accordingly will achieve better performance than by equally weighting all strategies. All else equal, a better performing strategy allocation would necessitate a lower number of managers to be included in the portfolio.
3. *Manager selection.* Manager selection has a major impact on portfolio performance as Reddy et al. (2007) show. A FoFs manager who can predict and overweight outperforming managers can achieve better performance. Superior manager selection would imply a portfolio with a lower number of managers could still meet the benchmark.
4. *Rebalancing.* The simulation study used the same portfolio composition for the entire five-year period. An investor (or a FoFs manager) has the opportunity to rebalance the portfolio (via strategy allocation or manager selection), which can lead to better performance. All else equal, a better rebalancing investment decision would necessitate a lower number of managers to be included in the portfolio.
5. *Survivorship bias.* As mentioned previously, the study considers only live funds. If such losses are considered, it would affect portfolios of smaller sizes more so than those of larger sizes. For example, a loss of −20 percent would result in 2 percent loss in a 10-fund portfolio as opposed to 0.5 percent loss in a 40-fund portfolio.

FUND-OF-FUNDS UNIVERSE

The previous section examined the performance of a FoFs portfolios created synthetically via simulation. This section looks at an available FoFs database. Exhibit 28.12 compares the yearly performance of two hedge fund indices—the DJCS Hedge Fund Index and a HFR hedge fund index with that of a HFR FOFs index from 2000 to 2011. The DJCS Hedge Fund Index is an asset-weighted noninvestable index; the HFR hedge fund index is an equal-weighted noninvestable index of several hundred hedge funds reporting to the HFR database.

The HFR FOFs index is an equally weighted index of different FoFs reporting to the HFR database. As Exhibit 28.12 shows, the performance of the DJCS Hedge Fund Index and the HFR hedge fund index track each other for most of the time of the comparison. What is more striking is the lower performance by the FoFs index

Exhibit 28.12 Performance of Hedge Fund Indices

	Hedge Fund Index		FoFs Index
Year	**DJCS (%)**	**HFR (%)**	**HFR (%)**
2000	5	5	4
2001	4	5	3
2002	3	−1	1
2003	15	20	12
2004	10	9	7
2005	8	9	8
2006	14	13	10
2007	13	10	10
2008	−19	−19	−21
2009	19	20	11
2010	11	10	6
2011	−3	−5	−6

This exhibit shows yearly performance of different hedge fund and FoFs indices. The DCJS is an asset-weighted hedge fund index; the HFR hedge fund index is an equal-weighted index of hedge funds; and the HFR FoFs composite index is an equal-weighted index of FoFs.

as compared to the hedge fund indices. For example, in 2009, the HFR FoFs index yields an 11 percent return, while the hedge fund indices show a much higher yield. The DJCS Hedge Fund Index performed 20 percent and the HFR hedge fund index performed 19 percent. Similarly in 2010, the FoFs index shows returns of 6 percent, and the hedge fund indices returns are much higher. The DJCS Hedge Fund Index performed 11 percent and the HFR hedge fund index performed 10 percent.

Two important observations can be made at this point:

1. The FoFs index is an equally weighted index of about 800 funds that represents a fund of fund of funds (F3) and not a single FoFs.
2. The hedge fund index is closer to the performance of a FoFs portfolio, but it is over-representative because it contains several hundred hedge funds, which is more than what a typical FoFs portfolio needs (as illustrated in the previous section).

About 1,600 FoFs report to the HFR database with data that have been updated through the end of 2011. These FoFs belong to more than 300 distinct managers. A manager could have multiple funds of different strategies or could have different share classes that are reported separately.

As of February 2012, about 800 fund-of-hedge funds were part of HFRI FoFs index. Instead of looking at the average performance of FoFs (as illustrated in Exhibit 28.12), analyzing the performance of its constituents is worthwhile. Exhibit 28.13 shows the performance of the current index constituents in different years. For each year the performance is separated out in different percentiles.

Because the reported FoFs performance data are net of performance and management fees, the results may seem lower than the simulated portfolio

Exhibit 28.13 Fund-of-Funds Performance in Different Percentiles

Year	5th Percentile (%)	25th Percentile (%)	50th Percentile (%)	75th Percentile (%)	95th Percentile (%)
2000	−14	5	11	15	25
2001	−5	2	6	9	16
2002	−6	−1	2	5	10
2003	4	8	11	15	28
2004	2	5	7	10	14
2005	2	6	8	11	19
2006	5	9	11	14	22
2007	3	8	11	16	29
2008	−37	−26	−20	−14	4
2009	−3	7	12	18	32
2010	−2	3	6	8	14
2011	−14	−8	−4	−2	3

The exhibit shows different performance percentile by year of FoFs.

performance. Comparing 95th percentile performance of simulated portfolios in Exhibit 28.6 to the 95th percentile of FoFs data in Exhibit 28.13 suggests that FoFs have about 30 to 40 managers. Comparing the 5th percentile data, the simulated performance is much higher in 2008. This finding may be due to the fact that actual FoFs are typically not overweighting the hedging strategies (managed futures and short bias) as applied by the simulation methodology.

Exhibit 28.14 shows the interquartile range (IQR) of fund-of-hedge funds performance. The first IQR plots the difference between 50th percentile and 25th percentile, and the second IQR plots the difference between 75th percentile and 25th percentile. This exhibit shows that investors investing in a fund in the 50th percentile instead of the 25th percentile would realize a performance gain of about 200 bps per year. In the same way, investors investing in a 75th percentile fund would realize a performance gain of around 600 bps per year.

Derman (2007) finds persistency in hedge fund performance. This persistency should flow through to a portfolio of hedge funds, implying that FoFs should also exhibit persistency as long as the turnover of hedge funds in the portfolio is low. The challenge for investors is to find FoFs managers who can consistently stay in the upper quartile.

Exhibit 28.15 shows the average correlation among FoFs for different years. The average correlation coefficient has typically been high for most years (> 0.5) implying little diversification benefit by including more FoFs in a portfolio.

SUMMARY AND CONCLUSIONS

FoFs represent about 31 percent of the total assets managed by hedge funds, which is lower than the historical peak of 42 percent reached in 2006. Investors criticize the double layer of fees that FoFs managers charge. Thus, many investors prefer to invest directly with hedge funds.

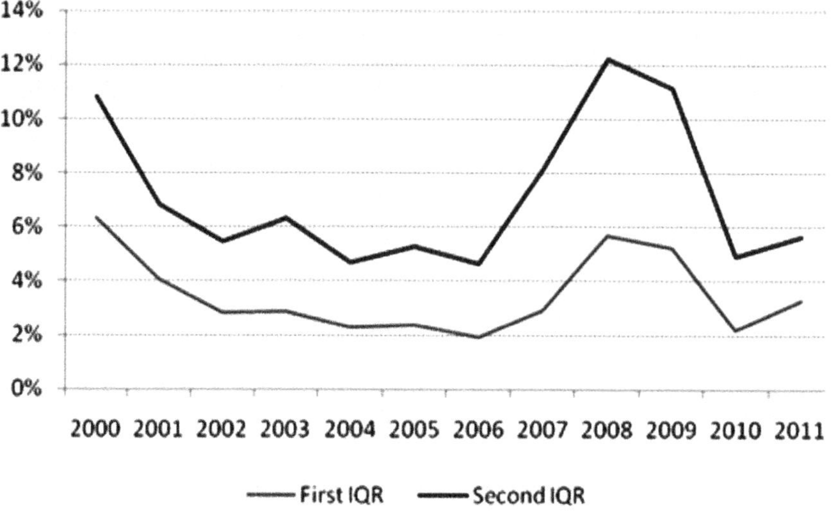

Exhibit 28.14 Interquartile Range of FoFs Performance

The exhibit shows the interquartile (IQR) performance in the FoFs universe by year. For example, a 6 percent first IQR in 2000 means that the difference between the 50th percentile and 25th percentile is 6 percent. Similarly, an 11 percent second IQR in 2000 means that the difference between the 75th percentile and 25th percentile is 11 percent.

The Madoff scandal highlights the importance of detailed due diligence. The Madoff investment scandal broke in December 2008 when Bernard Madoff admitted that the wealth management arm of his business was an elaborate *Ponzi scheme.* As such, Madoff used capital inflows from new investors to meet payments due to existing investors. The original estimated size of loss based on account balances was around $64 billion. A fraction of investments was made via fraudulent

Exhibit 28.15 Average Correlation of Fund-of-Funds

Year	N	Average Correlation
2000	212	0.46
2001	244	0.25
2002	296	0.38
2003	353	0.44
2004	425	**0.69**
2005	481	**0.73**
2006	542	**0.73**
2007	602	**0.65**
2008	651	**0.63**
2009	697	0.44
2010	647	**0.68**
2011	534	**0.55**

The exhibit shows the average cross-sectional correlation within the FoFs universe. The correlation values greater than or equal to 0.5 are indicated in bold.

"feeder" hedge funds that directly made their investments in Madoff securities. These hedge funds on the surface were audited by large and respected audit firms. However all the assets were in custody of Madoff Securities, which, in turn, was audited by a little-known, three-person auditing firm.

Large FoFs are capable of building strong infrastructure and operational due diligence teams that can identify operationally weak or fraudulent hedge funds. Brown, Fraser, and Liang (2008) show that vigilant operational due diligence is a source of alpha for FoFs. FoFs have the capability to offer products by creating customized hedge fund portfolio solutions. These complement existing investments to meet the overall investment objective and constraints for investors.

The decision to invest directly or indirectly raises the question of whether institutional investors have the necessary expertise and infrastructure to identify the best hedge funds and to monitor them on an ongoing basis. An important question in portfolio construction concerns the number of managers required to create the hedge fund portfolio. Selecting the number of funds in a portfolio depends on the risk appetite of investors. While a small number of funds in a portfolio have the potential of earning high returns, a risk of underperforming the benchmark required for institutional mandates exists. Better investment decisions (e.g., strategy allocation and manager selection) can also reduce the number of managers used for diversification in a portfolio. As the number of managers required in a portfolio increases, so does the task of conducting due diligence and monitoring for investors directly investing in hedge funds compared with a FoFs.

Persistence in the performance of FoFs exists over time. Selecting a FoFs depends on identifying funds with a strong operational due diligence team (capable of rejecting operationally weak hedge funds) as well as a capable investment team that can deliver above average performance through superior manager selection and strategy allocation process.

DISCUSSION QUESTIONS

1. Explain why dispersion in long-only managers is typically lower compared to hedge funds.
2. Identify several factors contributing to the variability of beta to the S&P 500 Index of long/short managers over time.
3. Using stratified sampling, explain why the average performance of portfolios of different sizes would be the same.
4. Identify the main factors that can justify investing in hedge funds using a FoFs.

REFERENCES

Agarwal, Vikas, and Narayan Y. Naik. 2004. "Risks and Portfolio Decisions Involving Hedge Funds." *Review of Financial Studies* 17:1, 63–98.

Amo Anne-Valere, Helene Harasty, and Pierre Hillion. 2007. "Diversification Benefits of Fund of Hedge Funds: Identifying the Optimal Number of Hedge Funds." *Journal of Alternative Investments* 10:2, 10–22.

Brown, Stephen, Thomas Fraser, and Bing Liang. 2008. "Hedge Fund Due Diligence: A Source of Alpha in a Hedge Fund Portfolio Strategy." NYU Working Paper No. FIN-07-032.

Brown, Stephen, William N. Goetzmann, and Roger G. Ibbotson. 1999. "Offshore Hedge Funds: Survival and Performance: 1989–1995." *Journal of Business* 72:1, 91–118.

Derman, Emanuel. 2007. "A Simple Model of Expected Premium for Hedge Fund Lock Ups." *Journal of Investment Management* 5:3, 5–15.

Fung, William, and David A. Hseih. 2000. "Performance Characteristics of Hedge Funds and Commodity Funds: Natural vs. Spurious Biases." *Journal of Financial and Quantitative Analysis* 35:3, 291–307.

Hedge Fund Research. 2011. Global Hedge Fund Industry Report—Year End 2011. Available at www.hedgefundresearch.com.

Lhabitant, Francois-Serge, and Michelle Learned. 2002. "Hedge Fund Diversification: How Much is Enough?" *Journal of Alternative Investments* 5:3, 23–49.

Markowitz, Harry. 1952. "Portfolio Selection." *Journal of Finance* 7:1, 77–91.

Park, James, Stephen J. Brown, and William N. Goetzmann. 1999. "Performance Benchmarks and Survivorship Bias for Hedge Funds and Commodity Trading Advisors." *Hedge Fund News*. Available at www.hedgefundnews.com.

Patel Kartik. 2008. "How Many Fund Managers Does a Fund of Funds Need?" *Pensions: An International Journal* 13:1–2, 61–69.

Reddy Girish, Peter Brady, and Kartik Patel. 2007. "Are Fund of Funds Simply Multi-Strategy Managers with Extra Fees?" *Journal of Alternative Investments* 10:3, 49–61.

Statman, Meir. 1987. "How Many Stocks Make a Diversified Portfolio?" *Journal of Financial and Quantitative Analysis* 22:3, 353–363.

ABOUT THE AUTHOR

Kartik Patel is Vice President of Risk and Technology at Prisma Capital Partners LP, a fund of hedge funds. At Prisma, he is responsible for building and managing risk and portfolio management systems. Before joining Prisma, he worked as a signal processing engineer in the wireless industry working for companies such as AT&T Wireless and Lucent Digital Radio. He earned a B.Tech in Electrical Engineering from I.I.T Bombay, an MS in Electrical Engineering from the University of Maryland, and an MS degree in Financial Engineering from Columbia University. He holds the Chartered Financial Analyst (CFA) designation.

Answers to Discussion Questions

CHAPTER 2 ROLE OF ALTERNATIVE INVESTMENTS IN STRATEGIC ASSET ALLOCATION

1. The risk-return profile of alternative investments, especially private equity, is distorted by appraisal smoothing, quarterly data availability, and stale pricing. Additional biases can exist because of illiquidity due to irregular price determination, long periods between price determination, and using book value instead of market prices.
2. The return distribution of alternative investments shows significantly higher moments (i.e., skewness and kurtosis). The mixed-normal distribution is a flexible and tractable method to capture asymmetric return distributions. Combining two normal distributions permits representing any higher moments and therefore adequately captures the return distribution of alternative investments.
3. Some alternative investments are only accessible by institutional investors. These investors have different incentive structures that are inadequately represented by standard utility functions such as quadratic utility. Therefore, alternative utility functions should be used such as min-max utility, which maximizes the probability of outperforming some benchmark return while minimizing the probability of underperforming another benchmark return.
4. Both traditional investments (e.g., stocks and bonds) and alternative investments (e.g., hedge funds and private equity) are represented in investor portfolios across different levels of risk aversion. Therefore, only the combination of the two asset classes leads to maximized investor utility. For that reason, they are complements because otherwise traditional or alternative investments would dominate the other in the portfolio.

CHAPTER 3 TRENDS IN ALTERNATIVE INVESTMENTS

1. With respect to fees, investors in hedge funds had few choices before 2008. For the most part, only one standard fee structure was available: a 2 percent management fee and a 20 percent performance fee. During and shortly after the financial crisis, experts forecasted that fees would decline. Although fees did not immediately decline overall, hedge fund managers soon began offering choices to investors in the years after the crisis. Investors could choose the standard 2/20

structure or lock up their money for a longer period and pay a lower fee. Despite no overall decline in fees in the years immediately after the crisis, the general level of fees started to decline slightly by 2011.

2. UCITS are funds that institutions offer in Europe that primarily target retail investors. The funds comply with the Undertaking for Collective Investment in Transferable Securities (UCITS). To be in compliance, such funds must offer greater liquidity and transparency. In 2010, UCITS funds made up only 7 percent of the hedge fund universe but accounted for 20 percent of the inflow. Thus, UCITS funds reflect the trend toward offering investors products with more transparency and liquidity. They may also reflect the possibility that investors who choose products with such properties may pay a price with respect to return. In 2010, UCITS funds had lower average returns than hedge funds: 6.9 percent versus 11 percent, respectively.
3. The historical record is favorable for smaller funds. According to Per Trac (2011), over 1996 to 2010, small funds (assets less than $100 million) generally outperformed midsized funds (assets between $100 and $500 million), which outperformed large funds. The explanation for this result is that managers of small and midsized funds can be more flexible and move into profitable deals more easily than those of larger funds. Investors show a preference for small and midsized hedge funds.
4. The following are three reasons that earning high returns in private equity has become difficult: (1) competition has increased for available deals, (2) fewer deals exist with adequate turnaround prospects to generate high returns, and (3) banks have restricted lending, which lowers the possibility of using leverage to increase return on equity.
5. Several factors that occurred in 2011 have important implications for the trends in the commodities and managed futures sectors. First, the poor performance in this sector led to a dramatic drop in inflows. This drop is important because it reflects that investors in these sectors are looking for more than diversification potential. Investors are increasingly demanding return. Second, the poor performance came despite higher volatility in 2011. Historically, these sectors have better performance in times of higher volatility. The 2011 anomaly may be indicative of a structural change, but it will take many more years to determine if that is true.

CHAPTER 4 ALTERNATIVE INVESTMENTS AND DUE DILIGENCE

1. Alternative funds are private investment vehicles that are usually subject to less regulation than traditional asset classes. From an investment perspective, managers of alternative investments typically use sophisticated and opaque investment strategies, trade complex instruments such as derivatives, use leverage, and invest in illiquid assets. Hence, alternative investments demonstrate risk-return characteristics that differ from those of traditional investments. These factors make analyzing and assessing alternative investments challenging and elevate the importance of thorough due diligence. Additionally, the entrepreneurial nature of many investment advisers coupled with a lack of

transparency necessitates an extensive business or operational due diligence examination.

2. Investment due diligence is the quantitative and qualitative examination conducted on an alternative investment fund to analyze its investment philosophy, strategy and process, historical performance record, volatility, drawdowns, and correlations with other asset classes and market indices. The objective behind investment due diligence is twofold. The first objective is to ensure that the manager has an established, replicable investment process that will create excess returns (i.e., alpha) and provide diversification benefits for an investor's portfolio. The second objective is to quantitatively verify the expected alpha and diversification benefits by analyzing past returns, volatility, correlations, and risk metrics. By examining the investment process and performance history, investors will try to get to the story behind the numbers and understand how the manager creates value. Further, investment due diligence will reveal how the prospective fund ranks in comparison to its peers.
3. Business or operational due diligence involves investigating the non-investment aspects of an alternative investment firm including the organization, management team, corporate governance, infrastructure and technology, business continuity and disaster recovery planning, middle- and back-office operations, legal and compliance, service providers, and investor reporting aspects. The objective of business due diligence is to ascertain that the investment firm has a stable organization, robust infrastructure, requisite investment and risk management process, efficient operations, and complies with all laws, rules, and regulations, as well as industry best practices. Business due diligence is a labor-intensive effort and requires extensive document review, onsite visits, interviews with operational personnel, background searches, and reference checks.
4. An investment mandate is initially created to describe the investment's objective and the criteria sought in prospective funds. In the idea sourcing and initial screening phase, a search is launched to identify a smaller set or a short list of prospective managers who will satisfy the broad quantitative and qualitative criteria of the mandate. These criteria include firm and strategy assets under management, length of the fund's track record, historical returns and volatilities, transparency, and liquidity terms. Others include firm-related requirements such as the existence of independent risk management or use of reputable third parties (e.g., a Big 4 accounting firm as auditor) to reduce the risk of fraud and enhance reliability. Further analysis is conducted on the managers in the short list to remove those with less desirable characteristics and identify the one that will undergo a full review or a "deep dive." A full review involves an in-depth investment due diligence and extensive operational or business due diligence, including onsite visits, interviews with operational staff, and third-party reference and background checks.

CHAPTER 5 REITS AND THE PRIVATE REAL ESTATE MARKET

1. The historical development of research on the connection between public and private real estate markets went through several phases. Early research focused

on comparing stock market returns, as well as bond and commodity returns, to the performance of private real estate portfolios. Studies show that tax advantages and leverage considerations explain some of the performance differential. Other findings to emerge reveal the low apparent volatility of real estate returns and the low or negative correlation with other asset classes. The next phase focused on comparing the investment performance of REIT returns to the returns of private real estate portfolios as well as stock market returns. The evidence led to a greater understanding of systematic and idiosyncratic (unsystematic) risk of REITs and discounts to net asset value for REITs. Early research on this topic was limited to private real estate portfolios or commingled real estate funds. The development of the NCREIF index facilitated more rigorous empirical research compared to earlier studies. Subsequent research comparing NCREIF returns to REIT returns examined the issue of price discovery in public real estate markets and whether private and public real estate markets were cointegrated.

2. REITs may be expected to behave substantially like the direct real estate market because, by regulation, REITs are required to have 75 percent of their assets in real estate. Furthermore, 75 percent of the gross income for the REIT must come in the form of rents or mortgage interest payments. These restrictions create a security where the underlying assets and cash flow are closely connected to real estate assets.
3. The results indicate that REITs have more than twice the variation of the transactions-based index (TBI), while REITs are slightly less volatile than the control group. The quarterly average standard deviation of REITs is 0.110 compared to an average of 0.057 for the TBI from the MIT Center for Real Estate, and an average of 0.115 for the control group. Substantial variations also exist among different property types in the REIT market but not as much for the TBI indices. The results also show that the correlation between the aggregate REIT and TBI indices increases from 0.06 for quarterly returns to 0.24 for annual returns, indicating that REITs behave more like real estate over longer time horizons. The results are similar at the property-type level. The average correlation between the TBI and the four different REIT property types grows from 0.04 for quarterly returns to 0.30 for annual returns. Even though REITs correlate more with real estate over the longer time horizon, REITs do not necessarily correlate less with financial assets.
4. Cointegration techniques are used to identify long-run statistical relationships between economic time-series data, even though the series may apparently move independently over short-time periods. The significant β coefficients presented in the chapter suggest long-run equilibrium relationships exist among the public real estate market, the private real estate market, and the financial market. Other results indicate that REITs and the private real estate market adjust to a long-run equilibrium relation when they are in disequilibrium. The evidence may also suggest that the financial markets lead public and private real estate markets.

CHAPTER 6 COMMERCIAL REAL ESTATE

1. Tenants are households that decide to rent versus to own a home. As tenants, their cost is the effective rent. The effective rent is the full service gross charge

multiplied by one minus the vacancy rate. Full service gross means that the landlord pays all the operating costs. As owners, households' costs are for mortgage interest after tax and operating expenses, less capital gains. When interest rates, operating expenses, and house price appreciation all decline, households tend to rent.

2. An industrial building with a long-term operating lease provides a stream of cash flows to the owner. These cash flows carry the credit rating of the tenant or lessor, even if the operating lease does not oblige the liability to be reported on the balance sheet. Because the tenant is closer to the property and has incentives for maintenance, the tenant bears the operating cost. The lease becomes triple net, or effective rent less operating expenses, and offers bumps or inflation protection. The series of indexed cash flows is sold to an investor as a bond. The lessor or landlord has no responsibility for maintaining the property and is buying the lessee's credit rating.
3. Agency issues occur in multitenanted office buildings. The tenant is closer to the space and the business, but is unsure about the landlord. The tenant is moving into a building where other tenants already exist. Tenants have incentives to overuse and to increase expenses if they are not paying them.

   The uncertainty about the landlord is addressed by tenant improvements. These are upfront payments made by the landlord to the tenant as incentives to move into the building. The landlord makes larger payments to better-credit tenants. The expenses from previous tenants are not passed on to existing tenants because leases use base stops. Only increases in rent above previous expenses are charged to the tenant. The operating expense incentives are addressed by billing tenants back.
4. The after-tax comparison of rent versus ownership for one lease or tenant is no longer effective if an anchor tenant such as a supermarket brings traffic. The lease on the large tenant is a loss-leader for the landlord. For example, in the limit, the supermarket rent covers only variable marginal costs such as utilities. The landlord must cover the fixed costs, both of operating expenses such as property taxes and insurance and of capital expenses on the remaining tenants. The mechanisms to charge higher rents to smaller tenants include reduced upfront capital expenses, increased base rents, and charges as percentages of sales. The landlord is measuring the total cost and benefit of owning and renting. The tenant is making only its own lease calculations, which generate losses if large and gains if small for the landlord.
5. The return to commercial real estate is the sum of a yield and capital gain, making it similar to other investments such as stocks. The yield is the cap rate, or ratio of net rent to the price of the property. Net rent is the net operating income, or collections less operating expenses. In longer-term studies, yields on commercial real estate have ranged between 5 and 9 percent annually. Capital gains have increased at the rate of inflation. As a result, the return to real estate has an expected long-run component of the cap rate, and a short-run, zero-expectation term for the capital gains–inflation differential. This condition differs from stock returns in two ways. Stocks do not have a readily similar decomposition of dividends and capital gains. The return to real estate has lower apparent volatility than stock returns, which is partly attributable to a failure to incorporate the time to sell.

CHAPTER 7 REAL ESTATE INVESTMENT TRUSTS

1. The four tests that determine whether a company is eligible for REIT status are:
   - Ownership tests: At least 100 different shareholders, with the largest five owning no more than 50 percent.
   - Assets test: At least 75 percent of assets qualify as real estate.
   - Income test: At least 75 percent of income is real estate related.
   - Distribution test: At least 90 percent of taxable income is distributed to shareholders.
2. The main arguments for including REITS are:
   - Returns are derived from ownership of real estate assets.
   - Correlation with unlisted real estate is higher over longer investment horizons.
   - Correlation with the stock market is lower over longer investment horizons.
   - Correlation with unlisted real estate is higher when a lag of four to five quarters is considered.
   - Correlation is higher when unlisted property returns are unsmoothed.
   - Volatility is more comparable when unlisted property returns are unsmoothed.
   - Volatility is nearly identical when unlevered transaction-based returns are compared.

   The main arguments against including REITs are:
   - Lack of illiquidity.
   - Traded through the stock market.
   - Low measured correlation with unlisted real estate returns.
   - Relatively high measured correlation with the stock market.
   - Higher measured volatility than unlisted real estate.
3. Illiquidity smoothing, also called temporal aggregation, results because property transactions occurring over a discrete time period (one month or one quarter) are aggregated to produce an index for that period. In contrast, REIT returns over a comparable period are measured by comparing end-of-period index values. Appraisal smoothing results from two major factors: (1) typically appraising only a portion of the portfolio during a given quarter and (2) having appraisers subject to the behavioral bias of anchoring, resulting in a lack of recognition of all of the actual changes in market value during that period. Both sources of smoothing cause measured volatility of unlisted real estate investments to be substantially lower than true volatility. The example in the chapter suggests that unsmoothing increased the measured volatility of unlisted real estate by 250 percent.
4. *Illiquidity lag* refers to the passage of time before a change in property values is revealed by a completed transaction, while *appraisal lag* refers to the passage of additional time before the information revealed by transactions is incorporated into appraisals on nontransacting properties. Taken together, illiquidity smoothing and appraisal smoothing cause the measured correlation between listed and unlisted real estate to be substantially lower than the true correlation. Oikarinen, Hoesli, and Serrano (2011) use cointegration analysis to find that the long-horizon correlation between listed and unlisted real estate approaches one.

5. The following aspects of the REIT business model may cause REIT returns to differ from unlisted real estate returns:
   - Transparency imposes capital market discipline, reduces capital costs, and promotes superior investment performance.
   - Liquidity imposes capital market discipline, reduces capital costs, and promotes superior investment performance. Little empirical evidence supports the notion of the existence of an illiquidity premium, especially in the real estate asset class.
   - Investor-oriented governance imposes capital market discipline, reduces capital costs, and promotes superior investment performance.
   - Alignment of interest between investors and investment managers promotes superior net returns to investors at an appropriate level of risk.
   - Limited free cash reduces the opportunity for shareholder wealth destruction through investments that serve the interests of investment managers to the detriment of investors. The free cash problem may have caused enormous net purchases by unlisted real estate investment managers during the market peak in 2007.
   - Financing through public equity and debt markets as well as private equity and debt markets enables asset purchases during market troughs, as REITs demonstrated during 2010. REIT stock sales do not entail redeeming shares, which might force REITs to hold uninvested cash or to sell properties.

CHAPTER 8 MORTGAGED-BACKED SECURITIES

1. The first consideration in creating a CMO is determining the number and type of securities that are to be created from the mortgage pool. Typically, creating the tranches of a CMO includes the following considerations: (1) demand at various points on the yield curve, (2) credit risk protection, and (3) reinvestment risk protection. The next consideration in creating a CMO security is to determine the total face value of the tranches that will be issued from the mortgage pool. If a government agency such as the FHA or VA backs the mortgages that are being securitized, then the mortgage pool is insulated from the possibility that mortgage default will decrease the value of the pool and the entire face value of the mortgage pool could be issued as CMO tranches. If a high possibility exists for mortgage default, the face value of the CMO tranches will likely need to be less than the face value of the mortgages.
2. In a PAC, the securities are structured such that principal payments are passed to security holders on a regular schedule, eliminating excess prepayment risk. The scheduled payments are designed to be maintained within a certain range of prepayments, known as the PAC band. In contrast to a PAC, a TAC has a fixed prepayment rate as opposed to a prepayment range. Thus, TAC securities will have greater cash flow variability relative to a PAC. IO tranches receive only interest payments and PO tranches receive only principal payments. An inverse floater is an IO security that pays out the difference between the interest rate cap level and the promised rate on the floater. Inverse floaters are risky securities and tend to be sold to sophisticated investors such as hedge funds.
3. In the 1880s, agricultural mortgage brokers in the United States placed mortgages in trusts and sold securities that used those mortgages as collateral. Today,

this type of security would be known as a mortgage-backed bond. Two financial innovations that helped fuel the mortgage debt boom in the 1920s, both of which are familiar features in today's mortgage market, are private mortgage insurance and participation certificates. Private mortgage insurance provided the financial guarantee that allowed mortgage lenders to sell mortgages to create liquidity and then issue more mortgages. Participation certificates gave holders the rights to the interest and principal payments made on those loans. These securities were very similar to the mortgage pass through securities that exist today.

4. Besides the growth in complex financial structures, three factors helped trigger the 2007–2008 financial crisis. First, the 1999–2000 recession prompted the Federal Reserve to cut interest rates to what, at that time, were at historically low levels. Second, the creation of REMICs after the 1986 Tax Reform Act allowed institutions that were securitizing assets to legally remove those assets from their balance sheets. Finally, a liberal regulatory climate characterized the period before the crisis. The deregulation of banks, including the removal of interstate branching restrictions and the allowance of bank holding companies to own securities firms, led to massive consolidation in the banking industry and spurred the growth of incredibly complex financial institutions.

CHAPTER 9 MEZZANINE DEBT AND PREFERRED EQUITY IN REAL ESTATE

1. Senior lenders and rating agencies generally prohibit mortgage borrowers from further encumbering the underlying real property with additional junior mortgages. Hence, mezzanine loans are preferred over traditional junior mortgages.
2. Mezzanine loans are structured to satisfy requirements imposed by the senior mortgage lender in the intercreditor agreement and the rating guidelines imposed by the national rating agencies. Accordingly, a mezzanine lender makes a loan to a newly formed limited liability company (LLC) that indirectly owns the mortgage borrower and the underlying real property. In return for the mezzanine lender's investment in the mezzanine borrower (in the form of the loan proceeds), the mezzanine lender receives a promissory note (debt instrument) and collateral to secure its loan. This collateral consists of the mezzanine borrower's equity interest in the underlying mortgage borrower. Rating agencies and senior lenders view this mezzanine loan structure as a hybrid debt/equity investment. A mezzanine lender is not a direct creditor of the underlying mortgage borrower.

   Some of the characteristics classifying mezzanine loans as debt investments include the existence of a promissory note evidencing the debt obligation, monthly interest payments at a stated rate and maturity date, foreclosure rights upon mezzanine loan default, and other typical lender's rights and obligations under the intercreditor agreement with the senior mortgage lender. Conversely, if the mezzanine borrower defaults, the mezzanine lender may foreclose upon the equity collateral and become the new indirect equity owner of the mortgage borrower. Because of this unique structure, senior mortgage lenders, rating agencies and the capital markets often treat mezzanine loans similar to equity investments from an underwriting and business perspective.

3. Developers of the underlying commercial real estate project generally seek mezzanine loans because the additional capital increases the developers' loan-to-value (LTV) ratio. They can use the added funds to fund the acquisition of, or major capital improvements to, the underlying real property. The additional funds and improvements not only increase the developer's leverage and rates of return, but also increase the value of the underlying property. As a result, senior lenders generally accept mezzanine loans made to separate borrowing entities, so long as the mortgage borrower is not further encumbered by any additional loan obligations. Although senior lenders are receptive to mezzanine loan investments, senior lenders limit and restrict the mezzanine lender's actions through an intercreditor agreement governed by state contract law. Also, senior mortgage lenders generally consent to mezzanine loan investments because the additional capital provides the necessary funds to cover the developer's gap in the LTV ratio and helps complete the underlying commercial project.
4. Upon a default under a mezzanine loan, a mezzanine lender can enforce its foreclosure rights under the Uniform Commercial Code (UCC). Generally, a mezzanine lender provides notice to interested parties and markets the pledged equity interests at a public sale as defined in the UCC. If the mezzanine lender is the successful bidder at a public sale, the mezzanine lender becomes the indirect owner of the mortgage borrower and the underlying property. Thereafter, the mezzanine lender has the power to control the mortgage borrower and to make major decisions about the underlying property, such as whether to sell, renovate or enter into leases.

   Because of the mezzanine lender's subordinated position in the capital stack of the project, the mezzanine lender is at risk that the senior mortgage lender may foreclose its mortgage and sell the underlying property to a third party. If this occurs the mezzanine lender's collateral becomes worthless because the mezzanine borrower no longer indirectly owns the underlying real property. As a result, in order to protect the value of its collateral (the equity interests), the mezzanine lender must be prepared to buy out the senior mortgage loan or purchase the property at foreclosure to prevent the transfer of the underlying property indirectly owned by the mezzanine borrower. Similarly, in order to protect its collateral in the event of a bankruptcy of the mortgage borrower, a mezzanine lender should have the available financial capital to make an advance payment to cure defaults under the mortgage loan or to negotiate a buyout of the senior loan. The mezzanine lender's rights and obligations would be set forth in the intercreditor agreement with the senior mortgage lender.

   Mezzanine lenders face many challenges in enforcing its UCC foreclosure rights, marketing and selling its equity collateral, and complying with the many restrictions imposed by the intercreditor agreement. Upon a default under the mezzanine loan, the mezzanine lender needs to make certain that the marketing and sale of the equity collateral complies with the "commercially reasonable" standards as set forth under the UCC. Further, the intercreditor agreement requires that the purchaser of the pledged equity interests at a UCC foreclosure sale be a "qualified transferee." This requirement typically limits the number and types of entities that are permitted to become indirect equity owners of the mortgage borrower.

5. Preferred equity investors contribute capital either to the mortgage borrower (direct owner of the underlying property) or to a borrowing entity (holding company that indirectly owns underlying property). Unlike a mezzanine lender, a preferred equity investor does not take collateral in return for its investment or possess any UCC foreclosure rights. As an alternative, a preferred equity investor receives an equity membership interest in the underlying property and the right to regular cash flow distributions. In many instances, the preferred equity investor ("preferred member") forms a joint venture partnership with the mortgage borrower ("common member"), who assumes the majority of the managerial control. In the event that the common member fails to make preferred rate of return payments or fails to repay the preferred equity investment before the period of redemption, this could trigger a "change in control event." Accordingly, a preferred member can enforce any available contract remedies to initiate a takeover of the underlying property and a removal of the common member's managerial control. Thus, although a preferred member cannot use Article 9 of the UCC to protect its investment, the structure of preferred equity transactions nevertheless provides the preferred member with an ability to quickly gain control of the underlying property.

CHAPTER 10 REAL ESTATE APPRAISAL AND VALUATION

1. Market value is typically estimated for the purpose of a real estate loan. *Market value* is an estimate of the most likely price that the property will sell for if the lender has to foreclose on the property in the event of default.
2. A *capitalization rate* is the ratio of the first year net operating income (NOI) to the value of the property. A *discount rate* is the rate that is used to discount the NOI for the entire holding period and the estimated sale price for the property at the end of the holding period to calculate the value of the property. The two rates are related because the capitalization rate that a buyer is willing to accept depends on what the NOI will be in the future. Thus, expected future growth in the NOI is implicit in the capitalization rate. The difference between the two rates is the expected growth in NOI and property value over the holding period.
3. DCF analysis requires a realistic estimate of future cash flows from the property, including those from operating and selling the property at the end of a holding period. The property could be overvalued by assuming NOI will be too high, the resale price is too high, or the discount rate is too low. The NOI might be overestimated by assuming rents are too high, vacancy is too low, or expenses are too low. The resale price might be overestimated by assuming a terminal capitalization rate that is too low or assuming the NOI the year after sale is too high.
4. The sales comparison approach relies on having comparable sales (comps) that are representative of the value of the property being appraised (subject). The more that the comps differ from the subject, the more adjustments have to be made to the comp, which can lead to errors in estimating the value. When few

sales of properties located near the subject property are available around the time the property is being appraised, the result may be a poor estimate of the value of the subject.

5. The three relevant types of value for a development project are the value as is, the value upon completion, and the value upon stabilization. The value as is requires estimating the value of whatever is on the site before the start of development, which is usually a vacant site. The value upon completion is the value after development is complete but before the property is leased up. The value upon stabilization is the value after the development is complete and the property has been leased up to a normal level of occupancy.
6. Risk is highest for a development project after construction has begun and a substantial amount of money has been spent but additional funds are needed to complete the project and lease it up. This occurs because the developer has committed to a particular development plan and changing what is being developed is costly if market conditions change such that what was originally planned is no longer as feasible. As development is being completed and the project is being leased up, the risk should begin to decline until the project is leased to a stabilized level of occupancy.

CHAPTER 11 PERFORMANCE OF REAL ESTATE PORTFOLIOS

1. The three types of commercial property price or return indices are appraisal based, transaction price based, and stock market based. Their names reveal their information sources. Appraisal-based indices use professional appraisals of individual properties aggregated across portfolios or populations. Transaction price–based indices use transaction prices filtered through econometric models. Stock market–based indices use share prices of REIT equity filtered through a pure play target portfolio model.
2. News relevant to property values is likely to be reflected in the three types of indices in the following order: (1) the stock market–based index, (2) the transaction price–based index, and (3) the appraisal-based index. The stock market based–index leads because the stock market is more informationally efficient than the private property market (i.e., the stock market more quickly and fully reflects in stock prices news that is relevant to the values of the shares). This is due to the nature and functioning of the stock market, with dense trading of homogeneous shares in a public double-auction format structured to provide rapid price discovery and constant liquidity, with very low transaction costs and the general possibility for short-selling (in all these respects differing from the private property market). The appraisal-based index lags behind actual sales because appraisers must first gather information about the sales prices of properties that have sold in the private market and then filter that information for comparability to subject properties. The sales of comparable properties typically have occurred in the past, and appraisers can only partially and conservatively adjust for private market movements since the comps' sales. Also, appraisal-based indices typically include stale appraisals (i.e., valuations that are not up-to-date or current).

3. In the traditional official NCREIF Property Index, the capital return is net of capital expenditures. Hence, it reflects only market effects without including landlord upkeep of the property, thus falling below average same-property price growth. In the repeat-sales transaction based index, the capital return is the same-property price appreciation as actually experienced by round-trip property investors. In the stock market–based index, the capital return reflects the stock market's valuation of the REITs' property value changes, including both same-property value growth plus some scale expansion of the REITs attributable to plowback of retained cash flow not distributed to stakeholders.
4. Tradability or investability in a price or return index of commercial property could allow real estate investors to sell short, to hedge unwanted "beta" (market risk) exposure, to more rapidly balance or adjust portfolios, or to invest synthetically in real estate with lower transaction or management costs than direct physical investment. Stock market–based indices are advantageous for such a role because they are based on potentially investable and tradable portfolios of actively traded REIT stocks. They are updated daily based on observable REIT share prices, allowing more transparent pricing and smaller margin requirements for derivatives based on the indices.

CHAPTER 12 VENTURE CAPITAL

1. Venture capital investors fill an important niche in the financing of young, entrepreneurial companies. Their comparative advantage over other investors, such as banks, relates to their relative efficiency in selecting and monitoring investments characterized by high informational asymmetries and high uncertainty and in writing adequate contracts. Amit, Brander, and Zott (1998), Ueda (2004), and Winton and Yerramilli (2008) provide excellent insights into how venture capital investors differ from banks.
2. Obtaining funding through venture capital might be a key milestone for company development as many entrepreneurs are unsuccessful in moving through the highly selective filter of venture capital investors. Probably as important is the source used by entrepreneurs to raise financing. Venture capitalists are not a homogenous group of investors. High-quality venture capital investors with more industry-specific experience and broader networks are likely to provide more and/or higher quality value adding services to their portfolio companies. For instance, venture capital investors with more industry-specific experience may be more active in professionalizing their portfolio companies. They are perceived by entrepreneurs as more valuable sounding boards and provide stronger signals to outside stakeholders that reduce uncertainty. Low-quality venture capital investors may be unable to provide their portfolio companies with a network of relevant contacts and may even repel high quality investors from providing follow-on financing in the future. Thus, entrepreneurs are often willing to pay a premium in order to affiliate with more reputable venture capital investors.
3. Most venture capital firms are organized as management companies responsible for managing several pools of capital, each representing a legally separate limited partnership. The economic life of most funds is 10 years although provisions are often included to extend the life of the funds by two years. Venture

capital investors are further interested in exiting their investments some three to seven years after an initial investment and realize a return. When approaching prospective venture capital investors, entrepreneurs should keep this structure in mind because it influences the incentives of venture capitalists. Entrepreneurs of a young biotechnology company may find raising finance from funds that are already five years old difficult if not impossible. Hence, when entrepreneurs want to increase their odds of raising venture capital, they should especially target young funds, which may be managed by very experienced and well-networked venture capital firms that are still looking for investment opportunities. This arrangement further decreases the exit pressure by venture capital investors on their portfolio companies.

Venture capital investors also have a tendency to specialize in certain industries, certain stages of development, or geographical areas. Industry publications often highlight the stated investment preferences of venture capital investors. Entrepreneurs may use this information to target the most relevant investors for their proposal. For instance, entrepreneurs with an early stage project may find targeting investors with a stated preference for providing growth capital as unproductive. Moreover, a due diligence of potential venture capital investors by entrepreneurs may not only increase their odds of raising venture capital but also highlight who the most relevant venture capital investors (e.g., those with most potential to contribute value-adding services) are for a specific investment proposal.

Finally, entrepreneurs should be aware that exit is an essential step in the venture capital investment process. Hence, they should be willing to either participate in an initial public offering (IPO), which is only feasible if the venture is extremely successful, or a trade sale. Buybacks by entrepreneurs, while possible, are not the preferred exit route for venture capital investors because buybacks do not provide the best return possible. An exit route that is increasingly popular and may mitigate concerns of both entrepreneurs and investors is the sale to a financial partner, often another (later-stage) venture capital investor.

4. Preinvestment venture capital investors may try to actively influence their deal flow in order to obtain more high-quality investment proposals. They may also actively engage in due diligence activities to select the best entrepreneurial companies from the pool of investment proposals they receive. Writing adequate contracts might further provide entrepreneurs with an incentive scheme that pushes them towards value creation. Postinvestment, venture capital investors may monitor the progress of portfolio companies and avoid the wasteful use of resources. They may also actively influence how their portfolio companies are run, for instance, by adding experience to the entrepreneurial team and providing entrepreneurs access to their network and reputation to open doors that would not open without being venture capital backed.
5. Evidence indicates that returns in venture capital persist strongly across subsequent funds of a partnership, with the best partnerships having a higher probability to continue to outperform. Thus, investors in venture capital should select the best funds. Nevertheless, access to these top funds is challenging because they can choose between numerous eager investors. According to Phalippou and Gottschalg (2009), limited partners tacitly obtain the right to participate in future, more successful funds by participating in inexperienced, often poorly

performing funds. This right is valuable because funds by successful and established general partners tend to be oversubscribed and prior investments receive privileged access.

CHAPTER 13 MEZZANINE CAPITAL

1. Mezzanine securities represent the privately negotiated instruments located in the middle of a company's capital structure, senior to common or preferred equity but subordinated to senior secured bank debt. Generally, mezzanine securities take the form of privately negotiated subordinated debt and, to a lesser extent, senior notes or preferred stock, with some form of equity participation either through common or preferred stock, options, or warrants. Mezzanine securities are structured to generate substantial current income for investors while at the same time creating opportunities to generate meaningful capital gains. The return on a mezzanine loan typically is composed of cash and PIK interest, equity participation, and fees.
2. The relative stability and seniority of the debt component of a mezzanine investment, when combined with the potential gains from the equity component of the investment, offer the opportunity to earn attractive risk-adjusted returns. Transactions involving mezzanine securities generally involve a single or limited number of investors who negotiate directly with issuers and their respective sponsors, allowing for more nimble execution and a higher degree of certainty when compared to public debt financing that requires capital markets syndication and an accessible market.
3. The ongoing dislocation in the credit markets has created an environment where liquidity and capital resources are scarce. The senior secured loan market has contracted substantially. Both the second lien bank debt and high-yield markets are generally only available to seasoned issuers typically raising large amounts with very conservative capital structures. These events create a particularly attractive environment for mezzanine investors as mezzanine capital will be required to complete transactions. Also mezzanine investing may be safer as more equity capital will sit beneath mezzanine tranches and mezzanine capital will participate in less levered capital structures. Mezzanine capital is more attractively priced and capital providers are able to secure better covenant packages and potentially better governance terms
4. Mezzanine financing is predominantly used in financing new buyouts but it also can be used to help refinance both existing buyouts and provide capital to non-LBO corporates (often referred to as "sponsorless" mezzanine deals). A strong deal flow is expected for both sponsored and sponsorless mezzanine loans given numerous supportive factors. First, a substantial amount of private equity capital commitments, estimated to be about $450 billion globally, is available for investment. Even assuming a very conservative leverage percentage on new transactions of 50 percent of the purchase price, this would imply potentially over $900 billion of transactions, by enterprise value, over the next several years. Second, a backlog of potential M&A investments is available that has been put on hold due to the volatile market conditions during the global financial crisis. In many cases, sellers of businesses have refrained from coming to market in light of a very weak buyer appetite driven by the paucity of credit available and

the uncertain macroeconomic environment. Many corporations, having experienced exceptionally difficult trading conditions, will redouble their efforts to focus on core activities and deleverage their balance sheets via disposals providing further deal flow. Third, refinancing requirements will drive demand for mezzanine capital as about $1 trillion of leveraged loans and high yield bonds reach maturity and will need to be refinanced. Fourth, many companies will have to undergo comprehensive balance sheet changes involving new equity capital, reductions to existing debt, and the provision of new subordinated capital, potentially in the form of mezzanine debt.

CHAPTER 14 BUYOUT FUNDS

1. The three value-creation measures are management monitoring, operational engineering, and governance intervention. Management monitoring describes the process in which the buyout fund managers monitor the performance of the portfolio firms' management. Installing reporting structures in which the portfolio companies' managers have to submit monthly or quarterly profit, loss, and cost indicators about the portfolio company allows the fund managers to track any changes in the companies' management performance.

   In the operational engineering process, fund managers focus on weaknesses in the actual operating business of a portfolio company. Most actions are directed at cost cutting. Examples of potential measures taken might include employee layoffs and improving the efficiency of supply, production, and distribution of a product. In drastic cases, fund managers might decide to sell off underperforming parts of the portfolio company.

   Governance intervention describes the process aimed at improving the portfolio companies' governance structures. Buyout fund managers either actively replace incumbent managers or install new governance features, such as audit and compensation committees, to improve the overall management efficiency.
2. The three major problems the buyout industry had to handle during the financial crisis were the distress of the banking sector, the economic downturn, and the turmoil in the capital markets. The distress of the banking system caused what is now known as the "credit crunch." Banks reduced their lending, especially high-risk loans to industrial small and medium-sized enterprises (SMEs) and debt as a buyout funding source. As a result, buyout funds faced two problems: banks lowered their capital commitments to the buyout funds and banks were unwilling to provide debt as a funding source for buyout deals.

   The economic downturn caused three major problems for buyout funds. The biggest problem was how to restructure a portfolio company in an adverse economic environment. The U.S. economy slid into a recession in late 2007, which lasted until mid-2009. Strengthening a portfolio company's operating business was challenging during this period.

   Another problem of the economic downturn was that strategic buyers for trade-sale exits of portfolio companies were almost nonexistent. Many companies had to deal with their own crisis-related problems and therefore had insufficient cash or capital to purchase other companies.

   The third problem, the turmoil in capital markets, affected two aspects of the buyout business model, namely, the exit via IPO and the debt funding of the buyout deals. Markets were at historically low valuation levels, making an IPO highly unattractive. The lack of potential buyers was another reason to avoid going public during this period. Because the crisis also adversely affected debt markets, many funding structures could not rely on bond issuances as part of the total debt funding structure.

3. The free operating cash flow of a company is the actual cash generated from the company's operations, as opposed to accounting profits. It is usually calculated by adding all non-cash-based deductions, such as depreciation and amortization, back to the net income and deducting all cash-based expenditures, such as capital expenditures or negative changes in net working capital, from the net income. A company can use its free cash flow to service debt payments resulting from the leverage structure the buyout fund applies to the portfolio companies. As its free cash flow increases, a company can more easily service its debt payments. A leverage buyout investment structure can only be applied to companies with sufficient free cash flow. If the cash flow is too low, fund managers can take actions to create more free cash flow such as reducing capital expenditures, selling off assets, and reducing cash-based costs.
4. The Volcker Rule argues along the lines of Glass-Steagall for separating high-risk proprietary trading in banking from safer and economically more important functions of banks to increase their overall stability. Section 619 in the Dodd-Frank Act of 2010 implemented the rule. The Volcker Rule prohibits banks from any kind of proprietary trading activities in any kind of securities. It also prohibits banks from investing in, managing, or sponsoring any type of private equity and hedge fund, including buyout funds.

   Although determining the long-term effects of the Volcker Rule on the buyout industry will take time, several preliminary effects have emerged. Large banks have not only begun to sell off their shares in third-party managed funds but also have sold off or closed their own in-house private equity programs. These actions might have two direct effects: (1) buyout funds might lose one of their major funding sources in banks because banks are no longer allowed to invest in buyout funds and (2) buyout funds might face lower competition in the market for desirable target portfolio companies. Because some banks with active in-house private equity programs were among the major players in the buyout industry, this competition is now gone for the buyout firms.

CHAPTER 15 DISTRESSED DEBT INVESTING

1. A *distressed security* is a security of a company that is, or may appear to be, insolvent, may be unable to pay its debts, and whose equity may have no value. As a result, its debt or equity may be worth less than face value. Investments in such instruments, while speculative, may present opportunities for returns based on the issuer's performance, but also based on the results of in- or out-of-court restructuring negotiations.
2. In general, a potential investor in distressed company securities seeks either to realize a short-term return based on increased value in those securities, or to capture potentially greater value if the investment proves to provide an opportunity to control the restructuring company. In the latter case, and if the investor has

correctly identified the "fulcrum" security, substantial litigation or protracted transaction negotiations may be involved, all resulting in large transaction costs.

3. If a company files for Chapter 11 bankruptcy reorganization, investors face many considerations including whether to participate in the formation of an official unsecured creditors' committee. The investor also may anticipate avoidable transfer litigation and inquiries regarding how, at what price, and from whom it acquired its position in the debtor's capital structure.
4. The still-emerging distressed securities market is generally unregulated. If and when the issuer files a bankruptcy case, the sole "policeman" is the bankruptcy court. Nonetheless, legal and regulatory concerns arise including potential claims disallowance and antitrust approval for "strategic" investors that may seek to acquire a competitor though an investment in distressed securities.

CHAPTER 16 PERFORMANCE OF PRIVATE EQUITY

1. Measuring performance is difficult for private equity funds because of their illiquidity. In the absence of true secondary markets, periodic-value observations are unavailable. Therefore, the time weighted return-metrics applied in the public markets arena cannot directly be applied to private equity.
2. Various types of performance measures are available. Performance measures can be separated into absolute versus relative performance measures as well as net asset value (NAV) versus cash flow–based performance measures. By using NAVs and interpreting them as value proxies, a time-weighted return for a private equity fund can be calculated. Alternatively, cash flows serve as a basis for measuring performance. The internal rate of return (IRR) as well as the money multiple are the two most important absolute performance measures. The public market equivalent (PME) is frequently used as a relative performance measure.
3. Measuring performance of private equity as an asset classes offers several challenges. One challenge is data availability because private equity data are not disclosed on a regular basis. Another problem is that a cash flow–based measure can theoretically be calculated only after the fund is fully liquidated. Because a fund's lifetime is typically 10 years or more, younger funds are frequently integrated in such an analysis in order to have a larger number of observations. In that case, the residual NAV is often interpreted as a final hypothetical cash flow of the fund. To the extent that this residual NAV is not an unbiased estimate of the future cash flow, such a calculation will lead to biased results. Moreover, private equity performance measurement becomes very intriguing once a risk-adjustment process takes place.
4. Public market equivalent methods have several advantages and disadvantages. The traditional index comparison method (ICM) generates the only true equivalent of investing in public equity and results in an IRR or money multiple spread compared to the index investments. However, in its original version, the ICM can run into a short position when the private equity fund outperforms the public market. To get around this problem using the modified version ("nonshort"), one simply stops further distributions when the index investment reaches zero value. The PME+ method downscales all distributions by a certain factor but eventually tends to understate the IRR of the public

market equivalent and thus the spread of the private equity fund. The index-adjusted multiple (PME) method is comparably simple to calculate but does not result in an annualized figure of outperformance or underperformance.

5. Risk-adjustments are needed to better benchmark buyout funds against public equity. Starting with a public equity index that matches the size and industry characteristics of the buyout fund or a portfolio of funds, the fund's overall performance would have to be adjusted for the higher beta inherent in its investments. As the beta changes over the lifetime of a fund, such adjustments would be needed at the level of individual cash flows as they occur over time.

   Beyond accounting for the exposure to market risk, an adjustment for funding and illiquidity costs should be incorporated. However, such costs can vary for different types of limited partnerships (LPs) and institutional investors depending on the structure of the existing private equity program as well as the availability and requirements of liquidity.

CHAPTER 17 PRIVATE EQUITY: RISK AND RETURN PROFILE

1. Typically, returns on portfolio companies are earned over a 7- to 10-year period. Analyzing changes over time and variation across industries is difficult. When evaluating the risk and return of financing rounds, more financing rounds are available than in venture capital funds. Studying financing rounds enables using more observations than by analyzing venture capital funds.
2. IRR is the standard performance measure employed in situations in which only a stream of cash flows (but no market valuations) can be observed. In more specific terms, the IRR of an investment is the discount rate at which the net present value (NPV) of the cash flows equals zero. For a private equity investment i with start date t_i and final liquidation date T_i, the IRR_i can be found as a solution to

$$\sum_{t=t_i}^{T_i} \frac{R_{it} - I_{it}}{(1 + IRR_i)^{t-t_i}} = 0$$

   where I_{it} denotes the amount invested at time t and R_{it} denotes the repayments at time t.
3. The standard IRR approach does not allow inferring the abnormal returns of private equity investments and their exposure to market risk. However, this approach can be extended by using a time-varying discount rate. This extension is accomplished by assuming that the rate of return R_{it} of investment i in period t is generated by the single-factor market model. Under this condition, the NPV of the cash flows of a sufficiently large sample of N private equity investments can be approximated by:

$$\frac{1}{N}\sum_{i-1}^{N}\sum_{t=t_i}^{T_i} \frac{R_{it} - I_{it}}{\prod_{s=t_i+1}^{t} (1 \mid r_f \mid \alpha \mid \beta \; R_{Ms})}$$

Using this result, the abnormal return α and the systematic risk β can be estimated from a cross-section of private equity investment cash flows by a numerical optimization of:

$$\min_{\alpha,\beta}\left(\sum_{i=1}^{N}\sum_{t=t_i}^{T_i}\frac{R_{it}-I_{it}}{\prod_{s=t_i+1}^{t}(1+r_f+\alpha+\beta\cdot R_{Ms})}\right)^2$$

4. The empirical evidence shows that the systematic risk measures (betas) for the venture and buyout segments are significantly different from 1.0, while abnormal returns (alphas) are significantly positive for both segments. The results also reveal differences in systematic risk and abnormal performance between venture capital and buyout investments. Buyout investments are characterized by lower systematic risk and higher abnormal performance than venture capital investments.

CHAPTER 18 INVESTING IN COMMODITIES

1. Direct investment means investing in physical goods. Investors can take advantage of this opportunity if they know the physical goods market and can manage and store the physical goods. However, investing in commodities has disadvantages. In fact, if investors buy commodities, they need to understand the quality of the goods and the problems that can exist due to asset quality. Another problem is the presence of different costs relating to storage, insurance, and cash opportunity costs. These costs affect the management of the physical good. Unlike stocks and bonds, commodities are an asset class without cash flows over time. Because commodities earn no current income, managers can only measure the return on the asset if they decide to sell the physical good. These costs reduce an investment's value.

   An indirect investment refers to selecting stocks of natural resource companies or structured products or with a commodities derivative. These investment vehicles offer the opportunity to earn the potential appreciation of each segment of the financial markets, so that investors can select various commodities without entering directly into the commodities markets. Exchange-traded funds (ETFs) offer a low cost structure and diversification benefits, providing the opportunity to gain potential returns for a specific market segment without the risk of single stock position. Investors can choose between many different instruments in energy, natural resources, precious metals, and agricultural products in the ETF market, avoiding the direct management of physical goods. Commodity index funds promise to mimic a commodity index. While these instruments were originally introduced as private investment funds for high-net-worth individuals and institutional investors, the market has evolved into one that includes exchange-traded retail products such as commodity index ETFs.
2. Soft commodities are divided into agricultural produce (e.g., cocoa, coffee, corn, cotton, oats, soybeans, sugar, and wheat) and livestock (e.g., cattle, hogs, and pork bellies). Their price depends on the weather in different parts of the world

at different times. Hard commodities are the products in energy, precious metals, and industrial metals sectors. They react to industrial drivers. The best choice depends on the prospects of the economic cycle. Energy, livestock, and meat perform especially well during the start of a recession. Agricultural commodities and metals exhibit the worst returns at the beginning of the recession. Energy performs poorly at the end of the recession.

3. Passive investment in commodities indices represents one of the best-known solutions to improve the risk-return relationship by adding alternative investments to a portfolio. Such an investment offers a large exposure to commodity assets and investors can choose to select different kinds of indices making up future contracts in different sectors of commodity markets. The return of the commodity index depends on changes in spot prices of an underlying commodity, the interest rate gained from government bonds used to collateralize the future contract, and the roll yield. Many asset managers favor commodity future indices because they are transparent and liquid. Also, two different uses of these indices are to speculate on the expected returns from commodities and to provide passive portfolio diversification. Speculators can use a tactical bet on the future performance of a commodity compared to stocks and bonds. Otherwise, they choose commodity futures indices to provide passive portfolio diversification without any view as to the current state of the business cycle. Asset managers can choose many different commodity future indices in terms of their intrinsic composition.
4. If investors choose to invest in commodities, they are exposed to counterparty risk at the maturity of the contract. If they decide to invest in commodity futures, they avoid counterparty risk because of the clearinghouse and margins rules. If investors choose commodity-based ETFs or ETNs, these products offer low structure costs and diversification benefits. Investors would take a long or short position according to the characteristic of the chosen product without taking encountering counterparty risk.
5. Financial and commodity markets follow the same trend as a "market of one" during extreme events. Büyüksahin, Haigh, and Robe (2010) find that the comovements between equities and commodities did not increase from June 2003 through May 2008 suggesting that commodities retain their role as a diversification tool. The correlation between equity and commodity indices was weak during the period 1997 to 2003 and even negative in the period between June 2003 and May 2008. The benefits in selecting commodities in a portfolio decreased from May to November 2008 when the correlation was positive during the financial crisis. This analysis relates to six subindices: agricultural, energy, industrial metals, livestock, nonenergy, and precious metals. The S&P 500 Index had a low, positive correlation with all commodity returns, and this relationship increased during the period 2003 to 2008. Precious metals represent the only exception during this period having a correlation with the S&P 500 Index close to zero.

CHAPTER 19 PERFORMANCE OF COMMODITIES

1. Commodity futures and options on commodity futures are themselves leveraged securities. The amount of leverage varies from commodity to commodity

but it is the thread that runs through all commodity trading. Various tradeoffs are associated with leverage. First, a bare position (i.e., one that is entirely speculative in nature) exposes the trader to the maximum gain (and the maximum risk) that comes from being levered. Second, as leverage underlies much of commodities trading (leverage is the basis of any futures contract), it provides the broadest and deepest entry to the trading of most if not all commodities. Third, the risk of commodity trading is the most visible and amplified because of leverage. Fourth, to reduce the risk inherent in the leveraged contracts, traders can use some of their initial investment to purchase highly rated liquid debt as a way to manage their "pain threshold" or risk aversion.

2. Before hiring a CTA, the most important information to obtain in a CTA's disclosure document is the worst peak-to-valley drawdown. The worst drawdown shows both the worst performance and the amount of time needed to recoup the loss. Disclosure documents also detail incentive fees and year-to-year rates of return. Other information that investors will want is the type of trading in which the CTA is engaged (e.g., directional or nondirectional), and the risk-adjusted return, sometimes known as the dispersion of losses. Investors often use the Calmar ratio to compare the risk-adjusted return between CTAs.
3. Cost of carry can be defined as the cost of carrying or holding a position. In the securities markets, cost of carry is the difference between the interest generated on a cash instrument such as a bond or a Treasury bill and the cost of funds to finance the position. In commodity markets, it is the cost of storage and insurance. Two important aspects of the cost-of-carry model are convenience yield and storage costs (and its associated return). Convenience yield is the benefit or premium associated with holding an underlying product or physical good rather than the associated contract or derivative. The convenience yield is meant to compensate investors for any expected rate of return shortfalls. Associated with convenience yield are storage costs and its associated return. The expected return on storage is defined as the sum of the expected growth rate in the spot price and the convenience yield.
4. The hedging pressure hypothesis contends that investors will receive a risk premium that is a positive excess return for going short in normal contango futures markets. The theory of storage emphasizes the role of inventories and links inventories to futures' prices. This theory predicts an inverse relationship between the level of inventories and the convenience yield. In other words, when inventories are low, backwardation occurs and when levels are high, contango occurs.
5. A futures margin is the amount of money that must be put up to control a futures contract. A commodity futures trader encounters three types of margin. Initial margin is the amount of money that must be deposited in a futures account before any trading takes place. Maintenance margin is the amount of money that must be maintained in a futures account. If the margin balance in the account falls below the maintenance margin as a result of a change in the contract price for the underlying asset, additional funds called variation margin must be deposited to bring the margin balance back to the initial margin amount.

CHAPTER 20 COMMODITY FUTURES AND STRATEGIC ASSET ALLOCATION

1. The popularity of investing in commodities can be attributed to their attractive risk-return profile and their abilities in effectively hedging against inflation.
2. Three proxies that can be used to estimate the exposure to commodities are (1) direct physical investment, (2) a weighted index of commodity-related stocks, and (3) commodity futures.
3. The major challenge in estimating the demands for a new asset class is the fact that exact analytical solutions are generally unavailable. Thus, finding a closed-form solution is essential for discriminating the demands for various asset classes.
4. The Campbell et al. (2003) approach has two main advantages: (1) it can accommodate multiperiod portfolio choice problems with a large number of asset classes and (2) it can decompose intertemporal hedging demands into components associated with individual asset classes.

CHAPTER 21 MANAGED FUTURES: MARKETS, INVESTMENT CHARACTERISTICS, AND ROLE IN A PORTFOLIO

1. Based on the Alphametrix study, an investor should expect to breakeven under worst conditions in two to three years and to experience positive returns after three to five years. While guaranteeing performance is impossible with any investment, the Alphametrix study, while general in nature, highlights an important conclusion: short-term horizons and performance chasing will probably not be rewarded. Any investment in managed futures should follow a methodical approach in the setting of the investment horizon.
2. While alternative investments generally seem to provide positive uncorrelated performance with traditional asset classes, an increasingly common occurrence is for most alternative strategies to correlate with traditional asset classes during times of substantial market stress. This strategy seems to be due to the classic drivers of crises and the performance drivers of most alternative investments. Many other alternative strategies usually profit from a combination of two elements: an illiquidity risk premium and some anomalies existing within the context of normal economic growth. For example, private equity is expected to outperform traditional stocks due to its illiquidity but its success is linked to positive credit conditions and a receptive stock market in order to monetize any exit strategy. In a market breakdown, the risk premium for illiquidity rises exponentially, credit conditions usually deteriorate gravely, and opportunities for exit strategies disappear.
3. Managed futures indices are often not investable and suffer from large survivorship and backfill biases. While most studies on asset allocation regard including managed futures as a way to optimize risk-adjusted performance, all alternative investment indices usually used to draw conclusions in such studies suffer from certain deficiencies. Most indices are not practically investable as too many

programs are included making closely replicating index performance impossible for even very large accounts. Such indices also tend to overstate returns and understate risks because failed programs are dropped by the index and the resulting performance represents only the survivors. Another problem deals with the timing of reporting. Often a manager will start reporting performance numbers after a major positive period and then backfill the index with past performance numbers (backfill bias).

4. Due to the difficulty in replicating index performance, being able to choose the proper CTA or the proper blend of CTAs is of critically importance. Choosing a CTA involves performing at least three levels of analysis: (1) quantitative analysis, (2) qualitative screening, and (3) organizational overview. A quantitative approach requires the investor to analyze performance in depth including the level of leverage, maximum drawdown, recovery speed, risk and return, and more. However, numbers and formulas alone cannot tell the whole picture. A detailed process also requires a qualitative approach in order for the investor to fully understand where the program's edge lies and how risk management is implemented. The third level of analysis concerns the operational aspect of the CTA, including how the different aspects of the business are handled and separated (e.g., trading, compliance, and marketing); how dependent the program is on key personnel; and how prepared the outfit is in dealing with a sudden departure.
5. While the bankruptcy of MF Global will be an evolving matter, it is already influencing how the futures market in general is perceived and operates. A weaker perception of the sanctity of segregation of customers' funds may lead to inefficiencies and lower trading volume in the sector. Changes in the regulatory framework are very likely. For example, a stricter monitoring of FCMs' activities and more stringent safeguards for customers' funds should be implemented. Another possibility is that hedging activities previously implemented via the futures and options exchanges may migrate to the over-the-counter market.

CHAPTER 22 AN OVERVIEW OF MANAGED FUTURES' PERFORMANCE: 1983 TO POST-2008 CREDIT CRISIS

1. The development of the managed futures industry can be traced back to the mid-nineteenth century, following the official opening of the Chicago Board of Trade (CBO) in 1848, where futures contracts started to trade with grains as the underlying commodity. Subsequent developments included the introduction of the world's first financial futures contracts (foreign currency futures) by the Chicago Mercantile Exchange (CME) in 1972. Because these new futures contracts made markets increasingly complex, users of the futures markets sought more specialized professional advice in managing their futures market assets. Investors can participate in managed futures in three ways. First, they can buy shares of public commodity funds. Public funds enable small (retail) investors to participate in managed futures because these funds offer the lowest minimum investment requirements. Second, investors can place funds with a private CPO who pools all investors' funds together and retains one or more professional traders. These

pools have higher minimum investment requirements than public funds. Third, investors can place their funds directly with one or more CTAs to manage their funds on an individual basis. CTAs typically require a larger minimum investment than the other two methods of investing in managed futures.

2. The possible sources of returns can be traced back to the risk transfer function of the futures market itself, highlighting how the interactions and motives between the commercial market participants (e.g., hedgers) and the noncommercial participants (e.g., investors) contribute to the determining the returns for futures' investments. The numbers and the types of the CTAs and hedgers in the future markets can also affect the sources of returns.
3. The merits of the strategies adopted by managed futures are favored in time of market crisis. Managed futures mainly rely on the divergent strategies that are often based on trend-following strategies, which could benefit from directional moves that reflect information gaps, changes in sentiment, and supply and demand imbalances in the markets Therefore, the pattern and trend of the price movements tend to differ from those in the stock markets. This relationship explains the low correlations compared to those of the stock markets.
4. The diversification benefits of managed futures are due to the low correlations with the stock and bond portfolios. However, investor preference is also another aspect to consider when deciding whether to include managed futures as part of equity portfolios. Tee (2009) relates the allocated proportion of managed futures to reflect investors' risk tolerance level. His results show that the potential diversification benefits of managed futures may deteriorate after reductions in downside risk tolerance levels. This finding appears to reinforce the importance of risk (tolerance) perception, particularly downside risk, when making decisions to include managed futures funds in equity portfolios as the empirical analysis suggests that this could also negatively affect portfolio returns.

CHAPTER 23 INVESTING IN HEDGE FUNDS

1. A satisfactory definition for a hedge fund does not exist because each hedge fund is unique. Further complicating the issue is the fact that hedge funds are legally allowed to be somewhat secretive. Thus, identifying the various investment, legal, and compensation structures in current hedge funds can be challenging. However, a few general requirements exist within most hedge funds. From an investment perspective, most hedge funds are structured to provide either higher risk-adjusted returns or a consistent level of return regardless of market volatility. From a legal perspective, most hedge funds are lightly regulated and are privately managed for accredited investors. From a compensation perspective, hedge funds usually include both a management fee and a performance fee.
2. Two important performance fee provisions structured into many hedge fund contracts are hurdle rates and high-water mark provisions. The hurdle rate creates an out-of-the-money option for the fund manager each year in that the manager does not receive any performance fees unless the fund reaches or exceeds the stated hurdle rate for that year. The high-water mark provision also provides an out-of-the-money option if the fund incurs losses during the current year or if the fund's returns are insufficient to cover past losses. Simply stated,

the high-water mark provision incentivizes hedge fund managers to constantly exceed the current maximum share value. As a result, both the hurdle rate and the high-water mark provisions protect investors from paying performance fees on poorly performing funds.

Empirical evidence suggests that high-water mark provisions can lead to superior fund performance (Agarwal, Daniel, and Naik, 2001). These findings further suggest that the high-water mark provisions are highly effective in motivating managerial effort and in alleviating agency problems. However, Goetzmann, Ingersoll, and Ross (2003) provide evidence that these provisions can create agency problems because managers have an adverse gambling incentive to increase risk when the fund is not far below the high-water mark. Both Fung and Hsieh (1997) and Brown, Goetzmann, and Park (2001) contend that reputation costs offset this adverse gambling incentive.

3. Besides the potential for double counting funds that are listed on more than one database, the main reasons for inaccuracies in hedge fund databases are biases. Besides illiquidity bias and serial correlation, hedge fund databases reflect four major biases: selection bias, survivorship bias, backfill bias, and liquidation bias. However, research shows that only the first three create significant bias within database performance data. Selection bias arises because hedge funds are not required to disclose asset or return information to any database. Consequently, hedge fund databases create biased samples because inclusion of hedge funds into databases is at the discretion of the hedge fund manager. Survivorship bias occurs when funds are excluded from databases because they stop reporting their returns. Finally, backfill bias arises from the tendency of databases to allow recently listed funds to backfill their historical returns.
4. The primary difference between nondirectional and directional investment strategies is market exposure. Simply stated, nondirectional hedge funds fully hedge market exposure, while directional hedge funds do not. As a result, nondirectional hedge funds concentrate on providing investors with a consistent return regardless of the performance of the broader market. Specific strategies include market-neutral and arbitrage hedge funds. In contrast, directional hedge funds have the potential to earn relatively higher returns, without using leverage because of their added market risk exposure. Examples of directional hedge funds include managed futures, global macro funds, emerging market funds, dedicated short funds, and active-extension long/short portfolios.

CHAPTER 24 PERFORMANCE OF HEDGE FUNDS

1. Modern portfolio theory, developed by Harry Markowitz, relies on a mean/variance framework. Normally distributed returns are fully described by the mean and variance of returns. These are the first and second moments of the return distribution. Stock and bond returns are typically assumed to be normally distributed. However, hedge fund returns are not normally distributed. Hedge fund returns exhibit negative skewness and positive excess kurtosis. Skewness refers to the asymmetry of the return distribution and kurtosis refers to the "peakedness" of the distribution. As a result the higher moments of the distribution must be considered when assessing the risk/return profile of a hedge fund.

2. Several reasons help to explain why both the number of hedge funds and the dollars invested in funds have grown dramatically. These reasons include:
   - Hedge fund returns have low correlation with traditional asset returns, making them a popular choice for reducing portfolio risk.
   - Investors have expressed increased interest in hedge funds in recent years due to their reported high returns.
   - An increasing number of sophisticated, high-net-worth investors, known as "accredited investors" have entered the market.
   - The 1990s bull market created additional wealth and some of those investable funds went to hedge fund investments.
   - Institutional investors have shown a willingness to consider hedge funds as an appropriate alternative asset class since the late 1990s.
   - Investors began searching for ways to diversify holdings in the early 1990s in the wake of falling equity values and lower bond yields.
3. Many academic studies examine the biases inherent in hedge fund databases. The biases include:
   - *Survivorship bias.* Hedge funds experience, on average, a 10 percent attrition rate each year. For new funds, managers may be unable to attract sufficient external capital to achieve the economies of scale required to make the fund a viable business. For older funds, performance may be lackluster and cause investors to redeem their shares. Studies contend that survivorship bias implies higher than actual returns because the funds that survive are likely to have higher returns than defunct funds or funds that quit reporting because of underperformance.
   - *Selection bias.* Because hedge funds are largely unregulated, fund managers decide to report performance to hedge fund databases. If the database is not representative of the universe of hedge funds, it may suffer from selection bias. Selection bias results in databases reporting upwardly biased returns because only high-performing funds have an incentive to make their performance public.
   - *Backfill bias.* Backfill bias, also called instant history or incubation bias, is the result of the "waiting period" before a new fund can establish a track record to report to a database. If the fund performs well, the manager will report to a database in order to attract outside capital. When the fund enters the database, the prior performance history is "backfilled." This instant history bias causes hedge fund performance to be overestimated.
   - *Liquidation bias.* Fund managers stop reporting returns to databases before the final liquidation of the fund. This results in liquidation bias, which biases returns upward.
4. The seven significant asset-based style factors identified by Fung and Hsieh (2004) are:
   - The excess return of the S&P 500 Index (i.e., the S&P 500 Index return minus the risk free rate).
   - The small cap stock returns minus large cap stock returns. These two equity factors were most important to the long/short equity funds which, according to Fung and Hsieh, account for 30 to 40 percent of all hedge funds.
   - The excess return of the 10-year Treasury bond relative to the risk-free rate.

- The excess return of Baa bonds relative to the 10-year Treasury bond. These two risk factors are most important to fixed-income funds.
- Call and put options on bonds.
- Call and put options on currencies.
- Call and put options on commodities.

According to Fung and Hsieh, the seven factor model explains 80 percent of the variation in the monthly returns in the HFR Funds of Funds Index.

CHAPTER 25 HEDGE FUNDS AND RISK MANAGEMENT

1. The different types of hedge fund risk exposures can be classified into two broad categories: (1) risks hedge funds share with other investment classes and (2) risks more specific to hedge funds. Major risks that hedge funds share with other investment classes include:
   - *Market risk.* Relates to adverse market factor shifts.
   - *Credit risk.* Relates to default probability on counterparty obligations.
   - *Liquidity risk.* Relates to illiquid markets or inability to raise necessary funds.
   - *Common factor risk.* Relates to specific characteristics of stocks or sectors.
   - *Operational risk.* Relates to operational failures.
   - *Event risk.* Relates to important and unexpected adverse events.
   - *Corporate event risk.* Relates to events affecting corporate value.
   - *Model risk.* Relates to model misspecification.

   Major risks that are more specific to hedge funds include:
   - *Lack of transparency risk.* Relates to lack of transparency in investment strategies, fund management, and nondisclosure.
   - *Manager idiosyncratic risk.* Relates to fund management power concentration by one or few managers.
   - *Leverage risk.* Relates to volatility and financing.
   - *Capacity risk.* Relates to potential capacity limits of investment strategy
   - *Fraud risk.* Relates to manager defrauding investors.
   - *Valuation risk.* Relates to pricing and net asset valuation (NAV) calculation by varying standards.
   - *Concentration risk.* Relates to large individual position exposures.
   - *Regulatory risk.* Relates to changing regulatory framework.
2. The expected shortfall (ES) approach can be employed as an alternative risk measure in hedge funds in order to support overcoming certain limitations of the VaR approach. ES, like VaR, is a function of two parameters: the time horizon in days (N) and the confidence level (x percent). ES is the expected loss during an N-day period, conditional that the loss is greater than the xth percentile of the loss distribution. ES is more conservative than VaR and more sensitive to the shape of the loss distribution in the tail of the distribution. Its attractive properties include scalability, correct risk ranking, and accounting for diversification.

   ES investigates "what the expected loss should be if things get bad" in a portfolio, producing more specific results relative to VaR. In other words, ES supports the assessment of portfolio performance, if certain extreme events occur, and identifies the likelihood of experiencing some sort of loss on one or more of those assets. Evaluating the return potential of each asset and paying attention to anticipating the shortfall and the possibility of incurring losses enables the portfolio manager to assess the overall impact on the portfolio and to make a decision of whether to hold onto those assets before the expected decrease in value should take place. Although ES has appealing features relative to VaR, it has certain practical drawbacks.

3. The three main elements of standard risk measure estimation are: (1) mapping the portfolio positions to risk factors, (2) calculating the risk factor covariance matrix based on historical prices, and (3) determining the model for the risk and calculating the risk measure. Risk factor mapping refers to the decomposition of the risk components of individual securities in a portfolio into exposures under the control of the fund manager and exogenous factors. Following the identification of portfolio risk factors, estimating the dependence structure between the risk factors is important. The correlation matrix determines the distribution of portfolio returns and therefore the portfolio risk measures. The dependence between risk factors is usually nonlinear and time varying. The assumption of normally distributed returns is restrictive in the case of hedge funds that often exhibit non-normal, nonlinear behavior, and extreme outcomes.

   Empirical models to calculate portfolio variance (volatility) and covariance (correlations) include: (1) εqually weighted moving average (EWMA), (2) εxponential moving average of squared returns and cross products with specified decay parameter, and (3) autoregressive conditional heteroskedastic (ARCH) and generalized ARCH (GARCH) models.

4. Copulas represent a general way of modeling dependence between random variables. They are incorporated in financial risk management because they can account for a wide range of dependence structures. The marginal behavior of the individual risk factors is separated from their dependence structure. Models for the single risk factors can then be combined with those for the dependence structure, without the very restrictive assumptions imposed by linear correlation (i.e., probability distribution being elliptic). This is particularly useful for hedge funds with significantly skewed and heavy-tailed returns.

   Consider an n-dimensional random vector $X = (X_1, \ldots, X_n)$. The information on the distribution of a vector X is fully described by the following joint cumulative distribution function:

$$F_X(x) = F_X(x_1, \ldots, x_n) = P(X \leq x) = P(X_1 \leq x_1, \ldots, X_n \leq x_n)$$

where F_{X_i} describes the marginal distributions of X_i that is calculated through the joint distribution function. Copulas decompose the above representation of the joint distribution function into two parts: the dependence structure and the marginal distributions. The fact that copulas functions apply to uniform distributions over the interval [0, 1] requires the extensive use of probability-integral and quantile transformations.

CHAPTER 26 HEDGE FUNDS AND THE FINANCIAL CRISIS

1. While some blame hedge funds for causing the financial crisis of 2007–2008, little evidence to date suggests that hedge funds actually caused the crisis. As some studies, such as Brown, Karperczyk, Ljungqvist, Lynch, Pedersen, and Richardson (2009), point out, hedge funds did not cause the growth in subprime mortgage market, make housing prices fall substantially, or result in banks taking risks in those subprime mortgage-backed collateralized debt obligations. Instead, hedge funds actually helped reduce the impact of the crisis by providing liquidity to the market, correcting fundamental mispricing in the market, increasing price discovery through their trading, and providing investors access to leverage and to investment strategies that perform well.
2. Systemic risk usually refers to the risk of broad-based breakdown in the financial system. A classic example of this is the massive number of bank failures during 1930 to 1933 in the United States. In order to measure systemic risk, the following six characteristics of the financial system need to be captured: leverage, liquidity, correlation, concentration, sensitivities, and connectedness.

   In their testimonies before the U.S. Congress, several hedge fund managers claim that hedge funds "are unlikely as a single class to be a substantial contributor to systemic risk" (Simon, 2008, p. 5). Yet, some researchers contend that despite little evidence suggesting that hedge funds caused the crisis, their role as "shadow banks" contributes to systemic risk.
3. Mutual funds are subject to rigorous regulatory oversight under four federal securities laws, specifically the Securities Act of 1933, the Securities Exchange Act of 1934, the Investment Company Act of 1940, and the Investment Advisers Act of 1940. In contrast, until the passage of the Dodd-Frank Act, hedge funds typically relied on the exclusions from registration under the federal securities laws that apply to hedge funds and their securities offerings to avoid regulation. The exclusions include (1) the exclusion from registration of the fund under the Investment Company Act of 1940, (2) the exemption from registration of the fund's securities under the Securities Act of 1933, (3) the exemption from registration of the hedge fund manager under the Investment Advisers Act of 1940, and (4) the exception from reporting requirements under the Securities Exchange Act of 1934. As a result, hedge funds were subject to much less regulation than mutual funds before the Dodd-Frank Act.

   Evaluating whether hedge funds require more or less regulations requires considering the tradeoff between the costs and benefits of heightened regulation. Hedge funds should be subject to more rigorous regulatory oversight in order to protect investors and to reduce systemic risk. Conversely, increased regulation would impose compliance costs on hedge funds and investors as well as the economy as a whole. Ultimately, regulators must balance the costs and benefits of increased hedge fund regulation and strike a balance so that the new regulation does not diminish incentives and opportunities while fulfilling its missions to protect investors and to reduce systemic risk.
4. The Dodd-Frank Act has important implications for hedge fund performance in three main areas. First, under the Act, more money would flow into the hedge fund industry. Thus, funds face greater difficulty in generating the same

superior returns as they used to due to liquidity and organizational diseconomies. Second, costs incurred in the process of complying with the new legislation would further reduce hedge fund profitability. Third, the new regulation subjects hedge funds to mandatory disclosure of material information about their trades and portfolio, which might reveal the funds' proprietary trading strategies and also raise front-running costs by other investors such as mutual funds, and thus reduce the profitability of hedge funds. In summary, hedge fund performance, on average, is expected to decline under the Dodd-Frank Act.

CHAPTER 27 HEDGE FUNDS: REPLICATION AND NONLINEARITIES

1. Academic studies provide evidence that hedge fund manager alpha has been diminishing over the last two decades (Fung and Hsieh, 2007; Naik, Ramadorai, and Stromqvist, 2007) and certain styles such as fund-of-funds have not delivered alpha (Fung, Hsieh, Naik, and Ramadorai, 2008). Although the majority of the studies estimate alpha net-of-fees, no evidence suggests that alpha before fees is consistently negative for all styles. Therefore, if investors could eliminate hefty hedge fund fees and inexpensively replicate all hedge fund returns (both alpha and beta), such strategies could create additional value to investors.
2. Apart from saving large fees for investors, hedge fund replication strategies provide at least three other advantages over investing directly in hedge fund. First, the clones are more liquid because clone strategies are constructed by design using liquid securities. Second, clones are transparent to investors. The precise composition of replicating portfolios is known all the time. This transparency simplifies hedge funds' risk assessment and the risk management process. Third, clones are less prone to capacity constraints (i.e., replication strategies are scalable as long as they employ liquid securities). In contrast, hedge funds often have arbitrary redemption rules, reducing the liquidity of investments, and do not disclose their positions. Further, their return-generating ability deteriorates with capital inflows (Naik et al., 2007).
3. Hedge funds' risk exposures are likely to have nonlinear patterns for several reasons. First, hedge funds are free to trade derivatives. Since many derivatives, such as options, have asymmetric payoff profiles, hedge fund returns may also be asymmetric functions of underlying risk factors. Second, hedge fund managers actively manage their portfolio. Accordingly, Merton (1981) demonstrates that dynamic trading induces nonlinear patterns in risk relations. For example, perfect market timing results in an asymmetric risk-return profile. Finally, the optionlike nature of incentive contracts (sharing profits and not penalizing for losses) might also lead to nonlinear patterns.
4. Arbitrage pricing theory (APT) assumes that risk factor payoffs are linear, which contradicts the fact that hedge funds trade securities with inherently nonlinear payoff profiles such as options. Therefore, APT is theoretically unsuitable in the context of hedge funds. Also, the capital asset pricing model (CAPM) assumes that asset returns are normally distributed, which is also false for hedge funds (Malkiel and Saha, 2005). CAPM provides the motivation for nonlinear hedge fund models.

5. The two main sources of alpha for an active manager are security selection skill and market-timing skill. Clones are unlikely to be able to replicate alpha due to manager's superior security selection skill because clones do not attempt to identify the exact holdings of individual funds. From this perspective, cloning alpha is impossible. However, theoretically accurate hedge fund replication models can detect and follow managers' decision about the dynamic portfolio allocation between different asset classes. For example, clones might imitate managers' decisions to reallocate capital from equity to bonds. In other words, alpha due to the market-timing skill, which Merton (1981) refers to as "macroforecasting," potentially can be replicated.

CHAPTER 28 FUND-OF-FUNDS: A TALE OF TWO FEES

1. Long-only managers typically use a benchmark such as the S&P 500 Index that they attempt to mimic. Conversely, hedge fund strategies are absolute-return based. As a result, the performance of long-only managers is clustered around the index returns and hence has lower dispersion.
2. Several factors contribute to the variability of beta to the S&P 500 Index of long-short managers over time. For example, long-short managers change their total exposure over time (market timing) depending on whether they perceive the market conditions to improve or deteriorate. Also, the overall beta depends on the security selection on the long side and the short side, leading to a change in the composition over time.
3. The central limit theorem helps to explain why the average performance of portfolios of difference sizes would be the same using stratified sampling. Creating thousands of portfolio drawing an equal number of funds from each strategy and then equally weighting them should yield average performance equal to equally weighting all strategies, which is computed by equally weighting the funds within each strategy.
4. A FoFs can be justified if it can avoid investing in operationally weak hedge funds via a vigilant due diligence process and if it has a superior strategy allocation and manager selection process.

Index

Printed and bound by CPI Group (UK) Ltd, Croydon, CR0 4YY

23/04/2025

14660930-0005